Globalization and the world of large cities

Note to the reader from the UNU

The United Nations University Institute of Advanced Studies Programme on Mega-cities and Urban Development was initiated to examine the growth and management of large metropolitan agglomerations, especially in the developing world. This volume is the fifth in a series of studies that began in the early 1990s. It follows the release of *Mega-city Growth and the Future* (Tokyo: UNU Press, 1994), *Emerging World Cities in Pacific Asia* (Tokyo: UNU Press, 1996), *The Mega-city in Latin America* (Tokyo: UNU Press, 1996), and *The Urban Challenge in Africa: Growth and Management of Its Large Cities* (Tokyo: UNU Press, 1997). The contribution of this book includes discussions of the key elements of globalization and the role that cities play in the economic restructuring process. Chapters in the volume present analyses in five crucial areas for large cities: new technologies; global finance; transportation and telecommunications; rural–urban relations; and urban food supply.

Globalization and the world of large cities

Edited by Fu-chen Lo and
Yue-man Yeung

**United Nations
University Press**

TOKYO · NEW YORK · PARIS

United Nations University Press
The United Nations University, 53-70, Jingumae 5-chome, Shibuya-ku, Tokyo 150, Japan
Tel: (03) 3499-2811   Fax: (03) 3406-7345
E-mail: mbox@hq.unu.edu

UNU Office in North America
2 United Nations Plaza, Room DC2-1462-70, New York, NY 10017
Tel: (212) 963-6387   Fax: (212) 371-9454   Telex: 422311 UN UI

United Nations University Press is the publishing division of the United Nations University.

Cover design by Andrew Corbett

Printed in the United States of America

UNUP-999
ISBN 92-808-0999-7

Library of Congress Cataloging-in-Publication Data

Globalization and the world of large cities / edited by Fu-chen Lo and Yue-man Yeung.
    p. cm.
  Includes bibliographical references and index.
  ISBN 9280809997
  1. Metropolitan areas. 2. Urbanization. 3. International economic relations. I. Lo, Fu-chen. II. Yeung, Yue-man.
  HT330.G56 1998
  307.76—dc21
                            98-19736
                              CIP

Contents

v

Tables and figures

Figures

Preface

The publication of this book marks the end of one stage of the support and efforts that have been directed by the United Nations University (UNU) towards the phenomenon of mega-cities in the last two decades of the twentieth century. The initiative of mounting research projects on these cities began in October 1990, with a Symposium on the Mega-city and the Future held in Tokyo co-sponsored by the United Nations University and the Population Division of the United Nations. This was followed by a number of multi-country projects that focused on mega-cities and world cities in the major regions of the developing world.

In order to carry this momentum one step further, the United Nations University contributed to the Second United Nations Conference on Human Settlements (Habitat II), held in Istanbul in June 1996, by taking stock of what had transpired in the regional projects and by anticipating what the urban future might hold for the world. A Pre-Habitat II Conference was held in Tokyo, on the theme of World Cities and the Urban Future, on 23–25 August 1995. This conference had the support not only of the United Nations University but also of the Japan Habitat Society and the National Institute for Research Administration (NIRA).

At Habitat II, a UNU Panel on Globalization and the Urban Future was organized on 7 June 1996, with the participation of five of the contributing authors of this book. They presented some of the major findings of the project. The Panel was chaired by Professor Heitor Gurgulino de Souza, Rector of the United Nations University. Dr. Wally N'Dow, Secretary-General of Habitat II, graced the Panel with his presence and was presented with two volumes of the earlier findings on mega-cities published by the UNU Press.

The papers in this volume originated from the Pre-Habitat II Conference. They have since been revised and expanded. In completing the task of editing this volume, we are grateful for the assistance rendered by many individuals. First of all, in carrying out the substantive editing of the chapters, frequent communication between Tokyo and Hong Kong was necessary. At the Tokyo end, thanks are due to Jacob Park and Peter Marcotullio, Research Associates of the United Nations University, for their efficiency and efforts. In actually communicating with all the contributing authors, Daisy Chung, of Shaw College at the Chinese University of Hong Kong, helped us by carrying this additional load to her normal work with grace and devotion. She was also responsible for transcribing the original papers, by mastering different word processing formats and ensuring consistency and accuracy in all the changes made. Joanna Lee, Research Assistant of the Urban and Regional Development in Pacific Asia Programme of the Hong Kong Institute of Asia-Pacific Studies of the same university, was meticulous in proofreading and verifying reference materials. S. L. Too, of the Department of Geography, assisted in redrawing most of the maps and figures.

Despite the convenience of the fax and the internet, communication with the contributors across the continents was not entirely easy. We wish, none the less, to extend our appreciation to them for their contribution to this project and for their meeting our requests for new data and amendments with cooperation and forbearance. In addition, we thank an anonymous referee for helpful comments, to which we have responded as far as we could. We are responsible for any remaining errors and shortcomings.

The editors
Tokyo and Hong Kong
October 1997

1

Introduction

Fu-chen Lo and Yue-man Yeung

The twentieth century is noted for humankind's numerous cultural advances and scientific achievements that have significantly changed and improved the quality of life for people everywhere. Probably nothing, however, can be compared with the speed of change since the 1980s in how goods are manufactured, how people, ideas, and capital travel, and how nations and cities perform their roles. The last two decades of the twentieth century have witnessed fundamental changes to our way of life, to our perception of our home, our workplace, and the world, and indeed to our future.

Underlying much of the far-reaching transformation of our time has been economic structural change on a global scale that has left hardly a single person or a single nation untouched. This has been accompanied by waves of technological innovation. These two tendencies have been mutually reinforcing, such that the world has become much more interdependent in its parts and globalization processes of diverse kinds have been penetrating every nook and corner of the world. These powerful and omnipresent changes have, as well, seen the ascendancy of large cities, particularly mega-cities and world cities, in the global political economy. Mega-cities are simply very large cities by virtue of their population size and world cities can be distinguished by the functions they perform in the new

1

global economy. The present global economy is underpinned by a functional world city system (Lo and Yeung, 1996).

The primary purpose of this volume is, within the context of global economic restructuring, to survey how large cities in different parts of the world have changed and reacted to the new challenges and opportunities. This survey covers all the major regions of the world, with the selection of several cities for more in-depth analysis and illustration. It is recognized that cities are viewed in different ways by authors in different geographical and socio-economic settings. For example, "global city" is used synonymously with "world city," and within the world city rubric there may be shades of differentiation between a world national city, a world regional city, and so on. Where a world city is only in the making, such as Johannesburg, its inclusion is primarily to highlight its process of becoming one. The sample of individual large cities is selected from the developing regions of Africa and Latin America, where problems of recent economic integration with the world economy have been especially acute. The present book project may be seen as an extension of recent related projects supported by the United Nations University (Fuchs et al., 1994; Lo and Yeung, 1996; Gilbert, 1996; Radoki, 1997). In addition, this volume takes one more step in reflecting on a number of key issues that are likely to exert a paramount influence on large cities in the future. These key issues will critically affect our urban future, although the authors dwell more on the past and the present, with implications for the future that can be readily drawn. The organization of the chapters follows the simple structure that has been adumbrated.

Trends of globalization

Since the 1980s the world economy has changed, rapidly and fundamentally, in its nature, operating modes, and relationships among countries and cities. These changes have been driven by several emerging mega-trends that have led to global structural adjustments.

First, a debt crisis emerged among the resource-exporting developing countries owing to the precipitous drop in the prices of primary commodities and fuel in the early 1980s and the corresponding advances in material sciences leading to a sharp reduction in the use of raw materials in manufacturing production. This created unprecedented difficulties for the developing countries, which have traditionally depended on the export of these products to finance their

2

national development. Countries in Africa, whose export earnings are dependent upon up to 90 per cent of these primary goods exports, have been severely affected. They were, moreover, increasingly burdened by fast-growing national debts. Similarly, South-East Asian countries that had hitherto depended heavily on the export of primary products for their export income were adversely affected. They were able to free themselves from the impasse because the period fortuitously coincided with a phase of rapid manufacturing development, propelled by Japan's readiness to search for foreign locales to decentralize its industrial plants and secure its competitive edge in world markets in the wake of the Plaza Accord in 1985 (table 1.1). That event caused the Japanese yen to double in value against the US dollar almost overnight. This led to a massive flow of foreign direct investment to the large cities and new industrial locations in South-East Asia, but not to Africa and Latin America.

Table 1.1   **Shares of manufacturing in GDP, 1970–1993**

	1970	1993	% change
USA	25	18[a]	−26.80
UK	33	25	−24.24
France	29[b]	22	−21.43
Germany	38	27	−28.95
Australia	24	15	−37.50
Japan	36	24	−33.33
Korea	21	29	38.10
Hong Kong	29	13	−55.17
Taiwan	35[c]	39[c]	11.40
Singapore	20	37	85.00
Malaysia	12	19[d]	58.33
Indonesia	10	22	120.00
Thailand	16	28	75.00
Philippines	25	24	−4.00
China	30	38	26.67
Argentina	32	20	−37.50
Brazil	29	20	−31.03
Mexico	22	20	−9.09

Source: World Bank, *World Development Report*, 1995.
a. 1991 figure, from *Survey of Current Business*, 1993.
b. 1965 figure.
c. Share of industry in GDP, from *Asian Development Outlook*, 1994.
d. 1985 figure.

Secondly, the relative decline in traditional raw materials in manufacturing has been accompanied by a commensurate increase in the importance of capital, especially transnational capital, as a determinant in economic development. Nations and cities are in the race for foreign direct investment (FDI). Transnational corporations, on the other hand, are basing their decisions on the selection of locations for investment largely on the comparative advantage of factors of production, namely, land, labour, and capital.

In the 1990s, the inflow of FDI from mostly America and Europe, accompanied by new technologies, increased its momentum in the Asia Pacific region. This has further intensified the structural interdependency of the world economy, linking cities in Europe, North America, and Asia. The movement of FDI has also strengthened the structural interdependency of production and marketing in cross-country linkages of city networks.

Thirdly, a key factor that has permitted breathtaking changes since the early 1980s has been technological innovations. Rapid advances in micro-electronics, telecommunications, robotics, biotechnology, and new materials have come in rapid succession in developed countries and selected newly industrializing economies. All these are, by nature, resource saving and reinforce the relative decline in material inputs in manufactured products mentioned above. Increasingly, the world economy is facilitated by the new information technologies, in which ideas, capital, and people move rapidly and in large numbers (Lo, 1994).

The impact of these mega-trends has varied within the different regions of the world. The traditional factors affecting the location decisions of industry have been greatly weakened and they have been superseded by new considerations of access to information through the latest technologies, the availability of capital, and changing comparative advantage. The location of industry is now based on a flexible mode of production at convenient points on information highways, challenging the Fordist techno-economic paradigm that dominated manufacturing before the 1980s (Lo, 1994). The rise of the information economy has the effect of lessening the importance of boundaries, including national boundaries – so much so that a borderless global economy has emerged (Ohmae, 1990). In other words, telematics and globalization have neutralized place and distance. The geography of globalization is characterized by a dynamic of dispersal and centralization (Saskia Sassen, chap. 14 in this volume). There is a new geography of rapid development and of marginality (Salah El-

Shakhs, chap. 10), highly conditioned by new information technologies, service intensity, and new kinds of spatial correlates. New forms of centrality are constituted by electronically generated spaces. Cities have emerged as elevated economic entities by virtue of their heightened centrality. Consequently, at the national and international levels there is keener competition among cities and, at the city level, intrametropolitan decentralization, first of residences, then jobs, occurs (Peter Hall, chap. 2). Specifically in North America, economic trends experienced globally affect intrametropolitan distribution of activities, including the shift towards services, the pull of an increasingly suburbanized labour force, the diffusion of agglomeration economies, and the effect of changes in the level of congestion. All this has resulted in firms being more footloose than ever (Peter Gordon and Harry W. Richardson, chap. 4). Increased economic and cultural polarization within world (or global) cities has also been observed (Sassen, 1991; Yeung, 1996).

The new dynamics of global production and changing comparative advantage have been conducive to the formation of regional trading blocs. Essentially, the present world economy is dominated by three trading blocs, namely the North American Free Trade Area, the European Union, and the loosely structured Pacific Asia entity. Together, they accounted in 1995 for 84.5 per cent of the world's GDP. It is clear that they form, by and large, more integrated regions of sustained development, although country and city economies within Western Europe and North America have been undergoing basic restructuring. Blue-collar jobs have been lost rapidly in such cities as Detroit, Pittsburgh, Manchester, Liverpool, Belfast, and Naples. OECD countries have adjusted their economies, such that between 60 and 70 per cent of their GDP is derived from the service sector (table 1.2). By contrast, the Western Pacific Rim has emerged as the fasting-growing region, supported by expansion of the manufacturing sector. The countries within it are at different stages of economic development and are able to capitalize on their varied factor endowments for effective complementarity and cooperative development for industrialization. A so-called "flying geese" pattern of industrialization has been noted for light manufactured goods, involving the staged development of Japan, the Asian newly industrializing economies (NIEs) of Hong Kong, South Korea, Singapore, and Taiwan (otherwise known as the Four Little Dragons), the countries of the Association of South-East Asian Nations (ASEAN), and China. One expression of rapid economic development has been

Table 1.2   **Shares of service sector in GDP, 1970–1993**

	1970	1993	% change
USA	63	75[a]	19.05
UK	52	65	25.00
France	52[b]	69	32.69
Germany	47	61	29.79
Australia	55	67	21.82
Japan	47	57	21.28
Canada	59	71	20.34
Italy	51	65	27.45

Source: World Bank, *World Development Report*, 1995.
a. 1991 figure, from *Survey of Current Business*, 1993.
b. 1965 figure.

the formation of urban corridors and growth triangles, which are highlighted by Sang-chuel Choe (chap. 7).

Uneven development has been an inevitable outcome of the new global economy. Regions, countries, and cities that are not heavily crossed by cyber-routes and digital highways are not active participants in the evolving patterns of development. In fact, for most of the period since 1980, countries in Africa and Latin America have been undergoing a painful process of structural adjustment under the twin burden of falling commodity prices and accumulating national debts. Alan Gilbert (chap. 8) has portrayed the situation in Latin America. He maintains that the debt crisis that has befallen most countries in the region would not have occurred without financial globalization. The Mexican financial crisis in December 1994 turned a paragon of economic success into a basket case overnight. The Mexican crisis poignantly reveals the economic and social volatility of economic globalization. It has also deepened economic inequality and social polarization. However, the upshot of a period of economic stagnation and social protest has prompted several countries in the region to seek a new path of rapid economic development. They have pursued export-oriented industrialization very much along the lines of the Asian NIEs. This provides a more positive prospect for the future.

Of all the regions, Africa appears to have been most adversely affected by processes of globalization. Notwithstanding the euphoric expectations of rapid development following the wave of independence movements in the 1950s and the 1960s, the disenchantment began to be felt in the 1970s. By the 1980s, most African countries were badly hit economically by the sharp fall in commodity prices. Historically, they have evolved a relationship with the world economy by depending on export earnings from primary products for more than 90 per cent of their GDP. By 1990, national debts in African countries became the heaviest among developing countries, as measured in relation to exports of goods and GDP. The structural adjustment programmes administered by the International Monetary Fund and the World Bank in fact created more immediate difficulties, despite their good intentions. The sub-Saharan countries have been most seriously affected by widespread poverty and economic stagnation. Globalization has thus failed to generate positive impulses in Africa; rather, it tends to marginalize the competitive edge of African countries, leading Carole Rakodi (chap. 12) to conclude that no world cities as yet exist on that continent.

Mega-cities and world cities

Although great cities emerged as a global phenomenon in the nineteenth century, attracting scholarly attention (Weber, 1899), the world of large cities grew ever more strongly as the twentieth century proceeded. In the 1960s, some scholars portrayed the future metropolis of man-made environments. At the beginning of the twentieth century, there were only 11 cities with over a million inhabitants. By the year 2000, it has been projected that the world will have 400 "million" cities.

In the twentieth century, one of the most striking phenomena is not just the rapid growth of population and of cities in developing countries since 1945, but the rise of very large cities, or mega-cities, in these countries since 1975. Mega-cities are defined as those with populations exceeding 8 million, following the United Nations definition (Chen and Heligman, 1994). By 1990, 14 mega-cities were located in developing countries, as opposed to 6 in more developed countries (counting Moscow in Russia). Within the developing world, the level of urbanization and the size of urban population vary sharply among the major regions. In 1994, there were 1,653 million urban dwellers in developing countries, at a level of urbanization of 37.0 per cent. Africa was the least urbanized at 32.4 per cent, with a total urban population of 240 million. Latin America reached an exceedingly high level of urbanization at 73.7 per cent, with 349 million urban dwellers. Asia was slightly above Africa at 33.4 per cent urbanized, but its urban population was huge at 1,064 million (United Nations,

1995: 23). In Asia, age-old agricultural practices oriented to food production have been holding population in the rural areas, but the situation is apparently changing fast.

Take the extreme example of China. Temporary migration of population towards the coastal cities, largely since 1984 when population migration controls relaxed as a feature of economic reforms, had already reached an estimated total of 70 million in 1988 (Li and Hu, 1991). The potential is even more staggering when one notes the estimated rural labour force of 450 million, with 300 million likely to leave the rural areas for lack of jobs by 2000 (Shen and Zhang, 1985: 75). Looked at from this perspective, it is vitally important to improve population-holding capacities in the rural areas in Asia, and hence the importance of such concepts as extended metropolitan regions (Ginsburg et al., 1991; McGee and Robinson, 1995). Indeed, rural–urban relations have undergone visible and substantive change as a result of globalization. Space–time collapse has resulted from transactional space change. Globalization processes at first affect the cities, then economic interactions, population mobility, and remittances radiate influences to as far as 150 km in the rural areas in Asia. The "new" rural–urban dynamics have blurred the traditional rural–urban divide, whereby people, commodities, and capital move ever more freely and imperceptibly than before (T. G. McGee, chap. 17). What is unquestioned is that Asia is still, on the whole, in the early stages of the urban transition. However, in parallel with rapid economic development in this region, a massive rural-to-urban migration is emerging as a mighty trend. Asia's present mega-cities are not simply big; they mirror a telescoped process of urbanization.

Because of the growing number of mega-cities that have mushroomed in developing countries, city governments have to contend with a host of problems, which have attracted scholars and policy makers. Because most of these cities are also hamstrung by limited financial and other resources, issues such as urban poverty, lack of jobs, governance, crime, and the environment have overwhelmed many of their administrators. At least increasing international resources and attention have been focused on them in recent years (Fuchs et al., 1994; Stren and Bell, 1995; Yeung, 1997).

In the present era of globalization, certain mega-cities are at a particularly sensitive stage of transition. Johannesburg, for one, is still in the delicate state of metamorphosis, after South Africa became a new multiracial country in 1994, into a city that can reflect the aspirations of a new nation. As Keith Beavon (chap. 13) has portrayed, the transition is difficult and incomplete. Downtown Johannesburg, despite its well-built infrastructure, is not yet redeveloped as a financial and commercial hub because crime and racial rivalries have driven business elsewhere. If there are one or two cities that have the greatest potential of becoming world cities in Africa, they are Johannesburg and Cairo.

Another strand of sensitivity is involved in dealing with Islamic cities. Muslims account for one-fifth of the world's people, and 7 of the 30 largest cities in the world are located in Muslim countries. Cairo, for example, is a pre-eminent Islamic city with a population of 12 million in 1994. For centuries, it has been the crossroads for trade and commerce in the Arab world and a crucible of civic and religious conflicts. Public policy has to tread a tightrope between tradition and modernity. If globalization influences are to be incorporated into Cairo's daily life, the indigenous values of its people must be fully taken into consideration (Mahmoud Yousry et al., chap. 11).

Salah El-Shakhs and Ellen Shoshkes (chap. 10) further argue that Islamic cities are distinct in a special way: they bear the imprint of modernization, Westernization, and globalization. In addition to Cairo, he chooses Istanbul and Tehran as case-studies and shows how local responses in those cities have been made to global economic restructuring. There is little doubt that globalization has sharpened the basic conflicts between the old and the new, secularism and religion, the West and the East, the haves and the have-nots. One outcome of rising inequities is for the rich to create their own basic services under schemes of privatization. Essentially, the rich and the poor are building their own environment. This may sow the seeds of possible future confrontation.

Although mega-cities have become a global phenomenon and have acquired national importance in the countries in which they are located, there is another class of cities that are critical to the new global economy. These are called world cities or global cities, because they perform certain functions that differentiate them from others and that help drive the global economy. In a recent book, Lo and Yeung (1996) have developed the concept of the functional world city system, which began to grow and network countries in the world through trade and commerce in the thirteenth century. However, it is primarily since the 1980s, when globalization processes gathered momentum in a new international division of labour, that world cities have come to the fore.

One key element of the functional world city system is that new networks and linkages are created in the system and world cities are at the points of convergence of these networks and thus acquire growing centrality and importance. Network functions are engendered through financial flows, headquarter–branch relations, high-tech service intensity, and telecommunications networks. The new wave of technologies since the late 1980s in electronics, robotics, telecommunications, new materials, and biotechnology has given rise to a new technology paradigm that accentuates the role of world cities (Lo, 1994). Innovation and continuous technological change are used to create new growth markets as demand for outdated products declines. The commercialization of many more innovations based on this new techno-economic paradigm awaits the economic incentives to create new mega-demands. According to UN sources, it is estimated that the potential from information technology will increase 10 times more in the 1990s than in recent decades. It should be noted that the Asian NIEs have been investing heavily in high-technology industries in recent years and are beginning to take a growing share of world trade.

World cities are extremely complex but constitute, historically, points of international articulation. Consequently, in the present era of large-scale and rapid exchange of goods, people, and ideas, the importance of ports, airports, and teleports (indeed infrastructure as a whole) cannot be overemphasized. In order to prepare a world city to perform the functions it is supposed to discharge, there is a need for cities to plan, invest, and carry out a process that may be briefly described as world city formation. Many of the world cities in Pacific Asia have spared no effort and expense to do precisely this, so that they are better prepared for the continued rapid economic growth that has been forecast for this region in the twenty-first century (Yue-man Yeung and Fu-chen Lo, chap. 6). Tokyo, for instance, has emerged as a dominant world city since the 1980s. It has been actively reaching out to Asia and beyond through joint ventures and direct foreign investment through scanning of global markets and technologies by its transnational corporations (Masahiko Honjo, chap. 5).

As linkages of cities assume greater importance, there is increasing tension and competition between them within countries and regions. Certainly, in many European cities there is concern about the trade-off between efficiency and equity. Two metaphors are commonly used to depict the relation of cities in Europe. On the one hand they are likened to *grapes*, which captures the essence of multicentrality, but leaves out the sense of spatial polarization or the centre of power. Alternatively, European cities have been compared to a bunch of *bananas*, whereby the sense of centrality is vividly conveyed (Klaus Kunzmann, chap. 3).

One of the effects of globalization on world cities is rapidly growing social and economic polarization. This impact, as alluded to before, is most pronounced in mega-cities in Latin America. Rio de Janeiro is a world city that has suffered through economic recession and a wave of social unrest. However, it still has some specialized financial services with which the city has maintained its comparative advantage. Given that the revenue base of the city is constrained and circumscribed, social infrastructure investment appears to be an avenue by which the urban poor can be materially assisted (Hamilton Tolosa, chap. 9).

The urban future

Cities have always been centres of civilization and vitality that have through the years led to human progress and material and scientific advances. As the twenty-first century is about to dawn, mega-cities and world cities, the focus of this volume, are no different in their nature and character. The processes they are subjected to, however, are different. Whatever the outcomes of these processes, the urban future of humankind will be much influenced by them.

The single most important factor that will bear heavily on the future of mega-cities in developing countries is overall population growth and the related extent of rural–urban migration. This issue should be viewed against the backdrop of the world population being estimated to be more urban than rural in the early years of the twenty-first century and more heavily concentrated in developing countries. The inexorable growth of population in these countries is already difficult to deal with because of their often large population base, but the prospect of sizeable rural–urban migration will create problems of gargantuan proportions. As noted earlier, the urban population share for most countries in Asia and Africa is only 30–40 per cent. Any major shift of population from the rural areas will play havoc in the cities in unimaginable ways.

One potentially critical problem already being faced by some mega-cities is food supply. Hal Kane (chap. 18) has called attention to the continual decline in cropland per capita relative to population growth. Increased production in food grains as a result of improved

11

seeds and fertilizer use has fallen off since 1984. Biotechnology is not likely to provide any agricultural panacea and no scientific break-through comparable to the green revolution of the 1960s is in sight. What is more, with rapidly modernizing and developing countries such as China changing their food habits and losing their arable land, the implications in terms of a dwindling supply of grain to feed their cities are serious and must be confronted. Overall, the world population must be able to stabilize at a certain level such that sustainable development can be achieved. It is expected that the world population will be over 10 billion by the year 2050, allowing modest growth from the 1995 figure of 5.68 billion.

Given their hypermobility in capital, ideas, and people, large cities of the future will perforce be centres of transport, telecommunications, and increasing connectivities. Peter Rimmer (chap. 16) has identified city networks that are connected to freight, telecommunications, and air passengers. By 2010, the 25 largest urban agglomerations will have a population of more than 10 million each and, as such, improved access by transport and telecommunications will be vital. Improved city networks should be a general target and should be premised by three principles: planned inter-city division of labour, strengthening of the comparative advantage of individual cities, and greater co-operation and synergy among cities.

Finally, the sustainability and stability of the urban future depend on, among other things, one key factor that figures very prominently in the present global economy – the financial flows around the world and their effect on the regional, national, and subnational economies. In this respect, the importance of world cities as financial centres merits careful analysis. Indeed, David Meyer (chap. 15) demonstrates the rapid expansion of international finance, reflecting the growth in exports and imports of commodities in the period 1970–1992. Financial intermediaries have grown in tandem and have faced up to competition in different ways. Thus, the keenest competition among financial centres is over acquiring the world regional and branch offices of global intermediaries. All these new developments will be important trends in world city formation for years to come.

References

Chen, Nancy Yu-ping and Larry Heligman (1994), "Growth of the World's Mega-lopolises." In: Roland Fuchs et al. (eds.), *Mega-city Growth and the Future*. Tokyo: United Nations University Press, pp. 17–31.

Fuchs, Roland et al. (eds.) (1994), *Mega-city Growth and the Future*. Tokyo: United Nations University Press.

Gilbert, Alan (ed.) (1996), *The Mega-city in Latin America*. Tokyo: United Nations University.

Ginsburg, Norton, Bruce Koppel, and T. G. McGee (eds.) (1991), *The Extended Metropolis: Settlement Transition in Asia*. Honolulu: University of Hawaii Press.

Li Mengbai and Hu Xin (eds.) (1991), *Impact of the Floating Population on Large Cities and Relevant Strategies*. Beijing: Economic Daily Press (in Chinese).

Lo, Fu-chen (1994), "The Impacts of Current Global Adjustment and Shifting Techno-economic Paradigm on the World City System." In: Roland Fuchs et al. (eds.), *Mega-city Growth and the Future*. Tokyo: United Nations University Press, pp. 103–130.

Lo, Fu-chen and Yue-man Yeung (eds.) (1996), *Emerging World Cities in Pacific Asia*. Tokyo: United Nations University Press.

McGee, T. G. and Ira Robinson (eds.) (1995), *The Mega-Urban Regions of Southeast Asia*. Vancouver: UBC Press.

Ohmae, Kenichi (1990), *The Borderless World: Power and Strategy in the Interlinked Economy*. New York: McKinsey & Co.

Rakodi, Carole (1997), *The Urban Challenge in Africa: Growth and Management of Its Large Cities*. Tokyo: United Nations University Press.

Sassen, Saskia (1991), *The Global City: New York, London, Tokyo*. Princeton, N.J.: Princeton University Press.

Shen, Bingyu and Zhang Suping (eds.) (1985), *Construction and Development of Medium Cities*. Economic Research Centre of China's Rural–Urban Construction (in Chinese).

Stren, Richard and Judith K. Bell (eds.) (1995), *Perspectives on the City*. Toronto: Centre for Urban and Community Studies, University of Toronto.

United Nations, Department of Economic and Social Information and Policy Analysis (1995), *World Population Prospects: The 1994 Revision*. New York: United Nations.

Weber, Adna (1899), *The Growth of Great Cities in the Nineteenth Century*. New York: Macmillan.

Yeung, Yue-man (1996), "An Asian Perspective on the Global City." *International Social Science Journal* 147: 25–31.

―――― (1997), "Geography in the Age of Mega-cities." *International Social Science Journal* 151: 91–104.

13

Part 1
Regional surveys and selected world cities

2

Globalization and the world cities

Peter Hall

World cities are not a new phenomenon. Patrick Geddes recognized them and defined them as long ago as 1915, in a book that has become a classic of the planning literature, *Cities in Evolution* (Geddes, 1915). And some 30 years ago I published a book entitled *The World Cities* (Hall, 1966), defining them in terms of multiple roles: they were centres of political power, both national and international, and of the organizations related to government; centres of national and international trade, acting as entrepôts for their countries and sometimes for neighbouring countries also; hence, centres of banking, insurance, and related financial services; centres of advanced professional activity of all kinds, in medicine, in law, in higher learning, and the application of scientific knowledge to technology; centres of information gathering and diffusion, through publishing and the mass media; centres of conspicuous consumption, both of luxury goods for the minority and of mass-produced goods for the multitude; and centres of arts, culture, and entertainment, and of the ancillary activities that catered for them. And, I argued, these kinds of activities tended to grow in importance; so, in the twentieth century, the world cities went from strength to strength: even as they shed some kinds of activity, from routine manufacturing to routine paper-processing, so they took on new functions and added to existing ones.

This definition, I would argue, still applies 30 years later. But it does need amplification and modification, because of the phenomenon of globalization and its impact on the urban system, coupled with what can be called the informationalization of the economy – the progressive shift of advanced economies from goods production to information handling, whereby the great majority of the workforce no longer deal with material outputs. John Friedmann was the first to suggest this relationship to a global hierarchy, in which London, New York, and Tokyo are "global financial articulations," Miami, Los Angeles, Frankfurt, Amsterdam, and Singapore are "multinational articulations," and Paris, Zurich, Madrid, Mexico City, São Paulo, Seoul, and Sydney are "important national articulations," all forming a "network" (Friedmann, 1986; Friedmann and Wolff, 1982; Smith and Timberlake, 1995: 294). Manuel Castells (1989) has characterized this as the fundamental economic shift of the present era, as momentous as the shift from an agrarian to an industrial economy in the eighteenth and nineteenth centuries. The process was already recognized half a century ago (Clark, 1940); by the 1980s, 30–40 per cent of the workforce in advanced countries were engaged in informational industries. Some argue that these activities still depend on production (Gershuny and Miles, 1983; Cohen and Zysman, 1987); but evidently, as the combined effect of globalization and informationalization, the production of services becomes increasingly disarticulated from production itself. As Saskia Sassen (1991) has put it:

The spatial dispersion of production, including its internationalization, has contributed to the growth of centralized service nodes for the management and regulation of the new space economy ... To a considerable extent, the weight of economic activity over the last fifteen years has shifted from production places such as Detroit and Manchester, to centers of finance and highly specialized services.

Thus, as production disperses worldwide, services increasingly concentrate into a relatively few trading cities, both the well-known "global cities" and a second rung of about 20 cities immediately below these, which we can distinguish as "sub-global." These cities are centres for financial services (banking, insurance) and headquarters of major production companies; most are also seats of the major world-power governments (King, 1990; Sassen, 1991). They attract specialized business services such as commercial law and accountancy, advertising and public relations services, and legal services, themselves increasingly globalized and related to controlling headquarters locations. In turn, this clustering attracts business tourism and real estate functions; business tourism allies with leisure tourism because both are in part drawn to these cities because of their cultural reputations, with effects on the transportation, communication, personal services, and entertainment and cultural sectors. There is intense competition between cities both at a given level in the hierarchy and also between levels in the hierarchy; however, there is also a great deal of historic inertia.

Further, these informational industries locate in order to gain access to their central raw material and information. To understand the significance, we need to understand how the informationalization of the economy has occurred.

Long waves of development and the growth of the information economy

More than 50 years ago, in his book *Business Cycles*, Joseph Schumpeter (1939) borrowed and interpreted the theory of the early Soviet economist Nikolai Kondratieff: that, throughout its history, the capitalist economy had shown a profound and regular tendency to develop in long waves of some 50 years' duration. Specifically, Schumpeter argued that the Kondratieff waves were 57 years long and that shorter cycles, such as the familiar business cycle of 9 years' duration, nested within them. But, of equal importance, he produced evidence that each Kondratieff wave was technology driven: the starting-point was a bunched series of innovations, the "carrying out of new combinations," whether in technology or in industrial organization, that generated new industrial complexes: cotton textiles, coal, iron, and steam in the first Kondratieff (1785–1842), Bessemer steel, railways and steamships, and machine tools in the second (1843–1897), cars, electrical goods, and chemicals in the third (1898–1954). Each of these bunches of innovation would come in a period of recession at the end of a Kondratieff wave, when the industries of the previous wave had in effect saturated the market – as in the subtitle of the book by the German economist Gerhard Mensch (1979), "Innovations overcome the Depression." Mensch, reinterpreting Schumpeter, argued that such innovation peaks could indeed be precisely dated: in 1764, 1825, 1881, and 1935. He claimed that the process was a regular one (though with a complex periodicity, because the waves themselves shortened progressively); thus, the next innovation wave would come in 1987.

Ever since the first appearance of *Business Cycles*, the notion of the Kondratieff waves has excited huge controversy, some observers denying their existence or arguing for alternative cyclical schemes, others reaffirming their validity. An important contribution, from the geographer Brian Berry (1991), argues that they are systematically related to the construction waves first identified by Simon Kuznets as an alternative to the Kondratieff cycles, and that these are related to major transport investments, which in turn shape urban growth generally. This is highly persuasive; it suggests that economists generally have ignored the effects of transportation innovations, though one distinguished economist, Colin Clark (1957, 1967), certainly did not. Certainly, each long wave seems to have been associated with a distinct advance in transportation technology: the first with turnpike roads and mail coaches, the second with the first long-distance railways and steamships, the third with subways, electric commuter railways and tramways, and motor buses and airplanes, and the fourth with cars, expressways, and jet airplanes. And, quite apart from their fundamental role in influencing patterns of world trade and movements of people on business, each of these revolutions – at any rate, from the second Kondratieff onward – just as profoundly helped shape the subsequent growth of cities.

If the relationship of the Kondratieff waves and transport investment had been underplayed before Berry's work, the relationship to information technology seems to have been ignored almost completely. Yet it is evident enough. As revealed in the path-breaking work of the Canadian scholar Harold Innis, and of others who have worked in the same tradition, there were momentous achievements in information technology before capitalism: notably, the discovery of papyrus by the ancient Egyptians, of cuneiform and hieroglyphic scripts by the ancient Babylonians and Assyrians, of the alphabet by the ancient Greeks, of paper by the ancient Chinese, and of printing during the Renaissance (Innis, 1950, 1951; Crowley and Heyer, 1991). But after 1800 the innovations become distinctly cyclical, and each is clearly related to a Kondratieff wave: photography, the electric telegraph, the penny post, and Pitman's shorthand at the start of the second Kondratieff; the typewriter, telephone, phonograph, duplicating machine, linotype, high-speed press, cinematography, and radio at the start of the third; television, the photocopier, tape recording for sound and then pictures, and the computer at the start of the fourth; and, very evidently coming out of Mensch's innovation peak of the 1980s, networked computers, multimedia, and convergent informa-

20

tion technology without doubt being the basis of the fifth Kondratieff long wave, which can be expected to begin its upward phase some-time around the end of the first decade of the twenty-first century.

A significant feature can of course be noticed: with each successive Kondratieff, the information content of the innovation wave becomes more and more pronounced. In the first Kondratieff, it was negligible: the only contribution was indirect, through transport technology in the form of the turnpike roads and the fast mail coach, which significantly speeded the exchange of letters. In the second, as well as transport technology in the form of the railway and the steamship, came the significant innovation of the electric telegraph, for the first time (experiments in semaphore and similar telegraphy apart) effectively separating the message from the human carrier. The third Kondratieff saw one of the greatest bursts of information technology innovation; yet oddly, since electrical generation and transmission were also an outcome of this innovation wave, most of the innovations were not electrical but mechanical in character. The real marriage of electricity and information through electronics had to await the fourth Kondratieff just after World War II, though of course the innovations themselves were made before and during the war. And in this wave, though there were also significant developments in transport technology (for instance, the jet engine), the fundamental innovations were informational. Information for the first time drove the economy, both through innovations in production technology (the computer, the copying machine) and also through developments in consumer technology (the transistor radio, the television, audio and video recording). The fifth wave will undoubtedly see the effective convergence of these technologies into one, which will have the interesting characteristic of being simultaneously a producer and a consumer technology in a way that no previous technology has been.

The historical background is important, because – though the informational economy is still everywhere dominant – information is still communicated in two different ways: by direct face-to-face communication or by electronic transfer. Face-to-face communication, as long ago recognized, encourages agglomeration in the global cities, because of their historically strong concentrations of information-gathering and information-exchanging activities and their position as nodes for national and international movement, especially by air and now also high-speed train (Hall, 1991, 1992a, 1992b, 1993). And this is fortified by the remarkable recent growth of the arts, culture, and entertainment sector, where, for instance, employment grew by 20

21

per cent in London during the 1980s (Kennedy, 1991), with further indirect impacts on associated personal services including hotels, restaurants, and bars. This group, too, clusters within the urban core and is subject to considerable locational inertia; but this can be modified by revitalization projects such as London's South Bank and Barbican, or the *Grands Projets* in Paris.

However, it was never feasible to operate an informational economy simply on the basis of dense agglomeration. Even at the end of the Middle Ages, Florentine bankers were engaged in dense networks of activity between the major cities of Europe and into the Far East. And, as global activity increased under capitalism, so transport networks multiplied in the form of railway systems and steamship lines. During the nineteenth century, the growth of global cities such as London, New York, and Tokyo was supported by their position as centres of national rail networks and of international steamship lines (though the latter might operate through subsidiary ports connected by railways, such as Liverpool and then Southampton for London, Le Havre for Paris, Hamburg for Berlin, or Yokohama for Tokyo). Then, to some extent in the inter-war period but overwhelmingly after it, air travel supplanted trains and ships for all intercontinental business travel and a substantial proportion of local inter-city travel over a certain threshold (typically about 300 km). Since this revolution, which was more or less complete by the end of the 1950s, the technology of air travel has remained remarkably stable, though increases in size and range of aircraft have had a significant impact in eliminating the need for intermediate stops on long-haul flights, with some notable urban impacts – particularly over the Pacific, the world's largest ocean (O'Connor, 1995). Recent studies of the interconnectivity of cities by air suggest that London is top, followed by Paris, New York, and Tokyo (Smith and Timberlake, 1995: 298; Cattan, 1995: 304–308).

The really new element, constituting a further transport revolution of profound significance, has been the arrival of the high-speed train, first in Japan in 1964 (and thus a fourth Kondratieff technology), then in Europe in the 1970s and 1980s. Experience shows that it competes effectively with air transportation in the range up to about 700 km, and may supplant it for much shorter-distance traffic between major urban centres, particularly if these centres are disposed in axial or corridor fashion (as is the case, for instance, on the Tokaido corridor in Japan between Tokyo and Osaka, or in Europe between Paris,

Lyon, and Marseilles, or between Hamburg, Hanover, Frankfurt, Stuttgart, and Munich, or more recently between London, Paris, and Brussels). The significance of the trains is not merely that they compete effectively, but that they are likely to alter the delicate geographical balance within metropolitan areas: with the exception of some services deliberately designed to interconnect with longer-distance air routes (as for instance through Paris Charles de Gaulle), they essentially connect traditional central business districts, and thus powerfully help to correct any tendency on the part of business to migrate from these centres to suburban locations close to the airports – a trend long observed in the United States but now becoming evident in Europe too, in developments around London Heathrow, Paris Charles de Gaulle, Amsterdam Schiphol, or Stockholm Arlanda.

Electronic communication, it is often argued, works in the opposite direction, as an agent of dispersal: as telecommunications costs drop dramatically, informational activities should be free to locate away from the old central locations. Not only can they migrate to lower-cost back offices in the outer suburbs – a tendency observable worldwide in such concentrations as Greenwich (Connecticut) and the New Jersey "Zip Strip," or Reading west of London, or the Paris New Towns, or Omiya and Kawasaki outside Tokyo; they may also migrate to quite distant provincial cities offering even greater savings in rents and salaries, such as the new financial centres of Bristol or Leeds in England, or such locations as Salt Lake City or Omaha (Nebraska) in the United States. Eventually, there is always the prospect that some such activities can be transferred to even lower-cost offshore locations, as has happened with so much manufacturing. But there are limits: telecommunications are not costless, and (unlike the traditional arrangements with mail) the costs are not uniform regardless of distance; world cities create their own demand for state-of-the-art telecommunications services (such as all-digital systems); linguistic and cultural boundaries, especially in Europe, create powerful barriers to the transfer of any activity based on direct voice communication, whether direct telephone sale of insurance or international television transmission. Even in Europe, studies show that the diffusion of advanced information technology is far more rapid in the largest metropolitan regions than elsewhere (Goddard and Gillespie, 1987; Batty, 1988). And so, as the informational economy grows, the largest global cities retain their key role.

The urban consequences: A global urban hierarchy?

The urban consequences can be treated at two separate though related levels: first, the national and international urban system, and the competition among cities at different levels of this system; second, the internal impacts on activity and land-use patterns within each metropolitan area.

It is now a familiar point that cities increasingly tend to compete and to market themselves as attractive locations for inward investment. However, in this they are obviously constrained by a sense of realism as to possibilities. It is useful conceptually to distinguish three levels of city: international or global; a category that we can term sub-global, especially prevalent in Europe; and regional.

The global cities have already been defined and need not detain us: they are cities whose business consists mainly in the production of specialized informational services, such as financial services, media services, educational and health services, and tourism including business tourism; but, following the central place schema laid down by Walter Christaller in the 1930s, they also perform lower-order functions for more restricted areas, notably at the national level. They lost certain functions during the 1970s and 1980s, either to their own peripheries or to overseas; consequently, they have exhibited the paradox of substantial job losses in traditional sectors such as manufacturing, goods-handling, and routine services, and large gains in others such as financial services and specialized business services. A major question in the 1990s is whether they are now exhibiting equally large losses of these latter functions also; certainly there have been substantial reductions in employment in both London and New York, in both cases accompanied by out-movements to other locations.

The most interesting question concerns the relationship between the global cities and the next level in the hierarchy, above all in Europe. Here, the only indisputably global cities are London and, perhaps, Paris; below this level is a rich array of national capital cities – Amsterdam, Brussels, Copenhagen, Stockholm, Oslo, Bonn/Berlin, Vienna, Prague, Budapest, Warsaw, Rome, Madrid, Lisbon, Dublin – as well as a number of rather special commercial cities that effectively perform as commercial or cultural capitals, such as Barcelona, Milan, Zurich, Geneva, and Frankfurt. These try to compete with the global cities, to some real effect in specialized sectors, such as Brussels, Rome, and Geneva for government, Frankfurt and Zurich for banking, or Milan for design. Similar functions are performed by a very few American cities in relation to New York: Washington for government, Chicago and San Francisco for financial services, Los Angeles for culture and entertainment. In Japan, Osaka performs a similar role in relation to Tokyo, especially as a trade centre. Here, however, because of the long political and economic union and homogenization of the country concerned, the regional cities perform a smaller role than their European equivalents. A major question for Europe, therefore, is whether the Single Market and the impacts of the Maastricht treaty will progressively assist the higher-order cities at the expense of the lower national-order ones. Related to this is the question whether cities with a distinct function within the European Union – Brussels, Luxembourg, and Frankfurt – will increasingly assert their role at the expense of London and, to some extent, Paris. This is an open question; but it should be noticed that the Euro-cities form a tight inner circle surrounded by a wider group of national capitals – London, Paris, and Amsterdam – all within convenient radius for face-to-face contact by air and, increasingly, by high-speed train (which, on present plans, should connect all of them by approximately 2010). So it seems certain that they will constitute an effective central core of the European urban system, connected by air services to a number of key regional cities that form an outer ring some 500–700 km distant: Copenhagen, Berlin, Vienna, Zurich, Milan, Madrid, Dublin, Edinburgh.

Rather confusingly, with a typical population range of 500,000 to 4 million, the national capitals and commercial capitals overlap in size with the major provincial capitals of the larger European nation-states (Manchester and Birmingham, Lyon and Marseilles, Hanover and Stuttgart, Florence and Naples, Seville and Valencia). These typically serve as administrative and higher-level service centres for prosperous mixed urban–rural regions, and have shown considerable dynamism even while they too have lost traditional manufacturing and goods-handling functions. Similar functions, of course, are performed by major American regional capital cities such as Boston, Atlanta, Dallas-Fort Worth, Minneapolis, Denver, and Seattle, as well as their Japanese equivalents such as Nagoya, Sendai, and Kumamoto. These cities do not as a rule compete in any substantial respect, either nationally or still less internationally, with the higher-order cities, though they may occasionally occupy special market niches, such as Boston for financial services or Atlanta for media services. The important but subtle distinction is whether a city offers any significant presence or significant challenge at the global level; in this respect Brussels, Frankfurt, and Milan, Chicago and Los Angeles, and Osaka can be said to act as global contenders in specially defined spheres, though not of course across the board, and so can best be defined as sub-global; Manchester, Munich, and Copenhagen, Minneapolis and Denver, Sendai and Kumamoto, to take examples more or less at random, cannot.

Three special urban categories

Three questions are raised by this categorization. The first concerns regional cities that occupy a remote position at the periphery either of their national territories or of wider transnational groupings such as the European Union. Many of these tend to have been manufacturing cities dominated by industries that have exhibited serious long-term structural decline, such as Belfast and Glasgow, Saarbrücken or Lille or Cadiz, Duluth or Buffalo, Sapporo or Nagoya. They may suffer from the phenomenon identified by Cheshire and Hay (1989) as "peripheralization of the periphery": as transport and communications in effect shrink distances between more centrally located cities, these places may be perceived as becoming less accessible even when in an absolute sense they are not. Such cities have tended vigorously to compete by developing new roles, either in advanced manufacturing (a major thrust of the Japanese technopolis programme) or by developing a new cultural role (Glasgow in the 1990s).

A special sub-variant of this group consists of the capital cities of Eastern Europe, whose remoteness has been an artificial result of the Iron Curtain and the barriers thus created to movements of goods and, above all, people. Noticeably, despite recent improvements, these cities are still less well connected either to each other or to the cities of Western Europe than these latter cities are to each other. Nevertheless, they offer large potential advantages in having well-educated and technically well-trained workforces with much lower wages than in the European Union; so they should be able to engineer a rapid growth similar to that of some of their southern European equivalents during the 1970s and 1980s. Further, since the service sector has been relatively weak in these countries, we should expect rapid expansion of retailing and white-collar office work, which will precipitate a commercial construction boom in the hearts of these cities and, by analogy with Western cities, residential construction on the periphery. A precondition, however, will be improvement of their external connections through expansion of their air, road, and high-speed rail infrastructure.

A third distinct category comprises the cities of the Asia Pacific group, including Australasia. Since this is the single most dynamic area of the world, it is experiencing explosive urban growth concentrated especially in a number of sub-global cities, some of which – Sydney, Singapore, Hong Kong, and perhaps Shanghai – are actively competing for sub-global status while others – Bangkok, Djakarta, Guangzhou – operate effectively as major national or regional capitals. Such is the growth record and expectation of this region that the urban system is exceptionally unstable and unpredictable.

The pattern of intrametropolitan deconcentration

In the past 40 years, deconcentration, first of residences and latterly also of employment, has become a universal phenomenon in the world's metropolitan areas. Once unique to the Anglo-American–Australian group of cities, it has now become characteristic of the whole of Western Europe and of Japan. And in the largest of these areas, the global cities, it has become extremely complex, extending over very wide areas of territory in a dynamic process that results in a highly polycentric metropolitan system.

Broadly, one can say that down to about 1950 even the world's major cities had a much simpler pattern of living and working: there was a mass of white-collar employment in the centre, a wide (and increasing) ring of commuter suburbs outside, interspersed by industrial, port, and warehouse areas with their own much more localized residential areas immediately next to them; the entire complex was dependent primarily on public transport, plus walking and cycling for the most local journeys. Then, already in American cities before World War II but in European cities only on any scale from the 1960s, further residential suburbanization occurred outside the limits of effective public transport systems, and therefore was dependent on the private car. At the same time, employment began to decentralize: first, routine assembly manufacturing in search of spacious premises close to highway systems; second, R&D and associated small-batch high-technology production, which moved to high-amenity locations, often close to airports for international access; and third, back offices performing routine processing applications for national headquarters firms, which moved to local suburban centres with ample local supplies of clerical labour; all accompanied, of course, by local service employment in shops, schools, and other public and private services, dispersed across the region. And finally, in the late 1980s and 1990s, there was evidence from some American cities – New York, San Francisco – of a more general exodus of even headquarters offices to suburban locations, apparently impelled in some cases by high local taxes.

The result in extreme cases, represented by London, New York, and Los Angeles, is a pattern of extremely long-distance deconcentration stretching up to 150 km from the centre, with local concentrations of employment surrounded by overlapping commuter fields and served mainly by the private car. The precise spatial details vary from country to country according to culture and planning regime: in the United States, lower-density and less regulated, with "Edge Cities" or "New Downtowns" on greenfield sites exclusively accessed by the private car; in Europe, medium-density, regulated through green belts and other constraints, and centred on medium-sized country market towns or planned new towns. And the process has gone much further in some large metropolitan areas (for instance, London) than in others (for instance, Paris, where suburbanization has almost entirely been captured in the large new cities resulting from the 1965 regional master plan). However, the general outward trend, for both population and employment, is universal. An interesting consequence has been accelerated growth in and around smaller country towns in the wider metropolitan orbit, especially those adjacent to major national highway and/or railway lines (that is, in the "transport-rich, city-rich" sectors in the Lösch central place model). Thus, in some cases there is a distinct tendency to linear corridor growth, as in the so-called "M4 Corridor" west of London or the E4 "Arlanda Airport Corridor" north of Stockholm, both based on a combination of high-technology industry and back-office functions. Some regional plans, including the Stockholm plan of 1966 and the Paris plan a year earlier, made a deliberate attempt to guide development into such corridors; but the same phenomenon has occurred spontaneously in other cases, such as the I-405 "Aerospace Alley" in Los Angeles and Orange county, or the "Dulles Airport Corridor" in the Virginia suburbs of Washington D.C. And some observers purport to see the development of even more extensive growth corridors connecting cities along highways and high-speed train lines, such as the "Dorsale" or "Blue Banana" of Western Europe connecting London, Brussels, Frankfurt, Zurich, and Milan (Hall et al., 1973; Brunet et al., 1989). East of London, the UK government's Thames Gateway proposal is a discontinuous series of urban developments following the planned new high-speed line from London to the Channel Tunnel – the first attempt to create such a corridor on a conscious basis (GB Thames Gateway Task Force, 1994).

A vigorous debate has raged in academic print concerning the consequences of deconcentration for commuter travel and thus for sustainable urbanization. One school, represented by Peter Newman and Jeffrey Kenworthy in Australia (Newman and Kenworthy, 1989a, 1989b, 1992), has argued that low-density suburban deconcentration leads to substantially higher energy consumption; this has been supported in international work by Robert Cervero (1985, 1989, 1995). An opposite viewpoint comes from Peter Gordon and Harry Richardson, who argue that the entire process self-equilibrates: as jobs move out behind the homes, so local employment nodes and even a completely decentralized employment develop, leading to commute distances no longer than before (Gordon, Kumar, and Richardson, 1988, 1989a, 1989b, 1989c; Gordon and Richardson, 1989, 1995; Gordon, Richardson, and Jun, 1991). Brotchie and his colleagues in Australia report similar results for Australian cities (Brotchie, Anderson, and McNamara, 1995). In part, the difference seems to arise because the two sets of authors are analysing different facets: it seems likely that density is related to energy consumption, though not in any simple or direct way; but that decentralization of jobs does reduce aggregate travel compared with a pattern of central jobs and dispersed homes. And this is intuitively plausible, of course. It is interesting that in a careful analysis Breheny (1995) concludes that Great Britain moved marginally away from a pattern of sustainable urban development between 1961 and 1991, but that the effect was not very substantial.

World cities and the developing world

Historically, the major cities of the middle-income world have played a disproportionately large role in their countries' development, either because these countries were small (in extreme cases, such as Singapore or Hong Kong, city-states), or because they were the principal ports and industrial cities, or both. Starting in almost every case as colonial cities, they channelled the supply of raw materials to the metropolitan country and the reverse supply of manufactured goods from that country. After independence, they developed their own industrial base. They invariably became the capital cities of their new countries, and the system of nation-states that then arose has proved remarkably resilient, in most parts of the world, since independence was obtained (in the early nineteenth century in the case of the Spanish empire, in the mid-twentieth century in the case of the British, French, and Dutch empires). Around the government and commercial functions developed the usual apparatus of finance, business services, the media, education, and health services. Thus, almost inevitably, a pattern of uneven development occurred: modernizing influences concentrated in the primate city, labour and capital were attracted to it both from outside and from the national periphery, and the national élite became heavily concentrated in this city. The city remained the chief point of articulation between the emerging nation and the world, and critical infrastructure, in the form of telecommunications or airport investment, was laid down here. This indeed was the conclusion that John Friedmann (1973) reached in his now classic study of the urban development process.

As Friedmann recognized, the pattern of development reflects the nature of the urban economies and the relationships between these cities and the remainder of the world. Whether they are city-state entrepôts like Singapore and Hong Kong, or the leading cities of continental-scale countries like Rio or Mexico City, they are central points for the exchange of information. They possess sophisticated banking systems and usually stock exchanges, some of which are of sub-global rank. They are the seats of national or continental headquarters offices of major transnational corporations. They have major hub airports, connecting national and international networks and sometimes performing important international exchange functions. A recent study of the interconnectivity of cities based on air travel, for instance, placed Hong Kong in fifth position, Singapore seventh, Mexico City eleventh, Seoul seventeenth, and São Paulo twenty-second (Smith and Timberlake, 1995: 298). This evidence, though so far fragmentary, strongly suggests that a small number of these middle-income cities perform a sub-global or even global role in relation to other parts of the world system of cities. Further, because of the rapid economic growth of those parts of the world in which these cities are located, over the next decade we should expect them to improve their positions in the league table while others join them: Bangkok, Kuala Lumpur, Djakarta, Saigon, and Shanghai are the most obvious candidates.

Many urban experts, especially those coming from a Marxist

standpoint, have been openly critical of this pattern with its heavy dependence on transnational capital. And a major theme in the literature, especially in Friedmann's World City hypothesis, was that such cities became increasingly disarticulated from their own national peripheries, resulting in hyper-urbanization and increasing internal income disparities. Others have questioned these conclusions, finding little systematic bias in inward investment towards the primate mega-cities; certainly, this is an unresolved issue in the literature, and transnational investment is only one element among many in their growth (Lin, 1994: 10–12).

Since 1950, propelled by high rates of natural increase and internal migration, many cities in this group have grown to be numbered among the world's largest. Whereas 9 of the world's 19 mega-cities were in developing countries in 1960, the projection for 2000 is that 50 out of 66 will be (Setchell, 1995: 2, UNDP, 1991: 12–15). In general, differentially high infrastructure investment in public services has allowed them to keep pace, but the performance has been very variable in key areas such as housing, utilities, and urban transport. Further, the size and complexity of these agglomerations – several of which exceed 10 million in population – have required extremely sophisticated urban management, which has not always been available. Specifically, whereas some middle-income cities have developed enviably efficient management systems, underpinned by generous urban investment, in others the performance has lagged well behind the needs of the population. Michael Cohen has identified this as one of the key problems for urban policy in the 1990s: he contrasts Abidjan with Lagos, Singapore, and Cairo (Cohen, 1990: 52–53). In Ibadan, Nigeria, water supply investments were made to produce 108 million litres of water a day, but poor maintenance cut this to 36 million litres (Cohen, 1990: 54). So "urban management" had developed as a new priority for the World Bank. It is significant that some of the most successful cases of urban management were also the ones that achieved the highest rates of sustained growth of per capita income; growth both underpinned the investment effort, and was in turn assisted by it. As a result, starting as low-income cities only 40 years ago, a select few Asian city-states have now entered the ranks of the advanced world. However, detailed per capita income data will show this to be equally true for other large cities in the more advanced middle-income countries such as Mexico City, Rio de Janeiro, São Paulo, or Caracas. The striking feature about these countries is the contrast between the modernity and affluence (albeit with extremely unequal income distribution) of the primate city, often fully comparable with cities of the developed world, and the rural periphery. In effect, these cities belong to the developed world; the rural areas around them do not.

Bangkok is a representative case. Its Metropolitan Region, with 9 million people, is the fifteenth mega-city in the world; it is the hub of one of the world's fastest-growing national economies, which grew by an average of 11.2 per cent during 1987–1990; it accounts for over 50 per cent of national GDP and nearly 80 per cent of output. GDP in the Metropolitan Region in 1990 was approximately US$4,290, equivalent to South Korea in 1986; in the rest of the country it was less than US$820, equivalent to Papua New Guinea. But, because growth has been in effect unplanned, there are huge and growing problems of environmental degradation and traffic congestion: at 8.1 km per hour, the traffic problem is probably the worst of any city in the world (Setchell, 1995: 2–3, 5, 7).

Equally, the mega-cities of the middle-income world tend to be internally segregated into rich and poor sections, ironically reflecting and reinforcing patterns first laid down by colonial governments before independence, but now corresponding to a division between the modern and informal sectors of the economy (Balbo, 1993: 27–31). Jakarta is a classic case, where luxury new developments constitute a Western-style suburbia in effect shut off from the *kampungs* all around (Leaf, 1994: 343–348).

The sustainability of the developing mega-cities

The central question remains the one that urbanists first posed over 20 years ago: does the growth of these great primate cities represent a positive development or a huge problem? The answer seems to be: some of both. It is true that the planning and management systems are daunting. But, just as in the cities of the developed world already considered in this paper, it appears likely that continued growth is accompanied by deconcentration of both homes and jobs, so the process may be self-equilibrating – when a city reaches 15 or 20 million people, major sub-centres develop, forming the basis for local short-distance commuter fields. And this is even more important for these cities than for their equivalents in the developed world, because these sub-centres may provide jobs and services for the less affluent, therefore car-less, section of the population.

The pursuit of sustainable urban development is governed by the same principles in every large metropolitan area: jobs should be decentralized from the central business district and brought closer to homes, though not necessarily next door to them; provision should be made for local jobs to be reached on foot or by bicycle, through specially protected route systems; jobs should be clustered in sub-centres around public transport interchanges where buses connect with other buses and also (where such systems exist) rail networks; public transport networks should be structured so as to provide a seamless web of services, both traditional radial ones and also orbital or circumferential ones connecting one suburb with another. The principles are similar in New York and Los Angeles, London and Paris, Djakarta and Bangkok, Mexico City and São Paulo. However, they need to be applied sensitively to take account of local geographies and cultural traditions. Tightly structured cities based on generous public housing, such as Hong Kong and Singapore, offer better potentials for investment in high-density rail corridors than do loosely structured shantytown cities such as Bogotá or Caracas. Experience in affluent, sprawling low-density western American cities such as Phoenix or Houston, which have pioneered high-occupancy vehicle lanes or para-transit systems or bus hubs, may be more relevant for their Latin American equivalents. It might be more virtuous to propose higher-density redevelopment; but, if such a proposal has little prospect of implementation, then it is better to adapt the means of transportation to the urban structure that exists.

References

Balbo, M. (1993), "Urban Planning and the Fragmented City of Developing Countries." *Third World Planning Review* 15: 23–35.

Batty, M. (1988), "Home Computers and Regional Development: An Exploratory Analysis of the Spatial Market for Home Computers in Britain." In: M. Giaoutzi and P. Nijkamp (eds.), *Informatics and Regional Development*. Aldershot: Avebury, pp. 147–165.

Berry, B. J. L. (1991), *Long-Wave Rhythms in Economic Development and Political Behavior*. Baltimore, Md.: Johns Hopkins University Press.

Breheny, M. (1995), "Counter-Urbanisation and Sustainable Urban Forms." In: J. F. Brotchie, M. Batty, E. Blakely, P. Hall, and P. Newton (eds.), *Cities in Competition: Productive and Sustainable Cities for the 21st Century*. Melbourne: Longman Australia, pp. 402–429.

Brotchie, J. F., M. Anderson, and C. McNamara (1995), "Changing Metropolitan Commuting Patterns." In: J. F. Brotchie, M. Batty, E. Blakely, P. Hall, and P. Newton (eds.), *Cities in Competition: Productive and Sustainable Cities for the 21st Century*. Melbourne: Longman Australia, pp. 382–401.

Brunet, R. et al. (1989), *Les Villes "Européenes": Rapport pour la DATAR*. Paris: La Documentation Française.

Castells, M. (1989), *The Informational City: Information Technology, Economic Restructuring and the Urban-Regional Process*. Oxford: Basil Blackwell.

Cattan, N. (1995), "Attractivity and Internationalisation of Major European Cities: The Example of Air Traffic." *Urban Studies* 32: 303–312.

Cervero, R. (1985), *Suburban Gridlock*. New Brunswick, N.J.: Rutgers University, Center for Urban Policy Studies.

────── (1989), *America's Suburban Centers: The Land Use–Transportation Link*. Boston: Unwin Hyman.

────── (1995), "Changing Live-Work Relationships: Implications for Metropolitan Structure and Mobility." In: J. F. Brotchie, M. Batty, E. Blakely, P. Hall, and P. Newton (eds.), *Cities in Competition: Productive and Sustainable Cities for the 21st Century*. Melbourne: Longman Australia, pp. 330–347.

Cheshire, P. C. and D. G. Hay (1989), *Urban Problems in Western Europe: An Economic Analysis*. London: Unwin Hyman.

Clark, C. (1940), *The Conditions of Economic Progess*. London: Macmillan.

────── (1957), "Transport: Maker and Breaker of Cities." *Town Planning Review* 28: 237–250.

────── (1967), *Population Growth and Land Use*. London: Macmillan.

Cohen, M. (1990), "Macroeconomic Adjustment and the City." *Cities* 7: 49–59.

Cohen, S. and J. Zysman (1987), *Manufacturing Matters: The Myth of the Post-Industrial Economy*. New York: Basic Books.

Crowley, D. and P. Heyer (eds.) (1991), *Communication in History: Technology, Culture, Society*. New York: Longman.

Friedman, J. (1973), *Urbanization, Planning and National Development*. London: Sage.

────── (1986), "The World City Hypothesis." *Development and Change* 4: 12–50.

Friedmann, J. and G. Wolff (1982), "World City Formation: An Agenda for Research and Action." *International Journal of Urban and Regional Research* 6: 309–344.

GB Thames Gateway Task Force (1994), *Thames Gateway Planning Framework: Consultation Draft*. London: Department of the Environment.

Geddes, P. (1915), *Cities in Evolution*. London: Williams & Norgate.

Gershuny, J. and I. Miles (1983), *The New Service Economy: The Transformation of Employment in Industrial Societies*. London: Frances Pinter.

Goddard, J. B. and A. E. Gillespie (1987), "Advanced Telecommunications and Regional Economic Development." In: B. Robson (ed.), *Managing the City: The Aims and Impacts of Urban Policy*. London: Croom Helm, pp. 84–109.

Gordon, P. and H. W. Richardson (1989), "Gasoline Consumption and Cities – A Reply." *Journal of the American Planning Association* 55: 342–346.

────── (1995), "Sustainable Congestion." In: J. F. Brotchie, M. Batty, E. Blakely, P. Hall, and P. Newton (eds.), *Cities in Competition: Productive and Sustainable Cities for the 21st Century*. Melbourne: Longman Australia, pp. 348–358.

Gordon, P., A. Kumar, and H. W. Richardson (1988), "Beyond the Journey to Work." *Transportation Research* 22A: 419–426.

────── (1989a), "Congestion, Changing Metropolitan Structure, and City Size in the United States." *International Regional Science Review* 12: 45–56.

——— (1989b), "The Influence of Metropolitan Spatial Structure on Commuting Time." *Journal of Urban Economics* 26: 138–151.

——— (1989c), "The Spatial Mismatch Hypothesis – Some New Evidence." *Urban Studies* 26: 315–326.

Gordon, P., H. W. Richardson, and M. Jun (1991), "The Commuting Paradox – Evidence from the Top Twenty." *Journal of the American Planning Association* 57: 416–420.

Hall, P. (1966), *The World Cities*. London: Weidenfeld & Nicolson; 3rd edn, 1984.

——— (1991), "Moving Information: A Tale of Four Technologies." In: J. Brotchie, M. Batty, P. Hall, and P. Newton (eds.), *Cities of the 21st Century: New Technologies and Spatial Systems*. Melbourne: Longman Cheshire, pp. 1–21.

——— (1992a), "Britain's Cities in Europe." *Town and Country Planning* 61: 7–13.

——— (1992b), "Cities in the Informational Economy." *Urban Futures: Issues for Australia's Cities* 5: 1–12.

——— (1993), "Cities and Regions in a Global Economy." In: P. Hall, R. de Guzman, C. M. Madduma Bandara, and A. Kato (eds.), *Multilateral Cooperation for Development in the Twenty-First Century: Training and Research for Regional Development*. Nagoya: United Nations Centre for Regional Development, pp. 6–26.

Hall, P., R. Thomas, H. Gracey, and R. Drewett (1973), *The Containment of Urban England*, 2 vols. London: Allen & Unwin.

Innis, H. A. (1950), *Empire and Communication*. Oxford: Oxford University Press.

——— (1951), *The Bias of Communication*. Toronto: University of Toronto Press.

Kennedy, Richard (1991), *London: World City Moving into the 21st Century. A Research Project*. London Planning Advisory Committee et al. London: H.M.S.O.

King, A. (1990), *Global Cities: Post-Imperialism and the Internationalization of London*. London: Routledge.

Leaf, M. (1994), "The Suburbanisation of Jakarta: A Concurrence of Economics and Ideology." *Third World Planning Review* 16: 341–356.

Lin, G. S.-S. (1994), "Changing Theoretical Perspectives on Urbanisation in Asian Developing Countries." *Third World Planning Review* 16: 1–23.

Mensch, G. (1979), *Stalemate in Technology: Innovations Overcome the Depression*. Cambridge, Mass.: Ballinger.

Newman, P. W. G. and J. R. Kenworthy (1989a), *Cities and Automobile Dependence: A Sourcebook*. Aldershot and Brookfield, Vt.: Gower.

——— (1989b), "Gasoline Consumption and Cities: A Comparison of U.S. Cities with a Global Survey." *Journal of the American Planning Association* 55: 24–37.

——— (1992), "Is There a Role for Physical Planners?" *Journal of the American Planning Association* 58: 353–362.

O'Connor, K. (1995), "Change in the Pattern of Airline Services and City Development." In: J. F. Brotchie, M. Batty, E. Blakely, P. Hall, and P. Newton (eds.), *Cities in Competition: Productive and Sustainable Cities for the 21st Century*. Melbourne: Longman Australia, pp. 88–107.

Sassen, S. (1991), *The Global City: New York, London, Tokyo*. Princeton, N.J.: Princeton University Press.

Schumpeter, J. A. (1939), *Business Cycles*. New York: McGraw Hill; reprinted 1982, Philadelphia: Porcupine Press.

Setchell, C. A. (1995), "The Growing Environmental Crisis in the World's Mega Cities: The Case of Bangkok." *Third World Planning Review* 17: 1–18.

Smith, D. A. and M. Timberlake (1995), "Conceptualising and Mapping the Structure of the World's City System." *Urban Studies* 32: 287–302.

UNDP (United Nations Development Programme) (1991), *Cities, People and Poverty: Urban Development Cooperation for the 1990s*. New York: UNDP.

3

World city regions in Europe: Structural change and future challenges

Klaus R. Kunzmann

Background and scope

In recent years world cities (synonymously called global cities) and globalization have become key concepts of social scientists and economic geographers observing, experiencing, and describing the profound changes that new communication technologies have been causing for worldwide economic and spatial development (Friedmann, 1986; King, 1990). Planners and policy advisers soon followed the academic interest and explored ways and means of promoting cities and city regions to world cities (e.g. London), followed in turn by social scientists analysing and criticizing the negative local and regional impacts of such globalization (Sassen, 1991, 1994; Marcuse, 1994).

After two decades of hope that decentralization and rural development policies could bring about more spatial equity and narrow economic, social, and spatial disparities in countries and regions, cities, and particularly large cities, are back on the global research and policy agendas. Large cities are again being considered as command centres and key engines for economic growth and development, despite rhetorical concerns about the endangered sustainability of the planet earth. Worldwide competition and economies of scale are again being

Table 3.1 **The world's 10 largest cities in the sixteenth, seventeenth, and twentieth centuries**

1500–	1700–	Around 1900	Mid-1980s
Paris	London	London	Tokyo
Naples	Paris	New York	New York
Venice	Lisbon	Paris	Mexico City
Lyon	Amsterdam	Berlin	Osaka
Granada	Rome	Chicago	São Paulo
Seville	Madrid	Philadelphia	Seoul
Milan	Naples	Tokyo	London
Lisbon	Venice	Vienna	Calcutta
London	Milan	St. Petersburg	Buenos Aires
Antwerp	Palermo	Manchester	Los Angeles

Source: Chase-Dunn, quoted in King (1990).

used to justify the concentration of tertiary and quaternary institutions, headquarters, or services, the promotion of sports and cultural events, and the development of large flagship projects at a few urban nodes. The negative social and spatial repercussions of such priorities remain a concern of a few academics, critical media, environmental international non-governmental organizations, and local and regional grass-roots action groups.

Whereas, five centuries ago, Europe used to be the unchallenged continent of world cities (King, 1990; Brunet, 1989), most large cities in the world are now in other world regions, in Asia, America, and Africa. Only Paris and London have remained as symbols of cities dominating the global economy (King, 1990). However, the ranking of the largest world city regions at different periods in the past five centuries shows significant shifts within the world city region system: between 1500 and 1700 the 10 largest cities were all in Europe; only London remains on such a list for the late twentieth century (table 3.1).

Europe, however, is different. The continent is characterized by a dense network of medium and large cities, based on strong national and regional economies and closely linked by efficient transeuropean transportation and communication networks (Kunzmann and Wegener, 1992). Partly drawing on potentials built up over centuries, all these cities have their function in the European urban system. At the most accessible nodes of this dense European urban network a few large city regions have evolved to challenge Greater London and

Greater Paris (Ile-de-France): the Greater Frankfurt region (Rhine–Main), the Rhine–Ruhr conurbation (with Bonn, Cologne, Düsseldorf, and the Ruhr), and the Randstad, comprising Amsterdam, The Hague, and Rotterdam.

Although the two obvious world cities in Europe, London and Paris, are said to compete with world cities in Asia and America, the three European polycentric world city regions are their most powerful economic contenders in various ways. When dealing with world cities from a European perspective, three dominant questions emerge:

- How have world cities in Europe changed their spatial configuration through new waves of technology and structural changes in the global economy, and what are the implications of such changes for the civil societies living there?
- How will European world cities contribute to the urban future of other European cities?
- How are European world cities linked to the world city system?

The chapter will explore these questions. However, it will also illustrate that these world city regions are now trapped between global competition and sustainability, between improving their worldwide competitiveness and the urge for more sustainability. It will demonstrate that the day-to-day policies of the key actors in these city regions are constantly required to compromise between improving their global accessibility and protecting the local environment, between improving metropolitan efficiency and meeting the democratic quest for more local participation, and to choose whether they should invest in flagship projects and international events or rather target growing social disparities. It is in the end a difficult choice between speeding up or slowing down. Obviously global market forces and vested financial interests leave little choice for the city regions, though the number expressing concern over unlimited urban economic growth is growing.

What really makes a world city?

Since the worldwide discourse on world cities started, efforts have been made to define what it really takes to make a large city be or become a world city. It is widely acknowledged today that the mere population size of a city says little about its importance in the world economy. African cities are usually quoted as pertinent examples (King, 1990).

Varied concepts of financial, economic, and political power over global systems are used to assign the label "global" to a city. Global cities are usually defined as key locations for financial services, which are necessary for the implementation and management of global economic operations, and as cities that also tend to attract the head-quarters of multinational corporations (Sassen, 1991, 1994). More comprehensive definitions assign to world cities additional character-istics such as centres of political power, national transportation cen-tres, centres of science and education, arts, media, and entertainment, and also the favoured residential locations of the nation's rich and poor (Hall, 1966).

According to the initiator of the world city debate (Friedmann, 1986), global cities are cities that "articulate" larger regional, national, and international economies and serve as *centres* through which flow money, workers, information, commodities, and other economically relevant variables. As centres defined by dense patterns of inter-action rather than by political administrative boundaries, they extend their influence into a surrounding field or region, whose economic relations they articulate into the global economy or *space of global accumulation,* as centres of representation, social interaction, and innovation. Spaces of global accumulation are defined as a set of national and regional economies that serves the purposes of capital accumulation on a worldwide scale. As commanding nodes of the global system, world cities reflect the economic power they command or have a specific place in the hierarchy of spatial articulations.

I will use the term "world city region" instead of "world city" throughout this chapter in order to reflect the larger regional dimen-sion of world cities in Europe. This is best justified by looking more closely at the city of Frankfurt. This city has a population of less than 700,000 and a narrow administrative boundary. It is the well-known financial centre of Germany and has the third-busiest airport in Europe. All these central functions serve a densely urbanized hinter-land of more than 1 million people with a set of cities specializing in different functions.

World city regions in Europe: Paris and London and what else?

The above criteria result in more or less well-justified though still arbitrary selections of world cities, with an unquestioned core group of world cities such as Tokyo, New York, London, and Paris, and additional lists of potential members of the prestigious virtual world

Table 3.2 **World cities in Europe according to various sources**

City	Hall 1966	Friedmann 1986	Brunet 1989	Conti and Spriano 1991
Greater London	*	*	*	*
Paris (Ile-de-France)	*	*	*	*
Rhine–Main (Frankfurt)		*		
Rhine–Ruhr	*	*		
Randstad	*	*		*
Moscow	*			
Vienna		*?		
Munich		*?		
Milan				*

Source: Hall (1966); Friedmann (1986); Brunet (1989); Conti and Spriano (1991).

city club – lists, however, that reflect differing macro-regional, cultural, or disciplinary perspectives and regional knowledge, and the respective choice of indicators (table 3.2).

When referring to the defined characteristics of world city regions, the decision as to which city to include, and which to omit, is extremely difficult. Which European cities, according to these criteria, could be considered as world city regions in Europe? I suggest the following approach.

First, there are **London** and **Paris**. There is no doubt that these two city regions are the two top-ranking city regions in Europe, representing the economic, political, and cultural headquarters of two of the major players in Europe, France and the United Kingdom.

Secondly, there are a few polycentric urban conurbations in Europe that exert a similar economic influence. Their influence and power, however, are divided among a few cities that, viewed individually, are not large enough to articulate into the European let alone a global economy. As conurbations where functions are divided among the individual cities, they exert an economic and political weight that is not far below that of London and Paris. These conurbations are the **Rhine–Main** conurbation, with Frankfurt as its global urban flagship, the **Rhine–Ruhr** conurbation (with Bonn, Cologne, Düsseldorf, Essen, Duisburg, and Dortmund), and the **Randstad**, the Dutch conurbation with Amsterdam, Rotterdam, and The Hague as the urban centres known worldwide.

Thirdly, there are two cities in Europe that, for the time being, do not really qualify as world city regions – **Moscow** and **Istanbul** –

41

though each has a population of more than 10 million and shows considerable growth rates. There is some evidence that their size will exceed that of all other European urban regions by mid-2100 at the latest. Since the demise of the Soviet Union and its economic repercussions, Moscow has lost its former role as a global decision-making centre. Greater Istanbul, owing to its geopolitical location at the historic point of exchange between European and Asian cultures, is probably the fastest-growing conurbation in Europe.

Fourthly, there is the special case of **Berlin**. Since the reunification of Germany in 1989, the now reunited city, with a population of more than 3 million, has rejoined the club of Europe's large cities. However, the special status of Berlin as a divided city has been a serious impediment to economic development. West Berlin was a heavily subsidized city, difficult to reach and economically weak. East Berlin in turn was trapped in the socialist system, and hence could never really become a dominant city. In the long run, the reunited Berlin may have some potential for returning to the club of world city regions. This, however, will take at least a generation, if not two, certainly much longer than optimistic Berlin promoters would like to accept, and it will largely depend upon the economic development of Eastern Europe and its cities (Moscow, Warsaw, Minsk, St. Petersburg, Wroclaw, and Prague). The faster the socialist economy of Eastern Europe transforms, the more Berlin will benefit from the resulting interaction with the economies of Western Europe (Kunzmann, 1994).

Fifthly, there is another city that at first sight does not really qualify as a world city region: **Brussels**, the capital of the European Union. Given the political power of the European Union, the city may be seen as a kind of political spider in the web of the European urban system, hence having a similar worldwide importance to the other conurbations. In this city, the rules and regulations of internal European cooperation are developed, compromised, moderated, enacted, and, increasingly, enforced. With a population of 1 million, however, Brussels is not a large conurbation. It remains an international island in a national context, with considerable social polarization, negative impacts on a speculative local real estate market, and social exclusion.

In addition, a few large city regions (e.g. Padania in Italy, Rhône-Alpes in France, and Copenhagen) exert essential complementary functions in the dense European urban system, though they are certainly less global than the other five world city regions.

Finally, it should be mentioned that some European cities exert selected global functions in certain domains. Zurich is such a case. Among bankers and insurance companies it is a key location for interaction, as is Vienna as an exchange for cultural affairs and interests, Stockholm for the paper industry, or Heidelberg for American students.

This chapter focuses only on the first two categories of city regions. It is important to state, however, that these cities could not perform their global function if they were not closely linked to the densely interwoven European urban system. The other cities are equally important players in the European urban concert. Their close observation remains a task for future European urban monitoring.

European world city regions in their historical, spatial, and political context

Over more than 2,000 years, Europe has experienced continuous waves of nation building and disintegration. The continent has suffered from continuous feudal and territorial conflicts, and has benefited from civic urban pride, considerable feudal investments in certain sites and urban infrastructure, and implementation on earth of ecclesiastical dreams of heaven. Europe has seen some cities grow, flourish, and expand and others decline, being neglected and forgotten. The capitalist societies of Europe's nation-states and city-states have benefited from centuries of internal and external colonialism and imperialism, and from exploiting their colonies in Asia, Africa, and America. Europe dominated the world economy into the nineteenth century, when the United States, and later Japan, entered the system as new global players.

Obviously, these 2,000 years of history of smaller and larger little kingdoms and fiefdoms, of city-states and regional governments, and of ecclesiastical domains have shaped the urban system in Europe (Braudel, 1979). Some cities function as administrative headquarters, others play a role as military headquarters. The favourable geopolitical and logistical location of European warlords, traders, and merchants at one of the various crossroads, the local availability of resources such as coal and iron or water power, the local commitment of the feudal aristocracy and civic societies were the major reasons for the evolution of these cities. However, over the two millennia the functional importance of some European cities has changed. Rome was undoubtedly a world city 2,000 years ago and meanwhile has lost

Table 3.3   **The degree of urbanization in selected European countries, 1950 to 2020 (%)**

Country	1950	1990	2025
United Kingdom	84.2	92.1	93.8
West Germany	72.3	86.4	88.6
France	56.2	73.8	77.3
Italy	54.3	68.3	75.8
Netherlands	82.7	88.5	89.6
Switzerland	44.3	59.6	69.5
Spain	51.9	78.0	86.3
Japan	50.3	76.9	80.6
United States	64.2	74.1	77.0
China	11.0	21.4	43.7

Source: United Nations (1987).

much of its former glory, though it is still a capital city, in contrast to Trier, a Roman world city that is today no more than a sleepy provincial town. Augsburg, Venice, and Antwerp were at one time European world cities, dominating financial and trade markets; today they have fallen considerably in the European urban hierarchy.

Continuous rural–urban migration flows swell the population of the cities over centuries. "Stadtluft macht frei" ("urban air liberates") was already a slogan in the fifteenth century pulling rural population to the cities. Security concerns in war-affected regions and productivity gains in agriculture were the push factors. Hence the regions and nations of Europe are almost fully urbanized, with urbanization levels ranging between 60 and 92 per cent in the 1990s (table 3.3).

Two thousand years of nation-building processes and the resulting scattered system of cultural regions and nations have shaped an urban system in Europe that is, with few exceptions (France, Hungary, Austria), extremely polycentric. Traditional polycentric nations with strong urban traditions are Germany, Italy, and Switzerland, perfectly proving Christaller's theory of central place hierarchies. The proportion of the respective national populations living in the world city regions of Europe demonstrates the national differences (table 3.4).

The visible result of these 2,000 years of urban history is a dense and (in comparison with most other mega-regions in the world) relatively balanced system of urban settlements throughout Europe,

Table 3.4 **The concentration of national population in world city regions in Europe, 1987**

World city region	World city population (million)	National population (million)	World city population as % of national population
London	12.0	57.7	20.9
Paris (Ile-de-France)	9.6	57.3	16.8
Rhine–Main	3.9	80.5	4.9
Rhine–Ruhr	10.8	80.5	13.4
Randstad	7.6	15.1	50.3

Sources: World city population – NUREC (1994); national population – The Economist (1994).

with thousands of economically viable small and medium-sized cities amidst rich agricultural production spaces, with numerous regional and national capitals, with cities accumulating knowledge, experience, and reputation over centuries in such areas as trading and logistics, industrial production and producer services, the arts, science, and education, or health and tourism. The roughly 350 million inhabitants of Europe are evenly distributed over the macro-region.

This multicentric European urban network represents an immense potential, protected by strong culturally based regionalism and by more than 100 languages still spoken in Europe. Though English is on the verge of becoming the unchallenged lingua franca of European business and science communities, the indigenous languages still dominate local, regional, and national information and communication processes. German is spoken by 89 million, French by 52 million, Italian by 58 million, and Polish by 39 million inhabitants. The fact that many European regions maintain their own "missions" in the European headquarters of Brussels illustrates their strong regionally rooted cultures. They do this in order to acquire first-hand information, to lobby for their regions, and to bypass the political censorship of national governments.

Since the 1970s, Europe has been in a process of political and economic reorientation, a process that received a surprising stimulus in 1989 with the fall of the Berlin Wall and the demise of the Soviet Union. With the gradual formation of a single market, Europe is strengthening its regional competitiveness in a global economy, particularly *vis-à-vis* Japan and North America, though also towards South-East Asia and China. This economic competition is at the centre of a political and economic debate. It dominates thinking and action, influences attitudes, and inspires and drives activities. Industrial corporations and business communities are driven by this global competition, banks organize the related financial transactions, and developers benefit from the resulting demand for property.

The logic of the globalization paradigm and the evolution of a single European market have been leading to new intra-European competition among cities and urban regions, with considerable implications for urban and national politics. This in turn has triggered a series of studies on the evolution and hierarchy of the European urban system, on growth and decline, on the ranking of cities in Europe, and on their competitiveness (Brunet, 1989; Cheshire and Hay, 1989; Conti and Spriano, 1991; Kunzmann and Wegener, 1992; COM, 1992; Saillez, 1993; BMBau, 1994). These studies point to various hierarchies of the European urban system, reflecting differing definitions of urban administrative boundaries (so far an unsolved problem of comparative urban studies in Europe), the individual selection of indicators measuring the ranking of cities, and the national bias (and information base) of the authors. One of these studies, promoting a European urban belt from London to Milan in the form of a (blue) "banana" (Brunet, 1989), has had considerable influence on geographers and planners, and even more so on developers searching for profitable locations for property development. The reality of the urban system in Europe, however, is much more complex. It has the form of a bunch of grapes rather than a banana. This visual metaphor explains both the existing urban systems of smaller and larger, though overall fairly balanced, urban regions in Europe, and the desirable policy direction to keep this system functioning (fig. 3.1).

Strengthening the polycentric urban system of Europe is also the overall objective of two documents of the European Commission on spatial development in Europe: Europe 2000 and Europe 2000+ (COM, 1993, 1994). These are the first documents to contain comparable and reliable up-to-date information on the whole territory of Western Europe, hence their reception among geographers, planners, and desk officers in planning and economic promotion agencies has been unusually enthusiastic. A far from powerless European Commission, with considerable funds for regional development and social cohesion in Europe, has rediscovered cities as engines for economic development. The result of this new renaissance of cities (and city regions) is that in Europe in the mid-1990s there is much political concern about the future of cities and about their national, European,

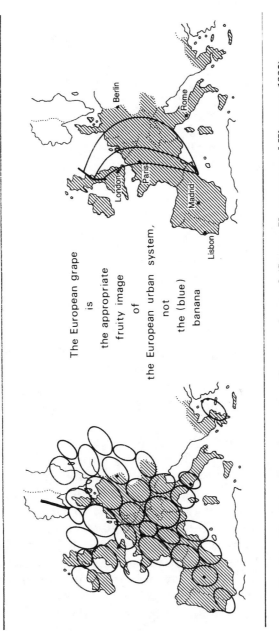

The European grape
is
the appropriate
fruity image
of
the European urban system,
not
the (blue)
banana

Fig. 3.1 **The European urban system: Grapes or banana? (Source: Kunzmann and Wegener, 1992)**

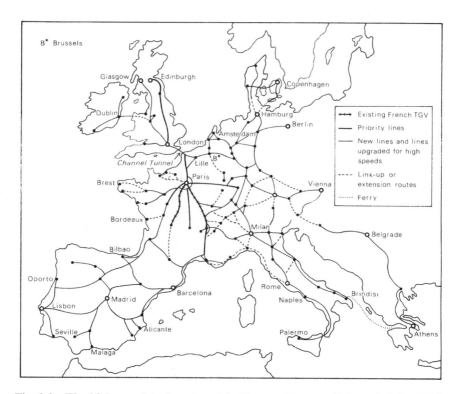

Fig. 3.2 **The high-speed train network in Europe (Source: Cole and Cole, 1994)**

and global competitiveness, though also about the negative social, cultural, and environmental impacts of policies promoting urban competitiveness.

In this context one project requires particular attention: the promotion of transeuropean (transport) networks (COM, 1994). This aims at improving transeuropean accessibility, mainly by high-speed trains. This project is intended to accelerate the completion of the single European market (and, explicitly, to create employment all over Europe) by filling in those missing links that still hinder the flow of goods and persons in Europe, from East to West and from North to South (fig. 3.2). Being a stop in the high-speed rail system is a must for all European cities that wish to participate in European or global competition. Great efforts are being undertaken locally to win the respective regional or national battles. In this process the linking of the high-speed train network with an international airport is seen as a most significant and desirable step (fig. 3.3).

The world city regions in Europe are an intrinsic part of the well-

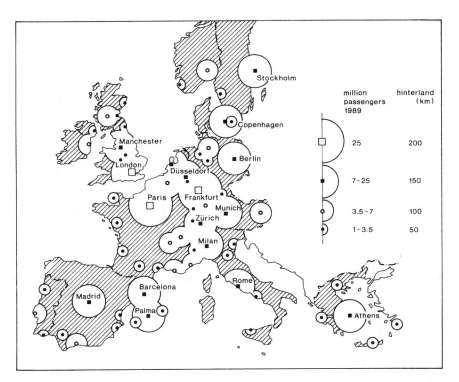

Fig. 3.3 **Airports in Europe (Source: Kunzmann and Wegener, 1992)**

developed European urban system. Without being linked into the filigree network of cities, with their respective single or multiple functions, the world city regions would not be able to perform their global function, be it as a centre of global financial transactions, of global services, of worldwide information and communication exchange, or just of attracting urban tourists to Europe. The European world cities are not spiders in the European web of cities; rather they are nodes in the European system that take over indispensable global functions for other cities in the network.

World city regions in Europe: Structural change and future challenges

London and Paris, as well as the conurbations Rhine–Main, Rhine–Ruhr, and Randstad, have been identified in this chapter as European world city regions of global importance. Selected development features of these regions are described below, focusing on features that illustrate their spatial and structural change and demonstrate their future challenges. Only selected aspects can be covered, such as population, economic change, unemployment, public transport, and media.

Population development

A large proportion of the national populations lives in the European world city regions. According to the administrative definitions of the Network on Urban Research in the European Union (NUREC, 1994), the proportions are: more than 20 per cent in Greater London, not much less (17 per cent) in Ile-de-France, and over 13 per cent in the Rhine–Ruhr region (see table 3.4 above). This concentration of people, together with the fact that with one exception (Frankfurt and, although only to a certain extent, Rhine–Ruhr) all the world city regions similarly execute the function of the capital cities, means a concentration of power and media presence.

The population change in European world city regions over the past two decades has been negligible, in contrast to many world cities in Asia and Latin America, and in contrast to their growth from 1880 to 1960 (table 3.5). It just reflects the minimal change in the national population as a whole (table 3.6). This stagnation of population figures is a great relief to the responsible authorities.

Although the city regions are spatially growing and expanding into their wider hinterland, this extension is not a consequence of overall population growth in the region. It is rather one of affluence, the demise of the traditional family, the growth of office space per job, the growing demand for floor space per person, and particularly an increasing number of smaller households (it is anticipated that at the beginning of the twenty-first century almost 50 per cent of all house-

Table 3.5 **Population growth of European world city regions, 1800 to 1960 (%)**

World city region	Around 1800	Around 1950	Around 1960
London	0.85	10.96	11.55
Paris	0.55	6.74	7.81
Rhine–Main[a]	–	–	–
Rhine–Ruhr[b]	0.28	8.14	10.42
Randstad	0.40	3.30	3.94

Source: Hall (1966: 11 and 23).
a. Not included.
b. Ruhr only.

Table 3.6 **World city regions in Europe: Population development, 1980 to 1990 ('000)**

	1980		1990	
Britain	56,314		57,411	
Greater London[a]		16,993		17,458
France	53,859		56,735	
Ile-de-France		10,008		10,692
West Germany	61,566		63,254	
Rhine–Ruhr		11,538		11,655
– Düsseldorf		5,210		5,200
– Cologne		3,915		3,996
– Münster		2,413		2,459
Rhine–Main:[b]				
– Darmstadt		3,431		3,522
Netherlands	14,150		14,950	
Randstad		6,309		6,641
– Utrecht		902		1,021
– North Holland		2,312		2,387
– South Holland		3,095		3,233
EUR 12	317,906		328,038	

a. Figures for South East England.
b. EUROSTAT does not give any figures for the region.

holds in world city regions will be one-person households). One aspect deserves a mention in this context: the number of elderly people (over 65) is rising constantly, as is the number of immigrants, people born abroad, and foreigners, who already comprise 25 per cent of the population in Frankfurt city, almost 20 per cent in Rotterdam, and 8 per cent (which represents 1.4 million, or about one-third of all foreigners residing in France) in Ile-de-France.

Economic change and employment

The GDP of world city regions in Europe is far above the European average (London 141, Ile-de-France 171, Darmstadt/Frankfurt, 172) and also above the national average (table 3.7), although higher figures might have been expected. This reflects the fact that the concentration of population in world city regions includes disproportionately large numbers of people living near or even below the poverty line.

The non-German world city regions are pertinent examples for de-industrialization theorists. In 1991, an average of 75 per cent of the

Table 3.7 **World city regions in Europe: Gross domestic product**

	GDP (EUR 12 = 100)		Employment in industry (%)[a]		Employment in services (%)[a]	
Britain	93		31.2		66.5	
Greater London		141		–		–
France	115		30.0		63.9	
Ile-de-France		171		25.3		74.3
Germany	128		40.3		55.5	
Rhine–Ruhr:						
– Düsseldorf		135		42.5		55.7
– Cologne		124		38.3		60.1
– Münster		105		41.6		54.5
Rhine–Main:						
– Darmstadt		172		36.0		62.7
Netherlands	124		28.9		67.6	
Randstad:						
– Utrecht		96		17.3		80.6
– North Holland		119		20.1		77.3
– South Holland		110		21.3		74.7
EUR 12	100		33.3		60.3	

a. Figures for 4/1991.

city regions' labour force could be attributed to the broad sector of services comprising both highly skilled and knowledge-intensive producer-oriented services and low-wage personal services, including huge numbers of "bad" jobs. Only the two German world city regions, Rhine–Ruhr and Rhine–Main, still show a comfortable average of about 40 per cent of jobs in industries, a figure that is similar to the national figure for West Germany.

Whether the figure is only 25 per cent or even 40 per cent, the world city regions are still important locations of large industrial complexes. Automobile production is to be found in the Ile-de-France (Renault), Rhine–Main (General Motors), and Rhine–Ruhr (Ford, Mercedes-Benz, General Motors). Similarly, chemical production is still a major industry in the two German world city regions, as it is in the Randstad, while defence industries are concentrated in Greater London and Ile-de-France. The regions are also the unchallenged national production centres for printing and media industries. Moreover, the large numbers of households living in the world city regions require a multitude of household-related small-scale production in all types of construction, maintenance, and repair, which further adds to the considerable absolute numbers of industrial jobs. Hence the usual image of world city regions as exclusively centres of global finance and sophisticated information services is too simple. It is true and visible only in those inner-city districts where financial institutions and their related forward and backward linkages and services are concentrated. The majority of districts in world cities do not differ in their spatial structure from any other large urban agglomeration in Europe.

Unemployment

In the past decade or so unemployment has become a major concern in Europe. Meanwhile, it is generally acknowledged that high unemployment is not a temporary problem, just being an interim consequence of economic change and adjustment. In Europe it is a structural problem mainly caused by technological change. Female unemployment is a concern, as is foreign unemployment, and youth unemployment is alarming. In France, almost one out of five persons under 25 does not have a formal job; in Britain one out of seven (there is some evidence that official unemployment statistics are manipulated down). In Germany, in comparison, with its traditional dual education system, the figures are less frightening, although trends do not allow anyone to be too optimistic (table 3.8).

Understandably, employment is high on the agenda of European policy makers. However, there are no easy solutions. The hopes and the related policies range from huge public sector financed employment initiatives to drastic reductions in wages. Britain is set on cheaper, unorganized labour, whereas Germany and the Netherlands prefer to rely on better education, shorter working hours, and job-sharing initiatives.

It is hardly comforting that unemployment in world city regions tends to be somewhat lower than the national average. This may be explained partially by the larger number of "bad' jobs available in the huge service industries for unqualified persons, partially by the large informal economies in European world city regions, which represent a huge grey zone between part-time and short-term employment and "black" labour. The vicious circle of poor education and training, youth unemployment, and crime is a particular threat in the world city regions, with their wide opportunities for escaping from social control.

Table 3.8 **World city regions in Europe: Unemployment (%)**

	Total		Women		<25 years old	
Britain	8.8		7.6		14.1	
Greater London[a]		7.6		6.8		11.5
France	9.0		11.4		19.1	
Ile-de-France		7.6		8.2		12.8
West Germany	8.7		8.8		11.0	
Rhine–Ruhr:						
– Düsseldorf		6.2		7.3		5.3
– Cologne		5.3		6.5		5.1
– Münster		5.5		6.8		5.0
Rhine–Main:						
– Darmstadt		2.8		3.3		2.5
Netherlands	7.0		9.3		10.5	
Randstad:						
– Utrecht		6.2		7.9		10.8
– North Holland		7.1		8.8		9.7
– South Holland		6.7		8.1		9.9
EUR 12	8.5		10.6		17.0	

a. South East England.

Social polarization

Social polarization in world city regions is a phenomenon that is arousing growing concern (Sassen, 1991). It was thought to have been overcome by the modern European welfare state. Now it is re-appearing in all European cities, although it is more obvious in world city regions. Within the regions there are growing income disparities of ever-smaller urban households. An increasing number of individuals are living below the poverty line. The growing number of homeless is a visible sign of the demise of social housing. Districts of ethnic minorities and an urban underclass are emerging that are distinct from the urban districts shown in global city promotion brochures. Security issues are becoming the prime concern of city dwellers and investors. The mainstream deregulation spirit in Europe is accelerating these processes of social erosion in cities. Constrained by public sector deficits, the cities will not be able to compensate for national or regional policies, which deny the need for some form of public intervention, redistribution, and social cushioning. Urban pockets of organized crime and power and urban poverty will appear side by side with offices and middle-class housing. Images of fragmented American cities have always been seen as non-transferable to Europe. Now the first signs of similar developments can be observed in the suburbs of Paris and in London, and they may also emerge even in Rotterdam and Frankfurt.

There is much empirical evidence that the ongoing economic development tends to favour spatial polarization within the world city regions. In this context, polarization means that there are territorial units that benefit from certain trends and urban regional competition, and others that have to bear some or all of the negative implications of specialization and spatial differentiation. Spatial differentiation processes as sketched above separate the world city region into urban glamour and backwater areas with their respective privileged and underprivileged urban classes. Land values and property prices tend to explode in certain locations within the world city region. Whereas land values in some socially and aesthetically privileged districts of a central city or of selected high-income suburbs grow to exclusive heights, they tend to stagnate in other parts of the region, where environmental pollution or social erosion deter middle- and high-income households from investing and settling. The result is a growing social fragmentation of city regions, where single urban districts tend to become virtually or even physically walled social and ethnic communities like isolated islands in an urban archipelago.

Thus the overall trends determining spatial development in European world cities are increasing spatial specialization, a resulting spatial differentiation, and a growing intraregional polarization (fig. 3.4).

Administrative structure and metropolitan governance

Metropolitan governance in world city regions in Europe is highly politicized. The obvious reason is that the politico-administrative structures in these regions are very complex. In three of the regions there is an urban centre (Paris proper, Frankfurt, the City of London) that represents the global image, while numerous medium-sized and small local governments in rings around the core city provide the preconditions for the global flag-city to function. In the other two regions, polynucleated structures add intraregional competition among the larger cities (Rotterdam/Amsterdam, Cologne/Düsseldorf/Essen/Dortmund/Duisburg) to the complex decision-making structures. The large number of smaller politico-administrative units (Ile-de-France:

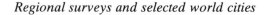

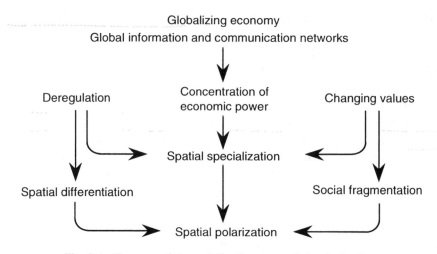

Fig. 3.4 **From spatial specialization to spatial polarization**

514, Greater London: 56, Rhine–Main: 182, Rhine–Ruhr: 135, and Randstad: 212) and their established participatory power in West European democracies make it difficult to develop joint visionary strategies for the world city region as a whole (table 3.9).

In politico-administrative environments where party politics and election periods play a crucial role, these regions are like large tankers drawn by pilot boats, the flag-cities, as a whole, being difficult to steer. Changing their general course can be done only by charismatic political leaders. Internal tax redistribution is, as a rule, one of the controversial issues; the financing of joint facilities (e.g. theatres, museums) and public utilities (e.g. waste disposal, water provision) is another one. In order to avoid open conflict, decisions are made through down-to-earth and day-to-day incrementalism and continuous bargaining processes among the communities concerned.

Only in centralist France was the creation of a joint regional authority possible; in all the other world city regions the establishment of effective and powerful regional authorities with clearly assigned functions and tasks has remained the planners' pet postulation. One consequence of such conditions is that the central government is a key player in local politics. This is undoubtedly the case in the London and Paris world city regions, although to a much lesser extent in the Randstad. Where national and regional tiers of administration and/or of democratically legitimized regions (as in Germany) are established, an additional layer of time-consuming decision-

Table 3.9 **World city regions in Europe: Population, area, and administrative units**

World city region	Population, 1987	Area (km^2)	Administrative units
London	12,043,400	14,578.80	56
Paris (Ile-de-France)	9,647,649	3,675.79	514
Rhine–Main	3,931,381	3,946.77	182
Rhine–Ruhr	10,754,554	9,935.57	135
Randstad^a	7,594,923	7,877.17	212

Source: NUREC (1994).
a. Excluding The Hague.

making processes makes it even more difficult to join forces. This may be why neither the Rhine–Main nor the Rhine–Ruhr regions have a single metropolitan authority promoting and controlling their regional development. For some metropolitan observers the absence of such bodies is considered to be fortunate, because it may avoid globally justified flagship policies at the cost of local communities.

Public transport

In all European world city regions public transport is, as a rule, well organized. The traditional metro and suburban rail networks of London and Paris have developed and expanded over decades. The two German regions, despite much lower population densities, have fairly modern and well-functioning intraregional rail transportation networks, with efficient regional transport authorities, together with the water boards, being the spearheads of intraregional cooperation. The Randstad in the Netherlands is served by an equally efficient national rail authority.

As a result of changing attitudes, more flexible working hours, environmental concerns, and improving organizational measures, public transport use in Germany and the Netherlands is growing. In the other world city regions, security issues and comfort tend to discourage public transport use, at least for those who have access to alternative modes of transport and the means to pay high parking fees. Parking policies are still the predominant key to public transport policies. All regions do little to restrain the use of private cars within the region as a whole. However, there are increasing pockets of traffic restrictions and constraints on car use within the more attractive inner districts of the city regions.

To what extent new information and communication technologies already do or may in the future substitute for intraregional mobility and movements is still unknown. The expectation is that such technologies will contribute to the spatial extension of the metropolitan region and to a further gentrification of the more attractive parts of the regional hinterland, strengthening the development of the smaller urban cores in the outer rings of the world city regions. They present or further improve opportunities to combine a cheaper and more relaxed way of life in smaller communities outside the global core with short-term accessibility to global infrastructure and metropolitan face-to-face contacts.

Major concerns of the regions are the smooth linking of public transport to the international transportation nodes, to airports and central high-speed train stations, passenger security issues, and continuous technical modernization.

The metropolitan public transport networks are highly subsidized by the public sector. Hence their condition and their passenger security depend on the willingness of national governments to raise money for modernization, for automation, for acceleration and regional extension, for raising comfort and frequency, for security control, and for preventing vandalism. Paris, again, seems to do better in this respect than London, where the Underground is in a deplorable state, while the more recent German systems are, as a rule, in a good shape. However, mainstream deregulation policies in all West European countries may further constrain the necessary modernization of tracks, stations, and rolling stock, which in turn will polarize the metropolitan population into those who are forced to use cheap public transport and those who are able to pay for more comfortable and safer substitutes.

Information power

It is not surprising that world city regions in Europe are the centres of European if not global information power and, as a rule, also the headquarters of international and national media corporations (table 3.10). They are the location of international correspondents and news agencies, and of global publishers. Owing to the concentration of financial (global exchange markets) and political power, the European world city regions are prime information sources for international news. The concentration of media (with their armies of journalists and news and information producers) in such locations usually

Table 3.10 **World city regions in Europe: Media power**

World city region	Journals	Media corporations (rank among the world's 100 largest media corporations)[a]
London	*Financial Times* *The Times* *The Economist*	Reed International (18) Maxwell (28) BBC (30) Reuters (35) Pearson (42) United Newspapers (48) Thorn/EMI (54) Associated Newspapers (66) Thames Television (100)
Paris (Ile-de-France)	*Le Monde* *Figaro*	Hachette (6) Havas (34) Socpresse (50) Groupe de la Cité (77) TF1 (79) Cal Plus (84)
Rhine–Ruhr	*Handelsblatt*	Bertelsmann/RTL 2 (2)[b] ARD/WDR (10) WAZ (56)
Rhine–Main Randstad	*Frankfurter Allgemeine*	ZDF (69) Elsevier (78) Polygram (27) Wolters/Kluwer (75)

a. 38 of the 100 largest corporations are North American corporations.

b. Bertelsmann has its corporate headquarters near the Rhine–Ruhr agglomeration (in Gütersloh), though its activities are highly decentralized all over the world.

has two effects: the information complexes serve as screening, analysing, and redistribution centres for global news, and they select, formulate, and feed European news into the wider global information network. Both processes are highly arbitrary and selective.

Conclusion

Other aspects of structural change in world city regions are not discussed in this chapter, such as the gradually changing housing sector, where public housing is gradually replaced by subsidized owner-occupied housing in various forms, or the growing attention culture in all forms is receiving in the metropolitan region, illustrated by the gradual privatization of cultural facilities and events. Sustainability and environmental concerns have become an extremely important policy area in Europe, though more at the European, national, and local level than at the world city region level. The provision of water and the reduction of energy consumption will certainly be major challenges for the European world city regions, as will be personal security matters and the future of a rapidly ageing population. These and other aspects of structural change and future challenges may require additional thought and attention when monitoring the development of world city regions in Europe and comparing it with development in other global cities.

Two further aspects would be worth exploring in more depth when assessing the relative achievements and failures of European world city region development. First, history matters, because it best explains the cultural attitudes and geopolitical dimensions of political decision-making processes. Secondly, a knowledge of national tax and insurance systems is essential, because these systems ultimately determine the locational behaviour of firms and households.

Patchwork city: Global economic trends and local consequences

For many reasons, though mainly owing to faster information and transportation flows, world city regions in Europe are becoming patchwork cities of functionally specialized spaces. The whole city region is a mosaic of spaces, some with global functions (e.g. international finance), some of European importance, and others with a solely local function. These functions, however, are highly interrelated. One functional space cannot survive without the others.

In order to strengthen their profile within international competition, and benefiting from their respective local potentials, world city regions promote the development of those outward-oriented global or European functions, usually at the expense of other functions (e.g. specialized producer-oriented services), the establishment of specialized research and training institutions, and the development of global transport centres. They promote hard and soft location factors in order to be competitive in the global market. They try to improve their accessibility and infrastructure standards, they fight to attract international and national institutions and enterprises to complement the local complex, they feel forced to initiate flagship projects to improve the visual quality of the city, and, finally, they sponsor events to attract global visitors, to demonstrate a commitment to culture, and to serve a demanding well-qualified local labour force. The presence of international media is essential.

The result is specialized spatial/territorial spaces within the world city regions and it is the global function that is causing intraregional spatial differentiation. This in turn requires a larger territory to accommodate the various requirements of actors in the global economy. Hence, global specialization and intraregional differentiation lead unavoidably to a further growth of the urban region in Europe, which is expanding more and more into a wider hinterland.

These gradually growing city regions are dominated and managed by functional networks of people, actors, and political players who formulate subregional development goals and regional decision-making processes. Within this process the groups that usually set the region's development priorities are those that use their global information power to influence the city region's opinion leaders and decision makers. Here they are supported, as London and Paris perfectly demonstrate, by the politico-administrative machinery of the state as a whole residing in the world city region. To challenge the global priority-setting, the intraregional losers in disadvantaged world city spaces can use only their negative power.

The trends sketched above are paralleled by changing value systems and behavioural patterns in Western society. They are additionally driven by more and more privatized or corporate decision-making systems in deregulated politico-administrative milieus. Such development trends bring about a growing spatial differentiation of urban and regional functions and land uses within world city regions (Ache et al., 1992). The scaling up of functions to adapt the world city region continuously to global standards leads to growing intraregional specialization of single territorial spaces.

International finance and services centres

International finance and services centres are those inner urban districts of world city regions in Europe where a great variety of institutions of international finance and services, their forward and backward linkages (media, printing, travel agencies, etc.), and the related life spaces of their labour forces and clienteles are concentrated. In London, Paris, or Frankfurt, such centres can be easily identified. They can also be found in Düsseldorf and Amsterdam, although in somewhat smaller versions. These international finance and services centres are globally interlinked and form part of the much-quoted global city network.

Franchise worlds

Complexes of glass-covered inner-city shopping malls and fancy shopping streets in world city regions are the urban context of international franchise chains, from Armani via Benetton to the Body Shop. They allow privileged global travellers to buy their Armani suit or their Dior cosmetics whenever they have the time to do their shopping, and the window shopper to dream the consumer dream, or just to stop over in a Pizzaland or Burger King restaurant. As a rule, the urban and architectural design of such districts is global, not local, unless the local conservation officer can reckon on political support to keep at least the original façade.

Gentrified urban islands

Re-urbanization processes in Europe, a consequence of, among others, changing value systems, altered lifestyles, smaller households, and the higher incomes of young households, have resulted in continuous development pressure on centrally located urban districts with a traditional housing stock and cultural milieus. Strong land-use control and conservation acts protect such districts from housing demolition and modern property development. Rising property values force the former owners and users from such areas, while professional people, artists, and design boutiques occupy these spaces and maintain their exclusivity. Chelsea is only one such area in London, and in Paris, as in Amsterdam, only a few inner-city districts remain untouched by gentrification pressure. Similar inner-city districts can be found in Düsseldorf and Cologne, in Frankfurt and The Hague.

Global tourist circuits

The historical inner urban districts in European world cities are favourite targets of the European and the global tourist. Visits to Paris are "musts" in the life of any American, Japanese, or European citizen if he or she can afford a stay in the city. London has a similar attraction for Arabs and Africans. For the average European tourist, visits to Amsterdam and Cologne can be added to the list, on which only Frankfurt has a very low rank, unless nearby Heidelberg is the traveller's target. As a rule, world city tourists "occupy" only selected urban areas of the world city, where historic monuments and modern plazas, a variety of first-class museums, fancy waterfront developments, a wide range of open-air restaurants, bars, and clubs, a large choice of tourist and luxury hotels, and indigenous boutique-type shopping precincts allow the tourist a relaxing mixture of cultural learning and local shopping.

Modern R&D spaces ("technopoles")

"Technopoles" are urban districts or intraregional territories and spaces where public and private R&D institutions are located, where they carry out basic and applied research, and where a variety of institutions of higher education and permanent education provide the required skilled labour force for laboratories and training establishments. Located around such spaces are high-income housing areas, leisure clubs, and sports facilities for the R&D workforce. The prototype model of such R&D spaces is Silicon Valley around Stanford University. European examples of such specialized districts are technopole districts in outer Paris and large science parks in Rotterdam, Darmstadt, or Dortmund.

Traditional industrial complexes

All European world cities have large traditional industrial areas that are in a process of gradual restructuring. Some city regions are more successful than others in changing their obsolete or continuously subsidized economic base (e.g. the Ruhr or to some extent the London Docklands). Some of these spaces have become the favoured location for power plants, waste disposal facilities, and marginalized scrap and recycling industries. Some are still producing basic industrial products that require neither a sophisticated labour force nor easy access to airports or modern logistics centres. Others make use of the abundance of derelict industrial space for storage and logistical operations that would be more costly elsewhere.

Modern production complexes ("just-in-time regions")

In contrast to old industrial areas, modern industrial complexes are characterized by modern infrastructure, new production plants in a

63

key sector (mainly highly sophisticated production such as defence and aerospace, multimedia and printing, or health industries), and a variety of smaller and medium-sized supplier plants. The complexes are additionally complemented by all kinds of producer-oriented public and private services, from education and training to insurance and logistics.

"Edge" cities

At the edge of the densely built-up inner-city areas in world cities, edge cities have emerged. Half way between the city core and the outer residential areas, they are close to ring roads and junctions of the metropolitan rail systems, complexes of office buildings, and apartment blocks. Whereas property development in the inner city is controlled by strong conservation concerns (for both cultural and tourist reasons), edge cities allow almost unlimited bargaining for development rights. Docklands is one such complex in London; La Défense and the centre of Marne La Valle are two of the many edge cities in Paris; Eschborn is an example for Frankfurt. Given the financial power behind such projects, planning and urban design considerations play hardly any role. The result, as a rule, is that public space is neglected. Only in the public sector led development of La Défense in Paris has public space received satisfactory attention.

Aerovilles ("airport cities")

The need for immediate accessibility to international airports has caused airport development corporations and private developers to invest in large airport cities, a specialized type of edge city where airport-related services and firms requiring fast access to global transport networks find suitable locations for their business activities. Such airport cities, which are simultaneously centres of global logistics, have been developed or are under development in Amsterdam, Paris, and Frankfurt.

Interregional distribution centres

Driven out by inner-city traffic restrictions and favoured by just-in-time production technologies, interregional centres of logistics and wholesale distribution are emerging at suitable out-of-town locations, linked to the global or European hubs and to interregional transportation corridors. Examples are strategic centres of European-wide logistical operations, or out-of-town centres for consumer goods distribution within the city region. Transport-related production and services such as filling stations, truck selling and maintenance operations, cheap accommodation, but also wholesale distribution and tele-shopping and home delivery enterprises, tend to locate in their vicinity.

Urbanized transportation corridors

Along transeuropean motorways, developments are taking place that accelerate the gradual urbanization of the corridor. Their accessibility (by car) favours firms and households driven out by inner urban restructuring and unaffordable rents to locate at one motorway exit site after the other. Enterprises benefiting from the flexible labour force living at such locations, and from generous local government subsidies, follow. As a consequence the former rural landscape is gradually being urbanized. The corridor along the Rhine valley in Germany is one such example; others are the M4 corridor linking London to Bristol, or the corridor from Paris to Lille in France.

Urban backwaters

All world city regions in Europe have their disadvantaged backwaters where those urban functions are concentrated that are considered potentially to spoil the attractive global image of the city, but are indispensable for the functioning of the world city region. These are urban spaces where for whatever reasons (industrial dereliction, social erosion, etc.) land values and housing rents are low, where the land market does not raise speculative hopes, where an outdated urban infrastructure is in bad shape, and where environmental conditions are deplorable. Such urban areas are "ideal" locations for low-cost urban operations and marginal businesses. But for many urban dwellers they are the only remaining affordable urban space. Hence they are the districts of the urban underclass, of ethnic minorities and businesses, and for any urban functions that require an inner urban location.

Leisure worlds ("Disney Worlds")

Eurodisney, recently renamed Disneyland Paris, is a prominent example of the kind of leisure complexes that seem to be emerging all over Europe with greater or lesser economic success. Another project under development is the MGM Park in the Ruhr. These complexes offer easily accessible and affordable short-term holidays in a relaxed but organized atmosphere. They may be entertainment parks for a carefree and safe weekend visit with children, or areas of organized sport and recreation for short- and longer-term holidays (e.g. yachting, golf, horse riding, or skiing).

Gentrified green belts

Rural areas within world city regions tend to become gentrified by well-off urbanites aiming for rural lifestyles in easily accessible nearby locations. The more attractive the rural landscape, and the more local production is threatened by lower world market prices, the more likely it is that agricultural production is given up. Apart from a few remaining city farms selling untreated natural products at higher prices to local consumers, such regions tend to be gradually taken over by citizens who wish to live in an environmentally sound rural environment, initially only at weekends, then maybe permanently after early retirement. New communication technologies may eventually speed up this rural gentrification process.

Rural industrial complexes

Future agricultural production in Europe will be industrial in character, where soil conditions and topography are favourable. Such areas will be dominated by large privately owned farms and related agro-businesses with all the required forward and backward linkages and agricultural services. Such spaces are even to be found in world city regions. The glasshouse agro-industries in the Randstad are one example, and agricultural areas in outer Paris another.

Marginalized rural regions

As a result of mainstream European integration policies, rural regions with low agricultural production, located in the shadow of major transeuropean transportation corridors, or with limited accessibility to the core of the world city region, will become further marginalized, unless they are discovered by mobile freelancers as cheap production spaces with global accessibility. Otherwise few economic prospects remain for such regions: they may become the world city region's nature reserves, if there is a certain ecological potential; they may have the chance of becoming areas for second and third homes for inner-city dwellers; and they may sell their remoteness for all kind of activities that do not require centrality or that are not welcome in central locations (e.g. nuclear power plants, defence-related facilities, biogenetic experimental laboratories, or industrial waste disposal facilities).

All such spatial categories, and probably still others, are identifiable in one form or another in all European world city regions (fig. 3.5). Knowing the economic pattern of a particular world city region, these categories can be easily mapped. These spatial categories are linked into interregional, international, or even global information networks, they develop their own dynamics and infrastructural requirements, and they perfectly reflect the growing fragmentation of Western society, where spatial competition is clearly in charge. As a rule, the functional specializations are mutually reinforced once the particular image of such spaces is established. The world city function, with all its local spatial requirements, is, as a rule, accelerating the spatial segregation as sketched above.

World city regions in Europe: Between competition and sustainability

At the end of the twentieth century, world city regions in Europe are bound to find it difficult to achieve a balance between competition and sustainability, a compromise between satisfying the requirements of their global economic clientele and their dependent urban complexes and milieus on one side, and commitment to sustainability on the other. The conflicts between the two options and the various local compromises dominate public debate and academic discourse in all European urban regions, though more so in the European world city regions. These controversies are sketched for three policy areas.

Global accessibility vs. local environmental concerns

Speeding up or slowing down – that is the conflict between those who wish to see the world city region as an economic winner in the global competition and who perceive economic growth as a prerequisite for social redistribution policies, and those who place environmental concerns above economic development. This conflict is best illus-

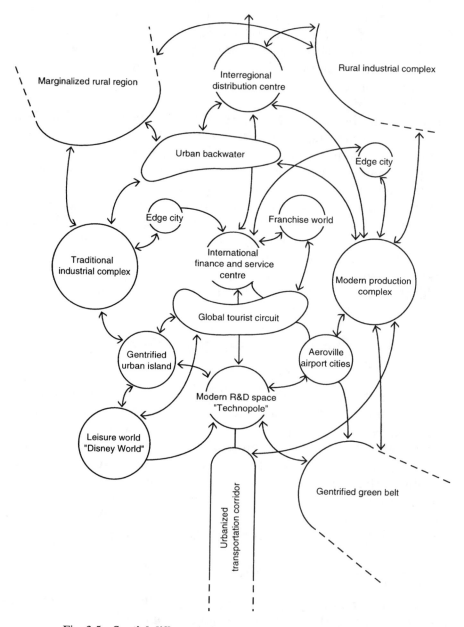

Fig. 3.5 **Spatial differentiation in European world city regions**

trated by the debates over airport extensions. Airport development is a major concern of all large conurbations in Europe; it best demonstrates the tough competition among world city regions in Europe for global accessibility.

Familiar with the considerable growth rates of air traffic, for both passengers and goods, all airport authorities wish to extend their airport facilities, by building additional runways, simultaneously fighting for 24-hour take-off and landing rights, and harbouring plans to link up with the European high-speed rail network. In their efforts they are supported by industrial institutions, conservative politicians, and various economic promotion agencies, but they are attacked by pressure groups, green parties, and ecological non-governmental organizations with considerable democratic and legal power to intervene in airport development.

In 1994, in order to exchange information and to join strategic forces, airport regions in Europe even established a cooperative network, in which London and Paris as well as Amsterdam and Frankfurt are represented. London is weighing a further extension of Heathrow, whose capacity is near to exhaustion, against a fifth international airport. Amsterdam is investing heavily to extend its airport (named "mainport") to make it a key hub on the continent, in competition with Paris and Frankfurt. It aims to attract more passengers from Rotterdam, from Brussels, and even from the Rhine–Ruhr conurbation, already with some success. Düsseldorf suffers from considerable operational constraints, which hinder any further development of its services and operating hours. Cologne may have better prospects if linked to the new high-speed train networks after 2000. These latter two options are opposed by environmental interest groups who are fighting with some good arguments for a general decline in air mobility. Paris has by far the best airport operational conditions. The ultra-modern Charles de Gaulle airport lies far outside the densely built-up area, and has recently even been linked to the TGV high-speed network. Given the favourable location, there is comparatively little opposition to airport operations. (See table 3.11.)

In a participatory context, as is the case in the five world city regions presented here, such conflicts between powerful airport authorities and local action groups, which are constantly improving their professionalized counter-strategies, require extremely long decision-making processes. As a rule, opposition to such projects is rarely successful. It does, however, considerably reduce negative en-

Table 3.11 **World city regions in Europe: Airports, passengers, and freight volumes, 1990**

World city region	Airports	Passengers embarked	Freight and post loaded (tonnes)
London	Heathrow Gatwick Stansted Luton	68,404,000	462,836
Paris	Charles de Gaulle Orly	23,127,000	–
Rhine–Main	Frankfurt (Rhine–Main)	14,331,000	628,399
Rhine–Ruhr	Düsseldorf Cologne Dortmund	13,131,000	133,133
Randstad	Amsterdam Rotterdam	–	–

vironmental impacts by forcing the authorities to reassess their plans and projects.

Flagship projects and gentrification vs. squatting and homelessness

The development of large and prestigious flagship projects is one of the significant features of European world cities. Large projects that symbolize the dominance of the world city are to be found in all these city regions. In Paris there is a long tradition of modern bourgeois "grands projets." It started with the cultural "Centre Pompidou," followed by the grandiose Grand Arche in La Défense and the Opera Bastille. These projects, now favoured goals for the global tourist, are objects of both local and global identification and they are prestigious symbols of the capital city against the rest of the country. London seems to be less ambitious, though the Docklands have become a flagship project, at least for the media and for architects and planners. Learning from the Docklands, Rotterdam is in the process of implementing a huge waterfront development scheme, "Kop van Zuid." Frankfurt has invested in the construction of 11 new museums along Museumsufer to get rid of its Manhattan image. Investment in cultural facilities has also occurred in Cologne and Düsseldorf. The flagship projects in the Ruhr are different. Here, large industrial structures are being either converted or used as they are for cultural and leisure activities. The overall purpose of all these projects is the same: they should add accessible modern sites of global interest to the local environment. They are regional conversation pieces for the global traveller. As a rule all these developments are government led, with more public control and intervention in France and Germany, and somewhat less in Britain and the Netherlands.

However, the development of these urban flagship projects has anticipated and undesired implications. First, they usually trigger and accelerate gentrification processes in their immediate local environment (Paris is a pertinent example) and force minority or disadvantaged groups in the lower echelons of the urban classes to leave the locality because they cannot afford rising rents and property values. Their new locality in the urban region is the declining urban (as in London) or impoverished suburban (as in Paris) area. Such gentrification processes are for various reasons less obvious and on a somewhat smaller scale in the other three world city regions (the Randstad, the Rhine–Ruhr, and the Rhine–Main areas).

Secondly, these flagship projects contrast with the growing visible appearance of homelessness and squatting, and also of the new urban poverty, which is one consequence of worldwide mainstream deregulation and privatization policies, proclaiming the end of the welfare state. Again this is felt more in monocentric Paris and London than in the other polycentric conurbations. Only where the scenic values of the world city region are endangered by growing signs of dereliction, squatting, and poverty are efforts being undertaken to shift the nuisance out of the inner city to less accessible urban districts.

Metropolitan efficiency vs. local independence

All the European world city regions covered in this chapter suffer from weak intraregional cooperation. Usually there is a large number of administrative units within the metropolitan area (in Paris, in London, or in Rhine–Ruhr), which compete among themselves for almost everything – to attract (tax-generating) facilities, high-tech firms, and affluent households, for large international institutions and corporate headquarters, for water, and for recreation spaces. They also compete not to have the facilities they would prefer not to be built within their local boundaries, such as dumps, incineration plants, nuclear power plants, or large traffic-generating out-of-town hypermarkets. This results in constant political conflicts between the metropolitan centre and the metropolitan periphery, between the global spaces of the city region and its local complements. Apart from their various substantive aspects, these conflicts have, as a rule, considerable ideological and tactical dimensions. Moreover, the local solution may depend on election periods and public awareness, on the media, and on individual personalities involved in such projects. There are many possible hindrances to the formulation of joint strategic efforts in response to the challenges that the metropolitan region faces as a whole. Local communities, however, fear with some justification that their independence and their interests are sacrificed on the altar of global competitiveness, their needs and requirements remaining unheard and unfinanced.

Strategic planning for the whole conurbation is convincingly done only in centralistic France, where a well-established LAPTC is constantly developing comprehensive and sectoral strategies for spatial development of the Paris region (Ile-de-France). Since the dissolution of the Greater London Council, London has been struggling for a new form of metropolitan government to look after all regional concerns. As an interim substitute, a committee was established to think about the future of the conurbation, here competing to some extent with the established SERPLAN, a regional planning agency with strategic planning responsibilities for the whole of South East England. Both agencies, however, have little power in the political environment. If they wish to convey messages to the political arena, their only chance is to get the ear of the media and of the informed public. No joint efforts of strategic planning are being undertaken in the Rhine–Ruhr conurbation; not even the powerful *Land* government has ever seen the necessity to initiate such a move. The once-powerful Siedlungsverband Ruhrkohlenbezirk, covering almost half the area of the Rhine–Ruhr conurbation, was deprived of its planning functions in 1975. Intraregional competition and jealousy also explain why neither the Greater Frankfurt conurbation nor the Randstad has entered into any form of serious strategic planning. However, the inner segment of metropolitan Frankfurt has its own joint land-use planning agency, the Umlandverband Frankfurt, which can claim some success in containing metropolitan sprawl. The local governments assigned to the Randstad by the Dutch physical planners show little interest in joining forces through joint strategic planning. Rather they leave it to the national physical planning agency, which for some decades has tried to promote the Randstad concept, with very little success (Faludi and van der Valk, 1994).

Such conflicts have considerably changed the role of planners in world city regions, making it even more difficult. Given the complexity of planning problems in world city regions, and the information power of those who wish to invest and to develop, extremely qualified and specialized planners are required, planners who think globally and act locally but are specialists in a selected field. The world city region needs planners who understand how to moderate between interest groups, planners who know how to communicate planning visions to the informed and general public, planners who monitor social and environmental changes and analyse their implications for spatial development, planners who have the capability to define and design public spaces in ways that simultaneously attract and constrain the private sector to develop their properties, and finally planners who continue to do what planners always did in the past, that is, traditional land-use planning, zoning, and planning control. Traditional land-use planning and zoning become a routine activity only after the time-consuming and power-related political bargaining processes have successfully been concluded. The spatially differentiated world city region requires highly specialized communicative planners who can flexibly adapt to local conditions in a global context.

At the end of the twentieth century, Europe, with its long urban and industrial history, has reached the point where it may pass the baton to rapidly urbanizing Asia. The mega-cities of the future will certainly evolve in Asia. Their problems will exceed those with which European world cities are confronted today. European world cities have some experience to share – their polycentric structure and their visions for longer-term spatial development linked to a public machinery that can control private land utilization to achieve such visions, i.e. their growing commitment to sustainability. Urban innovations in Europe, however, do not seem to be emerging from world city regions. They originate rather from the dense network of creative medium and larger cities in Europe, which do not have the burden of global competition. Whether European experience is transferable to Asia or elsewhere can be explored only by those who are responsible for planning, developing, and managing the cities in Asia.

Acknowledgements

I am most grateful to Graham Cass, Klaus Spiekermann, and Kirsten Opitz, who helped me in preparing this paper.

References

Ache, Peter, Hans-Jürgen Bremm, and Klaus R. Kunzmann (1992), *Auswirkungen des europäischen Binnenmarktes auf die Raum- und Siedlungsstruktur in Westdeutschland*. Schriftenreihe Forschung des Bundesministeriums für Raumordnung, Bauwesen und Städtebau, Band 488 (Raumordnerische Aspekte des EG-Binnenmarktes). Bonn-Bad-Godesberg.

BMBau (Bundesministerium für Raumordnung, Bauwesen und Städtebau) (1994), *Raumordnungspolitischer Orientierungsrahmen*. Bonn.

Braudel, Fernand (1979), *Sozialgeschichte des 15.–18. Jahrhunderts*. Munich: Kindler.

Brunet, R. (1989), *Les Villes Européennes*. Rapport pour la DATAR. Paris: Documentation française.

Cheshire, Paul C. and Dennis G. Hay (1989), *Urban Problems in Western Europe*. London: Unwin Hyman.

Cole, John and Francis Cole (1994), *The Geography of the European Community*. London: Routledge.

COM (1992), *Urbanization and the Functions of Cities in the European Community*. Regional Development Studies, vol. 4. Brussels: Commission of the European Union.

——— (1993), *Europa 2000. Perspektiven der künftigen räumlichen Entwicklung in Europa*. Brussels: Commission of the European Union.

——— (1994), *Networks of Cities*. Brussels, Directorate-General XI, mimeo (EDH.Im.622).

Conti, Sergio and Giorgio Spriano (1991), "Urban Structure, Technological Innovation and Metropolitan Networks." *Ekistics: The Problems and Science of Human Settlement* 58, 350/351.

Economist, The (ed.) (1994). *Pocket Europe: Profiles, Facts and Figures about Europe Today*. London: Penguin Books.

Faludi, Andreas and Arnold van der Valk (1994), *Rule and Order. Dutch Planning Doctrine in the Twentieth Century*. Dordrecht: Kluwer Academic Publishers.

Friedmann, John (1986), "The World City Hypothesis." *Development and Change* 17(1): 69–84.

Hall, Peter (1966), *The World Cities*. London: World University Library.

King, Anthony D. (1990), *Global Cities: Post-imperialism and the Internationalisation of London*. London: Routledge.

Kunzmann, Klaus R. (1994), "Europäische Städtenetze." *Stadtforum Journal* 14: 6–8.

Kunzmann, Klaus R. and Michael Wegener (1992), "The Pattern of Urbanization in Europe," *Ekistics*, Special Issue: "Urban Networking in Europe I and II," 59, 352/353.

Marcuse, Peter (1994), "Glossy Globalization: Unpacking a Loaded Discourse," mimeo.

NUREC (Network on Urban Research in the European Union) (1994), *Atlas of Agglomerations in the European Union*, vols. 1–3. Duisburg.

Saillez, Allain (ed.) (1993), *Les Villes, lieux d'Europe*. Mouchy/Champagne: Datar/ Éditions de l'aube.

Sassen, Saskia (1991), *The Global City: New York, London, Tokyo*. Princeton, N.J.: Princeton University Press.

—— (1994), *Cities in a World Economy*. Thousand Oaks: Pine Forge Press.

United Nations (ed.) (1987), *The Prospects of World Urbanization, Revised as of 1984–85*. New York: United Nations, Population Studies No. 101.

4

World cities in North America: Structural change and future challenges

Peter Gordon and Harry W. Richardson

Introduction

The past two decades have witnessed increasing interdependence of national economies and intensified globalization. Although the United States has a relatively low dependence on international trade (as measured by indices such as ratio of total trade, exports and imports, to GNP), the large size of its economy means that its international impact is immense. Moreover, because increasing global inter-dependence has been accompanied by dramatic changes in the composition of both exports and imports, and because economic structure varies widely among metropolitan areas, globalization has had a major influence on metropolitan development patterns.

The globalization of economic activity has been a raging topic of discussion in recent years, and its impact on urbanization has been widely debated. For example, the increase in capital mobility has made it as easy to transfer productive resources interregionally as internationally. The consequences for cities, both large and small, in manufacturing regions have been serious. Another trend has been the internationalization of financial markets. This has strengthened and reinforced the dominance of the already powerful financial cen-tres (e.g. New York, London, Tokyo), but the long-term impact is unclear because fund managers and other financial specialists have increasing capacity to locate ubiquitously. Yet another interesting hypothesis, associated with Paul Krugman, is that openness (in terms of international markets) is associated with dispersion down the national urban hierarchy, whereas autarky reinforces primacy. An examination of this (Richardson, 1994) yielded mixed results, but certainly the argument rarely applies to spatially large countries (e.g. the United States, Brazil, India, China), which tend to have low trade/GNP ratios and very dispersed spatial distributions in national urban hierarchy terms.

In most of this chapter, we focus on how economic trends experienced globally are affecting the *intra*metropolitan distribution of economic activity. These trends include: the continued shift toward services; the pull of an increasingly suburbanized labour force on the location of new and relocating firms; the spatial implications of the telecommunications revolution; the diffusion of agglomeration economies over metropolitan space; and the effects of changes in the level of congestion. Mainly, we explore the locational effects of these issues in 12 Consolidated Metropolitan Statistical Areas (CMSAs) of the United States, but we expect similar trends to be observed in large Canadian metropolitan areas, as well as in cities outside North America (such as Paris, Mexico City, and Seoul). We do not consider how far down the national urban hierarchy these trends are observed, although we do believe that restricted definitions of "world city" are outdated. Increasingly, all cities are world cities.

The growth and transformation of cities

The growth of nations is very much explained by their stock of knowledge. This involves "intellectual spillovers," most of which take place in cities (Glaeser, 1994). Cities, then, are not simply places that grow if and when their local industries grow; rather, they can be thought of as the "engines of growth." In the increasingly integrated global economy, efficiently functioning large cities have impacts far beyond national borders.

The concentration of economic activities in cities involves trade-offs between the inevitable costs of congestion and the prospective benefits of agglomeration. Much of the deconcentration can be explained by falling transportation costs, including the substitution of communications for travel, which allows some congestion costs to be avoided, making agglomeration benefits available over larger geo-

77

graphic spaces. Our work on commuting has shown that worsening trip speeds are *not* necessarily associated with city size or growth (Gordon and Richardson, 1994).

It follows that the extent to which cities are able to transform themselves spatially has much to do with growth and economic success. This idea is increasingly important in an age of steeply falling information transmission costs. In a previous paper, we documented the employment decentralization trends in major US metropolitan areas in the 1980s (relying on data from the 1982 and 1987 Economic Census; Gordon and Richardson, 1996). We noted that these trends were consistent with the hypothesis that households now move towards the metropolitan edges in search of amenities, followed by suburbanizing firms seeking access to suburban labour pools. This scenario is consistent with the idea that firms have become more footloose, reversing the traditional locational orientation from one where most residences were compelled to be near industries to one where industries are more likely to follow the locational choices of households. The dramatic shift from manufacturing dominance to the modern service economy has contributed to this change. In the 1979–1992 period, total employment in the United States grew by 1.4 per cent per year; services grew by 4.1 per cent; all business services grew by 6.3 per cent; of these, computer and data-processing services grew by 9.0 per cent. The fastest-growing industries are the most footloose.

The growth of US cities

Table 4.1 is helpful to an appreciation of how the 1980s affected population growth in individual cities (the drawback of the table is that the data refer to individual cities not to metropolitan areas [MAs], a necessary limitation because most of the fastest-growing areas are cities that are often not parts of MAs). Few of the large cities grew significantly, not surprisingly in view of the continued decentralization out of cities. However, growth during the decade exceeded 15 per cent in several large cities (San Diego, Austin, Phoenix, Jacksonville, San Jose, El Paso, Los Angeles, Forth Worth, and San Antonio), all of them in the West or the South. The fastest-growing cities were predominantly suburban jurisdictions, although a few freestanding cities (e.g. Bakersfield, Fresno, Modesto, Stockton, Las Vegas) have attracted some industrial activities. Moreover, the overwhelming majority of the fastest growers were in California,

Arizona, and Texas; the only exceptions were Las Vegas and Reno (Nevada), Virginia Beach (Virginia), Aurora (Colorado), and Overland Park (Kansas). Finally, the right-hand columns of table 4.1 show the biggest losers, ranked in terms of rate of population loss. Most of the heaviest losers (the exception is New Orleans) were industrial cities in the heartland, many of which were severely affected by international competition (e.g. the automobile cities such as Detroit, Flint, and Warren). On the other hand, a few of the cities (e.g.

Table 4.1 **The growth and decline of US cities, 1980–1990**

		Largest cities		
		1980	1990	Change (%)
1.	New York	7,071,639	7,322,564	3.5
2.	Los Angeles	2,968,528	3,485,398	17.4
3.	Chicago	3,005,072	2,783,726	−7.4
4.	Houston	1,617,966	1,630,553	0.8
5.	Philadelphia	1,688,210	1,585,577	−6.1
6.	San Diego	875,538	1,110,549	26.8
7.	Detroit	1,203,369	1,027,974	−14.6
8.	Dallas	905,751	1,006,877	11.2
9.	Phoenix	790,183	983,403	24.5
10.	San Antonio	813,118	935,933	15.1
11.	San Jose, CA	640,225	782,248	22.2
12.	Indianapolis	700,974	741,952	5.8
13.	Baltimore	786,741	736,014	−6.4
14.	San Francisco	678,974	723,959	6.6
15.	Jacksonville, FLA	540,920	672,971	24.4
16.	Columbus, OH	565,021	632,910	12.0
17.	Milwaukee	636,298	628,088	−1.3
18.	Memphis	646,170	610,337	−5.5
19.	Washington	638,432	606,900	−4.9
20.	Boston	562,994	574,283	2.0
21.	Seattle	493,846	516,259	4.5
22.	El Paso	425,259	515,342	21.2
23.	Nashville	477,811	510,748	6.9
24.	Cleveland	573,822	505,616	−11.9
25.	New Orleans	557,927	496,938	−10.9
26.	Denver	492,694	467,610	−5.1
27.	Austin, TX	372,536	465,622	25.0
28.	Fort Worth	385,164	447,619	16.2
29.	Oklahoma City	404,551	444,719	9.9
30.	Portland, OR	429,400	437,319	1.8

Source: US Censuses of Population.

Table 4.1 **(cont.)**

		Fastest-growing cities		
		1980	1990	Change (%)
1.	Moreno Valley, CA	28,309	118,779	319.6
2.	Rancho Cucamonga, CA	55,250	101,409	83.5
3.	Plano, TX	72,331	128,713	77.9
4.	Irvine, CA	62,134	110,330	77.6
5.	Mesa, AZ	163,594	288,091	76.1
6.	Oceanside, CA	76,698	128,398	67.4
7.	Santa Clarita, CA	66,730	110,642	65.8
8.	Escondido, CA	66,709	108,635	62.8
9.	Arlington, TX	161,872	261,721	61.7
10.	Las Vegas, NV	165,304	258,295	56.3
11.	Bakersfield, CA	113,193	174,820	54.4
12.	Mesquite, TX	67,053	101,484	51.3
13.	Glendale, AZ	98,418	148,134	50.5
14.	Ontario, CA	88,820	133,179	49.9
15.	Virginia Beach, VA	262,199	393,069	49.9
16.	Modesto, CA	112,790	164,730	46.1
17.	Scottsdale, AZ	89,577	130,069	45.2
18.	Santa Ana, CA	204,014	293,742	44.0
19.	Pomona, CA	92,742	131,723	42.0
20.	Stockton, CA	149,555	210,943	41.0
21.	Irving, TX	109,943	155,037	41.0
22.	Fresno, CA	252,031	354,202	40.5
23.	Aurora, CO	158,588	222,103	40.1
24.	San Bernardino, CA	120,333	164,164	36.4
25.	Vallejo, CA	80,303	109,199	36.0
26.	Overland Park, KA	82,487	111,790	35.5
27.	Salinas, CA	80,479	108,777	35.2
28.	Santa Rosa, CA	84,402	113,313	34.3
29.	Sacramento, CA	275,741	369,365	34.0
30.	Reno, NV	100,756	133,850	32.8

Atlanta, Denver) were central cities located in expanding metropolitan areas. Figure 4.1 locates the 100 largest US cities in 1990.

Turning to the metropolitan areas, table 4.2 shows that the national metropolitan area size class distribution remained remarkably stable between 1970 and 1990. The only notable change is a slight decline in metropolitan population share of the 2,500,000+ size class combined with very small increases in the shares of all other size classes (somewhat more marked in the 500,000–1,000,000 size class). Thus,

Table 4.1 **(cont.)**

	Most rapidly declining cities		
	1980	1990	Change (%)
1. Gary, IN	151,968	116,646	−23.2
2. Newark, NJ	329,248	275,221	−16.4
3. Detroit	1,203,369	1,027,974	−14.6
4. Pittsburgh	423,960	369,879	−12.8
5. St. Louis	452,804	396,685	−12.4
6. Cleveland	573,822	505,616	−11.9
7. Flint, MI	159,611	140,761	−11.8
8. New Orleans	557,927	496,938	−10.9
9. Warren, MI	161,134	144,864	−10.1
10. Chattanooga, TN	169,514	152,466	−10.1
11. Louisville, KY	298,694	269,063	−9.9
12. Peoria, IL	124,813	113,504	−9.1
13. Macon, GA	116,896	106,612	−8.8
14. Erie, PA	119,123	108,718	−8.7
15. Buffalo	357,870	328,123	−8.3
16. Birmingham, AL	288,297	265,968	−7.7
17. Richmond	219,214	203,056	−7.4
18. Chicago	3,005,072	2,783,726	−7.4
19. Atlanta	425,022	394,017	−7.3
20. Kansas City, KA	161,148	149,767	−7.1
21. Baltimore	786,741	736,014	−6.4
22. Akron, OH	237,590	223,019	−6.1
23. Toledo, OH	354,635	332,943	−6.1
24. Philadelphia	1,688,210	1,585,577	−6.1
25. Dayton, OH	193,549	182,044	−5.9
26. Knoxville, TN	175,045	165,121	−5.7
27. Memphis	646,170	610,337	−5.5
28. Cincinnati	385,410	364,040	−5.5
29. Denver	492,694	467,610	−5.1
30. Washington	638,432	606,900	−4.9

in aggregate terms the internationalization of the US economy appears to have had little influence on the national urban hierarchy.

When the United States is split into macro-regions (North, South, West), a different picture emerges. Table 4.3 illustrates the major regional trends by large metropolitan areas (defined as larger than 1 million), small MAs, and non-metropolitan areas. In the country as a whole, the large MAs grew faster than the other two categories in the 1960s and in the 1980s; non-metropolitan areas grew fastest of

81

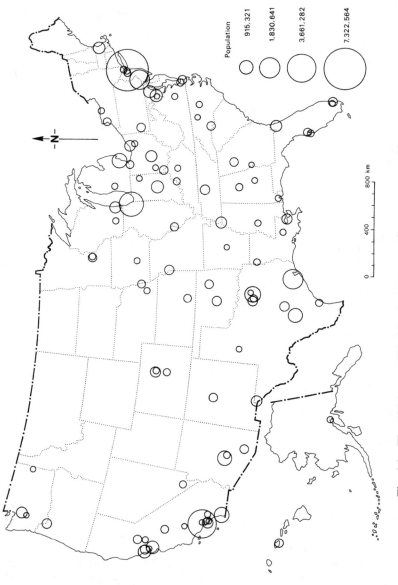

Fig. 4.1 The 100 largest US cities in 1990 (Source: US Census of Population)

Table 4.2 **Metropolitan population (CMSAs and MSAs) by size class in 1990, 1970–1990**

		1970		1980		1990	
Size class	No. (1990)	Population (million)	Share (%)	Population (million)	Share (%)	Population (million)	Share (%)
2,500,000 or more	15	79.0	49.5	84.3	47.7	94.1	47.6
1,000,000–2,499,999	25	30.4	19.0	34.4	19.4	38.8	19.6
500,000–999,999	33	18.2	11.4	21.4	12.1	24.3	12.3
250,000–499,999	63	17.3	10.8	19.8	11.2	22.0	11.1
<250,000	132	14.7	9.2	17.0	9.6	18.5	9.4
Total	268	159.6	100.0	176.9	100.0	197.7	100.0

Source: US Censuses of Population.

all the categories in the 1970s but slowest in the 1960s and the 1980s; and the smaller MAs were buoyant throughout. These trends were more or less mirrored in the individual regions, but there were striking interregional differentials in terms of growth rates. Particularly after the 1960s, growth in all categories almost disappeared in the North while remaining strong in the South and the West. Assuming that population shifts generally (but not always) reflect changing economic opportunities, and taking account of both the historical role of the North as the industrial heartland and the growth of export activities in the South and the West, these interregional changes are a direct indication of how different urban regions responded in demographic terms to increasing globalization. Figure 4.2 shows the locations of the 50 fastest-growing metropolitan areas in the 1980s.

These overall trends can be clarified by examining the performance of individual cities. Table 4.4 displays the population growth rates for the 25 largest MAs by region. The drastic deceleration in the growth rates (in some cases turning negative) of the large Northern MAs is almost across the board. Kansas is a partial and Minneapolis–St. Paul a striking exception (in the latter case a partial reflection of the success of several large internationally oriented companies such as 3M and Cargill). The Southern MAs performed well, with the exception of the border metropolises (Baltimore and, to a lesser extent, Washington, D.C.), but in at least two cases (Miami and Tampa–St. Petersburg) the reasons are non-economic. Dallas–Ft. Worth and Atlanta are the strongest performers in the region, while the deceleration of Houston (in the 1980s compared with the 1960s and 1970s, and within the 1980s in the latter half of the decade) primarily reflects the problems

Table 4.3 **Percentage population change for regional and metropolitan categories, 1960–1990**

Region and metropolitan category	1990 size (million)	Percentage 10-year change			Percentage 5-year change	
		1960–70	1970–80	1980–90	1980–85	1985–90
North						
Large MAs	62.9	12.0	−0.9	2.8	1.3	1.5
Other MAs	25.6	11.1	5.2	3.3	0.9	2.4
Non-MAs	22.6	2.6	8.0	0.1	0.7	−0.6
South						
Large MAs	28.2	30.9	23.4	22.3	12.3	8.9
Other MAs	31.9	15.5	20.9	13.4	8.8	4.2
Non-MAs	24.9	1.1	16.3	4.6	4.4	−0.3
West						
Large MAs	33.8	29.1	20.0	24.2	10.9	11.9
Other MAs	10.8	24.8	32.2	22.8	11.4	10.2
Non-MAs	8.1	9.0	30.6	14.1	9.1	4.6
US totals						
Large MAs	124.8	18.5	8.1	12.1	6.0	5.8
Other MAs	67.9	14.6	15.5	10.8	6.1	4.4
Non-MAs	56.0	2.2	14.3	3.9	3.6	0.3
Regional totals						
Large MAs	111.0	9.8	2.2	2.4	1.1	1.2
Other MAs	84.9	14.2	20.1	13.3	8.6	4.3
Non-MAs	52.8	24.6	24.0	22.2	10.7	10.3
Total	248.7	13.4	11.4	9.8	5.4	4.1

Source: Frey (1993) based on data compiled at University of Michigan Population Studies Center from decennial Census data and estimates prepared by the Census Bureau Population Division.

in the world oil market. In the West, all the large MAs experienced moderately strong growth. However, the fastest-growing MAs were Phoenix and San Diego, neither of which was closely involved internationally, despite their relative proximity to the Mexican border. But it was Los Angeles that showed the most dramatic acceleration in the 1980s, and here global influences were paramount: the dominance of the twin ports of Long Beach and Los Angeles in US international trade; the massive immigration from Latin America and Asia, which helped to prolong Los Angeles' position as a major manufacturing centre (e.g. in the garment industry); the growth of Japanese invest-

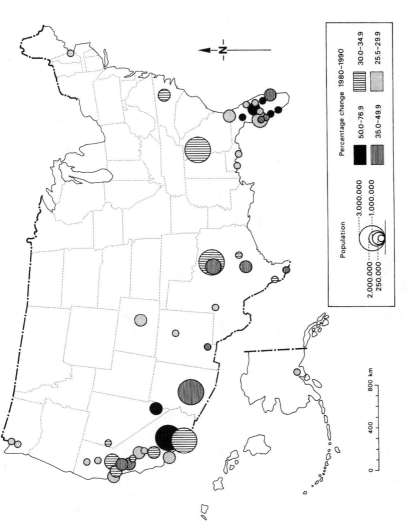

Fig. 4.2 **The 50 fastest-growing US metropolitan areas, 1980–1990 (Source: Paul E. Knox,** *Urbanization: An Introduction to Urban Geography,* **Englewood Cliffs, N.J.: Prentice Hall, 1994)**

Table 4.4 **Percentage change in the 25 largest metropolitan areas in North, South, and West regions, 1960–1990**

Region and metropolitan area	1990 size (million)	Percentage 10-year change			Percentage 5-year change	
		1960–70	1970–80	1980–90	1980–85	1985–90
North						
New York CMSA	18.1	11.8	−3.6	3.1	2.9	0.2
Chicago CMSA	8.1	12.2	2.0	1.6	1.9	−0.2
Philadelphia CMSA	5.9	12.1	−1.2	3.9	1.7	2.1
Detroit CMSA	4.7	13.4	−0.7	−1.8	−3.6	1.8
Boston CMSA	4.2	12.7	0.8	5.0	2.0	3.0
Cleveland CMSA	2.8	9.8	−5.5	−2.6	−2.0	−0.6
Minneapolis–St. Paul CMSA	2.5	23.0	7.8	15.3	5.9	8.9
St. Louis MSA	2.4	12.4	−2.2	2.8	1.5	1.3
Pittsburgh CMSA	2.2	−0.7	−5.2	−7.5	−3.6	−4.1
Cincinnati CMSA	1.7	9.9	2.9	5.1	1.2	3.8
Milwaukee CMSA	1.6	10.9	−0.3	2.4	−1.3	3.7
Kansas City MSA	1.6	14.2	4.4	9.3	4.2	4.8
South						
Washington MSA	3.9	37.3	6.9	20.7	7.3	12.5
Dallas–Fort Worth CMSA	3.9	37.1	14.6	32.6	19.8	10.7
Houston CMSA	3.7	38.1	43.0	19.7	16.8	2.4
Miami CMSA	3.2	48.8	40.1	20.8	8.9	10.9
Atlanta MSA	2.8	35.0	27.0	32.5	15.6	14.6
Baltimore MSA	2.4	14.8	5.3	8.3	2.4	5.7
Tampa–St. Petersburg MSA	2.1	34.8	46.0	28.2	15.8	10.7
West						
Los Angeles CMSA	14.5	28.8	15.2	26.4	10.8	14.1
San Francisco–Oakland CMSA	6.3	27.7	12.9	16.5	8.2	7.6
Seattle CMSA	2.6	28.6	14.0	22.3	7.4	13.9
San Diego MSA	2.5	31.5	37.1	34.2	14.6	17.1
Phoenix MSA	2.1	46.4	55.4	40.6	22.4	14.9
Denver CMSA	1.8	32.6	30.7	14.2	12.9	1.2

Source: Frey (1993) based on data compiled at University of Michigan Population Studies Center from decennial Census data and estimates prepared by the Census Bureau Population Division.

Table 4.5 **Metropolitan areas with greatest 1980–1990 increases: Total population**

Metropolitan area	Increase ('000)
Areas with greatest total increase	
Los Angeles CMSA	3,034
Dallas–Fort Worth CMSA	955
San Francisco CMSA	885
Atlanta MSA	695
Washington D.C. MSA	673
Areas with greatest White increase	
Dallas–Fort Worth CMSA	487
Atlanta MSA	414
Phoenix MSA	412
Tampa–St. Petersburg MSA	345
Seattle CMSA	324
Areas with greatest minority increase	
Los Angeles CMSA	2,795
New York CMSA	1,398
San Francisco CMSA	787
Miami CMSA	635
Houston CMSA	484

Source: Frey (1993).

ment (now disinvestment) in commercial real estate; and (until the late 1980s) defence-related economic activities.

Changing populations

Table 4.5 shows that the largest increases in minority population (mainly because of immigrants) between 1980 and 1990 occurred in Los Angeles, New York, San Francisco, Miami, and Houston. This growth accounted for most of each area's population growth in three cases (92 per cent in Los Angeles, 88 per cent in San Francisco, and 79 per cent in Houston) and more than offset non-minority declines in two cases (860,000 in New York and 85,000 in Miami). Four out of these five metropolitan regions (the exception is New York) grew rapidly in the 1980s, almost all of the growth being the result of immigration.

The growth of minority populations in the United States MAs in the 1980s was primarily associated with recent immigration (the national increase in the African-American population was only 13.2 per cent, compared with a 53.0 per cent increase in the Hispanic population and a 107.8 per cent increase in the Asian population; see table 4.6). Table 4.6 also sheds light on how the growth of different races varies by region and type of area. The growth was widely dispersed, especially for the Hispanic population. However, the growth of Asian population in the West was three times higher in the large MAs than in the other areas, while the growth of the African-American population was much higher in the small MAs and in the non-metropolitan areas than in the large MAs in the West and much higher than elsewhere in the country. Of the almost 13.5 million increase in the population of large MAs between 1980 and 1990, 64.5 per cent was accounted for by Hispanics and Asians. The growth of large MAs in the 1980s was largely fuelled by new or recent immigration. Although the quickening pace of immigration largely reflected the relaxation in US immigration laws, this relaxation occurred in an environment of increasing internationalization.

Table 4.7 examines central-city–suburban differentials in racial composition in the 25 largest metropolitan areas. As expected, in all cases minorities are much more concentrated in the central cities than in the suburbs. In many instances, such as Detroit, Baltimore, Atlanta, Chicago, Washington D.C., Cleveland, and Miami, the differentials are colossal. Yet, perhaps surprisingly, in every case except Milwaukee, the minority population grew faster in the suburbs between 1980 and 1990 than in the central city, in many metropolitan areas (e.g. Dallas–Fort Worth, Atlanta, Boston, Washington D.C., Tampa–St. Petersburg, Miami, and Seattle) much faster. Furthermore, in most metropolitan areas (the exceptions are Detroit, Cincinnati, Milwaukee, and Phoenix) the central-city–suburb differential in favour of the suburbs was wider for minorities than for non-Hispanic whites. These data are significant because they explode the myth of central-city populations of colour surrounded by white suburbs. However, in addition to this, the spilling over of minorities into the suburbs is a reflection of their increasing affluence and mobility. Furthermore, the 1990 suburban minority share tended to be particularly high in those metropolitan areas that showed the highest metropolitan-wide increases, largely reflecting the growth of immigrant populations.

Economic change

The above comments refer to population data. Employment indicators provide a more direct measure of how internationalization affects the economic performance of economic areas. Table 4.8 shows the

Table 4.6 1990 population and 1980–1990 percentage change of total population: Non-Hispanic whites, all minorities, Blacks, Hispanics, and Asians by regional and metropolitan categories

Region and metropolitan category	Total population		Non-Hispanic whites		All minorities		Blacks		Hispanics[a]		Asians	
	1990 population ('000)	1980–90 percentage change	1990 population ('000)	1980–90 percentage change	1990 population ('000)	1980–90 percentage change	1990 population ('000)	1980–90 percentage change	1990 population ('000)	1980–90 percentage change	1990 population ('000)	1980–90 percentage change
North												
Large MAs	62,897	2.8	47,184	−2.1	15,712	21.2	9,590	10.3	4,634	40.1	1,721	123.5
Other MAs	25,524	3.5	23,107	1.5	2,416	28.2	1,473	15.6	586	56.3	281	127.1
Non-MAs	22,581	−0.2	21,679	−1.0	901	26.4	339	21.8	272	33.5	108	85.2
South												
Large MAs	28,168	22.3	18,210	13.8	9,957	41.5	5,673	24.0	3,617	70.4	697	159.3
Other MAs	31,895	13.4	23,553	10.9	8,342	21.3	5,646	12.3	2,217	41.1	325	120.9
Non-MAs	24,857	4.6	19,165	4.1	5,692	6.3	4,434	1.2	919	19.1	91	81.5
West												
Large MAs	33,843	24.2	21,350	10.1	12,493	59.0	2,376	21.9	7,191	67.8	2,899	123.0
Other MAs	10,828	22.9	7,491	14.9	3,336	45.9	368	42.3	1,970	53.6	904	49.0
Non-MAs	8,114	13.9	6,384	10.1	1,729	32.4	83	56.8	944	37.7	243	40.4
Met. Classes												
Large MAs	124,908	12.1	86,745	3.8	38,163	37.0	17,640	15.9	15,443	58.9	5,318	127.3
Other MAs	68,247	10.8	54,152	7.1	14,095	27.6	7,487	14.1	4,774	47.8	1,511	72.1
Non-MAs	55,553	3.8	47,230	2.4	8,322	12.8	4,857	3.1	2,136	28.5	443	57.0

Table 4.6 (cont.)

Region and metro-politan category	Total population		Non-Hispanic whites		All minorities		Blacks		Hispanics[a]		Asians	
	1990 population ('000)	1980–90 percent-age change	1990 population ('000)	1980–90 percent-age change	1990 population ('000)	1980–90 percent-age change	1990 population ('000)	1980–90 percent-age change	1990 population ('000)	1980–90 percent-age change	1990 population ('000)	1980–90 percent-age change
Regions												
North	111,002	2.4	91,971	–1.0	19,030	22.2	11,403	11.3	5,493	41.3	2,111	121.6
South	84,921	13.3	60,929	9.5	23,991	24.5	15,754	12.6	6,754	51.2	1,114	138.8
West	52,786	22.2	35,228	11.0	17,559	53.4	2,828	25.0	10,106	61.6	4,047	94.5
Total	248,709	9.8	188,128	4.4	60,581	30.9	29,986	13.2	22,354	53.0	7,273	107.8

Source: Frey (1993) based on data compiled at University of Michigan Population Studies Center from 1980 and 1990 US Censuses.
a. Hispanics can be of any racial group (black, white, Asian, etc.).

Table 4.7 **1990 percentage for minorities, and 1980–1990 percentage change for non-Hispanic whites and minorities in primary central cities and surrounding suburbs of the 25 largest metropolitan areas in North, South, and West regions**

Region and metropolitan area	1990 percentage for minorities			1980–90 percentage change non-Hispanic whites			1980–90 percentage change minorities		
	Central city	Suburbs	Diff.	Central city	Suburbs	Diff.	Central city	Suburbs	Diff.
North									
New York CMSA	56.8	23.4	−33.4	−13.8	−4.1	9.7	22.2	34.7	12.5
Chicago CMSA	62.1	18.2	−43.9	−18.7	1.2	19.9	1.3	44.8	43.5
Philadelphia CMSA	47.9	15.8	−32.1	−14.3	4.7	19.0	4.8	30.2	25.4
Detroit CMSA	79.4	9.2	−70.2	−47.2	0.5	47.7	1.8	27.2	25.4
Boston CMSA	41.0	8.8	−32.2	−11.4	0.1	11.5	30.2	114.1	83.9
Cleveland CMSA	52.2	11.6	−40.6	−19.4	−2.4	17.0	−3.6	19.8	23.4
Minneapolis–St. Paul CMSA	21.3	4.3	−17.0	−10.1	19.8	29.9	69.8	101.9	32.1
St. Louis MSA	49.9	13.6	−36.3	−16.9	4.6	21.5	−7.5	19.3	26.8
Pittsburgh CMSA	28.4	5.6	−22.8	−15.9	−7.0	8.9	−3.6	5.8	9.4
Cincinnati CMSA	39.9	6.2	−33.7	−12.3	7.4	19.7	6.8	23.2	16.4
Milwaukee CMSA	39.2	5.5	−33.7	−15.8	3.5	19.4	34.9	33.1	−1.8
Kansas City MSA	35.0	10.3	−24.7	−7.4	13.0	20.4	6.6	33.8	27.2
South									
Washington MSA	72.6	30.9	−41.7	1.2	13.6	12.4	−7.0	72.1	79.8
Dallas–Fort Worth CMSA	49.6	18.7	−30.9	−3.5	35.1	38.6	36.1	154.5	118.4
Houston CMSA	59.4	28.6	−30.8	−20.6	25.1	45.7	27.2	87.0	59.8
Miami CMSA	87.8	47.7	−40.1	−34.9	−4.1	30.8	12.6	79.9	67.3
Atlanta MSA	69.7	23.4	−46.3	−11.9	29.9	41.8	−5.1	107.9	113.0
Baltimore MSA	61.4	14.5	−46.9	−16.8	12.7	29.5	1.5	45.8	44.3
Tampa–St. Petersburg MSA	33.1	11.4	−21.7	−4.1	35.5	39.6	15.6	95.0	79.4

Table 4.7 (cont.)

Region and metropolitan area	1990 percentage for minorities			1980–90 percentage change non-Hispanic whites			1980–90 percentage change minorities		
	Central city	Suburbs	Diff.	Central city	Suburbs	Diff.	Central city	Suburbs	Diff.
West									
Los Angeles CMSA	62.7	46.3	−16.4	−8.4	6.5	14.9	41.3	72.9	31.6
San Francisco–Oakland CMSA	59.7	34.3	−25.4	−6.5	4.0	10.5	20.0	62.1	42.1
Seattle CMSA	26.3	12.3	−14.0	−1.7	22.7	24.4	27.2	81.3	54.1
San Diego MSA	41.3	29.3	−12.0	8.3	27.0	18.7	67.7	90.0	22.3
Phoenix MSA	28.2	18.2	−10.0	14.5	53.2	38.7	60.3	86.3	26.0
Denver CMSA	38.6	14.0	−24.6	−12.1	18.3	30.4	8.8	58.3	49.5

Source: Frey (1993) based on data compiled at University of Michigan Population Studies Center from decennial Census data and estimates prepared by the Census Bureau Population Division.

Table 4.8 **Average annual growth rates in employment: 17 CMSAs, 1972–1992**

Sector	Average annual growth rates		
	CMSA	Core	Ring
Private	**0.02024**	**0.01772**	**0.02583**
Agricultural services, forestry, fisheries, and other	0.03845	0.03363	0.04451
Mining	0.03115	0.03173	0.02882
Construction	0.01652	0.01398	0.02146
Manufacturing	−0.00737	−0.00966	−0.00285
Transportation and public utilities	0.01027	0.00746	0.01743
Wholesale trade	0.01874	0.01278	0.03494
Retail trade	0.01970	0.01711	0.02482
Finance, insurance, and real estate	0.02220	0.01929	0.02968
Services	0.03985	0.03726	0.04597
Government and government services	**0.01049**	**0.00895**	**0.01356**
Federal, civilian	0.00428	0.00272	0.00884
Military	−0.00772	−0.00905	−0.00569
State and local	0.01502	0.01351	0.01785
Total	**0.01873**	**0.01640**	**0.02380**

Source: US Bureau of Economic Analysis, Regional Economic Information System data files.

average annual employment growth rates of individual sectors in the 17 CMSAs (the Boston CMSA is excluded because of complex boundary changes) between 1972 and 1992 (using 1992 CMSA boundary definitions), based on US Department of Commerce Bureau of Economic Analysis (BEA) data. The most salient features are that the range of growth rates varies from a decline of 0.74 per cent per annum in manufacturing to an increase of 3.99 per cent per annum for services (the total employment growth rate is 1.87 per cent per annum). Moreover, manufacturing is the only declining sector (with the exception of military employment). Furthermore, the typical core–ring growth differentials are observed in both manufacturing and services. To the extent that the deteriorating performance of manufacturing reflects the increasing intensity of international competition over this period, globalization has accelerated the to-be-expected shifts toward services in the largest metropolitan areas.

For example, one measure of the United States' increasing international interdependence is the threefold expansion in exports of producer services in the 1980s (producer services are defined as communications, banking, security and commodity brokers and services, insurance carriers and agents, holding and other investment companies, business services, film production, legal services, and miscellaneous professional services). By 1990, producer services accounted for 8.2 per cent of total US exports, and grew in the 1980s at $2\frac{1}{3}$ times total exports (13.3 per cent per annum compared with 5.7 per cent). Based on earnings data (neither output nor exports data are directly available), four CMSAs (New York, Los Angeles, Chicago, and San Francisco) accounted for 35 per cent of the US total in this sector (excluding communications, for which data are not fully available because of disclosure problems) compared with 25 per cent of total economic activity. Also, producer services accounted for one-quarter of economic activity in these four "gateway" CMSAs. These cities were the headquarter locations for each of the six largest accounting firms, 97 per cent of the 35 largest advertising firms, and 73 per cent of the 50 largest law firms (Drennan, 1992).

Table 4.9 uses BEA data to illustrate changes in economic structure in the 12 CMSAs examined in detail below between 1972 and 1992. They show specialization in the service sectors (especially wholesale trade, the FIRE (finance, insurance, and real estate) sector, and business and personal services) in most of the large metropolitan regions. Also, specialization increased in services between 1972 and 1992 in 8 of the 12 cities. On the other hand, despite the shift from manufacturing to services, 6 of the 12 cities (mainly in the Midwest) continued to specialize in the manufacturing sector.

Spatial change

While growing and changing in terms of economic activity, cities have also been reshaping themselves. Mostly, they have been growing outward. Table 4.10 shows population change from 1960 by macro-region for the 25 largest cities in their central cities and suburbs. Northern central cities lost population in all three decades with the exceptions of New York and Kansas in the 1960s and New York and Boston in the 1980s. In the South, there was brisk 1980s central-city population growth in Dallas–Fort Worth, slower growth in Houston, Miami, and Tampa–St. Petersburg, and decline in Washington, Atlanta, and Baltimore. The cities of the West all grew in the 1980s with the exception of Denver; San Francisco–Oakland and Seattle showed more modest growth than Los Angeles, San Diego, and Phoenix, but the former actually reversed 20 years of decline.

Table 4.9 **Specializations of 12 CMSAs by major economic sector**

CMSA	Construction	Manufacturing	Transportation & public utilities	Wholesale	Retail	Finance, etc.	Services
Chicago		X	X*	X		X*	X*
Cincinnati	X*	X	X	X*	X*		
Cleveland		X		X*	X*		X*
Detroit		X		X	X*		X*
Houston	X*		X	X			X
Los Angeles		X*		X*		X	X*
Miami			X	X*	X*	X	X
Milwaukee		X*		X*		X*	X*
New York			X	X		X*	X*
Philadelphia				X		X*	X*
San Francisco			X	X		X	X*
Seattle	X*			X		X	X*

Source: US Bureau of Economic Analysis, Regional Economic Information System file.
Note: X indicates share of jobs greater in the CMSA than in USA, 1992.
* indicates specialization greater in 1992 than in 1972.

Table 4.10 Percentage change in primary central cities and surrounding areas of the 25 largest metropolitan areas in North, South, and West regions

Region and metropolitan area	Age of area	1990 size ('000)		Primary central-city percentage 10-year change			Surrounding area percentage 10-year change		
		Metropolitan area	Primary central city	1960–70	1970–80	1980–90	1960–70	1970–80	1980–90
North									
New York CMSA	1800	18,087	7,323	1.5	−10.4	3.5	21.3	1.7	2.8
Chicago CMSA	1860	8,066	2,784	−5.1	−10.8	−7.4	30.3	11.8	7.1
Philadelphia CMSA	1810	5,899	1,586	−2.6	−13.4	−6.1	21.5	5.1	8.0
Detroit CMSA	1870	4,665	1,028	−9.3	−20.5	−14.6	28.2	8.4	2.5
Boston CMSA	1830	4,172	574	−8.0	−12.2	2.0	17.8	3.4	5.5
Cleveland CMSA	1870	2,760	506	−14.3	−23.6	−11.9	21.1	0.5	−0.3
Minneapolis–St. Paul CMSA	1890	2,464	641	−6.5	−13.8	−0.1	51.8	20.8	21.9
St. Louis MSA	1850	2,444	397	−17.1	−27.2	−12.4	28.1	6.5	6.4
Pittsburgh CMSA	1870	2,243	370	−13.9	−18.5	−12.8	3.3	−1.8	−6.3
Cincinnati CMSA	1850	1,744	364	−9.7	−15.1	−5.5	20.2	10.0	8.3
Milwaukee CMSA	1870	1,607	628	−3.2	−11.3	−1.3	26.2	8.9	4.8
Kansas City MSA	1880	1,566	435	6.5	−11.6	−2.9	19.3	13.8	14.8
South									
Washington MSA	1860	3,924	607	−0.9	−15.7	−4.9	57.5	14.4	27.0
Dallas–Fort Worth CMSA	1910	3,885	1,454	19.5	4.2	12.8	63.9	47.3	48.2
Houston CMSA	1910	3,711	1,631	31.6	29.3	2.2	47.8	61.1	38.1
Miami CMSA	1930	3,193	359	14.7	3.5	3.4	58.9	47.9	23.4
Atlanta MSA	1890	2,834	394	1.6	−14.1	−7.3	56.3	44.1	42.4
Baltimore MSA	1820	2,382	736	−3.5	−13.2	−6.4	34.3	19.4	16.5
Tampa–St. Petersburg MSA	1920	2,086	519	8.3	3.3	1.7	67.8	80.4	40.4

West

Los Angeles CMSA	1890	14,532	3,485	13.6	5.4	17.4	35.9	19.0	29.5
San Francisco–Oakland CMSA	1860	6,253	1,096	-2.8	-5.4	7.6	40.6	18.3	18.6
Seattle CMSA	1900	2,559	516	-4.7	-7.0	4.5	49.8	22.4	27.7
San Diego MSA	1920	2,498	1,111	21.6	25.6	26.8	43.7	49.2	40.7
Phoenix MSA	1940	2,122	983	33.0	35.2	24.5	72.5	85.8	58.3
Denver CMSA	1890	1,848	468	4.2	-4.3	-5.1	64.3	55.6	22.6

Source: Frey (1993) based on data compiled at University of Michigan Population Studies Center from decennial Census data and estimates prepared by the Census Bureau Population Division.

The suburban growth story is somewhat different. With the exception of Pittsburgh, all of the Northern suburbs grew significantly in the 1960s. This growth slowed substantially in the 1970s and the 1980s. Pittsburgh's suburbs declined in both decades and Cleveland's declined in the 1980s. In contrast, all of the Western and Southern suburbs grew substantially in all three decades. A more detailed examination of suburbanization using employment data follows.

Metropolitan jobs dispersion

The US Economic Census contains some of the most accurate and detailed data on US industrial location. In our previous paper (Gordon and Richardson, 1996) we focused on the 12 metropolitan areas that had been classified as CMSAs (Consolidated Metropolitan Statistical Areas) in 1982 and in 1987 (and without major redefinition). We analysed the employment data in terms of the central city (not to be confused with the CBD), the immediately surrounding PMSA (Primary Metropolitan Statistical Area, mostly the inner and older suburbs, referred to here as Ring I), and the remaining contiguous PMSAs (the outer and newer suburbs, Ring II). We did this in order to go beyond the standard central city vs. suburb dichotomies utilized in our population discussion. We were not evoking the idea of monocentric cities. Rather, we were testing the hypothesis of the previous section as best we could with data not available in less aggregated form (only some of the Census data were made available for postal Zip codes). With our approach, trends within each metropolitan area can be studied, but intermetropolitan comparisons must be made carefully because local county boundaries are the building blocks of the CMSAs and the rings.

The findings of the previous paper emphasized the almost ubiquitous decentralization of employment for the large US metropolitan areas in the 1980s; this was true for all major employment sectors, including services. We now carry the analysis forward into the 1990s, using data from the 1992 Economic Census (for the retail, wholesale, and services sectors; metropolitan-level data for the manufacturing sector were not yet released at the time of writing) as well as from the Bureau of Economic Analysis' Regional Economic Information System (REIS) file. The latter includes annual data from 1969 to 1993. It includes more sectors than the Economic Census but does not go below the county level; we can examine outer suburbs but we cannot separate inner suburbs from central cities. Also, employment

Table 4.11 **Shares of sectoral employment: Combined (12) major CMSAs, 1982, 1987, 1992**

Sector	Central city			Ring I			Ring II		
	1982	1987	1992	1982	1987	1992	1982	1987	1992
Manufacturing	0.302	0.258	–	0.349	0.377	–	0.349	0.365	–
Retail	0.281	0.258	0.231	0.368	0.379	0.396	0.351	0.364	0.373
Wholesale	0.377	0.319	0.273	0.336	0.360	0.380	0.287	0.321	0.347
Services	0.416	0.361	0.310	0.300	0.327	0.355	0.284	0.313	0.335

Source: Calculated by authors from US Economic Census data.

totals from the two sources are not consistent because the BEA includes part-time workers.

Table 4.11 shows that the 1982–1987 trends continued to 1992. Combining all 12 metropolitan areas, the shares of jobs in central cities continued to fall in all three sectors. Likewise, all three sectors' shares of Ring I employment rose, as did the corresponding shares in Ring II. In 1992, Ring II employment shares were about equal to Ring I shares.

Table 4.12 shows sectoral growth rates by metropolitan location. The 1987–1992 period included an economic recession; all growth rates were lower than in the previous five years. For the central cities this meant that only one of the three sectors (services) showed positive growth, though at just more than one-tenth the pace in Rings I and II. Retail and wholesale jobs grew in both Rings; retail growth was highest in Ring I whereas wholesale growth was highest in Ring II.

Growth rates during the period 1982–1992 include times of economic expansion as well as contraction. Ten-year population growth for the group of 12 CMSAs was 0.9 per cent per year. The Los Angeles CMSA grew fastest at 2.3 per cent per year; only the Cleveland CMSA experienced negative population growth. Los Angeles also led in Ring II population growth at 3.4 per cent; only Chicago experienced negative population growth in Ring II. Ring I population growth was greatest in Houston (3.0 per cent) and least in Cleveland (0.1 per cent). Most central cities had negative population growth (Milwaukee, Houston, Miami, Cincinnati, Philadelphia, Chicago, Cleveland, Detroit); only 4 of the 12 central cities (Los Angeles, Seattle, San Francisco, New York) reported positive population growth, though the rates were low, ranging from 0.3 per cent per year (New York) to 1.4 per cent per year (Los Angeles).

Table 4.12 **Average annual sectoral employment growth rates: Combined (12) major CMSAs, 1982–1992**

Sector	Central City			Ring I			Ring II			CMSA		
	1982–87	1987–92	1982–92	1982–87	1987–92	1982–92	1982–87	1987–92	1982–92	1982–87	1987–92	1982–92
Manufacturing	−0.0388	–	–	0.0075	–	–	0.0012	–	–	−0.0078	–	–
Retail	0.0215	−0.0126	0.0043	0.0454	0.0179	0.0316	0.0468	0.0140	0.0303	0.0394	0.0090	0.0241
Wholesale	−0.0029	−0.0211	−0.0121	0.0445	0.0213	0.0328	0.0535	0.0255	0.0394	0.0304	0.0099	0.0201
Services	0.0397	0.0068	0.0231	0.0885	0.0555	0.0719	0.0904	0.0518	0.0710	0.0698	0.0378	0.05369

Source: Calculated by authors from US Economic Census data.

Overall 10-year job growth for the group of 12 CMSAs can be summarized as follows: Ring I led Ring II in retail and services growth; Ring II led Ring I in wholesale jobs growth; the growth differences between the two rings were small; and the growth rates in Rings I and II greatly surpassed central-city growth rates.

Looking at 10-year job growth for individual areas (table 4.13), only 3 of the 12 central cities (Milwaukee, Seattle, Los Angeles) showed positive growth in wholesale jobs. All central cities but Detroit showed positive growth in services jobs. Only two central cities (Seattle and San Francisco) had retail job growth above 1 per cent per year; three declined (Cleveland, Milwaukee, Detroit); the other central cities grew but at less than 1 per cent per year.

Ten-year job growth in Ring I was positive in all CMSAs in all three sectors but growth rates varied widely. Ring I wholesale growth leader Seattle grew at six times the pace of lagging San Francisco (6.5 per cent per year vs. 1.1 per cent). Ring I services growth leader Houston grew at 13.3 per cent per year whereas last place New York grew at 4.7 per cent. Ring I retail growth leader Chicago (5.3 per cent) grew at almost 10 times the rate of lagging New York (0.6 per cent).

The range of growth rates was greater for Ring II. In the wholesale sector, Detroit's growth was 16.5 per cent per year, far greater than second-place Houston (6.4 per cent). Chicago's Ring II wholesale jobs actually declined in the decade. An even greater contrast is apparent in services growth: Detroit again led with 16.3 per cent per year; Chicago was again last with negative growth. The retail growth ranking was similar: Detroit was first (13.1 per cent); Cleveland and Chicago both showed negative growth.

Within the services sector, those subsectors that fall into the business services category (SIC 73) had employment growth that was much faster than the group in the personal services subsector (SIC 72; table 4.14). This reflects modern business practices that avail themselves of new information transmission opportunities, reduced transaction costs, more outsourcing, etc. As we would expect, of the metropolitan areas that led in 1987–1992 business services growth (Houston, Seattle, Cleveland, Miami, Chicago, Detroit, Los Angeles, San Francisco, Milwaukee), most (Houston, Seattle, Miami, Detroit, San Francisco, Milwaukee) experienced most of that growth in the outer suburbs. Cleveland and Los Angeles show Ring I and Ring II business services growth rates that are almost the same.

However, with respect to the four "gateway" metropolitan areas (Drennan, 1992), producer services remained much more centralized

Table 4.13 Average annual job growth rates: 12 CMSAs, 1982–1992

	CMSA	Central city	Ring I	Ring II
New York				
Wholesale	0.016	−0.012	0.019	0.036
Retail	0.025	0.001	0.006	0.040
Services	0.047	0.016	0.047	0.076
Los Angeles				
Wholesale	0.027	0.003	0.021	0.060
Retail	0.021	0.009	0.017	0.033
Services	0.055	0.031	0.062	0.073
Chicago				
Wholesale	0.019	−0.019	0.046	−0.060
Retail	0.021	0.005	0.053	−0.059
Services	0.052	0.026	0.091	−0.007
San Francisco				
Wholesale	0.032	−0.012	0.011	0.046
Retail	0.021	0.014	0.017	0.023
Services	0.054	0.030	0.060	0.063
Philadelphia				
Wholesale	0.009	−0.026	0.026	0.001
Retail	0.020	0.002	0.025	0.026
Services	0.059	0.023	0.064	0.093
Detroit				
Wholesale	0.029	−0.029	0.032	0.165
Retail	0.040	−0.013	0.035	0.131
Services	0.060	−0.009	0.063	0.163
Houston				
Wholesale	−0.012	−0.019	0.012	0.064
Retail	0.014	0.004	0.020	0.076
Services	0.055	0.021	0.133	0.100
Miami				
Wholesale	0.031	−0.014	0.035	0.057
Retail	0.022	0.006	0.029	0.021
Services	0.055	0.033	0.055	0.065
Cleveland				
Wholesale	0.013	−0.026	0.036	0.005
Retail	0.018	−0.001	0.035	−0.008
Services	0.048	0.015	0.074	0.033
Seattle				
Wholesale	0.039	0.006	0.065	0.041
Retail	0.049	0.016	0.048	0.093
Services	0.075	0.041	0.091	0.107
Cincinnati				
Wholesale	0.034	−0.007	0.057	0.064
Retail	0.033	0.008	0.043	0.026
Services	0.061	0.036	0.081	0.070
Milwaukee				
Wholesale	0.024	0.006	0.034	0.047
Retail	0.020	−0.004	0.034	0.018
Services	0.052	0.026	0.071	0.061

Source: Calculated by authors from US Economic Census data.

Table 4.14 **Average annual service sectors job growth rates: 12 CMSAs, 1987–1992**

	CMSA	Central city	Ring I	Ring II
New York				
Personal services	0.016	−0.015	−0.003	0.034
Business services	0.003	−0.042	0.048	0.038
Los Angeles				
Personal services	0.017	−0.014	0.020	0.039
Business services	0.037	0.015	0.048	0.043
Chicago				
Personal services	0.023	0.003	0.080	−0.142
Business services	0.044	0.022	0.069	−0.003
San Francisco				
Personal services	−0.006	−0.062	−0.025	0.015
Business services	0.033	0.001	0.032	0.044
Philadelphia				
Personal services	0.021	0.000	0.036	−0.004
Business services	0.003	−0.069	0.041	−0.056
Detroit				
Personal services	0.025	−0.013	0.006	0.272
Business services	0.039	−0.056	0.039	0.153
Houston				
Personal services	0.044	0.037	0.069	0.031
Business services	0.130	NA	−0.076	0.052
Miami				
Personal services	0.033	−0.042	0.060	0.026
Business services	0.047	0.007	0.049	0.059
Cleveland				
Personal services	0.033	0.024	0.065	−0.028
Business services	0.052	−0.009	0.078	0.074
Seattle				
Personal services	0.052	0.000	0.054	0.133
Business services	0.066	−0.016	0.119	0.175
Cincinnati				
Personal services	0.026	−0.008	0.044	0.000
Business services	−0.011	0.001	0.005	−0.011
Milwaukee				
Personal services	0.016	0.006	0.016	0.046
Business services	0.026	0.017	0.027	0.052
12 CMSAs				
Personal services	0.021	−0.006	0.038	0.025
Business services	0.031	NA	0.037	0.039

Source: Calculated by authors from US Economic Census data.

than other sectors. About 63 per cent of the CMSA totals were located in the core county (1988 data). Moreover, although suburban firms are much more prevalent than central-city firms, they tend to depend on central-city firms for externally provided financial services (actuarial services, auditors, banks, investment banks, and legal counsel), the percentages ranging from 53 per cent to 71 per cent (averaged over three CMSAs – New York, Los Angeles, Chicago; Schwartz, 1992). However, even financial services are now decentralizing as the revolution in information technologies reduces the need for face-to-face contacts, although the rate of decentralization lags behind that for other professional and business services (Stanback, 1991).

As already mentioned, the BEA employment data are not strictly comparable to the economic census data. Yet, they do include 1992 manufacturing employment (not yet fully available from the Census). Also, because the BEA data are available from 1969, we studied their 20-year (1972–1992) performance in order to test the longer-term durability of trends seen in the previous 1982–1992 analysis. Table 4.15 shows the shares of CMSA jobs in each of the outer suburbs (Ring II) at five-year intervals for seven major sectors as well as their total (All Private). Substantial employment decentralization occurred *almost* everywhere, in fast-growing Los Angeles but not in almost-as-fast-growing Seattle, in fast-growing Miami but also in slow-growing Philadelphia. Where rapid spatial dispersion occurred, it applied to services at least as much as to manufacturing, suggesting that in the aggregate the two sectors are similarly footloose. In fact, the 1972–92 trends for the combined CMSAs show all of them dispersing to Ring II. Population-following retail and construction were most suburbanized in 1992; those that had been least suburbanized in 1972 (wholesale, transportation and public utilities, FIRE) showed the fastest Ring II growth.

Conclusion

It is not possible to discern conventional regional patterns of growth and decline (e.g. "sunbelt"–"frostbelt") in these results. Rather, the major consistency appears to be the continued decline of the central cities and the industrial strength of the suburbs, with the outer suburbs reaching levels of employment that had previously been achieved by the inner suburbs. Where growth took place at all, it was mostly (not always) in the outer suburbs. These results appear to affect all three

Table 4.15 Shares of jobs in outer suburbs: Selected sectors, full-time and part-time employment, 1972–1992

	All private	Construction	Manufacturing	Transportation & public utilities	Wholesale	Retail	FIRE	Services
New York								
1972	0.494	0.599	0.591	0.425	0.412	0.563	0.362	0.441
1977	0.526	0.651	0.628	0.457	0.485	0.599	0.401	0.469
1982	0.540	0.620	0.658	0.488	0.529	0.616	0.407	0.483
1987	0.561	0.642	0.678	0.550	0.579	0.642	0.442	0.499
1992	0.566	0.634	0.677	0.550	0.609	0.651	0.459	0.520
Los Angeles								
1972	0.235	0.323	0.201	0.190	0.149	0.279	0.260	0.235
1977	0.273	0.404	0.236	0.218	0.185	0.318	0.317	0.257
1982	0.299	0.399	0.259	0.251	0.209	0.356	0.337	0.286
1987	0.326	0.474	0.284	0.278	0.250	0.379	0.333	0.307
1992	0.360	0.485	0.321	0.301	0.329	0.408	0.371	0.340
Chicago								
1972	0.091	0.105	0.124	0.079	0.037	0.093	0.055	0.073
1977	0.094	0.140	0.126	0.086	0.040	0.099	0.060	0.076
1982	0.086	0.124	0.118	0.080	0.038	0.099	0.051	0.075
1987	0.077	0.095	0.099	0.077	0.040	0.092	0.042	0.073
1992	0.081	0.115	0.099	0.086	0.054	0.101	0.444	0.072
San Francisco								
1972	0.607	0.635	0.749	0.454	0.486	0.656	0.512	0.588
1977	0.631	0.670	0.792	0.471	0.514	0.672	0.523	0.604
1982	0.645	0.642	0.817	0.496	0.554	0.680	0.514	0.616
1987	0.668	0.739	0.833	0.548	0.627	0.692	0.538	0.630
1992	0.682	0.751	0.834	0.552	0.688	0.706	0.570	0.650

Table 4.15 (cont.)

	All private	Construction	Manufacturing	Transportation & public utilities	Wholesale	Retail	FIRE	Services
Philadelphia								
1972	0.149	0.184	0.146	0.146	0.092	0.173	0.139	0.141
1977	0.152	0.192	0.155	0.155	0.106	0.172	0.138	0.141
1982	0.166	0.199	0.164	0.157	0.101	0.175	0.161	0.168
1987	0.176	0.174	0.169	0.142	0.103	0.187	0.172	0.172
1992	0.181	0.156	0.186	0.147	0.115	0.191	0.193	0.170
Detroit								
1972	0.146	0.139	0.177	0.092	0.115	0.144	0.118	0.130
1977	0.157	0.142	0.187	0.110	0.129	0.156	0.129	0.143
1982	0.165	0.180	0.201	0.110	0.144	0.162	0.141	0.151
1987	0.166	0.171	0.194	0.116	0.140	0.175	0.130	0.159
1992	0.166	0.191	0.196	0.117	0.116	0.176	0.131	0.161
Houston								
1972	0.087	0.080	0.131	0.094	0.028	0.095	0.077	0.078
1977	0.085	0.104	0.117	0.088	0.031	0.092	0.083	0.073
1982	0.071	0.076	0.114	0.074	0.028	0.080	0.061	0.065
1987	0.076	0.106	0.136	0.070	0.030	0.087	0.059	0.064
1992	0.077	0.111	0.128	0.064	0.036	0.091	0.070	0.063
Miami								
1972	0.286	0.425	0.217	0.178	0.186	0.336	0.340	0.265
1977	0.320	0.426	0.259	0.197	0.213	0.379	0.379	0.315
1982	0.344	0.412	0.307	0.208	0.254	0.401	0.399	0.339
1987	0.368	0.462	0.325	0.256	0.293	0.421	0.387	0.362
1992	0.381	0.450	0.326	0.277	0.315	0.432	0.400	0.384
Seattle								
1972	0.217	0.252	0.180	0.175	0.140	0.258	0.209	0.238
1977	0.214	0.263	0.166	0.165	0.151	0.247	0.209	0.242

1982	0.208	0.229	0.145	0.163	0.148	0.241	0.204	0.243
1987	0.206	0.241	0.128	0.168	0.145	0.254	0.191	0.233
1992	0.210	0.247	0.115	0.170	0.152	0.266	0.201	0.232
Cleveland								
1972	0.204	0.201	0.221	0.214	0.137	0.220	0.181	0.187
1977	0.201	0.195	0.209	0.214	0.143	0.221	0.184	0.193
1982	0.203	0.211	0.207	0.216	0.161	0.228	0.172	0.196
1987	0.207	0.227	0.218	0.223	0.182	0.228	0.172	0.191
1992	0.215	0.232	0.219	0.240	0.187	0.236	0.173	0.209
Cincinnati								
1972	0.117	0.124	0.149	0.073	0.064	0.111	0.122	0.099
1977	0.121	0.144	0.149	0.100	0.080	0.112	0.136	0.101
1982	0.118	0.152	0.145	0.083	0.085	0.111	0.133	0.105
1987	0.115	0.133	0.137	0.081	0.108	0.118	0.113	0.102
1992	0.113	0.143	0.121	0.091	0.118	0.117	0.098	0.108
Milwaukee								
1972	0.089	0.087	0.113	0.059	0.059	0.084	0.061	0.082
1977	0.095	0.089	0.125	0.071	0.066	0.091	0.063	0.082
1982	0.092	0.078	0.122	0.057	0.060	0.106	0.053	0.079
1987	0.092	0.085	0.129	0.073	0.055	0.105	0.057	0.076
1992	0.091	0.096	0.126	0.069	0.055	0.102	0.056	0.079
12 CMSAs								
1972	0.295	0.340	0.313	0.259	0.224	0.325	0.265	0.284
1977	0.309	0.348	0.326	0.273	0.257	0.339	0.285	0.297
1982	0.324	0.354	0.354	0.288	0.277	0.356	0.293	0.311
1987	0.340	0.407	0.362	0.313	0.307	0.371	0.305	0.321
1992	0.344	0.380	0.355	0.314	0.328	0.373	0.318	0.334

Source: Calculated by authors from REIS data.

of the major sectors studied, and also the seven sectors highlighted in the BEA file. Rapid spatial change in US cities appears to be accompanying rapid technological change. It is impossible to say which causes which. It is likely that they reinforce each other. We would expect similar interactions between global economic and technological trends and spatial changes to be observed in cities in other parts of the world. As a generalization, the *intra*metropolitan trends and their sources have received less research attention than the interregional and transnational trends.

References

Drennan, Matthew P. (1992), "Gateway Cities: The Metropolitan Sources of U.S. Producer Service Exports." *Urban Studies* 29(2): 217–235.

Frey, William H. (1993), "The New Urban Revival in the U.S." *Urban Studies* 30(4/5): 741–774.

Glaeser, Edward L. (1994), "Cities, Information and Economic Growth." Discussion Paper No. 1681. Cambridge, Mass.: Harvard Institute of Economic Research.

Gordon, Peter and Harry W. Richardson (1994), "Congestion Trends in Metropolitan Areas." In: Committee for Study on Urban Transportation Congestion Pricing, Transportation Research Board, Commission on Behavioral and Social Sciences and Education, National Research Council (eds.), *Curbing Gridlock: Peak-Period Fees to Relieve Traffic Congestion*, vol. 2: Commissioned Papers. Washington, D.C.: National Academy Press, pp. 1–31.

—— (1996), "Los Angeles among the Other CMSAs: Outlier or the Norm?" *Environment and Planning A* 28: 1727–1743.

Richardson, Harry W. (1994), "International Interdependence and Urban Concentration." OECD–Australian Government Conference on Cities and the New Global Economy, Melbourne.

Schwartz, Alex (1992), "Corporate Service Linkages in Large Metropolitan Areas: A Study of New York, Los Angeles, and Chicago." *Urban Affairs Quarterly* 28(2): 276–296.

Stanback, Jr., Thomas M. (1991), *The New Suburbanization: Challenge to the Central City*. Boulder, Colo.: Westview Press.

5

The growth of Tokyo as a world city

Masahiko Honjo

Introduction

This chapter describes the development of Tokyo as a world city, emphasizing changes after World War II.[1] The elements of this transformation include both urban growth and urban economic restructuring and are closely related to processes at the national level. Particularly important are the changes to Tokyo articulated through globalization processes that have occurred since the 1970s. These forces have helped to usher in Japan's new "post-industrial" stage of development. The principal change is the emergence of Tokyo as a location for central management functions that control the various activities of Japanese industries around the world.

Rapid metropolitan growth, especially that of capitals, has been a common phenomenon since 1950 all over the world. A growing number of cities around the world are reaching unprecedented size. The United Nations predicts that 21 cities will exceed 10 million in population by the end of the twentieth century (United Nations, 1995: 131). In less developed countries (LDCs), this urbanization is primarily due to the movement of people from rural areas to urban centres seeking opportunities for employment. In more developed countries (MDCs), large cities, although suffering from economic stagnation owing to the decline of their industries and resulting decay of inner cities, still continue to grow as a result of territorial expansion of their administrative boundaries and immigration. However, size alone does not make a world city. Tokyo, although holding the position of largest city in the world since 1960, is a world city because of the global functional linkages it has through business (commodities and securities trading, foreign direct investment, banking), telecommunications (media and Internet resources), and politics. Revealing the history of Japan's rise to global economic prominence is a major part of explaining the rise of Tokyo as a world city.

Japan's economic growth and the development of Tokyo

Japan's economic development can be characterized into distinct periods. Although within each economic era there were multifarious development activities, these periods can be categorized by a dominant type of development process. These stages, include (1) pre-war development; (2) rapid post-war national economic growth; (3) industrial restructuring; and (4) Japanese world economic development. The concentration of population and economic power in Tokyo proceeded over the course of all these periods, but became most prominent during the last stage.

Japan's pre-war development

During the Meiji period, Japan came out of political and economic isolation and, as a nation, experienced remarkable development. From the nineteenth century to about the 1950s, Japan accomplished rapid and intense industrialization. Specifically, traditional Japanese industries, such as textiles, modernized with the help of government policies. State policies were directed towards improving the physical infrastructure and the financial and monetary systems of the country. All industries benefited from these improvements. Even the heavy industries developed to such an extent that Japanese firms began to compete with nations in the industrialized world.

Japanese agricultural development also accelerated with the support of the government. Of great importance was the reformation of land distribution. Before the Meiji Restoration, Japan was run in a feudal manner. To liquidate the land assets of the ruling class, the government promulgated a variety of land taxes that more or less established land ownership and facilitated the disintegration of the peasant class.

The complementary establishment of land ownership and industrialization liberated the country from its feudalistic rules and facilitated the growth of commerce and wage labour. Domestic consumption grew and markets expanded around the entire country. The accumulation of capital was evident, not only in the concentration of farmland in the hands of landlords, but in the development of urban centres.

Japan not only experienced rapid industrialization during this period, but also underwent massive urbanization. In the course of one century the urban population rose from 15 per cent to 80 per cent of the total (fig. 5.1). This urbanization rate was twice as fast as that

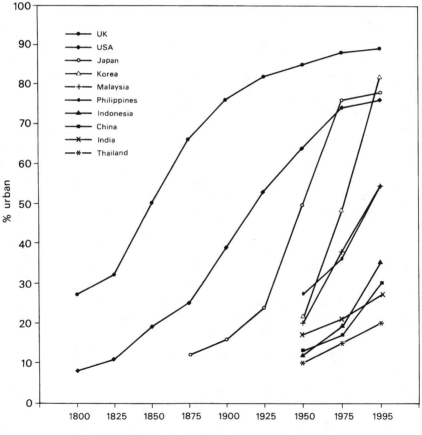

Fig. 5.1 **Urbanization trends in selected countries**

experienced in the United Kingdom and the United States. In parallel with the movement of large numbers of people to cities, the average family size shrank, average life expectancy increased, and the average level of education increased.

It was during the Meiji Restoration that the national capital of Japan was transferred from Kyoto to Edo (now Tokyo). At this point, in step with national trends, Tokyo began to grow into a city. The growth was so consistent that the Meiji government was forced to implement controls on development in the city through the Municipal Renewal Ordinance of 1888. This law regulated the construction of offices, roads, parks, and embankments to the Sumida River. Tokyo's growth was mainly based on its role as a political and cultural centre of Japan. Osaka was the original business centre. Notwithstanding this limitation, Tokyo continued to grow until World War II, despite the Great Kanto earthquake of 1923, which killed over 100,000 people and destroyed nearly 43 per cent of the city.

Right from the beginning of its growth, the development of Tokyo was not even. However, it was this uneven growth that helped to increase the physical size of the city. The dispersion of the city's population to suburban areas started early in the nineteenth century with the introduction of the electric streetcar and suburban railways. Population dispersion accelerated with the industrial boom accompanying World War I and as families and enterprises opted for the suburbs rather than return to the earthquake-ravaged central city in the mid-1920s. Once outlying communities gained population, they merged with the city proper, helping to expand the boundaries of the municipality. In 1932, for example, 23 new wards (*ku*) were added to the 15 existing ones. As a result of this growth, the government reorganized the city politically. During World War II, the old political boundaries of Tokyo were abolished. Instead, the Tokyo ward area became only one part of the new Tokyo Prefecture, or Tokyo-to. This political structure remains today. The Tokyo Prefectural government comprises the ward areas (23 *ku* in total) plus the Tama district, which contains an additional 26 cities, 7 towns, and 8 villages and the Izu and Ogasawara Islands (Nakamura and White, 1988).

Rapid post-war economic growth

The basis for Japan's present-day economy was secured in the late 1940s and early 1950s. Japan's national priorities centred on the

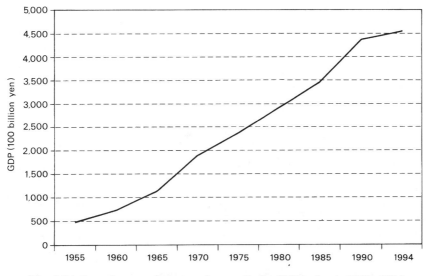

Fig. 5.2 **Japan's annual economic growth (in 1990 prices), 1955–1994**

development of energy resources and the re-establishment of the industrial base, which had been badly damaged during the war.

It took only a decade for Japanese industry to recover after the war. The economy began to grow again in the 1950s, stimulated by the Korean War. The demand for strategic goods lifted the Japanese economy into a boom. The "special procurements" (special demand for goods and services generated by the war) and rapid expansion of exports were particularly beneficial to Japan. By 1955 production output surpassed wartime peak levels, and the 1960s were the high point of rapid economic development for the country (figs. 5.2 and 5.3).

National economic growth was facilitated by government policies. The first National Five-Year Economic Plan of 1955 proposed an annual growth rate of 5 per cent, through the promotion of industrial development and foreign trade. In 1960, Prime Minister Hayato Ikeda instituted the Ten-Year Income-Doubling Plan, which aimed at a 9.1 per cent annual growth and proposed the quadrupling of annual production levels. Exceeding the original goals, the Ten-Year Income-Doubling Plan achieved 10.7 per cent average growth, and during 1961 growth peaked at 14.5 per cent. Rising incomes led to increased spending, which further stimulated the domestic market. This period

113

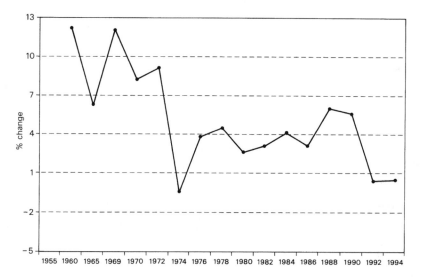

Fig. 5.3 **Japan's economic growth rate, 1960–1994 (annual percentage change)**

was the time of greatest growth for the country and is often referred to as the "rapid economic growth period."

From the start of the boom period, the movement of labour into the major urban areas around the country accompanied the increase in production. Until the mid-1970s, population movement into the three major metropolitan regions (Tokyo, Osaka, and Nagoya) followed urban industrial development. This movement was so great that it even outpaced the rate of economic growth. Much, if not all, of this labour was surplus from the agricultural sector (fig. 5.4). Including natural increases, in less than two decades the population net in-migration to the three main urban centres reached 10 million (8 per cent of the total Japanese population). Tokyo was an important recipient of the new migrants. The Tokyo Prefecture, after losing population during the war, grew to 8 million in 1955, 9.6 million in 1960, and 8.8 million in 1965.

In the middle to late 1960s the population trend shifted to dynamic suburban growth. During this phase of urbanization it was not uncommon to see 30–50 per cent annual increases in the suburban fringes of the three metropolitan areas. Population increases were also experienced in the smaller, regional metropolitan areas (Sapporo, Sendai, Hiroshima, and Fukuoka). By the early 1970s, some scholars noted that Japan's urban system had changed from being dualistic

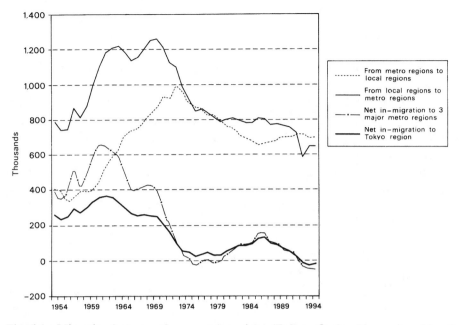

Fig. 5.4 **Migration between three metro regions (Tokyo, Osaka, Nagoya) and local regions, 1954–1994**

(urban and rural) to one that was monolithic (Takahashi and Suguira, 1996). The new monolithic urban system, which emerged in the early 1970s, consisted of the three major metropolitan areas (Tokyo, Osaka, and Nagoya) and four regional core metropolitan areas. Small and medium-sized cities and towns were no longer referred to as rural, but termed micropolitan areas (Takahashi and Sugiura, 1996).

This rapid and intense urbanization was the cause of much governmental concern. While the national government promoted economic growth it also promoted the decentralization of industries and population from large urban centres. The Ten-Year Income-Doubling Plan, for example, not only aimed at high economic growth but also intended to spread the growth more evenly within the country. Through the designation of 21 "special industrial development regions" or growth poles, the government attempted to direct both economic and population growth out of the three major cities, including Tokyo. As a result of this policy, there was a dramatic shift in public investment. In 1962, 60 per cent of total public investment was allocated to the three major urban centres; by 1975 the micropolitan areas received nearly half of all public investment. Although

115

this policy successfully decentralized the urban areas of Nagoya and Osaka, Tokyo continued to grow.

Major industries in Japan at that time included energy, steel, automobiles and ships, petrochemicals and chemicals, and transportation infrastructure. Before the decentralization programme many of these industries were located in the major urban centres, including Tokyo. However, these firms found the high land prices and the labour force in the city inadequate for their needs. They quickly took advantage of the government incentives and infrastructure provided through relocating to the micropolitan areas. As a result, a considerable proportion of manufacturing industries (such as steel, petrochemicals, shipbuilding, and heavy machinery industries) moved out and built their new plants in these areas.

During the initial stage of relocation, the sea front was developed for heavy chemical industries, particularly along the Pacific coastal belt. Manufacturing industries soon blossomed alongside. However, as industrial development proceeded, localities became aware of the negative externalities of industrial development. Especially serious was the problem of environmental disruption from the heavy chemical industries. Towards the late 1960s, these problems became a major national issue and public opinion began to regard industrial growth as negative. Among the most important environmental concerns were air pollution, water pollution, waste disposal, noise and vibration, and ground subsidence. Grass-roots outcry peaked with the "Big Four" court cases in the early 1970s (Barrett and Therivel, 1991).

However, while the Japanese public became more aware of the despoilation of the environment and the government was successfully decentralizing industries from urban areas, global politics, economic forces, and new technologies were already at work shaping the future of Japan and the role of Tokyo.

Oil shocks, economic slow-down, and industrial restructuring

A crucial turning-point for Japanese economic and urban development came in 1973 with the worldwide energy crisis. As a result of the tripling in the price of oil, the rate of economic growth dropped from 5.1 per cent in 1973 to −0.5 per cent in 1974. Not only did economic growth in Japan come to a halt, but the rural–urban population movement reversed for all urban centres in the country (except Tokyo).

The oil shocks of 1973/74 and then in 1978/79 led to a decline in the manufacturing sector. Heavy industries, such as steel and shipmaking, were hit hard. Steel production dropped from a peak of 119 million tonnes in 1973 to about 106 million tonnes in 1988, and this level was dependent on the government's public works projects. In the ship-building industry, after peak production of 17 million tonnes in the 1970s, production fell to 8.2 million tonnes in 1987. Automobile pro-duction continued to grow, but at a slower rate than before. Approxi-mately 8 million cars were produced in 1988, compared with slightly over 7 million in 1980 and 4.6 million in 1975. The production of chemicals and petrochemicals also lagged behind the forecasts of the 1970s, owing primarily to increased oil prices. Naphtha production declined steadily from the mid-1970s. Ethylene production, which stood at 5.3 million tonnes in 1977 and was predicted to be 15 million tonnes in 1985, was only 4.3 million tonnes in 1986 (Barrett and Therivel, 1991).

The oil and environmental crises enhanced the perception that the income-generating industries, ironically those relocated in the micropolitan areas because of their perceived growth potential, could no longer support Japan's future economic growth. The crises accelerated the replacement of these industries by newly emerg-ing high-tech industries such as micro-electronics (semiconductors, computers, and communications equipment) and other related manufacturing industries, such as automobile and consumer durable goods (Takahashi and Sugiura, 1996). Through industrial restructur-ing, heavy industry was replaced by high-tech-based, light, and knowledge-intensive industries. Whereas heavy industries moved out of the cities for more suitable locations in coastal industrial zones, high-tech industries moved inland to areas of clean air and water, high-speed transportation, and markets. The "Decade of Local Regions" from the 1970s to early 1980s is characterized by high industrial growth in the micropolitan parts of the country.

This relocation of industries also helped to change the move-ment of population. People migrated away from urban centres and towards less dense, but economically active areas of Japan. However, although Osaka and Nagoya lost population after 1970, the Tokyo Metropolitan Area continued to increase its population. And, owing to the in-migration of people of reproductive age, the population growth rate of the Tokyo Metropolitan Area during the 1980s was far greater than that in any other areas in the nation.

The anomaly of Tokyo's continued population growth during this and the previous period can be explained by the concomitant growth of new techno-economic-based industries, and then the rise of the service sector within the city. At one point the Tokyo Metropolitan Area accumulated the largest manufacturing agglomeration in the nation. However, like its counterparts, Tokyo lost 349 factories (with over 1,000 m² facilities) between 1975 and 1984. However, it remained a centre of high-tech industrial development and R&D investment (Takahashi and Sugiura, 1996).

The service sector had also traditionally been an important part of Tokyo's economy, but from the late 1970s onward it took on a special significance for the Tokyo Metropolitan Area. The service sector includes those activities associated with public, private, and voluntary services – the activities of banks, securities firms, investment banking offices, real estate development offices, accounting firms, advertising companies, law firms, research and development organizations, trucking, warehousing, and retail and wholesale trade, among other things. While the entire country was struggling through the restructuring of the manufacturing sector, urban areas, and in particular Tokyo, were becoming more dependent on services, i.e. the urban economy in Japan was undergoing a sectoral restructuring. This process was further enhanced by the globalization of Japan's economic activity and resulted in the ascendance of Tokyo as a premier world city.

The emergence of Japan as a world economic power

Whereas the traditional secondary (manufacturing) sector stagnated after its rapid post-war expansion, during this later period the tertiary (service) sector started to expand. From 1970 to 1994, while the manufacturing sector continued to account for approximately 26 per cent of GDP, the service sector (finance, real estate, and business services) rose from 26 to almost 34 per cent of the GDP of Japan during the same period. However, massive changes in the Japanese urban economy accompanied this transition. For example, the simple change from a manufacturing to a service economy does not explain why the service sector was concentrated in Tokyo, or how Tokyo rose to become one of the premier world cities. In order to understand these dramatic changes, it is important to view the economic activity within Tokyo as part of larger global economic forces and Japan's growing role within the new international division of labour.

Japan's emphasis on saving energy, pollution control, and automation devices provided dividends in improved productivity and resulted in increased competitiveness abroad. As a result, export surpluses increased and the Japanese trade volume quadrupled from 1970 to 1990. These surpluses contributed to the growth of financial reserves, which further enhanced Japan's commitment in international finance and assistance.

Japan's change from heavy industries to high-tech industries, such as robotics, automobiles, optics, electronics, and computers, allowed firms more production flexibility. These industries could "out-source" production to other localities. Hence Japanese high-tech industries could produce their products by having low-skilled, low-paid workers in other parts of Japan and in foreign countries do much of the production work. This flexibility allowed for the movement of Japanese investments to developing nations in Asia. The dominance of Japanese firms in the robotics field also helped them to compete successfully in foreign markets. They controlled the world's share of robots and put them to work successfully. For example, Toyota, using modern robotics, could produce an automobile using many fewer man-hours than its international competitors.

However, the real flight of Japanese foreign direct investment (FDI) was stimulated by the Plaza Accords (see chap. 1 in this volume). The result of the Plaza Accord in 1985 was to strengthen the dollar to the disadvantage of the yen. At this time the United States was suffering under a double deficit: government deficit (the government was spending more than it was taking in) and trade deficit (more American dollars were being spent on imports than other comparable monies spent on American exports). President Reagan wanted to keep the dollar strong and negotiated with the Japanese to devalue the yen. These talks resulted in the fall in the value of the yen from 221.68 in 1985 to 138.45 in 1987. The direct result of this change was that it was cheaper for the Japanese to buy American goods and Japanese goods became more expensive overseas.

The indirect result was the challenge to the Japanese industrial system to achieve even lower production costs. This stimulated the increased movement of Japanese investment into Asia in search of even lower production costs. The Japanese sought out places such as Indonesia and Malaysia to produce their products. Whereas in the past Tokyo was the centre of the Japanese national economy, after the movement of Japanese FDI out of the country the Japanese economy developed into a transnational system, with Tokyo at the centre. Hence a by-product of this new investment was the creation of a functional economic system within Asia with Tokyo as an important centre of its management functions.

At the same time that Japanese industries were decentralizing from urban centres and globalizing or relocating firms to areas outside of Japan, they were leaving behind their headquarters functions in Japanese urban centres, especially in Tokyo. A central dynamic of the new global economy was that the more globalized the Japanese economy became the higher the agglomeration of central functions within Tokyo (Sassen, 1991). Integral to these activities were the central managerial functions (CMF) for Japanese firms, including those related to finance, insurance, and wholesale and business services. CMFs are the top decision-making procedures in the planning and management of various sectors, public as well as private. CMFs are also closely linked to research/development and information functions and are supported by the work of myriad clerks, bureaucrats, and secretaries.

A growing number of national headquarters functions were locating in Tokyo as early as the 1960s, but Tokyo's position as the centre of the growing Asian urban functional city system and global economic system facilitated further CMF development. This activity was complemented by a complex of organizations dedicated to running the dispersed network of factories, offices, and service outlets as well as the production of financial innovations. The concentration of CMFs in Tokyo was enhanced by the development of the city's stock exchange, which joined New York's and London's as a major worldwide stock trading institution. The large national financial reserve and Tokyo's geographic location, which made it possible to operate a world stock market on a "round-the-clock" basis, increased the city's international importance. Tokyo's stock exchange opens shortly after New York's closes and it closes shortly before the stock exchange in London starts the day.

Figure 5.5 shows the concentration of functions and activities in the Tokyo Metropolitan Region. The area has a high and growing share of CMF and related functions. Tokyo became the centre of international business and financing for Japan: 90 per cent of all foreign companies doing business in the country were concentrated in the city; 70–80 per cent of financial transactions such as cheque exchange and stock sales also occurred there. More than half of bank loans provided by banks in Japan and about half of bank deposits in the country accumulated in institutions were located in the city.

Tokyo also became the centre of big enterprises (as defined by

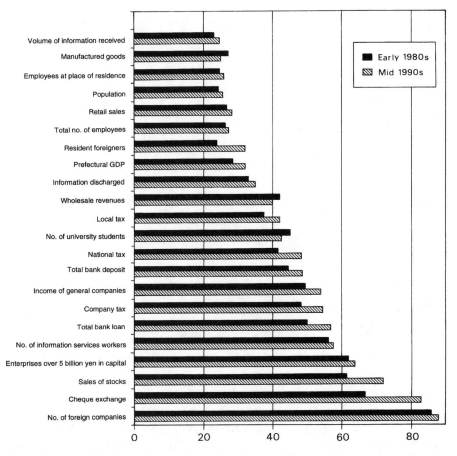

Fig. 5.5 **Concentration of command functions in Tokyo (% share of Japanese total), early 1980s and mid-1990s**

capital holdings of over 5 billion yen) in the country: 65 per cent of these large enterprises located their headquarters in Tokyo. Forty per cent of wholesale revenues and 55 per cent of general company income were concentrated in the city.

Tokyo also became the centre of information services and education in Japan. Over 55 per cent of workers in the information field, such as computer specialists and advertising workers, found employment in Tokyo. More than 40 per cent of university students are currently in Tokyo's tertiary institutions. This is despite the government's policy since the 1960s that restricted the siting of new universities in Tokyo's inner areas.

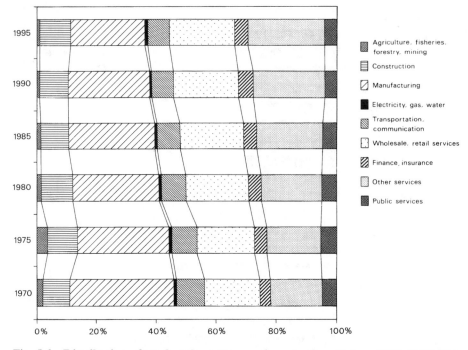

Fig. 5.6 **Distribution of workers by category of production: Tokyo, 1970–1995 (%)**

Whereas the Tokyo Prefecture has slightly over 9 per cent of Japan's total population, it generates over 18 per cent of national GDP. The large volume and concentration of productive energy indicates, by its sheer scale, Tokyo's capacity as a powerful consumptive market.

The resulting restructuring of Tokyo's economy can also be seen in the distribution of workforce energies and the number of workers in three areas – manufacturing, wholesale and retail trade, and communications and services. During this period, the largest and most rapidly growing area of the three sectors was activities involving the service economy. Figure 5.6 demonstrates the economic restructuring that has occurred in Tokyo since the 1970s. The changes in the percentage of workers by category of production can be summarized as follows. There was an evident shift in the workforce from the primary to secondary and tertiary sectors. Between 1970 and 1995 the percentage share of each sector changed from 6:40:54 to 2:38:60 in terms of production. The shift of production and manpower was from both the primary and secondary sectors to the tertiary sector. The manpower shift demonstrates the drastic shift in labour and productive activities within the city.

In the secondary sector there was a shift towards a higher degree of industrialization, namely from light industry to manufacturing and assembly-type industries. In the tertiary sector, although commerce and services continued to occupy an important share, CMF-related activities, namely finance, insurance, wholesale, and business services, showed a steady increase throughout every decade since 1960.

Regarding occupational status, the share of white-collar jobs (core administrative, professional/technical, and clerical support) increased from 16 to 29 per cent during these three decades. Blue-collar jobs decreased and this loss came mostly from the agriculture, fisheries, forestry, and mining industries. However, blue-collar jobs were retained in existing skilled production industries, infrastructure support, and transportation and communication. At present, more workers are needed for personal services. In the future, unskilled or semi-skilled workers will be needed for jobs in the construction and other primary industries. However, the attraction of high-level job opportunities may cause labour shortages in low-paying occupations for Japan.

In general, employment has shifted away from manufacturing (and handling goods) to corporate, public, and non-profit services. Occupations have similarly shifted from manual workers to managers, professionals, secretaries, and service workers. These transformations have also been identified in other cities moving towards the "post-industrial" society (Mollenkopf and Castells, 1991).

The Tokyo Prefecture remains an important economic entity. Tokyo's gross output accounted for almost 18 per cent of Japan's GDP for 1992 (Toyokeizai, 1996: 256). Although the bubble economy is almost over, Tokyo's share of Japan's GDP continues to rise. This is due to the continued concentration of high-tech service industries within Tokyo and such industries are among the most robust within Japan.

Tokyo's problems

Tokyo's continual population growth and dramatic economic restructuring did not occur without problems. Four important issues that remain high on the list of governmental priorities include: housing, waste management, the dependent population, and the environmental quality of the city.

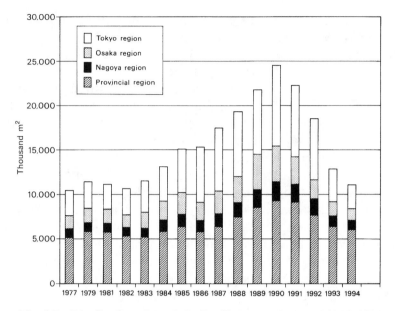

Fig. 5.7 **Distribution of newly built office space by area, 1977–1994**

Housing

The concentration of CMFs in Tokyo accelerated the race to acquire office space in particular areas of Tokyo's central business district (CBD). To meet this demand, construction of new offices was heavily concentrated in the Tokyo Region until 1991, and in particular in the 20 km² area within the three wards that cover the CBD (fig. 5.7).

A rise in land prices was triggered in 1986 by incoming foreign banks and other business and the prediction of increasing demand for office space. Incoming institutions could afford much higher rents and were attracted to the Tokyo CBD to be close to other regional and global corporate headquarters and business service providers. Speculation and corporate fluid capital played a role in rising land costs. The effect quickly diffused to neighbouring areas in Tokyo and to other big cities (figs. 5.8 and 5.9).

The rise in land prices created what was called the "land bubble." It was driven by speculation involving not only realtors and developers, but also financial institutions, politicians, and the government bureaucracy. Speculation escalated as winners in the game "revolved" land, i.e. bought cheap and sold dear. Firms had better access to the financial resources needed to buy property and were therefore in a

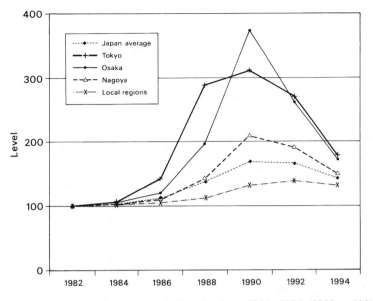

Fig. 5.8   **Increases in commercial land prices, 1980–1994 (1980 = 100)**

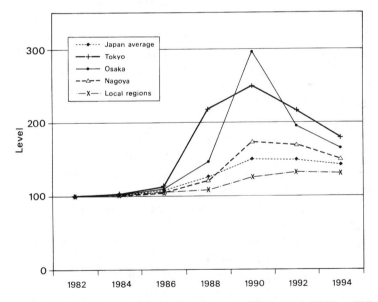

Fig. 5.9   **Increases in residential land prices, 1980–1994 (1980 = 100)**

much better position to obtain parcels than were individuals in the market. This promoted the expansion of "financial technologies," or the development of speculative branches within firms not usually involved in land development. Some of these firms claimed that it was easier to produce profits through these tactics than by working seriously in their business specialties. As a result of speculation, land values were estimated on the basis of the expected capital gain and increase in return from inflation, not on the basis of the expected return from utilization. This forced out most individual users. Tokyo's particular case of housing cost distortion was the worst in recent history.

Residential land uses were forced out by the pressure to develop commercial spaces. Whereas individuals felt the burden of property-based taxes, enterprises could find ways to reduce tax loads such as claiming business expense exemptions, assessing property at the lower-level book price, etc. Many house-owners were forced to give up their homes, especially those who inherited property. This induced a decrease in both residents and associated residential services in the inner-city areas. Elementary schools were closed as a result of falling rolls. Retail shops lost customers and were shut down. The rate of daytime population growth increased consistently from 1970 and in the latter half of the 1980s; in particular, the daytime population rose to 10 times the night-time population in the three central wards (TMG, 1994). Residences began to appear increasingly further away from the CBD in suburban regions. The commuting distance to Tokyo has extended to over 40–50 km along the major transportation routes. Those living in these areas and commuting to Tokyo experienced a miserable, long, overcrowded ride. For example, the Tokyo Metropolitan Government (TMG) estimated that railway line congestion, although falling as a result of increased construction of new tracks, was still over 200 per cent of capacity in 1994 (TMG, 1994). Meanwhile the periphery of the city was changing into a huge conurbation swallowing up other cities.

In 1991 the "land bubble" in Tokyo burst. Between 1991 and 1996 residential land prices in Tokyo fell by over 33 per cent while commercial land prices fell by over 60 per cent. Whereas in 1991 Tokyo had 37 per cent of all newly built office space, by 1994 its regional share had dropped to less than 25 per cent (see fig. 5.7).

The combination of the concentration of CMFs, speculation, and a large pool of liquid resources among firms in Tokyo helped to bring about the rapid rise in land prices in the inner city. The down-side of the process was that it forced individual residents further away from the city, causing them to suffer long, crowded journeys to work. Many Japanese citizens in the early parts of their careers failed to obtain adequate housing and therefore felt disappointed and anxious. Mass disappointment in the way housing was distributed may be a serious problem for Japan in the future.

Waste management

The garbage produced by the people of Japan in the course of their daily lives is referred to as general waste (excludes industrial and human waste) or household- and business-related garbage (Environmental Agency of Japan, 1994). These types of waste have been increasing both by total volume and in the amount produced per capita since the early 1980s. The garbage produced in Japan in 1991 amounted to 50,770,000 tonnes (about 136 times the amount that would fill the Tokyo Dome), an increase of 0.6 per cent from fiscal year 1990, which itself was an increase of 0.9 per cent over the previous fiscal year (Environmental Agency of Japan, 1994). Waste management is a national concern.

The waste problem is especially important to Tokyo. The average weight of daily waste per person has almost doubled in the past two decades. The Metropolitan Tokyo area, along with the Kanagawa Prefecture, Chiba Prefecture, and Saitama Prefecture, accounted for 24.4 per cent of all the garbage produced in Japan during 1991. However, whereas the production of garbage in the area is high, the capacity (expressed in terms of years) for final disposal is only 4.9, lower than the national average.

In Tokyo, 1.1–1.3 kg of waste per person is collected daily and the city burns approximately two-thirds (2.6 million tonnes per year) of this material (in 12 incineration plants), while the rest is landfilled (Takahashi and Sugiura, 1996). Tokyo currently has 199 hectares of remaining landfill available at its central breakwater landfill treatment site (the twentieth and last remaining landfill in operation is in Tokyo Bay). This was optimistically predicted to be exhausted by March 1996. Space limitations in Tokyo Bay mean that, even if new landfill sites are readied, the new sites will last for only 15–20 years. And there are no landfill sites in Tokyo's 23 wards. Because of the high price of land and growing concern over the location of waste treatment plants, it is becoming difficult to secure processing sites, imparting urgency to the implementation of reduction, recycling, and reuse policies. To deal with the current crisis Tokyo plans to reduce the waste stream in the wards by 23 per cent by the end of 2000. It is also planning to build 10 new incineration plants by 2010.

The dependent population

The Japanese society is rapidly becoming an ageing society. There are two important implications of the growth of the elderly dependent population (those over 64 years of age): (1) support of this population (i.e. the demand on the social welfare system); and (2) the allocation of physical amenities within the city (Tokyo was created for people who work). At present the proportion of elderly people is much higher in the micropolitan areas of the country than in the metropolitan areas.

In 1990, 10.5 per cent (1.24 million people) of Tokyo's population was elderly. Projections to the year 2015 are that the city's elderly will make up an increasingly larger proportion of the population, accounting for 24.2 per cent at that time. While this population continues to grow, the land uses allocated to social welfare and medical facilities continue to shrink in the 23-*ku* area. Between 1986 and 1991 the amount of land allocated to these services fell by 0.2 per cent, and accounted for only 0.7 per cent of the 1991 total urban space of Tokyo's inner 23 wards. Adding educational/cultural facilities, parks and playgrounds, outdoor land uses, forests, and sports and amusement facilities, the total land area put aside for all these activities still accounts for only approximately 17.9 per cent of the total urban space in the 23-ward area. The rest of the space is devoted to residential areas, work (or work-related) activities, or inaccessible areas (rivers, unused land, and undeveloped fields) (TMG, 1996).

Environmental quality

The Tokyo Metropolitan Government believes that the key to the quality of Tokyo's urban space and the continued competitive ability of the city in an international arena is the development of its infrastructure, specifically transportation, water, and parks. However, a 1994 study suggests that the development of these three basic urban infrastructures is at half or slightly better than half of the necessary level (TMG, 1994). No doubt, environmental quality, defined as the delivery of basic services, will continue to be a concern of municipal officials. Indeed, the most recent Tokyo White Paper was focused on how to create "the city suited for everyday living" (TMG, 1996: 6).

Conclusion

Japan is a small nation, approximately 380,000 km² in area, equal in area to the state of California in the United States. Its population of 126 million is highly concentrated (332 person per km²), making Japan one of the most densely populated countries in the world. Moreover, because Japan is a mountainous country with only 30 per cent habitable area, the real density (persons per habitable area) is closer to 1,100/km². Within Tokyo proper, "overconcentration" has been considered one of Japan's national problems; 25 per cent of the country's population is concentrated into 3.6 per cent of its total land area.

The development of the Japanese economy and the decentralization of Tokyo's population have been the pillars of national policies. Whereas the first has been dramatically achieved, the second remains a stubborn problem. For a variety of reasons that can be differentiated by development-stage, the population of Tokyo has experienced consistent growth. In order to understand the response of Tokyo's development to national policies, it is important to place the city's development within the larger perspective of national economic restructuring and growth. Tokyo has consistently played a unique and important role within Japan's economic development.

Currently, global economic trends and Japanese urban economic restructuring are leading to a reconcentration of population in urban centres. Remote areas are losing population while cities as sub-regional and regional centres gain. Within metropolitan regions, the population in inner-city areas is falling while that in outer suburbs is growing. In the Tokyo region, the population of the inner city has been stable at approximately 8 million people, while surrounding cities such as Yokohama continue to grow. This particular suburb increased by 2–3 million people in a matter of 15 years. This type of urban development is the reality of Japan's post-industrial society.

The continued concentration of people and activities within the city is due, in large part, to the role of the service sector and Tokyo's integration in the global economy. Tokyo is an important nodal point for the management of Japan's world economy. Because of the strength of Japan within the global economic system and the importance of Tokyo within the Japanese system, the city remains economically vital despite the tragic bubble fiasco. The number of service-related CMFs located in the city is a testimony to its importance.

Needless to say, much effort should be made to continue to secure Tokyo's premier position within the global system of cities. In order to keep the city competitive, two important policies should be followed. One is to continue to develop the infrastructure (transportation, port, and communications) needed to enhance the relative attractiveness of the city to both domestic and foreign capital; the other is to promote the creation of a habitable living and working environment. Tokyo needs to provide a healthy and attractive environment to both capital and its citizens. Such consideration of human aspects may be the most crucial issue in the future development of this world city, which will lead Japan into the twenty-first century.

Acknowledgements

This paper was updated and rewritten by Peter J. Marcotullio and Yuko Nishida, Research Associates at the Institute of Advanced Studies, United Nations University.

Note

1. The Greater Tokyo Region, considered in this discussion, includes the Tokyo-to (Special Prefecture) and three surrounding prefectures covering an area of roughly 60–80 km^2.

References

Barrett, Brendan F. D. and Riki Therivel (1991), *Environmental Policy and Impact Assessment in Japan*. London: Routledge.

Environmental Agency of Japan (1994), *Quality of the Environment in Japan, 1994*. Tokyo: Planning Division, Global Environment Office.

Mollenkopf, John H. and Manuel Castells (eds.) (1991), *Dual City: Restructuring New York*. New York: Russell Sage Foundation.

Nakamura, Hachiro and James W. White (1988), "Tokyo." In: Mattei Dogan and John D. Kasarda (eds.), *The Metropolis Era: Mega-Cities: Volume 2*. Newbury Park, Calif.: Sage, pp. 123–156.

Sassen, Saskia (1991), *The Global City: New York, London, Tokyo*. Princeton, N.J.: Princeton University Press.

Takahashi, Junjiro and Noriyuki Sugiura (1996), "The Japanese Urban System and the Growing Centrality of Tokyo in the Global Economy." In: Fu-chen Lo and Yue-man Yeung (eds.), *Emerging World Cities in Pacific Asia*. Tokyo: United Nations University Press, pp. 101–143.

TMG (Tokyo Metropolitan Government) (1994), *Urban White Paper on the Tokyo Metropolis, 1994*. Tokyo: Bureau of Planning.

——— (1996), *Urban White Paper on the Tokyo Metropolis, 1996*. Tokyo: Bureau of Planning.

Toyokeizai (1996), *Data Bank, 1997*. Tokyo: Toyokeizai.

United Nations (1995), *World Urbanization Prospects: 1994 Revision*. New York: United Nations.

6

Globalization and world city formation in Pacific Asia

Yue-man Yeung and Fu-chen Lo

Globalization and Asian cities

Any United Nations or similar projection of the urban world future would suggest that urban population in the next few decades will continue to increase rapidly, most notably in developing countries. The world's urban population could well double from 2.6 billion in 1995 to 5.2 billion in 2050. Much of this increase will be concentrated in the developing world: its urban population of 1.5 billion, representing 37 per cent of the total population in the early 1990s, will likely soar to 4 billion (or 57 per cent of the population) by 2025. At the same time, the growth and concentration of very large cities, or mega-cities of 10 million or more inhabitants in developing countries, are noteworthy. In 1990, there were only 13 mega-cities in the world; but, by the year 2000, it is expected that 17 of the 21 mega-cities in the world will be located in the developing world (OECD, 1995).

Many factors can be advanced for the rapid growth of cities, especially of mega-cities in developing countries. One contributing factor is related to the pervading forces of globalization that have been affecting the nature and tempo of daily life in many parts of the world during the past two decades. The world economy has changed in fundamental ways with a new international division of labour; an age of globally integrated production and the transnational corporation has dawned. What has contributed to the ascendancy of globalization in recent years? At least three mega-trends may be identified (Lo and Yeung, 1996).

First, the early 1980s saw the sudden collapse of the prices of oil and other primary commodities, an outcome that may be attributable to the long-run decline of material inputs in production in industrially advanced economies. This contributed to the precipitous decline in the share of fuels and non-fuel primary commodities in world trade from 43.5 per cent in 1980 to 28.4 per cent in 1987 (Lo and Nakamura, 1992). In fact, Drucker (1987: 21) was the first to call attention to three basic changes in the fabric of the world's economy since the 1970s: the "uncoupling" of the primary products economy from the industrial economy, thereby diminishing the role of resources; the "uncoupling" of production from employment in the industrial economy itself; and the emergence of the "symbol economy" of financial flows and transactions to overshadow the "real economy" of the production and trade of goods and services.

Secondly, the decline in the role of material resources in production has been accompanied by the rise of capital, in particular the internationalization of capital, as a major driving force in the global economy (Wallace, 1990: 6). Similarly, production processes, services, even domestic currency and the state have vital international dimensions in order to be in tune with the global economy. The Plaza Accord of 1985, with the resultant dramatic appreciation of the Japanese yen against the US dollar and other currencies, had an especially far-reaching effect in the spread of foreign direct investment (FDI) from Japan across the globe. Capital mobility has become an important facet in the new international division of labour (NIDL), in which cities play pivotal roles in an interconnected network of multinational firms and cities (Friedmann and Wolff, 1982; King, 1990). The world of capitalism is both a worldwide net of corporations and a global network of cities (Smith and Feagin, 1987: 3).

Thirdly, underlying most of the trends noted above is technological change, which is seen to be a determinant of structural change. In this respect the range and speed of innovations in micro-electronics and communications since the late 1980s have been breathtaking. The cluster of new innovations in computers, electronics, robotics, telecommunications, new materials, and biotechnology has been facilitating production processes, speeding up and revolutionizing business transactions, and permitting creativity. A new era of telecommunications, information technology, and widened opportunity is considered to have arrived (Lo, 1994). This technological frontier is predicted to expand rapidly in the years ahead into the twenty-first century.

Against this background of structural adjustments in the global economy, the countries in the Asia Pacific region have fared extremely well. Collectively and individually, they have grown rapidly and have provided classic examples of economic transformation. Economic miracles have been said to characterize the post-war economic growth of Japan and the "Four Little Dragons" of Hong Kong, South Korea, Taiwan, and Singapore. The economies of the Association of South-East Asian Nations (ASEAN) and China have also seen rapid growth in recent years, and the prospects into the twenty-first century are distinctly robust (Yeung, 1993).

The sustained and rapid growth of the Asian economies may be related to three waves of regional economic development. The first one was triggered by Japanese offshore industrial relocation to the Asian newly industrializing economies (NIEs) in the 1960s and 1970s. During that period the Asian NIEs provided favourable locales for Japanese industrial relocation offshore, because, on the one hand, Japan was experiencing escalation of factor costs, including labour, and the need to search for overseas markets and, on the other hand, the Asian NIEs were in great need of Japanese investment in providing local employment, capital infusion, and technological uplift. The second wave occurred in the 1970s and 1980s, when the comparative advantage of countries in ASEAN was such that Japanese investment was attracted to them in spectacular fashion. The collapse of commodity and fuel prices in the early 1980s spurred these capital flows, which were later pushed further by the sharp appreciation of the Japanese yen in 1985. Equally, the appreciation of their currencies by South Korea and Taiwan in 1986 and 1987, respectively, had a similar knock-on effect on offshore industrial relocation from these countries to ASEAN and other parts of the world. Hong Kong and Singapore, as the other two Asian NIEs, likewise had a centrifugal tendency of capital outflows to countries in Asia and elsewhere for investment purposes during this period. The third wave of rapid foreign investment and development has occurred since the mid-1980s when, with China's open policy gathering momentum, FDI converged on China's coastal areas in major ways. At first, the four Special Economic Zones in Guangdong and Fujian saw rapid development because of their special privileges in setting policies to make foreign investment attractive and propitious, but such policy prerogatives were also extended later to other coastal areas and other parts of China. Since 1990, when Pudong was declared open as a major thrust of China's next phase of openness, Shanghai and its surrounding areas have undergone rapid economic development and social change.

During the past two decades there have been many developments in Pacific Asia (defined here as the Western Pacific Rim inclusive of East and South-East Asia) that have drawn the countries towards greater interdependency from the standpoint of linkages in production and marketing. By the mid-1980s, Japan had already outstripped the United States in inter-industrial relations with the Asian NIEs and ASEAN in finished goods and raw materials. After 1973 ASEAN countries became net exporters of non-durable consumer goods and have continued to expand rapidly in this direction. The NIEs that first began with the export of non-durable consumer goods in the 1960s have since the 1970s developed with considerable success an export market in durable consumer goods. Japan, on the other hand, began to import non-durable consumer goods in the 1970s, while capital goods and durable consumer goods continued with their consistent and high export performance. This pattern of regional functional specializations represents part of the NIDL resulting from structural change and locational shifts of comparative advantage, which have the effect of increasing complementarity and structural interdependence among countries in the region (fig. 6.1).

The obvious leading position of Japan in Pacific Asia as a pace-setter of development and innovations and as the first of the "flying geese" pattern of development in the region is illustrated in figure 6.2, in which all pertinent countries in the region are arrayed along the GNP curve for Japan at the level they had reached in 1988. However, since the bursting of the bubble economy in Japan in the early 1990s, the Japanese economy has had to reposition itself and has been facing more acute competition from the countries in North America and Europe, which have redoubled their efforts to invest in the Asia Pacific region and reassert their technological and entrepreneurial leadership.

A connecting thread to much of the regional division of labour, structural change, and locational shifts has been FDI. It has been a major source of dynamism that has powered much of the economic restructuring and trade relations within the region. An indication of the attraction of Pacific Asia to FDI and of intra-Asia differentiation is that, in the period 1981–1985, 92 per cent of all FDI to Asia was

Induced Countries \ Inducing Countries / Industrial Sector	Japan						USA					
	India	Malaysia	Philippines	Singapore	Thailand	Korea	India	Malaysia	Philippines	Singapore	Thailand	Korea
Food, beverage & tobacco	∘											
Textile & leather products	○	○	○		∘	○		∘				∘
Lumber & wood products	○		∘	○	∘	∘			∘			∘
Pulp, paper products & printing	○			○	∘	∘			∘		∘	∘
Chemical products	○		∘	○	○	⊕			∘		∘	∘
Petroleum refining			○			⊕						
Rubber products				∘	∘	⊕			∘			∘
Non-metallic mineral products				∘								
Metal products	⊕	∘	⊕	○	○	⊕		∘			○	⊕
Machinery	⊕	○	○	○	○	⊕	∘			○	∘	⊕
Transport equipment	⊕	○	○	⊕	⊕	⊕			∘		∘	∘
Other manufacturing industries	○	∘	○	○	○	○		∘	∘			∘
Construction	○		○	∘	∘	∘				∘		∘

⊕ Inducement coefficient of more than 0.4.
○ Inducement coefficient of between 0.2 and 0.4.
∘ Inducement coefficient of between 0.1 and 0.2.

Fig. 6.1 **Comparison of Japanese and US inter-industrial linkage with East and South-East Asian countries (measured by induce-ment coefficient from an international input–output table) (Source: S. Furukawa, *International Input–Output Analysis*, Tokyo: In-stitute of Developing Economies, 1986)**

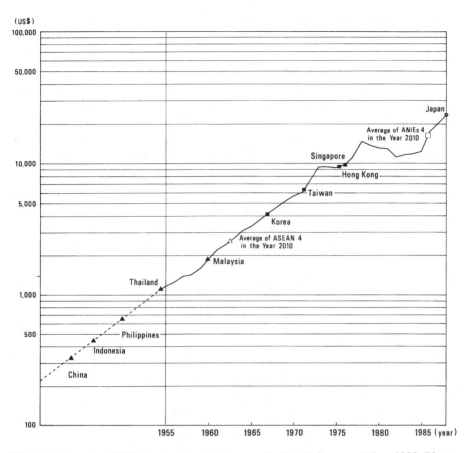

Fig. 6.2   **Trend of GNP per capita in Japan and other Asian countries, 1988 (Notes:
1. Based on IMF *International Financial Statistics* and other national statistics; 2.
Estimated figures in the year 2010 based on projection undertaken by EPA, Japan;
3. ANIEs 4 = Korea, Taiwan, Hong Kong, and Singapore; ASEAN 4 = Thailand,
Philippines, Indonesia, and Malaysia. Source: EPA (Japan), *Year 2010 Committee
Report*, 1991)**

destined for the Asian NIEs, the ASEAN countries, and China. Also,
more than 70 per cent of the annual flow of Japanese total FDI
is directed to the same countries (Panchamukhi, 1990). Investment
flows as a key indicator of growing regional interdependence offer
the opportunity of access to new technology, management, and marketing skills. Japan has become the largest single investor in Pacific
Asia, despite the importance of the United States and the European
Union in certain countries. Pacific Asia's catch of Japanese FDI has

137

declined in relative terms but still reached 11.7 per cent in 1988 at US$5.2 billion.

Another variant of the FDI flows is that the Asian NIEs themselves have begun to invest heavily in ASEAN since the mid-1980s. South Korea invested over US$250 million in cumulative stock in 1988 and Taiwan US$87 million in 1987 in ASEAN. South Korea's overseas investment worldwide hit a record of US$959 million in 1990, an increase of 68 per cent over the previous year (Clifford, 1991). Hong Kong has been reported to be a leading provider of FDI in the region, especially in the Pearl River Delta. Hong Kong's investment has also been substantial in South-East Asia, notably in Indonesia and Thailand (W. C. H. Yeung, 1994). Thus, the Asian NIEs have become exporters of capital in their own right, In particular, the importance of Taiwan (or Chinese Taipei) has come to the fore, reaching a climax in 1989 (table 6.1). Japan continued to be a major exporter of FDI, but the peak was reached in 1990. Since then, the

Table 6.1 **Direct investment in Pacific Asia from and into the economies of the Pacific Economic Cooperation Council (US$ million)**

Country	Flow	1988	1989	1990	1991	1992	1993
China	Outflow	850	780	830	913	4,000	−4,400
	Inflow	3,194	3,393	3,487	4,366	11,156	27,515
Indonesia	Outflow	*	*	*	*	*	*
	Inflow	576	682	1,093	1,482	1,777	2,004
Japan	Outflow	34,210	44,160	48,050	30,740	17,240	13,740
	Inflow	−520	−1,060	1,760	1,370	2,720	100
Korea	Outflow	151	305	820	1,357	1,047	1,056
	Inflow	871	758	715	1,116	550	516
Malaysia	Outflow	*	*	*	254	420	969
	Inflow	719	1,668	2,332	3,998	5,183	5,206
Philippines	Outflow	*	*	*	*	*	*
	Inflow	936	563	530	544	228	763
Singapore	Outflow	117	882	1,570	444	748	767
	Inflow	3,655	2,887	5,575	4,888	6,730	6,829
Chinese	Outflow	4,120	6,951	5,243	1,854	1,869	2,451
Taipei	Inflow	959	1,604	1,330	1,271	879	917
Thailand	Outflow	24	50	140	167	−147	−221
	Inflow	1,105	1,775	2,444	2,014	2,116	1,715
Viet Nam	Outflow	*	*	*	*	*	*
	Inflow	366	539	596	1,288	1,939	2,928

Source: PECC (1995: 69).

* Indicates less than US$1 million.

size of capital outflows has markedly shrunk. It should be noted that China and the ASEAN countries have emerged as major recipients of capital, exhibiting the shifting comparative advantage in their favour. Even Viet Nam increased its FDI inflows by eight times during the period 1988–1993.

The sizeable inflows of FDI to ASEAN countries have since the early 1980s led to sharp structural changes, particularly in the growth of export-oriented manufacturing. This is clearly reflected in the rapid rise of manufactures as a share of total exports from the countries in ASEAN (table 6.2). In the period 1980–1990, the rise of manufacturing industries in ASEAN may be seen from its export figures to the world (last column). While the ASEAN overall figure almost tripled from 21.8 per cent to 59.8 per cent in 10 years, Indonesia's percentage increase was 15.6 times, and Singapore and Thailand also recorded impressive gains. These figures certainly indicate that something akin to an industrial revolution had been taking place in ASEAN in the 1980s.

In terms of the relative importance of foreign investors in ASEAN, table 6.3 shows clearly that, by 1990, US FDI had already paled into insignificance. Asian NIEs' capital flows were already double those of Japan and are a force to be reckoned with. In any event, all these sizeable FDI flows emanating from within Pacific Asia have contributed markedly to growing regional economic integration and interdependence (Grosser and Bridges, 1990). A non-treaty trading bloc is fast becoming a reality in Pacific Asia, which may be viewed in stark contrast to trading bloc formation recently advanced elsewhere in the world.

One way of conceptualizing the rapid and interdependent changes that have been occurring in the Asia Pacific region in recent years centres on the emerging and critical roles cities have played in the new global economy. Certain types of city – world cities – have emerged to be important because, as network cities, various functions such as airports, banking, capital flows, waves of technology, and branches of multinational firms are performed through them in the regional and global economies. Cities do not grow in importance simply because of their demographic weight; their position in the global economy is judged by the number and range of functions being performed in the global economy. Put simply, globalization processes are enacted through world cities and a functional city system becomes a distinct expression of the global economy. A given functional city does not necessarily include certain cities within the same population size

Table 6.2 **Manufactures as a share of total exports: ASEAN countries, 1980–1990 (%)**

Country	Year	Destination						
		Indonesia	Philippines	Malaysia	Singapore	Thailand	ASEAN	World
Indonesia	1980	–	4.6	7.3	6.8	21.4	6.8	2.2
	1985	–	18.1	49.4	22.8	65.5	25.1	12.9
	1990	–	62.8	48.6	46.1	36.7	46.7	34.5
Philippines	1980	5.9	–	16.1	20.7	15.3	14.4	20.2
	1985	79.3	–	17.9	17.0	18.2	19.6	25.9
	1990	n.a.	–	n.a.	n.a.	n.a.	n.a.	n.a.
Malaysia	1980	59.6	25.1	–	17.5	14.5	18.3	18.6
	1985	35.4	13.0	–	27.3	7.9	23.5	26.8
	1990	n.a.	n.a.	–	n.a.	n.a.	n.a.	n.a.
Singapore	1980	19.0	53.8	55.1	–	33.7	50.5	45.6
	1985	51.1	42.9	54.8	–	41.3	51.5	50.3
	1990	53.6	63.9	71.6	–	49.0	63.9	70.8
Thailand	1980	9.5	37.0	25.3	44.9	–	31.4	24.2
	1985	29.0	12.8	22.2	57.8	–	41.8	37.1
	1990	46.6	51.2	38.4	75.4	–	63.9	62.6
ASEAN	1980	13.0	31.7	50.6	15.3	29.1	28.2	21.8
	1985	39.5	21.8	50.3	28.6	30.4	35.8	31.8
	1990	46.6	61.6	68.3	60.2	48.3	61.3	59.8

Source: United Nations, *Commodity Trade Statistics*, data tape; cited in Imada and Naya (1992: 57).
n.a. = data not available.

Table 6.3 **Direct investment in ASEAN, 1988–1990**

	1988		1989		1990[a]	
	US$ billion	% of total FDI	US$ billion	% of total FDI	US$ billion	% of total FDI
United States	1.6	13.4	1.1	7.3	1.2	4.8
Japan	3.6	30.4	4.8	32.8	5.5	22.6
NIEs	3.7	31.0	4.1	27.6	12.9	45.3

Source: Jaw-yann (1994: 107).
a. The data for 1990 are for January to August.

range, nor will it coincide with an entire national urban hierarchy. The collation of different functional networks of a city serves to define that city's external linkages with the world economy and its status within the world city system. A city grows in importance if it performs effectively and efficiently a number of key functions that another one does not. For example, Singapore serves as a hub of several functional networks, including imports and exports, tele-communications, international airlines, and international finance, thereby determining its extensive and key external linkages. In the global economy where national boundaries are becoming of decreasing importance in economic interactions, or simply in a borderless economy, it is the acquisition and accumulation of functions that determine the centrality and role of a city in the regional and global economies. In Pacific Asia, a regional functional city system is emerging, which is superimposed on cities. World cities in the region are being woven together into a mutually reinforcing, interdependent web.

The emerging urban system in Pacific Asia

The extent to which globalization has affected individual cities as well as national urban systems can be examined through their differential responses to the changing global economy and their own shifting positions within it. The relationships between the economic structural adjustments experienced in individual countries, on the one hand, and globalization forces and urban transformation, on the other, are reflected in a number of selected studies of world cities and national urban systems within Pacific Asia.

The clearest expression of the changing roles of a city in the region

141

over time can be exemplified by Tokyo. Three stages of development may be distinguished. In the 1960s, Tokyo evidently emerged as a national magnet in the Japanese economy, to which population and development were forcefully drawn. Then, in the 1970s Tokyo developed and strengthened, with greater contributions to the national economy, by developing as a financial, telecommunications, and transnational corporation centre. At the same time, decentralization of its manufacturing capacity, while keeping central managerial functions, began to be evident within Japan. All these developments, however, were played out largely within the constraints of the national economic system. With the advent of the 1980s, forces of globalization began to impinge on Tokyo, which was rapidly transformed into a world city having economic articulation with the global economy, not simply with the national or even regional economies. Tokyo, responding to the demands of a world city, gradually developed an NIDL and industrial restructuring by relocating manufacturing production to cities abroad, particularly in the Asia Pacific region, again retaining key central managerial functions and R&D within Japan. The comparative advantage of Tokyo and cities within Pacific Asia was being capitalized in the process. Japan emerged as one of the leading economies in the world. Tokyo's status as a world city grew as a consequence, for it had become increasingly integrated with the global and regional economies. Its importance within the Japanese urban system has also been enhanced, having become a giant urban agglomeration of more than 30 million inhabitants within its daily commuting distance of some 50 km from the city centre.

The recent development of Seoul and Taipei further epitomizes the regional response to economic globalization and the seizure of new economic opportunities as the Asian NIEs are in a position to seek development beyond their shores. In both cases, labour-intensive manufacturing has been decentralized to offshore locations, such as ASEAN countries, coastal China, and, recently, Viet Nam, where labour and other factors of production are lower, leaving capital-intensive types of production within their countries.

Seoul, whose population has quadrupled in the past three decades, has emerged as the overarching urban agglomeration within South Korea. It has exhibited a functional and economic dominance rarely seen in Asia. Although a decentralization policy put in place since the 1980s, designed to halt its unwanted growth, has been only partially successful, it has assiduously restructured its economy and prepared for its internationalization. The establishment of the Capital Region has been one mechanism to channel the future growth of the Seoul region in a more structured manner. Similarly, Taipei has since the 1980s repositioned its economy in relation to the growing effects of globalization and the internationalization of business. Like South Korea, Taiwan has positively nurtured its manufacturing sector towards technological progress and innovation, with explicit government support in the establishment of industrial estates and science parks. Taiwan has become the thirteenth-largest trading entity in the world. In comparison with Seoul, Taipei has been growing at a more modest pace. With the port city of Kaohsiung in the south, Taipei forms one end of a north–south urban corridor across the island, along which economic activities and facilities are more spread out than in South Korea.

Since the 1980s, waves of foreign investment have been reaching ASEAN countries and China, and their influence on the growth of these economies and their large cities has been strong. ASEAN countries presented just the right mix of conditions as hosts for offshore manufacturing to take place during this period. As a result, foreign direct investment in ASEAN countries increased sharply and this facilitated a major economic restructuring of these countries from being commodity exporters to manufacturing exporters. Structural reorientation also occurred in the early 1980s, when commodity prices collapsed, giving the ASEAN countries timely and critical relief from their previous overdependence on primary commodity exports for their national income. This infusion of growth impulses has given renewed strength to their large cities. Thus Bangkok, Kuala Lumpur, and Jabotabek have grown rapidly and in new directions. Growing international contacts and economic globalization have led to rapid growth, which in the context of the cities concerned has favoured the suburban areas rather than the central-city areas. These urban fringe areas have experienced the fastest rates of growth and the most rapid physical transformation (see table 6.4). These areas have relatively more land and somewhat less stringent regulatory controls on manufacturing-related growth and investment by transnational corporations. This process of rapid growth around urban agglomerations in Asia has been described as extended metropolitanization (Ginsburg et al., 1991). By virtue of their traditional and newfound importance, these emerging world cities within ASEAN have become better integrated among themselves and have become well articulated with the new global economy.

In large measure, very much the same globalization processes have

Table 6.4 **Varying rates of population growth in Jakarta, Hong Kong, and surrounding cities**

	Population ('000)		Annual growth rate (%)
	1980	*1990*	
Jabotabek	11,893	17,099	3.7
Jakarta	6,480	8,223	2.4
Bogor	2,739	4,007	4.1
Tangerang	1,529	2,765	6.1
Bekasi	1,143	2,104	6.3
	1978	*1988*	
Hong Kong–Zhujang Delta	7,810	12,166	4.5
Hong Kong	4,703	5,736	2.0
Shenzhen	23	322	30.2
Guangzhou	2,065	3,891	6.5
Macau	268	444	5.2
Zhuhai	13	191	30.8

Source: Lo and Yeung (1996: 38).

been bringing about rapid economic development in China since 1978. With the country having been isolated for decades from the mainstream of development, only China's coastal areas first came to be the foci of foreign investment. In this respect, it should be noted that foreign investment sources were initially largely from Asia, despite a trend recently to open up to Western industrially advanced countries. Even in the rapidly developing and changing coastal areas, the gradual and painful shift from a socialist to a market economy has prevented foreign investment from being immediately effective (Yeung and Hu, 1992). By trial and error, some of China's coastal cities are being brought into the global economy but no Chinese city, whatever its population size, has yet reached the stage of playing key network roles in the global economy. Thus a truly world city is yet to emerge in Mainland China.

Finally, in contrast to the fast-growing countries and cities in Pacific Asia that have been briefly touched upon, the Philippines has been experiencing slow rates of growth over decades. Political instability and other problems have not made the island nation conducive to foreign investment compared with its neighbours, which received massive foreign investment in the second half of the 1980s. In fact, because of economic stagnation, sustained emigration and labour migration to the Middle East countries have occurred for two decades. Consequently, Manila has been bypassed by some of the positive effects of globalization, and until recently persistent neglect of social and economic infrastructure had resulted in the deterioration of the quality of life, particularly for the urban poor. For Manila, whatever influence globalization has been brought to bear on it, its former economic and functional dominance over the country has been reported to have declined.

World city formation

In order to be effective in the new global and regional economies, world cities in Pacific Asia have been preparing themselves in different ways, in a process that may be called world city formation.[1] Many have not spared any effort or expense in infrastructure investment, creating space within their territory and improving themselves, physically and economically, so as to be able to play their roles as command posts, financial centres, headquarters locations, and transport hubs.

Many Asian cities have recently invested massively in physical infrastructure to be able to cope with rapidly growing traffic and telecommunications in a new global age. One example is the construction of huge and futuristic airports in many global cities, such as Changi in Singapore, Chek Lap Kok in Hong Kong, Kansai in Osaka, the Seoul Metropolitan Airport, and Nong Ngu Hao in Bangkok. The Kansai, Chek Lap Kok, and Seoul airports are all built on reclaimed land, which serves to highlight the need to create new space from the sea where existing land space poses a constraint for development. Examples of land creation through reclamation may be found in many Asian world cities. In Singapore, much of the east coast has been reclaimed over the past two decades, giving rise to new commercial and business centres such as Marine Parade. Tokyo, too, has been expanding through landfills along the Tokyo Bay since the 1960s for its booming industries and a new airport. The Haneda airport, only 15 km from the city centre, was originally built as an international airport but has remained only a domestic one after the opening of Narita airport. In the same way, the insatiable demand for land since the mid-nineteenth century has forced Hong Kong to reclaim land from its beautiful deep-water harbour, particularly in the post-war years. The speed and scope of recent and proposed reclamations, due in part to the new airport construction, have brought about a recent public debate on the subject (Man, 1995).

145

Because world cities are network dependent and technologically oriented, the establishment of infrastructure for information networks is viewed as indispensable in the trend towards a post-industrial society or an "information society." This trend is best exemplified by the Teleport project in Tokyo, built on a landfill in Tokyo Bay, only 5 km from downtown. It is conceived as a futuristic information city consisting of elegant apartment blocks for 60,000 people and high-tech companies offering 110,000 jobs, in fields such as tele-communications, business information functions, international business, information networking, advertising, printing, etc. These will be featured in a telecommunications centre and a business intelligence centre, designed to assist in the globalization of flexible production and transnational corporations (Fujita, 1991: 280).

Along with the general trend to computerize and automate, many Asian cities have striven to construct intelligent buildings with "beauty and brains," following similar innovations in American cities. The Mitsui New No. 2 Building in Tokyo, completed in 1985, is regarded as the first to be built in Asia. Since then, many intelligent buildings have mushroomed in Tokyo and elsewhere in Japan. Manila's 32-storey Stock Exchange Centre, completed in 1992, is run by an electronic nerve centre able to monitor the weather and regulate air-conditioning and lighting. Seoul's Sixty-four Building, Hong Kong's Central Plaza, and Kuala Lumpur's Petrona Towers are tall buildings of similar construction. All these tall buildings not only vie for prestige but create, at considerable cost, the much-needed office and other space for global cities to consolidate and expand their functions.

In a drive towards technology and knowledge, many global cities in Asia have invested in focused development of R&D, often in conjunction with tertiary institutions. In Japan, the government has encouraged the construction of a number of intelligent cities or "technopolises." These are small cities built for high-tech industries, research institutes, and colleges. The best example is Tsukuba Science City located some 60 km north-east of Tokyo. In Singapore, Taipei, and Seoul, science parks with substantial investment by government and industry have operated with distinct success, although Hong Kong is still to catch up with the other Asian NIEs in this respect.

Land reclamation and vertical development of space through tall and intelligent buildings are ways to increase space production, but world cities have also intensified urban renewal for the same reason. This process has taken different forms in different cities, but the redevelopment of much of the central city area of Singapore since the 1960s has been facilitated by legislation and the cooperation of the public and private sectors. Hong Kong only recently moved with vigour in this direction with the establishment of the Land Development Corporation. On a smaller scale, many cities have witnessed neighbourhood gentrification, whereby the physical and economic uplift of the area has been realized. The revitalization of Lan Kwai Fong on the fringe of Hong Kong's town centre as an upbeat recreation and commercial area is a classic example.

Urban redevelopment on any sizeable scale depends critically on a successful public–private sector partnership, as the experience of Japan has shown. Since the 1970s, private capital has been attracted to public development through incentives such as low taxes, large subsidies, and deregulation. Even some nationally owned land within central Tokyo was sold to private real estate companies. Consequently, the urban space of Tokyo has become an arena for capital accumulation on a huge scale (Machimura, 1992: 120). This explains in part the rapid and sustained escalation of land prices in Tokyo for more than a decade until the bubble economy burst in the early 1990s. By the same token, world cities in Asia have strenuously sought FDI through relaxation of restrictive regulations and market opening. The stage is set for them to be more active players in the global and regional economies.

As world city formation proceeds in Pacific Asia, most world cities are subject increasingly to the forces of international migration of population. Tokyo, for example, has for the first time experienced legal and illegal immigration of sizeable magnitude from neighbouring Asian countries, including those of South Asia. Immigration has become a new factor in Japanese urban life, providing needed labour for menial and other jobs and occasionally involved in the shady underworld of crime. Even in Hong Kong, as a result of its greater international orientation in recent years, the rise of foreign populations has been very rapid. Between 1980 and 1992, the resident Thai, Filipino, and Canadian populations more than tripled (Yeung, 1995a). Another manifestation of sizeable international migration within Pacific Asia has been the presence of Filipino domestic servants in many of its world cities. This is a form of NIDL within the region. Within the countries in the region, considerable rural–urban migration has occurred where enhanced employment opportunities are provided by the presence of export-oriented manufacturing industries, such as those that have been established in export-processing zones in Malaysia, Taiwan, and the Philippines, or in the suburban areas of world cities. The economic and social impacts of these migration streams on the cities and countries concerned are profound.

Indeed, within the Asia Pacific region a new climate of economic globalization has spurred subregional economic cooperation in several locales and others are being planned for implementation. Called growth triangles, these localized economic zones involving several countries can be viewed as an expression of a borderless economy, where the international division of labour is developed to its advantage (Thant et al., 1994). One such example is the cross-border cooperative development, involving capital, technological, and managerial inputs from Hong Kong and Taiwan, in China's southern provinces of Guangdong and Fujian, which have the comparative advantage in cheap land and labour. Natural complementarities of the territories in question have enabled the rapid development of this part of China since the early 1980s and the gradual economic integration of the three territories in many ways (Yeung, 1995b).

One sub-area of the Southern China Growth Triangle is the Hong Kong–Zhujiang Delta, representing a smaller area of intense economic cooperation between Hong Kong and the smaller cities in the delta region. Obvious economic disparity exists between Hong Kong and the delta region, but the lucrative symbiosis between the two lands is a powerful economic motivation for greater integration. To echo a point made earlier about the more rapid growth of suburban areas in Jakarta and, indeed, Bangkok, Taipei, and other world cities in Pacific Asia, this phenomenon is repeated in the Hong Kong–Zhujiang Delta area. If Hong Kong is viewed as the centre of the Hong Kong–Zhujiang Delta region, its annual population growth of 2.0 per cent is only a fraction of the more than 30 per cent per year in neighbouring Shenzhen and Zhuhai, two Special Economic Zones, in the period 1978–1988 (see table 6.4). However, the trend of growing integration within the region will be further reinforced by the return of Hong Kong to Chinese sovereignty in 1997. It has been forecast that the Hong Kong–Zhujiang Delta will continue to grow as a physical and economic entity in the years ahead and will likely evolve into a huge urban agglomeration of 40 million inhabitants in the twentieth-first century.

Another successful subregional economic entity is one in which Singapore, Malaysia (Johore), and Indonesia (Riau Islands) participate. Like the Southern China Growth Triangle, which has Hong Kong as its pivot, SIJORI (named after Singapore, Johore, and Riau Islands) revolves around Singapore, another world city. The three territories display excellent economic complementarities, making a clear division of labour possible. Population movement within the area is strictly controlled by territorial boundaries.

Future outlook and policy implications

The subregional cooperative entities focused on one world city, as described above, are one form of the urban-regional pattern that is emerging in Pacific Asia. They represent a new spatial form of cross-border urban region, which may or may not be centred on a world city. Such cooperative development regions reflect the new international division of labour being compressed and concentrated in the territories surrounding them, with nevertheless strong links to the global economy.

At an even larger level are economic development zones and urban corridors, which tend to extend over a wider territory and to be centred around a number of world cities or mega-cities. A number of urban corridors representing the highest level of interconnectedness among the cities they encompass within the delineated area as part of a regional restructured economy may be identified as follows:
· Pan-Japan Sea Zone
· Pan-Bohai Zone
· South China Zone
· Indo-China Zone
· Jabotabek
It should be recognized that these urban corridors are at varying stages of formation, some exhibiting but incipient development whereas others are quite advanced in form and connectivity among the cities. Certain urban corridors are already being formed in countries within the region, such as those connecting Pusan and Seoul, Taipei and Kaohsiung, Hanoi and Ho Chi Minh City, Johore Bahru–Kuala Lumpur–Penang, Jakarta and Surabaja. However, the best illustration of a mature urban corridor is one called BESETO, which consists of the region focused around Beijing, Seoul, and Tokyo. This will be discussed in detail in the following chapter by Choe. As the countries strive to improve infrastructure development within and among themselves, this urban corridor has every possibility of assuming greater importance within Pacific Asia (Choe, 1996). Given the rapid development of the Asia Pacific region forecast for the future, one future outlook for the Western Pacific Rim is to conceive of it as a more or less continuous urban belt linking a number of

urban corridors and economic development zones stretching from Japan and North Korea to West Java focused on Jabotabek. In this new urban age, world cities in Pacific Asia are playing increasingly important roles for the global and regional economies (Y. M. Yeung, 1994).

Globalization has transformed many Asian cities, providing them with new functions and heightened roles. At the same time, nations have found themselves having to contend with globalization forces in making their development plans. In the new global economy, the pivotal role of some cities, such as world cities, has come to the fore. Knight (1989: 327) has succinctly summed up the emerging global society and the growing influence of cities within it:

Now that development is being driven more by globalization than by nationalization, the role of cities is increasing. Power comes from global economies that are realized by integrating national economies into the global economy, and cities provide the strategic linkage functions. Activities related to the creation of global linkages, such as identifying opportunities, advancing and implementing technology, financing and handling transactional flows, structuring and serving global markets, are located primarily in cities and are expanding rapidly.... To wit, as global society expands, the role of cities increases and the role of the nations decreases.

Indeed, the present is being envisaged as a historic period, in that cities are now able to position themselves in the global society. To be more specific, Knight (Knight and Gappert, 1989: 12) maintains: "Once cities become aware of the possibilities created by the global society, they can begin positioning themselves to capture selected opportunities and thereby secure a role in the global society." If Knight's analysis and prognosis of global development are accurate, the omens are good for world cities in Pacific Asia in the twenty-first century with its predicted healthy economic outlook.

In reflecting on the future of world cities in Pacific Asia, several critical issues having a bearing on policy implications should be tackled. The extent to which these issues can be resolved will significantly determine how world cities in the region will evolve and position themselves in the global economy.

First, as world cities evolve and change to enable them to discharge both their old and their new functions, they are experiencing urban restructuring – spatially, economically, and socially. In terms of spatial outcome, a concentration of control and management functions in a world city leads to the transformation of urban functions and land-use patterns. The NIDL has redefined the employment structure of world cities. Whereas control, management, and service functions have increased, the relative importance of manufacturing has declined. Socially, the internationalization of Asian world cities has led to expensive housing and sharpened social inequalities and tensions. Traffic jams, growing pollution, and escalating crime are some of the negative consequences of rapid growth (Yeung, 1996).

Urban decision makers are confronted with certain critical choices, which have grave implications for energy consumption, pollution abatement, and financial burdens. One basic issue, for example, is the choice of intra-city transport. Many world cities in Pacific Asia do not have a mass transit system and are struggling to cope with the rapidly increasing number of automobiles that have come with growing affluence. Bangkok, Taipei, Manila, Kuala Lumpur, and Jakarta at best have plans for mass transit systems of sorts but, until they actually come into operation, traffic jams in these cities will go from bad to worse. Chinese cities are also having to contend simultaneously with "bicycle pollution" and a rapid increase in automobiles. Whereas the twentieth century for China has been a period of civil war, revolution, and strife, car-makers are confidently predicting that the twenty-first century will be one of cars, roads, and more traffic jams (Foo, 1995). To cope with their teeming populations, mass transit appears to be indispensable as the primary mode of urban transport in world cities. This will require the inculcation of certain values so that a desirable lifestyle can be maintained. Reliance of large cities on mass transit will result in less air pollution, reduced energy consumption, and a more efficient use of road space.

A second issue relates to the broad question of how world cities can be fed. A study on the food supply of China against the backdrop of its booming economy has thrown up some searching questions about the vulnerability of some Asian cities and countries (Brown, 1994). In Japan, soaring demand for grain ascribable to prosperity and the heavy loss of cropland to industrial development since World War II had pushed dependence on grain imports to 77 per cent of total grain consumption in 1993. Over the past few decades, active industrialization leading to the conversion of grainland to non-farm uses has caused Japan to lose 52 per cent of its grainland, South Korea 42 per cent, and Taiwan 35 per cent. These statistics are indeed disquieting for China, which, with rapidly rising per capita income, is already seeing signs of a change in people's diet. At the same time, China's cropland is shrinking fast, lost to industrial and other uses. Based on the experience of more developed Asian countries, the future fall in China's grain production is estimated conservatively at one-fifth. Translated into numbers, the deficit by 2030 will rise to 305 million tonnes of grain, which will not be capable of being borne by the world (Brown, 1994). The concerns raised by this study of China's food supply should be kept in mind by policy makers in world cities in the region. Although the functions of these cities are changing and intensifying in technology and complexity, this does not in itself help the food supply. These cities must therefore work within their national and regional economies to ensure that their food supplies are within certain margins of safety.

The third and final issue broadens the question of food supply to encompass the whole concept of sustainable development. Are world cities in Pacific Asia sustainable cities? This is not an easy question to answer because the concept of sustainable development is still rather new and complex. By one definition, "sustainable development is the ability to ensure the needs of the present without compromising the ability of future generations to meet their own needs" (WCED, 1987: 43). As the food supply issue illustrates, a city can be very vulnerable to the carrying capacity of near or distant lands. Other pressures on a city involve job opportunities, poverty, health, housing, waste management, and the environment (especially global warming). Sustainable development involves a holistic approach to the restructuring of our global society, including international relations. Two knowledge gaps exist in our understanding of sustainable cities: the link between carbon dioxide build-up and global warming, and how to reduce global population growth to replacement levels in the near future (Stren et al., 1992: 8–51). For world cities in Pacific Asia to be sustainable, all of the pressures mentioned above will have to be alleviated. Two questions in particular are of special relevance to policy makers. One has to do with the sustainability of the evolving roles and functions of world cities in the new global economy, taking into consideration their restructured economy, continued population growth through international and internal migration and natural increase, and heightened social tensions. The other pertains to the responsibility city governments have to shoulder the choice of energy-efficient systems of transport and electricity, minimizing the emission of "greenhouse" gases, and educating citizens in the good practices of environmental protection. If these questions are adequately addressed, sustainable world cities, in the sense of economic development along with environmental protection, will add to the collective strength of the Asia Pacific region.

Note

1. This section is adapted largely from Yeung (1996).

References

Brown, Lester (1994), "Who Will Feed China?" *World Watch*, September/October: 10–19.

Choe, Sang-Chuel (1996), "The Evolving Urban System in North-East Asia," In: Fu-chen Lo and Yue-man Yeung (eds.), *Emerging World Cities in Pacific Asia*. Tokyo: United Nations University Press, pp. 498–519.

Clifford, Mark (1991), "A Trickle, Not a Flood." *Far Eastern Economic Review*, 28 December: 67.

Drucker, Peter F. (1987), *The Frontiers of Management*. London: Heinemann.

Foo, Choy-peng (1995), "Car Giants Set for China Race." *South China Morning Post* (Hong Kong), 2 July.

Friedmann, John and Goetz Wolff (1982), "World City Formation: An Agenda for Research and Action." *International Journal of Urban and Regional Research* 6(3): 309–344.

Fujita, Kuniko (1991), "A World City and Flexible Specialization: Restructuring of the Tokyo Metropolis." *International Journal of Urban and Regional Research* 15(2): 269–284.

Ginsburg, Norton, Bruce Koppel, and T. G. McGee (eds.) (1991), *The Extended Metropolis: Settlement Transition in Asia*. Honolulu: University of Hawaii Press.

Grosser, Kate and Brian Bridges (1990), "Economic Interdependence in East Asia: The Global Context." *The Pacific Review* 3(1): 1–14.

Imada, Pearl and Seija Naya (eds.) (1992), *AFTA: The Way Ahead*. Singapore: Institute of Southeast Asian Studies.

Jaw-yann, Twu (1994), "East Asian Economic Perspectives on the New Triangular Network among Three Chinas and the New Phase of US–Japan Relations." In: Francois Gipouloux (ed.) (1994), *Regional Economic Strategies in East Asia: A Comparative Perspective*. Tokyo: Maison Franco-Japonaise, pp. 97–111.

King, Anthony D. (1990), *Global Cities: Post Imperialism and the Internationalization of London*. London: Routledge.

Knight, Richard (1989), "City Building in a Global Society." In: Richard Knight and Gary Gappert (eds.), *Cities in a Global Society*. Newbury Park, Calif.: Sage, pp. 326–333.

Knight, Richard and Gary Gappert (eds.) (1989), *Cities in a Global Society*. Newbury Park, Calif.: Sage.

Lo, Fu-chen (1994), "The Impacts of Current Global Adjustment and Shifting Techno-economic Paradigm on the World City System." In: Roland Fuchs et al. (eds.), *Mega-City Growth and the Future*. Tokyo: United Nations University Press, pp. 103–130.

Lo, Fu-chen and Yoichi Nakamura (1992), "Uneven Growth, the Mega-Trends of Global Change and the Future of the Asia-Pacific Economies." In: S. P. Gupta and S. Tambunlertchai (eds.), *The Asia Pacific Economies: A Challenge to South Asia*. Bangalore: Macmillan, pp. 25–64.

Lo, Fu-chen and Yue-man Yeung (eds.) (1996), *Emerging World Cities in Pacific Asia*. Tokyo: United Nations University Press.

Machimura, Takashi (1992), "The Urban Restructuring Process in Tokyo in the 1980s: Transforming Tokyo into a World City." *International Journal of Urban and Regional Research* 16(1): 114–128.

Man, Chi-sum (1995), "Reclamation and Its Negative Impacts on Navigation Safety and the Ecological Environment." *Hong Kong Economic Journal Monthly*, June, no. 219: 80–82 (in Chinese).

OECD (1995), "Towards an Urban World." *OECD Future Studies Information Base Highlights*, May, no. 11.

Panchamukhi, V. R. (1990), "UNCTAD in Asia: Issues in the 1990s." *IDS Bulletin* 21(1): 72–78.

PECC (Pacific Economic Development Council) (1995), *Pacific Economic Outlook, 1995–1996*. Singapore: PECC.

Smith, Michael Peter and Joe R. Feagin (eds.) (1987), *The Capitalist City: Global Restructuring and Community Politics*. Oxford: Basil Blackwell.

Stren, Richard, Rodney White, and Joseph Whitney (eds.) (1992), *Sustainable Cities: Urbanization and the Environment in International Perspective*. Boulder, Colo.: Westview Press.

Thant, Myo, Min Tang, and Hiroshi Kakazu (eds.) (1994), *Growth Triangles in Asia: A New Approach to Regional Economic Cooperation*. Hong Kong: Oxford University Press.

Wallace, Iain (1990), *The Global Economic System*. London: Unwin Hyman.

WCED (World Commission on Environment and Development) (1987*), Our Common Future*. Oxford: Oxford University Press.

Yeung, W. C. H. (1994), "Hong Kong Firms in the ASEAN Region: Transnational Corporations and Foreign Direct Investment." *Environment and Planning A* 26: 1931–1956.

Yeung, Yue-man (ed.) (1993), *Pacific Asia in the 21st Century: Geographical and Developmental Perspectives*. Hong Kong: Chinese University Press.

——— (1994), "Pacific Asia's World Cities in the New Global Economy." Paper presented at the OECD–Australian Government Conference on Cities in the New Global Economy, Melbourne, 20–23 November.

——— (1995a), "Hong Kong's Hub Functions." Paper presented at the Conference on Planning Hong Kong for the 21st Century, Hong Kong, 12–13 April.

——— (1995b), "Growth Triangles in Pacific Asia: A Comparative Perspective." In: S. J. Lew (ed.), *Tumen River Area Development Project: The Political Economy of Cooperation in Northeast Asia*. Seoul: The Sejong Institute, pp. 57–80.

——— (1996), "An Asian Perspective on the Global City." *International Social Science Journal* 48(1): 25–31.

Yeung, Yue-man and Xu-wei Hu (eds.) (1992), *China's Coastal Cities: Catalysts for Modernization*. Honolulu: University of Hawaii Press.

7

Urban corridors in Pacific Asia

Sang-chuel Choe

Introduction

Although terms such as "urban corridor" and "Pacific Asia" have never been precisely defined, they reflect an unprecedented sense of a community and opportunity on the Asian Pacific Rim. The 1995 *Time* magazine in its 11 January and 22 February editions ran two exciting cover stories relevant to the theme of this chapter. The subject of the cover stories was as follows: mega-cities, the world's sprawling urban centres, are rife with problems and filled with promise. The ambitious and the down-trodden of the world come by the millions, drawn by the strange magnetism of urban life.

For centuries, the progress of civilization had been defined by the inexorable growth of cities. Now the world is about to pass a milestone. More people will live in urban areas than in the countryside. Does the growth of mega-cities portend an apocalypse of global epidemics and pollution? Or will the remarkable stirrings of self-reliance that can be found in some of them point the way to their salvation? Trade across the Pacific Ocean already surpasses its transatlantic counterpart. With the apparent dawning of the Pacific Age years ahead of schedule, East Asia will continue to set the world pace for prosperity.

Certainly, Pacific Asia, which includes East Asia and South-East Asia, has been passing through great socio-economic transformations and a new era of urban revolution. Urbanization in Pacific Asia is not simply the upsurge of rural-to-urban migration. It is the surprising growth of mega-cities, the shaping of megalopolises, and the emergence of urban corridors across national borders. Mega-cities and megalopolises in Pacific Asia are not completely new but the concepts of urban corridor, growth triangle, and/or natural economic territory began to appear in the literature from the late 1980s. This chapter addresses these new urban phenomena. It begins with a review of the urbanization pattern in general and highlights the emerging urban corridors in Pacific Asia and how the urban system may be changed by the globalization of the Pacific Asian economy. Finally, it draws attention to the promises and disenchantments of the urban corridor phenomenon and the policy implications for urban development.

The urbanization pattern in Pacific Asia

In 1920, less than one-fifth of the world's population lived in urban places. By 1980, the urbanization level had reached more than two-fifths, and by 2000 it is projected to exceed one-half. Although there are great variations in the size and growth rates of urban population among countries in Pacific Asia, the proportion of the population living in urban areas is the lowest in the region as a whole, with the exception of highly urbanized countries such as Japan, South Korea, Taiwan, and the city-states of Hong Kong and Singapore (table 7.1). In 1990, the proportions of urban population in East Asia and South-East Asia were 38.6 and 28.1 per cent, respectively, compared with the world average of 45.9. However, the momentum for rapid urbanization has just begun in Pacific Asia. The urbanization level is related to the level of industrialization. In this regard, Japan and the Asian newly industrializing economies (NIEs – South Korea, Taiwan, Hong Kong, and Singapore) led economic growth and concomitant urbanization until the 1980s, but the rate of urbanization is beginning to stabilize. Instead, China and some countries of the Association of South-East Asian Nations (ASEAN) – Indonesia, Malaysia, the Philippines, and Viet Nam (the ASEAN-4) – will experience rapid urbanization along with recent economic development. The Asian NIEs are now facing new problems and challenges in global competition. The challenges include ever-soaring wages, labour shortages, price and exchange

Table 7.1 **Urbanization profile of East and South-East Asia**

	Mid-1994 population (million) (A)	Urban population (%) (B)	Population in urban areas of 1 million or more		Per capita GNP, 1992 (US$)
			As % of (A)	As % of (B)	
World	5,607.0	43	17	38	4,340
China	1,192.0	28	9	35	380
Hong Kong	5.8	100	95	100	15,380
Indonesia	199.7	31	11	36	670
Japan	125.0	77	37	47	28,220
Korea	44.5	74	53	73	6,790
Malaysia	19.5	51	10	24	2,790
Philippines	68.7	44	15	36	770
Singapore	2.9	100	100	100	15,750
Taiwan	21.1	75	20	27	4,709
Thailand	59.4	19	13	60	1,840

Sources: 1994 World Population Data Sheet and Carnegie Endowment for International Peace, *Defining a Pacific Community*, 1994.

rate fluctuations, increasing competition in export markets, and a protectionist tendency in major world markets. The rise of the low-cost economies of China and the ASEAN countries is starting to have visible effects.

Of the total urban population in 1950, Pacific Asia accounted for 19.1 per cent, with 15.6 per cent in East Asia and 3.5 per cent in South-East Asia. As of 1975, the urban population in Pacific Asia accounted for 22.6 per cent of the world's urban population. By 2000, it is projected to reach 27.4 per cent. This trend suggests the rapidity of urbanization, although the overall urbanization level is still lower than that in other parts of the world (table 7.2). The low level of urbanization has largely been caused by China and the ASEAN countries, which have remained among the least urbanized countries in the world. China is entering a new phase of development since new economic policies and the opening of coastal cities for foreign investment ventures were introduced in 1978. In these circumstances, controlling migration into urban areas may become much more difficult. It is clear that, with a policy of less controlled migration, the level of urbanization will accelerate and urban problems will become even more severe. The ASEAN-4 countries will tend to outpace the NIEs in terms of economic growth rate and will become major recipients of foreign direct investment from NIEs, eventually contributing

157

Table 7.2 **The urban population in East and South-East Asia**

	1950		1960		1975		2000		2025	
	No. ('000)	As % of world urban population	No. ('000)	As % of world urban population	No. ('000)	As % of world urban population	No. ('000)	As % of world urban population	No. ('000)	As % of world urban population
World total Pacific	724,147	–	1,012,084	–	1,538,346	–	2,926,444	–	5,065,334	–
Asia	138,506	19.1	232,748	23.0	347,849	22.6	803.781	27.5	1,415,723	27.9
East Asia	112,812	15.6	194,734	19.2	276,635[a]	17.9	607,110[a]	20.7	1,020,397[a]	20.2
South-East Asia	25,694	3.5	38,014	3.8	72,214	4.7	196,671	6.7	395,326	7.8

Sources: United Nations, *Patterns of Urban and Rural Population Growth*, 1980; UNCHS, *An Urbanizing World: Global Report on Human Settlements*, 1996.

a. Excluding Taiwan.

158

to the massive relocation of rural population into a few urban areas. The ASEAN-4 countries, as well as China, are also projected to experience robust growth, with China's growth in GDP and its share in regional importance being the most notable of all Asian Pacific countries (Yeung, 1993: 54). In promoting the national economies of Pacific Asia, foreign direct investment, which tends to be attracted to large urban centres, will also accelerate the growth of mega-cities in the recipient countries.

A second characteristic of Pacific Asian urbanization is the concentration of population in a few large cities, especially in mega-cities. With the enormous expansion of urban population, the largest urban centres grew to unprecedented sizes. Because the urban revolution started in Western Europe and North America in the nineteenth century, most of the largest cities were located in those regions. But the current phase of the urban revolution is marked by the urbanization of less urbanized regions, and many of the largest cities are now in Pacific Asia. The nature of this phenomenon can be seen vividly in table 7.3, which lists the 25 largest urban agglomerations from 1960 to 2000. In the year 2000, 9 of the 25 mega-cities in the world will be in Pacific Asia, from 6 in 1960.

Urban corridors, growth triangles, and natural economic regions

Urbanization does not appear everywhere and all at once. Taking advantage of the initial spatial system and natural endowments, urban corridors have many historical antecedents. Urban growth depends largely on the configuration of transportation routes and the geographical sequence of sources, junctions, and markets along a specific route. In the classical and medieval world, the Silk Road cities such as Luoyang, Changan (Xian), Tunhuang, Kashgar, and Tashkent, the Mediterranean and Aegean urban civilizations extending from Asian Minor through Greece to southern Italy, and the Hanseatic League cities during the Crusades would be the counterparts of the modern urban corridor. The concept of the urban corridor has been used interchangeably with "megalopolis" (Gottmann, 1961), "extended metropolitan region" (Ginsburg et al., 1991), and "ecumenopolis" (Papaioannou, 1970). Urban corridors, although they have different morphologies, are commonly characterized as absorbing an increasing proportion of their countries' population and economic growth. The historical juxtaposition of port cities and high-

159

Table 7.3 Ranking of city agglomerations by population, 1960, 1980, and 2000

	1960		1980		2000	
	Agglomeration	Population (million)	Agglomeration	Population (million)	Agglomeration	Population (million)
1	New York/NE New Jersey	14.2	*Tokyo/Yokohama	17.7	Mexico City	25.8
2	London	10.7	New York/NE New Jersey	15.6	São Paulo	24.0
3	*Tokyo/Yokohama	10.7	Mexico City	14.5	*Tokyo/Yokohama	20.2
4	*Shanghai	10.7	São Paulo	12.8	Calcutta	16.5
5	Rhein–Ruhr	8.7	*Shanghai	11.8	Greater Bombay	16.0
6	*Beijing	7.3	London	10.3	New York/NE New Jersey	15.8
7	Paris	7.2	Buenos Aires	10.1	*Seoul	13.8
8	Buenos Aires	6.9	Calcutta	9.5	Tehran	13.6
9	Los Angeles/Long Beach	6.6	Los Angeles/Long Beach	9.5	*Shanghai	13.3
10	Moscow	6.3	Rhein–Ruhr	9.5	Rio de Janeiro	13.3
11	Chicago/NE Indiana	6.0	Rio de Janeiro	9.2	Delhi	13.2
12	*Tianjin	6.0	*Beijing	9.1	*Jakarta	13.2
13	*Osaka/Kobe	5.7	Paris	8.7	Buenos Aires	13.2
14	Calcutta	5.6	*Osaka/Kobe	8.7	Karachi	12.0
15	Mexico City	5.2	Greater Bombay	8.5	Dhaka	11.2
16	Rio de Janeiro	5.1	*Seoul	8.5	Cairo/Giza	11.1
17	São Paulo	4.8	Moscow	8.2	*Manila	11.1
18	Milan	4.5	*Tianjin	7.7	Los Angeles/Long Beach	11.0
19	Cairo/Giza	4.5	Cairo/Giza	6.9	*Bangkok	10.7
20	Greater Bombay	4.2	Chicago/NE Indiana	6.8	*Osaka/Kobe	10.5
21	Philadelphia	3.7	*Jakarta	6.7	*Beijing	10.4
22	Detroit	3.6	Milan	6.7	Moscow	10.4
23	Leningrad	3.5	*Manila	6.0	*Tianjin	9.1
24	Naples	3.2	Delhi	5.9	Paris	8.7
25	*Jakarta	2.8	Baghdad	3.9	Baghdad	7.4

Source: United Nations, *Urban and Rural Population Projections 1950–2025: The 1984 Assessment*, New York, 1986.
Note: Cities in Pacific Asia are denoted by asterisks.

density regions creates the necessary preconditions for global linkage and readily available surplus labour (McGee and Yeung, 1993: 59).

There are already two well-known urban corridors. On the north-eastern Atlantic seaboard, from Massachusetts Bay to the valley of the Potomac, there is an almost continuous chain of impressive cities along the old highway known as U.S.1. Over a distance of about 800 km are five of the largest metropolitan areas in America: Boston, New York, Philadelphia, Baltimore, and Washington. Between them and in the interior immediately west of this axis, there are a dozen other metropolitan areas, each with populations ranging from 200,000 to 800,000 (Gottmann, 1961: 17).

As figure 7.1 shows, the axis containing most of Europe's major cities has a north-west to south-east orientation from the United Kingdom, through Belgium, the Netherlands, north-eastern France, and Germany to northern Italy. Within this vital axis are two major focuses: (a) a north-western focus concentrated upon the historic capitals of the former colonial powers (London, Paris, Randstad in Holland) and (b) a south-eastern focus concentrated upon cities in southern Germany, Switzerland, and northern Italy (Munich, Stuttgart, Milan). The faster relative growth of these cities has pulled the centre of gravity of the axis southwards (Dunford and Perrons, 1994). Jean Gottmann, who coined the term "megalopolis," accurately predicted in his seminal book subsequent developments on the urbanized north-eastern seaboard of the United States. It would certainly have immensely pleased the Founding Fathers of cities in the megalopolis to find that the way of life and the economic organization developed in that part of North America would serve as a model for many other parts of the world undergoing the process of urbanization (Gottmann, 1961: 776). It is exactly what has been happening in Pacific Asia.

The most dramatic is the Beijing–Seoul–Tokyo (BESETO) urban corridor in East Asia, which transcends national boundaries. It encompasses five mega-cities (Beijing, Tianjin, Seoul, Tokyo–Yokohama, Osaka–Kobe), each with a population of 10 million or over. It is larger than the European and North American counterparts in terms of population size. In an inverted S-shape, the corridor from Beijing to Tokyo via Pyongyang and Seoul comprises some 98 million urban inhabitants, and 112 cities each with a population of over 200,000. The cities are almost contiguous along a 1,500 km strip of densely populated land (as shown in table 7.4 and fig. 7.2), becoming a so-called "ecumenopolis," to use the term used by the Greek urban planner,

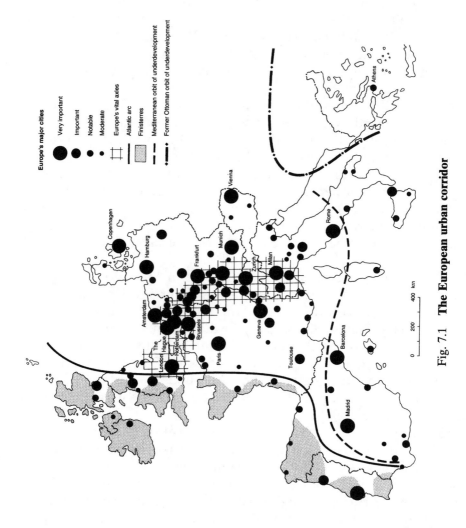

Fig. 7.1 The European urban corridor

Table 7.4 **Urban population and number of cities in the BESETO urban corridor**

	Population ('000)	No. of cities over 200,000
Bohai rim corridor, China	31,556	36
Shinuiju–Kaesong corridor, North Korea	4,997	9
Seoul–Pusan corridor, South Korea	22,642	15
Tokaido corridor, Japan	39,269	52
Total	98,464	112

Source: Choe (1996: 507).

C. A. Doxiadis. An ecumenopolis is defined as a unified settlement system spanning the entire habitable area on a global or continental scale. An urban corridor from the Tokaido megalopolis to Fukuoka in Japan is extending across the Korea Strait, via stepping stones of islands such as Tsushima and Iki, to Korea's south-eastern region centred on Pusan, which covers the most industrialized parts including Pohang, Ulsan, and Masan. This borderless urban corridor further extends from Pusan to Taegu and Seoul in South Korea and to Pyongyang and Shinuiju in North Korea. It then continues to China's Bohai rim cities such as Shenyang, Dalian, Tianjin, and Beijing. This region can be traversed in only one and half hours by air and would be within 10 hours' commuting distance if a high-speed train were introduced and the Korea Strait between the Korean peninsula and the Japanese archipelago were connected by an under-sea tunnel. In fact, the bullet train from Tokyo to Fukuoka is already in operation and a high-speed railway from Pusan to Seoul is scheduled for completion by 2002. The region covers the most developed parts of the respective countries, with bundled lines of railroads and expressways. Also, the region is connected by four distinctive megalopolises in each country, becoming an integrated natural economic region (Choe, 1996).

In other parts of Pacific Asia, smaller urban corridors are also developing in southern China, Malaysia, far north-eastern Asia, Taiwan, and the Indo-China peninsula. Among the most prominent ones are the Pearl River Delta (Guangzhou–Shenzhen–Dongguan–Hong Kong), the Taiwan–Fujian region (Taipei–Taichung–Kaohsiung–Xiamen–Fuzhou), the Singapore–Johor–Riau Triangle, the Yangzi River region, and the Tumen River Delta. The common features of these transnational groupings are the participation of two and more countries and the inclusion of only parts of these countries.

163

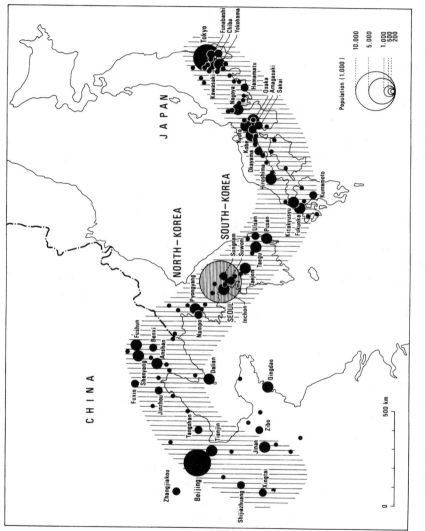

Fig. 7.2 **The Beijing–Seoul–Tokyo urban corridor (Source: Choe, 1996, fig. 14.2)**

164

They are what Robert Scalapino (1992) has termed a "natural economic region." This is an entity that crosses political boundaries, often encompassing only portions of states, but with its *raison d'être* resting upon the combination of natural resources, manpower, technology, and capital that can be pooled to maximum advantage. Again, Scalapino (1992) calls this phenomenon "soft regionalism." It is the growth of economic interaction among and between nations. It has had no solid institutional structure for largely political reasons nor has it necessarily encompassed entire nations.

The Southern China Growth Triangle, which can be subdivided into two distinct entities (the Pearl River Delta and the Taiwan–Fujian region), consists of Hong Kong, Taiwan, and four Special Economic Zones (Shenzhen, Zhuhai, Shantou, and Xiamen). The members operate under different political and economic frameworks, with their cooperation and integration being driven solely by mutual need and private sector initiatives. The massive inflow of investments into the southern China region has been promoted by a number of factors. On the part of the People's Republic of China, these include the open door policy and subsequent liberalization of economic policies and limited linkages with Taiwan after the Statute for Relations across the Taiwan Strait in 1992. In the case of Taiwan, a rapid and major appreciation of the currency was an added reason for offshore investment. Cultural and linguistic affinities and geographical proximity added to the formation of South China as an urban agglomeration.

Among the growth triangles in South-East Asia, the most celebrated is the Singapore–Johor–Riau (SIJORI) region, which includes Singapore, the neighbouring southern Peninsular Malaysian state of Johor, and the Indonesian province of Riau. SIJORI covers a land area of about 23,000 km^2 and has a total population of more than 5 million. The basic rationale is that it makes possible the joint development of the region by capitalizing on factor complementarities in the three participating territories. Geographical proximity keeps down transaction costs and facilitates the flow of resources, labour, and products. SIJORI is largely an outgrowth of Singapore and is expected to become an eventual cross-border urban agglomeration of Singapore. The formation of the SIJORI Growth Triangle has been in part a response to the phenomenon of the globalization of production by multinational corporations. The subregional economic grouping and urban agglomeration should be seen as an attempt to attract these investment funds and direct them to labour and land surplus areas in Riau as well as in Johor.

Recently, one of the most active natural economic regions has been the Tumen River Delta region. The Tumen River, which marks the border of three countries (North Korea, China, and Russia), flows into the East Sea (the Sea of Japan). The three countries have agreed, in principle, to lease their land around the estuary of the Tumen River for 70 years to an international corporation. Within the larger Tumen River Delta region there are the three cities of Vladivostok in Russia, Chongjin in North Korea, and Yanji in China, as well as many smaller cities such as Rajin and Sonbong in North Korea, Pos'yet and Zarubino in Russia, and Hunchun and Fangchuan in China. They will become an extended metropolitan region if the Tumen River development programme is carried out as planned.

In this era of globalization, many schemes in the name of growth triangles or natural economic regions have been devised in academic and political circles and are waiting to be developed into physical entities. The concept of the Yellow Sea Rim Economic Region, which includes China's Bohai rim cities and provinces (Tianjin, Beijing, Shandong, and Liaoning provinces), South Korea's southern and western coastal cities and provinces (Inchon, Kunsan, Mokpo, Yosu, and Pusan), and the south-western area of Japan centred on Fukuoka and Kitakyushu, has been widely discussed but is still in an embryonic stage, except for the inter-city coalition for fraternal exchange between Kitakyushu, Pusan, and Dalian.

Another natural economic region is the East Sea Rim (the Sea of Japan Rim) region, which covers the Japan Sea littoral prefecture and cities, the eastern coastal provinces of Korea, China's Jilin Province, and Far East Russia, although it has not progressed beyond wishful thinking. The most active cities in the cause of transnational cooperation are Niigata in Japan, Pohang in South Korea, Chongjin in North Korea, and Vladivostok in Russia. Inter-city networks such as the opening of direct air links and shipping lines are rapidly developing.

At present, many other subregional economic regions are developing in Pacific Asia. One of them is the Northern Growth Triangle, encompassing the contiguous subregions of northern Peninsular Malaysia centred on Penang, southern Thailand, and northern Sumatra. Another proposed natural economic territory links Davao on Mindanao in the southern Philippines, Manado in northern Indonesia, and Sandakan in Sabah, Malaysia, although this is far

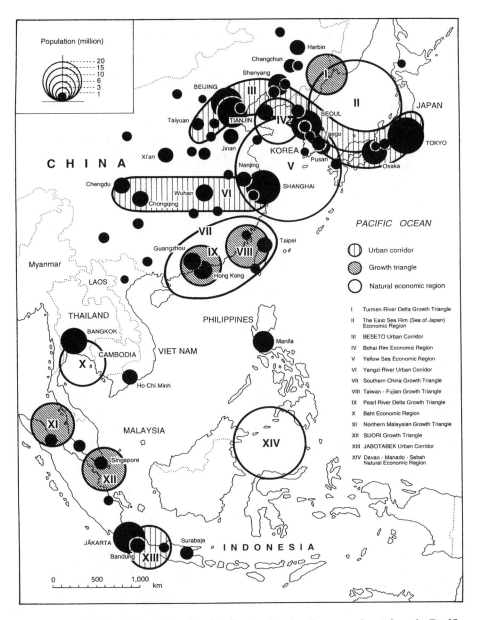

Fig. 7.3 **Urban corridors, growth triangles, and natural economic regions in Pacific Asia**

from being an urban agglomeration (Sobrepena, 1995). The urban corridors, growth triangles, and natural economic regions mentioned above are depicted in figure 7.3 in a schematic manner.

167

Similar trains of thoughts have been suggested by other scholars. Peter Rimmer (1990) has identified four emerging corridors within the Western Pacific Rim: (1) Japan's Pacific Belt, stretching from Tokyo to Kyushu, (2) the Eastern Australia corridor, reaching from Cairns to Adelaide, (3) the South-East Asian corridor, running between Chiang Mai and Bali, and (4) the East Asian corridor, spanning Seoul via eastern China to Hong Kong, with a possible extension to Hanoi (as shown in fig. 7.4). Naidu (1994) also drew attention to the evolving subregional economic zones in Pacific Asia

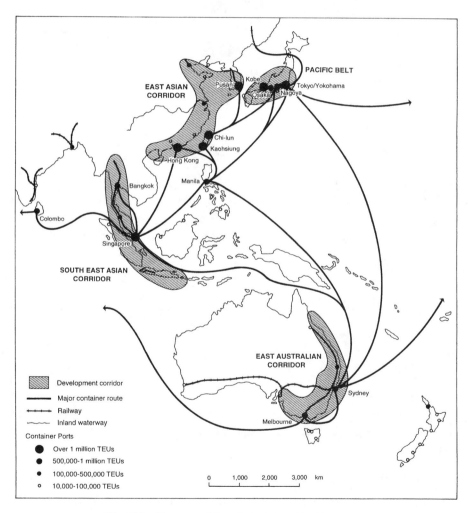

Fig. 7.4 **Four corridors in western Pacific Asia**

(as shown in fig. 7.5). After all, explosive population growth and a flood of migration from rural areas are creating unprecedented pressure on the great cities of the region. In Pacific Asia, a new order in the organization of inhabited space is to be created.

Globalization and a changing urban system

Cities now increasingly perform in ways that are transnational. They compete for mobile capital, employment, institutions, and events, as evidenced by foreign direct investment and the competitive hosting of international sporting events in recent years. Seoul and Nagoya bid for the 1988 Summer Olympic Games, and Seoul won. Seoul and Tokyo seriously competed to host the 2002 World Cup, but eventually they agreed to co-host the event. In the future, although intra-regional trade and investment in Pacific Asia will continue to expand and lead to less reliance on extraregional exports for sustainable growth, the source of growth will remain global. Economic dynamism has transformed the Asia Pacific region into a major player in world trade and technology. Most cities in Pacific Asia are still national cities, except for Hong Kong and Singapore. There is also no hierarchical order in terms of functional roles; each city is in competition with others in their respective areas. Competition among cities is likely to increase rather than diminish. Competition now is between cities across national borders and not between countries, as it used to be. Cities represent countries in the global economic system; they depend on global capital transfers and the new economic order. In turn, governments can assist urban institutions to prosper and compete globally. Urban productivity is becoming a catchword. It is based on the premise that the macro performance of the economy is critically determined by the productivity of individual households and firms in urban areas. Growth strategies have been introduced to remove constraints that inhibit the efficient functioning of the urban system and, hence, productivity growth in urban areas.

To this end, urban coalitions across national borders are commonly accepted without much hesitation. Super-infrastructure investment in airports, seaports, teleports, and convention and trade centres is being made to gain a competitive edge in the global economy. State-of-art airports have been built or are under construction, such as the Kansai International Airport in Osaka, the new Seoul International Airport in Youngjongdo, and the Chek Lap Kok Airport in Hong Kong. They are all located offshore and aim to become international

169

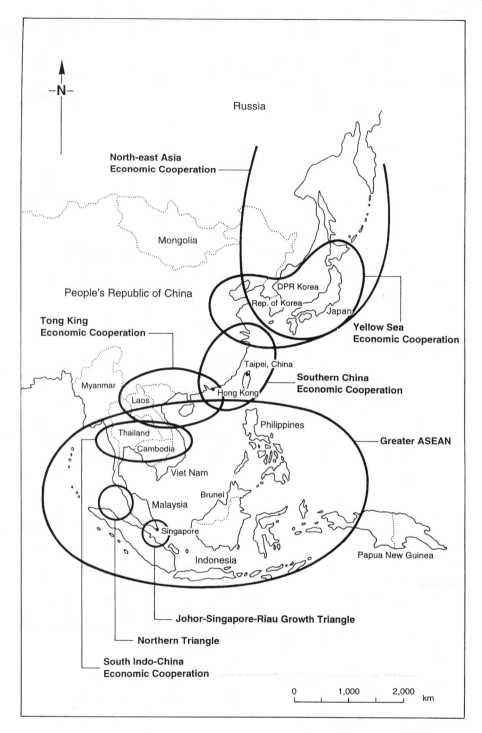

Fig. 7.5 **Regional economic zones in Asia and the Pacific**

hubs accommodating supersonic, intercontinental air services. The Pacific Asian Rim lies over a great land mass and is separated by the seas and it is, therefore, difficult for passenger traffic to rely on means of transport other than air transport. It is quite natural that air transport will become increasingly important. As Rimmer points out, the Western Pacific Rim provides an ideal laboratory for exploring the changing interrelationships between ports, inland transport, and regional development. Collectively, ports and inland transport reflect the Rim's emergence as a major focus of world trade and economic activity rivalling Europe and North America as a centre for capital accumulation (Rimmer, 1990: 3).

The surge of foreign direct investment (FDI), the globalization of financial and real estate markets, the international migration of labour, and the opening of overseas construction industries are all contributing to the changing pattern of the urban system in Pacific Asia. They have been key agents in integrating national urban centres into the global networks of the urban system with the transnationalization of business organization, production, and investment. Foreign direct investment is basically urban oriented, and South Korea's foreign direct investment is no exception. Since the mid-1980s, intraregional trade and investment growth within Pacific Asia have accelerated. Current trends in the foreign direct investment pattern can be summarized as follows: (1) the introduction of new home countries, diminishing differences in volumes between the established home countries of FDI, and the declining relative importance of Japanese total outward intraregional FDI; (2) the gradual appearance of a more balanced pattern of FDI flows in several bilateral relations as a result of growing Taiwanese, South Korean, and Singaporean investment in Japan, and Malaysian investment in Taiwan and Singapore; (3) a gradual shift of investment from labour-intensive sectors to market-oriented FDI in technologically advanced industries; (4) a rapid growth of labour-intensive investment in Chinese inland provinces; and (5) a continuous increase of investment in the service sectors (Alvstom, 1995: 126).

Conclusion: Promises and challenges

There is no alternative to cities. Cities have no choice but to live with and catch up with others that are already more developed. However, the phenomenal growth of the urban population in Pacific Asia brings its own blessings and poses grave challenges. The process of urbanization must be understood as a basic condition in economic, social, and technological development. But urbanization that outstrips the absorptive capacity of cities, the mega-city phenomenon, and its off-spring of urban corridors have offered promises as well as challenges. Yue-man Yeung (1990) has articulated some important urban challenges.

The first is the international impact of urbanization in Asian countries. As economic growth becomes more interdependent among nations, cities with specific functional complementarities begin to become linked across national boundaries.

Secondly, excessive concentration of population and economic activities has brought serious environmental problems, leading to questions about the sustainability of urbanizing the Asian continent. Environmental problems are also becoming transnational. Acid rain caused by the heavy use of fossil fuel in the Chinese provinces of Hebei, Shandong, and Liaoning and the cities of Beijing and Tianjin, which are densely populated and the most industrialized parts of China, has been of great concern to people in the Korean peninsula and the Japanese archipelago. The semi-enclosed Yellow Sea, surrounded by the densely populated littoral regions of China and Korea, is threatened with death. Environmentally hazardous industries have been relocated to escape stringent environmental regulations in their home countries under the disguise of foreign investment.

The third issue is that the emergence of urban corridors has accentuated ongoing disparities at international, national, and inter-urban levels. On a macro-geographical scale, there is a core of advanced areas and major mega-cities that extends from the BESETO corridor through the Chinese coastal cities of Shanghai, Xiamen, and Guangzhou, and Hanoi and Ho Chi Minh City to a great arc of Indo-China and Malaysian peninsulas. At increasing distances from this developed zone lie orbital areas of relative under-development. Depressed areas in each country are mostly located away from these developing urban corridors. In Japan, regional disparities do not disappear between the Tokaido megalopolis and other parts of the country. Korea's depressed regions lie in south-western and north-eastern areas, which are a long way from the Seoul–Pusan megalopolitan influence. China is no exception. In the process of national development after 1949, priority was given to inland areas over coastal cities, where the colonial and imperialistic imprint persisted. However, the opening of China's coastal cities since the 1980s has reinforced the development of the coastal regions at the expense of inland regions, which have experienced sizeable outflows of population to the coastal cities. Similarly, South-East Asian countries, including Viet Nam, Thailand, Malaysia, and Indonesia, will experience the peripheralization of regions outside urban corridors and growth triangles.

References

Alvstom, Claes (1995), "Integration through Trade and Direct Investment: Asian Pacific Patterns." In: R. Le Heron and Sam Ock Park (eds.), *The Asian Pacific Rim and Globalization*. Aldershot: Avebury.

Choe, Sang-Chuel (1996), "The Evolving Urban System in North-East Asia." In: Fu-chen Lo and Yue-man Yeung (eds.), *Emerging World Cities in Pacific Asia*. Tokyo: United Nations University Press, pp. 498–519.

Dunford, Michael and Diane Perrons (1994), "Regional Inequality, Regimes of Accumulation and Economic Development in Contemporary Europe." *Transactions of the Institute of British Geographers* 19: 165.

Ginsburg, Norton, Bruce Koppel, and T. G. McGee (eds.) (1991), *The Extended Metropolis: Settlement Transition in Asia*. Honolulu: University of Hawaii Press.

Gottmann, Jean (1961), *Megalopolis: The Urbanized Northeastern Seaboard of the U.S.* Cambridge, Mass.: M.I.T. Press.

McGee, T. G. and Yue-man Yeung (1993), "Urban Futures for Pacific Asia." In: Yue-man Yeung (ed.), *Pacific Asia in the 21st Century*. Hong Kong: Chinese University Press, pp. 47–67.

Naidu, G. (1994), "Johor–Singapore–Riau Growth Triangle: Progress and Prospects." In: Myo Thant, Min Tang, and Hiroshi Kakazu (eds.), *Growth Triangles in Asia*. Hong Kong: Oxford University Press, pp. 219–220.

Papaioannou, John G. (1970), "Future Urbanization Pattern: A Long-range Worldwide View." *EKISTICS* 175, p. 372.

Rimmer, Peter J. (1990), "Ports, Inland Transport Linkages and Regional Development: A Western Pacific Rim Conspectus." Paper presented at the 2nd Korea Maritime Institute Symposium on the Public Sector's Role in Logistics for the 21st Century, 2–7 July, Seoul, Korea.

Scalapino, Robert A. (1992), "The Politics of Development and Regional Cooperation in Northeast Asia." In: Won Bae Kim (ed.), *Regional Economic Cooperation in Northeast Asia*. Honolulu: East–West Center, pp. 22–28.

Sobrepena, Aniceto M. (1995), "Regional Cross-Border Cooperation: Towards Higher Forms of Economic Integration." In: Gun Young Lee and Yong Woong Kim (eds.), *Globalization and Regional Development in Southeast Asia and Pacific Rim*. Seoul: Korea Research Institute for Human Settlements, pp. 179–201.

Yeung, Yue-man (1990), *Changing Cities of Pacific Asia: A Scholarly Interpretation*. Hong Kong: Chinese University Press.

——— (ed.) (1993), *Pacific Asia in the 21st Century: Geographical and Developmental Perspectives*. Hong Kong: Chinese University Press.

8

World cities and the urban future: The view from Latin America

Alan Gilbert

Let me begin by admitting that I am very uncertain about the usefulness of the concepts "world cities" and "mega-cities" in analysing what is occurring in Latin America. After a brief introduction to the process of urbanization as it has occurred in Latin America, this chapter will examine the meaning of these terms. It will then proceed to consider the far-reaching but highly uneven process of globalization. What is globalization and what implications does it have for life in the major cities of Latin America? The chapter ends by sketching the major parameters that are likely to determine the future of Latin America's major cities.

My conclusion is that there is no single Latin American urban future but many futures. Local outcomes will be determined by the interaction of international and local forces. There can be no simple prognosis: what will happen in Mexico City will not happen in Bogotá or São Paulo. The only generalization that can be made is that globalization will lead to greater inequality and greater instability. Latin American cities are becoming more unequal and more unstable. Both processes are occurring because those cities are now firmly linked into an increasingly inequitable and volatile world economy.

Table 8.1 **Urban population in Latin America (settlements with more than 20,000 inhabitants), 1940–1990 (%)**

Country	1940	1960	1980	1990
Argentina	n.a.	74	83	86
Bolivia	n.a.	24	33	51
Brazil	31	46	64	75
Chile	52	68	81	86
Colombia	29	53	68	70
Cuba	46	55	65	75
Ecuador	n.a.	36	44	56
Mexico	35	51	66	73
Peru	35	47	65	70
Venezuela	31	63	79	91
Latin America	33	44	64	72

Sources: Wilkie et al. (1991); UNDP (1992).

Latin America's cities

Although Latin America has had urban civilizations for centuries, relatively few people lived in the cities until comparatively recently. In 1950, only Argentina, Chile, Cuba, and Uruguay contained an urban majority and, as table 8.1 shows, less than one-half of Latin Americans lived in urban areas as recently as 1960. Nevertheless, the process of urbanization was well under way by that time and, between 1940 and 1990, Latin America changed from a rural to an urban society. The transformation was wrought by a combination of falling mortality rates, rapid internal migration, economic development, and changing technology.

Population growth was critical. In 1930, Latin America had just over 100 million inhabitants; 60 years later, its population had passed the 425 million mark. Average life expectancy almost doubled from an average of 34 years in 1930 to 65 years by the early 1980s. With death rates plummeting, fertility continued at a very high level. Excluding Argentina and Uruguay, where average birth rates per thousand population were in the low 20s, fertility rates in the 1960s averaged around 45. It was not until the 1970s and 1980s that fertility rates began to fall substantially.[1] In the interim, Latin America's population exploded.

Because most people lived in the countryside, it was the rural areas that bore the brunt of the population explosion. Rapid growth created

175

a problem in so far as Latin America's land tenure system was very unequal and few families ever had sufficient land to nourish their children. A common response was for individuals, and sometimes whole families, to move to the cities. They moved because economic growth was generating jobs in the cities. The work might not be well paid but it was much better than remaining in the countryside. Young people, and especially young women, moved in huge numbers to the urban areas (Gilbert, 1994).

The newcomers were accommodated in large part by their own efforts, a majority eventually constructing self-help housing. But this kind of shelter solution was possible only because of new technology. The arrival of the bus allowed people to settle in areas distant from the central city; the improvement of electricity and water systems gave the authorities the power to service the sprawling shanty areas. Without the new technology, urban development would have been much less successful.

As a result of these processes, most Latin American cities grew very quickly after 1940 and some grew at quite spectacular rates. During the 1940s, for example, Caracas grew by 7.6 per cent annually, Cali by 8 per cent, and São Paulo by 7.4 per cent; during the 1950s, Guadalajara was growing by 6.7 per cent per annum. Although the populations of Latin America's cities all grew very rapidly at one stage in their development, that is no longer the case in the majority of cities. Table 8.2 shows that the region's major cities were growing much more slowly during the 1970s than they had been during the 1960s, and by the 1980s the pace of growth was sometimes lower than

Table 8.2 **Major Latin American cities: Annual population growth rates, 1950–1990 (%)**

City	1950–60	1960–70	1970–80	1980–90
Bogotá	7.2	5.9	3.0	n.a.
Buenos Aires	2.9	2.0	1.6	1.1
Caracas	6.6	4.5	2.0	1.4
Lima	5.0	5.3	3.7	2.8
Mexico City	5.0	5.6	4.2	0.9
Rio de Janeiro	4.0	4.3	2.5	1.0
Santiago	4.0	3.2	2.6	1.7
São Paulo	5.3	6.7	4.4	2.0

Source: Villa and Rodríguez (1996).

national rates of population increase. During the 1980s, only Lima grew by more than 2 per cent per annum and Buenos Aires, Rio de Janeiro, and Mexico City were growing annually by only 1 per cent.

The slower pace of expansion has been brought about by a combination of factors. First, rapid declines in fertility rates have been very important. In Brazil, the gross fertility rate fell from 6.2 in 1962 to 2.7 in 1980; in Colombia, from 6.8 in 1962 to 2.9 in 1990; and in Mexico from 6.8 in 1962 to 2.6 in 1986. With fewer children being born in the countryside, there were fewer potential migrants. Recently the number of people living in the countryside has begun to fall absolutely; in many countries there is no longer a huge surplus of rural people (Villa and Rodríguez, 1996). Fertility rates in the cities fell even faster, lowering the rate of natural increase in the metropolitan areas. Secondly, the pace of migration slowed during the 1980s because the economic recession hit most of Latin America's cities very hard. Urban employment was badly affected by the combination of recession and structural adjustment policies. By contrast, structural adjustment policies sometimes stimulated agricultural production. Slower urban growth was a clear outcome of the declining differential between urban and rural living standards. During the 1980s, more people moved out of some metropolitan centres than moved in (Villa and Rodríguez, 1996). Finally, slower metropolitan growth was encouraged by the process of spatial deconcentration. Faced by urban diseconomies, many companies decided to expand production beyond the boundaries of the metropolitan areas, albeit within the wider metropolitan region. This process was very marked in the vicinity of São Paulo, where "many branch and assembly plants are locating in industrial towns within a 200-km radius of the city of São Paulo such as São José dos Campos, Piracicaba, Americana, Limeira, Rio Claro, and Campinas.... In other words, we are witnessing the extension of the localization economies of existing industrial complexes from a strictly 'urban' to a somewhat broader 'regional' scale" (Storper, 1991: 61–62). There are now clear signs of an emergent polycentric urban form in many metropolitan regions in Latin America (Richardson, 1989; Gilbert and Gugler, 1992; Gilbert, 1994).

The interesting question is whether the slowing pace of urban growth is an outcome of globalization or whether it is more the outcome of shifts in the structure of Latin American society, for example owing to declining rates of fertility. This is one of the principal issues discussed in the rest of the chapter.

177

What are world cities and mega-cities?

According to UNDIESA (1986: iii), mega-cities are "cities that are expected to have populations of at least 8 million inhabitants by the year 2000." Like so many thresholds used in the social sciences, this figure seems to have been plucked from the air. There is no theoretical basis for asserting that a city with 8 million people is qualitatively different from one with rather fewer inhabitants (Gilbert, 1996: chap. 1). Perhaps for this reason different writers use widely differing definitions of a mega-city. Whereas Richardson (1993) and UNDIESA/ UNU (1991) use the 8 million benchmark, UNCHS (1987: 29), Ward (1990: xvii), and the World Bank (1991: 16) use 10 million, while Dogan and Kasarda (1988: 18) implicitly use 4 million.

Nor is it clear how the term "mega-city" differs from several similar terms. The word is frequently used as a synonym of "super-city," "giant city," "conurbation," "megalopolis," and "world city." Unfortunately, there is little agreement about what any of those terms mean either. Entry to the world of giant cities or metropolises is granted by Dogan and Kasarda (1988: 18) at 4 million, and the rank of super-city by Lowder at 5 million (1987: 5); the term "megalopolis" is attributed by Mayhew and Penny (1992) to "any continuous built up area of more than ten million inhabitants." That there is no adequate definition of a mega-city was recognized by a United Nations' seminar, which concluded that "there is a need to work out some sort of definition" (UNDIESA/UNU, 1991: iii).

Equally vague is the concept of the "world city." At one level I have no problem with Hall's (1977: 1) statement that: "There are certain great cities, in which a quite disproportionate part of the world's most important business is conducted." Similarly, Gilb's (1989: 96) description is not unhelpful: "Global cities are multifaceted centers of world trade, finance, and industry. They need not be the cities from which the power comes, but at least they are the cities through which the power flows." The problem comes when we try to move from this broad recognition that some major cities have real international significance to the point of distinguishing why they are different from other lesser cities. We can all agree that size is not terribly important; whereas several giant cities, Shanghai and Calcutta, are clearly not world cities, certain relatively small cities, such as Washington and Geneva, probably are (Hall, 1977: 3; Friedmann, 1986; Gilb, 1989; Simon, 1992: 185; Fuchs et al., 1994: 3).

So what transforms an ordinary city into a "world city"? According to Gilb (1989: 97): "A city cannot achieve global status on the basis of industry or size ... it must also provide essential services to foreign markets.... [T]o achieve global status it also has to be able to export its know-how, which requires building communication networks." Unfortunately, such a reasonable statement probably means that Hollywood and the Vatican automatically win world city status whereas Frankfurt and Milan do not. According to Dieleman and Hamnett (1994: 358), "in addition to the management of a New International Division of Labour in manufacturing, world cities are the key hubs for the control and coordination of global finance and producer and business services." Fine, but how key is key? Does this include Frankfurt and Paris or not?

According to these definitions Latin America probably contains several mega-cities. In 1990, Latin America contained four cities with more than 8 million people and another six with more than 3 million (table 8.3; fig. 8.1). But do any of these cities warrant inclusion as world cities? According to Gilb's definition, the only cities that might

Table 8.3 **Latin America's giant cities, 1990**

City	Population (million)
São Paulo[a]	15.18
Mexico City[a]	15.05
Buenos Aires[a]	10.89
Rio de Janeiro[a]	9.60
Lima[a]	6.42
Bogotá	4.85
Santiago (Chile)[a]	4.68
Belo Horizonte[a]	3.42
Pôrto Alegre[a]	3.02
Guadalajara[a]	3.01
Caracas[a]	2.97
Monterrey[a]	2.59
Recife	2.49
Salvador	2.40
Brasília	2.36
Santo Domingo	2.20
Havana	2.10
Fortaleza	2.09
Curitiba	2.03

Sources: UNDIESA/UNU (1991: 187–194); Villa and Rodríguez (1996).

a. In the light of recent census figures, these figures are clearly overestimates and have been modified.

179

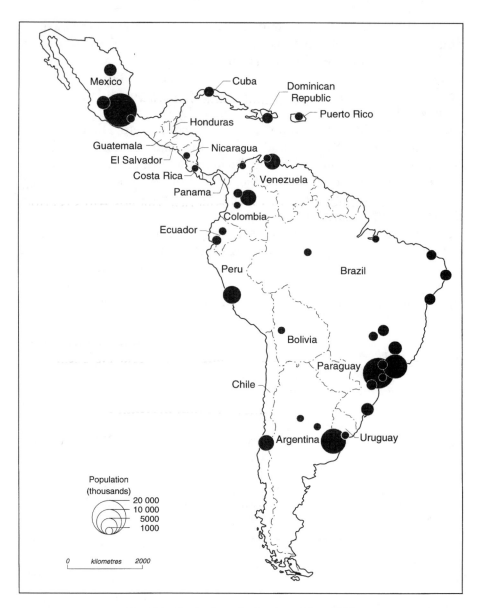

Fig. 8.1 **Latin America's giant cities, 1990**

justify inclusion are Cali and Medellín, the centres of Latin America's only major transnational corporations, the drug cartels. These are the only cities that have transferred their know-how to the developed world and established sophisticated communication systems both within Latin America and in Europe and the United States. The more obvious candidates for world city status in Latin America – Buenos Aires, Rio de Janeiro, Mexico City, and São Paulo – really do not perform that many international roles. If they do achieve world city status, then it is because within Latin America they act as "hubs for the control and coordination of global finance and producer and business services." Without them, transnational capital could not operate within the region. However, these cities are most certainly not performing world functions. São Paulo is producing cars and television soaps for an international market, but most of its "manufactures" go to other parts of Latin America. Buenos Aires is critical in integrating Argentina, Paraguay, and Uruguay into the global economy, but it performs few international functions beyond this limited region. Rio de Janeiro attracts millions of tourists but so do the Iguaçu Falls.

London, Paris, and New York differ in so far as economic decisions made there have a profound influence on what happens in the financial markets of Latin America. By contrast, decisions made in Buenos Aires, São Paulo, and Mexico City have very limited effects on the stock exchanges of London, Paris, and New York. As such, Latin America's mega-cities hardly rate as world cities.

Globalization and the new international division of labour

For reasons of convenience, I am going to label the changes that have taken place in the world economy as "globalization." It would be sensible to begin with a definition of the process that I am examining, although this is easier said than done. For, although recent writing in the social sciences has been fascinated with what is claimed to be a radical change in the way the world operates, it is less than clear on what precisely has changed. Most writers are specific only about those elements of the process that they are interested in. As such, the globalization of one writer is different from that of another. Similarly, the period over which globalization has been operating is anything but clear. Of course, I am not alone in questioning the meaning of globalization; Thrift (1994) has declared that the term has been "devalued" and Simon (1994: 3) that "it has little meaning."

In so far as there has been a fundamental process of global change, I think Mittelman (1994: 427) defines its form as well as anyone:

The manifestations of globalization include the spatial reorganization of production, the interpenetration of industries across borders, the spread of financial markets, the diffusion of identical consumer goods to distant countries, massive transfers of population within the South as well as from the South and the East to the West, resultant conflicts between immigrant and established communities in formerly tight-knit neighbourhoods, and an emerging worldwide preference for democracy.

Hamnett (1994: 402) links this change into the world city literature when he points out that:

the last 40 years have seen the emergence of a new international division of labour in which multi and transnational corporations have freed themselves from national constraints and established a global network of production and distribution. This has required greater control and coordination and reliance on financial and associated producer services which are concentrated in a number of large global cities.

What effect does this process have on the lives of ordinary people living beyond those global cities? What is certainly true is that the fate of Latin American populations is greatly affected by decisions made in the world cities. If globalization means anything, it is that life in one part of the world is heavily influenced by events elsewhere. The reduction in state autonomy (see below) is an important manifestation of this globalization. Free trade and global competition mean that the state is less able to protect its citizens from outside pressures.

Of course, if the level of integration and competition has increased in recent years, the process is hardly new. In so far as there are stronger global links, they have been superimposed on an already internationalized economy (Walton, 1985; Gilbert, 1990; Mittelman, 1994). In some respects, Africa, Asia, and Latin America are not much more global today than they were in the nineteenth century. Africa and most parts of Asia surely had little local autonomy when they were economic and political colonies of Europe. Decisions were made in London and Paris in the nineteenth century that had a direct impact on life in the periphery. Maybe the decisions took longer to implement, modern communications and technology have guaranteed that, but to what extent does the impact of decision-making on the periphery today differ from that of yesterday? We need to explore more fully how the supposed "global economy" differs from older international divisions of labour. Chase-Dunn (1985: 273) is surely correct in pointing out that:

certain trends that have been increasing for 500 years have continued to increase (the internationalization of capital, the increase in labor productivity), while several cycles that have long been operating (the rise and fall of hegemonic core powers, long waves of economic growth and stagnation) have continued to operate, and certain stable structural features (the inter-state system, the core–periphery hierarchy) have been reproduced.

In consequence: "The system of world cities ... did not appear in the 1950s, with cities having been 'national' before that time. Rather cities have long been both national and international."

Globalization and the Latin American city

If I have difficulty in defining clearly what I mean by "globalization," then I am going to have severe problems in distinguishing the effects of that process on Latin American cities. For this reason, I am going to look at individual elements of the so-called globalization process and explore their impact on Latin America. In so far as it is possible to generalize, my argument is that global forces are operating but their local manifestations are highly diverse. Globalization has not created world cities in Latin America although it has profoundly affected both the quality and the predictability of urban life in that region.

Technology and new production systems

Kaplinsky (1994: 337) asserts that the literature demonstrates "an increasingly widespread belief that the ground-rules of industrial competitiveness have altered since the 'golden age' of the postwar boom." Industrial competitiveness has been increased by the lowering of trade barriers, by improved transport and communications, and by a new ethos of competition encouraged by neo-liberalism. In practice, this new competitiveness has forced transnational corporations to modify their behaviour. According to Dicken (1994: 106), that involves:

(1) reorganizing the coordination of production chain functions in a complex realignment of internalized and externalized network relationships; (2) reorganizing the geography of their production chains internationally and, in some cases, globally; (3) redefining their core activities and repositioning themselves along the production chain, with a particular emphasis on downstream, service functions.

The most obvious form of industrial globalization in Latin America has occurred along the US–Mexican border. The setting up of export-

oriented *maquila* plants in Mexico has been a classic case of relocation of activity from the Rust Belt to the Sun Belt. Labour-intensive
activities have been moved from areas of expensive and inflexible
manufacture in the United States to the low-wage, non-unionized
environment of borderland Mexico. The number of workers in the
maquiladoras increased from 75,000 in 1976 to 550,000 in 1994
(INEGI, 1995). Elsewhere in Latin America industrial globalization
has been occurring for centuries. It started with the exploitation of
silver under the Spanish and accelerated with the massive expansion
of multinational investment during the import-substitution phase of
industrialization.

What has happened recently is that transnational enterprise has
modified its behaviour under the newly competitive conditions of the
world economy. Certainly, the structure of the corporation has seen
many changes both in developed economies and in Latin America.
Considerable numbers of corporate workers have been laid off. As
Roberts (1994: 13) puts it: "The large firm has ... become leaner,
concentrating on essential and profitable functions through a core of
stable workers, while less profitable or more volatile functions are
subcontracted or performed by temporary workers. These trends
have created spatial contexts, particularly in the large cities, that
encourage the informal economy and family strategies." From the
1970s on, Latin American cities have seen an expansion in the size of
the informal sector fuelled in part by this kind of process. More
workers have been engaged in part-time or casual work; more firms
have been subcontracting to small producers in the shanty towns.

Globalization, as manifest in the form of structural adjustment,
has led to considerable labour shedding. Falling aggregate demand
and the opening up of previously protected domestic markets have
created major problems for many companies producing for Latin
American markets. The 1980s saw huge numbers of industrial workers being laid off in the region's major cities (Hirata and Humphrey,
1991; Gilbert, 1993, 1994). Unemployment levels in Argentina's
second major manufacturing centre reached 26 per cent in 1994.
Between 1985 and 1988, Mexico City lost around one-quarter of its
manufacturing jobs; the latest crisis will lead to many more jobs being
lost. Mexicans can no longer afford to buy local products, so many of
the producers of those goods will go out of business.

Even for those who have kept their jobs, the outcome of globalization has been less than favourable. As Browne (1994: 4) puts it:
"In most cases the shift to new, globally-oriented plants enabled

184

corporations to weaken labor unions, cut wage costs, and increase managerial control over the organization of work. As globalization progressed both workers and governments found themselves in more direct international competition for a limited pool of capital and technology." In Mexico, the heavily unionized plants of central Mexico have lost out to the new, generally non-unionized, plants of the north. Most corporations have managed to reduce the rights of their existing workers. Simultaneously, governments have been modifying their labour and social security legislation, increasing the power of the companies over that of their unions (Arriagada, 1994). Although there have been strikes and protests about this shift, the union movement has been strangely muted in its reaction (Roxborough, 1989).

In addition to this deliberate strategy of reducing the power of organized labour, many industrial workers have experienced savage cuts in the value of their wages. In those countries that suffered from hyperinflation in the 1980s, real wages often plummeted. In Lima, the average real wage of manual workers fell by 61 per cent between 1980 and 1991 (UNECLAC, 1992). Whether this is a direct result of industrial globalization is open to question. None the less, it is part of the reality of labour conditions in Latin American cities after structural adjustment and the debt crisis.

Investment flows

Globalization has been associated with a major increase in foreign direct investment (FDI). Indeed, Dicken (1994: 109) asserts that FDI "has become a more significant integrating force in the global economy than the traditional indicator of such integration, trade." Growing foreign investment has generated new manufacturing facilities in formerly far-flung parts of the globe. In Latin America, the expansion of *maquila* plants on the Mexican–US border is the classic example. But, increasingly, such investment has focused less on manufacturing and more on services: "During the 1950s, FDI was concentrated in primary and resource-based manufacturing but by 1990 services accounted for close to 50% of all FDI and absorbed almost two-thirds of annual flows" (Watts, 1994: 372). The most significant branch of investment has been in producer services and, in Latin America, the expansion of major international hotel, communications, transport, accounting, and banking systems is very obvious. No major city in Latin America lacks a Hilton or a Hyatt Hotel, none is without the

185

subsidiaries of the major international banks, all contain offices of the major accounting and consulting companies. Perhaps most significant of all has been the expansion of financial services with the development of electronic transfers and 24-hour trading.

The integration of Latin America into the world financial community has been in evidence for many years. During the 1970s, the recycling of eurodollars led to vast sums of money pouring into the region. The problem is that this huge inflow of funds was invested poorly, sometimes even corruptly, and led directly to the debt crisis of the 1980s. What poured in during the 1970s flooded out in the 1980s; between 1982 and 1989 Latin America lost the equivalent of 4 per cent of its gross regional product (Altimir, 1994: 8). Without financial globalization, the debt crisis could not have occurred. Although Latin American decision makers bear their own share of the responsibility for that nightmare, it could not have occurred without the OPEC oil price rises, the development of the eurodollar currency market, and the manifest incompetence of the international banking community (George, 1988).

Latin America is supposed to have changed as a result of the debt crisis. Structural adjustment during the 1980s transformed its economy. Market forces were re-established and the amount of government meddling reduced. The aim of the International Monetary Fund (IMF) was to make the region a safer place in which to invest. Certainly, the 1990s saw an important expansion in foreign investment, both in productive enterprise and in portfolio investment. A series of stock exchange booms in Argentina, Brazil, Chile, and Mexico were evidence of the money pouring into the region as the spectre of a debt-laden Latin America was replaced by a much more business-friendly and open economy.

The downside of this process was demonstrated by events in Mexico in December 1994. From a paragon of neo-liberal economic virtue, Mexico changed into a basket case. A combination of guerrilla activity in Chiapas, an increasing balance of payments deficit, a new president with a less-than-deft political touch, and a bungled devaluation led to portfolio funds suddenly flooding out of Mexico. Almost overnight Mexico lost some US$4 billion trying to maintain the value of the peso. The Mexico City stock market dropped in dollar terms by 50 per cent; investors may have lost US$20 billion (*Sunday Times*, 5 January 1995). Mexico's banks are now in a precarious state. Having gone through a long, painful stabilization programme after the debt crisis of 1982, the Mexican economy is going through another

186

sustained period of belt-tightening. As before, it is the poor and the middle class who will bear the brunt of the adjustment. It was estimated that, during the first three months of 1995, car sales plummeted by 74 per cent and residential construction by 80 per cent (*Mexico Update*, II, 25). The Finance Ministry estimates that 436,000 jobs were lost during the same period (*Mexico Update*, II, 30).

The damaging impact of this loss of confidence has not been confined to Mexico. The so-called "tequila effect" hit stock markets and foreign exchange markets throughout the region. In the three weeks after the Mexico peso crisis of 20 December 1994, the São Paulo stock market fell by 34 per cent and that of Buenos Aires by 29 per cent (*The Economist*, 7 January 1995). No doubt Latin America's integration into the global financial system is excellent when foreign traders have confidence in the local economies. But what the recent Mexican crisis shows is that economic and social volatility is part of the new form of globalization. When Mexico got into trouble, Wall Street, London, and Tokyo immediately removed huge sums of portfolio investment from that country. That, at least, was understandable. But, the same investors immediately began to question the safety of their investments in the rest of Latin America. The "tequila effect" caused major problems in Argentina, Brazil, and even Chile.

The worry is that the new global financial community, with its reliance on the latest communications technology, reacts instantly to any local change in political or economic expectations. The extent of fluctuations in international exchange rates during 1995, which bore little relationship to real economic changes, suggests that the financial world is living constantly on a knife-edge. Mere hints of a change in interest or exchange rates send billions of dollars cascading around the financial circuits.

Not only the changing financial system but the whole process of international competitiveness seems to encourage volatility. As Quandt (1994: 3) puts it: "Despite the high level of concentration in the leading global industries, competition appears to be increasing as the international structure of production changes. Accordingly, comparative advantages tend to be a fleeting phenomenon." One day, Brazil may be producing most of Latin America's cars, the next day it may have lost its comparative advantage and be struggling to sustain its competitive edge because of a shift in the external value of the real. Internally, a crisis such as Mexico's will plunge domestic production into turmoil.

The internationalization of capital markets brings with it economic instability. It also restricts what governments can do in terms of local economic management. Macroeconomic planners can now take only limited action to remedy local problems such as high levels of un-employment. If they take what are perceived by the international moneybrokers to be inappropriate measures, that will precipitate an outflow of funds. This is hardly a new phenomenon (recall the trials and tribulations of the Wilson government with respect to devalua-tion in the United Kingdom in the 1960s – Pimlott, 1992), but the sensitivity of international capital markets has greatly increased with the development of modern communications and 24-hour trading systems.

Neo-liberalism and macroeconomic management

The debt crisis in Latin America ushered a new development model into Latin America. Import-substituting industrialization gave way to export-oriented industrialization. Neo-liberal economic thought and the lessons of the debt crisis have convinced one Latin American state after another that it should follow similar kinds of policy. In crude terms, practically every Latin American state has taken on the underlying logic of external orientation. This has required major transformations to the domestic economy. It has required the dis-mantling of trade tariffs and quotas, opening up the national economy to foreign investment, establishing a realistic exchange rate, reducing public expenditure and the role of the state, restructuring labour regulations and financial markets, and modernizing the country's infrastructure. Adoption of the "new economic model" has meant that macroeconomic policy has become increasingly similar through-out Latin America. Although different governments have embraced the new conventional wisdom with differing levels of enthusiasm, most have taken on the substance of the "new economic model." The new policy was embraced first in Chile, and later taken up in Argen-tina, Mexico, Bolivia, and Peru. Today, there are few countries that have not experienced some measure of structural adjustment and economic "reconversion" of the economy.

Table 8.4 shows that, by the early 1980s, this new development model had already had a profound influence on both the level of export orientation in most of the larger Latin American countries and the degree to which manufactures were developing. The irony is that, after the reforms of the 1980s and the virtual institutionalization of the export-based model, exports have fallen in most countries. Of this

Table 8.4 **Latin America: Export performance of selected countries, 1965–1992**

Country	Exports as % of GDP			Manufactured exports as % of total merchandise exports		
	1965	1983	1992	1965	1983	1992
Argentina	8	13	5	6	24	28
Brazil	8	8	10	8	39	58
Chile	14	24	23	4	8	15
Colombia	11	10	14	7	25	31
Mexico	9	20	8	16	12	50
Peru	16	21	16	1	14	21
Venezuela	31	26	23	2	3	10

Sources: World Bank (1985, 1994).

reduced export total, of course, much more is contributed by manufactures, although the table exaggerates the extent of change in so far
as the terms of trade have shifted against primary exports and in
favour of manufactures. Nevertheless, Latin America, like most parts
of the so-called third world, has shifted from an almost total dependence on primary products to a position where it has become a significant exporter of manufactures.

Neo-liberalism and structural adjustment have also brought other
changes. In an attempt to reduce the dangers of inflation, a major
attack has been made on the government budget deficit. This has led
to the privatization or closure of substantial parts of the state apparatus. In Mexico and Chile, the state has sold most of its productive
activities (PEMEX being a major exception), and manufacturing,
hotels, banks, and transport companies have all been privatized. In
Bolivia, the huge COMIBOL mining enterprise has been savagely
cut, the labour force falling from 28,000 in 1985 to 5,000 in 1992. The
changes have been slower in Brazil, Colombia, and Venezuela, but
even there the rhetoric of privatization and reduced governmental
action is deafening.

The recent changes have undoubtedly changed the development
model in Latin America, although whether or not the level of international influence on local governments is greater than before is
debatable. In the 1960s, the conventional wisdom was import substitution, national planning, land reform, and birth control. Every
country set up similar kinds of institution to manage the reform process, much of the intellectual initiative coming from Washington.
Today, Washington is still helping to influence policy but the message

is very different: the old interventionist model does not work, and a new market-based model must replace it. The fact that the new conventional wisdom was concocted in the same place as the old is worrying. At least, "the irony of the international agencies advocating the dismantling of the publicly-owned institutions that they themselves created in the 1960s, has not gone unnoticed" (Cook and Kirkpatrick, 1988: 30).

Selling the city

According to Browne (1994: 1), "the economic systems of advanced and developing countries alike are being restructured to meet the needs of global traders and investors." Globalization has brought greater competition between cities and regions. As Peck and Tickell (1994: 319) put it:

> In this harsh environment localities have, to borrow a phrase from Marx, become 'hostile brothers,' flinging themselves into the competitive process of attracting jobs and investment by bargaining away living standards and regulatory practices. ... In a situation of continuing global crisis and deregulation, in which there is not enough investment to go around, localities are resorting to beggar-thy-neighbour strategies.

The most negative side to international salesmanship of this kind is the way in which foreign companies are being attracted to the region. The authorities are guaranteeing to ask no questions if companies pollute the environment. Alternatively, the local authority will clear up the mess. Transnational corporations are not expected to house their labour force, and infrastructure will be provided by the state. Again, the example *par excellence* comes from the US–Mexican border, where the development of *maquila* plants has produced serious environmental problems. According to Browne (1994: 37), "maquila-based development has accentuated the planning and infrastructural problems faced by Mexican cities."

Latin America has also sought to compete in another way. Like urban areas across the globe, each Latin American city has been restructuring itself in an attempt "to make it more comfortable and appealing to foreigners, particularly those with high-level business or diplomatic credentials" (Cybriwsky, 1991: 113). In Latin America, this process has been under way for years both to attract tourists and to encourage visiting businessmen to invest in the region. But it has also occurred because Latin Americans like to live at international

190

standards. Buenos Aires is known as the Paris of Latin America because Argentines moulded their capital to look like Paris. Similarly, the country clubs and yacht clubs, so imitative of the United States, that have been built in all of the region's larger cities are not there primarily to attract foreigners; they are there because rich Latin Americans like to relax in sumptuous surroundings.

Consumption

Felix (1983: 7) argues that: "The 'international demonstration effect' is not a recent creation of Hollywood and Madison Avenue, but has been a behavioural trait of the Latin American affluent classes since the Conquest that ... has probably been unmatched in intensity by the behaviour of the affluent of other LDC regions." Latin America has aped the consumption habits of Europe and the United States for years. Import-substituting industrialization intensified this tendency as international companies started to produce and market goods locally. Recent forms of globalization have accentuated this tendency by reducing barriers to imports. Prices of imported goods have fallen and made the latest products available to Latin American consumers. The growing numbers of BMWs on the streets of Bogotá and other Colombian cities are testimony to this trend. The effect has been to worsen the balance of payments as more and more Latin Americans demand foreign-produced goods, a tendency that was extremely marked in the build-up to the latest Mexican peso crisis.

Of course, the degree to which consumption has followed international patterns varies considerably from place to place. Tijuana is much more international than La Paz, both because it is on California's doorstep and because it is much more affluent. Of course, the literature has often exaggerated the extent of globalization in this respect. As Simon (1994: 2) puts it: "globalised consumerism and industrial production for global markets often occur to very different extents in particular regions. Africa is a case in point: its increasing marginalisation within the world economy reflects the paucity of inward foreign direct investment and exports of secondary or tertiary output."

In Latin America, the desire of most households to become global consumers has been whet by the ubiquitous television set and by the advertising campaigns of international companies. Tastes have been affected further by the opening up of new branches of international consumer culture – McDonald's has just opened branches in Bogotá.

However, the wish to buy foreign "sophisticated" products and services is not the same as the ability to do so. With the value of local currencies often falling spectacularly against the dollar and with real incomes falling in many countries, the effective demand for internationalized forms of consumption has declined recently among the masses.

F.

Inequality and social polarization

The recession of the 1980s made Latin America's cities both poorer and more unequal (Altimir, 1994). The gap between the top 10 per cent of the population and the rest increased during the 1980s. Those who could put their money in dollars did very well from the recession; they were protected from the effects of inflation. Inflation hit the poor particularly hard and both the minimum wage and real incomes fell in most cities – in some, such as Lima, spectacularly so. Highly unequal cities became even less fair. They also became much poorer. By 1990, 35 per cent of the population of traditionally affluent Buenos Aires was living in poverty (Ainstein, 1996). In Lima, the proportion of households living below the poverty line rose from 17 per cent in 1981 to 44 per cent in 1985/86; after a single year of structural adjustment, the proportion had risen to 49 per cent in 1991 (Riofrío, 1996). In Brazil's major cities both absolute and relative poverty got worse during the 1980s. Rio de Janeiro was particularly badly affected and absolute poverty increased dramatically; by 1991, some 3.5 million people were living below the poverty line (Tolosa, 1996).

With economic recovery, the number of people living in poverty has fallen in most countries (Altimir, 1994). Evidence from Argentina suggests that control of hyperinflation during the late 1980s substantially cut the number of people living in poverty. The "indigent" population, which made up a startling 12.7 per cent of the total urban population in October 1989, had fallen to 2.4 per cent by May 1992. Unfortunately, even if the new economic model is cutting poverty levels (when it is successful), it is probably accentuating inequality. Indeed, some would argue that this is inherent in the new global model. As Mittelman (1994: 440–441) puts it: "life is marked by a deepening divide between rich and poor. The mosaic of globalization reflects a transformation of poverty in which three continents were most adversely affected by globalization to the marginalization primarily of a single world region and of enclaves in other regions."

The process is probably causing polarization even within successful urban regions. This, of course, is Sassen's (1991) contention about London, New York, and Tokyo, an idea shared by Friedmann and Wolff (1982: 320) when they argue that "the primary social fact about world city formation is the polarization of its social class divisions." In practice, it is uncertain whether polarization is an inevitable outcome of world city status in the developed world, even if it were wholly clear what Sassen meant by it (Hamnett, 1994). But, in Latin American cities, there seems to be little doubt: the new economic model is accentuating existing levels of inequality.

The effects of such growing inequality are aggravated by the structures of large Latin American cities. The rich are more likely to get jobs, the poor less likely to; service provision for the rich is excellent, that for the poor problematic. Critically, the rich are able both to benefit from the advantages of large cities and to escape from most of the diseconomies. There may be excellent hospitals, clubs, restaurants, and universities in large cities, but most are open only to those with money. The poor might as well be living in a different city as far as these kinds of facility are concerned. Similarly, the availability of better-quality jobs in the largest cities benefits the poor only so far as these jobs create more work in lower-paid activities. The poor, lacking university education and social skills, cannot expect to gain access to highly paid forms of employment.

If the poor gain few of the advantages offered by the mega-cities, they reap most of the disadvantages. In so far as levels of car ownership are much higher in large cities, traffic congestion is worse. Of course, the rich are also delayed by heavy traffic but, whereas the poor are held up in crowded buses, the affluent can listen to their car stereos. Similarly, pollution is likely to hit the poor much harder than the rich. Indeed, those with enough money can buy accommodation in the least polluted areas. I know of Latin American cities where pollution reaches high-income areas, but I know of no Latin American city where the rich do not live in the least affected areas. At weekends, the rich can also escape more easily from the noise and pollution.

Arguably, too, the privatization of services and the increasing practice of cost recovery may reduce the chances of poor neighbourhoods obtaining infrastructure. In Santiago, there have been strong signs that the privatized water and electricity agencies have been disconnecting households that are unable to pay their bills. Where privatization works well, it may improve service capacity, but where it works badly it will slow service delivery and hit the poor very hard. As such, it will accentuate levels of social polarization.

6. Politics and state autonomy

Browne (1994: 2) argues that "economic integration involves a reduction in the importance of national boundaries in the decisions of consumers, workers, and investors. This does not mean that national characteristics such as labor markets, infrastructure, and climate matter less. On the contrary, such characteristics become *more* important with integration because more people and corporations are freer to cross borders to take advantage of them." Latin American governments have been forced to make their economies more competitive and have sought to woo foreign investors. They have been required to reduce the barriers to foreign trade and investment and to remove many of the measures, instituted during the 1950s and 1960s, intended to protect their societies from exploitation by transnational companies. Mittelman (1994: 431) paraphrases the change that has occurred as follows: "In a globalized division of labour, the state no longer serves primarily as a buffer or shield against the world economy. Rather,... the state increasingly facilitates globalization, acting as an agent in the process." As a result, a form of neo-liberalism has been adopted throughout Latin America.

Just as the state removed many of the controls that it had painstakingly instituted during the phase of import substitution, it also began to reform itself. Reform of the state was hastened by the great shift towards democratic government that occurred in Latin America during the 1980s. In the late 1970s, virtually the whole of Latin America was controlled by military regimes. Only Costa Rica, Venezuela, and, much less clearly, Colombia and Mexico had democratically elected leaders. One of the ironies of Latin America is that the debt crisis was created by military governments and left to civilian leaders to clear up.

Today, virtually every government is democratically elected and many of these administrations have been embracing the ethos of decentralization and participation. They have tried to reduce centralized control and to give greater voice to the majority of the people. Of course, because this has occurred during a time of structural adjustment it has often been associated with deteriorating living conditions. As Mittelman (1994: 433) puts it: "Whereas in theory, democracy means accountability to the governed, in practice leaders are accountable to market forces, most notably debt structures and structural adjustment programmes."

One example of the difficulties that the combination of decentralization and neo-liberalism produces in practice lies in the field of infrastructure and services. Increasingly, more authority is being given to municipal and provincial governments to run services such as water and electricity. The problem is that local people have been given responsibility without the means to take advantage of their new powers. Public budgets have been slashed. One of the clear advantages of decentralization for central governments is that democratically elected local leaders now take the blame for the non-provision of services (Gilbert, 1992).

According to some observers, the new economic model has raised the level of social protest in Latin America. It is often argued that a wave of "austerity riots" swept through the region as governments instituted structural adjustment packages (Walton, 1989). As social polarization increased and poverty suddenly became widespread, the local population is supposed to have spilled out into the streets to protest. According to Mittelman (1994: 434):

The globalization of civil society precipitates resistance from disadvantaged strata in a changing division of labour. The losers in global restructuring seek to redefine their role in the emerging order. In the face of the declining power of organized labour and revolutionary groups, the powerless must devise alternative strategies of social struggle. They aim to augment popular participation and assert local control over the seemingly remote forces of globalization. New social movements – women's groups, environmentalists, human rights organizations, etc. – are themselves a global phenomenon, a worldwide response to the deleterious effects of economic globalization.... In sum, not only production and the state, but also civil society itself is being globalized.

Interesting though it is, I believe this hypothesis to be hopelessly overgeneralized. I do not believe that there has been any generalized rise in social protest or social movements in Latin America due to globalization (Gilbert, 1994). Indeed, for me one of the strangest features of political life in Latin American cities during the 1980s was how placidly most Latin Americans accepted structural adjustment. There were extreme forms of protest in Caracas in 1989 and riots in some Brazilian, Mexican, and Peruvian cities earlier in the decade, but, in general, the poor did not protest a great deal. Indeed, the election successes of presidents Cardoso (Brazil), Fujimori (Peru), and Menem (Argentina) suggest that the poor are prepared to reward the instigators of tough macroeconomic policies for removing the "poverty tax" of inflation.

The global reach of the media no doubt produces some kind of international demonstration effect: if they can riot in Caracas why not here in Mexico? But, on the whole, there is little sign of growing social activism or protest in Latin America's cities. Indeed, the whole process of weakening trade unions, reducing labour rights, and casualizing labour has met with surprisingly little protest (Roxborough, 1989). In the poorest neighbourhoods, the poor have been too busy working longer hours to make up the family budget to protest (Gilbert, 1994). Rather than being destroyed by austerity, clientelism seems to be making a come-back (Gay, 1990). Globalization may have created objective conditions under which protest should have appeared, but, so far at least, there are relatively few signs of its having done so.

The future prospects for Latin America's cities

World roles

Latin America's largest cities prospered during the era of import-substituting industrialization. They gained over the region's secondary cities because they attracted most of the new manufacturing plants. Large capital cities also benefited from the huge expansion in the government bureaucracy, part and parcel of the import-substitution developmental model.

During the 1980s, the pace of growth of the major cities throughout the region slowed because of changes in the wider economic and social environment. As the basis for development changed during the 1980s, many of the advantages of the major cities were removed. The manufacturing plants that were so favoured by the import-substituting industrialization model suffered badly during the 1980s. Structural adjustment and the new export-oriented model of development decimated much of Latin America's domestic industry. Recession and the removal of urban subsidies hit producers and consumers hard. Trade liberalization allowed foreign manufacturers to compete in Latin America's previously protected markets. The result has sometimes been terrible for the major cities.

The future of each of the giant cities depends in part on the prospects for the respective national economies; it is difficult for a major city to prosper in a declining national economy. In fact, recent

Table 8.5 **Economic growth in selected Latin American countries, 1980–1993**

Country	Annual growth in GDP (%)		
	1980–84	1985–89	1990–93
Argentina	−3.0	−2.3	5.9
Brazil	−0.5	2.5	0.0
Chile	−0.1	4.8	6.0
Colombia	−1.5	3.0	3.5
Mexico	−0.6	−1.2	2.9
Peru	−2.4	−2.5	0.1
Venezuela	−3.5	−0.9	5.7

Sources: UNECLAC (1992, 1993).

national records of economic growth show considerable differences. As table 8.5 reveals, some Latin American economies have been expanding, while others have been standing still. In per capita terms, Brazil and Peru are still in decline. It will be difficult for Lima to prosper if the Peruvian economy continues to suffer.

But the large cities also need to adapt so that they can maintain or improve upon their share of national production, can compete successfully with foreign imports, and can increase their output of manufactured exports. Some major cities in Latin America look well placed to do this. There is little doubt that the São Paulo metropolitan region will thrive because it contains Brazil's most efficient industries and most of its research and information technology capacity. Similarly, Bogotá seems to be thriving on trade liberalization, whereas Colombia's traditional industrial centre, Medellín, is doing less well. But the futures of Caracas, Lima, and Rio seem much less assured. Rio may be able to take on some of the dimensions of a "world city," particularly in terms of media, communications, and tourist functions, but it is rather unlikely that Lima ever will (Tolosa, 1996; Riofrío, 1996).

The shape and size of the city

I have already shown that metropolitan growth has slowed markedly in recent years. Whether this slowing in metropolitan growth will continue in the future is less certain. Continuing declines in fertility rates will help, but other features of the 1980s may well change. The resumption of economic growth could well stimulate the economies of some of the larger cities, which might reactivate cityward migra-

197

tion. In-migration might also be stimulated by some kind of rural crisis. Should trade liberalization and the removal of guaranteed agricultural prices lead to rural crisis, there could be a massive exodus of people from the countryside. In Mexico, some observers worry that entry into the North American Free Trade Area will undermine the viability of maize production; some 3 million peasant producers could become potential migrants. Rural violence may also lead to greater flows of cityward migrants. In Colombia, the urban growth rate has slowed much less than in other parts of Latin America, partly because of drug-related and political violence in the countryside. Something similar occurred in Peru during the period of Shining Path violence, when large numbers of families were forced to flee to Lima.

Coping with urban problems

Whether Latin America's cities grow slowly or rapidly, urban living conditions will ultimately depend upon how those cities are managed. Clearly, economic growth is an important element here; without economic growth, decently paid work will be scarce and there will be fewer resources for governments to provide services. Even if there is growth, governments have to manage the major cities better than they have in the past. Whether that will happen is anything but clear.

In so far as good governance clearly requires both political stability and democratic participation, Latin America's potential has improved greatly in recent years. First, few countries in the region are suffering from political instability and, for good or ill, there is little possibility of a social revolution in most parts of the region. Secondly, it is a long time since democratic government was quite so well established in the region. Thirdly, there are incipient signs of greater participation in government decision-making. More power is being given to local government and more ordinary people are being consulted about their needs and desires.

There are also some signs that some Latin American governments are managing to rectify some of the problems that have faced their metropolitan areas for decades. Mexico City, for example, has begun to control its air pollution and to curb traffic congestion. Despite the recession, the authorities managed to increase coverage of water and electricity during the 1980s (Davis, 1994). Unfortunately, these examples of improved urban government are still exceptions. Competent administration is anything but obvious in most cities of Latin

America. It is certainly lacking in Buenos Aires, where industrial and domestic waste is pouring into the River Plate (Ainstein, 1996). It is less than evident in São Paulo, where increasing levels of crime in the streets and a generalized lack of confidence in the justice and police systems led Kowarick (1991) to designate Brazil's largest city the "metropolis of industrial underdevelopment." It is far from obvious in Lima as the state of public services deteriorates in the nation's capital (Riofrío, 1991).

Another respect in which we cannot be wholly optimistic concerns the distribution of income and social segregation. During the recession, Latin American cities became hugely more unequal, particularly when hyperinflation was rampant. In the near future, a resumption of economic growth would improve living conditions for both the poor and the middle class. However, the overall result of liberalization and the rolling back of the "welfare" state is likely to be an accentuation of existing inequalities. Unless current efforts to target social expenditure are successful, conditions for the very poor may well deteriorate during an era of reduced social spending. Even with faster rates of economic growth, job creation will occur in an increasingly casualized labour market. Fewer jobs are likely to offer either security or decent incomes. In this sense, the future of Latin America's giant cities in a globalizing world is highly problematic.

Finally, there is the issue of economic stability. The early 1990s suggested that Latin America was emerging from the lost decade with good prospects for future growth, and there are still good reasons to believe that. However, the spectre of what happened in Mexico now hangs over Latin America. If a paragon of neo-liberal orthodoxy can be turned so quickly into a basket case, where else might disaster strike? Perhaps this is the greatest fear in this seemingly global era. A botched devaluation, a peasant uprising, or the election of a left-wing leader may suddenly hit international confidence. The achievements derived from years of hardship and economic reform could be swept away in a few days. And, when international confidence is damaged, one can be sure that it will be the poor and the middle class who will pay most of the price. In this age, when making money is once again a noble ambition, equity ranks low among the aims of most Latin American governments. Whatever the future holds for Latin America, therefore, it is likely to be less stable and less equitable than in the past. Given Latin America's past record, that hardly constitutes grounds for real optimism.

Note

1. The average birth rate fell from 42 per 1,000 in the early 1960s to 33 in the early 1980s.

References

Ainstein (1996), "Buenos Aires: A Case of Deepening Social Polarization." In: A. G. Gilbert (ed.), *Megacities in Latin America*. Tokyo: United Nations University Press.

Altimir, O. (1994), "Distribución del Ingreso e Incidencia de la Pobreza a lo Largo del Ajuste." *Revista de la CEPAL* 52: 7–32.

Arriagada, I. (1994), "Transformaciones del Trabajo Feminino Urbano." *Revista de la CEPAL* 53: 91–110.

Browne, H. (1994), *For Richer; for Poorer*. London: Latin American Bureau.

Chase-Dunn, C. (1985), "The System of World Cities, A.D. 800–1975." In: M. Timberlade (ed.), *Urbanization in the World-Economy*. New York: Academic Press, pp. 269–292.

Cook, P. and C. Kirkpatrick (1988), *Privatisation in Less Developed Countries*. New York: Harvester Wheatsheaf.

Cybriwsky, R. (1991), *Tokyo*. London: Belhaven.

Davis, D. E. (1994), *Urban Leviathan: Mexico City in the Twentieth Century*. Philadelphia: Temple University Press.

Dicken, P. (1994), "Global–Local Tensions: Firms and States in the Global Space-Economy." *Economic Geography* 70: 101–128.

Dieleman, F. M. and C. Hamnett (1994), "Globalisation, Regulation and the Urban System." *Urban Studies* 31: 357–364.

Dogan, M. and J. D. Kasarda (eds.) (1988), *The Metropolis Era. Volume One: A World of Giant Cities. Volume Two: Mega-cities*. Beverly Hills, Calif.: Sage.

Felix, D. (1983), "Income Distribution and Quality of Life in Latin America: Patterns, Trends and Policy Implications." *Latin American Research Review* 18: 3–34.

Friedmann, J. (1986), "The World City Hypothesis." *Development and Change* 17: 69–83.

Friedmann, J. and G. Wolff (1982), "World City Formation: An Agenda for Research and Action." *International Journal of Urban and Regional Research* 6: 309–343.

Fuchs, R. J., et al. (1994), *Mega-City Growth and the Future*. Tokyo: United Nations University Press.

Gay, R. (1990), "Community Organization and Clientelist Politics in Contemporary Brazil: A Case Study from Suburban Rio de Janeiro." *International Journal of Urban and Regional Research* 14: 648–666.

George, S. (1988), *A Fate Worse than Debt*. Harmondsworth, Middlesex: Penguin.

Gilb, C. L. (1989), "Third World Cities: Their Role in the Global Economy." In: R. V. Knight and G. Gappert (eds.), *Cities in a Global Society*. Beverly Hills, Calif.: Sage, pp. 96–107.

Gilbert, A. G. (1990), "Urbanisation at the Periphery: Reflections on the Changing Dynamics of Housing and Employment in Latin American Cities." In: D. Drakakis-

Smith (ed.), *Economic Growth and Urbanisation in Developing Areas.* London: Routledge, pp. 73–124.

―――― (1992), "Third World Cities: Housing, Infrastructure and Servicing." *Urban Studies* 29: 435–460.

―――― (1993), "Third World Cities: The Changing National Settlement System." *Urban Studies* 30: 721–740.

―――― (1994), *The Latin American City.* London: Latin American Bureau; New York: Monthly Review Press.

―――― (ed.) (1996), *Megacities in Latin America.* Tokyo: United Nations University Press.

Gilbert, A. G. and J. Gugler (1992), *Cities, Poverty and Development: Urbanization in the Third World*, 2nd edn. Oxford: Oxford University Press.

Hall, P. (1977), *The World Cities*, 2nd edn. London: Weidenfeld & Nicolson.

Hamnett, C. (1994), "Social Polarization in Global Cities: Theory and Evidence." *Urban Studies* 31: 401–424.

Hirata, H. and J. Humphrey (1991), "Workers' Responses to Job Loss: Female and Male Industrial Workers in Brazil." *World Development* 19: 671–682.

INEGI (Instituto Nacional de Estadística, Geografia e Informática) (1995), *Mexican Bulletin of Statistical Information.*

Kaplinsky, R. (1994), "From Mass Production to Flexible Specialization: A Case Study of Microeconomic Change in a Semi-Industrialized Economy." *World Development* 22: 337–353.

Kowarick, L. (1991), "Ciudad & Ciudadanía. Metrópolis del Subdesarrollo Industrializado." *Nueva Sociedad* 114: 84–93.

Lowder, S. (1987), *Inside the Third World City.* London: Croom Helm.

Mayhew, S. and A. Penny (1992), *The Concise Oxford Dictionary of Geography.* Oxford: Oxford University Press.

Mittelman, J. H. (1994), "The Globalization Challenge: Surviving at the Margins." *Third World Quarterly* 15: 427–443.

Peck, J. and A. Tickell (1994), "Jungle Law Breaks Out: Neoliberalism and Global–Local Disorder." *Area* 26: 317–326.

Pimlott, B. (1992), *Harold Wilson.* London: HarperCollins.

Quandt, C. (1994), "New Opportunities in the Big Emerging Markets." *Enfoque*, Fall: 1–3.

Richardson, H. W. (1989), "The Big, Bad City: Mega-City Myth?" *Third World Planning Review* 11: 355–372.

―――― (1993), "Efficiency and Welfare in LDC Mega-Cities." In: J. D. Kasarda and A. M. Parnell (eds.), *Third World Cities: Problems, Policies, and Prospects.* Beverly Hills, Calif.: Sage, pp. 32–57.

Riofrío (1991), "Lima en los 90. Un Acercamiento a la Nueva Dinámica Urbana." *Nueva Sociedad* 114: 143–149.

―――― (1996), "Lima: Megacity and Megaproblem." In: A. G. Gilbert (ed.), *Megacities in Latin America.* Tokyo: United Nations University Press.

Roberts, B. (1994), "Informal Economy and Family Strategies," *International Journal of Urban and Regional Research* 18: 6–23.

Roxborough, I. (1989), "Organized Labor: A Major Victim of the Debt Crisis." In: B. Stallings and R. Kaufman (eds.), *Debt and Democracy in Latin America.* Boulder, Colo.: Westview Press, pp. 91–108.

201

Sassen, S. (1991), *The Global City: New York, London, Tokyo*. Princeton, N.J.: Princeton University Press.

Simon, D. (1992), *Cities, Capital and Development: African Cities in the World Economy*. London: Belhaven.

——— (1994), "Urbanisation, Globalisation and Economic Crisis in Africa," mimeo, UNU Project.

Storper, M. (1991), *Industrialization, Economic Development and the Regional Question in the Third World*. London: Pion.

Tolosa, H. (1996), "Rio de Janeiro: Urban Expansion and Structural Change." In: A. G. Gilbert (ed.), *Megacities in Latin America*. Tokyo: United Nations University Press.

Thrift, N. (1994), "Globalisation, Regulation, Urbanisation: The Case of the Netherlands." *Urban Studies* 31: 365–380.

UNCHS (United Nations Centre for Human Settlements [HABITAT]) (1987), *Global Report on Human Settlements 1986*. Oxford: Oxford University Press.

UNDIESA (United Nations Department of International Economic and Social Affairs) (1986), *Population Growth and Policies in Mega-Cities: Seoul*. Population Policy Paper No. 4. New York: United Nations.

UNDIESA (United Nations Department of International Economic and Social Affairs) and UNU (United Nations University) (1991), *Summary Report and Recommendations of the Symposium on the Mega-City and the Future: Population Growth and Policy Responses*, 22–25 October 1990, Tokyo.

UNDP (United Nations Development Programme) (1992), *Human Development Report 1992*. Oxford: Oxford University Press.

UNECLAC (United Nations Economic Commission for Latin America and the Caribbean) (1992), "Preliminary Overview of the Latin American and Caribbean Economy 1992." *Notas Sobre la Economía y el Desarrollo*, 537/538.

——— (1993), "Preliminary Overview of the Latin American and Caribbean Economy 1993." *Notas Sobre la Economía y el Desarrollo*, 552/553.

Villa, M. and J. Rodríguez (1996), "Demographic Trends in Latin America's Metropoli, 1950–1991." In: A. G. Gilbert (ed.), *Megacities in Latin America*. Tokyo: United Nations University Press.

Walton, J. (1985), "The Third 'New' International Division of Labour." In: J. Walton (ed.), *Capital and Labor in an Industrializing World*. Beverly Hills, Calif.: Sage, pp. 3–14.

——— (1989), "Debt, Protest, and the State in Latin America." In: S. Eckstein (ed.), *Power and Popular Protest: Latin American Social Movements*. Berkeley: University of California Press, pp. 299–328.

Ward, P. M. (1990), *Mexico City*. London: Belhaven.

Watts, M. (1994), "Development II: The Privatization of Everything?" *Progress in Human Geography* 18: 371–384.

Wilkie, J., et al. (1991), *Statistical Abstract for Latin America 28*. University of California, Los Angeles.

World Bank (1985), *World Development Report 1985*. Oxford: Oxford University Press.

——— (1991), *Urban Policy and Economic Development: An Agenda for the 1990s*. Washington, D.C.: World Bank.

——— (1994), *World Development Report 1994*. Oxford: Oxford University Press.

9

Rio de Janeiro as a world city

Hamilton C. Tolosa

Introduction

In a seminal book written more than 30 years ago, Richard Meier foresaw much of the present-day discussion on world cities. His basic argument states that an intensification of communications, knowledge, and controls tends to be highly correlated with urban growth (Meier, 1962: 43). Meier's views on the growth of cities in the third world are especially interesting. He observed that "the more optimistic projections indicate that urban regions will continue to grow well into the twenty-first century. A tapering off of the exponential growth must occur then, if only because of an insufficiency of space and essential resources, but the numbers to be added to the cities still reach astronomical levels" (Meier, 1962: 154).

As a matter of fact, contemporary metropolitan growth in middle-income countries can be seen as a process of adaptation to changes arising from massive urbanization and from insertion in a global network of cities. In other words, each metropolitan area is compelled to adapt its internal structure in response to demographic, economic, and technological changes.

Latin American countries tend to show higher urban primacy than other economies at similar development levels.[1] However, countries differ in the way spatial inequalities are perceived and lead to political action. The Latin American historical experience also evinces that the pioneer efforts to fight socio-economic inequalities have always carried some sort of spatial content. Especially in territorially large countries, local and regional equity policies precede personal income redistribution efforts at the national level. Moreover, this reveals the capacity of regional leadership and local élites to be politically organized in the sense of pushing the central government into some sort of spatial redistribution action. Other societal groups, such as the poor, do not seem to share the same drive towards political mobilization.

With those questions in mind, this chapter looks at the Rio de Janeiro Metropolitan Area (RJMA) as a node in the system of world cities. A significant cultural and services centre among Brazilian cities, the RJMA ranks second in demographic and economic size only to the São Paulo Metropolitan Area (SPMA). Because the two economies are closely intertwined, this chapter naturally emphasizes comparisons between the two cities and their joint domination over the Brazilian spatial distribution of economic activities. I first briefly examine demographic similarities and differences among major Latin American world cities, namely, São Paulo, Mexico City, Buenos Aires, and Rio de Janeiro. I then review some of Rio's major institutional and historical features, paying special attention to its functional role in the Brazilian urban system. The following section looks into some typical world city industries and services, and their contribution to globalization, internal restructuring, and adaptation of the RJMA economy to externally induced changes. Finally, I discuss alternative urban growth scenarios as well as the part played by the RJMA in Brazilian economic recovery over the next decade.

World cities in Latin America

Besides sharing certain similarities such as fast urbanization, high primacy, and persistent spatial inequalities, Latin American countries also show some meaningful differences as far as the urbanization process is concerned. Table 9.1 compares urbanization indicators in the three largest Latin American countries. On that account, Argentina shows urbanization ratios and a city size distribution similar to those found in industrialized European countries. Brazil is at an intermediate position and Mexico still retains some typically rural features. It is also worth noting that, in the past two decades, Brazil and Mexico have displayed some of the highest urbanization growth

Table 9.1 **Urbanization ratios in territorially large upper-middle-income Latin American countries, 1970–1990 (%)**

	Urbanization ratio[a]						
	Overall ratio			In localities $\geq 20,000$ inh.		In localities $\geq 100,000$ inh.	
Country	1970	1980	1990	1970	1980	1970	1980
Argentina	78.3	82.7	86.2	66.4	70.6	55.7	57.9
Brazil	55.8	67.5	76.9	40.8	52.2	32.3	42.0
Mexico	59.0	66.4	72.6	45.5	51.4	37.4	43.4

Source: Economic Commission for Latin America and the Caribbean, *Statistical Yearbook for Latin America*, various years.
a. Urbanization ratio = urban population/total population ×100.

rates among all developing countries, causing further spatial imbalances and poverty concentration in large cities.

According to Friedmann (1986: 71), "all but two primary world cities are located in core countries. The two exceptions are São Paulo, which articulates the Brazilian economy, and the city-state of Singapore, which performs the same role for a multi-country region in South-East Asia." Thus, primary cities are first-rank nodes in a global urban hierarchy and Rio de Janeiro is regarded as a secondary world city of the same rank as Buenos Aires, Caracas, and Mexico City in Latin America, Johannesburg in Africa, and Hong Kong, Taipei, Manila, Bangkok, and Seoul in Asian semi-peripheral countries.[2]

Friedmann's ranking criteria combine such functional variables as major financial centre, headquarters or high-ranking decision centre for multinational, transnational, and large national corporations, rapid growth of modern business services, important manufacturing pole, major transportation and communications nodes, and population size. I use most of these variables in order to study the Rio de Janeiro articulation with other nodes of a global system of world cities (see below).

Table 9.2 compares the demographic performance of some Latin American world cities over recent decades. Three facts deserve special attention. First, differences in population size among Latin American metropolises are quite significant. Both São Paulo and Mexico City are nearly 1.5 times larger than Rio de Janeiro or Buenos Aires. Secondly, demographic growth rates fell consistently between 1970 and 1990. Growth rates were cut by half in São Paulo,

Table 9.2 **World cities in Latin America: Population growth, 1970–1990**

| World city | 1970 | | 1980 | | 1990 | | Average annual growth rates (%) | |
	No. (million)	As % of total urban population	No. (million)	As % of total urban population	No. (million)	As % of total urban population	1970–80	1980–90
Greater Buenos Aires	8.5	35.6	9.7	34.8	10.8	33.4	1.6	1.1
Mexico City	9.3	18.5	13.9	20.7	15.4	18.7	4.2	0.9
RJMA	6.8	7.0	8.8	7.3	9.6[a]	6.0	2.4	0.8[b]
SPMA	8.1	8.3	12.5	10.2	15.2	10.3	4.4	2.0

Source: Economic Commission for Latin America and the Caribbean, *Statistical Yearbook for Latin America and Caribbean*, 1994.
a. 1991.
b. 1980–1991.

by two-thirds in Rio, and by three-quarters in Mexico City, as a direct result of economic recession and internal adjustments caused by the Latin American debt crisis. Thirdly and most important, the figures for city share in the total urban population clearly point to meaningful differences in each world city's dominance of its national city system. Although fairly stable over the two decades, the Buenos Aires share was almost double that of Mexico City.

The joint effect of Brazilian world cities definitely stands out as a special case among middle-income developing countries. Taken separately, Rio and São Paulo are not much different from other Latin American metropolises. Considered as a single and closely interdependent economic unit, however, they have a completely different impact upon the global system of cities. First of all, in 1990 their joint population reached nearly 25 million, produced more than 50 per cent of the national manufacturing value-added, and earned the largest per capita income among Brazilian metropolitan areas – in other words, a local market comparable in size to the largest world cities in the developed world.

In spite of Rio's and São Paulo's demographic and economic sizes, the primacy ratio, measured by their share in total urban population (table 9.3), is still relatively small when compared with that in Argentina, Mexico, and several other Latin American countries. Physical distance can be a significant variable in explaining economic interdependency among spatial units. According to the well-known gravity model, for instance, the mutual attraction coefficient between any pair of cities is inversely related to the square of the distance between them. In sum, the nearer the spatial units are, the more

Table 9.3 **The population of pairs of major metropolitan areas as a percentage of total urban population, 1970–1990**

Pairs of major metropolitan areas	1970	1980	1990	Average annual growth rates (%)	
				1970–80	1980–90
Greater Buenos Aires and Cordoba	39.1	38.2	36.7	1.6	1.2
Mexico City and Guadalajara	21.5	23.9	22.2	4.2	n.a.
RJMA and SPMA	15.3	17.6	16.6	3.6	1.8

Source: Economic Commission for Latin America and the Caribbean, *Statistical Yearbook for Latin America and Caribbean*, 1994.

interdependent their demand and productive structure will be. As a matter of fact, Rio is only 219 miles from São Paulo, which is the shortest distance between the city pairs examined in table 9.3, namely, 284 miles between Mexico City and Guadalajara and 398 miles between Buenos Aires and Cordoba.

The role of Rio de Janeiro in the Brazilian system of cities

One could briefly describe demographic and urbanization trends in Brazil as concentrated in time and important in magnitude.[3] The Brazilian population was 80 per cent rural in 1940 and became a predominantly urban society in less than 40 years, no matter which definition is used. According to official sources, the present urbanization rate is of the order of 77 per cent. This accelerated growth process reached its peak in the late 1950s and early 1960s; since then, the growth rate has decelerated, especially in the so-called "urbanized regions" and less so in the frontier and backward areas.

The rapid population redistribution also meant significant changes in the Brazilian system of cities. In the 1960s and early 1970s, demographic growth concentrated in intermediate-size cities with a population between 100,000 and 250,000 inhabitants. Later, in the 1980s, medium-sized cities kept their economic importance but lost relative position as far as demographic growth is concerned. In more recent years, the large metropolitan areas, especially those located in the lagging North-East, have shown the highest growth rates in the urban system as a whole.

In 1960, for geopolitical reasons, the Brazilian federal capital was moved from Rio de Janeiro to Brasilia, located in the State of Goiás highlands, the geometric centre of the country. In 1973, a federal law established the first group of eight metropolitan areas (São Paulo, Porto Alegre, Curitiba, Belo Horizonte, Salvador, Recife, Fortaleza, and Belém), and one year later a specific law created the Rio de Janeiro Metropolitan Area (RJMA). According to the 1991 Demographic Census, the nine official metropolitan areas encompassed 42 million inhabitants, roughly 29 per cent of the total Brazilian population in that year.

The RJMA, the second Brazilian seaport in economic importance, is located in the comparatively developed South-East region, 219 miles north-east of the São Paulo Metropolitan Area (SPMA), the core of Brazilian industrial power. Together, these two metropolitan areas account for more than 35 per cent of national industrial employment and value-added. In the 1980s, Rio de Janeiro and São Paulo's joint share in the country population remained fairly stable and is expected to show a modest increase from its present 17 per cent to a maximum of 18–20 per cent at the turn of the twenty-first century.

In reality, such apparent stability disguises divergent trends. Since the 1970s, the São Paulo population has grown at a much faster rate than that in Rio. Its economic performance was equally striking and São Paulo alone currently accounts for nearly 25 per cent of Brazilian manufacturing value-added.[4] In contrast, the RJMA has been consistently losing relative position, not only to São Paulo but also to other major metropolitan areas, such as Belo Horizonte. Many of Rio's former leading industries and banking and high-technology companies have either relocated to nearby states, such as Minas Gerais and São Paulo, or simply moved their headquarters to the SPMA. Over time, the gap between the two largest Brazilian metropolitan areas has been growing fast. As an example, the per capita household earnings ratio between São Paulo and Rio, which was 1.1 in 1970, increased to 1.2 in 1976, and to 1.3 in 1988.

Since their institutionalization in the early 1970s, the boundaries of the nine metropolitan areas have remained basically unchanged. The RJMA comprises 14 counties or municipalities, namely: Rio de Janeiro, Duque de Caxias, Itaboraí Itaguaí Magé, Mangaratiba, Maricá, Nilópolis, Niterói, Nova Iguaçu, Paracambi, Petrópolis,[5] São Gonçalo, and São João de Meriti (see fig. 9.1). In 1980, the RJMA had 8.8 million inhabitants and its present population is estimated at more than 10 million.

The RJMA has a total area of 6,464 km^2, of which 18 per cent (or 1,171 km^2) relates to the "município" of Rio de Janeiro, the core of the metropolitan area and the capital city of the state of Rio de Janeiro. In 1988, the average demographic density was 1,700 inhabitants per km^2 in the metropolitan area as a whole and 5,000 inhabitants per km^2 in the capital city itself. The land-use pattern is quite uneven, owing partly to topographical obstacles such as mountains, lagoons, swamps, and flooded areas.[6]

Environmental costs can be considered to be among the most relevant social costs generated by world cities. In the specific case of Rio de Janeiro, environmental problems also stem from its particular spatial shape, since most of the densely populated metropolitan counties are located along the shores of Guanabara Bay (see fig. 9.1), giving the city the overall shape of a large horseshoe. This

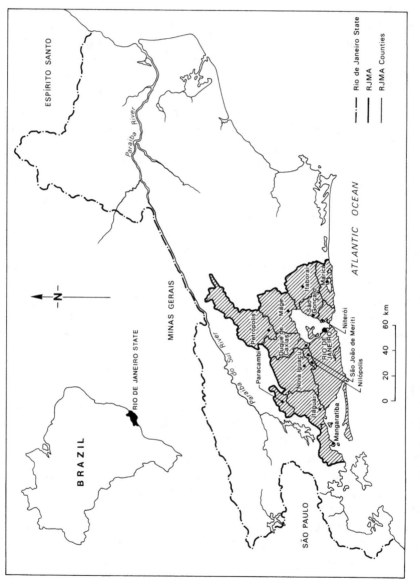

Fig. 9.1 **Rio de Janeiro state and Rio de Janeiro Metropolitan Area**

shape creates distinctive environmental problems, because domestic and industrial wastes produced in the metropolitan area naturally flow into the Bay waters.

Guanabara Bay itself covers an area of 381 km² and includes 44 km² of islands and islets. The whole basin area has 45 rivers and extends over 4,000 km² (*Rio de Janeiro Yearbook, 1992–93*: 5). It comprises a total population of 7.5 million, 80 per cent of whom are located along its western section. The slums or *"favelas"* (densely populated and illegally occupied residential areas) cause the basin's most serious social and environmental problems: over 1 million low-income people live in inadequate dwellings in the capital city alone.[7]

In 1980 the State of Rio de Janeiro's domestic product accounted for more than 13 per cent of the Brazilian gross domestic product; since then its share has dropped to 9 per cent (in 1994). According to recent estimates, services remain the dominant sector and their share has remained stable at 60 per cent. Industry comes next, its share having grown from 35 per cent in 1980 to 41 per cent in 1994.[8]

In the depths of the recession, per capita GNP declined at quite impressive annual rates: −5.7 per cent in 1981, −1.5 per cent in 1982, and −4.9 per cent in 1983. In 1987, after a short-lived export-led recovery, the Brazilian economy plunged into a new recession cycle that lasted into the first years of the 1990s. Although not as severe as the 1981–1983 recession, per capita GNP growth rates turned negative in 1987/88 (−2.3 per cent), 1989/90 (−4.2 per cent), 1990/91 (−0.8 per cent), and 1991/92 (−2.7 per cent). Once again, high-tech industries, strongly concentrated in São Paulo and Rio, were the most affected. For instance, in the 1986/87 period, electrical and communications equipment value-added decreased by 25 per cent, transport equipment by 23 per cent, pharmaceutical products by 21 per cent, and machinery by 18 per cent.

As table 9.4 shows, metropolitan population growth rates fell consistently from 1970, revealing the severe impact of the national economic recession. Nevertheless, the peripheries grew much faster than the capital cities. The highest absolute growth rates were observed in the SPMA during the 1970s and in the southern and northern metropolises in more recent years. São Paulo also leads the metropolitan areas as far as the fall in growth rates is concerned, followed closely by Greater Rio. The concentration of demand-elastic sectors in the two primate cities partly explains this, because such activities are highly sensitive to changes in income and prices. It is also worth noticing that São Paulo and Rio de Janeiro had the most significant drop in

Table 9.4 **Metropolitan population growth in Brazil, 1970–1991**

Metropolitan areas	Population						Average annual growth rates (%)	
	1970		1980		1991ᵃ			
	No. ('000)	Share of metropolitan total	No. ('000)	Share of metropolitan total	No. ('000)	Share of metropolitan total	1970–80	1980–91
RJMA	6,891	–	8,772	–	9,600	–	2.4	0.8
Rio de Janeiro	4,252	61.7	5,091	58.0	5,336	55.5	1.8	0.4
Periphery	2,639	38.3	3,681	42.0	4,264	44.5	3.4	1.3
SPMA	8,139	–	12,588	–	15,199	–	4.4	1.7
Capital city	5,924	72.7	8,493	67.4	9,480	62.3	3.6	1.0
Periphery	2,215	27.3	4,095	32.6	5,719	37.7	6.3	3.1
Southern metropolitan areasᵇ	4,053	–	6,334	–	8,451	–	3.8	2.7
Capital cities	2,729	67.3	3,929	62.0	4,600	54.4	3.7	1.4
Peripheries	1,324	32.7	2,405	38.0	3,851	45.6	6.2	4.4
Northern metropolitan areasᶜ	4,629	–	6,692	–	8,959	–	3.8	2.7
Capital cities	3,558	76.8	4,942	73.8	6,350	70.8	3.3	2.3
Peripheries	1,071	23.2	1,750	26.2	2,609	29.2	5.0	3.7
Brazil	93,165	–	119,002	–	146,154	–	2.5	1.9

Source: Brazilian Statistical Institute (IBGE), Demographic Censuses, 1970, 1980, 1991.
a. Preliminary results.
b. Belo Horizonte, Curitiba, and Porto Alegre.
c. Belém, Fortaleza, Recife, and Salvador.

periphery growth, perhaps an indication that migrants had temporarily loosened their grip on the two largest metropolitan areas.

As noted by Friedmann, world cities are destination points for large numbers of both domestic and/or international migrants. Furthermore, primary cities in semi-periphery economies tend to grow chiefly through internal migration (Friedmann, 1986: 75). In Brazilian metropolitan areas, incoming migrants are first absorbed by traditional services, the construction industry, and informal activities and temporarily settle in the metropolitan periphery. In the long run, migrants tend to perform better than natives, in terms of income and educational achievements.

Migrants comprise more than 40 per cent of the RJMA total resident population and their share tends to be much higher in the metropolitan periphery than in the core city. This indicates the role of the RJMA periphery as a major destination for migrants, not only from its immediate influence area (Rio de Janeiro State) but also from more distant states and regions. The highest migrant share (59.1 per cent) is found in a territorially small county, São João de Meriti, and is also high in densely populated counties such as Nilópolis (24.4 per cent). As far as recent migrants (less than five years of local residence) are concerned, the largest shares are observed on the eastern side of Guanabara Bay in the contiguous counties of Itaboraí (31 per cent) and Magé (26 per cent).

As a general rule, high population density and a shortage of land are characteristics common to world cities. Unfavourable topographical conditions in Rio de Janeiro further contribute to confine residential and industrial expansion, resulting in traffic congestion and an exponential rise in urban infrastructure costs. The very limited supply of new land is an especially acute problem, which in turn causes land prices to rise very fast not only in the centre but also in some of the peripheral counties. Moreover, high densities and poverty combine to produce large slums both in the core and in most of the metropolitan periphery.

Spatial restructuring and articulation with the global economy

From a global perspective, the world city economy performs a set of specialized functions and its growth is based upon a small number of rapidly expanding activities. Among those functions, five deserve special attention.

The first, already mentioned above, involves the articulation of the national economy with other nodes of a global system of world cities. The way such articulation takes place not only depends on global linkages among fast-growing high-tech productive activities, but also embodies local differences in history and cultural factors.

Recent studies of urban development, in both industrialized and third world economies, clearly indicate that technology- and knowledge-intensive industries often locate in large cities and metropolitan areas offering a rich variety of educational, research, and cultural opportunities. These areas become the birth places of new technologies and this capacity is closely related to the labour force competence profile[9] and the intensity of knowledge-oriented occupations in each region. In sum, metropolitan areas in general and world cities in particular have a definite competitive advantage as far as knowledge-oriented, research, and technical activities are concerned.[10] Likewise, agglomeration economies attract fast-growing business services, such as accounting, auditing, engineering, R&D, advertising, computer and data processing, and insurance and legal services.

The second group of world city specialized activities relates to the so-called "headquarters function," that is, the city as a high-ranking decision centre for multinational, transnational, and large national corporations.[11] It also includes regional (in the Latin American sense) corporate headquarters and local offices of multilateral institutions. The third function deals with a headquarters special case, that is, the city as a major decision centre for financial services, such as commercial and investment banking, savings and loans, foreign currency markets, international finance, and stock exchange. The fourth function concerns world cities as nodes of transportation and telecommunications networks and dissemination centres for news and cultural events. The fifth function refers to world cities as major poles of international tourism, that is, as the location of modern lodging and entertainment industries, airport facilities, museums, convention centres, and performing arts centres.

With these specialized world city functions in mind, table 9.5 compares the performance of some of the leading global industries and services located in the two largest and interdependent Brazilian metropolitan regions. First, one should mention the all-important regional and global technical linkages among fast-growing industries such as durables, chemicals, serial machinery, and some non-serial capital goods. These so-called high-tech manufacturing industries (see table 9.5 for definitions) are quite sensitive to demand changes and cycles,[12] as shown by the falls in employment (Rio, −2.7 per

Table 9.5 **World cities in Brazil: Performance of global industries and services, 1985**

World city	Employment			Labour share,[a] 1985 (%)	Change in non-labour share,[b] 1980–1985 (%)
	Number of employees ('000)	Central city as % of MA	Change, 1980–85 (%)		
RJMA	1,172.7		+1.4	–	–
Manufacturing	423.5	75	−12.3	22.8	+7.6
High-tech industries[c]	110.1	83	−2.7	20.5	+16.0
Commerce	381.8	72	+15.1	5.6	−0.3
Wholesale	46.3	83	+0.2	2.5	−0.2
Services	367.4	84	+7.6	25.0	−1.0
Lodging[d]	109.6	76	+12.0	15.8	−1.5
Finance[e]	3.2	97	−40.8	15.7	+5.1
Consultancy[f]	81.4	90	+8.0	30.0	+9.0
SPMA	2,657.4		−0.8	–	–
Manufacturing	1,564.0	60	−10.0	26.4	+3.6
High-tech industries[c]	447.3	57	−10.5	26.8	+2.5
Commerce	586.2	79	+25.8	5.0	−0.2
Wholesale	131.4	87	+32.3	2.6	0
Services	507.2	73	+6.8	25.1	−0.1
Lodging[d]	126.9	76	+4.7	19.4	−1.2
Finance[e]	11.0	64	+57.1	20.5	+6.0
Consultancy[f]	144.3	80	+11.6	32.0	+3.3

Source: Brazilian Statistical Institute (IBGE), Economic Census, 1985.

a. In manufacturing sectors the labour share is defined as the ratio between wages and salaries and industrial value-added; in commercial and service activities, it is defined as the ratio between wages and salaries and, respectively, total commercial sales and total services receipts.

b. See note 13.

c. High-technology industries comprise mechanical industries, electrical, electronic, and communications equipment, chemical and pharmaceutical activities.

d. Includes hotels, motels, other lodging facilities, and entertainment services.

e. Financial and insurance services.

f. Includes legal services, accounting and auditing, business services such as advertising, computer and data processing, engineering and economic consultancy.

cent; São Paulo, −10.5 per cent) over the 1980–1985 recession period. As indicated by their non-labour share positive signs, both manufacturing in general and high-technology industries in particular increased their capital content over the period.[13] Knowledge- and technology-oriented services usually show more volatile locational patterns and are attracted by research and higher educational facilities and access to a modern economic infrastructure (efficient seaports, warehousing, and teleports) and also are less dependent on local and national cyclical changes.

Table 9.5 examines four specialized "global" services, namely: wholesale, lodging and tourism facilities, finance, and consultancy and business services. In some cases, for instance wholesale and finance, it would be useful to have these sectors further disaggregated into domestic and international services; however, such information is not yet available.

Rather than trying to be precise in measuring non-labour variations over time, the final column merely indicates the direction of change in non-labour (mostly capital) factors.[14] A positive sign is associated with the adoption of new managerial methods, modern organizational procedures, and capital-intensive technologies. A reduction in employment might lead, for instance, to a more rational use of existing machinery and the elimination of uneconomical production lines, thus resulting in higher capital–labour ratios. The examples of manufacturing, high-tech industries, and consultancy in both cities, and of finance in São Paulo, illustrate this latter point quite well. In general, employment and labour shares are expected to change in the same direction.[15] In sum, economic recession caused a selective impact on both metropolitan economies. Over the examined five-year period, several manufacturing firms located in Rio and São Paulo were forced to lay off about 10 per cent of their workers and to modernize their productive processes.

In regard to headquarters site, the most recent Economic Census information shows that there were more than double the number of manufacturing firms with headquarters located in São Paulo as in Rio.[16] The difference tends to be even larger for high-tech industries (3.5 times larger), owing to the positive externalities offered by São Paulo. For most services, however, this difference drops significantly, being nearly non-existent in the case of financial institutions.

Wholesale trade can play a really meaningful part in strengthening economic linkages among world cities. In the fairly closed Brazilian economy, however, the significance of international wholesale trade is still relatively minor, especially if compared with world cities located in core countries and with its potential role in promoting the future globalization of Latin America. Total wholesale transactions in Rio amounted to US$7.5 billion in 1985 and represented 70 per cent of local commercial sales.[17] Table 9.5 also reveals striking differences as far as the impact of economic recession on wholesale trade is concerned. First, the entries in the final column indicate that wholesale trade, in both metropolitan areas, underwent neutral technological change over the 1980–1985 recession period. Furthermore, under such neutral conditions, employment tends to be strongly correlated with value-added, or, for that matter, with the level of economic activity. In other words, the large employment increase (+32.3 per cent) observed in the SPMA implies that the national economic recession caused wholesale agents to substitute São Paulo for Rio.[18]

Rio de Janeiro is well known for its natural beauty and busy tourism activity supported by reasonable hotel infrastructure, modern airports, adequate convention facilities, as well as artistic and all-year-round cultural events.[19] The city is also frequently chosen to host national and international business conferences and professional meetings (Gormsen, 1988).

In recent years, the international press has given notoriety to the rise in crime in Rio, which has severely affected the inflow of foreign tourists. The number of tourists, which had reached a peak of nearly 761,000 in 1988, dropped by almost half in 1989.[20] In fact, official crime statistics attest to an increase in so-called crimes against property (larceny, robbery, extortion, housebreaking, and fraud) over the 1966–1986 period. These are the kinds of offence that directly affect foreign visitors and, to some extent, this explains the persistent decline in tourism. On the other hand, both traffic accidents and crimes against the person (murder, attempted murder, abortion, and other minor offences) showed a downward trend over the same 20-year period.

Reliable statistical data on crime are difficult to obtain. Under-reporting is the rule and particular care should be taken as regards contiguous counties located within the same metropolitan boundaries. More often than not, crimes officially recorded as taking place in the core city can ultimately be traced to residents in the periphery. Besides, given the lack of comparable crime information in large Brazilian cities, it is not possible either to ascertain the impact of criminality upon local welfare or to compare metropolitan areas.

Of all the activities in table 9.5, financial services show the most distinctive performance as regards changes in employment and factor shares over the period 1980–1985. Increases in non-labour share point in the direction of modernization and reorganization of the finance sector in both cities.[21] Besides, it is worth noting that employment variations are not only large but also have opposite signs (+57 per cent in São Paulo and −41 per cent in Rio), which means that most of the São Paulo employment growth was obtained at the expense of corresponding reductions in Rio as well as in other large Brazilian cities. Two major factors explain this behaviour: first, a continuing industrial relocation process from Rio to São Paulo and, second, the worsening of the Brazilian external debt crisis, ultimately leading to drastic investment reductions in most federal government-owned companies located in Rio.

In spite of this process, which was aggravated during the 1980–1985 recession years, Rio still remains an important financial centre. The city hosts the open market operations of the Central Bank as well as the largest insurance and foreign currency markets in the country.[22] It is also the location of the headquarters of some of the most important federal government financing institutions, such as the National Economic and Social Development Bank (BNDES) and FINEP, the federal agency in charge of science and technology financing.

Table 9.6 breaks down the finance sector into seven different types of financial institution, each one performing a specific function in the Brazilian capital market. The table shows that there has been a consistent decrease in the number of leading financial institutions based in Rio. None the less, commercial and multiple banks, leasing operations, and insurance companies raised their local transaction values over the 1984–1993 period. Insurance companies, for instance, rank first in the country and managed to raise their share from 41 per cent in 1984 to 54 per cent in 1993. The net worth values of the five largest commercial and multiple banks located in Rio (US$468 million) and São Paulo (over US$7 billion) indicate that, as a result of financial deregulation, many small commercial banks and brokerage firms merged in the late 1980s and were transformed into either small multiple banks based in Rio or larger banks in São Paulo.

Investment banks, savings and loans companies, and finance companies also reduced their aggregate transaction values, both in São Paulo and in Rio, possibly as a direct result of unsuccessful stabilization policies and a lack of an organized long-term financial system. To some extent, the Rio-based finance companies fared better than those located in São Paulo, managing to raise their share from 14 per cent to 24 per cent of total financing.

A further indicator of local financial activity concerns stock market transaction values. Since 1985, the two largest stock exchanges, Rio and São Paulo, have accounted for nearly 97 per cent of negotiable stocks in the country. Lately, however, the Rio de Janeiro Stock Exchange has been losing position to São Paulo, from a 40 per cent

Table 9.6 The number of leading financial institutions with headquarters in Rio or São Paulo and their transaction values, 1984 and 1993

Leading financial institutions	Rio de Janeiro				São Paulo			
	Number		Value (US$ million)		Number		Value (US$ million)	
	1984	1993	1984	1993	1984	1993	1984	1993
Commercial and multiple banks[a]	4	2	1,749	2,183	15	18	6,261	41,621
% of Brazilian total	(13)	(7)	(8)	(3)	(50)	(60)	(28)	(59)
Investment banks[b]	5	2	1,237	331	11	12	3,521	931
% of Brazilian total	(28)	(11)	(23)	(20)	(61)	(67)	(66)	(56)
Finance companies[c]	4	3	404	215	13	10	2,190	415
% of Brazilian total	(20)	(15)	(14)	(24)	(65)	(50)	(75)	(47)
Savings and loans companies[d]	3	2	745	114	7	2	2,111	393
% of Brazilian total	(20)	(13)	(21)	(8)	(47)	(13)	(60)	(27)
Leasing companies[e]	n.a.	n.a.	645	1,681	n.a.	n.a.	955	3,025
% of Brazilian total			(39)	(32)			(58)	(57)
Brokerage firms[f]	20	12	189	58	9	22	83	537
% of Brazilian total	(50)	(33)	(56)	(43)	(45)	(40)	(32)	(71)
Insurance companies[g]	n.a.	n.a.	473	2,334	n.a.	n.a.	476	1,287
% of Brazilian total			(41)	(54)			(41)	(30)

Sources: Central Bank Annual Report, 1994; FGV, *Conjuntura Econômica*, 1994; *Revista Exame*, 1985 and 1994; and L. I. Legey, "Setor Financeiro," October 1994 (mimeo).

a. The 30 largest commercial and multiple banks ranked by total volume of deposits.
b. The 18 largest investment banks by total value of investment financing.
c. The 20 largest finance companies by total value of lending; data refer to 1992.
d. The 15 largest savings and loans companies by total value of housing financing.
e. The 20 largest leasing companies by volume of financial resources.
f. The 20 largest brokerage firms by total net worth.
g. The 20 largest insurance companies by total premium value.

share of the Brazilian stock market in 1985 to a low 13 per cent in 1993.

In spite of its recent poor performance, the RJMA still retains tangible comparative advantages as far as some specialized financial services are concerned. Among favourable local factors one can mention, for instance, a fairly sophisticated telecommunications infrastructure. An ambitious teleport project is presently under way in the decayed downtown area and involves 62,000 m^2 for building construction within a total of 250,000 m^2 with full urban infrastructure and facilities (including access to satellite ground station, fibre optic vertical transmission system, server for voice mail, e-mail, and telefax, hotels, restaurants, video conference room, and tele-centre for voice, data, and image terminals).

An equally significant comparative advantage pertains to the high local concentration of science and technology research facilities associated with concerns owned by the federal government in the oil industry, petrochemicals, telecommunications, and electric energy.[23] In this respect, the State of Rio de Janeiro compares favourably with the State of São Paulo and holds a leading position in the country.[24]

Existing research and consultancy capacity is better represented by the number of technical professionals involved in engineering projects, management consultancy, and economic viability studies. Along these lines, table 9.7 breaks down the number of business and consultancy firms by size classes defined according to the number of technical professionals holding university degrees. It is interesting to note that, although the total number of consultancy firms is nearly the same in both states, the São Paulo size distribution clearly favours those concerns employing more than 100 professionals, precisely the category comprising the most modern and experienced consultancy firms.

Prospective changes and public action

On the basis of the previous discussion, one may conclude that, as a world city, the Rio de Janeiro Metropolitan Area faces two basic economic and political challenges in the coming decades. First, at the macroeconomic level, the city will be compelled to define its future contribution to the national economic recovery effort. In addition, this role will definitely require internal economic adjustments to fit globalization trends and a new international order. The second challenge relates to local efforts to grapple with the accumulated social

Table 9.7 **Business and engineering consultancy firms, by number of graduates, 1987**

Number of professionals holding university degrees	State of Rio de Janeiro	State of São Paulo
Less than 30 (small)	52	44
30–100 (medium)	15	15
More than 100 (large)	15	25
Total	82	84

Source: FINEP, Science and Technology Ministry, 1987, and M. C. O. Schiller, "Novas Tecnologias e Reestruturação do Espaço: O Estudo do Caso do Estado do Rio de Janeiro," COPPE, Federal University of Rio de Janeiro, 1995 (mimeo).

debt caused by 15 years of severe economic recession and to avoid the social costs generated by future economic growth. Because the financial capacity of local governments is insufficient to deal with both aspects, broader institutional reforms and new revenue-sharing approaches are required in order to finance future urban investments in housing, sanitation, health, and education.

Economic recovery and globalization

In the year 2000, the Brazilian urban population is expected to reach 150 million inhabitants, implying an 80 per cent urbanization rate, that is, a pattern similar to that in mature economies. The absolute increase in the urban population will undoubtedly put enormous additional demands upon the already overburdened urban infrastructure.

According to estimates, the vast majority of the urban population will be located in the comparatively modern South-East (46 per cent) and the most notable economic changes are expected to occur in the frontier regions in the west of the country (Tolosa, 1992: 480). In addition, not only will the South-East display the highest urbanization rate (92 per cent) among Brazilian macro regions, but its two largest cities, Rio de Janeiro and São Paulo, will together account for nearly 37 million inhabitants.

By the turn of the twenty-first century, the RJMA is expected to have 14 million residents. The validation of this estimate, however, will strongly depend upon national economic performance over the next few years. Basically, one might conceive of two alternative scenarios. The first assumes zero growth rates – basically the same set of economic conditions that prevailed in the 1980s, that is, recession and economic stagnation. The second scenario is more optimistic and envisages a continuous and moderate economic recovery process led by a select group of export-oriented industries. Growth rates are expected to vary between 4 per cent and 5 per cent a year (below the 6 per cent historical trend). At this point, it is worth mentioning that Brazilian export-oriented industries have always shown a strong locational preference for large urban centres, in particular São Paulo and, to some extent, Rio de Janeiro. Despite generally falling investment rates, these two metropolises still hold a comparatively advantageous position among Brazilian cities as far as infrastructure services are concerned.

Along the zero-growth path, metropolitan areas and large cities are likely to have a demographic growth pattern similar to that of the 1980s (see table 9.4). Likewise, relative inequalities and absolute poverty are expected to increase owing to the lack of urban infrastructure investments. In short, the zero-growth hypothesis seems to be fairly consistent with the estimate of 14 million inhabitants in the RJMA at the turn of the twenty-first century.

Under moderate growth conditions, the recovery period ought to be divided into two stages. Throughout stage one, economic and demographic growth concentrates in primate cities and the hinterland lags behind. As a result, migration inflow to primate cities is reactivated and social inequalities are likely to improve slightly at the national level and to worsen considerably in the large centres. Afterwards, in stage two, growth trickles down to domestic sectors and migration spreads out to lagging regions and smaller cities.

In the real world, the zero-growth and the moderate recovery hypotheses share a common feature: mega-cities are expected to face overwhelming demand for urban services (water, sewerage, housing, health, education, and transportation). Hence, the major public policy challenge for Rio de Janeiro in the future certainly involves being able to provide the financial means to support new social infrastructure investments.

Social costs and local financial capacity

As a general rule, "world city growth generates social costs at rates that tend to exceed the fiscal capacity of the state" (Friedmann, 1986: 77). The 1988 Brazilian Constitution is the benchmark to which all public action ought to be referred. Basically, it embodies a fiscal reform involving the decentralization of public revenue from the federal level to local (state and municipal) governments. Municipalities are responsible for public health services and basic education and, in some cases, provide local public transportation, regulate land use, and protect the historical and cultural heritage.

In fact, most public services provided by the RJMA counties are centred upon health and basic education, that is, the sectors where direct cost recovery is not feasible. There is no practical way to charge those, especially the very poor, directly benefiting from public services. Hence, their costs ought to be financed by general taxes and transfer revenues. There are, however, other public services where cost recovery is not only possible but desirable. This is the case, for instance, with garbage collection and public lighting, two of the most costly local services, where the charges collected do not seem to cover one-fourth of their corresponding costs.

At present, local governments have little influence over some relevant urban prices, such as electricity, water, and sewerage. Electricity tariffs, for instance, are set by the federal government and are the same all over the country. A progressive tariff system is used, whereby low-income residents pay proportionally less. Water and sewerage services usually charge a minimum consumption tariff and tend to be regressive for small and medium consumers.

On average, roughly 34 per cent of Rio's total revenues[25] stem from local taxes and charges, 21 per cent from state government transfers, only 2 per cent from federal government transfers, and the rest from various sources, including credit operations. Local taxes comprise basically a services tax and a real estate tax, accounting for 70 per cent of Rio's tax revenue in 1992.

The services tax, the most significant revenue source, more than doubled its value from US$100 million in 1983 to US$250 million by 1992. As for the property tax, the problems of keeping the property values registry up to date under high inflation conditions led to a continuous reduction in revenues, to the point where the 1989 revenues represented about one-quarter of what was levied in 1980. After 1989, however, the property tax resumed its importance as a revenue source, reaching US$260 million in 1991, that is, an amount five times larger than the 1985–1989 average. Other municipal charges have also shown a fairly poor performance. The reduction in earmarked revenues for the purpose of financing garbage collection and public lighting, for instance, not only reflected a deterioration in public services but also raised the indebtedness of the municipal companies in charge of delivering these basic services.

Since the end of the 1970s, political pressures towards decentralization have been responsible for substantial increases in federal transfers to states and municipalities. Just as an example, the amount of funds transferred to municipal governments increased by 97 per cent in the 1980–1988 period alone.

Institutional and economic reforms at both the national and local levels can be considered an essential prerequisite to internal economic restructuring and globalization. At the institutional level, new global trends towards liberalization, deregulation, and increasing political participation will necessarily lead to further decentralization of economic decisions and new patterns in society's control over the political process.

Finally, given the present high levels of income concentration and metropolitan poverty, one should not underestimate the economic impact of socially oriented governmental policies. Besides being an important source of direct employment, social infrastructure investments also play a significant role in increasing the incomes of the urban poor and improving access to basic services such as health, education, housing, and transportation.

Notes

1. Based on a sample of 116 countries, both developed and developing, Richardson and Schwartz showed that three demographic variables (total population, urban population share, and a Latin American dummy) explain about 40 per cent of primacy (measured as the share of primate metropolitan area in urban population) variance. Economic variables such as gross national product per capita, manufacturing labour share, and the percentage of gross domestic investment in GDP do not appear to be important. See Richardson and Schwartz (1988: 471).
2. Semi-peripheral countries include, for the most part, upper-middle-income countries having a significant measure of industrialization and an economic system based on market exchange (see Friedmann, 1986: 72).
3. This section draws heavily on Tolosa (1996).
4. To be precise, according to the 1985 Industrial Census, the State of São Paulo accounted for 47 per cent and the SPMA for 27 per cent of the Brazilian industrial value-added. The corresponding shares of the State of Rio de Janeiro and of the RJMA were much smaller (10 per cent and 8 per cent, respectively).
5. Petrópolis has recently withdrawn from the RJMA. However, for the sake of official statistical data, all 14 municipalities are usually included.
6. Compared with Rio de Janeiro, the SPMA displays a more even land-use pattern and conforms fairly closely to the traditional radial city model.
7. The urban population living in the Bay basin is responsible for 300 tons per day of organic

sewage and 7 tons/day of domestic solid waste flowing directly into Bay waters. On the other hand, food-processing, chemical, and petrochemical industries and a busy seaport produce an organic load of 80 tons/day, oil discharges of 4.7 tons/day, and 0.4 tons/day of heavy metals. Since the mid-1970s, strong concern with environmental decay has led to comprehensive efforts to deal with water pollution, and the Guanabara Bay Master Plan defines a general strategy to fight water pollution at an investment cost of US$800 million financed by the Inter American Development Bank and Japanese capital.

8. In 1985 the RJMA accounted for 10 per cent and 81 per cent, respectively, of Brazilian and Rio de Janeiro State manufacturing value-added. For the sake of comparison, in that same year, the SPMA national share was 22 per cent and its share in the State of São Paulo amounted to 56 per cent.

9. A recent study for the United States shows that plants using the "most advanced technology pay the highest wages and employ the greatest fraction of non-production workers (who are generally regarded as more skilled than production workers)" (Dunne and Schmitz, 1995: 89; see also Bartel and Lichtenberg, 1987).

10. In fact, over 30 years ago Meier (1962: 152) observed that "most manufacturing in the large cities of the future would be classified as light industry, a type which can be carried on close to home in decentralized plants, mainly by female labour. The moderate quantities of medium to heavy manufacturing required would normally be carried out on industrial estates or on sites served by specialized cities, principally with male labour. But manufacturing need not occupy more than a tenth of the urban labour force. The vast majority would be employed in the services, even with allowance for construction and intensive agriculture to take a tenth apiece."

11. Several of the largest national and foreign companies have their Brazilian operations base in Rio de Janeiro.
    - *State-owned* companies: Petrobrás (oil), the largest company in Brazil; Vale do Rio Doce, the third-largest national company, operating iron and aluminium mining; Embratel (4th), telecommunications; Telerj Telecommunication (14th); Eletrobrás (26th), holding company for electrical energy investments.
    - *National private* companies: Siderúrgica Nacional (6th), steel production; Brahma (21st), beverages; Construtora Camargo Corriea (27th), construction; Petróleo Ipiranga (32nd), oil; Lojas Americanas (36th), retail trade; Cosigua (40th), steel mill; MBR (45th), mining; Emaq Verolme (48th), naval construction.
    - *Foreign* companies: Souza Cruz (17th), tobacco; Shell (34th); Olivetti; Dow Chemicals; Roche; Ishibrás Ishikawagima; Fiat Lux; White Martins; Merck; Texaco.

12. Machinery, for instance, reached its trough in 1983, with a striking 40 per cent reduction in output compared with 1980.

13. Assume an aggregated world city production function $Q = f(K, L)$, where Q stands for product, K for capital, and L for labour. Assume further that f is a linearly homogeneous function and long-run competitive conditions hold in the factor markets. Hence, by Euler's theorem, output can be rewritten as $Q \equiv r.K + w.L$, where w and r stand for wage and interest rates, respectively. In economic terms, this identity means that, under constant returns to scale, if each input factor is paid the amount of its marginal product, the total product will be exhausted by the distributive shares for all the factors. In other words, long-run equilibrium conditions assure that $(r.K + w.L)/Q \equiv 1$, meaning that, under pure competition, the capital share is the complement of the labour share. Under these conditions, the production function can be written as:

$$Q/w.L = f(r.K/w.L) \text{ or } w.L/Q = F(K/L; r/w),$$

that is, the labour share is a function F of technology (K/L) and relative prices (r/w). Likewise, the capital (or, broadly speaking, the non-labour) share is a certain function G of technology and relative prices, that is, $1 - F(K/L; r/w) = r.K = G(K/L; r/w)$ with partial derivatives $G_{K/L} > 0$ and $G_{r/w} >$ or < 0, meaning that, *ceteris paribus*, capital-intensive technologies are positively correlated with increasing non-labour shares.

14. As an example, consider the case of the commerce sector, where $CVA =$ commercial value-added; $TCS =$ total commercial sales, and $LWC =$ total wages paid to commercial workers. The commerce labour share is defined as: $s_c = LWC/CVA$. Since statistical information on LWC is not available, s_c is a non-observable variable. Instead, one defines a new variable, $v_c = LWC/TCS$, that is, the ratio between total commercial wages and total commercial sales. Hence, v_c can be accepted as a "proxy" for s_c only if: $v_c = g(s_c)$, where g is a monotonically non-decreasing function, and $v_c \geq s_c$. Under these conditions, the proxy v_c brings in an upward bias to the estimates of s_c and can be considered a reliable indicator of the labour share direction of change. This same reasoning applies to the services sector and its subsectors.

15. As a matter of fact, labour shares in manufacturing and in commerce and services are not strictly comparable for the reasons already discussed in note 14, which is why no figure is given for the aggregated metropolitan area in table 9.5.

16. In 1985, there were 25,000 manufacturing firms with local headquarters in São Paulo and only 10,000 in Rio. For high-tech industries, the corresponding numbers were 4,500 in São Paulo and 1,300 in Rio. It ought, however, to be pointed out that the size distribution of industries is more skewed to the right in São Paulo than in Rio. In the latter, 1.7 per cent of industrial establishments with more than 100 workers account for 66 per cent of the corresponding employment.

17. By the end of the 1980s, the city of Rio de Janeiro had nearly 10,500 wholesale firms, 84 per cent of them with local headquarters.

18. It is not clear how permanent this substitution effect will be. One should expect, however, a severe and long recession to cause lasting adjustments.

19. The 1991 Rio de Janeiro Statistical Yearbook listed 41 art galleries, 69 museums, 85 theatres for the performing arts, and 12,000 tourist rooms in hotels with three or more stars – nearly 58 per cent of the total number of rooms available in the area.

20. Namely, 472,000 in 1989, 438,000 in 1990, a low of 118,000 in 1991, and back to almost normal levels at 628,000 in 1992.

21. In fact, financial services are among the leading Brazilian sectors as far the adoption of data-processing and new automation methods is concerned.

22. In 1993, Rio accounted for 21 per cent of total foreign currency bought and 32 per cent of total currency sold in the country. In absolute terms this means a local currency market of US$14–16 million.

23. Of the existing 62 research centres in the metropolitan area, only 12 are totally private. Rio also plays a leading role in vocational training for industry, commerce, and services. In 1991, 208,000 students were enrolled on vocational training courses sponsored by entrepreneurial associations.

24. In 1986, the numbers of graduates (M.A., M.Sc., or Ph.D) per million inhabitants were very similar in Rio (697) and São Paulo (672) and much larger than the national average (285). Moreover, the ratio between the number of graduate students and manufacturing value-added is significantly larger in Rio (171) than in São Paulo (80) and than the national average (75).

25. Total revenues remained fairly stable up to 1992, varying from US$1.6 billion to US$2.1 billion.

References

Bartel, A. and F. Lichtenberg (1987), "The Comparative Advantage of Educated Workers in Implementing New Technology." *Review of Economics and Statistics* 69: 1–11.

Dunne, T. and J. A. Schmitz Jr. (1995), "Wages, Employment Structure and Employer Size–Wage Premia: Their Relationship to Advanced-technology Usage at US Manufacturing Establishments." *Economica* 62 (245): 89–107.

Friedmann, J. (1986), "The World City Hypothesis." *Development and Change* 17(1): 69–83.

Gormsen, E. (1988), "Tourism in Latin America: Spatial Distribution and Impact on Regional Change." *Applied Geography and Development* 32: 65–80.

Meier, R. L. (1962), *A Communications Theory of Urban Growth*. Cambridge, Mass.: M.I.T. Press.

Richardson, H. W. and G. Schwartz (1988), "Economic Development, Population and Primacy." *Regional Studies* 22(6): 467–475.

Tolosa, H. C. (1992), "Condicionantes da Política Urbana na Década de 90." In: *Perspectivas da Economia Brasileira 1992*. Rio de Janeiro: IPEA, pp. 471–485.

——— (1996), "Rio de Janeiro: Urban Expansion and Structural Change." In: A. G. Gilbert (ed.), *Megacities in Latin America*. Tokyo: United Nations University Press.

10

Islamic cities in the world system

Salah El-Shakhs and Ellen Shoshkes

Introduction

Islam as a way of life has increasingly become a political movement to reckon with, not only in Islamic nations but also internationally. As a result, major Islamic cities – Beirut, Tehran, Baghdad, Riyadh, and Kuwait, to name a few – have recently been thrust upon the world stage. This is not only changing the place and role of Islamic cities in the world system and in the Islamic city subsystem, but also leading to basic changes within these cities at the community and neighbourhood levels. Assorted Islamic groups, mosques, and associations are beginning to assume a far more active role not only in religious revival but also in providing basic services such as health care, education, nutrition, and welfare. There is a growing civil society and sense of community in Islam, particularly in low-income neighbourhoods.

This change in cities is taking place at the same time that globalization forces and information technology (computers and connectivity) are suspected of rendering central place hierarchies obsolete and replacing them with diffuse urbanized networks linked by a global communications system. Yet there are also indications that the changing nature of work and new technological imperatives are also reinforcing the value of agglomeration. Ironically, evidence seems to indicate that one of the impacts of the growing power of global and transnational organizations (which in effect subordinates nation-states) has been to strengthen the role of cities as the base from which local economic and political autonomy interests are expressed (Jacobs, 1985; Castells, 1994).

Most scholars and policy makers interested in cities and in the urban future seem to agree that a historical transformation of urban form is under way, in response to global processes. Some identify the basis of this transformation as changes taking place within world capitalism, whereas others locate economic restructuring in the broader context of societal evolution. In either case, the backbone of such change seems to be what has been termed "a technological informational revolution heralding an information age," which is triggering a restructuring of urban form as profound "as the onset of the industrial era marked for the nineteenth century" (Castells, 1994). We know that the impacts of this process of global change will be felt first and foremost in the major cities of advanced industrial nations as well as in the growing mega-cities of the third world. Most major Islamic cities seem to be no exception.

This chapter attempts to analyse the impacts of the increasing globalization of economic, technological, and cultural systems, along with the rising tide of Islamic movements and revival of traditional values in the Muslim world, on the development and integration of Islamic cities, particularly mega-cities. We will not address issues of architecture, aesthetics, and design here, because there is already an extensive literature devoted especially to the built environment, notably publications sponsored by the Aga Khan Award for Architecture organization. Rather than deal with the question of rank in global hierarchies, we chose to focus our attention instead on the emerging pattern of regional interactions within the Islamic city system and the local development processes that are restructuring Islamic mega-cities. The chapter is organized in five sections: the first is a general discussion of the impacts of globalization on third world cities; the second describes the Islamic world city system; the third summarizes the recent development history of major Islamic cities; the fourth analyses local responses to globalization; and the fifth section, in conclusion, considers the future of Islamic cities.

The impacts of globalization on third world cities

Any perceptive tourist can observe the visible impacts of the current global process of transformation on major cities in the third world, because airports, business districts, and luxury residential zones now look remarkably similar to those in advanced industrial nations, as a result of the standardization of urban systems. Parallel to this Westernization of built forms, consumption habits also reflect the spread of Western-style dress, music, dance, and fast food. In the new global mass society, however, members of local élites preserve their status by circulating in the exclusive network that links members of the educated, affluent, globe-trotting class in both rich and poor nations. In third world countries, these élites consist of the fortunate few who receive CNN, speak English, and listen to the BBC, have access to the Internet, and do lucrative business with international organizations. Their children are educated at select universities at home or abroad. And they guard their freedoms and privileges by controlling access to the information and opportunities opened up by globalization, and thus present no threat to existing, often authoritarian, governments.

To go beyond these readily apparent impacts of globalization, however, one has to dig deeper into the urban fabric, below the veneer of Westernization and rationalization imposed by modern technology. The two primary causes of the rapid change in the global system taking place today are economic growth and population growth. Therefore, a good place to look for more substantial impacts of globalization within major cities is in innovative local responses to the problems caused by growth, i.e. congestion, pollution, inadequate infrastructure, deficient housing, increasing poverty, and social welfare needs. We suspect that the most promising innovations will probably emerge in the marginal areas within large metropolitan regions, through informal experimentation, and the approaches pioneered by local groups, marshalling whatever resources are available to address the needs of the community in a pragmatic fashion.

The emerging role of world cities

One of the first observers of the magnitude of the global changes under way today was economist Kenneth Boulding, who concluded that "the twentieth century marks the middle period of a great transition in the state of the human race" (1964: 1), a process he viewed as driven by the growth of knowledge; in other words, the evolution of science, of technology, and of society is an interrelated process. Today, many theorists agree that revolutionary advances in information technology and biological science have forged an even tighter link between the economic forces and cultural capacity of society than existed in the past. For example, Castells (1994: 29) argues that, in the new post-industrial economy, "the productivity and competitiveness of regions and cities is determined by their ability to combine informational capacity, quality of life, and connectivity to the network of major metropolitan centres at the national and international levels."

Experts describe the phenomenon of global economic restructuring associated with the rise of the post-industrial economy as characterized by "regional shift, internationalization of the economy, growth of the informal sector, downgrading of manufacturing, flexible specialization of industry, decline of mass production industries, the hollowing out of the corporation, and the domination of central-city economies by financial and business services" (Fainstein and Markusen, 1993: 1468–1469). Global cities theorists explain that one consequence of this restructuring is that the command and control functions of the international economy no longer are concentrated in one place, but now reside in a system of major world cities (global cities) linked by an electronic grid (Friedmann, 1986; Sassen, 1991; Fainstein et al., 1992). The multiple locations within the global city system are not redundant, but serve specialized functions based on the new international division of labour. Moreover, the emergence of this network of decision-making and information-processing centres appears to be giving rise to a new urban form, which Castells (1994) has called the informational city.

Indeed "the potential ability of a city to have direct access ... to any other city or region of the world and the never abating concentration, in the city or around the city, of the most sophisticated intellectual, cultural, and service activities are giving today's city an unprecedented economic and social power" (Bugliarello, 1994: 134). As a result of these linkages, global cities have more in common with each other than with other cities in their national systems. And, as Castells has observed (1994: 29), "[s]uch globalization of urban forms and processes goes beyond the functional and the political to influence consumption patterns, lifestyles, and formal symbolism."

Globalization and convergence

To the extent that globalization triggers urban restructuring, one might expect to see a convergence in the resulting physical, social, and cultural patterns found in major cities worldwide. The ultimate result of such convergence, as suggested earlier, could be the creation of a uniform world culture and the loss of distinctive local identity. Crown Prince Hassan Bin Talal of Jordan expressed the concern of many when he lamented recently that "physically our Middle East cities are quickly losing their centuries old architectural character and beauty. The ravages of vulgar development has dwarfed and distorted the architectural treasures" (Saqqaf, 1987: xii). On the other hand, McNulty and Weinstein (1982: 67) have observed that "contemporary patterns reflect complex ecological balances between indigenous and foreign, old and new, inter-regional and inter-local forces." Rather than leading to homogenization, then, empirical evidence suggests that globalization will produce a rather multifarious urban environment, "filled with competitive conflicts" (Soja, 1991: 362). As a result, we can understand urban restructuring as an open-ended process that unfolds differently in each city, and that is not easily generalized.

Another way to think about convergence is in terms of how different cities resolve these competitive conflicts. In this way we can see convergent patterns of urban restructuring in response to globalization as a parallel trend to what political scientists refer to as "the third wave of global democratization" (Diamond, 1994: 5), and what planners refer to as "alternative development." Friedmann (1992) sees the emergence of alternative development approaches – by which ordinary people "transform the world around them for the better" in the face of increasing global integration – as a parallel intellectual movement to the rise of civil society as a collective actor worldwide and the corresponding rise of broad social movements, in particular the environmental and the women's movements. Alternative development theory essentially shifts attention away from business districts to urban neighbourhoods; and shifts the analytic perspective to concern with the needs of households and quality of life, as opposed to the needs of firms and economic growth. The objective of alternative development, like many ideologies of the 1990s, is empowerment of citizens through autonomy in community decision-making, local self-reliance, participatory democracy, and experiential social learning.

New approaches to local economic development

As a parallel trend to alternative development approaches in the third world, there has also been a transformation of local economic development approaches in the West, focused on enhancing a local community's ability to generate its own economic base. Michael Teitz (1994: 103) observes that "most of the tools put forward as part of the new economic development originated as local responses to particular problems." In other words, the fundamental shift in development activity that has been observed in both advanced and less developed nations has mainly been the outcome of grass-roots mobilizations to improve urban conditions – and innovation that emerged from the realm of civil society rather than from political élites.

In this context, values such as "a sense of place" and "commitment to the community" have become perhaps the most salient rallying cries for organized civic action in cities worldwide. In third world cities, alternative development strategies serve as a unique medium for the expression of the pressures for democratic change that come from "the 'resurrection of civil society,' the restructuring of public space, and the mobilization of all manner of independent groups and grassroots movements" (Diamond, 1994: 4). The implication here is that local politics *do* reflect global processes, and that examination of the impact of globalization on cities should focus on the role of civil society in local redevelopment politics, that is, social conflict over the use and management of urban resources, particularly land.

To the extent that grass-roots groups provide an alternative to the established party system as a vehicle for political participation, we can see the rise of civil society as the informalization of urban politics. Saskia Sassen suggests that studying how informal sectors emerge is an interesting arena in which to explore the limits of old forms and the viability of pre-existing structures; and that the place to look for these informal sectors is within the new geography of marginality created by globalization.[1] It is in the margins, she advises, that people can find room to manoeuvre, as well as opportunities for action. As Krooth and Moallem (1995) note, agitation for change develops at the margins, as a consequence of, or perhaps as resistance to, the Westernizing effect of modernization. These views support the premise of this chapter, that the study of grass-roots planning initiatives can help explain more complex developmental processes at higher levels of social organization.

Table 10.1 **Population size and percentage increase: World, more developed regions, less developed regions, and Muslim countries, 1995–2025**

| | Estimated population | | | | |
| | 1995 | | 2025 | | |
Area	No. (million)	%	No. (million)	%	% increase, 1995–2025
World	5,759.3	100.0	8,472.5	100.0	47.1
More developed regions	1,244.2	21.6	1,403.3	16.6	12.8
Less developed regions	4,515.1	78.4	7,069.2	83.4	56.6
Muslim countries[a]	1,130.0	19.6	1,779.2	20.9	59.3

Sources: United Nations (1993) and US Census, as reported in Funk & Wagnals (1995).
a. Does not include countries where the Muslim population is a significant minority (e.g. in China, India, Russia, the Philippines, and several African countries).

The internationalization of third world cities

The world population has been growing at an exponential rate and, despite recent declines in the overall rate of growth, even optimistic projections forecast an enormous increase of population in the future, particularly in less developed regions (see table 10.1). Furthermore, the world's population is becoming increasingly urban. Over half of humanity will live in urban areas by the end of the twentieth century. Urbanization on such a massive scale clearly has an enormous impact not only on urban areas but also on the world's changing ecosystems. The "'appropriate' carrying capacity" of mega-cities is satisfied not "only from their own rural and resource regions but also from 'distant elsewheres' ... In other words, they 'import' sustainability" (Roseland, 1992: 23). Furthermore, the "ecological footprint" of large mega-cities increasingly crosses national as well as municipal borders, reinforcing the interdependence of national economies.

One implication of this "irreversible globalization of national economies through networks of cities," is that any change in the global economy will be felt not simply within the global cities system in advanced industrial nations but also in the mega-cities of the third world, to the extent that these cities are linked internationally (CEDARE, 1994: 3). Such links include flows of people, goods, capital, and information as well as institutional, cultural, and political interactions over time. The nature and extent of such interactions determine the position and role of cities within global and regional systems, and can be assessed not only by the obvious direct impacts of such interactions but also by the local responses to problems caused by rapid transformations.

Islamic cities in the world system

Urbanization of the currently Muslim countries dates back to such ancient civilizations as those of the Indus Valley, Mesopotamia, Persia, and the Nile Valley. Currently, 7 of the 30 largest cities in the world are in Muslim countries (see table 10.2). These are Cairo, Istanbul, Tehran, Karachi, Lahore, Dhaka, and Jakarta. Although smaller in size, Algiers, Alexandria, Baghdad, Casablanca, Damascus, Riyadh, and Tunis round-up the dozen or so cities that in effect constitute the top layer of the Islamic world's city system. This urban system serves a Muslim population that was estimated at about 1.25 billion in 1995, and accounts for over a fifth of the world's total population. It is projected that the population of these cities will increase by some 59 per cent by the year 2025, to over 1.75 billion, or about 21 per cent of the world population. That is, Islamic countries will have more people than all the developed countries combined. Muslims currently constitute the predominant religious group in at least 45 countries (fig. 10.1). Of the world's large cities of 1 million or more population, 46 are Islamic cities accounting for an estimated total of 144 million people in 1995 and a projected 173 million in the year 2000 (see table 10.3, fig. 10.2).

The development of Islamic mega-cities

The fortunes of the largest Islamic cities are closely tied to those of their countries. In fact both Egypt and Cairo are referred to by the same name (*Misr*) not only in colloquial Egyptian but in most Arab countries as well. Not only are these cities the major economic, political, and cultural centres of their countries but they are also the gateways for most of their global interactions, and to the rest of the world they are in effect synonymous with them. Many of these mega-cities pre-date the formation of their countries as currently constituted, and even pre-date Islam.

The seven mega-cities cited above continue to exhibit a high degree of primacy over their systems. For example, the population of Jakarta is estimated to be 3.7 times that of the second-largest city Bandung; Tehran, 3.0 times that of Mashhad; Dhaka, 3.0 times that of

Table 10.2 **The world's 30 mega-cities by rank in the year 2010: Their growth and share of national urban populations**

Rank	Mega-cities by rank in the year 2010	1990 Population (million)	1990 As % of national urban population	2010 Population (million)	2010 As % of national urban population	Av. annual growth rate, 1995–2000 (%)
1	Tokyo	25.0	26.24	28.9	27.14	0.82
2	São Paulo	18.1	16.16	25.0	15.08	1.77
3	Bombay	12.2	5.66	24.4	6.07	3.68
4	Shanghai	13.4	4.45	21.7	3.58	2.76
5	Lagos	7.7	20.29	21.1	20.91	5.41
6	Mexico City	15.1	24.60	18.0	18.64	0.80
7	Beijing	10.9	3.60	18.0	2.97	2.89
8	**Dhaka**	**6.6**	**35.20**	**17.6**	**32.65**	**5.30**
9	New York	16.1	8.54	17.2	7.23	0.39
10	**Jakarta**	**9.2**	**17.35**	**17.2**	**15.77**	**3.49**
11	**Karachi**	**7.9**	**21.01**	**17.0**	**18.94**	**3.94**
12	Metro Manila	8.9	33.32	16.1	32.24	3.25
13	Tianjin	9.2	3.06	15.7	2.59	3.04
14	Calcutta	10.7	4.97	15.7	3.91	1.65
15	Delhi	8.2	3.78	15.6	3.88	3.36
16	Los Angeles	11.5	6.09	13.9	5.84	1.16
17	Seoul	11.0	35.09	13.8	32.41	0.92
18	Buenos Aires	11.4	41.14	13.7	37.57	1.02
19	**Cairo**	**8.6**	**37.48**	**13.4**	**33.38**	**2.17**
20	Rio de Janeiro	10.9	9.76	13.3	8.05	0.95
21	Bangkok	7.1	58.34	12.7	52.10	3.06
22	**Tehran**	**6.7**	**20.09**	**11.9**	**16.37**	**2.93**
23	**Istanbul**	**6.5**	**19.07**	**11.8**	**18.14**	**3.53**
24	Osaka	10.5	11.00	10.6	9.95	0.00

25	Moscow	9.0	–	10.4	–	0.69
26	Lima	6.5	43.05	10.1	41.26	2.43
27	Paris	9.3	22.65	9.6	20.87	0.15
28	Hyderabad	4.1	1.91	9.4	2.34	4.48
29	**Lahore**	**4.2**	**11.05**	**8.8**	**9.83**	**3.86**
30	Madras	5.3	2.44	8.4	2.08	2.13

Source: United Nations (1993).

Note: Bold type indicates the mega-cities in the Muslim world. Other important cities excluded from this table because of their smaller size include: Alexandria, Algiers, Ankara, Baghdad, Casablanca, Damascus, Esfahan, Kano, Tunis, and Riyadh.

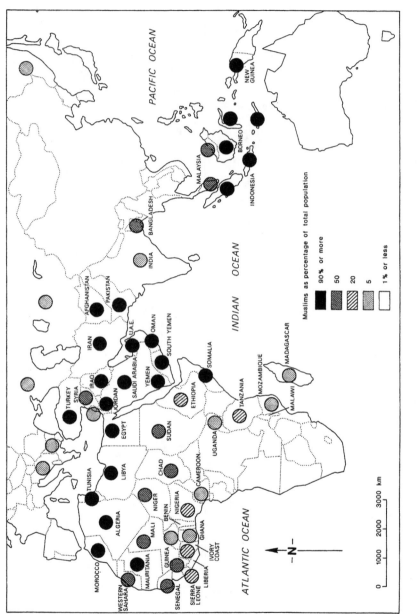

Fig. 10.1 **Muslims as a percentage of the total population, by country, 1982 (Source: adapted from Robinson, 1982)**

Table 10.3 **Total population, percentage Muslim, and large cities (1+ million in 1995) in countries where Muslims constitute the largest religious group**

Country	Estimated population, 1995 (million)	Percentage Muslim	Large cities (1+ million)	City's population (million) 1995	2000
Europe					
Albania	3.4	70.0	–		
Bosnia/Hercegovina	4.6	40.0	–		
Turkey	**62.0**	**98.0**	**Istanbul**	**7.8**	**9.3**
			Ankara	2.8	3.2
			Izmir	2.2	2.5
			Adana	2.0	2.4
Africa					
Algeria	28.6	99.0	Algiers	3.7	4.5
Chad	6.4	44.0	–		
Djibouti	0.5	94.0	–		
Egypt	**58.5**	**94.0**	**Cairo**	**9.7**	**10.8**
			Alexandria	3.6	4.0
Eritrea	3.2	50.0	–		
Gambia	1.0	90.0	–		
Guinea	6.7	85.0	Conakry	1.5	2.0
Libya	5.4	97.0	Tripoli	3.3	4.0
Mali	10.8	90.0	–		
Mauritania	2.3	100.0	–		
Morocco	28.3	99.0	Casablanca	3.3	3.8
			Rabat	1.6	1.9
Niger	9.1	80.0	–		
Nigeria[a]	126.9	50.0	–		
Senegal	8.4	92.0	Dakar	2.0	2.4
Somalia	10.2	99.0	–		
Sudan	29.0	70.0	Khartoum	2.5	3.0
Tunisia	8.9	98.0	Tunis	2.1	2.4
Western Sahara	0.3	n.a.	–		
Asia					
Afghanistan	23.2	99.0	Kabul	2.1	2.6
Azerbaijan	7.7	85.0	Baku	1.8	1.9
Bahrain	0.6	100.0	–		
Bangladesh	**128.3**	**83.0**	**Dhaka**	**8.8**	**11.5**
			Chittagong	2.9	3.8
Brunei	0.3	63.0	–		
Gaza/W.Bank	0.7	n.a.	–		

Table 10.3 **(cont.)**

Country	Estimated population, 1995 (million)	Percentage Muslim	Large cities (1+ million)	City's population (million)	
				1995	2000
Indonesia	**201.5**	**87.0**	**Jakarta**	**11.2**	**13.4**
			Bandung	3.0	3.6
			Surabaja	2.8	3.4
			Medan	2.3	2.7
			Semarang	1.5	1.8
			Palembang	1.5	1.8
Iran	**66.7**	**95.0**	**Tehran**	**7.5**	**8.7**
			Mashhad	2.5	3.2
			Tabriz	1.8	2.2
			Isfahan	1.8	2.2
			Shiraz	1.5	2.0
Iraq	21.2	97.0	Baghdad	4.5	5.1
Jordan	4.8	92.0	Aman	1.2	1.5
Kazakhstan	17.3	47.0	·Alm-Ata	1.3	1.4
Kuwait	1.6	95.0	Kuwait City	1.0	1.1
Kyrgyzstan	4.7	70.0	–		
Lebanon	3.0	70.0	–		
Malaysia	20.1	n.a.	Kuala Lumpur	2.1	2.5
Oman	1.8	75.0	–		
Pakistan	**135.0**	**97.0**	**Karachi**	**9.8**	**11.9**
			Lahore	5.0	6.1
			Faisalabad	1.9	2.3
			Peshawar	1.7	2.1
			Gujranwala	1.6	2.1
			Rawalpindi	1.3	1.6
			Multan	1.2	1.5
Qatar	0.5	95.0	–		
Saudi Arabia	17.6	100.0	Riyadh	2.6	3.3
			Jeddah	1.5	1.8
Syria	14.8	90.0	Damascus	2.1	2.9
			Aleppo	2.2	2.7
Tajikistan	6.0	90.0	–		
UAE	1.8	96.0	–		
Uzbekistan	22.6	95.0	Tashkent	2.2	2.4
Yemen	13.9	95.0	–		

Source: United Nations (1991); Robinson (1982); Funk & Wagnals (1995).

a. Although Nigeria's predominant religion is Islam, Muslims are concentrated in the north, and the largest cities with a majority Muslim population (Kano, Sokoto, and Kaduna) are smaller than 1 million in population size.

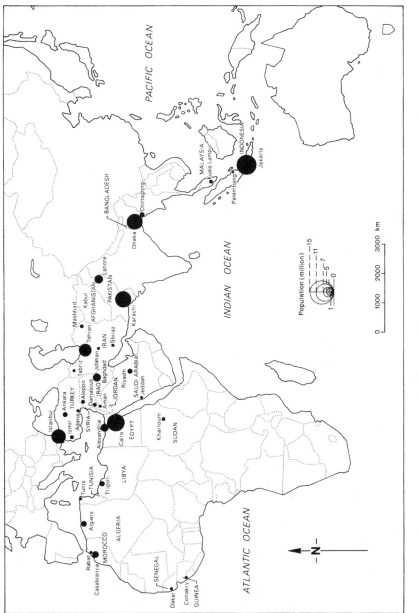

Fig. 10.2 **Major Muslim cities with a population of 1 million or more, 1982**

Table 10.4 **Population of the mega-city as a percentage of its country's national urban population, 1950–2010**

City/Country	1950	1960	1970	1980	1990	2000	2010
Cairo/Egypt	37.1	37.8	**38.2**	38.2	37.5	35.8	33.4
Istanbul/Turkey	**24.5**	21.3	20.5	22.6	19.1	18.3	18.1
Tehran/Iran	22.8	25.5	**27.6**	26.0	20.1	17.6	16.4
Karachi/Pakistan	14.9	16.7	19.1	20.1	**21.0**	20.3	18.9
Dhaka/Bangladesh	23.7	24.5	29.6	33.0	**35.2**	34.8	32.7
Jakarta/Indonesia	14.8	**19.1**	19.1	17.9	17.4	16.8	15.8

Source: United Nations (1993).

Chittagong; Istanbul, 2.8 times that of Ankara; and Cairo, 2.7 times that of Alexandria. However, the degree of concentration of national urban populations in these cities has recently been on the decline (see table 10.4). The degree of primacy of Istanbul seems to have peaked the earliest (in the 1950s), followed by Jakarta (1960s), and Tehran and Cairo in the 1970s. Karachi and Dhaka seem to have just peaked in the 1990s. However, Cairo and Dhaka continue to house more than a third of their nations' urban populations. These cities' primacy has been, at least in part, due to their role as the primary nodes of global interaction. They are the location of the most important or the only international airport and, in the case of Istanbul, Karachi, and Jakarta, the major seaport. They are also the cultural hubs and the major centres of industry, business, and finance as well as, in the case of capital cities, administration. The most sophisticated people and technology (particularly in communication and information systems) are concentrated in or around these cities.

The degree of concentration of population in the largest cities seems to increase with the extent of government centralization (Cairo and Tehran) and with greater overall population density (Cairo and Dhaka). Although the rates of population growth of all the cities have slowed down considerably since 1980 (see table 10.5), they are still growing rapidly. Of all the major Islamic cities, the Asian cities (Karachi, Dhaka, and Jakarta) continue to be the fastest growing, and are all projected to top 17 million by the year 2010. Although Dhaka's population growth rate has declined considerably, from a high of 8.4 per cent in the 1960s, it is still by far the fastest growing of all Islamic mega-cities, at an annual rate of 6.0 per cent. Dhaka is also one of the world's poorest and least-developed mega-cities (United Nations, 1987).

Table 10.5 **Average annual rate of growth of the Muslim mega-cities (%)**

City	1950–1960	1960–1970	1970–1980	1980–1990	1990–2000
Cairo	**4.3**	3.6	2.6	2.7	2.7
Istanbul	**4.8**	4.7	4.6	4.1	3.6
Tehran	**5.9**	5.6	4.4	2.9	2.3
Karachi	**5.9**	5.2	4.6	4.4	4.1
Dhaka	4.3	**8.4**	7.8	7.0	6.0
Jakarta	3.4	3.4	4.2	**4.4**	4.0

Source: Chen and Heligman (1994: 26).

The Islamic world city subsystem

Many of the current major Islamic cities served as seats of extensive empires at different points in their history. Damascus was the centre of the expanding Islamic world under the Omayyads in the seventh and eighth centuries, when Islam spread from China to Spain. Baghdad was the seat of the Abbasid caliphate from A.D. 730 to 1258. Cairo was the capital of the Fatimite dynasty, which ruled North Africa, Syria, Palestine, and the Hejaz (Arabia) from A.D. 909 to 1171. Constantinople, which was the centre of the Byzantine empire, became the capital of the Ottoman empire, and was renamed Istanbul in 1453. Two other Muslim empires coexisted with the Ottomans around 1700, one in India (the Mogul empire) and the other in Persia (the Safavid empire).

Islamic cities of the Middle Ages (Mecca, Damascus, Baghdad, Istanbul, Cairo, Alexandria, Isfahan, and Delhi) flourished with the great expansion of Islamic civilization as an interconnected world city subsystem in the pre-modern era. They were connected primarily by caravan and maritime routes. Most great cities originated as ports on the sea (e.g. Istanbul, Casablanca, Alexandria, Beirut, Jeddah, and Karachi) or along rivers (Cairo and Baghdad) and were well connected by maritime routes. In modern times, however, advances in transportation, aviation, and telecommunications technology gave interior cities that had been relatively isolated (e.g. Riyadh, Tehran, and Ankara) instant international access, visibility, and a role in the world system by connecting them into the international web. Aviation and telecommunications infrastructures are becoming defining elements in any city's world status and ability to assume leading roles in international business and finance (Bugliarello, 1994).

The predominant factor unifying the Islamic world city subsystem

243

continues to be Islam itself. All Muslims around the globe still face Mecca in their five daily prayers and, as the technology and safety of travel improve, they flock in greater numbers every year to that holy city for Hajj (pilgrimage) and Umrah visits. The number of visitors exceeded 2.5 million in 1983, and they pumped more than US$1 billion into Mecca's economy, which constituted more than a third of its annual consumer spending. Hajj is becoming a truly global event without parallel, drawing the community of believers (*Umma*) "from all major world regions and most cultural, racial, and national backgrounds" (Toulan, 1993: 38). It is the greatest global face-to-face gathering and expression of unity.

Other measures of unity of the Islamic city system include the multinational organizations and political movements that link the Muslim world. The Organization of Islamic Conference, headquartered in Jeddah, has the welfare of Muslims around the world as its primary focus. It often rotates its meetings among different cities in member states. The League of Arab Nations, headquartered in Cairo, is concerned not only with political questions but also with issues of trade, foreign aid, and economic development. Its concerns often extend to other Muslim countries. The Gulf Cooperation Council headquartered in Riyadh was established in 1981 to provide a framework for common actions for the Gulf oil countries in the face of the Iran/Iraq war. Finally, the Kuwaiti Fund for Development was created to provide aid for economic development to Arab and Muslim countries.

That sense of community (*Umma*) in Islam, based on faith rather than on kinship (Galantay, 1987), also manifests itself as an important unifying force at the grass-roots level in popular movements ranging from concern for the plight of the Palestinians to the political organization of the Muslim Brothers founded in Cairo in 1928. As a religious movement, the Muslim Brothers initially focused on educational, social, charitable, and religious work and engaged in some economic enterprises. Through a tumultuous history of conflict and appeasement with governments, particularly in Egypt, the Muslim Brothers movement spread into other Arab countries and beyond, and gained moral and material support at different times from conservative Muslim regimes, including the Saudi and Iranian monarchies (Lewis, 1993). The Muslim Brothers' experience spawned several other organizations in different countries. Several of these were more militant but most played a significant role in community development.

Economic linkages have once more become extremely important

with the advent of oil riches in the Muslim countries of the Middle East. The consequent upsurge in employment opportunities, particularly in construction, resulted in some of the largest migratory labour movements in post-war history. Although Muslim labour has moved in great numbers to the West (estimated at 1.3 million in 1977, including a third of a million Algerians in France and half a million Turks in Germany; Miller, 1981), labour moved in even greater numbers to the oil-rich but labour-poor Arab countries (Libya, Saudi Arabia, Iraq, and the Persian Gulf region). Migrant workers represented one-third of their labour force, or 4.5 million, in 1985 (Osman, 1987). They come primarily from the heavily populated poorer countries (Egypt, Pakistan, Bangladesh, Malaysia, Yemen, and the Palestinian West Bank and Gaza) (see table 10.6). Labour comes also from far-off Muslim communities in Africa or the Philippines, as well as much smaller numbers of non-Muslims from Korea and the West. This movement resulted in major transfers of resources in both labour and remittances.

In addition to the circulatory movements of migrant labour, the oil riches also resulted in movements of regional capital and tourists that further connected the Muslim city system. Branches of major Arab banks were opened in almost all major Arab cities. Bahrain took over the function of being the Arab world's financial centre from Beirut after the outbreak of the Lebanese civil war in the mid-1970s (Pepper, 1991). Arab real estate investments, which traditionally went to Beirut, promptly shifted to Cairo and other cities, as did Arab tourism. This is evidence not only that there are interactions in the Islamic city system but also of the substitutability of locations within it, particularly in its Arab component.

Players on the world scene

Thus far we have discussed the interactions within the Islamic city system itself. However, in the new globalism, cities, rather than nation-states or regions, are becoming the global nodes of interaction. Thus specific cities that are well connected in transnational information and exchange networks are likely to play multiple roles in national, regional, as well as global city systems. In order to assess the role that major Islamic cities play in the world system, and conversely the impact of globalization on them, we inevitably have to focus our investigation on a few cities.

We focus on the three mega-cities that have recently been most

Table 10.6 **Income, assistance, debt, and workers' remittances to selected Muslim countries**

Country	GNP/capita, 1992 (US$)	Development assistance, 1991		Total external debt, 1992 (US$ m.)	Migrant workers, 1987 ('000)[a]	Net workers' remittances, 1992 (US$ m.)
		US$ m.	US$/capita			
Egypt	640	4,988	93.1	40,018	586	5,430
Turkey	1,980	1,675	29.2	54,772	180	3,008
Iran	2,200	194	3.4	14,167	–	–
Pakistan	420	1,226	10.6	24,072	450	1,468
Bangladesh	220	1,636	14.6	13,189	180	848
Indonesia	670	1,854	10.2	84,385	45	184
UAE	22,020	–6	–3.7	–	–	–
Saudi Arabia	7,510	45	2.7	–	–	–

Sources: World Bank (1984, 1994).

a. Estimated by the authors based on various ILO and other sources.

visible on the world scene, namely: Cairo, Istanbul, and Tehran. Cairo plays a central role in both the Arab and Muslim worlds in addition to Africa. It is the seat of the League of Arab Nations, and the Islamic world's bridge to Africa. Istanbul has been the most liberalized and Westernized major Muslim urban centre, at least up to now, and is literally the link between Europe and Asia and between the Muslim world and the West. On the other hand, Tehran spearheaded the only successful Islamic revolution in recent history and continues to advocate a non-Western approach to development based on Islamic teachings and values. It acts as both a role model and a proactive participant in Islamic revival movements and in resistance movements in the region.

These three cities also represent the diverse emerging currents of religious, civic, and urban developments in the Muslim world. They embody the diversity of the ethnic and cultural roots of Islam: Arab/ African, Byzantine/Ottoman/European, and central Asian/Persian cultures and empires. Three of the largest Islamic cities – Dhaka, Jakarta, and Karachi – certainly deserve a detailed analysis of their own, which would require another paper.

Cairo at the crossroads

Cairo has been the capital of Egypt for over 1,000 years. Its roots actually go further back to the Arab invasion of Egypt in the seventh century. It served as the capital of the Fatimite and Ayubide dynasties (A.D. 969–1254), which expanded Cairo's influence greatly under Salah el-Din, over Syria, Palestine, and the Hejaz. Later Cairo was a principal provincial capital under the Ottoman empire. Since its establishment in the tenth century, Cairo has been a major crossroads for trade between the East and the West, particularly prior to the discovery of the Cape of Good Hope and the building of the Suez Canal.

At an estimated metropolitan area population of over 14 million in 1994 and a projected 17 million for 2000, Cairo is the largest metropolitan area in the Arab world, Africa, the Middle East, and the Islamic world (fig. 10.3) (Hassan and Atta, 1994; United Nations, 1990). As such it commands an important role in multiple and overlapping world city subsystems: African, Arab, Mediterranean, and Islamic. Khedive Ismael (1863–1879) sought to make Cairo a European city (Ibrahim, 1987). Since then and through the colonial period (British Occupation: 1881–1956), large numbers of foreigners from Europe settled in Egypt, mainly in Cairo and Alexandria. Much of

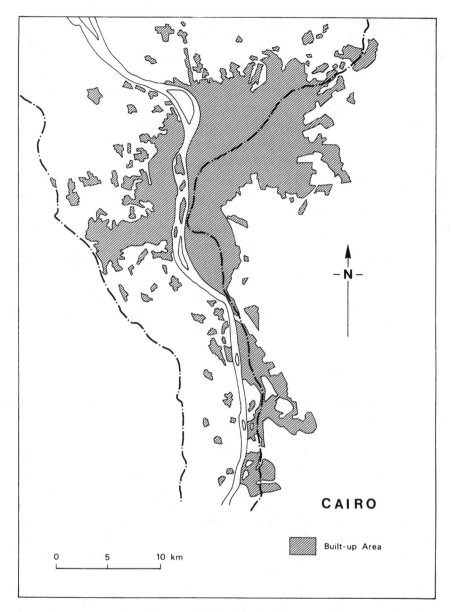

Fig. 10.3 **Cairo urbanized area (Source: adapted from General Organization for Physical Planning,** *The Greater Cairo Plan***, Cairo, 1992)**

modern Cairo (complete with European-like suburbs such as Garden City, Zamalek, Heliopolis, and Maadi) was built during that period by European companies and according to European plans.

248

After a period of experimentation with Arab socialism and public sector centralized planning, Egypt adopted an "open door" policy in the mid-1970s, designed to attract foreign investments. In addition, Egypt liberalized property laws to allow foreigners to own land. There were major increases in foreign assistance to the tune of US$5 billion a year (particularly from the United States following the 1979 Camp David accords). Workers' remittances from migrant labour in the Arab countries amounted to another US$5 billion in 1992 (see table 10.6). Over 3 million tourists brought in US$2.3 billion in foreign currency. In 1992, tourism revenue was more than twice as much as the revenue from the Suez Canal (US$1 billion), and almost as much as that from oil (US$3 billion) (El-Masry, 1992; UPS, 1994).[2]

Cairo became home to the world's largest American embassy, the largest AID mission, and a large number of branches of US multinational corporations, including GM, Coca-Cola, IBM, AT&T, John Deer, and Colgate. American fast food franchises multiplied in numbers, including KFC, Pizza Hut, and, at the last count, 25 McDonald's. Cairo is also home to branches of several international financial institutions. As mentioned above, tourism increased rapidly, accounting for the largest foreign exchange earnings after the oil revenues. Almost 44 per cent of the tourists in 1990 were from the Arab countries (Hassan and Atta, 1994).[3] Thus Egypt and Cairo have become greatly dependent on infusions of foreign assistance and vulnerable to the political whims of the West (Krooth and Moallem, 1995).

During the past 20 years, trade imbalances and the national debt multiplied and inflation became rampant, generally in double digits as high as 35 per cent. Disparities in income and in quality of life between the rich and the poor increased greatly. Eighty per cent of the "new millionaires" of Egypt live in Cairo, and at 200,000 constitute barely 5 per cent of the city's population but receive 50 per cent of its income (Sobhi, 1987: 237). On the other hand, it is estimated that 23 per cent of Egypt's population live in "abject poverty," 20 per cent of the labour force are unemployed, and another 20 per cent underemployed (Krooth and Moallem, 1995). The infusion of capital and remittances into housing drove land prices and construction costs in Cairo to unprecedented levels. Land values multiplied 10 times and construction costs five times between 1975 and 1982 (TAKAA, 1984: 97). Thus there was a disproportionate increase in the supply of luxury housing, while squatters and those living in old cemeteries multiplied at least four times. Poverty-stricken districts function like inward-looking cities unto themselves and house large populations, of up to 1 million in the case of Imbaba, primarily in informal housing.

Despite the fact that Cairo now has a relatively clean and well-run subway system, the number of private vehicles has been rapidly increasing at 17 per cent per annum, resulting in major congestion. Uncontrolled emissions from autos and industries (Cairo continues to be Egypt's primary industrial centre with 36 per cent of its manufacturing labour) contributed to worsening air pollution. Cairo is now second only to Mexico City as the most polluted capital city in the world (United Nations, 1990; Hassan and Atta, 1994).

All these problems notwithstanding, Cairo continues to be seen as the cultural centre of the Arab world, especially in terms of popular culture (Theroux, 1993), and is also the seat of a number of African economic, political, sporting, and social organizations. Egypt has been elected as head of the Organization of African Unity several times (twice in the past decade), and such functions are obviously located in Cairo. Cairo also continues to assume a primary responsibility for Islamic education through Al-Azhar University, which hosts a large number of foreign students and scholars from Islamic countries. Cairo attempts to maintain a leadership role in the Islamic world by steering a fine course between tradition and modernity, while suppressing those who are calling for either a Western-style democracy or an Islamic state. As a result, Egypt and Cairo are currently the scene of major civic and religious conflicts.

Istanbul's secularization

Founded around 667 B.C. as Byzantium by the Greeks, Istanbul has had a long history as the capital of three states: the Byzantine empire, the Ottoman empire, and the Turkish Republic. The present city, initially named Constantinople, was consciously created by Constantine the Great to be a world centre, which grew to be the largest city in medieval Europe with over 1 million inhabitants. It is the only city in the world that straddles two continents (Asia and Europe) across the Bosporus (Danielson and Keles, 1985) (fig. 10.4). This link is clearly not only geographic but social, cultural, and political as well. Istanbul's links with Europe greatly enhanced its economic dominance in the nineteenth century, and its development was strongly shaped by the influx of Europeans, their businesses, ideas, lifestyles, and foreign capital.

250

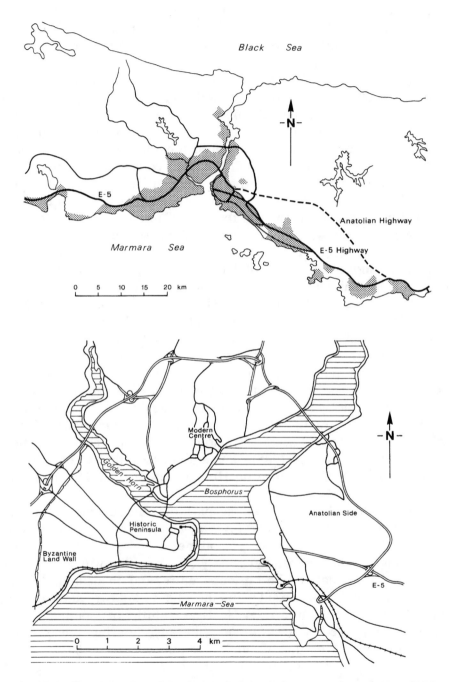

Fig. 10.4 **The expansion of the Istanbul metropolitan area (Source: Noe, 1991)**

251

The reform movements in Turkey started with the *Tanzimat* (reorganizations) towards equality in the mid-1800s. This continued through the Young Turks' pressures for modernization through Westernization at the end of the nineteenth century. It culminated with the Kemalist reforms in the 1920s, which established secular laws based on Western models, as well as a new capital, Ankara, in the interior. Turkey is the only officially secular country with a nearly 98 per cent Muslim population. It is one of only two Muslim countries (the other is Tunisia) that has replaced the Islamic Shariah personal status laws with a gender-equitable civil law code (Moghadam, 1993). It has had a functioning multi-party competitive democratic system since 1946, which provides a great leverage and voice to the urban population, particularly squatter residents. Turkey's democracy, however, has not been without turbulence (Danielson and Keles, 1985).

Though no longer the capital, Istanbul has regained its status as the premier cosmopolitan centre of Turkey. It is the largest port and the largest industrial centre (with a population of over 8 million). It is also the centre for intellectual, cultural, commercial, and tourist activities as well as the preferred residence of the members of the élite in modern Turkey. Istanbul's metropolitan area accounts for only 10 per cent of the population, but is home to 45 per cent of all industry, 40 per cent of all commerce, 24 per cent of all vehicles, 25 per cent of all transportation and communications activity, 44 per cent of the country's hotel rooms, and one half of Turkey's university students. It is the home of the Istanbul Technical University and School of Design, a major regional centre of higher education (Danielson and Keles, 1985). Istanbul hosted the second major international UN Conference on Human Settlements, Habitat II, in 1996.

Turkey often classified itself as part of Europe and eventually joined NATO. An extensive highway system and the Bosporus bridge facilitated greater flows of commerce and goods through the metropolis. The area expanded greatly on both sides, with about two-thirds of the population, the business centre, and financial and trade activities on the European side, and most heavy industry and squatter settlement on the Asiatic side. Nearly two-fifths of Istanbul's population are housed in *gecekondus* (literally, housing "thrown up overnight"), which occupy marginal and publicly owned land.

Recent plans have focused on: the construction of the second Bosporus bridge (1985), the metro project, a world trade centre, another harbour, and five big tourist hotels, along with a host of other environmental and infrastructure projects (IEMB, 1988). Istanbul retains its strategic importance by virtue of its location on the Bosporus, which provides the only access to the Mediterranean for Russia, Ukraine, Bulgaria, and Romania, among others. Land traffic across the Bosporus is also intense (Noe, 1991). This gives Turkey, and Istanbul, a pivotal role in the emerging geopolitical changes in the Black Sea and the Balkan regions.

Tehran under the Islamic regime

Tehran, like other major capitals of Iran, was located along the famous Silk Route of the ancient world linking China with the Syrian port of Antioch on the Mediterranean (fig. 10.5) (Kheirabadi, 1991). Though not Iran's oldest or most religiously revered city, Tehran consolidated its grip on the country. By the 1970s, Tehran had 54.5 per cent of all telephone services, 52.9 per cent of all banking units in the largest cities, and 82.7 per cent of all nationally registered companies. In addition, it had 60 per cent of the national employment in wholesale and 40 per cent in retail, 41 per cent of all insurance companies, and 47.2 per cent of all investment in construction activities (Amirahmadi, 1995).

Like Turkey and Morocco, Iran's Westernization started early in the twentieth century. Reza Shah (1925–1941) decided to modernize major cities by simply driving major networks of long straight roads through the heart of the traditional city (Clark, 1980).[4] In the 1950s the "CIA undercut the plebiscite putting Mosaddeq in power, picking the shah of Iran to replace him" (Krooth and Moallem, 1995: 125). The Shah dutifully aligned himself with the West and embarked on a road of élitist modernization of Iran and globalization of Tehran. By the late 1970s, hundreds of foreign companies were operating in Iran, located primarily in Tehran, in all fields including communication, transportation, computers, and banking.[5] Iran's modernization under the Shah was both alien and authoritarian.

Thus, the Islamic revolution in 1979 was a revolution against political repression, extreme economic inequality and deprivation, Westernization, and perceived Westernized decadence.[6] It was a move towards Islamism in its unadulterated form. Long after the revolution, however, the bazaar and the neighbourhoods around it continue to be the focus of the traditional city and of the poor. The wealthy still inhabit the higher neighbourhoods and, like their counterparts in Cairo, frequent the expensive restaurants where a

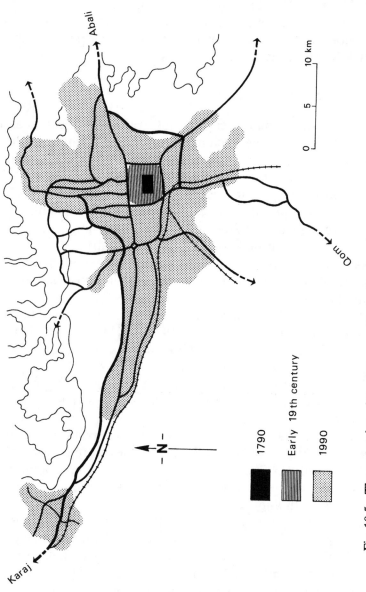

Fig. 10.5   The expansion of the Tehran urbanized area, 1790–1990 (Source: Neikpour, 1995)

family can spend 50,000 rials for one supper, which is a month's wage for the average person.

Following the 1979 revolution, Iran's, and by implication Tehran's, international connections took on a major regional focus, partly because of the severing of relations with the Western sources of capital, particularly from the United States, partly as a result of the Afghan war and the break-up of the Soviet Union, and partly from the desire to become a regional power in central Asia, the Islamic world, and the Persian Gulf. Currently the Iranian government's budget includes an official allocation for the Palestinian resistance movement, and unofficially it helps movements in Lebanon, Afghanistan, and the Sudan.

The headquarters of the Economic Cooperation Organization (ECO) is in Tehran,[7] and Iran plays an important role in the Caspian Sea Organization (Iran, Azerbaijan, Russia, Kazakhstan, and Turkmenistan), and in OPEC. A railroad linking Iran's northern borders with the Persian Gulf has finally made the Gulf accessible to the Russian and Central Asian republics. Iran is home to some 4 million Afghan, Kurd, and Central Asian refugees. Another million or so Afghan seasonal migrant labourers come to Iran for temporary work, and young Iranian migrant workers estimated in the tens of thousands prefer to go to Japan (Neikpour, 1995).

Iran's efforts to re-establish its global connections have shifted east to India, China, and Japan.[8] Tehran has recently inaugurated what is described as the largest telecommunications centre in the Middle East (Neikpour, 1995). The current government has also been attempting a liberalization and a wider open door policy since 1988. High government bureaucrats in Tehran routinely receive CNN in their offices, and an estimated 14 per cent of Tehranians listen to the BBC. The government sponsors a large number of conferences and symposia, inviting foreigners from all over the world, including Iranian expatriates.[9]

Islamic city roles in a global context

Cairo, Istanbul, and Tehran seem to have already developed major regional networks of interactions in which they play a pivotal role. They are likely to strengthen such regional roles in the future and thus command positions as important second-tier nodes in the global city system. This scenario is all the more likely because the Arab countries and Iran (a large part of the Islamic world) control a substantial part of the world's oil reserves, command major capital resources, and represent significant markets. As the Arab oil embargo (1973) and the Gulf War (1991) have shown, the world economies, particularly those of the West, have vital interests in that important Middle Eastern source of energy.

Furthermore, the Muslim world in general and major Islamic cities in particular command strategic locations and control major international transportation links. These include vital oil pipelines and critical sea, land, and rail routes. For instance, the Suez Canal and the Bosporus provide strategic maritime links between East and West and between the Black Sea and the Mediterranean. Also the north–south railroad in Iran provides crucial access to the Persian Gulf and the Arabian Sea for Russia and the newly independent Central Asian republics.

Of the three major Muslim world regional centres discussed above, Cairo appears to be the most likely candidate for a leading role in the Islamic world city system, provided that it maintains its relative economic openness and religious middle-of-the-road path. This seems to be in large part a function of Cairo's ability to resolve transformational conflicts through local developmental processes. Globalization in effect sharpens the basic conflict between the old (population), which embodies "tradition and Islamic values, indigenous culture and ways of life, and the new, which is the incarnation of secularism, modernity, the West, wealth, and power." This is becoming more dramatic in Cairo with the declining economy and the spreading disillusionment with everything Western (Ross, 1987: 58). The increasing frustration, alienation, and identity crisis fuel the resurgence of Islamicist movements, which see "an unholy alliance between the foreign world and the domestic elite" (Ross, 1987: 58), and attempt to resist widespread moral corruption and breakdown of traditional institutions (Jawad, 1994).

Local responses

Since there are no predetermined outcomes to the process of urban restructuring in response to global forces, investigation of restructuring in specific cities should focus more on the process of change instead of indicators of impacts. Rather than search for unambiguous evidence of the direction of change – which implies there is a continuum along which the emergent urban forms have been "more" or "less" achieved – the task becomes to specify what paths away from current practice are likely and what affects the probabilities that one or another of those paths will be followed.

However, in order theoretically to link observations at the micro level of local development to observations at the macro level of global processes, what is needed is a multidisciplinary, policy-oriented approach – a theoretical perspective referred to here as political ecology.[10] Political ecology provides an analytic framework to study urban restructuring on two levels, namely, the ecological and the political. The contemporary concept of the city as an ecosystem is based on a holistic vision of urban life. This view implies that change in one component of the urban system, say economic restructuring, resonates throughout the entire system, i.e. as social change, political reform, and shifts in organized religion. The political ecology framework allows us to explain the broader significance of local redevelopment projects by charting the dynamics of the planning and development process within the urban system. We discuss examples of local redevelopment projects in Cairo, Istanbul, and Jakarta that reveal evidence of restructuring in response to globalization, as viewed from the political ecology analytic perspective.[11]

Cairo: Cultural Park for Children

The Cultural Park for Children opened in 1990, in Abu al-Dahab, a poor neighbourhood in the community of Sayyida Zeinab, "the heart of medieval Cairo."[12] Inserted into this congested, derelict setting, the two and half acre park is like an oasis, filled with libraries, art studios, computer facilities, playgrounds, fountains, and stages. Monuments surrounding the site inspired the park's design, a complex arrangement of geometric patterns, but architect Abdelhalim Ibrahim Abdelhalim relied on the input of local residents to determine the final layout. Although the design of parks with citizen input is a common strategy for neighbourhood revitalization schemes in the West, this approach is still rare in Egypt. At one level, this project is yet another example of innovation diffusion through the agency of educated élites. In a larger context, however, we can see the adoption of this process innovation in Cairo as evidence of a fundamental change in response to globalization.

The Children's Park illustrates how communities in Islamic cities, like other major cities worldwide, seek to accommodate growth and change in a way that allows continuity with the city's past. In this case, the architect developed his proposal for the park around the theme of growth, basing the design concept on the spiral form, as a symbol of growth in nature, and on geometry. The spiral form is dominant in the local skyline, as there are several historic mosques, including in the vicinity. Together the spiral and geometric forms express the integration of the natural and the man-made world – a development objective now valued worldwide. The scheme also proposed that community residents participate in the planning of the park. In this way Abdelhalim is clearly influenced by the work of architect Charles Moore. Moore, an advocate of community involvement in design, has inspired a whole generation of planning and design professionals, particularly graduates of the University of California at Berkeley, where he taught, including Abdelhalim, who studied there. Ironically, popular involvement in design was actually the traditional pattern for urban growth in Sayyida Zeinab, long ago.

But of particular interest here is the way in which the architect mobilized popular support to overcome bureaucratic resistance that threatened to sink the project – a strategy that has been aptly described as "a perfect example of political rather than aesthetic innovation." After his firm won the competition for the commission, government officials kept delaying the signing of a contract. Apparently, "political interest groups in the Parliament" had blocked the project. Abdelhalim recalls: "[T]he people in the community, the real supporters of the project, had no contact with either ... the press [or] the power structure, which in any case [were] confused about the image of the project.... We realized that we would have to mobilize the community to get the project moving.... The opportunity [to do this] came when the Minister of Culture [the client] decided to lay the corner-stone of the project during the National Festival for Children."

The architect proposed that a life-size model of the scheme be built, rather than simply display drawings as is usually done on such occasions. He also suggested inviting artists to create works to be performed by local schoolchildren. "In this way we sought to restore the age-old function of the building ceremony that had been traditional in Egypt, from the Luxor Temple and mosque of Ibn Tulun almost up to the present day." The Minister agreed, and local officials then quickly contracted schools and artists, and transformed the vacant lot into "a fabulous scene." As he reports: "The children began to arrive to rehearse ... while a choreographer ... worked out the performance to follow the configuration of the scheme. When they could not, we changed the ... arrangement. This happened several times and each time the scheme was improved.... I came actually to believe what I had claimed to the Minister, that the great buildings of Egypt were always the result of ceremony."

In this way the traditional event gained new significance, as a way of stimulating the community's interest and engaging their active support for the project. Moreover, it led to the expansion of the project to include Abu-al-Dahab Street, symbolically extending the improvements into the neighbourhood. This was important because, without the help of local officials, the architect would not have been able either to stage the ceremony or to overcome bureaucratic resistance at higher levels of government. The completed park is an apparent success. For example, teachers use the park's historically inspired but boldly modern architectural forms to teach children about the surrounding monuments and local history. And they use the park's geometric features to teach al-Khwarazmi's contributions to mathematics. In this way, the park is the physical realization of the architect's view of tradition "as a living ... 'envelope' of culture." The most important impact of the park, perhaps, is as a testimony to the power of civic action to bring about positive change to help reverse neighbourhood decline, and how the redesign of a vacant lot can provide a dynamic, imaginative vision of a modern future comfortably linked with a proud past.

Istanbul: Community development

In Istanbul, as reported in the *New York Times*: "Room by room, Alawite Muslims in the Gazi Mahallesi district [which is on the European side of the Bosporus] are building their own community centre – a cross between a house of prayer, a social club, a funeral parlor and a neighborhood dining room that can serve 1,000 meals at a time."[13] In doing so the Alawite group is following a longstanding tradition, as the basic organizational units of the cities of the Ottoman empire were communities formed along religious lines.[14] From Belgrade to Damascus, these communities were linked with the rest of the city and society at large through locally controlled networks for the provision of essential services, such as fire protection, police, and education. Today, the old city centre in Istanbul – where churches, synagogues, and mosques, *medrese* and mission schools stand beside the bazaar and public buildings – provides a glimpse into this way of life, where diverse groups mingled while maintaining their own culture. But, as reported in the newspaper, this *cemavi*, as the Alawite community centre is called, "is more than a building. It reflects a newly awakened Alawite consciousness that is forcing its way through the cracks in Turkey's secular state and that burst onto the streets in March in several days of violent demonstrations."

The awakening of Alawite consciousness coincides with recent political gains by Sunni fundamentalists in Turkey, where 98 per cent of the population is Muslim. Alawite Muslims believe in a more liberal version of Islam than the strict Sunni majority. Today Alawites, who number around 20 million, a third of Turkey's population, are relatively free to pursue their way of life, as demonstrated by the opening of community centres such as the one in Gazi and the publication of books on Alawite history and culture. But "they are fully aware that their freedoms are guaranteed by the state under a secular system," according to Msutafa Timisi, an Alawite political leader, who is deputy chairman of the Republican People's Party. Having been persecuted by the majority Sunnis during the Ottoman empire, Alawites are very sensitive to renewed signs of discrimination and "they are ... fully aware that if ever a fundamentalist system was established in Turkey, their rights would be in danger." As a result, Alawite leaders hope to ensure that secularism remains a central tenet of the Turkish state, as it has been since Kemal Atatürk founded the republic 72 years ago.

Recently, however, Sunni Islam has again been on the rise in Turkey, particularly since the 1980 military coup. The Sunni resurgence has reached a point where the leader of the Gazi Mahallesi district, Newzat Altun, commented: "We don't believe that the state is secular because they finance only one strain of religious thought while trying to assimilate the rest." Alawite children are required to learn a Sunni brand of Islam in school, and mosques, which Alawites do not attend, are built with state money in their neighbourhoods, staffed by imams whose training was also funded by the state. And the Alawites, generally considered to be politically tolerant and progressive, feel they are being forced out of local government jobs, either because of their politics or because they do not observe Sunni practices, such as public prayer and, for women, the wearing of veils.

After Sunni fundamentalists won the municipal elections in Istanbul in March 1994, representatives of the new administration went directly to the community centre in Gazi, which was then under construction, and challenged its land and building permits. Eventually, according to the news account, "City Hall backed off, and construction continued." Soon afterwards, however, a group of gunmen opened fire on three outdoor cafés on the main street in Gazi

Mahallesi. When police did not respond promptly, Alawites from all over the city gathered to march in protest. Police attempting to turn back the crowds opened fire and, in the end, 34 people were dead. Huseyin Gulen, a leader of the cultural organization that runs the community centre, was quoted as saying: "Before we didn't feel the need to react to oppression. But firing bullets is something we could not accept."

The predicament of the Alawites can be understood in the context of the debate over the future of secularism in Turkey. One dimension of this understanding is to see the struggle over the community centre in Gazi as an example of how the pressure for democratization, one consequence of globalization, builds in a large cosmopolitan Islamic city such as Istanbul. Here, as in other cities worldwide, the realm of local development serves as the arena in which this pressure reshapes the urban environment. The way in which the community resolves competing claims for control of the use of urban land reflects the dynamics of social change taking place at higher levels of Turkish society. And once more we find groups reaching back to traditional patterns – in this case the neighbourhood organized around religion for service delivery and local governance – as a model for delegating a degree of autonomy to subunits in order to accommodate the coexistence of diverse groups within a crowded urban space and encourage greater political and religious tolerance.

Jakarta: Kampung greening and cleaning movement

The population of Jakarta grew to an astounding 9.2 million by 1990, and the city's metropolitan region now covers an area with a radius of roughly 70 km, extending from the downtown. Informal settlements surrounding Jakarta, known as kampungs, lack most municipal services and basic infrastructure such as paved roads, adequate drainage, and clean water. As a result of the lack of sanitation, frequent flooding, and overcrowding, the environment of many kampungs has suffered serious degradation. Yet kampung residents often lack the resources, organizational capacity, and political clout to improve conditions in their own neighbourhoods. The Indonesian government has attempted to address the problems that arise in the kampungs through centrally planned infrastructure projects. But not only did local governments and communities have little input in the process of planning these projects, they also lacked the resources to maintain them. To make matters worse, as the problems of the kampung grew more severe, owing to the continuing growth of the Jakarta metropolitan region, federal support for municipal infrastructure projects decreased.

In recent years the federal government has shifted its approach to the alleviation of the problems of kampungs. Since 1989 the federal kampung policy is to encourage the private sector and local communities to become more involved in devising local development activities, in order to promote more sustainable kampung improvements. In support of this new policy, "various packages of deregulation and debureaucratization policies have been launched."[15] But in order for communities to take more initiative in the development process, more attention must be paid to building the capacity of local leaders. The greening programme in the kampung Bidara Cina is one such local solution that planners hope will serve as a model for wider implementation throughout Jakarta.[16]

The Bidara Cina programme is very simple: local community council members organized and motivated residents to participate in a gardening and clean-up programme. The programme uses local resources and has produced immediate results. Community gardening programmes are commonplace in large Western cities today, but represent a significant process innovation in the low-income neighbourhoods of Jakarta, which are organized along traditional, hierarchical lines. In the words of one technical reviewer, it "transformed kampung residents from passive recipients of government assistance to active participants in their own development," thereby giving them valuable experience in organization and community action. This involves a substantial change in attitudes, given the local culture, and the design of new organizational structures in which local residents assume more responsibility and accountability for improving their surroundings, without extensive input from the central government.

In 1990, nearly 44,294 people lived in Bidara Cina's 126 ha, located along the Ciliwung River. These residents are illegally squatting on government-owned land and most are extremely poor. The average per capita income of residents of Bidara Cina is less than half of the national average. Bidara Cina is divided into 15 community organizations known as Rukun Warga (RW), which consist of approximately 300–500 households. RW 14, which is situated along the river bank, is the subject of this report. Frequent flooding, poor sewerage systems, and insufficient ventilation of the cramped, single-storey houses make RW 14 a particularly "dirty, squalid, unhealthy place to live." In 1992 a joint programme was launched by federal and provincial government agencies, focused on greening, cleaning, sanitation, and river cleaning. The local council for RW 14 became very involved in the promotion of the cleaning and greening component of this government programme, and eventually turned it into a project that was directed and funded by the community itself. The main objective of the programme, in which local leaders encouraged residents to cultivate plants or small gardens in their yards, is to "develop among residents habits conducive to creating and maintaining a clean and green living environment." It is hoped that this involvement will expand the capacity of the community organization to take on more complex programmes, such as solid waste management, home improvements, or riverbank development.

The RW 14 council has been effective in promoting the enthusiastic participation of residents, as evidenced by the large number of households willing to spend their own money on seeds. In addition the council conducted an information campaign, educating the residents about the importance of proper waste disposal. In doing so, the chairman of the RW council began to delegate tasks to other council members, a departure from past practice that helped make the operations of the council more transparent and accountable. In this way local leaders opened up the decision-making process and began to democratize community-based development activities.

The programme in RW 14 was accompanied by extensive coverage in local newspapers, in an effort to spread the word to other communities, and a competition for the cleanest area in the district enhanced the participation of local residents. This publicity resulted in considerable interest from the leaders of local communities, many of whom have visited RW 14 with the intention of beginning similar programmes. In addition, the federal kampung improvement project will assist the RW 14 council in launching a city-wide "Kampung Greening Movement." As the Mega-cities Project report (p. 20) notes, "Using Bidara Cina as an example, the Kampung Greening Movement is also designed to foster a democratized and community-led process which will eventually provide more comprehensive and sustainable improvements in low income settlements."

As noted in the Mega-cities Project team's evaluation of the Bidara Cina greening project (pp. 26–28), this project serves less as a transferable model than as a successful example of innovation.

The crux of this innovation is the way a traditional community organization, in this case the community council, took on a new role in the implementation of an environmental and developmental project.... [T]he government acted as the catalyst ... to promote local control and utilize local resources.... The Greening Program in Bidara Cina shows the capacity for development often lies within the communities themselves, in already existing, but underutilized groups. By adopting a new role and becoming community organizers, these groups can make development a more responsive and inclusive process, make projects cheaper and more successful, and expand and strengthen the role of an emerging civil society among the poor.

Conclusion: The future of Islamic cities

In summary, a review of the literature suggests that we can come to several conclusions about the general phenomenon of urban restructuring in response to global forces. The extent to which these trends are evident in Islamic cities is directly related to these cities' linkages to the regional and global systems through trade and information flows. First, the globalization of the economy and the emergence of the "information age" appears to be enhancing the role of the local community (particularly large cities) as the level at which local economic interests coalesce and are best promoted. Secondly, despite powerful macroeconomic forces and national political constraints that would appear to undermine local autonomy, there is room for cities to reclaim control over local development and shape their future environment. Thirdly, the degree of local autonomy – in many political systems – appears to be a function of the capacity of local interest groups to form coalitions and engage in collective action. This is a cumulative rather than a "revolutionary" process because social learning is involved. Finally, in order to improve urban conditions, local communities often find it is easier to undertake redevelopment programmes than initiatives in other areas of social policy, such as education or welfare. And the impact of redevelopment projects often extends, symbolically, well beyond the boundaries of a site. As Clarence Stone tells us (1993: 24), in an era when many people have lost faith in planned intervention, redevelopment projects offer opportunities for change that resonate "through concrete efforts that demonstrate how small steps can cumulate into larger moves."

In this context we can understand how the redevelopment process is both shaped by and influences the local outcome of global economic restructuring processes. But urban redevelopment in response to restructuring is an open-ended process – it unfolds differently in each city. And the changes we observe in Islamic cities cannot be characterized as simply the displacement of the traditional fabric by Westernized forms imposed by modernization. That fact that Muslim cities have a distinctive flavour and character is undeniable. However, alongside the symbols of Islamic culture and values, one also encounters the "overwhelming imprint of the modern era: unmistakable symbols of international architecture, modern transportation systems, shanty towns and squatter settlements, industrial complexes, informal markets, and satellite cities" (Amirahmadi and El-Shakhs, 1993: 1).

The emerging city-scape is full of complexity and contradiction, reflecting the complex and contradictory impulses associated with global forces. For example, on the one hand global restructuring appears to lead to the dispersal of activities, while on the other hand the process reinforces existing hierarchies and patterns of accumulation. Nevertheless, we can make some generalizations about the way in which the process is evolving in Islamic cities, which resembles similar patterns observed in the United States and Europe. For example, there appears to be a convergent emergence of similar organizational and process innovations to achieve mobilization of the non-government sector and democratization of local government. In every major city, we see the rise of civil society as a major social actor in local planning and governance. Moreover, we find progressive responses to redevelopment challenges occurring first and most robustly in the marginal neighbourhoods of diverse and dynamic cities, where a variety of other innovations are taking place and where the pressure for change is greatest.

To the extent that Islamic cities seek to preserve their introverted nature, *vis-à-vis* the global system, the visible evidence of restructuring may be hard to detect, as a function of the controlled flow of information into and out of those places. But we have seen that the sheer growth in the size of major Islamic cities, and the consequent added complexity of the structure of metropolitan regions, trigger seemingly universal patterns of change, such as decentralization and the need for greater autonomy for administrative subunits. And although large Islamic cities may be able to prevent or delay the superficial impacts of globalization – in terms of physical forms and patterns of consumption – we have seen that the most important impact of globalization has been the opening up of the decision-making process involved in local development. In other words, the process of urban restructuring in response to globalization appears to be irreversible, even if the outcome is not predetermined.

Acknowledgements

We would like to acknowledge the generous research help on this chapter provided by Anupa Varghese, Hassan Hegab, and Fereydoun Neikpour, all graduate students in Urban Planning at Rutgers University.

Notes

1. Remarks made during a lecture at Rutgers University, 1995.
2. According to Egyptian sociologist Saad El-din Ibrahim (1987), 300 new nightclubs opened in Cairo in the 1970s, double the number built over the previous 20 years. This was very likely a response to the demise of Beirut's entertainment role in the Arab world, and was made possible by the new open door policy in Egypt.
3. An invasion of Cairo by Russian ballerinas-turned-belly-dancers was reported by the *New York Times* (9 June 1995). As foreigners, such dancers are not subject to the moral dress code and performance restrictions that Egyptian dancers are, and thus attract more tourists.
4. Traditional Iranian cities have been greatly influenced by Islam, particularly its Shiite branch. The importance, arrangement, interaction, and use of major public buildings are determined by their religious function, and are usually integrated within the bazaar. The bazaar is an integral part or even the heart of Iranian cities. It usually includes the main Friday Mosque and other religious institutions, forms all or part of the main street, and "is the focus of public life as the major commercial centre, it is also the centre of social, cultural, recreational, religious, and political activities" (Kheirabadi, 1991: 49).
5. There were 25 to 30 companies in communication, 12 in computer services, and 45 suppliers of transmission and distribution equipment. These included General Electric, Honeywell, Westinghouse, General Telephone Electronics, and General Motors. In addition to General Motors there were nine other Swedish, German, Japanese, and American automobile licensing and assembly operations. In banking, some 40 foreign banks, including Chase Manhattan and Citibank, had major branches in Tehran (Amirahmadi, 1995).
6. According to Galantay (1987: 15), the ultimate irritant that triggered the riots against the Shah was the ambitious business project of *Shahastan Pahlevi* to be built on Shah's family land on the hills north of the city and supplied with a subway and modern infrastructure at public cost. It would have brought a tremendous windfall for land owners in the area. Such "accumulation of excessive profit is contrary to the egalitarian and charitable principles of Islam".
7. The ECO was initially founded by Iran, Pakistan, and Turkey as the Regional Cooperation for Development in 1964. After the collapse of the Soviet Union, the ECO was joined by Turkmenistan, Uzbekistan, Kyrgyzstan, and Tajikistan, and in 1993 by Afghanistan. The ECO decided to establish a trade and development bank in Turkey, an insurance company in Pakistan, and shipping and airlines in Tehran. It has an observer status with the United Nations (Neikpour, 1995).
8. International corporations that currently have branches in Tehran include Sony, Panasonic, National, Phillips, AEG, and Caterpillar.
9. An estimated 1.5 million relatively affluent Iranians live abroad, mainly in the West (Amirahmadi, 1995).
10. A concept proposed by Ellen Shoshkes, as described in several unpublished papers including "Political Ecology of Community Based Housing" presented at the ACSP annual conference, 1994, Phoenix, AZ.
11. The examples are drawn from recent publications and news articles, as noted.

12. Description of the Cultural Park for Children and all quotations in the text from Steele (1994: 29–32).
13. This example is based on an article by Celestine Bohlen, "A Sect of Muslims Feels Fundamentalist Threat," *New York Times*, 3 June 1995, p. 2, except where otherwise noted. No other citation will be provided.
14. Turkish national promotional brochure.
15. This account is based on the text of the case-study of Jakarta, as included in Janice Perlman et al., "Manuscript Outline, Case Study Abstracts, Analytic Abstract," Urban Environment–Poverty Case Study Series, Mega-Cities Project, working document for the United Nations Development Programme, New York, 1994. No other citation will be provided.
16. The Mega-Cities Project examined the critical relationship between human activity at the community level and the sustainability of metropolitan environmental policy in the world's largest cities. Case-studies included the Bidara Cina greening project in Jakarta, the source for this example.

References

Amirahmadi, H. (1995), "Local–Global Relations in Two Cities of the Muslim World: The Cases of Tehran and Cairo." Paper presented at an International Workshop on Local Cultures in the Global Cities, Istanbul, 29–30 April.

Amirahmadi, H. and S. El-Shakhs (eds.) (1993), *Urban Development in the Muslim World*. New Brunswick, N.J.: Rutgers University, Center for Urban Policy Research (CUPR).

Boulding, Kenneth (1964), *The Meaning of the Twentieth Century*. New York: Free Press.

Bugliarello, George (1994), "Technology and the City." In: R. Fuchs, E. Brennan, J. Chamie, Fu-chen Lo, and J. Uitto (eds.), *Mega-City Growth and the Future*. Tokyo: United Nations University Press, pp. 131–146.

Castells, M. (1994), "European Cities, the Information Society and the Global Economy." *New Left Journal* Spring: 18–32.

CEDARE (Centre for Environment and Development in the Arab Region & Europe) (1994), *Cedare Chronicle* (Giza, Egypt), 2(2), May–June.

Chen, N. Y. and L. Heligman (1994), "Growth of the World Megalopolises." In: R. Fuchs et al. (eds.), *Mega-City Growth and the Future*. Tokyo: United Nations University Press, pp. 17–31.

Clark, B. D. (1980), "Urban Planning: Perspectives and Problems." In: G. H. Blake and R. I. Lawless (eds.), *The Changing Middle Eastern City*. London: Croom Helm, pp. 154–177.

Danielson, M. N. and R. Keles (1985), *The Politics of Rapid Urbanization: Government and Growth in Modern Turkey*. London: Holmes & Meier.

Diamond, Larry (1994), "Rethinking Civil Society: Toward Democratic Consolidation." *Journal of Democracy* 5(3): 4–17.

El-Masry, A. (1992), *Marakat Al-Iqtisad Al-Islami: Bayna Al-Istismar wa Al-Tawgeeh*. Cairo: Wahbah.

Fainstein, Susan S. and Ann Markusen (1993), "The Urban Policy Challenge: Integrating across Social and Economic Development Policy." *North Carolina Law Review*, June: 1463–1486.

Fainstein, Susan S., Ian Gordon, and Michael Harloe (1992), *Divided Cities: New York and London in the Contemporary World*. Cambridge: Blackwell.

Friedmann, John (1986), "The World City Hypothesis." *Development and Change* 17: 69–83.

———— (1992), *Empowerment: The Politics of Alternative Development.* Oxford: Blackwell.

Funk & Wagnals (1995), *The World Almanac and Book of Facts 1995.* Mahwah, N.J.: St. Martin's Press.

Galantay, E. Y. (1987), "Islamic Identity and the Metropolis: Continuity and Conflict." In: A. Y. Saqqaf (ed.), *The Middle East City: Ancient Traditions Confront a Modern World.* New York: Paragon House, pp. 6–24.

Hassan, M. Y. and T. A. Aboul Atta (1994), "Challenge of Urban Growth in Cairo." Paper presented at the United Nations University's meeting on "The Challenges of Urban Growth in Africa," London, December.

Ibrahim, S. E. (1987), "Cairo: A Sociological Profile." In: A. Y. Saqqaf (ed.), *The Middle East City: Ancient Traditions Confront a Modern World.* New York: Paragon House, pp. 209–226.

IEMB (Institut d'Estudis Metropolitans de Barcelona) (1988), *Cities of the World: Statistical, Administrative, and Graphical Information.* Barcelona: IEMB.

Jacobs, Janet (1985), *Cities and the Wealth of Nations.* New York: Random House.

Jawad, Haifa A. (1994), "Pan-Islamism and Pan-Arabism: Solution or Obstacle to Political Reconstruction in the Middle East." In: H. A. Jawad (ed.), *The Middle East in the New World Order.* New York: St. Martin's Press, pp. 99–117.

Kheirabadi, Masoud (1991), *Iranian Cities: Formation and Development.* Austin: University of Texas Press.

Krooth, R. and M. Moallem (1995), *The Middle East: A Geopolitical Study of the Region in the New Global Era.* Jefferson, N.C.: McFarland & Company.

Lewis, Bernard (1993), *Islam and the West.* New York: Oxford University Press.

McNulty, M. and J. Weinstein (1982), In: S. El-Shakhs and J. G. Lutz (eds.), *Tradition and Modernity: The Role of Traditionalism in the Modernization Process.* Washington, D.C.: University Press of America, pp. 67–85.

Miller, M. J. (1981), *Foreign Workers in Western Europe: An Emerging Political Force.* New York: Praeger.

Moghadam, Valentine M. (1993), *Modernizing Women: Gender and Social Change in the Middle East.* Boulder, Colo.: Lynne Rienner.

Neikpour, Fereydoun (1995), "Tehran in the Global City System." Unpublished paper. New Brunswick, N.J.: Rutgers University, Department of Urban Planning.

Noe, Samuel V. (1991), "Public and Private Responses to Hypergrowth in Third World Metropolitan Areas." *Third World Planning Review* 13(3).

Osman, M. O. (1987), "Population Movement and Urbanization in the Arab World." In: A. Y. Saqqaf (ed.), *The Middle East City: Ancient Traditions Confront a Modern World.* New York: Paragon House, pp. 54–79.

Pepper, W. F. (1991), "Foreign Capital Investment in Member States of the Gulf Cooperation Council." *Arab Law Quarterly* 6: 231–266.

Perlman, Janice (1994), *Environmental Justice: Environment–Poverty Intersection.* Working document for the United Nations Development Programme, New York.

Robinson, F. (1982), *Atlas of the Islamic World since 1500.* Oxford: Equinox Ltd., Oxford University Press.

Roseland, Mark (1992), *Toward Sustainable Communities.* Ottawa: National Round Table on the Environment and the Economy.

Ross, T. (1987), "Cairo's Conflict between the Old and the New." *World Press Review*, March.

Saqqaf, A. Y. (ed.) (1987), *The Middle East City: Ancient Traditions Confront a Modern World*. New York: Paragon House.

Sassen, Saskia (1991), *The Global City: New York, London, Tokyo*. Princeton, N.J.: Princeton University Press.

Sobhi, H. M. (1987), "The Big Urban Bias." In: A. Y. Saqqaf (ed.), *The Middle East City: Ancient Traditions Confront a Modern World*. New York: Paragon House, pp. 227–242.

Soja, Edward W. (1991), "Poles Apart: Urban Restructuring in New York and Los Angeles." In: John Mollenkopf and Manuel Castells (eds.), *Dual City: Restructuring New York*. New York: Russell Sage Foundation, pp. 361–376.

Steele, James (ed.) (1994), *Architecture for Islamic Cities Today*. London: Academy Editions.

Stone, Clarence N. (1993), "Urban Regimes and the Capacity to Govern: A Political Economy Approach." *Journal of Urban Affairs* 15(1): 1–28.

TAKAA (The Aga Khan Architecture Award) (1984), *The Expanding Metropolis: Coping with the Urban Growth of Cairo*. Cairo.

Teitz, Michael (1994), "Changes in Economic Development Theory and Practice." *International Regional Science Review* 16(1&2): 101–106.

Theroux, Peter (1993), "Cairo: Clamorous Heart of Egypt." *National Geographic Magazine* 183(4): 38–69.

Toulan, N. (1993), "Planning and Development in Makkah." In: H. Amirahmadi and S. El-Shakhs (eds.), *Urban Development in the Muslim World*. New Brunswick, N.J.: Rutgers University, Center for Urban Policy Research, pp. 37–71.

United Nations (1987), *Dhaka*. Population policy paper No. 8, Population Growth and Policies in Mega Cities. New York: United Nations.

——— (1990), *Cairo*. Population policy paper No. 34, Population Growth and Policies in Mega Cities. New York: United Nations.

——— (1991), *World Urbanization Prospects 1990: Estimates and Projections of Urban and Rural Populations and of Urban Agglomerations*. New York: United Nations.

——— (1993), *World Urbanization Prospects: The 1992 Revision; Estimates and Projections of Urban and Rural Populations and of Urban Agglomerations*. New York: United Nations.

UPS (Ummah Press Service) (1994), *Annual Report on Egyptian Economy in Egyptian and Arab Press*. Cairo: UPS.

World Bank (1984), *World Development Report 1984*. New York: Oxford University Press.

——— (1994), *World Development Report 1994*. New York: Oxford University Press.

11

Cairo as a world city: The impact of Cairo's orientation towards globalization

Mahmoud Yousry, Tarek Abu-Zekry, and Ahmed M. Yousry

Introduction

Since the early 1970s, the world has been witnessing a continuous process of global transformation resulting in the international division of labour between developed and less developed countries. This transformation has been accelerated by keen competition among multinational and transnational corporations at the global level. As the life of new products became shorter and the cost of research and development increased, the only way to recover costs and ensure continuity was to establish larger markets for consumption and/or production. Multinational corporations moved towards globalization "by locating each phase of the new global enterprise where it is economically best to locate. They develop world-class resources that can supply global demand; they locate each particular manufacturing operation wherever in the world it is most economic to do so; they market products wherever in the world there is a significant demand; and they manage the entire operation where it is best to manage" (Harper, 1990: 29). To facilitate this process, multinational and transnational corporations directed their efforts to extend communications and transportation networks, to cultivate production and services technologies, to ease capital and skilled labour flows among

270

countries, and to develop sophisticated management systems (Peet, 1987; Smith and Feagin, 1987; Knight and Gappert, 1989; Haggard, 1990; Amirahmadi, 1990, 1991; Lipietz, 1992; Sayer and Walker, 1992).

The globalization process has resulted in the relocation and migration of many production and service activities from developed countries to new markets throughout the world. For many governments in less developed countries (LDCs) the globalization process offered an opportunity to recover their budget deficits and lead their development on the basis of an export-led strategy. Governments have been working on the formulation of the appropriate political, economic, and legislative contexts to attract global, market-based production and consumption activities. In addition, governments have promoted national and international industrialization and capitalist development. This welcome response to the needs of capital has reshaped the structure of national economies and their relationships to the world economy (Jenkins, 1984).

Because of its strategic situation in the Middle East as well as its leadership of both the Islamic and Arab worlds, it was inevitable that Egypt would be affected by, and attracted to, the globalization process. During the past two decades Egypt has been going through structural economic, political, and legislative transformations to cope with globalization requirements. Economic reforms, initiated by President Sadat's open door policy (1974) and prescribed by both the International Monetary Fund (IMF) and the World Bank, dealt with problems associated with capital formation, aimed at rectifying interest and exchange rates, and insisted on privatization and cutting subsidies on public services and goods. At present, Egypt is under heavy pressure from international financiers, including the IMF, the World Bank, the Club of Paris, and some OECD governments, to shift from inward- to outward-looking strategies with the emphasis on exports rather than import substitution, and with private entrepreneurship and market forces given a more prominent role to play in the Egyptian economy (Hansen, 1991).

Global transformations, however, have generated many problems in cities of LDCs that have been pulled into the process. These problems include urban deterioration, increasing unemployment rates, environmental pollution, and distortions and imbalances in urban systems as well as in regional development. These problems have indeed been aggravated in Cairo by its orientation towards globalization. This chapter explores the impact of the globalization process on the spatial configuration of Cairo and sociocultural changes in Cairo since the mid-1970s.

Egypt's orientation towards globalization

The adoption of the open door policy

The first legislative step towards the open door policy came with Law 65 of 1971 on foreign investment. The new code provided for a five-year corporate tax grace period and the establishment of free zones, and stated that joint ventures between foreign investors and public sector authorities would be considered autonomous. President Sadat's October Paper in 1974 stated the need for resolute steps towards the economic open door policy. With the issuance of Law 43 on Arab and foreign investment in Egypt in 1974, the legal underpinning for the open door policy was in place.

Law 43 introduced important provisions. First, the law set priorities for investment, encouraging projects that would be self-sufficient in foreign exchange and that would promote Egyptian exports, projects that would bring in advanced technology and management techniques, and projects that would enhance Egypt's strategic position. Secondly, foreign investors could take a majority interest in industries that had been reserved for the public sector such as basic metals, minerals, textiles, and chemicals. They were also allowed to move into the domain of public utilities and transportation services. Thirdly, Law 43 terminated the public sector monopoly of banking and provided for the establishment of private commercial banks. The law created an Investment Authority, within the Ministry of Economy and Foreign Trade, that was to screen investment applications and then obtain the approval of relevant governmental agencies (PADCO, 1982). Free zones, established in Cairo, Alexandria, and Port Said, attracted many projects because the free zones were not subject to Egyptian taxes, and capital transfers could be made without restriction between these zones and foreign countries. In-country projects were entitled to tax exemptions of five to eight years after starting operations and to the duty-free import of equipment and raw materials needed for production.

Later, Law 32 of 1977 introduced important modifications to Law 43 to further ease and encourage foreign investment. Law 32 made it possible for foreign investors to purchase foreign exchange with local currency and to sell products locally for foreign exchange. The open door policy and investment laws paved the way for a vast market for investment and commercial banking. By 1981, 62 international banks had been authorized, 40 had begun operating, and 13 had entered into joint ventures with public sector banks. These banks were joined by 129 investment companies (*Alahram Iqtisadi*, 23 March 1981).

The evolution of the private sector

The extension of a wide range of privileges and incentives for foreign investors under Law 43 prompted reciprocal measures for the Egyptian private sector. Law 73 of 1974 extended to local investors some of the tax incentives provided in Law 43. Egyptian businessmen were allowed to act as commercial representatives for foreign firms. Law 136 of 1974 provided for tax exemptions on capital transfers. Law 118 of 1975 broke the monopoly of the state over foreign trade. Except for strategic commodities, such as imported wheat and petroleum, or exported cotton, rice, or cement, the private sector was authorized to engage directly in foreign trade. Other decrees and laws have followed since the mid-1970s, opening the way to increased private sector activity. In 1975 the private sector was allowed to import building materials duty-free and housing projects in new development areas were exempted from taxes for five years (*Alahram*, 18 May 1975).

The most important legislation affecting the private sector was contained in Law 32 of 1977. It extended to the local private sector several of the privileges granted to foreign investments. These included exemption from prevailing labour legislation, the right to dispose freely of foreign exchange earned by the project, free importation of goods necessary to the production process, the right to export directly without permit, exemption from corporate profits tax for eight years, and exemption from taxes on all foreign currency loans (Arab and Foreign Investment Code, *Alahram Iqtisadi Supplement*, 1 February 1978).

Both the US Agency for International Development (USAID) and the World Bank had taken concrete steps to promote private sector activity since the issuance of Law 32. The World Bank played a major role in the creation of the Industrial Development Bank (IDB) in 1975. Designed to meet the credit needs of private sector industry, the IDB had committed US$100 million to about 3,000 projects by 1979, by means of loans from USAID and the World Bank. USAID has also established the Special Fund for Private Projects worth US$30 million (Waterbury, 1983). Liberalization laws and policies and economic reform steps imposed by the IMF and the World Bank have spurred private sector activities and led to significant Egyptian private investments in industry. Comparing aggregate public and private expenditure in the economy between the second half of the 1970s and the second half of the 1980s, it is evident that the private sector acquired an impressively larger share of the country's resources, expanding from 63 per cent of aggregate demand in the period 1975–1979 to 74 per cent in 1985–1987 (Handoussa, 1991).

Since the adoption of the open door policy, foreign trade has been additionally boosted by increases in petroleum exports and savings in foreign currency accumulated because of remittances from Egyptian workers abroad. Real economic growth occurred in the 1970s because of the country's transition from a socialist to a market-oriented economy. The gross domestic product (GDP) grew rapidly at a sustained 9 per cent per annum between 1974 and 1984, peaking at 10.9 per cent in 1976, compared with 5.3 per cent in the 1950s and 6.1 per cent in the 1960s (Aga Khan, 1985; Handoussa, 1991). The restructuring of the economy is reflected in the changing sectoral distribution of the GDP. Agriculture decreased from 32.2 per cent in the 1960s to 28.7 per cent in the 1970s, and housing decreased from 9.7 to 1.9 per cent, while industry rose from 17.6 to 24.1 per cent in the same period (Aga Khan, 1985).

Exogenous foreign currency earnings, augmented by generous foreign aid flows, however, led to a real depreciation of the exchange rate. The result was a serious misallocation of the country's investment expenditure, which averaged 30 per cent of GDP over the boom period (1974–1984). Further, an excessive bias in favour of the non-traded sectors (infrastructure, housing, electricity, transport, and other services) at the expense of the non-oil tradeables had negative repercussions on the growth and export performance of agriculture and manufacturing (Handoussa, 1991).

Economic reforms and structural adjustment

By the mid-1980s, major imbalances plagued the macroeconomic structure of the Egyptian economy. The balance of payments deficit on the current account peaked at US$5.3 billion in 1986 (15 per cent of GDP) and the budget deficit reached £E8.8 billion (23 per cent of GDP) (Handoussa, 1991). The ensuing recession was compounded by a reduction in foreign aid and capital inflows, making it increasingly difficult to service the foreign debt, which reached US$44 billion in 1986/87 (Handoussa, 1991; Awad, 1991).

In cooperation with international lending agencies, the Egyptian government has taken several steps towards economic reform in order to regain equilibrium in the national accounts. In 1987, an IMF/World Bank structural adjustment programme was adopted in order to reschedule the servicing of Egypt's foreign debt. The reform agenda focused on five major items: adopting fiscal policies to reduce aggregate expenditure and control inflation; reforming and unifying the exchange rate; increasing domestic interest rates to encourage savings, rationalize the allocation of investment, and attract a larger inflow of workers' remittances from abroad; promoting a structure of domestic relative prices through the elimination of price controls and subsidies as well as the adjustment of regulated prices in monopoly sectors so as to approach international prices; and reforming the public sector privatization process and increasing its autonomy (Handoussa, 1991).

The adoption of privatization policies was induced by the enactment of Law 111 of 1975. The government abolished public institutions and replaced them with diversified holding companies, which would be responsible for efficient and profitable operation. In theory, Law 111 weakened state control over holding companies and gave their management more flexibility and autonomy. In practice, abolishing public institutions has eliminated their role as intermediaries between the ministries and public enterprises and, therefore, concentrated power at the ministerial level and led to more bureaucratic bottlenecks (Dessouki, 1991). The structural adjustment programme specified privatization strategies for public sector reform such as direct selling or leasing of state-owned enterprises. In the 1990s, direct liquidation of the public sector through the sale of the shares or assets of state-owned enterprises is under way under the Business Sector Law 203 of 1991 (Yousry, 1992). It is also planned that public sector shares in joint venture companies will be sold to the private sector.

It is hoped that the adoption of the IMF/World Bank approach to structural adjustment, supported by the writing off of a considerable portion of the foreign debt, will result in reducing external as well as internal deficits. Uncertainty persists as to whether the government will manage the foreign indebtedness it has accumulated over the past decade, as well as continue to indulge in extensive domestic deficit financing that has cost the economy an ever-accelerating rate of inflation (Zaki, 1985; Handoussa, 1991).

Cairo's striving towards globalization

Cairo as a world city

Cairo is peripheral to core-country global cities despite its central importance as a gateway between Africa, the Middle East, and Europe. This marginality can be illustrated by "the level of foreign diplomatic representation, and the location of headquarters and secretariats of international organizations" (Simon, 1994: 9). Although Cairo comes top in Africa in terms of the number of diplomatic communities (109) and the number of secretariats of international organizations (75), these numbers are much smaller than in most developed countries. Cairo hosts principal secretariats of only 5 global, international, and intercontinental membership organizations (compared with 135 in Paris and 118 in London), and 63 regional, continental, and subcontinental membership organizations (compared with 563 in Paris and 397 in London) (Simon, 1994). Despite the location of a number of UN headquarters and other international agency headquarters in Cairo, Egypt plays a marginal role in the world economic system. No transnational banks and service firms have their headquarters in Cairo.

Within the hierarchy of global cities (Friedmann, 1986; Rakodi, 1994), Cairo could be considered to be on the second level after world cities. As a regional or continental city, Cairo "performs similar functions within the world's capitalist system to global cities, but within a more restricted geographical region" (Rakodi, 1994: 17). It is not yet agreed upon, however, that Cairo could be of relative global significance to the capitalist economic system as are those LDC cities that are transforming to newly industrialized cities (NICs) and are "increasingly integrated into functional networks of economic linkages with core global cities" (Rakodi, 1994: 17). Elkholei and Abu-Zekry (1993) argue that Cairo has the potential to be an NIC. They point to several essential elements that could lead to an economic take-off. Among these they stress the recent IMF-prescribed economic reforms, monetary policies, and privatization; the writing off of some foreign debts and the rescheduling of the remainder; and favourable foreign currency interest and exchange rates (Elkholei and Abu-Zekry, 1993).

On the *regional* level, Cairo is strongly interrelated with its surrounding world subsystems, namely the African continent, the Arab world, and the Muslim world (Yousry and Abulatta, 1994). In Africa,

Egypt has several times been elected head of the Organization of African Unity (OAU), twice in the past decade. Cairo is also the seat of many African political, economic, social, and sporting organizations. Deep-rooted economic and cultural relations tie Egypt with many African countries, particularly in the north of the continent. Cairo represents the heart of the Arab countries. Cairo is the seat of almost 50 per cent of Arab political, economic, social, and cultural organizations, most notably the Arab League. Egypt provides military support as well as a major labour market, in almost all fields, for neighbouring Arab countries. Cairo is considered the cultural centre of the Arab world; it is the Arab world's Hollywood. Arab tourism accounts for the highest proportion of tourism in Cairo. In 1990, Arab tourists represented 44 per cent of the total number of tourists and half of tourist nights spent in Egypt (Yousry and Abulatta, 1994). As for the Muslim world, Cairo has played the leading role because of the existence of Al-Azhar Mosque and University, which have disseminated Islamic knowledge and thought for centuries. A substantial educational exchange of students and scholars links Cairo with most Muslim countries.

As a *national* city, Cairo is indeed "the focus for national accumulation, and also provides a location for transactional offices and operations, banks and corporate services, and is thus linked into the world economic system" (Rakodi, 1994: 17). An active, yet small and local, stock market is emerging in Cairo. As of March 1994, the number of listed companies in Cairo's stock market was 674 and market capitalization amounted to US$1.5 million, compared with the well-established Johannesburg Stock Exchange with a market capitalization of US$216.7 million (Simon, 1994). Being the largest mega-city in Egypt, as well as in Africa and the Middle East, Cairo is a potential location choice for both transnational and domestic investment and the offices of transnational corporations (TNCs). Even though transnational investment in the country is limited, what there is occurs in Cairo, "the fulcrum of flows of international banking, commercial and industrial capital, travel and communications" (Rakodi, 1994: 18). Foreign direct investment is even more concentrated than domestic investment in Cairo, because of its executives' greater knowledge of the local economic environment and the presence of commercial facilities to intermediate between production and the international market where these are not contained within a TNC itself (Sit, 1993).

To adapt the investment environment to globalization trends and to provide the economic space for investors in the new global market, the Egyptian government adopted two major urban policies, each of which has predominantly changed both the physical fabric and the sociocultural pattern of Cairo. First, extensive foreign technical and financial assistance was acquired to upgrade the infrastructure and transportation and communication networks of Cairo to enhance its target role as a world city. Secondly, the government initiated the policy of building new cities to expand national economic space as well as to divert migration away from existing settlements.

Upgrading Cairo's infrastructure

Public investment trends
The October 1973 war represents a milestone and a breakthrough point in the investment pattern in Egypt. After the war and the sub-sequent 1979 Peace Treaty, considerable funds were transferred from the military budget to economic investment. This alteration in invest-ment is illustrated by figure 11.1, which compares committed public investment in Egypt in several five-year periods (1962–1987). In each

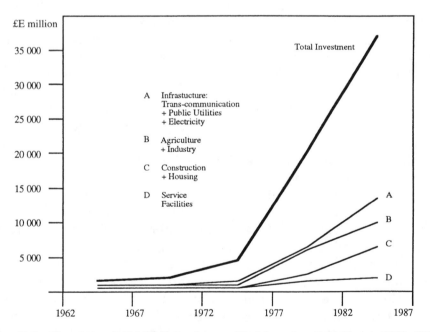

Fig. 11.1 **The sectoral distribution of committed investment in Egypt, 1962–1987 (Source: CIDC, 1990)**

278

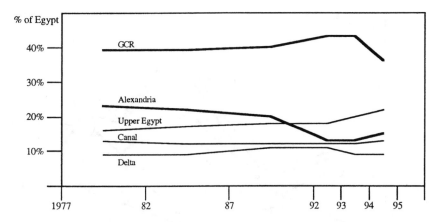

Fig. 11.2 **The regional distribution of invoiced investment in national five-year socio-economic plans (Source: Ministry of Planning, 1977–1995)**

of the two periods before the 1973 war, investments totalled only around £E1.7 billion. They then jumped to some £E20 billion in the period 1977–1982, and to more than £E35 billion in the period 1982–1987 (CIDC, 1990). It is worth noting that this jump was concurrent with the adoption of the open door policy. It is also noticeable that the post-war periods show increasing emphasis on infrastructure (more than productive sectors such as industry and agriculture as well as construction and housing) and decreasing emphasis on investment in service facilities.

Figure 11.2 shows the regional distribution of invoiced investment (actually spent) in Egypt since 1977. It shows a consistent bias in favour of the Greater Cairo Region (GCR), which accounts for about 20 per cent of Egypt's population and yet consumes over 40 per cent of total public investments. This share, however, varies from one sector to another. Figure 11.3 shows the sectoral distribution of invoiced investment in the GCR as a percentage of Egypt. It shows above-average (above 40 per cent) expenditures on infrastructure (public utilities, transportation, and communications) and on construction at the expense of social services. Considerable jumps in the share of infrastructure took place in the period 1987–1992.

Foreign loans and grants were also biased in favour of infrastructure projects. Table 11.1 shows a breakdown of investment into local investment, foreign loans, and foreign grants for both new and existing communities in the decade up to 1993. It shows that foreign loans

279

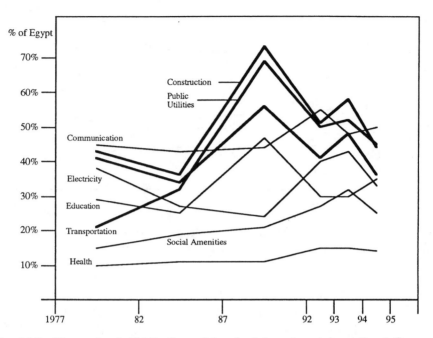

Fig. 11.3 **The sectoral distribution of invoiced investment in national five-year socio-economic plans (Source: Ministry of Planning, 1977–1995)**

Table 11.1 **Certified local investment and foreign loans and grants in the construction and public utilities sectors up to 1993 (£E million)**

Loans/grants	New communities	Existing communities	
		Housing	Public utilities
Certified local investment	4,011	10,247	4,881
Foreign loans (£E equivalent)	236	40	765
Foreign grants (£E equivalent)	34	85	3,300
Foreign investment as % of local investment	6.7%	1.2%	83.3%

Source: Ministry of Development, New Urban Communities, Housing, and Utilities (1993).

and grants for public utilities matched 83 per cent of local investment, whereas they reached only 1.2 per cent for housing.

Greater Cairo Project Implementation Agency
Transportation and communications were notorious bottlenecks in Cairo by the early 1970s. Inadequate maintenance and overloading

severely affected the quality and efficiency of trans-communication systems. In 1975, the Greater Cairo Project Implementation Agency (GCPIA) was established to implement a World Bank-supported Greater Cairo Urban Development Project. Since the late 1970s, the GCPIA has undertaken and coordinated new construction of high-ways, overpasses, housing, and community facilities in the GCR.

More than 10 overpasses were constructed at major intersections to solve traffic congestion problems. Both the 6th of October and the 15th of May elevated freeways have facilitated traffic flow between Cairo's CBD and Giza and have alleviated the congestion on existing bridges between Cairo and Giza. The Helwan–Heliopolis Freeway has provided a substantial alternative for GCR regional through traffic. It is hoped that the GCR Ring Road (GCRRR), to be fully completed by the turn of the century, will solve the problems caused by regional through traffic. In addition, four multi-storey car garages have been constructed to date and several off-street parking spaces have been provided to improve transport conditions in Cairo's CBD.

Extensions of both the 6th of October and the 15th of May ele-vated freeways are currently under implementation to link peripheral districts smoothly together with relatively shorter trip distances and times. All railroad–highway intersections are currently being replaced by free intersections in the GCR to ensure unhindered traffic flows and to decrease accident rates.

GCPIA investments in improving transportation and traffic situa-tions since the late 1970s, however, have far exceeded investments committed for housing and community facilities in the region. Table 11.2 shows this imbalance in investment distribution. Up to 1993, about 85 per cent of total GCPIA investments were spent on trans-portation projects (GCPIA, 1993).

Transport
Public transport facilities have improved remarkably since the 1980s. The Cairo Transport Authority (CTA), responsible for operating buses, trams, and river buses, has improved bus maintenance and overhaul facilities, extended bus routes to low-income areas, and renewed and expanded its bus fleet with new buses and minibuses. The intervention of the private sector with the shared-taxi system, in which 12-seater vans operate on specific routes, especially from densely populated areas, was supported by the Central Traffic Police and was well organized by a drivers' union (Cook, 1985). Growth in this service has taken some of the strain off conventional public

Table 11.2   **Accomplished investments in GCPIA projects, 1977–1993 (£E million)**

Project	1977/78–1981/82	1982/83–1986/87	1987/88–1991/92	1992–93[a]	Total
Regional freeways and GCRRR	12.1	69.2	148.0	28.5	257.8
Intersection overpasses	66.1	39.4	68.2	39.5	213.2
6th of October elevated freeway	60.0	45.0	55.0	55.0	215.0
15th of May elevated freeway	30.0	35.0	0.0	20.0	85.0
Tunnels	0.0	0.0	4.6	10.8	15.4
Total transportation projects	168.2	188.6	275.8	153.8	786.4
Housing	38.0	28.9	48.0	5.8	120.7
Schools	0.4	0.6	0.0	0.0	1.0
Health centres and hospitals	5.4	0.0	6.3	0.0	11.7
Social and cultural facilities	0.0	0.1	0.0	0.0	0.1
Commercial retail facilities	1.7	2.6	1.0	0.0	5.3
Public & administrative services	0.5	0.1	0.0	0.0	0.6
Total	214.2	220.9	331.1	159.6	925.8
Transportation projects as % of total	78.5%	85.4%	83.3%	96.4%	84.9%

Source: GCPIA (1993).
a. The first year of the 1992/93–1996/97 five-year plan.

transport facilities. The extremely high ridership of the Cairo transit system (80 per cent of urban dwellers within GCR), however, has led to the inevitable introduction and implementation of a rapid transit system that will bring added relief, particularly to Cairo's CBD. With the aid of French technical assistance the metro (part subway) system was embarked upon in 1982, the first subway system in Africa and the Middle East. The metro system consists of three lines with a total of 142 km of ground-level track and 30 km of underground track. The first metro line (connecting Helwan in the south with Elmarg in the north-east through Cairo's CBD, with a total track of 42.5 km, 5 km of which is underground in the CBD area) was completed in 1989 with a carrying capacity of 60,000 passengers per hour per direction, and work on the second line started in 1991 (NAT, 1993).

Public utilities
By the 1980s, large areas in the GCR were lacking basic public utilities such as sewerage and potable water networks. Existing util-

ities and networks were completely inadequate to meet the immense needs and increasing demands of the rapidly growing population. This increase in demand was caused not only by the increase in population size and geographical area, but also by the acute increase in density in inner and intermediate districts of the GCR. In high-income districts, sharp increases in land values resulted in the demolition of single-family houses and their replacement by high-rise buildings. The wastewater treatment system was handling a volume of 650,000 m^3 per day, whereas the city was generating about 1,250,000 m^3 daily (Aga Khan, 1985). About half of the volume of potable water was lost because of leaks in the deteriorating distribution network. Existing water and sewerage facilities were operating at 25–50 per cent beyond their design capacities (Neamatalla, 1985).

Several water-supply projects have been implemented since the 1980s. Projects included upgrading and constructing new water treatment plants, pump stations, water tanks, and water networks. The cost of water-supply projects is estimated to reach US$2.9 billion (Aga Khan, 1985). These projects have increased water-supply capacity by about 1.5 million m^3 per day (GOGCWS, 1993). In 1979 a Cairo Waterworks Master Plan was approved to increase the reliability of the existing system as well as to construct additional waterworks facilities to meet the needs of the GCR population. In 1981, the Cairo Waterworks Organization (CWO) was specially established to implement and coordinate the plan's wastewater projects, which represented one of the largest sewerage projects in the world. USAID, the British Overseas Development Administration, as well as some OECD countries have assisted with both funding and technical consultation for the Cairo Master Plan projects. Extensive projects, with an estimated cost expected to exceed £E10 billion, have focused on: improvement of existing wastewater systems; rehabilitation and renewal of existing major pumping and ejector stations; and expanding the wastewater system in the GCR in three sectors, namely, the East Bank (Cairo and Shubra Elkheima), the West Bank (Giza), and Helwan (CGOSD, 1992). Table 11.3, showing the detail of investments for these projects, demonstrates huge investments in both implemented and future wastewater projects.

Telecommunications

Telecommunications too have developed immensely. The number of telephone lines reached about 3 million in 1994, compared with only half a million lines in 1981/82 (see table 11.4). About half of these are

283

Table 11.3 **Investment in Cairo Waterworks Master Plan's wastewater projects (£E million)**

Project	Investment invoiced for executed projects, 1981 to March 1992	Investment certified for projects under construction as of March 1992	Investment committed for projects in the 5-year National Plan 92/93–96/97	Investment committed for projects not included in the 5-year National Plan 92–97	Total invoiced, certified, and committed investment
Existing system improvement	8	23	165	0	196
Existing system rehabilitation	249	0	0	0	249
East Bank system expansion	1,761	1,230	400	1,470	4,861
West Bank system expansion	1,964	407	660	1,375	4,406
Helwan wastewater project	338	114	91	280	823
Total investment	4,320	1,774	1,316	3,125	10,535

Source: CGOSD (1992).

Expansion of the telephone system in Egypt, 1982/83–1993/94

Indicator	1982/83[a]	1987/88[a]	1992/93[a]	1993/94[b]
Number of telephone lines ('000)	575	1,450	2,530	3,320
International-call volume (million minutes)	62	159	315	360

Source: NCA (1994).
a. The first year of the 1982/83–86/87, 1987/88–91/92, and 1992/93–96/97 five-year plans.
b. Committed.

in the GCR (see appendix table 11A.1). The number of public telephones increased from 250 to 4,570, and car phones from 400 to 7,500 between 1981 and 1994. In the same period, international telephone-call volume increased from 62 to 360 million minutes; the number of countries that could be dialled direct rose from 29 to 217; and the capacity of international central units leapt from 160,000 to more than 7.5 million telephone lines (NCA, 1994).

Urban development

Plans and policies for the Greater Cairo Region
The metropolitan area encompassing the cities of Cairo, Giza, and Shubra Elkheima and some small surrounding urbanized settlements forms the urban conurbation of the GCR (see fig. 11.4). The population of the GCR was estimated at more than 12 million in 1994, representing more than 20 per cent of Egypt's total population and about 40 per cent of its urban population (Yousry and Abulatta, 1994). In 1974, a Master Plan for the GCR was approved by a Ministerial Decree to tackle the ongoing and future problems of the urban agglomeration. The two main concepts governing the 1974 Master Plan were: (a) establishing self-sufficient new towns to act as relief poles to accommodate new migrants to the GCR, and (b) controlling the growth of the existing agglomeration in order to end urban encroachment on arable land and to keep the agglomeration to a manageable size (Gorgy, 1985). These two development concepts eventually led to, first, the establishment of the satellite cities of 6th of October, Elobour, 15th of May, and Badr (at a later stage), and, second, the construction of the ring road around the GCR. Subsequently the 1974 plan had to be updated to take into account the

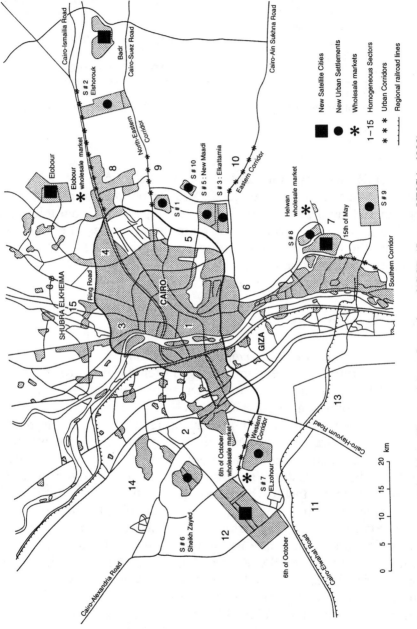

Fig. 11.4 The spatial configuration of GCR (Source: NUCA, 1993)

GCR-related recommendations of the National Urban Policy Study (NUPS) carried out in the early 1980s (Shorter, 1989; Cornu, 1985), as well as the important socio-economic changes that occurred after 1974 as a result of the open door policy, which drastically changed public and private investment patterns (Gorgy, 1985). A 1983 GCR Master Plan aimed at increasing the productive capacity of the economy by protecting agricultural land, directing industrial location, improving transport efficiency, maximizing the use of infrastructure, and protecting the archaeological and historical heritage. The Master Plan also aimed at improving the living environment in the Greater Cairo agglomeration by directing growth to new settlements, providing alternatives to informal areas, improving access to public services, rehabilitating old neighbourhoods, protecting water resources, and controlling air pollution (Aga Khan, 1985; Gorgy, 1985). To meet these objectives, four development and spatial concepts underlie past and current planning approaches:

1. The conceptualization of the GCR as an *urban region*, a heterogeneous entity to be dealt with on an integrated regional basis;
2. The subdivision of the GCR into *homogeneous sectors*, to restructure the agglomeration into contrasting autonomous geographic entities;
3. the establishment of *new settlements*, located beyond the GCR ring road, offering an alternative to informal settlements and taking advantage of existing employment in the GCR;
4. the fostering of development between the existing agglomeration and other existing and new economic centres and settlements by creating *development corridors* (see fig. 11.4).

Recent urban policies and actions illustrate these spatial concepts. Ten new settlements, with a target population of 250,000 each, have been planned, half of which are currently being developed (table 11.5). Development corridors are being delineated with respect to the planning of new centres and new settlements. Four development corridors have been determined and aim at the following population distributions: North-Eastern Corridor (Cairo–Suez and Cairo–Ismailia roads) 250,000; Eastern Corridor (Cairo–Suez and Cairo–Ain Sukhna roads) 750,000; Western Corridor (Cairo–Elwahat road) 700,000; and Southern Corridor (Maadi–Helwan road) 500,000 inhabitants (NUCA, 1993). Three new wholesale markets are being established to serve the GCR by the turn of the century. The markets are located on the outskirts of the GCR on urban growth corridors near newly

Table 11.5 **New urban settlements around the GCR, 1993**

New urban settlements	Master Plan target population ('000)	Master Plan built-up area (km²)	Distance from Cairo CBD (km)	Location in Cairo	Location on regional roads	Remarks[a]
S # 1	250	n.a.	30	East	Cairo–Suez	1
S # 2: Elshorouk	250	18.9	38	North-east	Cairo–Suez Cairo–Ismailia	2
S # 3: Elkattamia	250	7.6	25	East	Cairo–Ain Sukhna	2
S # 4	n.a.	n.a.	n.a.	North-east	n.a.	3
S # 5: New Maadi	250	9.1	23	East	Ring Road	2
S # 6: Sheikh Zayed	450	15.7	30	West	Cairo–Elwahat	2
S # 7: ELzohour	250	n.a.	25	West	Cairo–Elwahat	1
S # 8	250	n.a.	30	South	15th of May Ring Road	1
S # 9	250	n.a.	35	South	n.a.	3
S # 10	n.a.	n.a.	n.a.	East	Ring Road	3
Total	2,200	51.3				

Source: NUCA (1993).
a. 1 = planned, not yet implemented; 2 = in the implementation phase; 3 = in the planning stage.

established satellite cities: in the north-east near Elobour, in the south-west near 6th of October, and in the south near 15th of May (see fig. 11.4). The markets will reduce congestion in the GCR as well as improve the performance of wholesale activity in meeting GCR needs. Elobour wholesale market has been established and has started operations. Development costs have reached about £E100 million, and annual transaction activity is estimated at £E3 billion (NUCA, 1993).

New cities policy
The New Urban Communities Authority (NUCA) was established under Law 59 of 1979 on new urban communities. The area of land used or designated for new urban communities has reached about 2,535 km^2, representing 18 per cent of the built-up area of Egypt since 1978. The area of land supplied with infrastructure has reached about 70 km^2 and the population in new communities approaches 250,000 inhabitants (NUCA, 1993).

The new urban community movement started with the establishment of economically independent cities, away from the GCR, to provide new development poles (10th of Ramadan, Sadat, and Borg Elarab). By the mid-1980s, the trend had changed towards dependent satellite cities around the GCR (6th of October, Elobour, 15th of May, and Badr). Smaller in size and located near major urban centres, these cities would be able to rely on functions and services offered by the existing city. At the same time, they would relieve many of the urban-related problems associated with the existing city. Table 11.6 shows some data for the new cities.

Several incentives were used to stimulate industrial development in the new cities. Foreign investment laws discussed above provide 10-year tax exemptions on project land and profits located in new cities. Foreign investors can freely transfer foreign currency profits. Law 59 of 1979 and Law 186 of 1986 further exempted equipment needed for industries to be established in new cities from custom tariffs (NUCA, 1993).

Among the various industries established in new cities, the mechanical, electrical, electronic, chemical, pharmaceutical, textile, and food-processing industries are the most important for both local markets and international trade. Up to 1993, as table 11.7 shows, 1,059 factories had been built on 12.5 km^2, with capital investment approaching £E4 billion and yearly production of about £E4.7 billion. About 700 factories were under construction, covering an area of

Table 11.6 **Facts and figures on new cities in Egypt, 1993**

New cities	Master Plan target population ('000)	Residential & services area according to Master Plan (km²)	Industrial zone area according to Master Plan (km²)	No. of housing units constructed/under construction	Residential & services area provided with infrastructure (km²)	Industrial zone area provided with infrastructure (km²)
Independent new cities						
10th of Ramadan	500	45.0	11.0	23,947	7.3	10.7
Sadat	500	37.8	10.0	15,532	1.3	2.8
Borg Elarab	500	41.2	6.6	8,649	1.2	3.6
Satellite cities						
6th of October	500	40.5	19.5	24,155	20.3	10.4
15th of May	250	12.4	0.0	25,824	4.3	0.0
Elobour	250	18.2	2.8	13,976	5.6	0.0
Badr	250	12.6	3.0	19,394	0.7	0.5
New settlements around						
GCR	2,200	51.3	0.0	42,940	1.2	0.0
Total	4,950	259.0	52.9	174,417	41.9	28.0

Source: NUCA (1993).

Table 11.7 **Industries in new cities, 1993**

New cities	Established industries			Industries under construction		
	No. of factories	Capital investment (£E m.)	Yearly production (£E m.)	No. of factories	Capital investment (£E m.)	Yearly production (£E m.)
10th of Ramadan	531	2,542.4	2,850.0	263	9,040.5	1,289.3
Sadat	96	309.9	619.4	82	502.0	828.1
Borg Elarab	146	440.0	612.1	108	281.5	325.6
6th of October	286	664.7	654.2	245	378.5	795.2
Total	1,059	3,957.0	4,735.7	698	10,202.5	3,238.2

Source: NUCA (1993).

6 km^2, with capital investment of £E10.2 billion and yearly production of £E3.2 billion (NUCA, 1993).

Housing development in new communities has been mainly managed and financed through major governmental institutions. A pivotal role was played by the Building and Housing Cooperatives Authority (BHCA), which assists housing cooperatives in providing housing to their members through direct provision or subsidized housing loans (Yousry, 1992). BHCA's loans for housing in new communities reached £E2,904 million up to 1993, representing about 79 per cent of total housing loans in new communities, and 36 per cent of total housing loans for the entire country (NUCA, 1993). The Housing and Development Bank (HDB), established in 1979, has also participated in housing development in new settlements through offering subsidized and regular housing loans to individuals as well as to housing cooperatives. Since its establishment in 1979, NUCA has provided about £E540 million in subsidized housing loans. Total loans for housing development in new communities up to 1993 amounted to about 46 per cent of total housing loans in Egypt (see table 11.8).

Recently, Egyptian companies and businessmen have been investing in the development of high-quality housing compounds for the rich in new satellite cities and settlements around Cairo. Several compounds are being constructed in the 6th of October City, Sheikh Zayed, and Elshorouk, consisting of distinguished villas and mansions on large plots, vast green open spaces, and exclusive recreational and social amenities.

Table 11.8 **Distribution of loans for housing development in new communities, 1982–1993 (£E million)**

Governmental agencies providing loans for housing	1982/83– 86/87 Plan	1987/88– 91/92 Plan	1992–93[a]	1982–1993 total
BHCA	1,004	1,610	290	2,904
HDB: Subsidized loans		89	113	202
Regular loans		30	21	51
NUCA	100	350	90	540
Total loans for housing projects	1,104	2,079	513	3,696
Total housing loans in Egypt	2,341	4,742	895	7,978
New communities' housing loans as % of total loans in Egypt	47.2%	43.8%	57.3	46.3%

Source: NUCA (1993).

a. The first year of the 1992/93–1996/97 five-year plan.

Consequences and problems

Sociocultural polarization

The implementation of the open door policy within a Western economic dependency framework has led to large inequalities in the socio-economic structure of Egyptian society. It has also led to the emergence of parasite classes who benefited from the new economic dependency by linking their interests to the West. Later in the 1980s, with the implementation of privatization policies, influential upper-income groups exerted pressure to accelerate the public–private transformation process. USAID, one of the main architects in this process, relied heavily on business coalitions (USAID, 1991). The reliance of USAID on particular (upper) classes of society created exclusive relationships that negatively affected the interests of the other broad classes, whose basic needs had not yet been met. An acute sociocultural class polarization has occurred as a result of the structural changes in the Egyptian economy. Sociocultural groups espousing the new dominating Western culture were confronted by other groups calling for the upholding of traditional norms and values, resenting foreign cultural invasion, and opposing cultural submission with anger and occasionally with hostile resistance. The riots of January 1977 in response to IMF/World Bank austerity measures adopted by the government at that time are still vividly recollected (Awad, 1991).

Doubts about US assistance policies have often been raised at different levels and on various occasions. Between 1986 and 1990 USAID aid to finance local governmental and non-governmental organizations reached £E44 million and was directed to about 3,600 organizations (Kandil, 1993). A later American–Egyptian agreement (1991) concerning private voluntary associations (PVAs) committed US$9 million to support and assist self-help activities in PVAs that aim to improve the situation of the urban poor (USAID, 1991). On the one hand, financial support to some PVAs has led to splits in the non-governmental sector. On the other hand, dependence of PVAs on foreign finance has led to their endorsing the desires of the donor agency when drawing up lists of priorities. Conditional articles in the agreement further deepen dependency on the Americans. For example, the choice and registration of selected PVAs had to meet certain USAID criteria, regardless of the applicability of these measures to the associations (Kandil, 1993).

A quick look at different interest groups working in the Egyptian context sheds some light on the mechanism of Cairo's global orientation and the impact this orientation has on the sociocultural fabric of the mega-city. The interest groups in focus are business associations, labour and professional syndicates, and non-governmental and private voluntary organizations.

Business associations

From the mid-1970s, business organizations were being established to serve their investment interests in the open door policy era. Six organizations have been formed to date: the Egyptian American Council, the Egyptian Businessmen's Association, the American Chamber of Commerce in Cairo, the Economic Committee for Businessmen in Alexandria, the Investors' Association in the 10th of Ramadan, and the Investors' Association in the 6th of October City (Kandil, 1993). Business associations represent national élites and the bourgeoisie – those with economic as well as political influence. Members include not only private sector investors, but also many upper-management staff in the public sector and banks, because they are key personnel in decision-making. Individuals with influential positions and status, such as ministers, ex-ministers, or cabinet rep-resentatives, are pivotal members in such associations, because their personal contacts are instrumental in the pursuance of association objectives (Awad, 1991). Naturally, business associations exercise influence and exert pressure to accelerate the implementation of eco-nomic reforms and privatization. Because of the nature of their mem-bers as well as their financial and administrative independence, they have an effective say in decision-making and decision-taking.

Labour and professional syndicates

Labour syndicates reflect the interests of the working class, and operate under the umbrella of the General Union of Labour (GUL). Labour syndicates have directed their attention to the political and economic problems that affect the interests of the working class (such as the privatization process, unemployment, and inflation). Because of their affiliation with GUL, however, labour syndicates are under government control, which limits their effectiveness in expressing the interests and needs of the working class. In general, the Egyptian labour movement is characterized by dissension between workers and their syndicates on the one hand, and ongoing tension between the syndicates and GUL on the other (Kandil, 1993).

Professional syndicates are larger bodies with huge memberships of specialized professionals from the middle socio-economic classes in both the public and private sectors. They can also include upper socio-economic classes, especially in the case of doctors or engineers. Between the influential business associations, which encourage and expedite government moves towards capitalism, and the helpless, government-controlled labour syndicates, professional syndicates voice criticism and opposition to government trends.

From the 1980s, leading syndicates (in particular, of engineers, doctors, and lawyers) opposed government policy on issues of democ-racy, freedom of expression, and human rights. They were also dis-satisfied with government policies on education, health, and above all economic strategies towards capitalism, which have increased the country's dependency on the West and have caused it to fall into foreign debt. A religious ideology embracing traditional and indige-nous values in dealing with political, social, and economic problems has dominated the boards of these syndicates. The genuine organ-izational capabilities and skilful administrative procedures of these boards have led to notable successes in dealing with the concrete social and economic problems of their members. The syndicates have offered real solutions to the housing problem for new graduates, to the inflation problem by offering goods at reasonable rates of repayment, to the skyrocketing cost of health care through the adoption of subsidized health programmes, and to the unemployment problem by creating job opportunities and offering loans for small projects. Syndicates have succeeded in serving their members' needs, which could not possibly have been met either by them on their own, or by the government. The middle sociocultural classes, who had no stake in the political and economic national striving towards globalization, and who subsequently were the most to suffer because of the rapid structural changes, have flocked to the syndicates and given them their full support.

An alliance between syndicates and opposition political parties in the 1990s, however, widened the gap between the syndicates and the government and led to the government's issuance of a Unified Professional Syndicates Law (Law 100 of 1993), whereby the role of these syndicates was considerably reduced (Kandil, 1993).

Non-governmental organizations and private voluntary associations
Other types of interest group are local non-governmental organizations (NGOs) and private voluntary associations (PVAs). Law 32 of 1964 grants the government complete control over the formation, supervision, and dissolution of NGOs and PVAs. Despite the country's move towards political pluralism and the adoption of open door policies, Law 32 remains untouched. The domination of the state through the Ministry of Social Affairs is still in effect. PVAs in Egypt are classified into two categories according to the type of services they offer to their communities: social welfare associations (SWPVAs) and social development associations (SDPVAs).

In 1989/90, SWPVAs accounted for about 75 per cent of the total number of PVAs, offering a wide range of services in the fields of motherhood and child care, family planning and welfare, and social aid. As table 11.9 shows, about 45 per cent of all SWPVAs were located in Cairo (MSA, 1991). This bias in geographical distribution has been explained by Kandil (1993), who concluded that the concentration of SWPVAs in urban areas, and particularly in the GCR (see table 11.10), was the result of meeting the needs of low-income, poor, and vulnerable families (Korayem 1987; Kandil, 1993). Because

Table 11.9 **Number of private voluntary associations in the GCR and Egypt, 1990**

	SWPVAs		SDPVAs		Total PVAs	
Region	No.	%	No.	%	No.	%
GCR	4,358	87.2	639	12.8	4,997	100.0
Total (Egypt)	9,547	74.5	3,276	25.5	12,823	100.0
GCR as % of Egypt	45.6%		19.5%		39.0%	

Source: MSA (1991).

Table 11.10 **Number of beneficiaries of facilities offered by private voluntary associations, 1990**

	Social welfare facilities[a]			
	1	2	3	4
GCR	77,260	114,536	134,647	266,454
Total	162,094	560,864	192,106	414,159
GCR as % of total	47.7%	20.4%	70.1%	64.3%

	Social development facilities[b]			
	5	6	7	8
GCR	5,304	83,563	107,835	681,511
Total	19,717	103,512	141,635	1,036,516
GCR as % of total	26.9%	80.7%	76.1%	65.8%

Source: MSA (1991).
a. 1 = motherhood and childhood care; 2 = family planning and welfare; 3 = nursery and childhood care; 4 = social aid.
b. 5 = handicap care; 6 = vocational preparation; 7 = cultural facilities; 8 = mixed developmental facilities.

the needs of the poor were not being met by the government in its bias towards the rich, SWPVAs concentrated their efforts on service delivery.

SDPVAs represented only 25 per cent of total PVAs in Egypt (MSA, 1991). The fields of action of SDPVAs, which are directed to society as a whole rather than to local communities, include creating job opportunities and providing cultural facilities and activities (Elkhateeb et al., 1992; Kandil, 1993).

In an extensive study of PVAs in Cairo, White (1986) argued that their role could potentially be considerably broadened towards self-help and community transformation rather than providing only re-sponsive service delivery. She examined the extent to which PVAs' service delivery role enables them to develop community mobilization and grass-roots participation that would lead to the development of self-reliant community-based organizations. An important implication of her research is that PVAs "are providing a basis for development insofar as they are building an organization and bringing the commu-nity together around mutual concerns and needs" (White, 1986: 249).

A considerable number of SWPVAs are religious-based organiza-tions (35 per cent Islamic based and 9 per cent Christian based at the national level; 22 per cent Islamic based and 7 per cent Christian based in the GCR) (Kandil, 1993). The deep-rooted perception of these associations as helping the poor and the unprivileged on a reli-gious non-profit basis has reinforced their position and increased their number in poor urban areas. Many informal urban squatter settlements have rapidly spread around the area mosque (or church). Because social institutions and social infrastructure were almost com-pletely lacking in these areas, most social activities tended to rely on the neighbourhood religious institution (Steinberg, 1990). Yet the expansion of religious-based NGOs and PVAs and the augmentation of public participation are seen by the government as a curtailment of its power and authority. Despite the rhetoric about democracy and human rights, the government is intolerant of political diversity. Political affiliation of local groups is incompatible with government and the political situation is too uncertain and turbulent to allow the long-term development of local groups (Hassan, 1992). The govern-ment's fear of genuine grass-roots politics has driven it to issue new laws, such as Law 100 of 1993 on professional syndicates, or to enforce old ones, such as Law 32 of 1964 concerning PVAs, in order to ensure central control and domination. The intention of the government to stifle any opposition voice is evident in its issuance of Law 93 of 1995, which advocates severe measures against the freedom of publication and expression. Where control is held tightly by the central govern-ment, any local initiative that is allowed is like window-dressing, an exercise designed to foster an illusion of shared power.

Cairo's social inequalities

Cairo's location as "the place of residence of politicians, senior civil servants, and diplomats has helped to bias public expenditure on services and infrastructure towards them" (Rakodi, 1994: 7). This bias has caused sharp inequalities. Simon (1994) asserts that "the accumulation of capital, the sophistication and often ostentatious Western lifestyles of the national elites and bourgeoisie are built on exploitation. The majority of residents in Cairo have little stake in the globalizing, materialistic culture."

Cairo has social equity problems. There is no longer a relationship between education, occupation, and income. Open door policies have encouraged the emergence of a new capitalist class and resulted in an increasingly skewed distribution of income. This distortion was exacerbated by the development of inflationary pressures, which further widened the gap between fixed-income earners and the entrepreneurial class (Handoussa, 1991). Another aspect is the emergence since the 1970s of parallel service institutions, in particular private schools and hospitals, which cater for the top 5 per cent of the population, with vast differences in quality (Ibrahim, 1985). Similarly, much of the public expenditure on the city's transportation system has disproportionately gone to owners of private cars. In the 10 years between 1972 and 1982, the number of private cars tripled (from 80,000 to 250,000) while the number of public and semi-public vehicles only slightly more than doubled (from 17,000 to 45,000) (Ibrahim, 1985). New highways, overpasses, and the ring road obviously cater mainly to commuters with private cars.

The growing inequality in Cairo reflects the situation in the country as a whole. The richest 5 per cent of the population raised its share of national income from 15 to 24 per cent between the early and late 1970s, while the share of the lowest 20 per cent dropped from 17 to 13 per cent. In Cairo this inequality is particularly glaring: about 200,000 of Egypt's estimated 250,000 millionaires are residents of Cairo. They occupy spacious and luxurious waterfront apartments or private mansions on the outskirts of the city. Large areas in the new satellite cities and settlements have recently been developed for expensive villa complexes. In contrast, the poor crowd into older districts or cemeteries, or engage in unauthorized development. The *nouveaux riches* continue to be conspicuous, as long as their immediate districts and homes remain in good shape. It is the middle classes, especially those on the lower rungs, who are feeling the squeeze and who are bursting with frustration and anger (Ibrahim, 1985).

Spatial distortions

Government policies for upgrading infrastructure networks in Cairo and for establishing new cities have attracted huge governmental investments and many job-generating projects away from the populated areas. The result is a relative degradation of infrastructure and community facilities as well as higher unemployment rates in poor areas of Cairo. This degradation has aggravated social unrest and crime rates. It has also led to a disparity between the urban environment of poor and rich districts, because the rich districts have not relatively suffered from budget cuts.

The informal sector in Egypt plays a pivotal role in providing the poor, vulnerable, and unprivileged socio-economic groups not only with housing, but also with sustainable economic opportunities. Its methods and practices contrast with those in the formal sector. The informal sector is characterized by reliance on indigenous resources, small scale of operation, labour-intensive and locally adapted technology, and unregulated and competitive markets. Despite government neglect and opposition to this unofficial, unauthorized sector, the informal sector contributes to economic growth and is essential to the survival strategies of the urban poor (Rizk, 1991; Hassan, 1992). The spread of informal sector activities in the impoverished urban domain has created an environment of informality that has become the context in which the local community and community-based organizations operate. This informal culture has widened the gap between social classes and their spatial territories, hence aggravating socio-cultural polarization and spatial distortions. It has also led to an ongoing conflict between these unrecognized communities and the government.

Government withdrawal from poor areas, which was an inevitable outcome of the imbalance in resource allocation, has accelerated the growth of the informal economy, which is manifested in the expansion of informal sector housing. Housing informality has been defined in terms of the legal status of housing as regards land subdivision and occupancy as well as of the physical characteristics of building (Mayo et al., 1982; Lim, 1987). Informal sector housing includes a wide variety of illegal (unauthorized and/or unofficial) types of substandard housing. Squatter settlements, inner-city slums, cemetery housing, emergency shelter areas, rooftop shacks, and illegal alterations and transformations in public housing are some of the types that exist in Egypt and in the GCR in particular (Hassan, 1992).

299

The population of degraded urban areas in Egypt, as table 11.11 shows, is nearly 11 million, about 20 per cent of Egypt's total population and about 38 per cent of the total urban population in 1993. About half of this population lives in the GCR in below-standard conditions. In a comprehensive study of degraded urban areas (IDMSC, 1993), the Ministry of Local Government has identified 1,034 action areas, 81 of which are to be cleared and their population relocated and housed elsewhere. The estimated cost of projects in these action areas had reached £E5,337.7 million at the national level and £E2,153.7 million for the GCR alone in 1993. The 1993/94 budget, however, designated only £E336 million for infrastructure, service facilities, and new housing for degraded areas and the relocated population.

The highest population in degraded areas within the GCR can be found in Giza, where 2.3 million inhabitants (about 60 per cent of the city's population) live in 32 action areas, comprising about 63 per cent of the city area (IDMSC, 1993). Up to June 1993, £E10 million had been spent on street lighting, sewerage networks, road surfacing, and solid waste collection in several degraded areas. Yet the funds needed to upgrade some areas amounted to £E78.3 million for the 1993/94 fiscal year. The city of Cairo is in second place in terms of degraded-area population. About 2.2 million inhabitants (32 per cent of the total city population) live in 79 high-density, degraded action areas with a total area of 28 km^2. Twelve areas with a population of about 602,000 inhabitants have been designated for clearance and redevelopment (IDMSC, 1993). The Governorate of Cairo estimated that 15,327 housing units would be needed for the redevelopment of these areas, and that the upgrading of the rest of the areas would take about six years, beginning from 1993/94. Although the estimated cost of clearance and upgrading amounted to about £E950 million, only £E10 million had been approved and designated for Cairo's degraded areas up to June 1993 (IDMSC, 1993). About 64 per cent of Shubra Elkheima's population live in degraded areas in poor environmental conditions and lacking basic community facilities. Nearly £E280 million is needed for upgrading projects (IDMSC, 1993). A priority action plan has been assessed for the upgrading of the infrastructure networks of the city at a cost of £E33.9 million, of which only £E12 million was approved in the 1992/93 Socio-economic Plan.

Table 11A.3, in the appendix to this chapter, reveals the characteristics of degraded urban areas in the GCR and figure 11.5 shows

Table 11.11 **Degraded urban areas in the Greater Cairo Region and Egypt's regions, 1993**

Region	No. of action areas to be cleared	No. of action areas to be upgraded	Total no. of action areas	Area (km²)	Action area population ('000)	Population density ('000 inh/km²)	Action area population as % of region's urban population	Estimated cost of clearance & upgrading (£E m.)
Cairo	12	67	79	28	2,193	78.3	32.0	950.0
Giza	4	28	32	44	2,259	51.3	60.0	924.0
Shubra Elkheima	0	60	60	20	938	46.9	64.4	279.7
GCR total	16	155	171	92	5,390	58.6	52.0	2,153.7
Alexandria	21	89	110	63	1,548	24.6	46.0	705.0
Delta	6	305	311	41	1,651	40.3	40.4	586.8
Canal	29	92	121	66	562	8.5	25.2	336.1
N. Upper Egypt	0	109	109	17	535	31.5	34.6	187.0
Asyout	7	64	71	34	470	13.8	30.5	446.0
S. Upper Egypt	2	140	142	24	638	26.6	36.3	923.1
Total	81	954	1,035	337	10,794	–	–	5,337.7
Average	–	–	–	–	–	32.0	37.9	–

Source: IDMSC (1993).

1. Ain Shams, Mataria, & Elmarg
2. Elwayli & Zawia Elhamra
3. Manshiet Nasser
4. Ezbet Elhaggana
5. Elfustat
6. Elbasaleen
7. Dar Elsalam
8. Tora & Maasara
9. Arab Ghoniem & Arab Rashed
10. Kafr Elelw
11. Elhekr & Eltebeen
12. Begam
13. Behteem
14. Imbaba & Mounira
15. Boulaq Eldakrour
16. Faisal
17. Elharam
18. West Maryoutia & Elsamman
19. Sakeit Mekki
20. Elmonieb
21. Manial Sheeha
22. Elhawamdia
23. Elbadrasheen & Meet Rahina

-------- Regional railroad lines

Fig. 11.5   The location of degraded urban areas in GCR (Source: GOPP, 1993)

their location. None of the areas is served by paved roads. Most areas lack sewerage and potable water networks and most are only partially served by electricity. Almost all areas lack community facilities (GOPP, 1993). Local community associations (social welfare and/or social development PVAs) have evolved to offer the necessary services, especially in areas of nursery and child care and social aid (see table 11.10). The unemployment rate has risen to nearly 19 per cent in some areas, with an overall average much higher than the GCR average rate of about 10 per cent (CAPMAS, 1994). Illiteracy is widespread among parents, and 95 per cent of women are not in the labour force (Fahmy, 1986).

A 1989 study by the High Institute of Social Work in Cairo on the Imbaba and Mounira areas in Giza (see table 11A.3) provides some typical indicators (Elsamalouti, 1989). Illiteracy affected 42 per cent of family households (reaching 57 per cent among wives and 49 per cent among children above 10 years old). About 71 per cent of children had not enrolled in education or finished the primary stage. Solid waste disposal was causing serious environmental problems. Almost 64 per cent disposed of garbage on nearby vacant land or in drainage canals. Because of the lack of recreational facilities, 63 per cent of the population spent their leisure time on the street. Roughly 65 per cent of the interviewed sample confirmed the spread of drugs in the area. Only 10 per cent of the population were members of local PVAs – 4 per cent being members of SDPVAs (Elsamalouti, 1989). In other areas such as Elbasateen (see table 11A.3), the lack of both services and street lighting had resulted in high crime rates and provided shelter for outlaws (Elwali, 1993).

In 1992 and 1993, violent attacks by extremist religious groups aimed at tourism came as the result of the ongoing conflict between the government and these groups. Terrorist attacks on foreigners as well as on public figures by these groups have led to a series of clashes between them and the police. The scene of these clashes has always been degraded urban areas, where these groups flourish and are easily able to spread their radical thoughts and organize anti-government militant action. These recent incidents have brought to the surface the issue of government neglect of these degraded areas and their population. A report issued by the People's Assembly in 1993 mentioned that high rates of unemployment and the lack of community facilities in degraded areas had facilitated the growth of these groups (*Alakhbar*, 11 January 1993). Another aspect that did not attract

government attention was that the needs of the populations of degraded areas were partly being met by voluntary associations and
community-based organizations, many of which pursued their work
through a religious motivation to solve economic and social problems. The October 1992 earthquake alerted the government to the
inherent power of these organizations as they dealt with the disaster
in its early stages. The government immediately intervened and took
strict measures to ensure that all private donations and help to the
victims of the disaster were made through authorized channels such
as the Red Crescent Association (Elwali, 1993). Such action only
served to widen the gap between these organizations and the government, and provoked hostility and mistrust towards it.

Conclusions and recommendations

Cairo is definitely heading towards globalization and has gone an
appreciable distance along this path. According to the IMF/World
Bank structural adjustment programme, some severe measures still
need to be taken to reform the Egyptian economy (Wahba, 1995).
Among the most important are: accelerating privatization (four public sector companies to be privatized per month until the year 2000);
freeing foreign trade and conforming with the General Agreement
on Tariffs and Trade (GATT); raising the prices of energy and other
basic commodities to conform with world prices; removing rent controls and price subsidies; and devaluing the local currency. By the
turn of the twentieth century, Egypt is required to increase exports
from the domestic sector six-fold, decrease government expenditure
by 10 per cent, decrease public sector investments by 25 per cent, and
provide 3.6 million job opportunities (Wahba, 1995). Clearly, these
targets will be difficult to fulfil at the current pace of investment. In
addition, some of these measures could increase unemployment and
have a negative impact on local production. Vulnerable and poor
socio-economic groups in society will be the most affected by these
measures. Some of these measures will have hugely inflationary effects
while others, such as removing rent controls and price subsidies, are
socially unacceptable. Devaluation of the local currency is currently
being met with ferocious resistance.

A study of the consequences and problems arising in the process of
globalization is needed to focus the attention of decision makers and
society at large on taking the necessary measures and precautions to

alleviate the painful consequences and minimize the social cost of the process. The programming and timing of economic reform measures should allow for adaptation to the social, economic, and cultural changes resulting from structural adjustment. Price rises, changes in customs tariffs, and rent control policies should be gradual and well integrated with programmes of economic development. More attention should be given to the impoverished classes who are most affected by the harsh consequences of economic reform. The programme of upgrading degraded urban areas is under way, but it is suffering from slow implementation, inadequate funding, and a lack of results, especially in Cairo. More important than upgrading the physical environment and providing social services is generating employment opportunities. Not only could economic betterment policies mitigate social unrest, but they could also provide the poor with the economic means with which to cope with their bleak situation.

A balance in resource allocation is needed in policy planning to solve the equity dilemma. Most public and private investment has been used to upgrade Cairo's infrastructure and to improve the environment of those who are involved in the globalization trends. The move towards globalization has been at the expense of the middle- and low-income groups on fixed earnings. These powerless groups need urgent assistance to meet their pressing needs. NGOs and PVAs are potential resources that the government ought to rely on and utilize. The establishment and strengthening of community-based organizations should be promoted in a facilitating rather than in a dominating manner. Ways must be found to reduce community dependency on, or domination by, the government. Collaboration among public and private local institutions is also needed to achieve effective, efficient, and widespread urban development. The government's role in the development of local institutions and of interaction between them is crucial; devolution of power to local authorities and agencies is indispensable.

Social conflict and sociocultural polarization should be mitigated and tackled with sincerity. Notable incidents in times of crisis and disasters have shed glimpses of hope that may inspire pragmatic conflict resolution. Cairo's 1992 earthquake and Upper Egypt's 1994 floods have shown how socioculturally polarized groups can come together in dealing with a national catastrophe. Individuals, businessmen, and institutions showed enduring cooperation in reconstructing villages, schools, and social services. Yet such cooperation should be neither unexpected nor misunderstood. Between those whose slogan is "Islam is *the* solution" and those who are captivated by the West, lies a majority who encompass both modernity and tradition. It is necessary, therefore, that development, reforms, and all other ingredients of the move to globalization take into consideration the indigenous values of the population, which are deep rooted in their history and heritage and are part of their religion and culture.

So far, the reconstruction, improvement, and upgrading of degraded urban areas have been temporary remedial actions in the face of violence, terrorism, and intense social unrest. In regard to spatial planning policy, it is important that the government recognizes and deals with the informal sector. The informal sector should be seen not as an economic or physical liability (as it is indeed still perceived by the government), but rather as an asset that could be directed, upgraded, and recruited as an efficient stimulus to development. Informal sector systems and mechanisms have to be studied and incorporated in urban planning policy to achieve more practical and adaptive outcomes.

Appendix

Table 11A.1 **Service and community facilities in the GCR and Egypt as of 1993/94**

Service/community facility	GCR	Egypt	GCR as % of Egypt
Total length of surfaced roads (km)	7,544	35,663	21.2
Inhabitants per km	2,364	1,913	–
Number of telephone lines	1,469,462	2,806,252	52.4
Inhabitants per telephone line	16	33	–
Number of post offices	1,245	5,768	21.6
Inhabitants per post office	12,396	11,789	–
Number of higher education institutions	78	292	26.7
Number of higher education students	315,993	644,511	49.0
Number of hospitals and health centres	234	1,525	15.3
Number of health unit beds	35,623	96,717	36.8
Inhabitants per health unit bed	488	627	–
Number of physicians	16,436	53,411	30.8
Inhabitants per physician	1,064	1,037	–

Table 11A.1 **(cont.)**

Service/community facility	GCR	Egypt	GCR as % of Egypt
Number of nurseries	1,629	5,095	32.0
Number of social service associations	3,573	5,508	64.9
Number of family planning units (FPU)	469	3,345	14.0
Families per FPU	10,346	5,700	–

Source: CIDC (1994).

Table 11A.2 **Sectoral distribution of accomplished investments in new cities of Egypt, up to 1993 (£E million)**

Sector	Housing	Infra-structure[a]	Community facilities[b]	Industry[c]	Other[d]	Total
Independent new cities						
10th of Ramadan	234.5	368.4	53.4	2.4	25.5	684.2
Sadat	135.0	155.8	57.2	3.6	23.2	374.8
Borg Elarab	123.9	176.8	33.4	8.5	13.0	355.7
Total	493.4	701.0	144.0	14.5	61.7	1,414.6
Satellite cities						
6th of October	285.5	510.6	92.8	5.6	12.3	906.8
15th of May	275.0	196.4	63.1	3.6	19.7	557.8
Elobour	99.1	66.7	11.9	2.3	121.7	301.7
Badr	60.3	91.9	2.7	0.6	1.9	157.4
Total	719.9	865.6	170.5	12.1	155.6	1,923.7
New settlements						
S # 2: Elshorouk	84.9	11.8	0.0	0.0	1.4	98.1
S #3: Elkattamia	0.0	27.3	2.3	0.0	3.2	32.8
S # 5: New Maadi	71.2	11.4	0.0	0.0	0.1	82.7
S # 6: Sheikh Zayed	3.3	3.8	0.0	0.1	0.8	8.0
Total	159.4	54.3	2.3	0.1	5.5	221.6

Source: NUCA (1993).
a. Includes roads, water supply, wastewater disposal, electricity, and communication.
b. Includes public, educational, health, social, commercial, religious, and cultural services.
c. Includes industrial storage areas as well as management facilities.
d. Includes Master Plan Study cost, agriculture and land reclamation, and landscaping.

307

Table 11A.3 Characteristics of degraded urban areas in the GCR

Area	Area (km²)	Population ('000)	Population density ('000 inh/km²)	Served by road network	Served by public utilities	Served by community facilities	No. of local community associations	Unemployment rate (% of labour force)
Cairo								
Ain Shams, Mataria, & Elmarg	15.5	1,110	72	NS	S	NS	24	11.2
Elwayli & Zawia Elhamra	3.6	225	63	NS	S	NS	20	14.5
Manshiet Nasser	2.5	120	48	NS	PS	NS	5	9.8
Ezbet Elhaggana	2.5	108	43	NS	NS	NS	2	9.5
Elfustat	1.9	100	53	NS	PS	NS	10	18.7
Elbasateen	1.9	148	78	NS	PS	NS	16	14.4
Dar Elsalam	5.5	480	87	NS	PS	NS	21	10.4
Tora & Maasara	4.2	300	71	NS	PS	NS	16	15.7
Arab Ghoniem & Arab Rashed	2.9	126	43	NS	S	S	24	15.7
Kafr Elelw	1.1	52	47	NS	PS	PS	12	10.6
Elhekr & Eltebeen	1.9	48	25	NS	PS	NS	5	15.3
Giza								
Imbaba & Mounira	6.7	560	84	NS	PS	NS	42	17.1
Boulaq Eldakrour	5.5	455	83	NS	S	NS	32	14.1
Faisal	4.2	300	71	NS	S	S	33	12.3
Elharam	5.9	420	71	NS	S	NS	36	14.7
West Maryoutia & Elsamman	5.5	325	59	NS	PS	NS	29	12.7
Sakeit Mekki	0.7	53	76	NS	S	S	4	9.8
Elmonieb	0.6	45	75	NS	PS	NS	3	7.8
Manial Sheeha	0.4	30	75	NS	PS	NS	3	10.7
Elhawamdia	1.9	126	66	NS	PS	NS	12	7.6
Elbadrasheen & Meet Rahina	1.5	70	47	NS	S	S	9	9.9

Shubra Elkheima

Begam	5.8	350	60	NS	PS	NS	21	13.7
Behteem	5.0	300	60	NS	PS	NS	19	13.9

Sources: GOPP (1993); MSA (1994), CAPMAS (1994).
S = serviced.
PS = partially serviced.
NS = not serviced.

References

Aga Khan Program for Islamic Architecture, Harvard University and the Massachusetts Institute of Technology, Office of Special Programs (1985), "Cairo: 1800–2000, Planning for the Capital City in the Context of Egypt's History and Development." In: Ahmet Evin (ed.), *The Expanding Metropolis: Coping with the Urban Growth of Cairo*. Proceedings of Seminar Nine in the Series: Architectural Transformations in the Islamic World, Cairo, 11–15 November 1984. Singapore: Concept Media, pp. 91–120.

Amirahmadi, H. (1990), "Global Restructuring and Prospects for Third World Transformations." In: G. Lim and G. Lee (eds.), *Dynamic Transformation: Korea, NICs and Beyond*. Urbana: Consortium of Development Studies, pp. 511–528.

———— (1991), "Third World Economic Imbalances and Global Restructuring: Prospects for Medium-Term Growth." Paper presented at the Consortium on Development Studies Meeting, Seoul National University, Seoul, Korea.

Awad, I. (1991), "Socio-Political Aspects of Economic Reform: A Study of Domestic Actors' Attitudes Towards Adjustment Policies in Egypt." In: H. Handoussa and G. Potter (eds.), *Employment and Structural Adjustment: Egypt in the 1990s*. Cairo: American University in Cairo Press, pp. 275–294.

CAPMAS (Central Agency for Public Mobilization and Statistics) (1994), *1993 Statistical Yearbook*. Cairo: CAPMAS (in Arabic).

CGOSD (Cairo General Organization for Sanitary Drainage) (1992), *CWO Project Status Report 1992*. Cairo: National Organization for Potable Water and Sanitary Drainage.

CIDC (Central Information and Documentation Center), General Statistics Department (1990), *A Statistical Study of the Progression of Principal Indices of the Egyptian Economy*. Cairo: Ministry of Planning (in Arabic).

———— (1994), *A Statistical Map for the Governorates of Egypt*. Cairo: Ministry of Planning (in Arabic).

Cook, D. (1985), "Transport Problems in Cairo." In: Ahmet Evin (ed.), *The Expanding Metropolis: Coping with the Urban Growth of Cairo*. Singapore: Concept Media, pp. 152–157.

Cornu, J. (1985), "Planning for Cairo's Future Environment." In: Ahmet Evin (ed.), *The Expanding Metropolis: Coping with the Urban Growth of Cairo*. Singapore: Concept Media, pp. 188–191.

Dessouki, A. (1991), "The Public Sector in Egypt: Organization, Evolution, and Strategies of Reform." In: H. Handoussa and G. Potter (eds.), *Employment and Structural Adjustment: Egypt in the 1990s*. Cairo: American University in Cairo Press, pp. 259–274.

Elkhateeb, M., et al. (1992), *Areas for Developing the Capabilities of NGOs in Egypt*. Cairo: UNDP and Ministry of Social Affairs (in Arabic).

Elkholei, A. and T. Abu-Zekry (1993), "The Impact of Global Transformations on the Process of Urbanization in Newly Industrialized Countries: Lessons for Future Egyptian Urban Policies." Paper presented to the Third International Conference of Al-Azhar University. Cairo: Al-Azhar University, Faculty of Engineering.

Elsamalouti, E. (1989), *Toward a Developmental Model to Meet the Needs of*

Impoverished Urban Communities: Case Study of West Mounira. Cairo: High Institute of Social Work (in Arabic).

Elwali, M. (1993), *Shacks and Squatters Settlers.* Cairo: Rosalyousef Publishing (in Arabic).

Fahmy, N. (1986), *Socioeconomic Aspects of Spontaneous Growth in Residential Areas in Egypt.* First Conference on City and Regional Planning. Cairo: Association of Egyptian Engineers (in Arabic).

Friedmann, J. (1986), "The World City Hypothesis." *Development and Change* 17: 69–83.

GCPIA (Greater Cairo Project Implementation Agency), Central Development Agency (1993), *Reconstruction Report 1993.* Cairo: Ministry of Development, New Urban Communities, Housing, and Utilities (in Arabic).

GOGCWS (General Organization for Greater Cairo Water Supply) (1993), *Potable Water Supply Report 1993.* Cairo: Ministry of Development, New Urban Communities, Housing, and Utilities (in Arabic).

GOPP (General Organization for Physical Planning) (1993), *Urban Area Upgrading in Greater Cairo Region.* Cairo: Ministry of Development, New Urban Communities, Housing, and Utilities (in Arabic).

Gorgy, M. (1985), "The Greater Cairo Region: Land Use Today and Tomorrow." In: Ahmet Evin (ed.), *The Expanding Metropolis: Coping with the Urban Growth of Cairo.* Singapore: Concept Media, pp. 176–182.

Haggard, S. (1990), *Pathways from the Periphery: The Policies of Growth in Newly Industrialized Countries.* Ithaca, N.Y.: Cornell University Press.

Handoussa, H. (1991), "Crisis and Challenge: Prospects for the 1990s." In: H. Handoussa and G. Potter (eds.), *Employment and Structural Adjustment: Egypt in the 1990s.* Cairo: American University in Cairo Press, pp. 3–24.

Hansen, B. (1991), "A Macro-Economic Framework for Economic Planning in Egypt." In: H. Handoussa and G. Potter (eds.), *Employment and Structural Adjustment: Egypt in the 1990s.* Cairo: American University in Cairo Press, pp. 189–218.

Harper, R. (1990), "A New World Force: The Global Network of Major Metropolitan Management Centers." In: G. Lim and G. Lee (eds.), *Dynamic Transformation: Korea, NICs and Beyond.* Urbana: Consortium of Development Studies, pp. 29–35.

Hassan, A. (1992), "Housing the Urban Poor in Egypt: A Social Systems Approach." Ph.D. dissertation, Philadelphia, University of Pennsylvania.

Ibrahim, S. (1985), "Cairo: A Social Profile." In: Ahmet Evin (ed.), *The Expanding Metropolis: Coping with the Urban Growth of Cairo.* Singapore: Concept Media, pp. 25–33.

IDMSC (Information and Decision-Making Support Center) (1993), *Spontaneous Housing.* Cairo: Ministry of Local Government (in Arabic).

Jenkins, R. (1984), "Divisions over the International Division of Labor." *Capital & Class* 22: 28–57.

Kandil, A. (1993), *Democratization Process in Egypt.* Cairo: Ibn Khaldoun Center for Developmental Studies (in Arabic).

Knight, R. and G. Gappert (eds.) (1989), "Cities in a Global Society." *Urbana Affairs Annual Reviews* 35 (California: Sage Publications).

Korayem, K. (1987), *The Impact of Economic Adjustment Policies on the Vulnerable Families and Children in Egypt*. Cairo: UNICEF.

Lim, G. (1987), "Housing Policies for the Urban Poor in Developing Countries." *Journal of the American Planning Association* 53(2): 176–185.

Lipietz, A. (1992), *Towards a New Economic Order: Postfordism, Ecology and Democracy*, translated by M. Slater. Cambridge: Polity Press.

Mayo, S., et al. (1982), *Informal Housing in Egypt*. Cambridge, Mass.: Abt Associates.

Ministry of Development, New Urban Communities, Housing, and Utilities (1993), *Construction Report 1993*. Cairo (in Arabic).

Ministry of Planning (1977–1995), National Five-year Socioeconomic Plans.

MSA (Ministry of Social Affairs) (1987–1991), *Statistical Indicators in Social Welfare and Development 1985/86–89/90, Yearly Reports*. Cairo: MSA (in Arabic).

NAT (National Agency of Transit) (1993), *Greater Cairo Metro System Progression Report 1992/93*. Cairo: Ministry of Transportation and Communication (in Arabic).

NCA (National Communication Authority) (1994), *Communication Development Report*. Cairo: Ministry of Transportation (in Arabic).

Neamatalla, M. (1985), "Urban Service Delivery." In: Ahmet Evin (ed.), *The Expanding Metropolis: Coping with the Urban Growth of Cairo*. Singapore: Concept Media, pp. 165–168.

NUCA (New Urban Communities Authority) (1993), *New Urban Communities in Egypt*. Cairo: Ministry of Development, New Urban Communities, Housing, and Utilities (in Arabic).

PADCO (1982), *Egypt: Urban Growth and Urban Data Report*. National Urban Policy Study. Washington, D.C.: PADCO.

Peet, R. (ed.) (1987), *International Capitalism and Industrial Restructuring: A Critical Analysis*. Boston: Allen & Unwin.

Rakodi, C. (1994), *Globalism, Urban Change and Urban Management in Africa*. Tokyo: UNU Project, Challenge of Urban Growth in Africa.

Rizk, S. (1991), "The Structure and Operation of the Informal Sector in Egypt." In: H. Handoussa and G. Potter (eds.), *Employment and Structural Adjustment: Egypt in the 1990s*. Cairo: American University in Cairo Press, pp. 167–188.

Sayer, A. and R. Walker (1992), *The New Social Economy: Reworking the Division of Labor*. Cambridge, Mass.: Basil Blackwell.

Shorter, F. (1989), *Cairo's Leap Forward*. Cairo: American University in Cairo Press.

Simon, D. (1994), *Urbanization, Globalization and Economic Crisis in Africa*. Tokyo: UNU Project, Challenge of Urban Growth in Africa.

Sit, F-S. (1993), "Transnational Capital Flows, Foreign Investments, and Urban Growth in Developing Countries." In: J. Kasarda and A. Parnell (eds.), *Third World Cities: Problems, Policies and Prospects*. California: Sage Publications, pp. 180–189.

Smith, M. and J. Feagin (eds.) (1987), *The Capitalist City: Global Restructuring and Community Politics*. Cambridge, Mass.: Basil Blackwell.

Steinberg, F. (1990), "Cairo Informal Land Development and the Challenge for the Future." In: P. Baross and J. van der Linden (eds.), *The Transformation of Land Supply Systems in Third World Cities*. Aldershot: Gower, pp. 111–132.

USAID (United States Agency for International Development) (1991), *United States Economic Assistance to Egypt, Status Report*. Cairo: USAID.

Wahba, S. (1995), "The World Bank and the Embezzlement of Egypt." *Alahram*, 24 June (in Arabic).

Waterbury, J. (1983), *The Egypt of Nasser and Sadat: The Political Economy of Two Regimes*. Princeton, N.J.: Princeton University Press.

White, L. (1986), "Urban Community Organizations and Local Government: Exploring Relationships and Roles." *Public Administration and Development* 6(3): 239–253.

Yousry, M. (1992), "Urbanization and Human Settlement Policy in Egypt." *Regional Development Dialogue* 13(4): 62–78.

Yousry, M. and T. Abulatta (1994), *The Challenge of Urban Growth of Cairo*. Tokyo: UNU Project, Challenge of Urban Growth in Africa.

Zaki, R. (1985), *Rescheduling Debt and the Future of Economic Development in Egypt*. Cairo: Madbuli Press (in Arabic).

12

Globalization trends and sub-Saharan African cities

Carole Rakodi

Introduction

Phases of urbanization can be distinguished in Africa that are, in part, related to the shifting terms on which the continent has been integrated into the world economic system. The changing nature of global trends and their influence on sub-Saharan Africa (SSA) will be examined in this chapter, in relation to economic development, the pace and pattern of urbanization, and attempts to manage urban growth. First, the evolution of cities related to Africa's immediate post-independence history will be sketched. Secondly, the ways in which current global economic trends manifest themselves in and impact upon African economies will be explored in more detail, and related to patterns of urbanization since the mid-1970s. The management of urban growth in a situation of varied but generally limited economic prosperity and administrative capacity will be examined. Finally, international lending for urban development and its impact on African cities will be critically reviewed.

Integration or autonomy? The post-independence decade

The integration of Africa into the world economy throughout the lengthy mercantilist period and during the colonial era that followed had major implications for the development of urban centres, which, because of constraints on space, cannot be analysed here (Gugler and Flanagan, 1978; Mehretu, 1983; O'Connor, 1983; King, 1990; Coquery-Vidrovitch, 1991; Simon, 1992; Chandler, 1994). By 1950, at the beginning of the main decolonization period, Johannesburg was the largest city (915,000), followed by Cape Town, Lagos, and Accra. Overall, only a small proportion of SSA's population lived in urban areas and in most countries the urban population was heavily concentrated in one or two cities, normally including the colonial capital.

Politics and economic development

The great majority of African countries gained their independence in the 1960s. As this was also a decade of relative economic prosperity before major changes occurred in the world economy in the mid-1970s, it was significant for both national political economies and the process of urbanization. Independence implies autonomy to make political and economic decisions and the capacity to carry them out, but, although the newly independent states were strong in juridical terms, they were politically and socially weak. Nationalist movements had incorporated divergent interests and the initial problem for the inexperienced politicians who took power, on the basis of political systems modelled on those of the metropolitan powers, was to establish their legitimacy and balance conflicting ethnic and economic interests. The inherited bureaucracies were generally fairly well developed (except in the ex-Portuguese and ex-Belgian colonies) but costly to run and hard to manage without expatriate expertise. However, heavy demands were placed on both the political and bureaucratic structures, while the uncertain relationship between them gave rise to misunderstanding and conflict (Tordoff, 1984; Chazan et al., 1988). The apparent need for state economic development planning and, in the absence of foreign control of major economic sectors, for the state to take on productive roles led to the establishment of planning machinery and large parastatals, which further strained the capacity of the states to manage their affairs. A further problem has been the role of the military, and many countries have been subject to military repression, civil war, and ethnic pogroms.

For a variety of reasons, including economic management and resource allocation to fulfil developmental goals, the need to foster a sense of national unity, fear of strong or opposition-controlled local government, and scarcity of skilled and experienced public servants, strong government was equated with centralization. However, this facilitated the abuse of power, increased the propensity to error, slowed down and bureaucratized responses to changing circumstances, and made access to the central state the prime source of opportunities for personal accumulation. Except in "strong man" governments, there were attempts at decentralization, but these were typically flawed and unsuccessful (Wunsch and Olowu, 1990). Politics were characterized by personal rule. In some countries, a degree of continuity, stability, and accountability was achieved, but more commonly political processes were marked by repression, instability, inequality, dishonesty, and ineffectiveness (Chazan et al., 1988). In addition to state weakness, political autonomy was eroded by superpower interest, continued identification with the ex-colonial powers, external interference with national sovereignty originating within the continent itself, and the links between economic and political dependence. Although African regimes did exercise some political autonomy, their scope for doing so was limited by the ability of external powers to exert political influence based on economic dependency.

The economies inherited by African countries imposed considerable constraints on policy choices. Exports were overwhelmingly of raw materials and agricultural products, most economies depended on fewer than three products for over three-quarters of their export earnings, rendering them very vulnerable to fluctuations in world commodity prices, and trade was often monopolized by large European companies. In SSA, industry accounted for only 9 per cent of GDP and manufactured exports were unimportant. Trade was largely with the colonial powers, an industrial base was almost non-existent except in some of the settler economies, and education and training had been exceptionally poor.

The favoured development strategy during the independence decade was based on modernization, industrialization, economic diversification, and indigenization of the economy. Given the heavy reliance on imported manufactures, the logical place to start was with import substitution. Given the obstacles (inadequate infrastructure oriented mostly towards colonial trade, absence of an industrial workforce, small domestic markets, dearth of indigenous capital), high levels of protection, a substantial role for the state, and a search for external assistance were inevitable. External assistance was obtained mostly from transnational corporations (TNCs). Foreign direct investment (FDI) grew during the 1960s and by the mid-1970s investment was concentrated in Nigeria, Liberia, Zaire, Gabon, Kenya, and the Côte d'Ivoire, although it also grew rapidly in some other countries. Although a fifth of worldwide FDI was in Africa by the early 1970s, over half of the stock (excluding South Africa) was invested in the primary sector and only a third in the secondary sector, compared with just over a quarter in all developing areas (Cantwell, 1991).

What TNC investment there was in manufacturing had a number of disadvantages: restrictive practices often prohibited local subsidiaries from producing for export; the use of capital-intensive techniques generated relatively few jobs; and the goods produced were often considered to be inappropriate for local markets. Despite increasing insistence on local public or private sector participation, import-substitution industrialization (ISI) did not live up to its promise. It proved to be import intensive, quasi-monopolistic, inefficient, and a drain on what local capital was available for investment. Policies associated with ISI included an overvalued exchange rate, inefficient public ownership, and inappropriate choice of industries and technologies (Chazan et al., 1988). Although an increase in manufacturing output was recorded for the continent as a whole, economic diversification based on industrialization proved elusive.

The capital requirements of mineral extraction were also clearly beyond indigenous entrepreneurs or most of the smaller African governments and so mining was dominated by TNCs. From its traditional base in South Africa, multinational investment in mining rapidly grew after independence. Soon the disadvantages of TNC operations (repatriation of profits and reluctance to develop in-country processing) were seen to outweigh the supply of capital, technology, and export outlets. The only alternative open to governments appeared to be nationalization, either by expropriation or by acquisition of majority shareholdings. By no means discomfited by such moves, TNCs have maintained a high degree of control by licensing agreements, management contracts, provision of refining and manufacturing facilities, and overseas marketing.

Chazan et al. (1988) argue that agriculture in many African countries was relatively healthy at independence: although cash-crop production was widespread, it had in most places not been established at the expense of food crops and there was scope for increased production of both. However, the slow rise in agricultural production combined with rapid population growth turned a food surplus into a deficit by the mid-1970s. Explanations for the poor performance of the agricultural sector were complex: they included environmental constraints and anti-agriculture policies aimed at extracting surplus as taxes and subsidizing urban food. Exacerbating these were lack of recognition of the strengths of peasant agriculture, leading to disastrous experiments with large-scale mechanized state farming; bias towards plantation agriculture in research, allocation of inputs, and extension; and failure to develop adequate infrastructure (Chazan et al., 1988). Declining per capita food production led to increased dependence on food imports and, even more damagingly, on food aid.

Overall, the real value of many significant exports did not rise as rapidly as that of imported manufactured goods. In addition, continued reliance on one or two exports rendered countries particularly vulnerable to price fluctuations and Northern protectionism. The pattern of development in most newly independent countries was regarded as "neo-colonialist," signifying the impossibility of formulating and implementing development policy based on local resources when economic growth depended so heavily on external conditions of demand and foreign capital (Jamal and Weeks, 1993).

Urbanization and urban management

At the beginning of the 1960s, less than a fifth of Africa's population lived in urban areas. Although the proportion of southern Africa's population that was urban was twice this (42 per cent), the remainder of African countries, with few exceptions, had very low levels of urbanization (United Nations, 1993) (table 12.1). However, despite the extractive nature of colonial economies, the limited development of manufacturing, and attempts at influx control, urban areas had been growing at between 4 and 6 per cent per annum in the 1950s, except in southern Africa. The rate of urban growth, which had thus been accelerating prior to the main wave of countries attaining independence, continued to accelerate. Rates of natural increase also steadily increased, with the result that the urban growth rate reached 8 per cent a year or more during this period in a number of countries. The most marked increases in urban growth rates occurred, on the whole, in the least urbanized countries, including those that attained independence without significant urban centres, while, in contrast, slower rates of urban growth were experienced in some countries that inherited oversized capitals, for example Senegal, where Dakar had been the administrative centre for the whole of French West Africa (O'Connor, 1983).

In 1960, only Johannesburg had a population of more than 1

Table 12.1 Urbanization in Africa, 1950–1995

	1950–55	1955–60	1960–65	1965–70	1970–75	1975–80	1980–85	1985–90	1990–95
% urban at the beginning of period									
East	5.3	6.3	7.4	8.8	10.3	12.3	14.6	16.9	19.1
Middle	14.2	15.9	17.9	21.1	24.8	26.6	28.2	29.8	31.9
South	38.2	40.0	41.9	42.8	43.6	44.1	44.5	45.0	46.2
West	10.2	12.2	14.5	16.9	19.7	22.7	26.0	29.5	33.2
Average annual rate of growth (%)									
East	5.63	5.79	6.07	6.04	6.05	6.50	5.71	5.55	5.62
Middle	4.11	4.29	5.51	5.68	3.86	3.98	4.07	4.39	4.64
South	3.21	3.32	3.00	2.86	3.02	2.89	2.84	3.01	3.22
West	5.85	5.93	5.73	5.77	5.78	5.73	5.64	5.52	5.27

Source: United Nations (1993: 74).

million, whereas by 1970 there were four cities of this size, two in South Africa and only two elsewhere in SSA: Lagos and Kinshasa, which had grown, in so far as it was possible to tell in the absence of reliable census results, at about 10 per cent per annum consistently throughout the 1950s and 1960s. Other large cities with particularly rapid rates of growth (over 10 per cent p.a.) in the 1960s and early 1970s included Abidjan, Conakry, and Dar es Salaam, along with many of the smaller cities. A pattern of increased concentration of rural–urban migration in the largest city within a country was widely evident (Zachariah and Condé, 1981).

Any explanation of the rapid rates of urbanization and urban growth observed in African countries must take into account a wide range of structural factors. Incorporation of the African peasantry into the national and international economy started in the mercantilist era, was consolidated in the colonial era, and was desired both by governments reliant on extracting foreign exchange and revenue from cash-crop exports and food for their urban populations from food-crop surpluses and by farmers, who had become used to and dependent on cash purchases. The contribution of subsistence agriculture to the costs of reproduction of the migrant labour force enabled wages to remain low. However, Standing (1984) suggests that the effect was that surplus was withdrawn from the rural economy to maintain the urban labour force, with the result that eventually rural incomes were reduced to the point that out-migration occurred despite a lack of urban opportunities. In some areas population growth and environmental deterioration placed pressure on land and other means of production, while increasing life expectancy and larger families reduced the prospects of access to land through inheritance. Although migration was not the only response, it was a common one (Gugler and Flanagan, 1978). Elsewhere the rural economy broke down because of civil strife, for example in Zaire, where numbers in Kinshasa rose by 350,000 to nearly 1.7 million between 1955 and 1975 (O'Connor, 1983). Finally, government policies typically reduced producer prices in the interests of increasing the competitiveness of export crops and providing cheap urban food, reducing the returns to agriculture.

Meanwhile, a number of changes associated with independence increased the attraction of cities. The growth of civil services, attempts to industrialize, and the abandonment of remaining relics of influx control gave a boost to rural–urban migration. The centralization of politics and bureaucracy formed a further attraction to investors who needed access to the state machinery. The process of decolonization resulted in the emergence of many new states, each generating a new or enlarged national bureaucracy. Thus the former colony of French West Africa, for example, was dissolved into eight new states (Standing, 1984). What urban centres there were became the locus of power and investment and new states invested heavily in infrastructure and amenities in their capitals because of their international and national visibility (Gugler and Flanagan, 1978; Mehretu, 1983). The creation of additional subnational units gave further impetus to the development of administrative centres, while construction of the first of the new capitals was started in this period. Nigerian National Development Plans in the 1970s, for example, devoted over 80 per cent of non-agricultural public capital investment to urban areas (Salau, 1990: 163). The exploitation of new resources led to growth in cities such as Port Harcourt, centre of Nigeria's oil industry, while other mining centres declined in relative terms, for example in Zaire and Zambia.

Both the predominant migration model and the belief that urban bias accounts for the perpetuation of rural poverty rest on the concept of a labour aristocracy, paid above-market wages in a substantial formal sector. In some cities, for example Nairobi, Harare, and Lusaka, the large-scale sector dominated urban employment and the availability of wage jobs attracted migrants. In other cities, however, small and intermediate enterprises accounted for a large proportion of employment even at independence; for example, Kumasi with 60 per cent and Accra with 45 per cent in 1960 (O'Connor, 1983: 143). In Abidjan, whereas 44 per cent of workers in 1974 were in the informal sector, by 1984 58 per cent of urban jobs, following Côte d'Ivoire's relatively successful state-driven industrialization, centralization of administration, attraction of foreign capital, and concentration of public investment, were in the formal sector (Dubresson, 1997). However, despite the concentration of a large proportion of all manufacturing in countries' capital cities (a third in Accra and Lagos, half in Conakry, two-thirds in Abidjan, three-quarters in Freetown, 87 per cent in Dakar) (O'Connor, 1983), the empirical evidence that wages were higher and employment more secure than in the informal sector was scarce (Jamal and Weeks, 1993). Where colonial labour policies had resulted in an urban age–sex structure dominated by men of working age, the trend towards convergence with national age–sex structures that had begun with labour stabilization policies 20 or more years before intensified, as increasing numbers of women either joined their husbands in the cities or migrated in their own right. In South Africa, however, apartheid policies and the use of migrant labour from surrounding countries maintained its relatively slow rate of urban growth and gender imbalance. A secondary attraction in some places was the better access to social and educational facilities available in town, while transport improvements and greater awareness of opportunities because of better access to education and the media facilitated the process. Remittances by urban migrants to rural areas continued to be significant.

The inherited philosophy, legal and financial basis, and institutional system for planning and managing urban development changed only incrementally in most countries in the early years after independence. The balance between continuity and change, Simon (1992) suggests, was influenced by the nature of the anti-colonial struggle; the fate of the ex-colonial élite; the policies pursued by the new élite with respect to national integration and relations with the world economy; national modes of production and means of social reproduction; and the extent to which urban legislative change was instituted. Governments were preoccupied with national political and economic issues and generally paid relatively little attention to urban administration. Where centralized structures existed, these persisted, especially in francophone Africa (Stren, 1989a). Where urban local government on the British model had been established, apart from a rapidly enlarged franchise at independence, it was retained more or less intact. However, the scope of urban local government functions was reduced by the establishment of separate statutory bodies and the adoption by central government of responsibility for services such as education and the police (Rakodi, 1986a). The contradiction inherent in central–local government relations led to the erosion of local government autonomy in most post-colonial societies, although the extent to which this occurred and the form that it took varied between and even within countries. This erosion was exacerbated by the lack of administrative capacity and the use of political office to fulfil traditional social obligations, further personal interests, and increase popular support and power bases (Rakodi, 1986b).

An environment conducive to business and the maintenance of lifestyles for European residents had been achieved by infrastructure provision; by land-use planning in the parts of settlements used for trade, administration, and European residence (and sometimes manufacturing); and also, as mentioned above, in many settlements by the public sector provision of housing for African residents. The urban spatial structure and built environment that were inherited reflected the underlying ideology of separate development, based on racially segregated residential areas and radically different standards of service provision and construction. The imported land administration system survived independence; but the speed of urban growth far outpaced its capacity to cope, and the years after independence were marked by a proliferation of unauthorized residential developments. The problems arising from the superimposition of an imported system on indigenous tenure systems, its role in producing the segregated colonial built environment, its considerable administrative and skill requirements, and its function as one of the main bases for local revenue generation, were not resolved. The system of private individualized land tenure, with the opportunities it presented for accumulation, was extended on independence to many more indigenous urban residents, entrenching their interest in maintaining and extending private property ownership.

The extension of unauthorized development, central government expenditure constraints, and the lack of a buoyant revenue base together resulted in infrastructure provision and maintenance falling further and further behind demand. Even where inherited administrative structures were changed after independence, the change more often led to a deterioration than to an improvement in services. The philosophy underlying colonial housing policy in some countries, that of providing housing for temporary urban residents (Africans and in many countries Europeans too), which had led to a system of contractor-built tied subsidized rental housing, was apparently not reconsidered. Most post-independence housing policies were based on similar assumptions: they proved to a greater or lesser extent unable to keep pace with the housing needs of the growing urban population and rapidly gave rise to vested interests in their continuation (Rakodi, 1986a). In urban areas that pre-dated colonialism, the public sector had much less of a role and private sector construction was relied upon to a greater extent to provide houses for low-income residents, for example in Zaire, the Sudan, and Nigeria until the mid-1970s (Stren, 1989a). In almost all these settlements, the continuation of spatial planning as a technical/regulatory activity undertaken by a section of the bureaucratic élite and/or foreign consultants, as well as the failure to reconsider land administration, meant that a large proportion of urban development occurred without reference to any guiding framework. Resources that were available for investment in infrastructure, service provision, and regulatory activities, and that could have ensured basic environmental standards for all urban residents rather than high standards for a few, were not used to best effect.

Global forces in the past two decades of African development

The impress of mercantilist trade and above all of colonial control left an enduring political, economic, and spatial legacy that not only determined countries' room to manoeuvre on their attainment of independence, but also, as seen in the recent history of the continent, is far from spent. The global forces that affect African countries and cities today have their origins in the historical relationship between the continent and the world economic system. However, the character of globalization has continued to evolve and its differential effects to become more marked.

First, with respect to trade, by 1990, 91 per cent of Africa's export earnings were still from primary products, although fuels, metals, and minerals accounted for two-thirds of this compared with a quarter in 1965. Unlike low- and middle-income countries elsewhere in the world, which had increased the share of manufacturing in their export earnings from 26 per cent to 50 per cent, and had increased their share of world trade, Africa remained marginal to the world trade system. This was not, as often implied by the International Monetary Fund (IMF), for want of effort (export volumes from SSA grew at 6.1 per cent p.a. between 1965 and 1980 and at 0.2 per cent p.a. in the 1980s – World Bank, 1992), but because demand for primary commodities has weakened. In addition, even the IMF admits that the terms of trade for African countries as a whole deteriorated in six out of the eight years between 1984 and 1992. Imports have, inevitably, been dominated by manufactured goods, although food continues to constitute 16 per cent of imports and the volume of food aid in 1989–1990 was nearly three times that needed in 1974–1975 (World Bank, 1992). Although imports grew less rapidly than exports between 1965 and 1980, during the 1980s, while the volume of exports continued to grow slowly, imports fell by −4.3 per cent p.a. as countries came under pressure to use export earnings to repay their debts (World Bank, 1992). The reduced capacity to import in turn had adverse effects on growth throughout the later 1970s and 1980s (IMF, 1993).

Perhaps the most crucial incidents affecting Africa's trading position have been associated with oil prices. The price increases of

1973–1974 and the later 1970s improved the terms of trade for the oil exporters. For example, Nigeria's economy grew by 7.0 per cent p.a. between 1965 and 1975. The boom, however, stimulated extravagant investment and the use of the state machinery by members of the élite, civil servants, and intermediaries for foreign capital to further their own interests. The naira was allowed to appreciate, leading to a decline in agricultural exports, so that, when the oil-based boom came to an end at the end of the 1970s, not only did Nigeria have little other than increased inequalities, increased concentration of activity in the southern cities, and wasteful prestige projects to show for it, but also alternative sources of export earnings had not been developed. As a result, it rapidly entered the slow-growth group of economies and its GDP actually fell by −2.5 per cent p.a. between 1975 and 1986. Cameroon, although a smaller producer, was equally dependent on oil exports. Unlike Nigeria, its currency was allowed to depreciate, foreign exchange reserves were accumulated abroad, oil revenue was used to finance manufacturing, and coffee and cocoa producer prices were maintained despite lower world prices, so that it avoided the worst effects of the oil price falls (Nafziger, 1990). However, the terms of trade of the great majority of countries that were oil importers declined to 85 per cent of 1973 levels (Nafziger, 1990: 52). The immediate impact on transport, energy, and agriculture forced countries to borrow to foot the increase in import bills. At the time, the massive influx of petrodollars into the world financial system was resulting in negative real interest rates, and the strategy seemed both necessary and rational.

However, for the majority of African countries, their additional borrowing in 1973–1974 was to have adverse effects in the longer term, as real interest rate increases coincided with yet higher oil prices at the end of the decade, producing the debt crisis of the early 1980s. Commercial borrowing was dominated by a few countries, including Nigeria, Gabon, and the Congo, mainly for oil exploitation, and also Côte d'Ivoire. Another reason for borrowing has been to cover current account deficits. In the poorest countries, reliance on aid has been unavoidable. Thus Africa's indebtedness is variously a result of necessity, extravagance, and the opportunities offered by its past strategic importance. However, much of the money has been squandered, especially in countries such as Zaire, Ghana, and Nigeria (Nafziger, 1990). Repayments have consistently absorbed 25 per cent of export earnings since the mid-1980s, and even then much of the accumulated debt consists of arrears rather than new borrowing.

Although, by world standards, Africa is not a major borrower, the burdensome nature of this debt to the countries concerned is illustrated by comparing SSA, which had outstanding debt equal to 324 per cent of exports of goods and services and 109 per cent of GDP in 1990, with East Asia and the Pacific (91 per cent and 27 per cent, respectively) or Latin America and the Caribbean (257 per cent and 42 per cent) (World Bank, 1992). Commercial bank debt makes up, however, a much less significant proportion of the debt overhang (13 per cent) than official debt (78 per cent) (IMF, 1993: 187). Before considering official development assistance (ODA) in more detail, the ability of African countries to attract equity investment will be analysed.

Although between the early 1970s and mid-1980s, global FDI became less important than bank credit, it continued to grow in volume. Much was concentrated in a small number of countries with large domestic markets, rich natural resources, or advantages as a base for export-oriented production. By 1982, the proportion of global FDI that was in less developed countries (LDCs) had increased to 24 per cent but Africa's share of it had decreased from 21 per cent to 11 per cent (Cantwell, 1991: 187–189). Its share of new FDI was even less. Even when they offered substantial incentives and imposed few restrictions, acknowledged the IMF, the smaller resource-poor African countries were unsuccessful in attracting investment (IMF, 1985: 4). Thus between 1976 and 1986, significant net inflows occurred only to Nigeria, Liberia, Zaire, Gabon, Kenya, Cameroon, and Côte d'Ivoire. Most countries experienced net disinvestment, and in 1985 and 1986 SSA as a whole experienced net disinvestment, not least because of the effects of structural adjustment (Cockcroft, 1992: 337).

The sectoral composition of worldwide FDI changed over the period, initially away from oil, mining, and agriculture to manufacturing. Nationalizations and the effect of policies to restrict entry of new foreign capital lessened TNC interest even in oil and mining in Africa (IMF, 1985; UNCTC, 1991). Nevertheless, by the early 1980s, half the total stock of FDI was still in the extractive sectors, compared with about 20 per cent in non-African LDCs. To the extent that FDI occurred in manufacturing (about a quarter of the stock in Africa by the beginning of the 1980s, compared with half in Asia and over half in Latin America), it has been in low-value-added import-substitution and resource-processing industries in the larger, more developed economies (Cantwell, 1991). Although Africa's share of worldwide FDI remained stable, at just over 2 per cent throughout the 1980s, most of this originated in the former colonial powers rather than in Japan or the United States, and, even to industrial capital in the former colonial powers, Africa is now only of marginal and decreasing interest (Bennell, 1990). A further sectoral shift gathered pace in the 1980s, as services FDI grew to comprise over half of all annual flows of FDI and 40 per cent of FDI stock worldwide. Recent growth in services FDI in Africa has been concentrated in a few countries (mainly Nigeria) and in the traditional areas of trade and construction, rather than in the financial services sector, which has been so important globally. However, a very high proportion of the tiny but growing Japanese investment is in trade and financial services (UNCTC, 1989). Although Africa has shared in the increased global flows of investment in services, as with manufacturing, its position is marginal. Only South Africa has a well-developed capital market and a stock exchange dealing significantly in international stock (Simon, 1997). The limited volume of manufacturing and services FDI has exacerbated the difficulties experienced by African countries in generating sufficient wage jobs for growing urban labour forces.

External and internal shocks, a general deterioration in the terms of trade for many of Africa's most important products, and economic mismanagement have led to a continued need for foreign exchange that is not satisfied, by earnings from exports, commercial bank borrowing, or FDI. As a result, Africa became the largest recipient region of ODA by the 1980s. Aid receipts as a percentage of GNP were 9.6 per cent in 1990, but much more in the poorest and most aid-dependent countries (Mozambique 66 per cent, Tanzania 48 per cent, and Somalia 46 per cent). Although other countries were less aid dependent, in several between a fifth and a third of GNP came from aid. The recipients of the largest volume of aid per capita, however, were not the poorest countries (World Bank, 1992). In addition, it should be noted that, whereas net credits from the IMF were positive in the early 1980s, they were negative later in the decade (ODI, 1993).

The reliance of African countries on aid has rendered them vulnerable to policy conditionality, both by the multilateral donors, which supplied just under a third of ODA in the 1980s, and, in their wake, by the bilateral donors. Policy conditions have affected both general economic management and approaches to urban development. The latter will be considered in the next section. The difficulties caused for African countries by the external shocks of the 1970s and early 1980s were initially seen as temporary trade crises and tackled by IMF stabilization packages. However, endogenous shocks (drought, civil strife) and economic mismanagement, combined with external vulnerability, showed that the economic crisis had deeper roots, resulting in the addition of structural and sectoral adjustment programmes to the stabilization programmes. By the end of the 1980s, 30 African countries had adopted structural adjustment policies (SAPs), many implementing a succession of programmes, and others had introduced some kind of "home-grown" programme (Jesperson, 1992). The programmes adopted by most countries comprised three basic components: liberalization and measures to encourage exports, streamlining of the public sector by means of privatization and reduction of expenditure, and restructuring of external debt in order to increase repayments and attract new flows of aid and commercial investment (Seralgeldin, 1989). By the end of the 1980s, the World Bank's emphasis had shifted from stabilization and growth to place rather more emphasis on equity, stressing the need for programmes to foster the participation of the poor in the process of economic growth, by improving their access to jobs, income-generating assets, and basic services, and by introducing compensatory transitional provisions to protect vulnerable groups' access to services and to enable redundant workers to make a new start (Seralgeldin, 1989; Ribe et al., 1990).

African countries have pursued SAPs in difficult economic circumstances (fluctuating and/or declining terms of trade, high real interest rates exacerbating the debt burden, and droughts). Although the World Bank detected a number of positive experiences, especially in countries relatively little affected by unusual weather or external shocks (Seralgeldin, 1989), many assessments are less positive and others reach contrary conclusions (for example, Jesperson, 1992; Killick with Malik, 1992; Stewart et al., 1992; Mosley and Weeks, 1993). In partial recognition of this, the World Bank's most recent assessment (World Bank, 1994) is more measured in its conclusions. Despite privatization and the liberalization of prices and foreign trade, investment and GDP have generally fallen, and the share of manufacturing in GDP and export earnings increased little if at all. In the past few years, some signs of industrial recovery have emerged, but the picture is very mixed, with many countries showing a continued deterioration (Simon, 1997). It was hoped that increased producer prices and reduced food and services subsidies would benefit rural populations, especially small farmers, redressing the perceived anti-agriculture and anti-rural bias in government policy. However, in practice these impacts have been uneven and in many cases strongly negative, despite half-hearted compensatory programmes and attempts to integrate anti-poverty measures into SAPs (Gibbon, 1992). Many of the impacts have affected urban populations in particular and will be analysed in more detail below.

Although policy reform was needed in African countries, their increased dependence on external assistance in the 1980s made them susceptible to uniform policy prescriptions, determined, despite apparent opportunities for negotiation, largely by outside agencies. Although the donors claim that there is now evidence of improved macroeconomic performance as a result, few others are convinced. Instead, the hegemony of the colonial powers over policy formulation to which Africa was subjected in the first half of the twentieth century seems to have been substituted by a new hegemony, which no less clearly has the interests of transnational capital and Northern countries at heart. Such a hegemony, it is argued, is illustrated by the lack of influence of alternative agendas for reform, such as that of the United Nations Economic Commission for Africa (UNECA, 1989; Stewart et al., 1992).

Urban growth and change

What, in the context of Africa's external dependence and vulnerability, marginalization and aid dependence, has happened to cities? What effects has the economic deterioration precipitated by the first oil price increases and reinforced by subsequent exogenous and endogenous forces had on the rate of urbanization and on the economic structure of cities? One of the manifestations of the internationalization of capital has been the emergence of a hierarchy of cities with particular roles in the capitalist economic system. Although there is disagreement over the precise identification of levels in the hierarchy and which cities to include in each category, the general consensus seems to be that currently four levels can be identified, representing different functions with respect to capital accumulation.

At the apex of the system are the so-called "world cities," sites for the control and management of TNC operations, specialized business services to back these up, and nodes in the world banking and commercial system (Sassen, 1994). Not unexpectedly, given Africa's marginality to the world economic system, none of the world cities are located in Africa.

Second to these global cities are regional or continental cities, which perform similar functions within the world capitalist system to global cities, but within a more restricted geographical region (Sit, 1993). LDC cities of most obvious regional significance are those in the newly industrialized countries (NICs), which are increasingly integrated into functional networks of economic linkages with global or core cities, especially in Asia. Within these regional networks, "growth triangles" have been identified, based on complementarities across national boundaries, and urban corridors based on mega-cities (Yeung and Lo, 1996). Although one or two cities in sub-Saharan Africa have roles beyond their national boundaries, for example Nairobi (Simon, 1992), and the regional economic significance of others such as Johannesburg is growing, Africa is not even part of the semi-periphery, and the functional city systems linked across national borders that have begun to emerge in Asia are not evident in Africa except in so far as cities in the interior must use ports in other countries for trade. Abidjan in west Africa and Dar es Salaam in east Africa, for example, perform this function.

At the third level in the hierarchy are national cities, which are focuses for national accumulation but also, by providing a location for transnational offices and operations, banks, and corporate services, are linked into the world economic system (Simon, 1992; Sit, 1993). Some of the national cities that currently have only limited regional functions are competing with each other to attract external investment and extend their regional significance. In West Africa, for example, Accra and Abidjan foresee that they may be able to attract such investment in competition with larger Lagos, because of the more promising economic circumstances of the countries in which they are located (Ghana and Côte d'Ivoire) and an urban environment more conducive to economic efficiency. Finally, secondary cities within countries, which perform functions primarily for local capital, may also be integrated into the global system as channels for traded goods and locations for TNC production.

In 1970, there were only four cities with a population of over 1 million in sub-Saharan Africa (Lagos, Cape Town, Johannesburg, and Kinshasa), but by 1990 there were estimated to be 17, in 13 countries (United Nations, 1993). Only Lagos was said to have a population of over 5 million (estimated by the United Nations at 7.7

million in 1990, by the Lagos State Water Corporation at 7.9 million in 1990, and from the provisional census figures at 5.7 million in 1991). However, if Johannesburg's boundaries are defined to include the Pretoria–Witwatersrand–Vereeniging (PWV) metropolitan region, its population was 8.8 million in 1990 (Beavon, 1997). Possibly nine other cities have populations of between 2 and 5 million (Luanda, Abidjan, Addis Ababa, Nairobi, Maputo, Dakar, Cape Town, Khartoum, and Kinshasa) (see fig. 12.1).

In all but one of the countries containing a city of over 1 million (South Africa), the largest city was home to at least one-fifth of the country's urban population, but the range of concentration is very wide (from 20 per cent of Nigeria's urban population in Lagos to 76 per cent of Guinea's in Conakry). Large cities also dominate in the least urbanized countries: in the case of Ethiopia only 12 per cent of the population in 1990 was urban, but 30 per cent of this was in Addis Ababa (1.8 million) (United Nations, 1993). Even in countries that do not have very large cities, the proportion of the urban population living in the largest city is high and increasing, while secondary cities and small urban centres continue to be underdeveloped (Rondinelli, 1988).

Rates of urban growth and city size are not linked crudely to national economic trends or the economic functions of cities (Simon, 1997). Despite Africa's marginal position in the world economy and the economic difficulties experienced more or less consistently since the mid-1970s, urbanization has continued (table 12.1). By 1990, it was estimated that nearly a third of the population was urban compared with less than a quarter in 1975. According to a recent UN publication, the rate of urban growth was about the same in the 1980s as in the post-independence decade, running at just under 5 per cent p.a. As in the earlier period, rates of growth in the least urbanized regions (East and West Africa) were greater than those in the most urbanized region (southern Africa). However, there are major difficulties with these figures: the recency and reliability of censuses vary widely, with two of the largest countries (Zaire and Nigeria) failing to produce reliable figures. The inability of so many African countries to carry out regular and reliable censuses is a symptom of their poverty and underdevelopment, as well as a result of civil war and political instability. Many of the apparently precise figures are mere estimates, based on extrapolations of earlier trends, but, given the series of exogenous and endogenous shocks that have affected the development of most African countries, it is risky to make such assumptions.

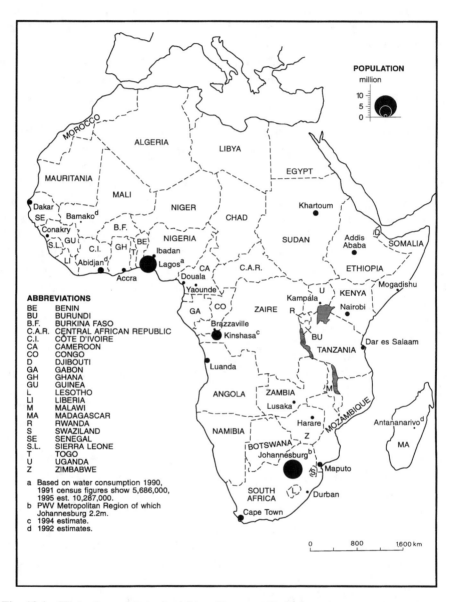

Fig. 12.1 **The urban pattern in Africa (Sources: United Nations, *World Urbanisation Prospects: The 1994 Revision (1995 Estimates)*; exceptions based on relevant chapters from UNCHS, *Global Report on Human Settlements*, draft, Nairobi: UNCHS, 1995, table 4)**

332

Accra, for example, was reputed to have experienced significant net out-migration during the worst period of economic hardship in the early to mid-1980s, as people returned to their traditional stool or family lands: certainly census data demonstrated that the national urban growth rate of 3.2 per cent p.a. for 1970–1984 was considerably less than the 1960–1970 growth rate of 4.8 per cent. This trend, it was suggested, reversed again once conditions improved under the second SAP in the late 1980s and early 1990s and its associated Programme of Actions to Mitigate the Social Costs of Adjustment, but data are not yet available to substantiate this (Simon, 1997). Similarly, the annual population growth of Abidjan, which averaged 10–12 per cent p.a. between 1960 and 1978, fell in the 1980s to 4–6 per cent, below that of middle-sized towns. The flow of migrants, especially from neighbouring countries, which made Abidjan one of the most cosmopolitan cities in the continent, has slowed down (Dubresson, 1997). Falling rates of urban growth reflect a decline in rates of in-migration and also a tendency for rates of "return" migration to increase (Potts, 1997). Flows of displaced people into Maputo, Luanda, Addis Ababa, and Monrovia as a result of rural conflict, or out of Mogadishu and Kigali in response to urban-based insurrections, also confound estimates based on previous trends and may or may not produce permanent changes in the urban population (Simon, 1997).

In the 1960s and 1970s, the proliferation of informal activities seemed to be sustained by the demand generated by formal sector enterprises and wages. However, in the 1980s, the implementation of SAPs, involving the slimming down of civil services and parastatals, privatization, relaxation of labour protection policies, and dismantling of trade protection, led almost universally to an absolute or relative decline in formal sector employment and a narrowing or reversal of the urban–rural income gap (Jamal and Weeks, 1993; Potts, 1997). Urban-based manufacturing suffered particularly badly from short-ages of imported materials, increased interest rates, reduced invest-ment, and declining effective demand. In some cities, nevertheless, formal sector employment continued to predominate. For example, in 1977 over half of all manufacturing establishments and 71 per cent of building and construction firms in Kenya were located in Nairobi. By 1988, over half of all urban wage employment was still in the city (63 per cent of formal construction employment, 72 per cent of that in finance, real estate, and business services) (Simon, 1992: 94–97). The 1992 census showed that in Kenya the loss of wage employment had been greater in secondary urban centres, with the result that the majority of those working in Nairobi were still in formal wage employment (Obudho, 1997). Even where formal sector manufacturing continued to be important, however, declines were registered. Beavon (1997), for example, describes the early mining and later manufacturing economic base of Johannesburg, which, together with its services functions, account for its growth and agglomeration into the PWV conurbation. However, industrial decline in the late 1980s and early 1990s has been caused by a decline in mining, cutbacks in military production, and the effect of decentralization policies on labour-intensive industries, especially clothing and textiles (Rogerson, 1997). Although some of those retrenched in African cities returned to the rural areas, unemployment rates also rose and many resorted to informal sector activities to earn a living. Thus, in Côte d'Ivoire since the beginning of the 1980s, the SAP has meant the loss of thousands of jobs in the public and parastatal sectors, manufacturing, and construction. In 1980 in Abidjan there were 383,000 jobs in the formal/modern sector and 330,000 in the informal sector, but by 1988 the economic activity rate had fallen to 42 per cent (compared with 59 per cent in 1978) and 58 per cent of jobs were in the informal sector, within which the proportion of self-employed had grown from 32 per cent to 41 per cent in 10 years (Dubresson, 1997: 263).

The most recently available data indicate that nearly two-thirds of the total African urban labour force is engaged in informal sector activities (ILO–JASPA, quoted in Rogerson, 1997) and almost all the new jobs are being created in the small-scale micro-enterprise economy. For those in employment, real wages usually fell, sometimes dramatically, and they also sought economic activities in the informal sector. In Kinshasa in 1986, the proportion of income derived from wages was only 33 per cent for civil servants, and no more than 45 per cent or so for other wage workers, with wages as a proportion of income decreasing as wages increase (Piermay, 1997). Findings in Tanzania (Tripp, 1992) and Uganda (Bigsten and Kayizzi-Mugerwa, 1992) were similar. Although some of those previously employed as wage workers lack the skills to become self-employed, many others use the basic working capital provided by wage employment, and the contacts and opportunities that their formal sector jobs provide, to establish successful businesses. The complexion of small-scale economic activities varies between cities, although in most places they are predominantly trade related (for example in Dakar and in the urban areas of Botswana, Malawi, Swaziland, Kenya, and South

Africa) and the extent of small-scale manufacturing is limited. Participation in small-scale enterprises does not mean that most of the workforce is self-employed – wage employment is widespread, even though most of the enterprises may be single-person businesses. However, constraints on accumulation and availability of credit have resulted in a pattern of replication rather than capital/skill/technology upgrading and increased enterprise size (Rogerson, 1997). One characteristic associated with the growth in significance of the small-scale sector is the increased participation of women both in the workforce and in informal sector activities, although the sexual division of labour tends to confine them to the less profitable activities. The key explanatory factor for the proliferation of small-scale and informal economic enterprise is the progressive emasculation of the formal economy. Although the exodus of skilled technicians to which this gives rise may create an opportunity for technological upgrading of the informal sector, especially where demand for modern manufactured goods is transferred from formal to informal sector firms (as appears to have happened in Côte d'Ivoire and maybe Kenya), the influx of new entrants may also exceed the capacity of the sector to absorb them, leading to overproduction and overtrading, declining profits, and the expansion of exploitative labour practices (Rogerson, 1997). A potentially important aspect of informalization relates to growing linkages between formal and informal enterprises, in which formal factory jobs are increasingly displaced by jobs in unregistered plants and home-working, in order to bypass labour regulations and reduce costs. This is, to date, limited in urban Africa (Rogerson, 1997). As yet, our understanding of the nature and scope of this burgeoning of the small-scale competitive sector is insufficient to make judgements, first on whether it is merely a refuge, enabling people to survive at or below the poverty line, or a dynamic flexible sector capable of generating economic growth, or, secondly, on how the changing nature of the urban economy will influence migration trends in future. However, Dubresson (1997) doubts that, without the stimulus of formal sector purchasing power, small-scale trade, services, and manufacturing can provide the economic dynamism required by large cities.

Despite Africa's economic difficulties and the apparent slow-down in rates of urban growth, large cities have continued to grow (at an estimated average of 4.5 per cent p.a. in 1990–1995) (United Nations, 1993). Rates of natural increase are high despite the spread of AIDS; these cities are communications and transport hubs, and often the seats of government. Their location as the place of residence for politicians, senior civil servants, and diplomats has helped to bias public expenditure in specialized health and other services and infrastructure towards them; this and the need for access to government offices have in turn made them the most likely locational choice for both transnational and domestic investment in manufacturing and for the offices of TNCs with mining or agricultural enterprises elsewhere in the country. Even though transnational investment in services in African countries is limited, what there is occurs in the largest cities. FDI is even more concentrated than domestic investment in the largest cities, because of executives' greater knowledge of the city's economic environment and the presence of commercial facilities to intermediate between extraction/production and the international market where necessary (Sit, 1993). The locational attractions of the city are often magnified by policy with respect to, for example, transport tariffs, energy and service prices, and incentives for industrial development. Official policies to encourage decentralization are often counteracted by the spatial effects of non-spatial policies. Lagos, for example, accounted for only 8.5 per cent of Nigeria's urban population in 1950, but has increased its dominance in succeeding decades and now is estimated to accommodate one-fifth of the country's urban population (United Nations, 1993). From its colonial origins as a port and administrative centre, a history of concentrated public and private sector investment underlain by poor communications with the rest of the country, political and administrative dominance combined with a politics of patronage, and dependence on imported inputs for industry and construction has reinforced its early dominance. Over 90 per cent of total net subsidies to industries benefited those located in the city (Oberai, 1993). Despite the removal of the national capital and federal civil service to Abuja, Lagos remains the economic and commercial hub of Nigeria and its main point of international access (Abiodun, 1997).

Many rural areas provide few economic opportunities for their growing populations, despite the pro-agriculture policy changes that have formed part of SAPs. Although the deterioration in infrastructure and services that has resulted from public expenditure cutbacks has been countrywide, rural areas started in a disadvantaged position. The chance of a better life in the cities, however much of a gamble, continues to attract migrants (Dogan and Kasarda, 1988). However, the unpredictable outcomes of economic reform programmes, the lack of reliable demographic information, and our limited understanding of the dynamics of urban economies following the virtual collapse of formal sector employment and wages make it difficult to foresee future urban growth trends.

Aid dependence and urban management

Rapidly growing urban populations place increasing demands on land, housing, services, and infrastructure, but weak revenue bases, lack of technological and administrative capacity amongst the agencies responsible for urban development, and vulnerability to evasion or exploitation by those with political and economic power prevent provisions keeping pace with need. The result is environmental damage, deteriorating living conditions, especially for the urban poor, and lack of the political legitimacy needed to improve revenue collection and regulatory processes. Investors have supported such aspects of urban administration as they perceive to be in their interest, especially the maintenance of private tenure, physical infrastructure provision, zoning, and development control. When affected by shortcomings in these administrative and service systems, however, it has served their interests better to make private provision, including private health care and education, private vehicle ownership, borehole water, diesel electricity generators, and radio equipment, rather than increasing their contribution to the development of comprehensive and effective urban services (Lee, 1993). Recognition by the 1970s of urban bias in both spatial investment and non-spatial policies led to an over-reaction. Aid flows switched almost entirely to rural development, with the partial exception of the World Bank and the United States Agency for International Development (USAID). Governments, despite the political power of urban populations, had declining volumes of resources and often misdirected them into ineffective or prestige investment. The result was that local administration and services deteriorated.

Despite continued struggles to improve urban planning and management, even in cities with substantial economies and formal political and administrative systems, the ability of land-delivery and physical and social services provision to provide an efficient urban environment for economic enterprise and a reasonable living environment for cities' residents has been inadequate (Stren, 1989b). Most successful in this regard have been the closely controlled cities of the recent settler economies, with their formal sector economic bases and substantial volumes of locally generated resources: South

Africa and Zimbabwe (Rakodi, 1995a). Even in these countries, however, the systems have been under pressure, and the influx of "illegal" migrants from the rural areas to the cities of South Africa, together with segregated and discriminatory administrative systems, resulted in widespread illegal land occupation and deterioration of services. In countries that had reasonably buoyant economies during the 1960s and early 1970s, such as Zambia, Kenya, and Côte d'Ivoire, inherited systems of urban administration survived and coped reasonably well, despite the pressures of rapid population growth. However, economic deterioration combined with the cumulative impacts of failure to change policies, reform administrative procedures, and ensure that revenue generation kept pace with growth and needs led to increasing incapacity to deal with urban planning and management needs.

The collapse of the formal economy, democratic politics, and administration and services has gone further in some societies than others. Zaire is generally considered to be at the opposite end of the spectrum from, say, South Africa or Zimbabwe, in terms of economic and public sector capacity. However, Kinshasa continues to grow, its inhabitants to obtain access to land and housing, and some urban services to function. Although there is a formal administrative structure, the state has a very weak role with respect to the urban development process. That the city has not collapsed in chaos is due to the functions performed by state officials in parallel systems (for example, informal land allocation), the powerful roles played by local leaders including traditional chiefs, and the initiatives taken by private sector agents including businessmen and the churches (Piermay, 1997). Ironically, it is perhaps in some aspects of this model that promising approaches to future urban management can be detected. Reliance on a weak local state has been shown to be misplaced and new provider/producer relations between the state and the private sector, non-governmental organizations (NGOs), and community-based organizations are being developed with respect to service provision and neighbourhood improvement (Wekwete, 1997).

Nevertheless, Africa's aid dependency has brought with it policy conditionality not merely for economic policies but also for spatial investment. The World Bank's first attempt to tackle urban problems started in the early 1970s (World Bank, 1972). Its search for appropriate locations for pilot projects based on the principles of affordability, cost recovery, and replicability coincided with the dawning realization in low-income countries that traditional methods of catering for newly formed urban households by the construction of complete conventional housing units for rent or sale were unrealistic. In Senegal and Zambia, the World Bank identified promising locations for its first projects, both based on sites and services, with the latter also incorporating upgrading of unauthorized areas. It envisaged these projects as both pilot and demonstration projects, and located them in the capital cities of the respective countries in the hope that they would later be replicated throughout the urban system. Neither were, although some of the lessons from them were fed into later projects of the same type in other African countries. Between 1972 and 1978 there were 12 such projects in SSA (Okpala, 1990) and by 1984 a further 13 (World Bank, 1986). Few, however, were wholly successful with respect to the three principles on which they were based: most sites and services projects were not affordable by the poorest, hidden subsidies were common, cost recovery problems were widespread, and replication was rare. Other funders, especially USAID, which was funding 14 projects in 1984, adopted similar approaches (World Bank, 1986). Thus in 1985, out of the 72 projects identified for the International Year of Shelter for the Homeless in 28 African countries, 60 per cent were externally funded (Okpala, 1990).

By the later 1970s, it was clear to many observers that there were problems associated with project-based lending, some of which resulted from the external funding and some from the process of project planning and implementation. The requirement for most significant decisions with respect to project design, implementation, and cost recovery to be agreed at the appraisal stage, prior to loan approval, and for agreed schedules of implementation to be adhered to, first, deterred participation in project planning even in unauthorized areas and where local political and official forces were sympathetic, and, secondly, made it difficult to modify project components that proved inappropriate or unworkable in practice. The establishment of separate project units to implement externally funded projects was a mixed blessing: they permitted external agencies to keep track of funds and insist on their correct use, and local implementors to avoid red tape and recruit appropriate staff, but they also led to problems of integrating newly serviced areas into ongoing systems of administration and service operation and maintenance. In addition, few of the projects resulted in an improved capacity with respect to land delivery, infrastructure provision, operation and maintenance, building materials production and supply, or housing finance (Rakodi, 1991).

By 1983, the World Bank had also begun to recognize some of these problems (World Bank, 1983; Cohen, 1983, 1990) and the emphasis of its lending programmes and those of USAID shifted. Major constraints on the larger-scale provision of serviced plots were perceived to be inadequate local revenue generation and the limited volume of mortgage funding that the public sector was able to make available. Attention was paid to the former from the mid-1980s, when, for example, a USAID study of local revenue generation in Burkina Faso was carried out (Mabogunje, 1990). A desire to tap into private sector funds for low-income housing, an ideological belief that private sector institutions would be more efficient in disbursing and recovering loans than public sector institutions, and an underlying desire to extend the reach of international and domestic large-scale capital led to a major focus on housing finance. USAID had established a Housing Guarantee programme in the early 1970s, which mobilizes private bank funding in the United States through a Congressionally sanctioned government loan guarantee. Attempts were made to create self-supporting financial intermediaries capable of making loans to low- and moderate-income households and to reduce and restructure housing subsidies (especially to eliminate subsidized interest rates) (World Bank, 1993). This was much easier in Asia and Latin America, with their more developed financial sectors, than in Africa and, although the worldwide volume of Bank shelter-related lending increased, it also shifted towards higher-income countries (World Bank, 1993: 57). The limitations of the approach and its vulnerability to economic downturn are revealed by the Zimbabwe experience (Rakodi, 1995b; see also Pugh, 1994). Following an overall review of experience (UNCHS, 1987), the new emphasis was nevertheless endorsed by the United Nations (UNCHS, 1990) and the World Bank (1993). In a strategy based on enabling the private sector to address the housing needs of all income groups, including the poor, the role of government is seen to be management of the housing sector as a whole rather than project-based support. The World Bank's approach is based on the use of various instruments designed to stimulate housing demand, facilitate supply, and provide an overall institutional framework (World Bank, 1993). This does represent a more coherent view of the proper role for government and also contains some recognition that the appropriate package of policies for a country will differ according to the level of development of its financial sector and the nature of the supply constraints on land and housing development (World Bank, 1993).

Parallel with this attention to the housing sector was a recognition that most cities were so poorly serviced that they could not maintain their roles in national economies as the centres of administration and suppliers of rural inputs (Stren, 1992), while the inhibiting effects on private sector investment of infrastructure neglect were also recognized (Peterson et al., 1991). In Tanzania, for example, while the economy stagnated, the per capita decline in expenditure on infrastructure and services was −11 per cent p.a. between 1978/79 and 1986/87. As a result, large firms had to lay off workers sporadically in response to irregular water and electricity supplies; these in turn resulted in lower production, lower profits, and lower yields from taxation (Stren, 1993: 128).

In 1990, a World Bank policy document set out a new agenda, designed:
1. to improve urban productivity by remedying infrastructure deficiencies, rationalizing regulatory frameworks, strengthening local government, and improving the financing of urban development;
2. to alleviate urban poverty by increasing demand for the labour of the poor, investing in health and education, and supporting safety nets and compensatory measures to deal with transitional problems caused by SAPs; and
3. to protect the urban environment by raising awareness, improving the information base, and developing city-wide environmental strategies and programmes of action (World Bank, 1991; Cohen, 1992; Cohen and Leitmann, 1994).

To implement this agenda, an increase in World Bank lending was anticipated, as well as a shift in emphasis from neighbourhood investments in shelter and infrastructure to city-level policy reform and institutional development and city-wide investment in infrastructure. The Urban Development Cooperation Strategy, "Cities, People and Poverty," of the United Nations Development Programme (UNDP) has similar goals but apparently places more emphasis than the World Bank on the need for social justice, participation, and support for NGOs (Cheema, 1992). The World Bank, together with the United Nations Centre for Human Settlements (UNCHS) and the UNDP and later some bilateral donors, agreed an urban management programme (1986–1996) that aims to work with developing countries to strengthen the contribution that cities and towns make towards economic growth, environmental quality, and the reduction of poverty. The programme now works in five areas: land management, infrastructure management, municipal finance and administration, environmental management, and poverty alleviation. It operates in Africa through a regional office in Accra, using city and country consultations as a basis for policy formulation and regional networks of expertise to provide technical advice on the implementation of action plans. The programme is underpinned by earlier World Bank research (for example, Bahl and Linn, 1992, on urban finance) and an ongoing research programme, as part of which a series of research and advisory publications is being produced. By the late 1980s, lending to strengthen municipal finance, infrastructure investment and management, and land management had increased (Wegelin, 1994).

As yet, there have been neither published in-house nor independent external evaluations of the World Bank's new urban agenda and the Urban Management Programme (UMP). However, concerns have been expressed about the assumptions upon which it is based, the gap between policy and implementation, and its relationship to the wider economic policies advocated by the same institutions (Jones and Ward, 1994). Harris (1992), for example, considers that the measures intended to increase urban productivity are not based on an adequate understanding of the structure or of the competitive advantages and disadvantages of city economies. Stren (1993) criticizes the agencies' failure to define what is meant by urban management, although he recognizes that this is in part to retain organizational flexibility. The term has become popular, Stren suggests, because of its ideological appeal, given its association with business management, and the desire of the funding agencies to harness private sector resources. Nevertheless, it can be used to incorporate conceptual and practical advances in approaches to planning for urban growth (Devas and Rakodi, 1993). There is also a certain political naïvety in the published documents (Jones and Ward, 1994), and the mentions of participatory approaches seem to be made with little understanding – as exemplified by the suggestion by UNDP's programme manager that "we [sic] must organize the urban poor at the community level to increase their capacity to make demands on the urban system" (Cheema, 1992: 27). Presumably he is referring to the domestic political system rather than the international urban lending programme, although the international donor agencies typically distance themselves from local demand-making. With respect to implementation, Harris (1992) points out that many World Bank and UMP projects are still concerned with traditional land management, household service provision, and housing, rather than city-wide institutional strengthening.

Structural adjustment lending, with its economic and political conditionalities, forms the context within which the new emphases in urban lending will be implemented. Although the municipal development funds being established in a number of countries as part of projects funded by the World Bank promise a more regular supply of capital funds, they do not of themselves solve all the difficulties in the political relationships between the central ministry responsible and local councils. The ability of local authorities and other agencies to achieve good yields from a variety of revenue sources is threatened by the pressure on them to lay off staff and the necessity for remaining staff, in a situation of declining real wages, to continue and diversify the survival strategies they have already developed. Without adequate administrative capacity, service delivery is not good enough to persuade users to pay their charges or taxes; poor service delivery in turn diminishes the political legitimacy of local authorities and makes it more difficult to enforce regulatory instruments and tax collection.

Real government expenditure per capita stagnated or fell in most countries in the region, as required by SAPs, and the pattern of expenditure also changed. The World Bank encouraged micro-credit schemes, expenditure on public works for upgrading and maintenance of urban infrastructure, and "shielding public expenditure on key health, education, nutrition and other basic welfare services" (Seralgeldin, 1989: 50) in order to protect those most vulnerable to cuts. In practice, spending on health care, education, economic services, and infrastructure was disproportionately cut (Stewart, 1991; Logan and Mengisteab, 1993). Such cuts reflected not government policy changes but the resources available once increased debt repayments had been allowed for (Jesperson, 1992). Some governments made efforts to redirect expenditure towards primary education and basic health care, but these efforts were threatened or negated by reduced resources and the introduction of user charges. In theory, prices for water, energy, health, education, etc. can be structured progressively. In practice, the balance of interests in most countries has militated against political commitment to progressive price structures (Jones and Ward, 1994), while measures to protect the poor from price increases have often been badly designed and under-resourced. As a result, and exacerbated by falling real wages and increased unemployment, defaults have increased, so that the flow of revenue is insufficient to build up local capacity to provide the quality of service people will be willing to pay for. Although evidence

343

is patchy, and sometimes contradictory and inconclusive, there is some indication of worsening nutritional and health status among vulnerable groups, declining school enrolment, and deteriorating basic educational achievements. The pressures have had a particularly adverse impact on women (Stewart, 1991). Reduced expenditure on education and training adversely affects the quality of the available workforce, as does the poor health associated with deteriorating infrastructure. These inhibit the mobilization of private sector investment in manufacturing, while poor health reduces the ability of children to absorb education (Harris, 1992; Stewart et al., 1992).

Programmes introduced to compensate the newly unemployed (severance payments, retraining, credit, etc.) have not reached the poor, while programmes to assist the chronically poor (public works schemes, nutrition supports, and targeting of subsidized education, health care, and food) may mitigate some of the immediate adverse effects of impoverishment but do not address its structural causes. Meanwhile, basic SAP policy packages have not been redesigned either to eliminate these adverse effects or to reduce poverty (Stewart, 1991).

The blanket faith in the private sector on which SAPs have been based has also been subject to criticism. I have noted above that FDI is unlikely to show any marked increase in volume. It cannot be relied on for the development of manufacturing, and foreign investors are unlikely to be interested in infrastructure and housing. Development will, therefore, depend on the level of domestic savings and investment, which, it is hoped, will increase with interest rate reforms. Some doubt, however, has been thrown on the expectation that higher interest rates will generate increased investment (Helleiner, 1992). It is by no means certain that the funds will be there for local authorities to borrow from the private sector, or that the housing finance system will be able to rely on private sector savings. Investment is partly a function of household income and, as long as incomes are depressed, it is unrealistic to expect savings (for investment in formal sector financial institutions, owner-occupied housing, or small enterprises) to increase at the cost of consumption (Jamal and Weeks, 1993).

The new approaches to housing and urban development are, in some respects, to be welcomed. This brief and incomplete assessment has shown that many of the assumptions on which they are based fit logically with the premises of SAPs. However, not only can many of these assumptions be challenged (Jones and Ward, 1994), but there are also notable inconsistencies between the effects of SAPs and the aims of the new urban agenda, as recognized even by some World Bank staff (Cohen, 1990).

Conclusion

The impact of mercantilist trade and above all of colonial control left an enduring political, economic, and spatial legacy that not only determined African countries' room to manoeuvre on their attainment of independence but also, as seen in the recent history of the continent, is far from spent. The colonial period was marked by a reorientation of urban patterns to serve the needs of trade and administration. A transitional period ensued, ending in most sub-Saharan African countries in the 1960s, in which the achievement of autonomous economic and political status was attempted by means of state-centred interventionist strategies paralleled by a regulatory approach to urban development. Since independence, there has been relatively little change to the pattern of urbanization, and what change did occur in the main post-independence decade was associated as much with administrative as with economic change. The rate of urban growth increased owing to expansion of public sector employment, attempts to industrialize, an increased rate of natural increase, and relative neglect of rural areas.

Global forces including trade, foreign investment, flows of international finance capital, and flows of official development assistance continue to have a major impact on the continent. Thus the failure of African economies to diversify and grow can be attributed partly to external factors: the terms of their integration into the global economy have produced continued dependence, vulnerability, and marginalization. In addition, the preconditions for successful competition in the new growth sectors of the global economy, especially export-oriented manufacturing, flexible production in both import-substituting and export industry, and specialist "niche" production, have been absent: infrastructure, a literate and numerate workforce, and a capacity for effective state intervention are lacking (Rogerson, 1997). Thus, a variety of domestic factors must also be taken into account.

None of the world cities are located in Africa. Nevertheless, despite its marginal position in the world economy and the economic difficulties experienced more or less consistently since the mid-1970s, urbanization has continued. In some cases, the most important factor driving urban growth has been a significant urban formal sector, providing wage employment in manufacturing, commerce, and administration. Increasingly, however, in many of the largest cities, this formal sector economic base has collapsed in the face of economic decline, liberalization, and political instability. Urban population growth has continued nevertheless, although perhaps less rapidly, driven by high rates of natural increase and the continued attractions of urban areas. Although small-scale informal sector economic activities have burgeoned, the evidence that these are dynamic rather than involutionary is scarce and appropriate support policies are rare (Rogerson, 1997).

Weak revenue bases, lack of technological and administrative capacity amongst the agencies responsible for urban development, and vulnerability to evasion or exploitation by those with political and economic power prevent land, housing, and infrastructure provision from keeping pace with need. However, even those cities where formal political and administrative systems and economies have been replaced by "informal" systems, notably Kinshasa, have not collapsed in chaos because indigenous political and social systems have been shown to be remarkably resilient and adaptable.

International lending for urban development, although influential in policy terms, has produced only limited results, at least in part because of agencies' lack of understanding of the very varied African political and social reality. A new aid agenda has resulted from the recognition, first, that structural adjustment lending has had adverse impacts on welfare and productivity, especially of the urban poor, and, secondly, that cities without adequate infrastructure and services do not provide an efficient location for economic activity. Although representing some advance on earlier thinking, some of the assumptions on which the new agenda is based can be challenged and achievement is likely to be threatened by the unresolved contradictions between its aims and wider structural adjustment policies. African countries' dependence on aid reduces their ability to resist policy conditionalities, even where these are perceived to be inappropriate. However, the picture is neither wholly nor universally gloomy. With respect to the cities of Africa, the seeds of a more autonomous future lie in the parallel economic and administrative systems of countries such as Zaire, in the confidence of South Africa and others that change can be achieved, and in the positive alliances that are being forged between local authorities and other agents in cities such as Lusaka.

Acknowledgements

The work on which this chapter is based was undertaken during the coordination and editing of a UNU project on the challenge of urbanization in Africa, reported in full in Rakodi (1997).

References

Abiodun, J. O. (1997), "The Challenges of Growth and Development in Metropolitan Lagos." In: C. Rakodi (ed.), *The Urban Challenge in Africa: Growth and Management of Its Large Cities*. Tokyo: United Nations University Press, pp. 192–222.

Bahl, R. W. and J. F. Linn (1992), *Urban Public Finance in Developing Countries*. Oxford: Oxford University Press for the World Bank.

Beavon, K. S. O. (1997), "Johannesburg: A City and Metropolitan Area in Transformation." In: C. Rakodi (ed.), *The Urban Challenge in Africa: Growth and Management of Its Large Cities*. Tokyo: United Nations University Press, pp. 150–191.

Bennell, P. (1990), "British Industrial Investment in Sub-Saharan Africa: Corporate Responses to Economic Crisis in the 1980s." *Development Policy Review* 8(2): 155–177.

Bigsten, A. and S. Kayizzi-Mugerwa (1992), "Adaptation and Distress in the Urban Economy: A Study of Kampala Households." *World Development* 20(10): 1423–1441.

Cantwell, J. (1991), "Foreign Multinationals and Industrial Development in Africa." In: P. J. Buckley and J. Clegg (eds.), *Multinational Enterprises in Less Developed Countries*. London: Macmillan, pp. 183–224.

Chandler, T. (1994), "Urbanization in Medieval and Early Modern Africa." In: J. D. Tarver (ed.), *Urbanization in Africa: A Handbook*. Westport, Conn.: Greenwood, pp. 15–32.

Chazan, N., R. Mortimer, J. Ravenhill, and D. Rothchild (1988), *Politics and Society in Contemporary Africa*. London: Macmillan.

Cheema, G. S. (1992), "The Challenge of Urbanisation." In: N. Harris (ed.), *Cities in the 1990s: The Challenge for Developing Countries*. London: UCL Press, pp. 24–33.

Cockcroft, L. (1992), "The Past Record and Future Potential of Foreign Investment." In: F. Stewart, S. Lall, and S. Wangwe (eds.), *Alternative Development Strategies in SubSaharan Africa*. London: Macmillan, pp. 336–367.

Cohen, M. A. (1983), "The Challenge of Replicability." *Regional Development Dialogue* 4(1): 90–99.

——— (1990), "Macroeconomic Adjustment and the City." *Cities* 7(1): 49–59.

——— (1992), "Urban Policy and Economic Development – the Agenda." In: N. Harris (ed.), *Cities in the 1990s: The Challenge for Developing Countries*. London: UCL Press, pp. 9–24.

Cohen, M. A. and J. Leitmann (1994), "Will the World Bank's Real 'New Urban Policy' Please Stand Up?" *Habitat International* 18(4): 117–126.

Coquery-Vidrovitch, C. (1991), "The Process of Urbanization in Africa (From the Origins to the Beginning of Independence)." *African Studies Review* 34(1): 1–98.

Devas, N. and C. Rakodi (eds.) (1993), *Managing Fast Growing Cities: New Approaches to Urban Planning and Management in the Developing World.* London: Longman.

Dogan, M. and J. D. Kasarda (1988), "Introduction: How Giant Cities Will Multiply and Grow." In: M. Dogan and J. D. Kasarda (eds.), *The Metropolitan Era. Vol. 1, A World of Giant Cities.* Newbury Park, Calif.: Sage, pp. 12–29.

Dubresson, A. (1997), "Abidjan: From the Public Making of a Modern City to Urban Management of a Metropolis." In: C. Rakodi (ed.), *The Urban Challenge in Africa: Growth and Management of Its Large Cities.* Tokyo: United Nations University Press, pp. 252–291.

Gibbon, P. (1992), "The World Bank and African Poverty, 1973–91." *Journal of Modern African Studies* 30(2): 193–220.

Gugler, J. and W. G. Flanagan (1978), *Urbanization and Social Change in West Africa.* Cambridge: Cambridge University Press.

Harris, N. (1992), "Productivity and Poverty in the Cities of the Developing Countries." In: N. Harris (ed.), *Cities in the 1990s: The Challenge for Developing Countries.* London: UCL Press, pp. 173–195.

Helleiner, G. K. (1992), "Structural Adjustment and Long-term Development in SubSaharan Africa." In: F. Stewart, S. Lall, and S. Wangwe (eds.), *Alternative Development Strategies in SubSaharan Africa.* London: Macmillan, pp. 48–77.

IMF (International Monetary Fund) (1985), *Foreign Private Investment in Developing Countries.* IMF Occasional Paper 33, Washington, D.C.: IMF.

––––––– (1993), *World Economic Outlook.* Washington, D.C.: IMF.

Jamal, V. and J. Weeks (1993), *Africa Misunderstood or Whatever Happened to the Rural–Urban Gap?* London: Macmillan for the ILO.

Jesperson, E. (1992), "External Shocks, Adjustment Policies and Economic and Social Performance." In: G. A. Cornia, R. Van der Hoeven, and T. Mkandawire (eds.), *Africa's Recovery in the 1990s: From Stagnation and Adjustment to Human Development.* New York: St. Martin's Press, pp. 9–90.

Jones, G. A. and P. M. Ward (1994), "The World Bank's 'New' Urban Management Programme: Paradigm Shift or Policy Continuity?" *Habitat International* 18(3): 33–51.

Killick, T. with M. Malik (1992), "Country Experiences with IMF Programmes in the 1980s." *The World Economy* 15(5): 599–632.

King, A. D. (1990), *Urbanism, Colonialism, and the World-Economy: Cultural and Spatial Foundations of the World Urban System.* London: Routledge.

Lee, K. S. (1993), "How Nigerian Manufacturers Cope with Infrastructural Deficiencies: Private Alternatives to Public Provision." In: G. S. Cheema (ed.), *Urban Management: Policies and Innovations in Developing Countries.* Westport, Conn.: Praeger, pp. 253–260.

Logan, I. B. and K. Mengisteab (1993), "IMF–World Bank Adjustment and Structural Transformation in Sub-Saharan Africa." *Economic Geography* 69(1): 1–24.

Mabogunje, A. L. (1990), "Urban Planning and the Post-colonial State in Africa: A Research Overview." *African Studies Review* 33: 121–203.

Mehretu, A. (1983), "Cities of SubSaharan Africa." In: S. D. Brunn and J. F. Williams (eds.), *Cities of the World.* New York: Harper & Row, pp. 243–279.

Mosley, P. and J. Weeks (1993), "Has Recovery Begun? 'Africa's Adjustment in the 1980s' Revisited." *World Development* 21(10): 1583–1606.

Nafziger, E. W. (1990), *The Economics of Developing Countries*. Englewood Cliffs, N.J.: Prentice-Hall.

Oberai, A. S. (1993), "Urbanization, Development and Economic Efficiency." In: J. D. Kasarda and A. M. Parnell (eds.), *Third World Cities: Problems, Policies and Prospects*. Newbury Park, Calif.: Sage, pp. 58–73.

Obudho, R. A. (1997), "Nairobi: National Capital and Regional Hub." In: C. Rakodi (ed.), *The Urban Challenge in Africa: Growth and Management of Its Large Cities*. Tokyo: United Nations University Press, pp. 292–334.

O'Connor, A. (1983), *The African City*. London: Hutchinson.

ODI (Overseas Development Institute) (1993), *Does the IMF Really Help Developing Countries?* London: ODI Briefing Paper.

Okpala, D. C. I. (1990), "The Roles and Influences of External Assistance in the Planning, Development and Management of African Human Settlements Systems." *Third World Planning Review* 12(3): 205–229.

Peterson, G. E., G. T. Kingsley, and J. P. Telgarsky (1991), *Urban Economies and National Development*. Office of Housing and Urban Programs, Washington, D.C.: USAID.

Piermay, J.-L. (1997), "Kinshasa: A Reprieved Mega-City?" In: C. Rakodi (ed.), *The Urban Challenge in Africa: Growth and Management of Its Large Cities*. Tokyo: United Nations University Press, pp. 223–251.

Potts, D. (1997), "Urban Lives: Adopting New Strategies and Adapting Rural Links." In: C. Rakodi (ed.), *The Urban Challenge in Africa: Growth and Management of Its Large Cities*. Tokyo: United Nations University Press, pp. 447–494.

Pugh, C. (1994), "Development of Housing Finance and the Global Strategy for Shelter." *Cities* 11(6): 384–392.

Rakodi, C. (1986a), "Colonial Urban Policy and Planning in Northern Rhodesia and Its Legacy." *Third World Planning Review* 8(3): 193–217.

—— (1986b), "State and Class in Africa: A Case for Extending Analyses of the Form and Functions of the National State to the Urban Local State." *Society and Space* 4: 419–446.

—— (1991), "Developing Institutional Capacity to Meet the Housing Needs of the Urban Poor: Experience in Kenya, Tanzania and Zambia." *Cities* 8(3): 228–243.

—— (1995a), *Harare. Inheriting a Settler-Colonial City: Continuity or Change?* Chichester: Wiley.

—— (1995b), "Housing Finance for Lower Income Urban Households in Zimbabwe," *Housing Studies* 10(2): 199–227.

—— (ed.) (1997), *The Urban Challenge in Africa: Growth and Management of Its Largest Cities*. Tokyo: United Nations University Press.

Ribe H., S. Carvalho, R. Liebenthal, P. Nichalos, and E. Zuckerman (1990), *How Adjustment Programs Can Help the Poor: The World Bank's Experience*. World Bank Discussion Paper 71. Washington, D.C.: World Bank.

Rogerson, C. M. (1997), "Globalization or Informalization: African Urban Economies in the 1990s." In: C. Rakodi (ed.), *The Urban Challenge in Africa: Growth and Management of Its Largest Cities*. Tokyo: United Nations University Press, pp. 337–370.

Rondinelli, D. A. (1988), "Giant and Secondary City Growth in Africa." In: M. Dogan and J. D. Kasarda (eds.), *The Metropolis Era. Vol. 1, A World of Giant Cities*. Newbury Park, Calif.: Sage, pp. 291–321.

349

Salau, A. T. (1990), "Urbanization and Spatial Strategies in West Africa." In: R. B. Potter and A. T. Salau (eds.), *Cities and Development in the Third World*. London: Mansell, pp. 157–171.

Sassen, S. (1994), *Cities in a World Economy*. Thousand Oaks, Calif.: Pine Forge Press.

Seralgeldin, I. (1989), *Poverty, Adjustment and Growth in Africa*. Washington, D.C.: World Bank.

Simon, D. (1992), *Cities, Capital and Development: African Cities in the World Economy*. London: Belhaven.

——— (1997), "Urbanization, Globalization, and Economic Crisis in Africa." In: C. Rakodi (ed.), *The Urban Challenge in Africa: Growth and Management of Its Large Cities*. Tokyo: United Nations University Press, pp. 74–108.

Sit, F.-S. (1993), "Transnational Capital Flows, Foreign Investments, and Urban Growth in Developing Countries." In: J. D. Kasarda and A. M. Parnell (eds.), *Third World Cities: Problems, Policies and Prospects*. Newbury Park, Calif.: Sage, pp. 180–198.

Standing, G. (1984), *Population Mobility and Productive Relations: Demographic Links and Policy Evolution*. World Bank Staff Working Paper 695. Washington, D.C.: World Bank.

Stewart, F. (1991), "The Many Faces of Adjustment." *World Development* 19(12): 1847–1864.

Stewart, F., S. Lall, and S. Wangwe (1992), "Alternative Development Strategies: An Overview." In: F. Stewart, S. Lall, and S. Wangwe (eds.), *Alternative Development Strategies in SubSaharan Africa*. London: Macmillan, pp. 3–46.

Stren, R. E. (1989a), "Urban Local Government in Africa." In: R. E. Stren and R. R. White (eds.), *African Cities in Crisis: Managing Rapid Urban Growth*. Boulder, Colo.: Westview, pp. 20–36.

——— (1989b), "The Administration of Urban Services." In: R. E. Stren and R. R. White (eds.), *African Cities in Crisis: Managing Rapid Urban Growth*. Boulder, Colo.: Westview, pp. 37–68.

——— (1992), "African Urban Research Since the Late 1980s: Responses to Poverty and Urban Growth." *Urban Studies* 29(3/4): 533–556.

——— (1993), " 'Urban Management' in Development Assistance: An Elusive Concept." *Cities* 10(2): 125–139.

Tordoff, W. (1984), *Government and Politics in Africa*. London: Macmillan.

Tripp, A. M. (1992), "The Impact of Crisis and Economic Reform on Urban Women in Tanzania." In: L. Beneria and S. Feldman (eds.), *Unequal Burden: Economic Crises, Persistent Poverty and Women's Work*. Boulder, Colo.: Westview.

UNCHS (United Nations Centre for Human Settlements – Habitat) (1987), *Global Report on Human Settlements, 1986*. Oxford: Oxford University Press for UNCHS.

——— (1990), *The Global Strategy for Shelter to the Year 2000*. Nairobi: UNCHS.

UNCTC (United Nations Centre for Transnational Corporations) (1989), *Foreign Direct Investment and Transnational Corporations in Services*. New York: UNCTC.

——— (1991), *World Investment Report 1991: The Triad in Foreign Direct Investment*. New York: UNCTC.

UNECA (UN Economic Commission for Africa) (1989), *African Alternatives to Structural Adjustment Programmes: A Framework for Transformation and Recovery*. Addis Ababa: UNECA.

United Nations (1993), *World Urbanization Prospects: The 1992 Revision*. New York: UN Department of Economic and Social Information and Policy Analysis.

Wegelin, E. (1994), "Everything You Always Wanted to Know About the Urban Management Programme (But Were Afraid to Ask)." *Habitat International* 18(4): 127–137.

Wekwete, K. (1997), "Urban Management: The Recent Experience." In: C. Rakodi (ed.), *The Urban Challenge in Africa: Growth and Management of Its Large Cities*. Tokyo: United Nations University Press, pp. 527–552.

World Bank (1972), *Urbanization Sector Working Paper*. Washington, D.C.: World Bank.

—— (1983), *Learning by Doing: World Bank Lending for Urban Development 1972–82*. Washington, D.C.: World Bank.

—— (1986), "Aid Flows for Urban Projects Remain Relatively Low." *Urban Edge* 10(2): 4–5.

—— (1991), *Urban Policy and Economic Development: An Agenda for the 1990s*. Washington, D.C.: World Bank Policy Paper.

—— (1992), *World Development Report*. Washington, D.C.: World Bank.

—— (1993), *Housing: Enabling Markets to Work*. Washington, D.C.: World Bank.

—— (1994), *Adjustment in Africa: Reforms, Results and the Road Ahead*. Oxford: Oxford University Press.

Wunsch, J. S. and D. Olowu (1990), *The Failure of the Centralized State: Institutions and Self-Governance in Africa*. Boulder, Colo.: Westview.

Yeung, Yue-man and Fu-chen Lo (1996), "Global Restructuring and Emerging Urban Corridors in Pacific Asia." In: Fu-chen Lo and Yue-man Yeung (eds.), *Emerging World Cities in Pacific Asia*. Tokyo: United Nations University Press, pp. 17–47.

Zachariah, K. C. and J. Condé (1981), *Migration in West Africa: Demographic Aspects*. Oxford: Oxford University Press.

13

"Johannesburg": Coming to grips with globalization from an abnormal base

Keith Beavon

Introduction

The City of Johannesburg is at the core of the major metropolis of sub-Saharan Africa and reflects most sharply South Africa's re-engagement with the rest of the world in a period of globalization. The ending of apartheid and the re-entry of South Africa into the world economy have also seen a popular take-over of large tracts of the inner city that both the old and new custodians of the city have been afraid to confront. As such, a sad irony will be exposed – that the net effect of the uncontrolled and unordered "occupation" of the downtown and inner-city residential areas has been to damage the capacity of the inner city either to accommodate or to prosper from the positive effects of globalization that are most likely to accrue to South Africa via Johannesburg and to the city's citizens via its central business district.

At the outset, a distinction must be made between the city of Johannesburg *per se* and its rapidly growing metropolitan region (fig. 13.1), itself composed of several autonomous but interconnected towns and cities (figs. 13.2 and 13.3), which will be referred to here collectively as Metropolitan Johannesburg or "Johannesburg" (note the use of quotation marks). No doubt, many would like Johannes-

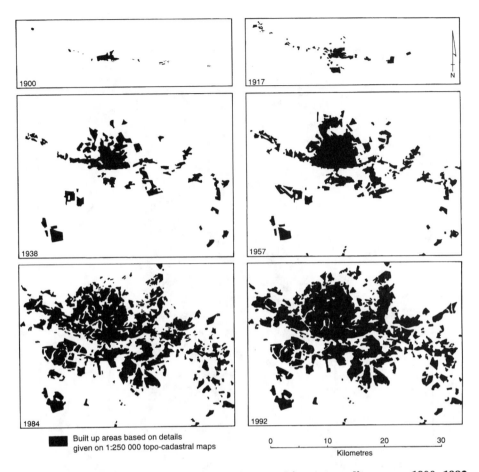

Fig. 13.1 **The rapid growth of Johannesburg and its metropolitan area, 1900–1992**
(Source: after Whitlow and Brooker, 1995)

burg to be seen as a "world city" but, within the combined range
of criteria that already constitute the increasingly strict definitions
of that category of city (see *inter alia* Cohen, 1981; Friedmann and
Wolff, 1982; King, 1990; Sassen, 1991; Hamnett, 1994; Shachar, 1994),
neither Johannesburg nor Metropolitan Johannesburg is as yet, or
ever likely to be, categorized unequivocally as one of the small élite
category of world cities.

Notwithstanding this, there are many aspects of Metropolitan
Johannesburg that, when taken in isolation, allow it to compare very
favourably with what is found in genuine world cities, and as such it
might aspire to being an important metropolis on the world stage.

353

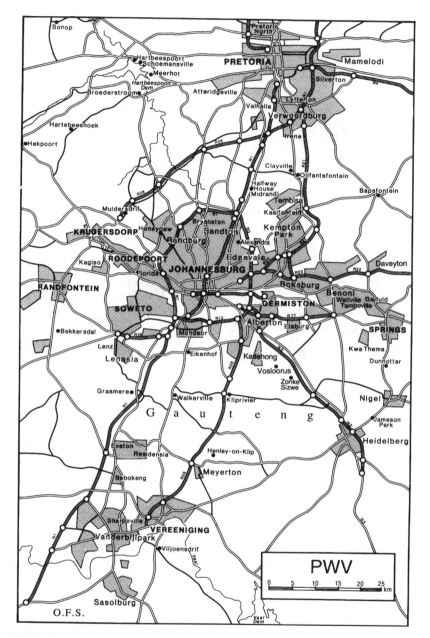

Fig. 13.2 **Components of the Johannesburg metropolitan area within the context of its metropolitan region**

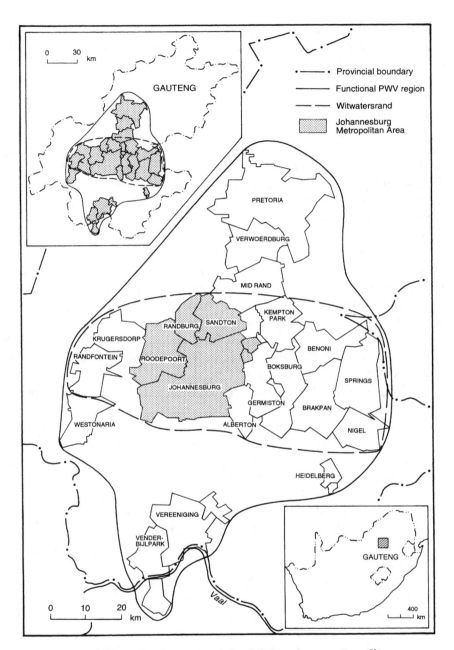

Fig. 13.3 **The Witwatersrand and the Johannesburg metropolitan area**

355

There is also no doubt that many people in various political and financial leadership positions in Johannesburg would like the "old" city to improve and increase those of its attributes that are necessary for some form of world status. They realize that, unless that route is followed, the city, and indeed even Metropolitan Johannesburg, could lose whatever status it presently enjoys outside of South Africa, and that will be to the economic detriment of all its citizens and entrepreneurs. As such the development path of Johannesburg should at first glance be obvious: at all costs modernize and make the central city the prime location sought by all major office-based, service, and retail activities. Yet, given the strange dichotomy that characterizes Johannesburg as both the product of a system of bitter racial segregation for its first 105 years and the financial key for post-apartheid reconstruction and restitution of some form of normality, at least within its own urban hinterland, then the economic trajectory and urban future of the whole metropolis become more complex and less obvious to outsiders. None the less, there can be no doubt that, if any South African city is to provide the point of articulation not only between South Africa and the rest of the world in general, but with the major cities of the world in particular, and if in addition any South African city is to provide a fulcrum for general upliftment in southern if not sub-Saharan Africa, then that city must be Metropolitan Johannesburg.

Consideration of how and why Johannesburg finds itself in the dual position of, on the one hand, being a potentially important link with the global economy, which begs a specific, virtually first-world style of development, and, on the other hand, being the perceived panacea for local poverty, which seeks a very different development path, will constitute the bounding parameters of this chapter. Selected aspects of the internal problems and opportunities that face the city, its metropolitan area, and the region to which it is central will be identified and examined.

It is important to state at this stage that Metropolitan Johannesburg stands at a crucial position in the space–time continuum of the world's important urban places. Ironically it was at least in part best equipped to join the ranks of the world's major cities in respect of its physical infrastructure when morally and correctly, as a South African city, it and the country were shunned because of the actions of the apartheid government. Now, as the world holds out a hand of welcome, it can be argued that the city of Johannesburg (as opposed to Metropolitan Johannesburg), as a consequence of internal socio-political trends and events over the duration of the apartheid years but particularly during the past decade, is probably less ready and able immediately to join the world community as an equal partner (in terms of the quality of its built environment) than at selected times in the past 100 years.

It is appropriate at this stage to sketch the framework of the chapter. To set the scene, a brief presentation will be made of some of the salient facts and figures that underscore the dominance of the city and its metropolitan region within the South African space economy. From that base it will be shown (admittedly more by implication than by concrete examples and data) why it is anticipated that "Johannesburg" is likely to profit from the current flurry of initiatives to re-engage South Africa and its economy with the rest of the world, and particularly with the part of the world that is already operating within the framework of globalization. Thereafter the point will be made that it is essential to take cognizance of aspects of the shady racist past of Johannesburg in order to gain at least a basic understanding of how and why a clutter of problems associated with its apartheid baggage threatens to trip the city as it elects to cross the threshold to a welcoming world. In drawing the chapter to a close, it will be shown that, despite the problems that confront the "old" city of Johannesburg, the potential for Metropolitan Johannesburg to grasp the opportunity of engaging with world cities and the global economy is much higher than for its core area alone. Yet, if that is to be the case, the decline of what has historically been the central business district (CBD) and inner-city zone of Johannesburg will probably accelerate, thereby diminishing the prospective role of the city in being the cash panacea to the problems created by apartheid in its immediate urban sphere.

"Johannesburg" and the local and national economy

"Johannesburg" is located on the high interior plateau of South Africa in the province of *Gauteng* (a colloquial African word meaning "The Place of Gold") (fig. 13.3). Within the province, Johannesburg lies at the mid-point of both the Central Witwatersrand region and the industrial and financial heartland of South Africa colloquially known as the PWV (the acronym for the Pretoria–Witwatersrand–Vereeniging region) (cf. figs. 13.2 and 13.3). The PWV comprises only 2.5 per cent of the area of South Africa but it contains approximately 22 per cent, or some 9 million, of the 41 million people that the Central Statistical Services now estimate are South Africa's population (*The Star*, 10 July 1995), without the addition of a probable 1 million illegal immigrants found in the PWV alone. With 93 per cent of the PWV population in effect classed as urban and notwithstanding that 16.4 per cent of its population were unemployed in 1991 (Hall et al., 1993), it is not surprising to find that almost 33 per cent of all formal employment in the country occurs in the region. The PWV is responsible for a little over 40 per cent of the gross domestic product (GDP) of the country (Hall et al., 1993), which stands at US$69.1 billion (African Development Bank, 1994).[1]

The Johannesburg metropolis is served by a combined international and major internal airport linked to all parts of the world by 53 airlines and now capable of handling 11 million passengers a year (Beavon, 1997). Metropolitan Johannesburg has four other regional airports for medium and light aircraft already handling 328,000 domestic passengers a year. Johannesburg is also the site of South Africa's major dry-port where the railway freight terminal shifts 300,000 containers each year. Because of its development history, Johannesburg is the principal point of a tightly integrated region served by 54 km of motorway, arranged in two concentric loops, one curling around close to its central business district (CBD) and the other through its outer suburbs and metropolitan neighbours, and 900 km of high-grade dual carriageway arterial roads (Wright et al., 1994). In 1991 the population of Metropolitan Johannesburg was in excess of 2.2 million (Central Statistical Services, 1992). Now apparently ranked the fourth-fastest-growing "city" in the world (Johannesburg, 1993), it was anticipated in 1990 that by the year 2020 Metropolitan Johannesburg would be the focal point of a PWV region containing an estimated 20 million people (Beavon, 1989). Recent in-migration trends, not least by foreigners from other southern African countries, give one reason to suspect that such may well be the case several years earlier.

The importance of financial and other tertiary services

Although founded and promoted on gold, actual mining of the precious metal now occurs further afield and is no longer directly part of the economic activity of Johannesburg itself (Fair and Muller, 1981; Beavon, 1997). The position of secondary industry, which expanded with the booms that occurred in 1925, the 1930s, the 1940s, and the 1950s, has subsequently declined in relative importance as tertiary services have increased. In Metropolitan Johannesburg, tertiary and office-based activities constitute almost 60 per cent of its gross geographic product (GGP) (Mabin and Hunter, 1993). It is therefore not surprising to find that Metropolitan Johannesburg contains some 6 million m^2 of good-quality office space. In national terms that is just over 1 million m^2 more office space, of the same quality, than occurs in the combined office buildings of Cape Town, Durban, and Pretoria (the three other major metropolitan areas of the country). The Johannesburg CBD alone contains just under 3 million m^2 of office space, or 57 per cent of what is available in the other three major metropolitan regions combined (Ampros, 1994a, 1994b).

Sited in the office space of central Johannesburg alone are the headquarters of 65 per cent of South Africa's Top 100 national public companies, controlling 72 per cent of the assets of that set of companies (Hunter et al., 1995). First and foremost of the financial institutions in the city is the Johannesburg Stock Exchange (JSE), founded in 1887 when the city was just a year old. In 1994, it was ranked 11th in the world on the basis of its market capitalization of US$260 billion (Beavon, 1997). The same year saw foreign trading (purchases and sales) total US$12.4 billion (JSE, 1995). In addition to South Africa's big-four commercial banks (with a combined market capitalization of US$11 billion in 1994) (Wright et al., 1994), there are currently some 30 foreign banks from the Americas, Europe, and Asia operating in Johannesburg. Significantly, over the past few years South African banks, most with Johannesburg-based headquarters, have been establishing close ties with banks beyond the borders of the country, and particularly within Africa, in order to service their corporate clients as they engage and re-engage with the African and world economy (*Business Times*, 9 July 1995). The South African Reserve Bank recently opened a branch in Johannesburg, in effect moving its main financial operations from Pretoria to a location alongside the Stock Exchange. And very significantly the African Development Bank has moved to Johannesburg from Abidjan. Those two developments have added significance for Johannesburg given the statement of the governor of the South African Reserve Bank (*The Star*, 10 July 1995) that the central banks of southern Africa now need to play a coordinated role in harmonizing interest and exchange rates, starting with a campaign to reduce the current vast difference in existing financial structures. It seems obvious that the role of the Reserve Bank in Johannesburg will be a leading one and will reinforce the city's role, through the national stock exchange and the commercial banks, as a financial leader at least in southern Africa.

The growing importance of tailgating on trade

From what has been outlined above, coupled with an inflow of US$555 million through the JSE in the first five months of 1995 (*The Star*, 22 June 1995), there can be little doubt that Johannesburg is the centre for capital flows not only in and out of the South African economy but for southern African capital markets. To add strength to this claim, bearing in mind the city's headquarter function, it is useful to present some illustrative data that reflect the extent to which South Africa, and by implication Johannesburg's tertiary services sector, has rapidly re-engaged in trade with the rest of Africa following the demise of the apartheid regime.

Exports to Africa, excluding those to members of the Southern African Customs Union, have increased more than five-fold off the 1987 base of approximately US$0.6 billion (R1.62 billion) to US$2.4 billion (R8.63 billion). In addition, 1994 saw exports worth US$3.9 billion (R13.8 billion) to members of the Southern African Customs Union (Botswana, Lesotho, Namibia, and Swaziland). Overall, the balance of trade is very much in South Africa's favour. With imports from Africa amounting to only US$1.6 billion, the trade surplus was US$4.6 billion in 1994. Total exports to African countries, amounting to US$6.2 billion, now constitute 31 per cent of all exports from South Africa (excluding some US$8.3 billion of unclassified, mainly gold, exports) and exceed exports to European Union countries that have "traditionally" been the largest market (*Business Times*, 18 June 1995). The importance of the African market extends beyond the mere volume of exports. South Africa, under the presidency of Nelson Mandela, sees itself, and indeed is seen by many of the sub-Saharan countries, as the gateway to African markets. Johannesburg in turn views itself as the hub of the gateway, with air freight arriving and leaving through its international airport and land and sea freight being received and dispatched through its container terminal, as a consequence of many of the country's exporting factories being located in the region of which Johannesburg is the centre. Consequently, an increasing number of specialized trade fairs, for the display of African goods to the world and for the display of goods aimed at sub-Saharan countries, are now being hosted by Johannesburg.

In keeping with the accelerating merger and acquisition (M&A) trend in the global market-place, South African M&A activity leapt in 1994. The level of transactions reached US$8.7 billion, approximately four times that of 1993. Companies recently involved with

South African associates, and all of which have a presence in the Johannesburg region, are Coca-Cola, Pepsi, Federal Mogul, Irish Independent Group, Ford Motor Company, and IBM (*Business Times*, 2 July 1995).

The influx of foreign trade delegates, bankers, and financiers, all eager to examine and get a feel for the South African economy, has seen Johannesburg scrambling for a large share of the action. For reasons that will be better understood later in the chapter, new hotels and new office blocks in which foreign-based firms are important tenants have opened not in and about the downtown of Johannesburg but elsewhere in its metropolitan region. There can be little doubt that the leafy-green character of the "suburbs," with their multitude of high-order shops in new and recently upgraded shopping malls, and the proximity of a large number of excellent golf courses have contributed to the emergence of a cosmopolitan flavour in the decentralized business nucleations.

There appears to be a clear realization that opportunity only knocks once and that those South African cities and metropolises that are most successful in establishing international links right now will be the places to prosper in the future. To what extent individual city initiatives, or the attempts of provincial premiers to secure commercial links for their provinces with near and distant states, are in violation of the spirit of regional cooperation to which South Africa is a party is debatable. In 1980, in the era of late-apartheid, the Southern Africa Development Coordinating Conference (SADCC) was established. It consisted of nine southern African states: Angola, Botswana, Lesotho, Malawi, Mozambique, Swaziland, Tanzania, Zambia, and Zimbabwe. Among the aims of the group was the desire to reduce their economic dependence on the pariah state of South Africa and thereby also to increase the isolation of its apartheid regime. What SADCC was attempting to do was to increase collective self-reliance. With the fall of apartheid the SADCC reconstituted itself as the Southern African Development Community (SADC) and the view is that, with South Africa as a full member, it will assist in correcting imbalances in regional economics and other business relationships (Ramsamy, 1995). Whether successful unilateral attempts to engage South Africa in the world economy will be seen as helpful to those medium- and longer-term goals remains to be seen. Such considerations aside, the premier of the Gauteng province has been actively seeking and closing business and investment deals as far afield as London, Seoul, and Beijing in competition with other South African provincial premiers. In addition, Johannesburg appointed a Director of Commerce and Industry a few years ago to develop corporate relationships between the city and others abroad. Already a series of international agreements are reported to have been signed with, *inter alia*, New York, Los Angeles, New Orleans, Baltimore, London, and Tokyo (Wright et al., 1994), with a view to making sure that significant amounts of the international business development that is being attracted to South Africa by the national and provincial governments is, in fact, located in Johannesburg and its metropolitan area. For example, the successful visit of President Mandela to Japan in mid-1995 clinched an aid package worth US$100 million for South Africa that will be used to fund national Reconstruction and Development Programme (RDP) projects, thereby also creating jobs and economic spin-off effects. Significantly, one of the three projects to be funded from the Japanese aid is a scheme for upgrading and improving the commuter rail links between Johannesburg and Soweto and other Black townships (*The Star*, 4 July 1995).[2]

Making up lost ground: The costs of apartheid on the economy

In the discussion above, reference has been made to the re-engagement of South Africa and "Johannesburg" with the world. Implicit in that statement is the fact that for between 19 and 35 years South Africa was progressively isolated because of its apartheid policy. Inevitably, because of the lack of contact with and the consequent decreasing necessity to keep abreast of changes in world business systems and markets, many aspects of the city's operations and the economy of its region were allowed to lag behind what one might loosely term "international standards." Some may naïvely believe that the abandonment of apartheid, and the successful transition to a democracy, will have made it easy for the country as a whole, and for "Johannesburg" in particular, immediately to re-engage with the world on a meaningful and competitive basis. Of course, it is not that simple.

During the apartheid years, and certainly in the later stages of the regime, the economy was seriously damaged. Admittedly in the middle phase of apartheid the economy boomed. For example, between 1960 and 1969 GDP grew at an average rate of 5.8 per cent. That was better than the industrial nations of the time achieved, and considerably better than for the countries of the developing world, including the Tigers of the Far East. Then in the 1970s, when South

Africa became involved in a conventional war against some of its neighbouring states, and at about the time of the Soweto uprising, growth dropped to 3 per cent, and for the 15 years from 1980 it averaged a mere 1.5 per cent at a time when the developing world was moving into higher gears. Indeed, the final years of apartheid, even following the announcement of its demise in 1990, saw GDP shrinkage approaching −1 per cent, with population growth running at about 2.8 per cent. In more specific terms, the post-1980 period saw US$25 billion, in capital and disinvestment by 709 foreign firms, leave the country. The decision by international financiers not to allow the apartheid regime to roll-over foreign loans resulted in South Africa becoming a net exporter of capital, and interest on foreign loans is still the second-largest item on the debit side of the national budget (Fallon, 1995).

In order to prop up the South African economy during the years when it was ostracized by the international community, the manufacturing component was protected by increased tariff barriers or duties on imports. With the advent of the South African democracy, the new government has realized that not only has the country been readmitted to the hurly-burly of international trade but the re-entry is subject to current international trade agreements. Notwithstanding attempts that are currently being made for South Africa to become a full member of the Lomé Convention, and simultaneous attempts to negotiate concessions with the European Union on exports directed to European countries (ERO and TPMP, 1995; *Sunday Times*, 2 July 1995), South African manufacturers and producers are already gearing themselves to conform to the stipulations that emerged from the Uruguay Round of the General Agreement on Tariffs and Trade (GATT) and that are now part of the World Trade Organization (WTO) (United Nations, 1994). The implications of reducing tariffs will have varied absolute and relative effects on the Johannesburg region and they are briefly considered below.

Tariffs, trade, and the implications for Johannesburg and its region

Amongst political leaders and the captains of manufacturing there is a general awareness that South African industry has to prepare itself to shift away from import substitution to export promotion. It has not gone unnoticed that such a move will favour the metropolitan and port cities of the coastal region. As such it can be argued that, to the extent that foreign markets will provide greater sales prospects than the local market, much of the advantage that Gauteng (or, loosely speaking, Metropolitan Johannesburg) industries enjoy from being adjacent to 22 per cent of the county's population will be significantly reduced. Consequently there has been a rather strong bias, across the local political spectrum, against directing production towards exports (Hunter et al., 1995). Part of the reluctance comes from the need to make rapid progress with the national Reconstruction and Development Programme (RDP). Even so, the determination to adhere to GATT will inevitably require greater concentration on export-oriented industries in the long term (Hunter et al., 1995). A closer examination of industrial trends in the Witwatersrand shows that there is a continued "drift" of motor manufacturers (foreign vehicles are manufactured under licence with a high level of local content) to the PWV, and, with the variety of other manufacturers already located in the same area, overall export growth will benefit the Johannesburg region even if individual coastal metropolises do benefit to a greater extent (Hunter et al., 1995).

Turning more specifically to the city of Johannesburg (as currently constituted), it seems likely that GATT will have positive implications for employment in industries engaged in the production of food and beverages (until internal economies pull them closer to the sources of raw materials), as well as for trade, accommodation, and financial and community services, and also for "government industries." On the other hand, employment implications for the metal, general machinery, and electrical machine manufacturers will be negative. Making use of the best available data, which unfortunately include information as old as 1988 and reflect conditions in the apartheid era, a recent study (Hunter et al., 1995) has shown that the immediate and overall employment effects of the GATT agreements for Johannesburg and its region will on balance be more positive than negative. Furthermore, the overall trend towards the increased agglomeration of tertiary activities in Johannesburg and its metropolitan area is likely to be boosted by GATT.

Other impacts of globalization on local economic activities

In addition to the increasingly international and outward-looking trends in the South African economy, there are other aspects of globalization that are likely to have an impact on the inner-city areas of the Johannesburg metropolis. In accordance with global trends, there is a general decline of "traditional" manufacturing, an expansion in local financial and service business sectors (already in part referred to above), and increased importance of subcontracting, self-employment, and expansion of the informal sector (reference to the last category follows later in the chapter).

Since the mid-1970s, there has been a steady decline in the share of the manufacturing component in the GGP of Johannesburg. Beginning in the mid-1980s, however, the decrease has been in relative rather than in absolute terms. In a compensatory sense the "slack" has been absorbed by expansion in local financial and business services with some major investments in the CBD, notably in the form of massively expanded national headquarter buildings for banks and insurance companies that now include some of the most technologically sophisticated complexes in the world (*The Star,* 5 February 1995). The explanation for that phenomenon is closely related to the apartheid legacy, which has affected the geography of the city (discussed in more detail below), which in turn supports the continued centrality advantages of the CBD over the suburbs in respect of large numbers of Black people employed in clerical and middle-management positions and still living in the old Black townships.

The decline of "traditional" manufacturing in Johannesburg, for a variety of reasons not least as a result of government industrial policy under the apartheid regime (Rogerson, 1994), looks set to be transformed by emerging strategies for small, medium, and micro enterprises (South Africa, 1994). Leaving aside the survival enterprises that are found mainly within the burgeoning informal sector, the state is anxious to promote micro enterprises and small businesses as a means of "absorbing" unemployed, mainly Black, people. One of the significant developments in recent years has been the growth of activity in the clothes-making sector. Here self-employed individuals and small groups of Black persons are seeking contracting work with formal components of the clothing industry despite the exploitation that goes with it (Hunter et al., 1995). In contradistinction to the micro enterprises that are run informally, there is a sector of growing formal small enterprises many of which are owned and managed by white people. It is also suggested that small-scale furniture manufacturing will prosper as the housing programme of the RDP gathers momentum.

There is evidence that the CBD of Johannesburg is increasingly offering an urban environment for Black entrepreneurs to get started in small-scale business (Hunter et al., 1995), one that will now be financially assisted by the US$100 million seed capital that the United States Agency for International Development is channelling through the Southern Africa Enterprise Development Fund (*The Star*, 25 July 1995). As such the CBD may well fulfil an incubator role for small Black industries and enterprises, many of which have chosen to locate in the vacant lower-grade office buildings. However, taking account of the high failure rate of new small enterprises, it remains a moot point whether the contribution to the GGP of Johannesburg by the small industries will offset what is being, and has been, lost.

Having provided a thumbnail sketch of some of the economic aspects of Johannesburg and its relationship to the national economy, attention will now be drawn to some of the inertial problems related to the past.

Reflections of a past that threatens the future

Apartheid not only caused decline and ostracism for the economy but created a racially divided society in Johannesburg, and indeed in all South African towns and cities. So much so, it can be argued that, even if the national economy, and Johannesburg's share of it, continue to pick up rapidly, the ability of the city of Johannesburg readily to assume the status of an important place in the world will remain severely impeded for some time. Yet before one can proceed to assess and make comments on the future of Johannesburg and of its metropolitan area, it is essential to bring some of its troublesome history into sharper focus.

Aspects of the racial geography of Johannesburg and the status of the city, 1886–1994

It is neither possible nor appropriate here to unpack the long and detailed "story" of the making of apartheid Johannesburg. Persons who wish more detail on that topic will have to consult other texts (*inter alia*, Kane-Berman, 1978; Proctor, 1979; Morris, 1980; Beavon, in preparation; Parnell, 1993). Virtually from its founding in late 1886, and certainly from 1887 to 1994, Johannesburg was characterized by the separation of racial groups other than white into ghettoes (colloquially termed Locations). As early as 1904, under the post-Boer War British Administration, the first forced removal of Black people from the inner areas of the emerging city took place and they were required to reside, outside the municipal limits, at a place called Klipspruit (the site of a municipal sewage farm) on the south-western periphery. With the passage of time, other Locations (also termed townships) for Black people would be established near Klipspruit and much later become officially known by the acronym Soweto (for *South*western *T*ownships).

Notwithstanding a continuous campaign that made use of various ploys to segregate black people on the distant boundaries of the urban area, a set of three Johannesburg suburbs (Sophiatown, Martindale, and Newclare), known collectively as the Western Areas, remained a predominantly Black enclave of freehold properties amidst the white suburbs on the western side of Johannesburg until the policy of apartheid was enforced in the 1950s. The removal of the Western Areas people to Soweto (Lodge, 1981) and much later the uprooting and relocation of Indian people (from the inner-city suburb of Pageview) to Lenasia, south of Soweto (Carrim, 1990; Beavon and Parnell, in preparation), saw the fulfilment of a large part of the apartheid planners' "dream": a city in which the only Black residents were domestic servants in the backyard rooms of white householders.

The effect of both early segregation and the later policy of apartheid on the city was to be substantial. Not only were Black people removed from the suburbs of the city and dumped in small, poorly constructed, rental houses in segregated Locations far from the urban core but the nature of tenure and economic opportunities available to the vast majority of them were also restricted. With a few paltry exceptions, Black people in particular were excluded from operating businesses and were able to earn a living only as labourers. A major effect of the racial laws was that the Johannesburg municipality for all intents and purposes became the preserve of white people. Entrepreneurial opportunities were limited to the whites, suburban residential areas were reserved for whites, the bulk of the municipal transport system in the form of trams and buses was for use by whites, and, because of the wage restrictions inherent in belonging to the Black labouring class, virtually all the shopping opportunities in Johannesburg catered for a white clientele and were geared to the incomes of whites. The most significant cleavages of the kind just indicated first occurred in the mid- to late-1930s.

Notwithstanding the industrial boom of 1925, associated with the promulgation of the South African Tariff Act (Martin, 1990), which created protection for many sectors of industry, and claims in 1926 that Johannesburg had become the great "Emporium" of Central and southern Africa, the most dramatic change in the status of the city came about in the years 1933–1938. It followed South Africa's decision to take itself off the international gold standard at the end of 1932. With the price of gold increasing by virtually 50 per cent overnight, marginal gold mines were made profitable and profitable mines massively increased their profits. The effect on the inflow of capital was dramatic. Between 1932 and 1938, some £63 million of new international capital flowed into Johannesburg through the banks and the stock exchange. That volume of capital inflow over six years was only £32 million less than the total capital inflow to Johannesburg over its first 46 years (Hobart Houghton and Dagut, 1973: 113–114)! Not surprisingly, a building boom without precedent was set in motion in the mid-1930s that saw substantial demolition, construction, and reconstruction of major buildings in retail and commercial zones of the Johannesburg CBD and in the adjacent industrial areas. Soon the skyline of the city was spiked with "skyscrapers." In 1937 alone, some 24,000 non-residential building plans were approved (City Engineer, 1967).

The 1930s' building boom in Johannesburg coincided with a period in international architecture that saw the emergence of a new style later tagged as Art Deco. Given the abundance of capital available, many fine examples of Art Deco soon graced the city and, it has been argued, helped transform it from a provincial mining centre into a world metropolis (Chipkin, 1993). The entertainment precinct of the downtown blossomed and, with neon signage cribbed from Radio City in New York, it was soon referred to as "the Great White Way." Not only did the main shopping streets of the city undergo physical changes but, concomitant with the increased fortunes of the city, which were rubbing off on many of the white inhabitants, the stores adopted a distinctly international style. Construction and reconstruction of retail frontages saw Art Deco mixed in with late-Victorian, Edwardian, and neoclassical styles. Along the principal shopping street were the great shops of South Africa, including major departmental stores (then the local equivalents of London's Harrods and Liberty's, or Paris's Bon Marche and Printemps) and a variety of other large and small retail establishments all offering up-market goods, including diamonds from De Beers, Savile Row suits, and women's fashions direct from Paris (Chipkin, 1993).

With the above pen-picture of central Johannesburg in mind, it is interesting to turn for a moment to the criteria that are today used to identify a "world city."

The evolution of the world city concept has recently been traced by Shachar (1994), who, after reviewing the works of a number of researchers, has listed the main characteristics of a world city. In brief, they are that a world city is an international management centre, it is the locus of advanced producer services, and it has a rich mix of urban infrastructure and urban amenities. Amongst the infra-structural components is office accommodation of the highest quality in a top location that is easily accessible. In addition, a world city should have a rich assortment of social and cultural amenities, in-cluding schools of the highest reputation and a large variety of meet-ing places that facilitate social and business networking through informal meetings (Shachar, 1994). Certainly Johannesburg of the late-1930s, with its then state-of-the-art office buildings, its links to the outside world via the Atlantic cable (the equivalent of today's e-mail), the headquarters of some 50 per cent of the world's gold production, and managing a virtual monopoly on world diamonds, was a financial centre of considerable status on a world scale. The city was also the seat of outstanding secondary schools and a university whose graduates were recognized and accepted worldwide. Its variety of sporting and social clubs, not least the influential Rand Club, cer-tainly facilitated the informal networking referred to above. If there had been an A-league of world cities in the late 1930s, then Johan-nesburg would certainly have deserved close consideration for being included – but only in respect of the white people's City of Gold.

The situation for the deprived

The situation for the Black population was the very antithesis of that for the whites. Not only had Black people been restricted to certain areas of the city and denied all political rights, but as their population increased so the conditions in those restricted areas became progres-sively worse. Forced by circumstances, many found themselves living "illegally" in the slumyards of suburbs that had been abandoned by the white élite in the previous century. The exclusively white local authority neither made sufficient funds available for Black housing, even if it was to be in peripheral areas, nor made an effort to seek those funds from the rates base that the ever-more opulent down-town generated. The decision in 1937 to raise funds for Black housing from the profits of the municipal monopoly the (white) Council had just placed on the brewing and sale of sorghum-based beer (Proctor, 1979), the only liquor that Blacks in urban areas were allowed to drink, was bitterly resented by the Black population. The surge of

369

industrialization in and around Johannesburg, sparked by the move away from the gold standard and the demand for manufactured supplies that accompanied South Africa's war effort in the period 1939–1945, saw a concomitant surge in Black people drawn to work in the growing numbers of factories increasingly located between the white urban periphery and the city-facing margins of the Black townships (Proctor, 1979; Stadler, 1979; Morris, 1980).

Inheriting a working blueprint for segregation, the National Party, which came to power on a platform of racial segregation in 1948, simply proceeded to enforce and extend separation through an increasingly ruthless and inhumane race policy called apartheid. For its own ideological reasons, the new central government in the 1950s readily made more money available for Black housing in the growing townships of Soweto (Morris, 1980, 1981) and in the other Black townships peripheral to the municipality that would later be part of the Johannesburg metropolitan area. Nevertheless, the pattern of poor-quality Black residential areas, with pitifully few amenities (see Morris, 1980; Beavon, 1997) and separated by open space from the more affluent and well-endowed white city, remained the norm.

The CBD maintains its importance, 1950–1975

Once the National Party had consolidated its hold on the reins of government, the lines of privilege and power, on the one side, and poverty and powerlessness, on the other, became ever more sharply drawn. The general economic boom of the early to mid-1960s and the improved economic prospects of the early 1970s saw massive changes and enhancements to the central business district of Johannesburg. Many new fingers of steel, glass, and concrete reached ever higher in the downtown as dysfunctional buildings of yesteryear, and even architectural gems of the 1930s, were demolished and replaced at an almost feverish rate. The levels of office sophistication grew apace. Many of the apartment blocks in the areas closest to the CBD were occupied by older but affluent white people who still wished to enjoy the amenity of the downtown. Selected residential suburbs that were relatively close to the CBD, as opposed to the zones of apartment blocks, began to experience gentrification as younger white people chose to live in older and more readily affordable houses close to the core of the city.

If the Johannesburg CBD of the 1970s had achieved its pre-eminence in a genuine democracy, then the role of Johannesburg as

370

the seat of financial and industrial power in southern Africa would once again have supported the city's claim to being the sub-Saharan contender for matching the requirements needed for a world city. Instead, the number of countries that had begun to isolate South Africa because of apartheid grew substantially when in 1976 Soweto erupted in protest, a revolt that many now see as the start of South Africa's successful revolution. By the 1980s, the number and effect of foreign boycotts on South African goods, services, industries, banks, and cities were substantial. Associated with South Africa's isolation, and for a number of other more local reasons, not least the construction of its intrametropolitan freeways and the advent of the shopping mall (see Beavon, in preparation), the relative importance and high status of the Johannesburg CBD as the preferred site of prime office space and the most important retail and entertainment centre of the country, let alone of its metropolitan area, declined, both absolutely and relatively, from the status it enjoyed up to the mid-1970s. This trend was exacerbated by a combination of white prejudice and the civil disobedience that characterized the last decade of the apartheid era when increasingly the downtown became the focus for mass protest marches by the oppressed Black population. The effect of those last apartheid years on the fortunes of the downtown and how that influences Johannesburg's attempt to come to grips with the implications of globalization will be partially clarified below. Before doing so it is instructive to examine the essence of the occupational and income geography of Johannesburg when the CBD of the apartheid city still reigned as the supreme retail and commercial centre.

The geography of occupations and incomes under apartheid

The steady decline of gold mining in the immediate vicinity of Johannesburg as the ores were worked out, combined with the decentralization of manufacturing industry encouraged by the central government in order to support its Bantustan policy, saw the tertiary activities of the CBD beginning to dominate the employment structure of the city and its region even in the era of late apartheid. As such, coupled with the race-based "job reservation" policy of the National Party, there was an increasing polarization of the city's occupational and income structures. Relatively well-paid white-collar clerical and service staff and well-paid top- and middle-management personnel worked in the downtown and lived in the white suburbs.

Labourers and members of the manufacturing workforce were largely Black and poorly paid, and lived on the periphery of the urban area. Although many white people's job descriptions and occupations would have designated them as part of the working class, the racial overtones that positively affected their incomes allowed them to live middle-class lives. The opposite was true for the small numbers of Black people doing white-collar jobs. The net result was that the overall occupation/income distribution of Johannesburg in the late-1970s was very polarized but, ironically, similar to the one described for current world cities by Hamnett (1994).

The significance of the socio-economic geography of Johannesburg, which has been merely hinted at here, should not be seen as an attempt to argue that the city in the 1970s was moving towards fulfilling the requirements for world city status. Rather, if one of the present characteristics of a world city is geographical and sectoral polarization of society into haves and have-nots, or groups of have-plenty and have-relatively-little, then one should not now expect it to be a sought-after product by popular leaders who have emerged from the have-not groups of the apartheid city.

Before any arguments can be considered about whether Johannesburg will enhance its standing in the ranks of cities that aspire to world city status, it is necessary, using what has been set out above as a backdrop, to look at the social and economic changes in the city that have marked the final years of formal apartheid.

The recent past and the blighting of the inner city

As the number of urban Black people increased during the bad days that characterized the era of grand apartheid in the 1970s, and even in the early 1980s, there was a concomitant increase in the number of residents per Black dwelling unit. In the "matchbox houses" of the townships, typically measuring 40 m^2, it was not uncommon to find between 9 and 10 people (Morris, 1980). As the population pressure continued to rise over time, thousands upon thousands of Black township dwellers were forced through circumstances to take up residence in shacks set up in the backyards of the formal rental houses. By 1989, the 412,000 formal houses in the Black townships of the PWV were exceeded by the 422,000 backyard shacks. In addition there were 635,000 shacks on vacant land, ranging from the Soweto golf course, where some 29,000 people lived on the 9-hole layout, to land that was "vacant" by virtue of being zoned for agricultural or industrial uses (Beavon, 1992). Similar population pressures on the limited formal housing stock were experienced by Coloured and Indian people (although the absolute numbers of the latter two groups were much less), who were also precluded from residing in what were the proclaimed white areas of the city and its suburbs.

In the mid-1980s, although the formal policy of apartheid was still in place, the will to enforce it began to crack as the absurdity of continuing with it became ever more clear to increasing numbers of white South Africans. Amongst the front runners who ignored the racist restrictions were Johannesburg's big businesses, which were increasingly employing people other than whites in shops and offices in clerical and other "white-collar" jobs. Yet the National Party, even once it realized that apartheid must go, continued to tinker with the details rather than grasping the nettle they had planted and simply "uprooting" or repealing the Group Areas Act, which was the cornerstone of the policy. Consequently, as more and more so-called "non-white" people began taking up city-based office jobs (Prinsloo, 1994), they also sought accommodation close to the CBD. From the mid-1980s, with population pressures beyond bursting point in the areally constrained black townships, Black people, preceded initially by Indian and Coloured people, took up vacant rental accommodation in the high-rise inner-city suburbs adjacent to the CBD (Crankshaw and White, 1994) and initiated the "greying" of the formerly all-white apartment areas. In a sense, black people were re-entering "their" city.

The immediate consequence of the perceived "greying" was an accelerating tempo of white flight towards the more distant, and still all-white, suburbs of the metropolitan area. As the needs for accommodation by black people grew, and they increasingly moved into the apartment zone, the white trickle outwards became a white stream, one that was inadvertently assisted by a state housing subsidy to first-time white home-buyers. With house prices cheapest on the edges of the existing white suburbs (mainly to the north of the metropolitan area), that is where young white couples moved to, instead of first taking an apartment in an inner-city apartment block as they had done in the past (Crankshaw and White, 1994). Both the initial and subsequent flight of white residents had an effect on the leasing decisions of small retailers in the CBD as well as on the owners of large fashion and speciality stores, prompting both to re-relocate their businesses to the emergent and booming suburban shopping malls in the white suburbs. The effect on the CBD was a growing number of vacant premises or lower-order businesses that catered for the lower paid and, consequently, for a more down-market mass clientele than before.

Despite the changes just described, the Group Areas Act was still in operation in the 1980s. It followed therefore that black people moving into the inner-city apartments were "illegal" residents in a group area reserved for whites. Unscrupulous landlords, who perceived the increasing demand for accommodation by black people to be an opportunity for making a "killing" on rents, proceeded to inflate accommodation charges and also shirk on maintenance (Crankshaw and White, 1994). The black residents, as a consequence of being in the wrong group area, were not able to take legal action against the rack-renting landlords without putting themselves in jeopardy with the South African race laws. As the rents went up, so subletting (as a ploy to reduce the rent burden) and consequent overcrowding became the order of the day. The net result was a fairly rapid decline in the physical conditions of apartment blocks occupied by black people. That situation in turn only exacerbated the trend of white flight and the ease with which new black tenants were lured to vacant inner-city apartments before the rents on those units were also racked upwards.

The combination of the changing tenant population in the apartment blocks and the flight of essentially white-oriented shops led to a rapid decline in the physical appearance and status of inner-city retailing in the CBD (Hunter et al., 1995), to the extent that certain buildings were closed and boarded up. In essence, the de facto desegregation of the inner-city zones of the city gave rise to a de facto shift of the *de jure* group area boundaries rather than to the creation of a multiracial mix of tenants, owners, and shoppers. As conditions in the apartment blocks continued to deteriorate, the residents resorted to rent boycotts in an effort to force landlords to maintain the units and the buildings as a whole. Almost inevitably, eviction notices were then served by the landlords on those who refused to pay, and broad-based tenant associations emerged to champion the cause of the occupants against the landlords. Not infrequently, the situation escalated into violent conflict, and boarded-up properties were broken into and "occupied" (in the aggressive sense of that word).

Even making allowances for the role that political uncertainty played in the period of negotiations that led to the general election and the transfer of government in April 1994, and not gainsaying the shortage of accommodation for black people caused by the apartheid system, the physical decline of formerly good-quality and at one time fashionable apartment stock has been extremely severe (MacGillivray, 1995). Even so there are now between 4,000 and 6,000 homeless persons in the inner city (Fraser, 1995), and some of its small parks have been taken over by people living in shacks made of corrugated iron, cardboard, and plastic sheeting. The grassed space of some parks has also been turned into terminals and repair areas for the myriads of minibus taxis that provide the long-distance transportation service for the new inner-city residents who also have homes in the far-off former bantustans of the apartheid era. It must be stressed that, whereas the initial wave of black people to the inner city was related to job opportunities in the CBD, many of the later arrivals were simply seeking accommodation regardless of where they were employed, if they were employed at all.

The changing character of the CBD and the inner-city apartment zone (to the immediate north and north-east of the CBD; fig. 13.4), together with a relaxation of the former almost Draconian by-laws against hawkers and pavement sellers, has led to a surge in the number of informal sector operators. It is estimated that the number of participants has grown from about 300 in the 1980s to some 5,000, who now share an annual turnover of approximately US$140 million (Fraser, 1995).

Unfortunately, in the chaotic conditions that characterize certain parts of the inner city, the apartment zone, and the congested pavements, criminal elements have also perceived new opportunities. Crime, vice, and drug trafficking, as well as muggings and car hijackings, have all reached alarming proportions. Figures for the 12 months ending in July 1994 show that 14,039 people were arrested for serious crimes in the inner city, 1,300 firearms were seized, 583 murder suspects were arrested, and 2,374 people were held for car theft and hijacking (Fraser, 1995).

Of the estimated 100,000 black people who now live in the inner-city areas, approximately 33,000 "arrived" between 1991 and 1992. So not only has the change been radical but it has also been swift. Most importantly, much of the swing occurred when the authorities of the old discredited regime were in the process of disengaging and when the office-bearers of the new transitional metropolitan government appeared to lack the confidence to undertake firm management (see Shiceka, 1995).

With the democratic national and provincial elections a thing of the past, it now remains to demarcate the boundaries of new metropoli-

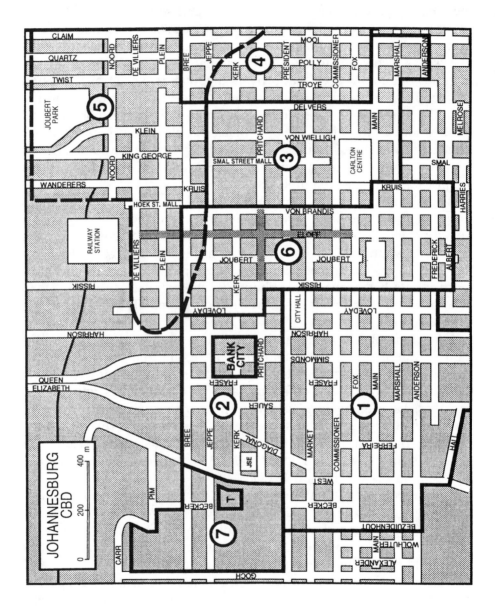

JOHANNESBURG CBD

Fig. 13.4 Functional zones and major components of the Johannesburg CBD (Notes: Zone 1 = the "old" financial and office area; Zone 2 = the new financial district, which includes the Johannesburg Stock Exchange (JSE) and the four-block consolidation of Bank City; Zone 3 = the retail district, with a focus at the Carlton Centre, which is linked to the railway station by the Smal Street Mall; Zone 4 = the wholesale and light-manufacturing district, also containing residential elements in the form of apartments; Zone 5 = the north-east inner-city apartment area, also containing some retail and offices functions; Zone 6 = the mid-town district, containing a mixture of land uses and an increasing number of vacant/construction sites; it also contains the former prime retail shopping streets (Pritchard and Eloff); Zone 7 = the cultural precinct, with theatres, museums, and restaurants as well as artists' workshops; not yet complete and the point of articulation with Zone 2 is supposed to be the Turbine Hall Shopping Mall (T))

tan substructures and to elect formally constituted councils. Those elections were held in November 1995, after political gerrymandering concerning the political boundaries. Even so, the uncertainties and lack of firm management that characterize the administration of the city by the Greater Johannesburg Transitional Metropolitan Council have continued. For example, no action is taken against "squatters" in the inner-city area, littering on a massive scale is tolerated, and petty and serious crime occurs on a scale that gives the impression that there is little or no policing. Up to 1,200 people have lived "permanently" in the concourse of the main railway station (*The Star*, 31 May 1995) and reports of up to 6,000 people sleeping in the concourse and on the platforms during cold winter nights appeared in the daily press during 1995.

With the background information provided above, it is now possible to take a broad overview of a CBD in trouble and flanked by burgeoning business developments in the suburbs (formerly open only to whites) lying to the north. Having done that it will only remain, for the purposes of this chapter, to draw some conclusions on how "Johannesburg's" increasing contact with the globalizing world might evolve in the immediate future and affect the new unfolding geography of the metropolis.

Big business and government in the CBD of the 1990s

As a consequence of decisions made within days of the first of Johannesburg's properties being put up for auction in 1886, and following the commercial patterns that were established in the first few years of the town's existence, Johannesburg's main financial quadrant and retail areas in the downtown were ever after largely separate from one another. The office-based functions were located in the south-west quadrant and retailing was best and most fully developed along the Pritchard Street and Eloff Street axes (fig. 13.4).

Although the decline in up-market retailing began to be noticeable as early as the late 1970s, the first signs of a major shift in the weighted centre of gravity for financial office space occurred in the late 1980s. What has now emerged and is in the process of being consolidated is a new financial district (also more generally termed a business improvement district, or BID) running from Rissik Street westward towards the Johannesburg Stock Exchange in Diagonal Street, and lying between President Street and Jeppe Street (fig.

13.4), with the east–west Kerk Street becoming a pedestrian spine through the whole.

The loss of high-fashion shopping along the north–south Eloff Street, which catered for clients of yesteryear, has in part been replaced by the parallel Smal Street Mall, a line of small shops catering for the new demand that lie athwart the popular pedestrian route between the former blacks-only railway terminus and the large in-city shopping complex known as the Carlton Centre.

With the delimitation of the "new" province of Gauteng, and following the national elections in 1994, places in the province were asked to "bid" for the seat of government. The bid made by Johannesburg (Central Johannesburg Partnership, 1994) was successful and the actual physical move of the legislature and its bureaucracy into the refurbished former Johannesburg City Hall (fig. 13.4) and buildings in the near vicinity took place in mid-1995. It is hoped that the arrival of the provincial government in the downtown, which is in close proximity to the new financial district, will not only lead to more and better policing of the area but increase investor confidence in at least the half of the CBD lying to the west of Rissik Street.

In addition to the recent and current developments described above, much effort and planning have gone into the further development of the area further westward known as Newtown (established in the late nineteenth century). Focused on the old fresh produce market, now partially converted into a cultural museum and theatres, Newtown is currently planned to be Johannesburg's premier cultural precinct and tourist attraction. If successfully developed, it is believed it should contribute to enhancing the quality of the environment for office workers in the financial district. Hopes aside, so-called plans for Newtown have come and gone for the past 25 years and, although it now boasts a clutch of theatres, a weekend flea market, and a cluster of museums and some restaurants, it is anything but the vital throbbing cultural area it is hoped it will be. The key point of articulation between the financial district and the Newtown cultural precinct, an old decommissioned power station, has yet to be developed into the key inner-city shopping mall that was "announced" in 1988!

The main reason a number of large South African banking, insurance, and financial institutions have, even in recent years, located their corporate headquarters in the new financial district of Johannesburg's CBD (fig. 13.4) is, as hinted earlier, the fact that, as a consequence of apartheid, the CBD is still more accessible for the large number of Black clerical employees, many of whom are still resident in the former Black-only townships, than are the suburbs to the north. There has been substantial investment in recent years in new headquarter blocks, which individually might have between 5,000 and 8,000 company employees at work each day (*The Star*, 12 October 1994), designed around their own pedestrian precincts and containing small but high-order speciality shops in an attempt to offset the general blight and crime that have become an everyday presence elsewhere in the CBD. One example is the headquarters of First National Bank (formerly Barclays Bank), which came on stream in 1995 at an estimated cost of US$300 million (a considerable amount within the framework of building prices in South Africa). The volume of capital now invested in new buildings already operating in the new financial district and in buildings in the process of construction exceeds the investment in any comparable sized area in South Africa (Hunter et al., 1995).

Those who have invested so heavily in buildings and real estate in the "new" part of Johannesburg's downtown obviously have very specific hopes for the future; namely that, as foreign tertiary sector business is attracted to Johannesburg, as it in turn tailgates on the revival of the national economy, the larger of the foreign corporations will also establish their own presence in the downtown. The likelihood of that occurring, however, needs to be seen against the perspective of what is already happening in the suburbs, particularly those to the north.

The attraction and increasing appeal of the north

Although the physical and functional decline of the CBD and the extraordinary changes that have occurred in the residential zone that sweeps about it have been most marked in the past few years, the disenchantment with the CBD, admittedly within the context of varied political and economic climates, can be traced over a much longer period. Office block and retail decentralization can be detected as far back as the 1950s, when the first of the substantial northern business nodes began to emerge. The construction of the M1 arm of the inner freeway and the upgrading of the arterial roads in the 1970s not only increased the accessibility of the CBD but made access to selected nodes in the northern suburbs easier than before. Data on the construction and supply of both apartment and office blocks show that no additional housing stock has been added to the inner city since 1973 (Fraser, 1995). Since 1975, the growth of office space in decentralized nodes (almost exclusively located in the northern suburbs of Johannesburg and the suburbs of the northern municipalities belonging to the metropolitan area; cf. fig. 13.2) has been almost double that in the CBD (Moross & Partners, 1995).

Although the total amount of good-quality office space in the CBD still far exceeds that in the suburbs, the point must be made that suburban office developments are no longer of the high-rise style. Instead, with large pieces of land still readily available in the low-density suburbs, developers have been able to satisfy the demand for medium-rise offices (three to five storeys), set in landscaped and green environments with generous space between buildings. In keeping with leading architectural designs in the world, the new office blocks have also been planned to allow tenants of individual sections to share no more than a common foyer, if they share the building at all. Office-based concerns that employ a relatively small staff, and particularly staff with technological skills, are finding that most of their employees already live in the suburbs or can afford to reach suburban work locations without difficulty, especially when the concepts of flexitime are utilized.

In the case of retailing the trend is also towards the suburbs. For example, the main shopping malls in the outer ring of such establishments comprise 345,000 m^2 of shops – an amount that is equal in gross area to 50 per cent of what is available in central Johannesburg. Furthermore, the quality of the shopping environment in the malls, let alone the quality and range of goods, is so high that the power of their areal extent and shopping mix to attract customers must far exceed that of downtown Johannesburg. In addition, the suburbs are served by many other malls, and, taking account of only the 29 that are 10,000 m^2 or larger, then in those shopping malls alone there is 1,104,000 m^2 of shopping (Sapoa, 1995), or 57 per cent more space than the 700,000 m^2 in downtown Johannesburg (Watt, 1995). Each day the chances of someone in the suburbs bypassing one of the suburban malls in order to make a purchase in the CBD grow slimmer if they exist at all. Between 1993 and 1995 suburban shopping areas in the malls alone increased by 42 per cent (Sapoa, 1993, 1995).

In late 1994, a study was undertaken to ascertain locational preferences for future retail and office nodes. Based on interviews with 15 of the top local and national property development companies and property managers, including those that still had CBD headquarters, it was found that there was an overwhelming preference from their

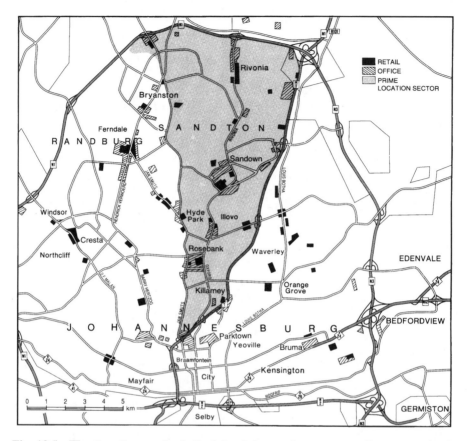

Fig. 13.5 **The "northern suburbs" of the Johannesburg metropolitan area with its business nucleations (Source: after Moross & Partners, 1995)**

clients for developments in the northern suburbs. Furthermore, it was ascertained that, of the 67 new constructions and upgradings of existing suburban nodes taking place in northern Johannesburg, 66 per cent were located in the sector north of the CBD and lying between the M1 (to the east) and the line of the major northern arterial road (to the west) (fig. 13.5). Furthermore, it is reported that 90 per cent of the enquiries for office space made to the developers and property managers interviewed were for offices in the sector just identified (Moross & Partners, 1995).

There can be little doubt that, with the exception of the massive national head-office type of developments that choose to locate in the new financial district of the CBD, the current preference by small and medium office-based organizations is to avoid what they perceive to be the congested, dirty, and crime-beset central business district. Instead, the latter category of businesses are either now located, or are actively seeking space, in the office clusters situated in the high-priced residential areas close to the up-market suburban shopping centres of the northern suburbs (fig. 13.5) (Moross & Partners, 1995).

It is not the purpose in this chapter to focus on local developments and trends *per se*. Rather the attention just given to the local situation is merely to set the scene for consideration of how local trends might be advanced or retarded by aspects of globalization. Returning, therefore, to the effects of globalization on the South African economy, it can now be noted that, as foreign investors and corporate agents move into the South African economy, they will need to establish offices. In accordance with the high concentration of GDP in the Witwatersrand, it is not unreasonable to expect a commensurate share of foreign firms to site their local head offices in Metropolitan Johannesburg. Because those offices will not be comparable in scale or employment profile to the national head offices of South African banks, other financial institutions, or the long-established mining houses, they will most likely take the options that small- and medium-sized office firms are currently selecting – to locate in the suburbs of the metropolitan area and not in downtown Johannesburg. For example, LG International, the giant South Korean electronics and industrial corporation, which has just acquired the Zenith Corporation in America, has now established its presence in South Africa. It hopes to be engaged in electronics and in other industrial engineering projects and has opened its offices in a Sandton suburb in the desired northern sector of the metropolis. IBM, on its return to South Africa, eschewed the modern black-glass and steel tower block it had designed and erected in the CBD of Johannesburg in the 1970s, and opted instead for accommodation in a custom-designed, technologically sophisticated, low-rise building in a Sandton office park. The chances of other foreign "returning" corporations or first-time foreign investors making the same choice appear to be very high.

Conclusion

In this chapter, material has been presented on Johannesburg as a place and on its position in the local and national economies. Glimpses have been provided of its past, and particularly of its recent past. In addition, there has been evidence of the changing fortunes of its downtown, and the present situation that confronts the CBD has been highlighted and contrasted with trends that now characterize the allure generated by the suburbs in the northern reaches of the metropolis.

In the introductory remarks, attention was drawn to the fact that Johannesburg finds itself in a dual position of being a potentially important link with the global economy, which begs a specific modern or first-world style of development, and at the same time being perceived as providing a cash panacea for local poverty, which seeks a different path.

In drawing this chapter to a close, and against the backdrop of the detail it has been possible to include, it now only remains to highlight more clearly the horns of the dilemma that the city faces. On the one hand, for Johannesburg and much of its metropolitan area, the survival of the CBD is more than a sentimental wish. The downtown area has for years generated a sizeable slice of the revenue needed to maintain the city. For example, until recently, and within the boundaries of the old Johannesburg municipality, rates collected from the CBD constituted 43 per cent of those collected in the whole municipality (Fraser, 1995). Those rates not only were used for maintenance and development but helped to keep the rates on residential properties within reasonable bounds. If the CBD declines any further, then the value of its properties, and its rate-generating ability, will also decline. Consequently, it can be argued that it is in the interests of the community at large to make the CBD as strong and viable as possible and certainly more so than is the case at present. On the other hand, there are those who take the view that the prime role of the downtown in a "new" Johannesburg is to provide living space for the masses of the urban poor flooding out of the overcrowded and violence-racked townships. Advocates of that view see the present occupation of downtown Johannesburg and many of the inner-city apartment areas as a victory for the people as well as an advance on the abnormal situation that prevailed under apartheid. And, in the highly charged and emotive atmosphere of the early post-apartheid period, particularly with the memories of mass deprivation caused by apartheid fresh in the minds of inner-city residents and in the minds of both popular and political-party leaders, it is hard to challenge the latter view without being labelled a racist. Such a cheap-shot response, however, simply masks the harsh realities of the problem. For, if the sheltering function of the Johannesburg core is given priority above all else, then there can be no doubt whatsoever that its commercial property values will drop dramatically, and that the drop will come sooner rather than later. With a declining rate base, the revenue generated from the inner city will fall and the implications for the cash-strapped community projects and even local government plans for delivering cheap housing to poor people will be placed in considerable jeopardy. Nor will a dead CBD provide any comfort for its inner-city residents.

Continued decline in the fortunes of the CBD will simply enhance the belief of those institutions that can relocate and operate perfectly well in the suburbs that the time to do so has come. Leading the pack could be the Johannesburg Stock Exchange. Already its members are of the opinion that, given the global technology of electronic mail and electronic banking and the other advantages of information technology that go with high levels of modern computerization, all of which are already operating in the world of the exchange and South Africa's financial institutions, then the exchange itself no longer needs to have a physical presence in the downtown of Johannesburg. Closure of the Johannesburg Stock Exchange (the only national exchange in the country), and its departure for the greener pastures of the suburbs or even a new town, would send a message to the rest of the international business world that would certainly be interpreted in one way alone. Not only would it be perceived that "Johannesburg" is in trouble but almost certainly it would be perceived that South Africa, of which Johannesburg and its region are the very heart, is dying. The consequences of such a message for the South African economy cannot be underestimated. If the disastrous scenario sketched here should eventuate, then, as indicated in the introduction to the chapter, everyone in Johannesburg, in its metropolitan area, and in Gauteng would be losers.

What is required above all else at the present moment, as Johannesburg gets to grips with globalization from its abnormal base, are cool heads and strong management by people who are fully informed of the dangers that are entailed if South Africa, through "Johannesburg," is not able firmly to grasp the friendly hand being offered to draw it and South Africa into the competitive world of the future. Just how Johannesburg manages to solve its dilemma is not a matter for concern here, but it remains the most urgent matter on the agenda of the new metropolitan council. If the councillors are wise they will attempt to embrace the positive benefits that are on offer from globalization and that can and should be absorbed in the city of Johannesburg as well as elsewhere in its metropolitan area.

Notes

1. For the sake of non-South African readers, wherever possible and wherever considered appropriate, sums of money have been given in US dollars. The South African currency is the rand and is designated by the letter R. The weakness of the rand has seen it steadily sliding against the dollar for some years and in the conversion of rands to dollars the appropriate rate for the date or period has been used. At the time of writing in mid-1995 the exchange rate was approximately R3.60 to US$1.00.
2. Because of the racial divisions in South African society that were emphasized in the apartheid era, it is necessary to refer to them in any analysis that includes that past. The word "black," with a lower case "b," is used when referring to people other than whites. The word "Black" is used when referring to African people who are not white, Coloured, or Asiatic.

References

African Development Bank (1994), *Selected Statistics on Regional Member Countries*. Abidjan: African Development Bank.

Ampros (1994a), "Vacancy Survey of Completed Office Buildings." Unpublished report. Johannesburg: Anglo-American Property Services.

——— (1994b), "Report(s) on the letting market(s) of (the) Commercial District(s) in Johannesburg." *Ampros Research*, July to November. Johannesburg: Anglo-American Property Services.

Beavon, K. S. O. (1989), "Mexico City and Colonias Populares: Hints for a South African Squatter Policy." *South African Geographical Journal* 71: 142–156.

——— (1992), "The Post-Apartheid City: Hopes, Possibilities, and Harsh Realities." In: D. M. Smith (ed.), *The Apartheid City and Beyond*. London: Routledge, pp. 231–242.

——— (1997), "Johannesburg: A City and Metropolitan Area in Transformation." In: C. Rakodi (ed.), *The Urban Challenge in Africa: Growth and Management of Its Large Cities*. Tokyo: United Nations University Press, pp. 150–191.

——— (in preparation), *Johannesburg*. World Cities Series. London: John Wiley.

Beavon, K. S. O. and S. Parnell (in preparation), "Pageview and the Origins of Lenasia." *Business Times*, supplement to the *Sunday Times*, Johannesburg.

Carrim, N. (1990), *Fietas: A Social History of Pageview, 1948–1988*. Johannesburg: Save Pageview Association.

Central Johannesburg Partnership (1994), "Greater Johannesburg: The Seat of Regional Government for the PWV Province." Unpublished report prepared as a submission to the provincial legislature. Johannesburg: Central Johannesburg Partnership.

Central Statistical Services (1992), *Population Census 1991: Geographical Distribution of the Population with a Review for 1970–1991*. CSS Report No. 03-01-02 1991. Pretoria: Central Statistical Services.

Chipkin, C. M. (1993), *Johannesburg Style: Architecture and Society 1880s–1960s*. Cape Town: David Philip.

City Engineer (1967), *Central Area Johannesburg*. Report by the Forward Planning Branch, City Engineer's Department. Johannesburg: Johannesburg City Council.

Cohen, R. B. (1981), "The New International Division of Labor: Multinational Corporations and Urban Hierarchy." In: M. Dear and A. J. Scott (eds.), *Urbanization and Urban Planning in Capitalist Society*. New York: Methuen, pp. 287–315.

386

Crankshaw, O. and C. White (1994), *Racial Desegregation and the Origin of Slums in Johannesburg's Inner City*. CPS Development Policy Series, Research Report No. 36. Johannesburg: Centre for Policy Studies.

ERO (European Research Office) and TPMP (Trade Policy Monitoring Project) (1995), *South Africa and the Lome Convention*. Johannesburg: Friedrich Ebert Stiftung.

Fair, T. J. D. and J. G. Muller (1981), "The Johannesburg Metropolitan Area." In: M. Pacione (ed.), *Urban Problems and Planning in the Developed World*. London: Croom Helm, pp. 157–188.

Fallon, I. (1995), "How Apartheid Brought SA to the Brink of Ruin." *Sunday Business*, supplement to *The Sunday Independent*, Johannesburg.

Fraser, N. (1995), "Overview: The Need to Revitalise the City of Johannesburg to Provide Formal Business Opportunities." Unpublished paper presented at the Conference on Commercial Opportunities in Rejuvenating Johannesburg. Johannesburg: AIC Conferences.

Friedmann, J. and G. Wolff (1982), "World City Formation: An Agenda for Research and Action." *International Journal of Urban and Regional Research* 6: 309–343.

Hall, P., G. Saayman, D. Molatedi, and P. Kok (1993), *A Profile of Poverty in the PWV*, 2 vols. Rondebosch: Southern Africa Labour and Development Research Unit, University of Cape Town.

Hamnett, C. (1994), "Social Polarisation in Global Cities: Theory and Evidence." *Urban Studies* 31: 401–424.

Hobart Houghton, D. and J. Dagut (1973), *Source Material on the South African Economy 1860–1970: Volume 3, 1920–1970*. Cape Town: Oxford University Press.

Hunter, R., M. Jonker, J. Rogerson, C. M. Rogerson, and R. Tomlinson (1995), "Johannesburg Inner-City Strategic Development Framework: Economic Analysis." Unpublished report prepared for the City Planning Department of the Greater Johannesburg Transitional Metropolitan Council. Johannesburg: Richard Tomlinson Consultants.

Johannesburg, City of (1993), *Johannesburg: A Special Study on the Conditions for Foreign Investment*. Milton Keynes: Reprint of a Corporate Location Report, Corporate Location.

JSE (Johannesburg Stock Exchange) (1995), "Monthly Report," May. Unpublished information sheet for JSE members. Johannesburg: Listings Department, Johannesburg Stock Exchange.

Kane-Berman, J. (1978), *Soweto: Black Revolt, White Reaction*. Johannesburg: Ravan Press.

King, R. (1990), *Global Cities: Post Imperialism and the Internationalisation of London*. London: Routledge.

Lodge, T. (1981), "The Destruction of Sophiatown." *Journal of Modern African Studies* 19: 107–132.

Mabin, A. S. and R. Hunter (1993), *Final Draft Report of the Review of Conditions and Trends Affecting Development in the PWV*. Johannesburg: PWV Forum.

MacGillivray, R. (1995), "Resolving Inner-City Housing and Urban Decay." Unpublished paper presented at the Conference on Commercial Opportunities in Rejuvenating Johannesburg. Johannesburg: AIC Conferences.

Martin, W. G. (1990), "The Making of an Industrial South Africa: Trade and Tariffs in the Interwar Period." *International Journal of African Historical Studies* 23: 59–85.

Moross & Partners (1995), "Johannesburg Nodal Development Study." Unpublished report prepared for the Johannesburg City Council. Johannesburg: Moross & Partners Inc.

Morris, P. (1980), *Soweto*. Johannesburg: Urban Foundation.

——— (1981), *A History of Black Housing in South Africa*. Johannesburg: South Africa Foundation.

Parnell, S. M. (1993), "Johannesburg Slums and Racial Segregation in South African Cities, 1910–1937." Unpublished Ph.D. thesis, Department of Geography and Environmental Studies, University of the Witwatersrand, Johannesburg.

Prinsloo, D. (1994), "Economic and Spatial Trends in the Johannesburg CBD." Unpublished report. Johannesburg: Urban Development Studies.

Proctor, A. (1979), "Class Struggle, Segregation and the City: A History of Sophiatown 1905–1940." In: B. Bozzoli (ed.), *Labour, Townships and Protest*. Johannesburg: Ravan Press, pp. 49–89.

Ramsamy, E. (1995), "South Africa and SAD(C): A Critical Evaluation of Future Development Scenarios." In: A. Lemon (ed.), *The Geography of Change in South Africa*. London: Wiley, pp. 197–214.

Rogerson, C. M. (1994), "Democracy, Reconstruction, and Changing Local and Regional Economic Planning in South Africa." *Regional Development Dialogue* 15: 102–118.

Sapoa (1993), *Shopping Centre Directory 1993*. Sandton: South African Property Owners Association Publications.

——— (1995), *Shopping Centre Directory 1995*. Sandton: South African Property Owners Association Publications.

Sassen, S. (1991), *The Global City: New York, London, Tokyo*. Princeton, N.J.: Princeton University Press.

Shachar, A. (1994), "Randstad Holland: A 'World City'?" *Urban Studies* 31: 381–400.

Shiceka, S. (1995), "The Future of Johannesburg CBD: A Gauteng Government Perspective." Unpublished paper presented at the Conference on Commercial Opportunities in Rejuvenating Johannesburg. Johannesburg: AIC Conferences.

South Africa (1994), *Strategies for the Development of an Integrated Policy and Support Programme for Small, Medium and Micro-Enterprises in South Africa: Discussion Paper*. Cape Town: Ministry of Trade and Industry.

Stadler, A. W. (1979), "Birds in the Cornfields: African Squatter Movements in Johannesburg, 1944–1947." *Journal of Southern African Studies* 6: 93–124.

United Nations (1994), *Trade and Development Report, 1994*. New York: Secretariat of the United Nations Conference on Trade and Development.

Watt, I. (1995), "Retail Opportunities: The Test for Developers and the Community." Unpublished paper presented at the Conference on Commercial Opportunities in Rejuvenating Johannesburg. Johannesburg: AIC Conferences.

Whitlow, R. and C. Brooker (1995), "The Historical Context of Urban Hydrology in Johannesburg. Part I: Johannesburg, 1900–1990." *Journal of the South African Institute of Civil Engineering* 27(3): 7–12.

Wright, C., R. Robinson, and R. Saxby (eds.) (1994), *Johannesburg: The Gateway to Africa*. Johannesburg: History of South Africa Community Publications.

Part 2
Key issues about the urban future

14

The impact of the new technologies and globalization on cities

Saskia Sassen

Telematics and globalization have emerged as fundamental forces shaping the organization of economic space. This reorganization ranges from the spatial virtualization of a growing number of economic activities to the reconfiguration of the geography of the built environment *for* economic activity. One outcome of these transformations has been captured in images of geographic dispersal at the global scale and the neutralization of place and distance through telematics in a growing number of economic activities. This raises a question of importance to the future of cities, especially regarding leading economic sectors that are intensive users of the new technologies and tend to operate globally.

In terms of their economic function, cities provide something we can think of as centrality–agglomeration economies, massive concentrations of information on the latest developments, a market-place. How do economic globalization and the new technologies alter the role of centrality and hence of cities as economic entities. The chapter shows that centrality remains a key feature of the global information economy, but that it can assume several spatial correlates, ranging from the central business district to a new global grid of cities.

Organizing much of the following discussion is the role of place and production in the global economy today. This is an important first step because so much analysis and general commentary on the global economy and the new growth sectors focuses on the neutralization of geography and on expertise.

A second major organizing argument is that the immediate future of major cities is being shaped by the intersection of two processes: (a) the shift to services, particularly the growing use of services in the organization of all industries – a much neglected aspect that I consider crucial; and (b) the globalization of economic activity. Both growing service intensity and globalization rely on and are shaped by the new information technologies. And both have had and will continue to have pronounced impacts on urban space.

The growing service intensity in economic organization generally and the specific conditions under which information technologies are available combine to make cities once again a key "production" site, a role they lost when mass manufacturing became the dominant economic sector. It is through these information-based production processes that "centrality" is reconstituted.

These are the subjects discussed in this chapter.

Place and production in the global economy

Globalization can be deconstructed in terms of the strategic sites where global processes materialize and the linkages that bind them. Among these sites are export-processing zones, offshore banking centres, and, on a far more complex level, global cities. This produces a specific geography of globalization and underlines the extent to which it is not a planetary event encompassing all of the world.[1] It is, furthermore, a changing geography, one that has changed over the past few centuries and over the past few decades[2] (and, most recently, has come to include electronic space).

This geography of globalization contains a dynamic both of dispersal and of centralization, a condition that is only now beginning to receive recognition (see Castells, 1989; Sassen, 1991: chap. 1; Frost and Spence, 1993; *Le Debat*, 1994; Knox and Taylor, 1995). The massive trends towards the spatial dispersal of economic activities at the metropolitan, national, and global level which we associate with globalization have contributed to a demand for new forms of territorial centralization of top-level management and control operations. The spatial dispersal of economic activity made possible by telematics contributes to an expansion of central functions *if* this dispersal is to take place under the continuing concentration in control, ownership, and profit appropriation that characterizes the current economic system.[3]

National and global markets as well as globally integrated organizations require central places where the work of globalization gets done.[4] Further, information industries require a vast physical infrastructure containing strategic nodes with hyperconcentration of facilities; we need to distinguish between the capacity for global transmission/communication and the material conditions that make this possible. Finally, even the most advanced information industries have a production process that is at least partly place-bound because of the combination of resources it requires even when the outputs are hypermobile.

One of the central concerns in my work has been to look at cities as production sites for the leading information industries of our time and to recover the infrastructure of activities, firms, and jobs that is necessary to run the advanced corporate economy.[5] These industries are typically conceptualized in terms of the hypermobility of their outputs and the high levels of expertise of their professionals rather than in terms of the production process involved and the requisite infrastructure of facilities and non-expert jobs that are also part of these industries.[6]

New forms of centrality

Today there is no longer a simple straightforward relation between centrality and such geographic entities as the downtown or the central business district (CBD). In the past, and up to quite recently in fact, the centre was synonymous with the downtown or the CBD. Today, the spatial correlate of the centre can assume several geographic forms. It can be the CBD, as it still is largely in New York City, or it can extend into a metropolitan area in the form of a grid of nodes of intense business activity, as we see in Frankfurt (Keil and Ronneberger, 1995). The centre has been profoundly altered by telematics and the growth of a global economy (both inextricably linked); they have contributed to a new geography of centrality (and marginality). Simplifying an analysis made elsewhere (Sassen, 1994), I identify four forms assumed by centrality today.

First, although there is no longer a simple straightforward relation between centrality and such geographic entities as the downtown or the central business district, as was the case in the past, the CBD remains a key form of centrality. But the CBD in major international

393

business centres is profoundly reconfigured by technological and economic changes.[7]

2. Secondly, the centre can extend into a metropolitan area in the form of a grid of nodes of intense business activity. One might ask whether or not a spatial organization characterized by dense strategic nodes spread over a broader region does constitute a new form of organizing the territory of the "centre," rather than, as in the more conventional view, an instance of suburbanization or geographic dispersal. In so far as these various nodes are articulated through cyber-routes or digital highways, they represent a new geographic correlate of the most advanced type of "centre." The places that fall outside this new grid of digital highways, however, are peripheralized. This regional grid of nodes represents, in my analysis, a reconstitution of the concept of region. Far from neutralizing geography, the regional grid is likely to be embedded in conventional forms of communications infrastructure, notably rapid rail and highways connecting to airports. Ironically perhaps, conventional infrastructure is likely to maximize the economic benefits derived from telematics. I think this is an important issue that has been lost somewhat in discussions about the neutralization of geography through telematics.

3. Thirdly, we are seeing the formation of a transterritorial "centre" constituted via telematics and intense economic transactions (Sassen, 1991). The most powerful of these new geographies of centrality at the inter-urban level binds the major international financial and business centres: New York, London, Tokyo, Paris, Frankfurt, Zurich, Amsterdam, Los Angeles, Sydney, Hong Kong, among others. But this geography now also includes cities such as São Paulo and Mexico City. The intensity of transactions among these cities, particularly through the financial markets, trade in services, and investment, has increased sharply, and so have the orders of magnitude involved.[8] At the same time, there has been a sharpening inequality in the concentration of strategic resources and activities between each of these cities and others in the same country.[9] For instance, Paris now concentrates a larger share of leading economic sectors and wealth in France than it did 15 years ago, while Marseilles, once a major economic hub, has lost share and is suffering severe decline.

4. Fourthly, new forms of centrality are being constituted in electronically generated spaces. Electronic space is often read as a purely technological event and in that sense a space of innocence. But if we consider, for instance, that strategic components of the financial industry operate in such space, we can see that these are spaces

where profits are produced and power is thereby constituted. In so far as these technologies strengthen the profit-making capability of finance and make possible the hypermobility of finance capital, they also contribute to the often devastating impacts of the ascendance of finance on other industries, on particular sectors of the population, and on whole economies. Cyberspace, like any other space, can be inscribed in a multiplicity of ways – some benevolent or enlightening, others not (see Sassen, 1994). My argument is that structures for economic power are being built in electronic space and that their highly complex configurations contain points of coordination and centralization.

In the next sections I discuss various aspects of these four forms of centrality, focusing particularly on cities as a way of showing the logic that produces centrality in a global information economy.

Concentration and the redefinition of the centre: Some empirical referents

The trend towards concentration of top-level management, coordination, and servicing functions is evident at the national and international scales in all highly developed countries. For instance, the Paris region accounts for over 40 per cent of all producer services in France and over 80 per cent of the most advanced ones. New York City is estimated to account for between a fourth and a fifth of all US producer services exports though it has only 3 per cent of the US population. London accounts for 40 per cent of all exports of producer services in the United Kingdom. Similar trends are evident in Zurich, Frankfurt, and Tokyo.

Elsewhere (Sassen, 1994), a somewhat detailed empirical examination of several cities served to explore different aspects of this trend towards concentration. Here there is space only for a few observations. The case of Toronto, a city whose financial district was built up only in recent years, allows us to see to what extent the pressure towards physical concentration is embedded in an economic dynamic rather than simply being the consequence of an inherited built infrastructure from the past, as one could think was the case in older centres such as London or New York. But Toronto also shows that it is certain industries in particular that are subject to the pressure towards spatial concentration, notably finance and its sister industries (Gad, 1991).

In the financial district in Manhattan, the use of advanced information and telecommunication technologies has had a strong impact on the spatial organization of the district because of the added spatial requirements of "intelligent" buildings. A ring of new office buildings meeting these requirements has been built over the past decade immediately around the old Wall Street core, where the narrow streets and lots made this difficult; furthermore, renovating old buildings in the Wall Street core is extremely expensive and often not possible. The new buildings in the district were mostly corporate headquarters and financial services industry facilities. These firms tend to be extremely intensive users of telematics, and the availability of the most advanced forms typically is a major factor in their real estate and locational decisions. They need complete redundancy of telecommunications systems, high carrying capacity, often their own private branch exchange, etc. With this often goes a need for large spaces. For instance, the technical installations backing a firm's trading floor are likely to require additional space equivalent to the size of the trading floor itself.

The case of Sydney illuminates the interaction of a vast, continental economic scale and pressures towards spatial concentration. Rather than strengthening the multipolarity of the Australian urban system, the developments of the 1980s – increased internationalization of the Australian economy, sharp increases in foreign investment, a strong shift towards finance, real estate, and producer services – contributed to a greater concentration of major economic activities and actors in Sydney. This included a loss of share of such activities and actors by Melbourne, for long the centre of commercial activity and wealth in Australia (Daly and Stimson, 1992).

At the international level, the case of the leading financial centres in the world today is of continued interest, because one might have expected that the growing number of financial centres now integrated into the global markets would have reduced the extent of concentration of financial activity in the top centres. One would further expect this given the immense increases in the global volume of transactions.[10] Yet the levels of concentration remain unchanged in the face of massive transformations in the financial industry and in the technological infrastructure on which this industry depends.[11]

For example, international bank lending grew from US$1.89 trillion in 1980 to US$6.24 trillion in 1991 – a fivefold increase in a mere 10 years. The United States, Japan, and the United Kingdom, mostly through their three premier cities, accounted for 42 per cent of all such international lending in 1980 and for 41 per cent in 1991, according to data from the Bank of International Settlements.[12] Beyond these three, Switzerland, France, Germany, and Luxembourg bring the total share of the top centres to 64 per cent in 1991, which is just about the same share these countries had in 1980. Yet another example of concentration is Chicago, which singlehandedly dominates the world's trading in futures, accounting for 60 per cent of worldwide contracts in options and futures in 1991.

In brief, with the potential for global control capability, certain cities are becoming nodal points in a vast communications and market system. Advances in electronics and telecommunication have transformed geographically distant cities into centres for global communication and long-distance management. But centralized control and management over a geographically dispersed array of plants, offices, and service outlets do not come about inevitably as part of a "world system." They require the development of a vast range of highly specialized services and of top-level management and control functions.

The intersection of globalization and the shift to services

To understand the new or sharply expanded role of a particular kind of city in the world economy since the early 1980s, we need to focus on the intersection of two major processes. The first is the sharp growth in the globalization of economic activity; this has raised the scale and the complexity of transactions, thereby feeding the growth of top-level multinational headquarter functions and the growth of advanced corporate services. It is important to note that, even though globalization raises the scale and complexity of these operations, they are also evident at smaller geographic scales and lower orders of complexity, as is the case with firms that operate regionally. Thus, although regionally oriented firms need not negotiate the complexities of international borders and the regulations of different countries, they are still faced with a regionally dispersed network of operations that requires centralized control and servicing.

The second process we need to consider is the growing service intensity in the organization of all industries. This has contributed to a massive growth in the demand for services by firms in all industries, from mining and manufacturing to finance and consumer services. Cities are key sites for the production of services for firms. Hence the increase in service intensity in the organization of all industries had a significant growth effect on cities in the 1980s. It is important to recognize that this growth in services for firms is evident in cities at different levels of a nation's urban system. Some of these cities cater to regional or subnational markets; others cater to national markets; and yet others cater to global markets. In this context, globalization becomes a question of scale and added complexity.

The key process from the perspective of the urban economy is the growing demand for services by firms in all industries and the fact that cities are preferred production sites for such services, whether at the global, national, or regional level. As a result we see in cities the formation of a new urban economic core of banking and service activities that comes to replace the older, typically manufacturing-oriented, core.

In the case of cities that are major international business centres, the scale, power, and profit levels of this new core suggest that we are seeing the formation of a new urban economy. This is so in at least two regards. First, even though these cities have long been centres for business and finance, since the late 1970s there have been dramatic changes in the structure of the business and financial sectors, as well as sharp increases in the overall magnitude of these sectors and their weight in the urban economy. Secondly, the ascendance of the new finance and services complex, particularly international finance, engenders what may be regarded as a new economic regime: although this sector may account for only a fraction of the economy of a city, it imposes itself on that larger economy. Most notably, the possibility for super-profits in finance has the effect of devalorizing manufacturing in so far as manufacturing cannot generate the super-profits typical in much financial activity.

This is not to say that everything in the economy of these cities has changed. On the contrary, they still show a great deal of continuity and many similarities with cities that are not global nodes. Rather, the implantation of global processes and markets has meant that the internationalized sector of the economy has expanded sharply and has imposed a new valorization dynamic – a new set of criteria for valuing or pricing various economic activities and outcomes. This has had devastating effects on large sectors of the urban economy. High prices and profit levels in the internationalized sector and its ancillary activities, such as top-of-the-line restaurants and hotels, have made it increasingly difficult for other sectors to compete for space and investments. Many of these other sectors have experienced considerable downgrading and/or displacement, as, for example, neighbourhood shops tailored to local needs are replaced by upscale boutiques and restaurants catering to new high-income urban élites.

Though at a different order of magnitude, these trends also became evident during the late 1980s in a number of major cities in the developing world that have become integrated into various world markets; São Paulo, Buenos Aires, Bangkok, Taipei, and Mexico City are only a few examples. Also here the new urban core was fed by the deregulation of financial markets, the ascendance of finance and specialized services, and integration into the world markets. The opening of stock markets to foreign investors and the privatization of what were once public sector firms have been crucial institutional arenas for this articulation. Given the vast size of some of these cities, the impact of this new core on the broader city is not always as evident as in central London or Frankfurt, but the transformation is still very real.

It is important to recognize that manufacturing remains a crucial sector in all these economies, even when it may have ceased to be a dominant sector in major cities. Indeed, several scholars have argued that the producer services sector could not exist without manufacturing (Cohen and Zysman, 1987). A key proposition for these and other authors is that producer services are dependent on a strong manufacturing sector in order to grow. There is considerable debate around this issue (Noyelle and Dutka, 1988; Drennan, 1992; Sassen, 1991). Drennan (1992), a leading analyst of the producer services sector in New York City, argues that a strong finance and producer services sector is possible in New York, notwithstanding decline in its industrial base, and that these sectors are so strongly integrated into the world markets that articulation with the larger region becomes secondary.

Sassen (1991), in a variant on both positions, argues that manufacturing indeed feeds the growth of the producer services sector, but that it does so whether located in the area in question, somewhere else in the country, or overseas. Even though manufacturing – and mining and agriculture, for that matter – feeds growth in the demand for producer services, its actual location is of secondary importance in the case of global-level service firms. Thus, whether a manufacturing plant is located offshore or within a country may be quite irrelevant as long as it is part of a multinational corporation likely to buy the services from those top-level firms. Secondly, the territorial dispersal of plants, especially if international, actually raises the demand for producer services. This is yet another meaning, or consequence, of globalization: the growth of producer service firms headquartered in New York or London or Paris can be fed by manufacturing located anywhere in the world as long as it is part of a multinational corporate network. Thirdly, a good part of the producer services sector is fed by financial and business transactions either that have nothing to do with manufacturing, as is the case in many of the global financial markets, or for which manufacturing is incidental, as in much merger and acquisition activity, which is centred on buying and selling firms rather than the buying of manufacturing firms as such.

Some of the figures on New York and London, two cities that experienced heavy losses in manufacturing and sharp gains in producer services, illustrate this point. New York lost 34 per cent of its manufacturing jobs between 1969 and 1989 in a national economy that overall lost only 2 per cent of such jobs, and there was actually manufacturing growth in many areas. The British economy lost 32 per cent of its manufacturing jobs between 1971 and 1989, and the London region lost 47 per cent of such jobs (Fainstein et al., 1993). Yet both cities had sharp growth in producer services and raised their shares of such jobs in total city employment. Further, it is worth noting the different conditions in each city's larger region: London's region had a 2 per cent decline compared with a 22 per cent job growth rate in the larger New York region. This divergence points to the fact that the finance and producer services complex in each city rests on a growth dynamic that is somewhat independent of the broader regional economy – a sharp change from the past, when a city was presumed to be deeply articulated with its hinterland.

The formation of a new production complex

According to standard conceptions about information industries, the rapid growth and disproportionate concentration of producer services in central cities should not have happened. Because producer services are thoroughly embedded in the most advanced information technologies, they could be expected to have locational options that bypass the high costs and congestion typical of major cities. But cities offer agglomeration economies and highly innovative environments. The growing complexity, diversity, and specialization of the services required have contributed to the economic viability of a free-standing specialized service sector.

The production process in these services benefits from proximity to other specialized services. This is especially the case in the leading and most innovative sectors of these industries. Complexity and innovation often require multiple highly specialized inputs from several industries. The production of a financial instrument, for example, requires inputs from accounting, advertising, legal expertise, economic consulting, public relations, designers, and printers. The particular characteristics of production of these services, especially those involved in complex and innovative operations, explain their pronounced concentration in major cities. The commonly heard explanation that high-level professionals require face-to-face interactions needs to be refined in several ways. Producer services, unlike other types of services, are not necessarily dependent on spatial proximity to the consumers (i.e. firms) served. Rather, economies occur in such specialized firms when they locate close to others that produce key inputs or whose proximity makes possible joint production of certain service offerings. The accounting firm can service its clients at a distance, but the nature of its service depends on proximity to specialists, lawyers, and programmers. Moreover, concentration arises out of the needs and expectations of the people likely to be employed in these new high-skill jobs, who tend to be attracted to the amenities and lifestyles that large urban centres can offer. Frequently, what is thought of as face-to-face communication is actually a production process that requires multiple simultaneous inputs and feedbacks. At the current stage of technical development, immediate and simultaneous access to the pertinent experts is still the most effective way, especially when dealing with a highly complex product. The concentration of the most advanced telecommunications and computer network facilities in major cities is a key factor in what I refer to as the production process of these industries.[13]

Further, time replaces weight in these sectors as a force for agglomeration. In the past, the pressure of the weight of inputs from iron ore to unprocessed agricultural products was a major constraint pushing towards agglomeration in sites where the heaviest inputs were located. Today, the acceleration of economic transactions and the premium put on time have created new forces for agglomeration. This is increasingly not the case in routine operations. But where time is of the essence, as it is today in many of the leading sectors of these industries, the benefits of agglomeration are still extremely high – to the point where it is not simply a cost advantage but an indispensable arrangement.

This combination of constraints suggests that the agglomeration of producer services in major cities actually constitutes a production complex. This producer services complex is intimately connected to the world of corporate headquarters; indeed, they are often thought of as forming a joint headquarters–corporate services complex. But, in my reading, we need to distinguish the two. Although it is true that headquarters still tend to be disproportionately concentrated in cities, over the past two decades many have moved out. Headquarters can indeed locate outside cities, but they need a producer services complex somewhere in order to buy or contract for the needed specialized services and financing. Further, headquarters of firms with very high overseas activity or in highly innovative and complex lines of business tend to locate in major cities. In brief, firms in more routinized lines of activity, with predominantly regional or national markets, appear to be increasingly free to move or install their headquarters outside cities. Firms in highly competitive and innovative lines of activity and/or with a strong world market orientation appear to benefit from being located at the centre of major international business centres, no matter how high the costs.

Both types of firms need a corporate services complex, but where this complex is located is probably increasingly unimportant from the perspective of many, though not all, headquarters. From the perspective of producer services firms, such a specialized complex is most likely to be in a city rather than, for example, a suburban office park. The latter will be the site for producer services firms but not for a services complex. And only such a complex is capable of handling the most advanced and complicated corporate demands.

The region in the information age

The massive use of telematics in the economy and the corresponding possibility for geographic dispersal and mobility of firms suggest that the whole notion of regional specialization, and of the region, may become obsolete. But there are indications that, as is the case for large cities, the hypermobility of information industries and the heightened capacity for geographic dispersal may be only part of the story. The evidence on regional specialization in the United States and in other highly developed countries, along with new insights into the actual work involved in producing these services, points to a different set of outcomes.

What is important from the perspective of the region is that the existence of, for instance, a producer services complex in the major city or cities in a region creates a vast concentration of communications infrastructure, which can be of great use to other economic nodes in that region. Such nodes can (and do) connect with the major city or cities in a region and thereby to a worldwide network of firms and markets. The issue from the regional perspective is, then, that somewhere in its territory the region should count on state-of-the-art communication facilities that connect it with the world and that bring foreign firms from all over the world to the region. Given a regional grid of economic nodes, the benefits of this concentration in the major city or cities are no longer confined to firms located in those cities.

Secondly, given the nature of the production process in advanced information industries, as described in the preceding section, the geographic dispersal of activities has limits. The importance of actual face-to-face transactions means that a metropolitan or regional network of firms will need conventional communications infrastructure, e.g. highways or rapid rail, and locations not further than something like two hours. One of the ironies of the new information technologies is that, to maximize their use, we need access to conventional infrastructure. In the case of international networks it takes airports and planes; in the case of metropolitan or regional networks, it takes trains and cars.

The importance of conventional infrastructure in the operation of economic sectors that are heavy users of telematics has not received sufficient attention. The dominant notion seems to be that telematics obliterates the need for conventional infrastructure. But it is precisely the nature of the production process in advanced industries, whether they operate globally or nationally, that has contributed to the immense rise in business travel in all advanced economies over the past decade, the new electronic era. The virtual office is a far more limited option than a purely technological analysis would suggest. Certain types of economic activities can be run from a virtual office located anywhere. But, for work processes requiring multiple specialized inputs, considerable innovation, and risk-taking, the need for direct interaction with other firms and specialists remains a key locational factor. Hence the metropolitanization and regionalization of an economic sector have boundaries that are set by the time it takes for a reasonable commute to the major city or cities in the region. The irony of today's electronic era is that the older notion of the region and older forms of infrastructure re-emerge as critical for key economic sectors. This type of region in many ways diverges from older forms of region. It corresponds rather to the second form of centrality posited above in this chapter – a metropolitan grid of nodes connected via telematics. But, for this digital grid to work, conventional infrastructure – ideally of the most advanced kind – is also a necessity.

The new marginality

The new growth sectors, the new organizational capacities of firms, and the new technologies – all three interrelated – are contributing to produce not only a new geography of centrality but also a new geography of marginality. The evidence for the United States, Western Europe, and Japan suggests that it will take government policy and action to reduce the new forms of spatial and social inequalities.

The new marginality has several components: the inevitable "creative destruction" that is part of growth; losses due to international and national competition; insufficient quality in factors of production; redundancy or excess capacity; and others (*Social Justice*, 1993; *Competition and Change*, 1995; King, 1995).

One critical component that is not sufficiently recognized, and where government policy could make a difference, is the misunderstanding that seems to prevail in much general commentary about what matters in an advanced economic system, the information economy, and economic globalization. Many types of firms, workers, and places (for example, in industrial services) that look as if they do not belong in an advanced, information-based, globally oriented economic system are actually integral parts of such a system. They need policy recognition and support because they cannot compete in the new environments where leading sectors have bid up prices and standards, even though their products and labour are in demand. For instance, the financial industry in Manhattan, one of the most sophisticated and complex industries, needs truckers to deliver not only software but also tables and light bulbs; and it needs blue-collar maintenance workers and cleaners. These activities and workers need to be able to make a decent living if they are to stay in the region.

Yet another dimension not sufficiently recognized is the new valuation dynamic. The combination of globalization and the new technologies has altered the criteria and mechanisms through which factors, inputs, goods, and services are valued and priced. This has had devastating effects on some localities, industries, firms, and workers. Thus the salaries of financial experts and the profits of financial services firms zoomed up in the 1980s while the wages of blue-collar workers and the profits of many traditional manufacturing firms sank. We can expect more of this. At times the devastation hits sectors that are part of a well-balanced economic system and hence it becomes counterproductive for economic growth.

The policy challenge

Beyond the multiplicity of policies called for by the complexity and diversity of the problems and potential associated with the new technologies and economic globalization, several policy innovations will be needed. In view of the intricacies of policy and the political frameworks within which policies operate, I will limit myself to itemizing some key issues that emerge from the discussion in this chapter.

1. Urban and regional economic development policy is in part international development policy – more so than in the past, owing to the formation of global markets and the growing importance of multinational corporations, all in a context of governmental deregulation; major cities and central regions interact directly with the world economy.
2. Economic development policy is deeply intertwined with developments in communications; this has always been the case, but today the complexity of many of the new technologies creates specific challenges. The most advanced forms of communication need to be harnessed to economic development goals that benefit a broad spectrum of economic actors.
3. Economic development policy will have to have a social equity dimension running through it. The 1980s made it clear that great wealth can be produced and high growth rates achieved without significant benefits for a large share of individuals and economic sectors. In the long run, the absence of equitable distribution appears to create a drag on overall economic growth.

Notes

1. Cf. Robertson's (1991) notion of the world as a single place or of the "global human condition." I would say that globalization is also a process that produces differentiation, only the alignment of differences is of a very different kind from that associated with such differentiating notions as national character, national culture, and national society. For example, the corporate world today has a global geography, but not everywhere in the world; in fact it has highly defined and structured spaces. Secondly, it also is increasingly sharply differentiated from non-corporate segments in the economies of the particular locations (a city such as New York) or countries where it operates. There is homogenization along certain lines that cross national boundaries and sharp differentiation inside these boundaries. We

405

can also see this in the geography of certain built forms – from the bungalow (King, 1990) to the corporate complex (Sassen, 1991) or the landscapes of American theme parks; we can see that these various built forms are both global yet highly localized in certain places. It is in this sense that globalized forms and processes tend to have a distinct geography.

2. We need to recognize the specific historical conditions for different conceptions of the international or the global (Sassen, 1996). There is a tendency to see the internationalization of the economy as a process operating at the centre, embedded in the power of the multinational corporations today and of colonial enterprises in the past. One could note that the economies of many peripheral countries are thoroughly internationalized owing to high levels of foreign investment in all economic sectors and to heavy dependence on world markets for "hard" currency. What the highly developed countries have is strategic concentrations of firms and markets that operate globally, the capability for global control and coordination, and power. This is a very different form of the international from the one we find in developing countries.

3. More conceptually, we can ask whether an economic system with strong tendencies towards such concentration can have a space economy that lacks points of physical agglomeration. That is to say, does power, in this case economic power, have spatial correlates?

4. I see the producer services, and most especially finance and advanced corporate services, as industries producing the organizational commodities necessary for the implementation and management of global economic systems (Sassen, 1991: chaps. 2–5). Producer services are intermediate outputs, that is, services bought by firms. They cover financial, legal, and general management matters, innovation, development, design, administration, personnel, production technology, maintenance, transport, communications, wholesale distribution, advertising, cleaning services for firms, security, and storage. Central components of the producer services category are a range of industries with mixed business and consumer markets: insurance, banking, financial services, real estate, legal services, accounting, and professional associations (for more detailed discussions see, e.g., Noyelle and Dutka, 1988; Daniels, 1991).

5. Methodologically speaking, this is one way of addressing the question of the unit of analysis in studies of contemporary economic processes. "National economy" is a problematic category when there are high levels of internationalization. And "world economy" is a problematic category because of the impossibility of engaging in detailed empirical study at that scale. Highly internationalized cities such as New York or London offer the possibility of examining globalization processes in great detail, within a bounded setting, and with all their multiple, often contradictory aspects.

6. Much analysis and general commentary on the global economy and the new growth sectors does not incorporate these multiple dimensions. Elsewhere I have argued that what we could think of as the dominant narrative or mainstream account of economic globalization is a "narrative of eviction" (Sassen, 1994). Key concepts in the dominant account – globalization, information economy, and telematics – all suggest that place no longer matters and that the only type of worker that matters is the highly educated professional. This account privileges the capability for global transmission over the concentrations of built infrastructure that make transmission possible; information outputs over the workers producing those outputs, from specialists to secretaries; and the new transnational corporate culture over the multiplicity of cultural environments, including reterritorialized immigrant cultures, within which many of the "other" jobs of the global information economy take place. In brief, the dominant narrative concerns itself with the upper circuits of capital, not the lower ones, and with the global capacities of major economic actors, not the infrastructure of facilities and jobs underlying those capacities. This narrow focus has the effect of evicting from the account the *place*-boundedness of significant components of the global information economy.

7. We may be seeing a difference in the pattern of global city formation in parts of the United States and in parts of Western Europe (Hall, 1988; Kunzmann and Wegener, 1991; Keil and

Ronneberger, 1995; Sassen, 1994). In the United States, major cities such as New York and Chicago have large centres that have been rebuilt many times, given the brutal neglect suffered by much urban infrastructure and the imposed obsolescence so characteristic of US cities. This neglect and accelerated obsolescence produce vast spaces for rebuilding the centre according to the requirements of whatever regime of urban accumulation or pattern of spatial organization of the urban economy prevails at a given time.

In Europe, urban centres are far more protected and they rarely contain significant stretches of abandoned space; the expansion of workplaces and the need for intelligent buildings necessarily will have to take place partly outside the old centres. One of the most extreme cases is the complex of La Défense, the massive, state-of-the art office complex developed right outside Paris to avoid harming the built environment inside the city. This is an explicit instance of government policy and planning aimed at addressing the growing demand for central office space of prime quality. Yet another variant of this expansion of the "centre" onto hitherto peripheral land can be seen in London's Docklands. Similar projects for recentralizing peripheral areas were launched in several major cities in Europe, North America, and Japan during the 1980s.

8. The pronounced orientation to the world markets evident in such cities raises questions about the articulation with their nation-states, their regions, and the larger economic and social structure in such cities. Cities have typically been deeply embedded in the economies of their region, indeed often reflecting the characteristics of the latter; and they still do. But cities that are strategic sites in the global economy tend, in part, to disconnect from their region. This conflicts with a key proposition in traditional scholarship about urban systems, namely, that these systems promote the territorial integration of regional and national economies.

9. In the case of a complex landscape such as Europe's we see in fact several geographies of centrality – one global, others continental and regional (see Sassen, 1994). A central urban hierarchy connects major cities, many of which in turn play central roles in the wider global system of cities: Paris, London, Frankfurt, Amsterdam, and Zurich. These cities are also part of a wider network of European financial/cultural/service capitals (some with only one, others with several of these functions) that articulate the European region and are somewhat less oriented to the global economy than Paris, Frankfurt, or London. And then there are several geographies of marginality: the East–West divide and the North–South divide across Europe as well as newer divisions. In Eastern Europe, certain cities and regions, notably Budapest, are rather attractive for purposes of investment, both European and non-European, while others will increasingly fall behind, notably in Romania, Yugoslavia, and Albania. We see a similar differentiation in the south of Europe: Madrid, Barcelona, and Milan are gaining in the new European hierarchy; Naples, Rome, and Marseilles are not.

10. Furthermore, this unchanged level of concentration has happened at a time when financial services are more mobile than ever before: globalization, deregulation (an essential ingredient for globalization), and *securitization* have been the key to this mobility – in the context of massive advances in telecommunications and electronic networks. One result is growing competition among centres for hypermobile financial activity. In my view, there has been an overemphasis on competition both in general and in specialized accounts on this subject. As I have argued elsewhere (Sassen, 1991: chap. 7), there is also a functional division of labour among various major financial centres. In that sense, we can think of a transnational system with multiple locations.

11. Much of the discussion around the formation of a single European market and financial system has raised the possibility, and even the need if it is to be competitive, of centralizing financial functions and capital in a limited number of cities rather than maintaining the current structure in which each country has an international financial centre.

12. There were compositional changes: Japan's share rose from 6.2 per cent to 15.1 per cent and the UK share fell from 26.2 per cent to 16.3 per cent; the US share remained constant. All increased in absolute terms.

13. The telecommunications infrastructure also contributes to concentration of leading sectors in major cities. Long-distance communications systems increasingly use fibre optic wires. These have several advantages over traditional copper wire: large carrying capacity, high speed, more security, and higher signal strength. Fibre systems tend to connect major communications hubs because they are not easily spliced and hence not desirable for connecting multiple lateral sites. Fibre systems tend to be installed along existing rights of way, whether rail, water, or highways (Moss, 1986). The growing use of fibre optic systems thus tends to strengthen the major existing telecommunication concentrations and therefore the existing hierarchies.

References

Castells, M. (1989), *The Informational City*. London: Blackwell.

Cohen, Stephen S. and John Zysman (1987), *Manufacturing Matters: The Myth of the Post-Industrial Economy*. New York: Basic Books.

Competition and Change (1995), *The Journal of Global Business and Political Economy* 1(1), October.

Daly, M. T. and R. Stimson (1992), "Sydney: Australia's Gateway and Financial Capital." In: E. Blakely and T. J. Stimpson (eds.), *New Cities of the Pacific Rim*. Institute for Urban & Regional Development, University of California, Berkeley, chap. 18.

Daniels, Peter W. (1991), "Producer Services and the Development of the Space Economy." In: Peter W. Daniels and Frank Moulaert (eds.), *The Changing Geography of Advanced Producer Services*. London and New York: Belhaven Press.

Drennan, Mathew P. (1992), "Gateway Cities: The Metropolitan Sources of US Producer Service Exports." *Urban Studies* 29(2): 217–235.

Fainstein, S., I. Gordon, and M. Harloe (1993), *Divided Cities: Economic Restructuring and Social Change in London and New York*. New York: Blackwell.

Frost, M. and Nigel Spence (1993), "Global City Characteristics and Central London's Employment." *Urban Studies* 30(3): 547–558.

Gad, Gunter (1991), "Toronto's Financial District." *Canadian Urban Landscapes-1*, pp. 203–207.

Hall, Peter (1988), *Cities of Tomorrow*. Oxford: Blackwell.

Keil, Roger and Klaus Ronneberger (1995), "The City Turned Inside Out: Spatial Strategies and Local Politics." In: Hitz et al. (eds.), *Capitales Fatales*. Zurich: Rotpunkt Verlag.

King, A. D. (1990), *Urbanism, Colonialism, and the World Economy. Culture and Spatial Foundations of the World Urban System*. The International Library of Sociology. London and New York: Routledge.

——— (ed.) (1995), *Representing the City. Ethnicity, Capital and Culture in the 21st Century*. London: Macmillan.

Knox, Paul L. and Peter J. Taylor (eds.) (1995), *World Cities in a World-System*. Cambridge: Cambridge University Press.

Kunzmann, K. R. and M. Wegener (1991), *The Pattern of Urbanisation in Western Europe 1960–1990*. Report for the Directorate General XVI of the Commission of the European Communities as part of the study "Urbanisation and the Function of Cities in the European Community." Dortmund, Germany: Institut für Raumplanung, 15 March.

Le Debat (1994), Special issue on "The New Paris," May–June.

Moss, M. (1986), "Telecommunications and the Future of Cities." *Land Development Studies* 3: 33–44.

Noyelle, T. and A. B. Dutka (1988), *International Trade in Business Services: Accounting, Advertising, Law and Management Consulting.* Cambridge, Mass.: Ballinger Publishing.

Robertson, R. (1991), "Social Theory, Cultural Relativity and the Problem of Globality." In: A. D. King (ed.), *Culture, Globalization and the World System.* Current Debates in Art History 3. Department of Art & Art History, State University of New York at Binghamton, pp. 69–90.

Sassen, Saskia (1991), *The Global City: New York, London, Tokyo.* Princeton, N.J.: Princeton University Press.

—— (1994), *Cities in a World Economy.* Thousand Oaks, Calif.: Pine Forge/Sage Press.

—— (1996), *Losing Control? Sovereignty in an Age of Globalization.* The 1995 Columbia University Memorial Schoff Lectures. New York: Columbia University Press.

Social Justice (1993), Special issue on "Global Crisis, Local Struggles," 20(3–4), Fall–Winter.

15

World cities as financial centres

David R. Meyer

The expansion of international finance

International financial centres house the pivotal intermediaries who control and coordinate the exchange of capital, such as investments (infrastructure, stocks, and bonds), payments arising from trade in commodities and services, and currencies (Meyer, 1986, 1991a). The livelihood of these centres rests on the expansion of national economies from both population growth and rising per capita incomes. That growth generates larger financial exchanges both within and among nations. Nations that participate actively in international economic exchanges offer greater opportunities for their financial intermediaries to control and coordinate capital flows. A supportive governmental regulatory apparatus confers advantages on financial intermediaries of the home nation, and they can draw on social networks within the nation to gain advantages *vis-à-vis* financial intermediaries from other nations.

The rapid growth of exports and imports of commodities between 1970 and 1992 provided one pillar for the expansion of international financial intermediaries (table 15.1). The rate of growth in that trade rose from an annual average of 4 per cent between 1970 and 1980 to 4.9 per cent between 1980 and 1992. However, the participation of

Table 15.1　**The average annual growth rate of merchandise trade in the world and selected nations, 1970–1992 (%)**

	Exports		Imports	
	1970–1980	1980–1992	1970–1980	1980–1992
World	4.0	4.9	4.0	4.9
High-income countries				
Germany	5.0	4.6	2.8	5.7
Hong Kong	9.7	5.0	7.8	12.6
Japan	9.0	4.6	0.4	6.6
United States	6.5	3.8	4.3	6.1
Upper-middle-income countries				
Brazil	8.5	5.0	4.0	1.5
Malaysia	4.8	11.3	3.7	7.9
Mexico	13.5	1.6	5.5	3.8
South Korea	23.5	11.9	11.6	11.2
Lower-middle-income countries				
Chile	10.4	5.5	2.2	3.5
Morocco	3.9	5.5	6.6	4.4
Thailand	10.3	14.7	5.0	11.5
Turkey	4.3	9.0	5.7	9.6
Low-income countries				
China	8.7	11.9	11.3	9.2
India	4.3	5.9	3.0	1.9
Nigeria	0.4	1.7	19.4	−10.5
Tanzania	−7.5	−1.2	−0.6	−1.3

Source: World Bank (1994: 186–187, table 13).

nations in this growth differed substantially both over time for a nation and among nations. The growth rates of exports of some high-income nations, such as Germany, Hong Kong, Japan, and the United States, slowed across the two time-periods, whereas their growth rates of imports rose. Rapidly industrializing economies, such as those of Malaysia, South Korea, and Thailand, achieved growth rates in exports and imports far above the world averages. Economic crises also affected the pace of growth in dramatic ways; for example, the growth rate of exports from Mexico virtually collapsed between 1970–1980 and 1980–1992. Low-income nations also followed significantly different trajectories. African nations such as Nigeria and Tanzania remained moribund or declined as participants in the global economy. India, in contrast, joined in trade modestly, especially com-

411

pared with lower-middle-income countries such as Turkey, whereas China acquired the trade characteristics of the rapidly industrializing economies such as Malaysia and South Korea.

This differential participation of nations in exports and imports affects the capacity of their international financial intermediaries to control and coordinate the exchange of capital. Expanding export and import sectors give financiers opportunities to underwrite trade through the provision of credit, and, if their domestic producers expand facilities outside the home nation, the financiers can follow the firms to provide loans and credits. Contracting or moribund trade economies, however, provide limited opportunities for financial intermediaries, except, perhaps, in the provision of loans to cover losses. These economies also experience a slow-down or contraction in the accumulation of capital; that hinders the capacity of domestic financial intermediaries to participate in capital exchanges. The absolute or relative decline in trade probably benefits financial intermediaries outside the home nation to a greater degree because they have greater capacity to fund loans.

The growth of international financial transactions partially mirrors this growth of trade, yet it also provides a broader perspective because loans and deposits for other purposes are included. The pace of expansion of these transactions exceeded the growth of trade by almost a two-to-one margin (table 15.2). The world annual growth rate of liabilities and claims against lending banks reached 11 per cent between 1980 and 1986; it declined slightly to 9 per cent between 1986 and 1993. This differential between financial and trade flows suggests that international transactions of financial capital may become more important to the viability of financial centres than the control of trade by their commodity brokers, wholesalers, and producers.

The industrial countries, along with rapidly growing Asian economic powers such as Hong Kong, Singapore, and Thailand, had the greatest consistency in the expansion of borrowing and lending by their banks (table 15.2). In contrast, nations in Africa, the Middle East, and the western hemisphere south of the United States had wildly fluctuating rates of growth and often collapsed into substantial declines in financial exchanges. This limited participation in financial exchanges undercuts the capacity of their financial intermediaries to accumulate capital and build expertise in financial intermediation. Consequently, external financial intermediaries will dominate the provision of capital, unless the nation-state intervenes with its own financial intermediation. The small scale of financial centres in these

Table 15.2 **The growth of international financial transactions by national groups and selected nations, 1980–1993**

Residence of bank	Compound annual growth rate (%)			
	1980–1986		1986–1993	
	Liabilities, borrowing bank	Claims, lending bank	Liabilities, borrowing bank	Claims, lending bank
World	11	11	9	9
Industrial countries	12	13	8	9
United States	19	17	8	3
Japan	24	28	10	14
Germany	4	17	14	13
Italy	10	9	12	8[a]
United Kingdom	11	12	6	5
Africa	9	−8	−1	8
Ghana	56	30	−34	−7
Kenya	−6	0	−13	−11[a]
Nigeria	−10	−22	−3[a]	1[a]
Tanzania	40	−11	2	12
Asia	20	20	14	11
Hong Kong	22	28	18	11
India	–	3	–	13
Singapore	24	21	11	9
Thailand	0	10	25[b]	36[c]
Middle East	5	0	3	4
Egypt	0	4	7	16
Israel	−1	0	−12	4
Western hemisphere	5	6	6	6
Brazil	14	2	34[d]	15[d]
Chile	9	−2	−7	1
Mexico	−2[e]	42[e]	−1	−5
Venezuela	0	−11	−6	4

Source: International Monetary Fund (1994: 64–67).
a. 1986–1992.
b. 1986–1991.
c. 1986–1990.
d. 1986–1987.
e. 1982–1986.

nations, therefore, mirrors the limited development of their international capital markets. The industrial countries, plus Hong Kong and Singapore, exert overwhelming dominance over financial exchanges

413

as the residence of the borrowing banks and of lending banks. Those nations accounted for 72 per cent of borrowing in 1980 and 84 per cent in 1993; similarly, they accounted for 70 per cent of lending in 1980 and 82 per cent in 1993 (International Monetary Fund 1994: 64–67). Over half of the relative gains of this group from 1980 to 1993 came from the expansion of lending and borrowing of banks in Hong Kong and Singapore. Nations outside this group of industrial countries and Hong Kong and Singapore, especially those in Africa, the Middle East, and parts of Asia, such as India, therefore, have declined relatively as participants in international financial exchanges. This implies that their financial centres will remain weak or decline relatively as pivots of global capital exchanges.

These changes in the exchange of commodity and financial capital suggest that simple assumptions that financial exchanges will increase as part of some seamless global flow of capital rest on a weak foundation. National differences in economic growth and welfare continue to loom large, and financial centres will not form a tightly integrated hierarchy of exchange. Financial centres in the leading economic powerhouses, including the longstanding financial centres in Asia, such as Hong Kong and Singapore, exert a disproportionate and increasing dominance over the global exchange of capital. Explanations of the future of world financial centres, therefore, must probe beneath the surface view of the seamless integrated global economy that draws all nations tightly into its web.

Paradoxes

Speculations about the future of world financial centres raise a bewildering array of paradoxes. On the one hand, observers argue that advances in global telecommunications obviate the necessity for face-to-face communications. Individuals with computers, faxes, and telephones can operate from any place, including their homes; financial centres, thus, lose their reason for existence (Selz, 1993; Whitney, 1993). On the other hand, observers claim that the global dispersal of economic activity requires centralized control and coordination. Sophisticated financial activities, therefore, increasingly concentrate in a few financial centres, such as New York, London, and Tokyo (Sassen, 1991; Irwin and Kasarda, 1994). Innovations in telecommunications, such as satellite transmission and fibre optics, permit vast quantities of information (data and voice) to exchange globally almost instantaneously. This capacity would seem to allow financial institutions to disperse among many world centres. The high fixed cost of these telecommunications networks and their infrastructure of a small number of high-capacity switching nodes nevertheless require that financial firms engaged in the greatest exchange of information locate at those nodes (Langdale, 1989; Warf, 1989, 1995). Finally, deregulation of national financial markets would seem to open up many world cities as sites for important financial firms. However, the experience of the deregulation moves of the 1980s, such as the "Big Bang" of 1986 that opened London financial markets, suggests that leading financial firms will concentrate in a few global cities (Hepworth, 1991; Sassen, 1991).

An explanation of the dynamics of world financial centres must resolve these paradoxes. That resolution faces two alternative paths. One path focuses on exploring the implications of new technologies, such as satellites and fibre optics, new organizational structures, such as multinational banks, and new political processes, such as deregulation. This approach has the advantage that it directs attention to the transformation of world financial centres. The disadvantage, however, is that the focus on newness disconnects the explanation from past changes in those centres. This reduces the chance of identifying broad generalizations that might allow prediction about the future trajectory of financial centres, such as the degree to which a few centres will dominate global finance or the impact of new technologies of information processing.

An alternative path to explain the dynamics of world financial centres starts with the premise that the exchange of capital comprises the core activity of financial intermediaries. To implement this exchange, they must first solve two distinct, yet related, problems: capture control over the exchange, and acquire the means "physically" to implement the exchange. As part of their ongoing exchange of capital, financial intermediaries react to competition in three ways: alter transaction costs, differentiate or dedifferentiate to control markets, and appeal to force (Meyer, 1991a,b). They invest in information-processing and telecommunications technologies as part of their strategy of reacting to competition.

Control and physical implementation of exchange

For financial intermediaries to control the exchange of capital, they must insert themselves between actors (individuals, firms, governments) who supply capital and actors who demand it (Meyer, 1980).

415

This process of insertion can take two forms: acquisition of ownership of capital as an intermediate step in exchange; or provision of essential services in the exchange of capital that buyers and sellers of capital cannot circumvent without developing the equivalent expertise. To implement this control of exchange of capital, financial intermediaries must acquire access to information about the demand for and supply of capital and have ownership of sufficient capital to underwrite ownership of additional capital.

The physical implementation of the exchange of capital requires that intermediaries have access to telecommunication technologies. Changes in ownership of capital must be communicated between buyers and sellers, and the provision of services in the exchange of capital also relies on those telecommunication technologies. These technologies, however, have their own infrastructural logic of fixed and variable costs, nodes, and "lines." The precise "physical" means that the exchange of capital follows does not have to match exactly the organizational ties that bind financial intermediaries, buyers of capital, and suppliers of capital (Meyer, 1980). Given that financial intermediaries acquire ownership of capital or provide essential services in its exchange, their long-term operations require that they react successfully to competition.

Reactions to competition

Alter transaction costs

To remain competitive, financial intermediaries alter their transaction costs through several mechanisms (Meyer, 1991a,b). Investments in information-processing technologies (hardware and software) raise the capacity to manipulate, store, and analyse information in greater quantities, with more sophistication, and at faster speeds. Similarly, investments in telecommunications technologies enhance the capacity to transmit greater quantities of information at faster speeds. Because volume, capacity, and speed rise in both types of technologies, these investments reap large economies of scale. To achieve these economies, however, requires substantial capital investment. This permits highly capitalized firms to gain much greater unit-cost savings than less well-capitalized firms, substantially widening the gap in the cost of business for the two types of firms.

These investments in information-processing and telecommunications technologies also introduce disequilibrium in the organization

416

of information processing and transmittal. The processing and transmittal of non-routine information stand as the hallmark of sophisticated financial intermediary activity. Yet technological advances in information processing often transform non-routine information into a routine form. For example, until recently, current information about stock and bond prices remained the specialty of firms with personal access to market makers. Those with this non-routine information gained advantages in controlling investment decisions. The advent of high-powered computers and high-capacity telecommunications media, however, opened this information to anyone with computers and the ability to pay a modest fee; the information becomes routine and highly decentralized. On the other hand, some highly capitalized financial intermediaries may make additional investments in information-processing technologies, such as sophisticated software programs to analyse price trends; these rest on complex proprietary mathematical models. These programs may give them advantages *vis-à-vis* those with access to prices but who lack the capacity to analyse them in the same way. At the same time as non-routine information processing and transmittal transform into routine forms, therefore, new non-routine forms may arise.

Financial intermediaries also alter transaction costs by reducing risk. They can accomplish this through internalizing intermediary transactions within a social group, family, ethnic group, or religious group. The trust that exists within these groups permits the intermediaries to engage in a wider range of secure transactions than they might otherwise participate in. In a somewhat similar way, internalizing intermediary transactions within an organization, when previously they occurred between organizations, reduces the risks of exchange. Finally, financial intermediaries may reduce transaction costs by agglomerating with other intermediaries. The face-to-face exchange within the agglomeration permits them to share complex, confidential information more easily, and the social networks that exist allow the intermediaries to build trust and thus reduce risk.

Differentiate or dedifferentiate

Financial intermediaries also may react to competition by differentiating or dedifferentiating to control markets (Meyer, 1991a,b). Differentiation, or specialization, provides a powerful mechanism because resources are focused on a narrower range of activities. Because specialization often means that financial intermediaries must reach larger market areas for transactions in order to have the requisite business to support the specialized activity, they need access to larger amounts of capital than do less specialized intermediaries. This greater capital requirement results because larger investments must be made in information acquisition through telecommunications and transportation. Furthermore, specialization often requires that financial intermediaries engage in large-scale transactions; this also adds to capital requirements to underwrite the transactions. Dedifferentiation, or the addition of functions to an organization, also raises capital requirements, assuming that the original activities are maintained at the same scale. Both differentiation and dedifferentiation, therefore, are strategies that larger-scale, more highly capitalized financial intermediaries can use to combat competition from smaller-scale, less highly capitalized intermediaries.

Appeal to force

Finally, financial intermediaries may appeal to force to counteract competition from others (Meyer, 1991a,b). Although they may make a direct appeal to the use of violence, more benign forms, though no less effective, are used. Those forms comprise an appeal to a political unit, such as the nation-state, to impose sanctions on competitors. These sanctions come in a variety of forms, such as outright prohibitions on operation within the nation, special restrictions on the types of financial transactions that competitors can engage in, and extra costs imposed on competitors, including taxes, fees, licences, and tariffs. Financial intermediaries who gain the support of their nation-state to impose these sanctions on competitors, however, pay a cost. If competitors are excluded from operating freely, the financial intermediaries who have the sanctions imposed may lose opportunities to cooperate with competitors. Such cooperation stands as a hallmark of financial intermediation. It includes the formation of syndicates to sell stocks and bonds and loan consortia to lend much greater amounts of capital than any one intermediary may be willing to risk in loans to large borrowers. Furthermore, these competitors are also sources of information gained face to face; their absence inhibits intermediaries from gaining access to this information.

Financial intermediaries make choices about reactions to competition that vary according to the type of exchange in which they engage. To simplify, these types are divided into two broad categories: changes in the ownership of existing assets, and exchanges that alter asset values. This distinction provides a means to resolve some of the paradoxes raised about the future of world financial centres.

Exchanges of assets

Changes in the ownership of existing assets

At any point in time, the global stock of existing assets vastly exceeds the investments that alter the stock of assets. These existing assets include stocks that reflect the ownership of a wide array of firms, such as an auto company and an employment agency, or infrastructure, such as a shopping centre and an office building. These assets also include instruments such as bonds or options that represent claims on assets. Other types of existing assets that are exchanged include precious metals, such as gold, silver, or platinum, and commodities, such as grain, copper, or timber. Currencies, such as yen, Deutschmarks, and dollars, are stores of value that represent existing assets that are exchanged. Over time, financial intermediaries have created instruments that are symbols of these assets to facilitate their exchange. The stock or bond certificate, for example, remains removed from the actual trading of these assets. Precious metals and commodities are stored in warehouses and only the ownership of them changes until someone buys them to use in a product. Financial intermediaries have also securitized many other assets, such as loans and real estate portfolios, that did not trade previously and transformed them into marketable securities that trade (Levich and Walter, 1989).

The trading of existing assets, therefore, increasingly occurs both separate from the actual physical movement of the assets and separate from the use of the assets. This transformation of the exchange of existing assets from physical to symbolic exchange, where ownership is the ultimate final concern, provides one girder for the tightening of the bond between telecommunications and financial intermediation. The creation of electronic exchanges for stocks, bonds, commodities, currencies, and other financial instruments, and the probable demise of fixed buildings where traders meet face to face in "exchanges," signify this bond. In modern exchange, financial traders are armed with computers, software, and telecommunications links. At its simplest conception, this type of exchange of assets seems to suggest that financial centres have no basis in the future. Such an implication, however, neglects the institutional framework within which these exchanges occur.

419

At the most elementary level, the telecommunications media over which these exchanges occur have a physical infrastructure that consists of heavy fixed capital investment in switching networks and high-capacity linkages that cannot be made ubiquitously available because they are expensive. Financial intermediaries, therefore, must agglomerate at these nodes to provide the demand that justifies their construction (Langdale, 1989; Warf, 1989, 1995). Future reductions in the cost of telecommunications, however, may make this structure obsolete; the trader of existing assets might have the capacity to operate from almost anywhere. The expansion of the internet globally suggests that this option may come sooner than many realize.

This technological interpretation of the exchange of existing assets, however, abstracts from the social institutional context within which these exchanges occur. Individual owners of existing assets may exchange from their home over the future global telecommunications network, but they need certification that they own the assets they exchange; this embeds them within the framework of financial institutions that testify to that ownership. In theory, individual owners may exchange their own assets, but in practice they defer that exchange to financial institutions because they lack sufficient information and time to trade; that is the essence of financial intermediation. This undergirds the existence of pension funds, mutual funds, and money management firms, as well as stock brokerage firms (Mizruchi and Stearns, 1994). Individual professional traders also operate within the framework of financial institutions. Those organizations provide the capital that finances the infrastructure of exchange, including computers, software, and telecommunications linkages. That infrastructure has substantial economies of scale and provides the basis for larger-capitalized firms to compete effectively against lesser-capitalized firms.

The importance of the institutional context for this exchange nevertheless extends beyond this infrastructure. The financial institution provides the capital that underwrites the exchange; this underwriting comprises the guarantee that the firm has the capital to cover losses. The greater the amount of capital available to underwrite the exchange, the greater the volume of exchange that can be implemented; that relation also generates economies of scale in that the transaction costs of large-scale exchanges rise at a slower rate than the volume of capital exchanged. Because the trader that implements the exchange uses the capital of the firm and these exchanges are typically highly leveraged, the firm must monitor the trader to reduce the possibility of malfeasance. Checks on that malfeasance therefore embed the trader within the social networks of the firm. Those personal networks are the arena for the production of trust and are a strategy that the firm uses to lower risks (Coleman, 1990).

The institutional framework of the collection of firms that trade among themselves either directly or through the medium of electronic or floor exchanges also requires that these firms produce trust among themselves. The high speed and large volume of exchanges of stocks, bonds, currencies, options, and derivatives preclude detection of malfeasance until it is too late to stop it. Elaborate methods of certification, the institutional staff of the exchanges, and the social networks of member firms are mechanisms that they use to verify the trustworthiness of the firms (Coleman, 1990). This production of trust could not work if every individual employee who operated from an isolated site had to be checked by the overarching institutional structure. The production of trust among financial intermediaries therefore nests hierarchically. Networks of firms monitor trustworthiness, and each firm has the responsibility to monitor that trustworthiness among its employees.

The social networks within and among firms influence the type of information traders have to implement exchanges (Powell and Smith-Doerr, 1994; Pryke and Lee, 1995). Because the price of existing assets includes information that is widely available, traders who operate in separate sites and whose only information comes from public sources have no basis for trading other than simply guesses about the future. Access to specialized, private information therefore provides the key to the exchange of existing assets (Pred, 1977). Financial firms have two means to collect and disseminate this specialized information; both mechanisms embed traders tightly within the social networks of firms. The first means is the sharing of information among traders within the same firm and their supervisors, symbolized by the trading floor of the firm, with its row upon row of traders operating at computers; strategic decisions are made and shared within this context. The second means is the institutionalization of units within firms whose task is to devise trading strategies. Those strategies are formulated both within group discussions and as tasks of specialists who develop sophisticated mathematical models to execute trades. The interfirm social networks of traders complement these intrafirm networks (Baker, 1984). The gatherings over meals, at clubs, and in homes become the vehicle for expanding access to specialized, non-public information. The exchanges that alter asset values have even greater embeddedness in social networks.

Exchanges that alter asset values

Exchanges that raise or lower the capital value of existing assets or investments in new assets comprise fundamental long-term decisions about the future value of the assets. Financial intermediaries who engage in these types of exchanges include investment bankers and corporate lenders. The types of financial instruments range from new stocks and bonds to short- and long-term loans for increases in asset values and bankruptcies and liquidations for decreases in asset values. Exchanges that alter asset values are riskier than exchanges of existing assets because there is no record of how the new level of assets will perform.

Financial intermediaries must engage in labour-intensive, face-to-face dialogue consisting of both strategic planning within the firm and complex negotiations among firms. Because these intermediaries place the capital of the firm at risk through underwriting the financial instruments or lending their own capital, they constantly seek strategies to reduce risk. They cooperate with each other, for example in underwriting stock issues or forming a loan consortium, as one powerful strategy to reduce risk (Mintz and Schwartz, 1985). Loan consortia, for example, comprise systematic, ongoing social networks of firms whose strength is continually affirmed and reinforced by the need to negotiate with each other to develop a common strategy *vis-à-vis* a borrower and to enforce structural constraint when the capacity of the borrower to repay the loan becomes jeopardized.

The social networks of individuals and of firms are therefore critical means that these actors use to ensure trustworthiness. Those who break that trust receive the sanction of the group. Given the necessity for these individuals and firms to cooperate in exchange, as well as to have trustworthiness in competitive settings, that sanction is tantamount to exclusion from participation in financial intermediation (Coleman, 1990). This means that financial intermediaries must invest substantial time and resources in the construction and maintenance of social networks, including country clubs, service on public and private boards of directors, church organizations, private schools, and friendship groups. These social networks are maintained over long distance through gatherings, but the locality-based social networks stand as some of the most powerful because every member has a home base that occupies the majority of the daily schedule.

The financial intermediaries who engage in exchanges that alter asset values also benefit from sharing information with those who exchange existing assets because both sets of intermediaries must analyse economic, social, and political information that affects the current and future value of assets. The ease of sharing within the social network of a firm therefore undergirds the internalization of these functions under one organizational umbrella. At the same time, diversification of risk and sharing similar support services might also motivate a dedifferentiation strategy. Intermediaries who engage in exchanges that alter the value of assets also require the support of sophisticated modellers of risk and economic trends and high-level information processing and telecommunications.

Advanced services

The increased scale and scope of financial intermediation at the global scale, coupled with the growing complexity and number of governmental units, even with deregulation, that intermediaries must deal with, has created a large demand for specialized firms to supply services that support exchange (Cohen, 1981; Sassen, 1991; Daniels, 1993). These services cover the range from international law, accounting, and management consulting firms, to computer consultants and operations to maintain the sophisticated systems, and real estate consultants to advise on investments in offices. Some of these, especially the law and accounting firms, provide such sophisticated advice during the process of strategic planning and negotiations of financial intermediaries that the principal employees must engage in face-to-face dialogue with members of other similar firms, as well as with the financial intermediaries. The need for trustworthiness among these service firms and with their clients, the financial intermediaries, provides strong incentives for them to participate in similar dense social networks.

Implications for world financial centres

Regulations

The growing global interactions of large financial intermediaries, coupled with the capacity of telecommunications systems to bypass national barriers, make government regulation of cross-border trans-actions increasingly problematic (Budd, 1995). In this fast-paced, high-volume environment of financial transactions, national govern-ments have few avenues for controlling these intermediaries. Fidu-ciary and reserve requirements can be established, but the malefactor can wreak havoc before any regulatory agency can stop the activ-ities. This places a growing burden on financial intermediaries to engage in self-regulation to control whom they exchange with; they certify trustworthy members. Ironically, this process of the late twen-tieth century represents, in many ways, a return to the self-regulation that prevailed before the nation-state expanded its regulatory appa-ratus, beginning in the late nineteenth and early twentieth centuries.

The most powerful regulatory apparatus of the nation-state com-prises restrictions on the entry of financial intermediaries to a national centre and restrictions on the types of financial transactions that the firms can carry out (Levich and Walter, 1989). These restrictions ben-efit indigenous financial intermediaries by limiting competition; the results are higher costs to consumers of their services. The dilemma for those firms, however, is that the restrictions reduce their access to the critical social networks of sophisticated foreign intermediaries. This limits their access to information about global financial oppor-tunities and risks and reduces their chances to cooperate on financial transactions. As a result, their profit opportunities are reduced and their risks are raised. The nation-state that chooses to restrict the entry of global financial intermediaries therefore both consigns its intermediaries to limited participation in global financial flows and hinders the access of its businesses to the lowest-cost capital.

A commercial legal code that provides the opportunities to punish malefactors, adjudicate disputes, and seek redress is the regulatory apparatus of the nation-state that confers the greatest benefits for its international financial centre. All of the leading world financial centres, such as New York, London, Tokyo, Frankfurt, Zurich, and Hong Kong, have legal protections. The threat of a reduction in that legal protection remains one of the potential handicaps that Hong Kong faces as a world financial centre. Although the legal protections have been formalized, financial intermediaries fear that the Chinese government might unilaterally end them after 1997. This fear is behind the move by many firms to transfer their legal domicile to other locations. The beginnings of a legal system with some removal from direct political control in China raises the possibility that Hong

Kong may retain the major elements of British legal protections (Brauchli, 1995).

Competition among centres

The growing globalization of finance raises paradoxical implications for the competition among world financial centres. Until the mid-twentieth century, competition among the leading world financial centres primarily consisted of selected overlap of financial inter-mediation in some world markets outside the national territories. For example, London and New York City banks competed with each other in parts of Latin America; in continental Europe, New York City banks with London branches competed with London banks (Meyer, 1986). To the extent that this competition emerged, it typi-cally was a by-product of the expansion of banks with their national corporate customers.

This bond between the international expansion of non-financial firms and their financial advisers and funding sources remains resilient because the volume of direct foreign investment continues to expand enormously (table 15.3). The outward flow of capital from the nations of the Organization for Economic Cooperation and Development (OECD) rose more than fourfold from US$71 billion during the 1960s to US$302 billion during the 1970s; this volume almost doubled again during the 1980s. The inward flow to the OECD nations also expanded enormously. It grew over fourfold from US$42 billion dur-ing the 1960s to US$188 billion during the 1970s; from that level it doubled again during the 1980s. The difference between the outward and inward flows nevertheless shows that the OECD countries were net exporters of foreign investment. Because these OECD nations loom so large in foreign direct investment, their financial inter-mediaries and the centres from which they operate have a com-petitive edge in the global exchange of capital. Not surprisingly, the United States, the United Kingdom, and Japan, which house the global financial centres of New York, London, and Tokyo, accounted for the overwhelming share of outward foreign direct investment by the 1980s. The United States and the United Kingdom dominated inward flows as well; Japan, however, fell much lower on those flows. The relatively high rank of the Netherlands in outward and inward flows of foreign direct investment is testimony to the continued re-silience of Amsterdam as a global financial centre.

Table 15.3 **Direct investment by OECD nations, including reinvested earnings, 1961–1988**

	1961–1970		1971–1980		1981–1988	
	US$ billion	% share	US$ billion	% share	US$ billion	% share
Outward						
United States	46.822	66.3	134.354	44.4	121.230	21.4
United Kingdom	7.398	10.5	55.112	18.2	120.520	21.3
Japan	1.438	2.0	18.052	6.0	93.672	16.5
Germany (W.)	4.091	5.8	23.130	7.7	47.745	8.4
France	2.641	3.7	13.940	4.6	40.556	7.2
Netherlands	2.692	3.8	27.829	9.2	36.926	6.5
Canada	1.483	2.1	11.335	3.7	29.437	5.2
Italy	1.667	2.4	3.597	1.2	18.805	3.3
Australia	0.493	0.7	2.510	0.8	17.592	3.1
Sweden	1.074	1.5	4.597	1.5	11.400	2.0
Switzerland	–	–	–	–	8.877[a]	1.6
Norway	0.060	0.1	1.079	0.4	5.379	1.0
Belgium–Luxembourg	0.323[b]	0.5	3.213	1.1	5.131	0.9
Finland	0.146	0.2	0.605	0.2	5.024	0.9
Spain	0.090	0.1	1.274	0.4	2.654	0.5
Austria	0.055	0.1	0.578	0.2	1.591	0.3
Denmark	0.103	0.1	1.063	0.4	0.476	0.1
Portugal	–	–	0.038[c]	–	0.070	–
Total	70.576	100.0	302.306	100.0	567.085	100.0
Inward						
United States	6.282	14.9	56.276	29.9	213.690	52.9
United Kingdom	4.310	10.2	40.503	21.5	53.940	13.4
France	2.804	6.7	16.908	9.0	24.127	6.0
Australia	5.402	12.8	11.295	6.0	20.329	5.0
Netherlands	2.294	5.5	10.822	5.8	17.771	4.4
Spain	1.201	2.9	7.060	3.8	16.870	4.2
Italy	3.634	8.6	5.698	3.0	16.148	4.0
Germany (W.)	6.270	14.9	13.957	7.4	8.716	2.2
Belgium–Luxembourg	1.358[b]	3.2	9.215	4.9	8.299	2.1
Switzerland	–	–	–	–	4.595[a]	1.1
Canada	5.489	13.1	5.534	2.9	3.665	0.9
Greece	–	–	–	–	3.481	0.9
Japan	0.624	1.5	1.424	0.8	2.582	0.6
Austria	0.360	0.9	1.455	0.8	2.061	0.5
Norway	0.372	0.9	3.074	1.6	2.045	0.5
Sweden	0.889	2.1	0.897	0.5	1.955	0.5
Portugal	–	–	0.535[c]	0.3	1.475	0.4
Ireland	–	–	1.659	0.9	0.919	0.2
Finland	0.081	0.2	0.376	0.2	0.754	0.2

Table 15.3 **(cont.)**

	1961–1970		1971–1980		1981–1988	
	US$ billion	% share	US$ billion	% share	US$ billion	% share
Denmark	0.698	1.7	1.561	0.8	0.308	0.1
Total	42.068	100.0	188.249	100.0	403.730	100.0

Source: Orr (1992: 179, fig. 8.2).
a. 1983–1986.
b. 1965–1970.
c. 1975–1980.

The largest-scale, most highly capitalized financial intermediaries that attempt to operate globally, that is, have operations in many world financial centres, produce a different competition among centres than occurred in the past, even though foreign direct investment remains as a critical component of capital flows. Now these firms choose a headquarters for their global operations and then develop a branch network to extend their global reach. The competition therefore becomes limited to the few centres that have an agglomeration of similar-level financial intermediaries, for example New York, London, and Tokyo (Sassen, 1991). This nest of social networks, with its information-rich environment and the opportunity to create co-operative ventures to reduce risk, becomes the key competitive feature of the centre. The infrastructure of global telecommunications and air transportation is an attractive feature, but this can be created by the demand of the firms and their investment of capital. The key in the provision of this infrastructure is a cooperative local political-economy of city and metropolitan government that provides the conditions for this infrastructure to be built (Lee and Schmidt-Marwede, 1993).

A financial intermediary that wants to operate a global service, such as investment banking, must therefore shift that operation to one of the leading global centres or buy such an operation in that centre if its corporate headquarters is located in another financial centre. For example, large German banks, such as Deutsche Bank and Dresdner Bank, headquartered in Frankfurt, look to the purchase of London investment banks, such as Morgan Grenfell and Kleinwort Benson, in order to become global intermediaries in that line of business (Milbank and Ascarelli, 1995; Whitney, 1995). Seen from this perspective, therefore, only a few financial centres can

427

acquire the headquarters of global operations. The key global firms in them cooperate as well as compete with each other. Furthermore, each of these firms has global operations in the other leading world centres. Rather than competition among this small number of global centres being the key characteristic, they actually are bound in a tight array of interactions that include both cooperation and competition. Most competition among centres is thus over acquiring the world regional and branch offices of the global intermediaries. This competition resembles the intranational competition of branches of national firms headquartered in the national metropolis. Those branches operate from the regional and subregional metropolises and compete with local branches of other firms.

A global hierarchy

The globalization of financial intermediaries suggests that a world hierarchy of financial centres is in the process of forming (Meyer, 1991a; Sassen, 1991; Smith and Timberlake, 1995). The global headquarters of the leading firms will concentrate in a few centres. World regional financial centres will house the branch offices of these global firms. These regional branches will concentrate in those cities that offer the greatest access to information about the world regional economy. The pivotal regional centres most likely will be those that house financial intermediaries headquartered there with long experience in the world region. Competition, therefore, will pit both the branches of the global firms against each other and these branches against the headquarters of firms in those cities. A similar rationale applies to subregional global centres.

Differences in levels of specialization and capitalization between the headquarters and branches of global firms and the headquarters of local firms in the "branch cities" undergird this hierarchy. The most highly specialized and capitalized operations will be based in the few leading world financial centres. Those operations will span much of the globe and include lending to the global headquarters of the largest non-financial corporations and investment banking and currency trading for them. The world regional branches will handle the financial intermediation services for the branches of these multinational non-financial firms. The branches of these global financial firms and locally headquartered financial firms will target the multinational non-financial firms headquartered in the world regional centres or in lower-level financial centres in the world region.

The significance of social networks of financial intermediaries and their institutional framework of firms precludes global firms from operating only from the leading world centres. The social networks within the few truly global cities, such as London, Tokyo, and New York, cannot suffice for financial intermediation within world regions or nations. The social networks in those areas must be penetrated for financial intermediaries successfully to capture control of exchange. Global telecommunications are no substitute for shared experiences in a local environment.

Small intermediary clusters

The continual advances in information processing and global tele-communications keep transforming non-routine intermediation into routine intermediation, at the same time that new non-routine inter-mediation activities are created. These non-routine activities, how-ever, do not employ large numbers of people, compared with many other economic activities. The large size of older world financial centres was based not on the non-routine financial activities but on the large "back-office" routine financial jobs and on the physical movement of commodities, such as ports and warehousing, and, later, on industrial activities. Back-office, routine financial jobs now decen-tralize to lower-wage areas distant from the world financial centres and are linked to the global centres by telecommunications. Similarly, major cargo ports and railroad operations can function better away from the congestion of large metropolises. The global financial inter-mediaries and their associated advanced service firms thus operate quite independently, in terms of spatial proximity, from those other economic activities. The headquarters of global non-financial firms have similar processes undergirding their location. The headquarters do not need a large staff; they need access to the financial inter-mediaries, but the large routine information-processing activities of the headquarters can locate elsewhere. Global financial intermediaries and their associated firms therefore comprise small clusters in world cities. By themselves, they contribute only modestly to large-city growth. Much of the back-office work still done at the headquarters and at large branch offices could be relocated to low-density sites. The retention of this employment in the financial centre reflects inertia and reasonably competitive office space, not a need for proxi-mity to the headquarters.

Conclusions

The control and coordination of capital by international financial intermediaries remain tightly bound to the ebb and flow of the world economy and the differential participation of nations in it. The often-noted expansion in international capital flows has not had a uniform impact. On the one hand, the highly developed industrial nations, along with the rising economic powers of Asia, such as Hong Kong, Singapore, South Korea, and Malaysia, have large and rapidly growing participation in global financial exchange. Their financial centres therefore stand as critical elements in the global hierarchy. On the other hand, nations in Africa, Central and South America, the Middle East, and parts of Asia that have weak economies or economies subject to wild fluctuations have financial centres that participate only modestly or very little in global exchanges of capital.

Recognition that this differential participation in the exchange of capital continues serves as a cautionary note to the casual prediction that the world is moving to a condition of seamless exchange. The global hierarchy of financial centres will continue to have an upper level of leading centres that dominate most flows and a lower level that participates little in that exchange. Large, poor nations will have minor financial centres that house weak intermediaries and low-level branches of global financial firms. The social networks of capital remain resilient; those networks rest on social ties within and among firms. Because these bonds stand strongest where economic exchange thrives, the tightest social networks of capital are found in the sinews of economic integration of the highly developed nations and those rising into that rank. These conditions of capital exchange suggest that the impressive advances in global telecommunication that make financial exchanges quicker, cheaper, and broader are more likely to reinforce existing capital exchange and the centres that dominate it than to permit new financial centres to rise to global importance. Only centres in those nations that significantly raise their level of economic development have the possibility of becoming important participants in this global exchange of capital.

References

Baker, Wayne E. (1984), "The Social Structure of a National Securities Market." *American Journal of Sociology* 89: 775–811.

Brauchli, Marcus W. (1995), "Beijing Eases up: China's New Economy Spurs Legal Reforms, Hopes for Democracy." *Wall Street Journal*, 20 June: A1 and A8.

Budd, Leslie (1995), "Globalisation, Territory and Strategic Alliances in Different Financial Centres." *Urban Studies* 32: 345–360.

Cohen, Robert B. (1981), "The New International Division of Labor, Multinational Corporations and Urban Hierarchy." In: Michael Dear and Allen J. Scott (eds.), *Urbanization and Urban Planning in Capitalist Society*. London: Methuen, pp. 287–315.

Coleman, James S. (1990), *Foundations of Social Theory*. Cambridge, Mass.: Belknap Press of Harvard University Press.

Daniels, P. W. (1993), *Service Industries in the World Economy*. Oxford: Blackwell.

Hepworth, Mark (1991), "Information Technology and the Global Restructuring of Capital Markets." In: Stanley D. Brunn and Thomas R. Leinbach (eds.), *Collapsing Space and Time: Geographic Aspects of Communications and Information*. London: HarperCollins Academic, pp. 132–148.

International Monetary Fund (1994), *International Financial Statistics Yearbook 1994*. Washington, D.C.: International Monetary Fund.

Irwin, Michael D. and John D. Kasarda (1994), "Trade, Transportation, and Spatial Distribution." In: Neil J. Smelser and Richard Swedberg (eds.), *The Handbook of Economic Sociology*. Princeton, N.J.: Princeton University Press, pp. 342–367.

Langdale, John V. (1989), "The Geography of International Business Telecommunications: The Role of Leased Networks." *Annals of the Association of American Geographers* 79: 501–522.

Lee, Roger and Ulrich Schmidt-Marwede (1993), "Interurban Competition: Financial Centres and the Geography of Financial Production." *International Journal of Urban and Regional Research* 17: 492–515.

Levich, Richard M. and Ingo Walter (1989), "The Regulation of Global Financial Markets." In: Thierry Noyelle (ed.), *New York's Financial Markets: The Challenges of Globalization*. Boulder, Colo.: Westview Press, pp. 51–89.

Meyer, David R. (1980), "A Dynamic Model of the Integration of Frontier Urban Places into the United States System of Cities." *Economic Geography* 56: 120–140.

——— (1986), "The World System of Cities: Relations between International Financial Metropolises and South American Cities." *Social Forces* 64: 553–581.

——— (1991a), "Change in the World System of Metropolises: The Role of Business Intermediaries." *Urban Geography* 12: 393–416.

——— (1991b), "The Formation of a Global Financial Centre: London and Its Intermediaries." In: Resat Kasaba (ed.), *Cities in the World-System*. New York: Greenwood Press, pp. 97–106.

Milbank, Dana and Silvia Ascarelli (1995), "Dresdner Bank Holds Talks to Buy Kleinwort Benson." *Wall Street Journal*, 16 June: A11.

Mintz, Beth and Michael Schwartz (1985), *The Power Structure of American Business*. Chicago: University of Chicago Press.

Mizruchi, Mark S. and Linda Brewster Stearns (1994), "Money, Banking, and Financial Markets." In: Neil J. Smelser and Richard Swedberg (eds.), *The Handbook of Economic Sociology*. Princeton, N.J.: Princeton University Press, pp. 313–341.

Orr, Bill (1992), *The Global Economy in the 90s: A Users Guide*. New York: New York University Press.

Powell, Walter W. and Laurel Smith-Doerr (1994), "Networks and Economic Life." In: Neil J. Smelser and Richard Swedberg (eds.), *The Handbook of Economic Sociology*. Princeton, N.J.: Princeton University Press, pp. 368–402.

431

Pred, Allan (1977), *City-Systems in Advanced Economies: Past Growth, Present Processes and Future Development Options*. New York: Wiley.

Pryke, Michael and Roger Lee (1995), "Place Your Bets: Towards an Understanding of Globalisation, Socio-financial Engineering and Competition within a Financial Centre." *Urban Studies* 32: 329–344.

Sassen, Saskia (1991), *The Global City: New York, London, Tokyo*. Princeton, N.J.: Princeton University Press.

Selz, Michael (1993), "More Small Firms Are Turning to Trade Intermediaries: Middlemen Enable Companies to Build International Sales Faster." *Wall Street Journal*, 2 February: B2.

Smith, David A. and Michael Timberlake (1995), "Conceptualising and Mapping the Structure of the World System's City System." *Urban Studies* 32: 287–302.

Warf, Barney (1989), "Telecommunications and the Globalization of Financial Services." *Professional Geographer* 41: 257–271.

——— (1995), "Telecommunications and the Changing Geographies of Knowledge Transmission in the Late 20th Century." *Urban Studies* 32: 361–378.

Whitney, Glenn (1993), "Taking Stock: Turmoil in Europe's Financial Markets Will Produce Both Big Winners and Losers." *Wall Street Journal*, 3 February: R3.

——— (1995), "Deutsche Bank Takes New Interest in Morgan Grenfell." *Wall Street Journal*, 8 June: B4.

World Bank (1994), *World Development Report 1994: Infrastructure for Development*. Oxford: Oxford University Press.

16

Transport and telecommunications among world cities

Peter J. Rimmer

> The world city hypothesis ... is primarily intended as a framework for research. It is neither a theory, nor a universal generalization among cities, but a starting point for a political enquiry. (Friedmann, 1986: 69)

Since the late 1960s, profound changes have occurred in firms associated with the movement of freight, passengers, and information. Enhanced cooperation between firms evident in strategic alliances, joint ventures, and consortia has highlighted the importance of *global networks* in ensuring sufficient scale economies, fast reaction capability, and, above all, continuous innovation capacity in an era of rapid technological change. The advantages of cooperative firm network strategies are that they avoid the high transaction costs resulting from resorting to the market, and reduce the high costs stemming from the internal development of a new technology or competence (Camagni, 1993). As these cooperative global organizational structures have occurred through innovations in telecommunications and air transport, they have been paralleled by an analogous development of transport and communications firms. They offer global network services, facilitating point-to-point interactions between many dispersed locations. Integrated transport and telecommunications are the prerequisite for corporate global activity. Thus we have to be concerned with changes permeating across interdependent transport and telecommunications networks.

Within this evolving situation, changes have occurred in the preferred mix of transport and communications modes. Individual or combined modes offering newer, faster, and more direct services are favoured over others (provided that they meet increasingly stringent energy and emission targets). Simultaneously, attention has been focused on the significance of logistical systems – the equipment and networks for transporting and distributing goods, information, and people (including the infrastructure within urban nodes). Analyses of the past development of transport infrastructure by Andersson and Stromquist (1989) have revealed three logistical revolutions in Europe that were accompanied by the fast growth of new centres and industrial expansion: *c*. A.D. 1000, associated with improvements in coastal shipping; the sixteenth century, linked to improvements in ocean transport; and the industrial revolution, based on the increased possibilities offered by sea, canal, and railway transport. An emerging fourth logistical revolution has been recognized that features a new, dense, multi-layered logistical network with fast, but thin, links and its associated urban forms. It is based on a road network incorporating travel guidance and control systems, advanced and efficient telecommunications networks, and an extensive and more competitive air transport system. Collectively, these networks serve firms exhibiting a strong trend towards cooperation and merger.

In discussing this new infrastructural arena, a global network perspective, not a continental one, is mandatory. Top-ranking city regions or *world cities* have become key nodes in this emerging network structure. Although nation-states retain their control over macroeconomic policy, the local and regional advantages possessed by world cities in accessing global technological, commercial, and financial networks are now the most critical factors in locational decision-making by multinational firms. Indeed, world cities have to be regarded as key elements of global networks in their own right rather than as subregional economies of nation-states. Because the world cities integrate local economies into the global economy, they have become centres of innovation. This function is the key to the designation of a "world cities system." Rapid transport and communications paths connecting these world cities have become critical links in global development patterns.

Two issues are raised by these global trends: how have transport and telecommunications interlinkages developed around the world cities; and what are their implications for urban policies directed towards using better external transport and telecommunications linkages to widen the markets of local firms, attract new functions, and enhance the local production fabric? Attention here is focused on the first issue; the second is addressed briefly in a conclusion.

Ideally, consideration of the initial issue requires international freight, telecommunications, and passenger flow indicators for a period of at least 10 years. A major problem, however, is that most measurements are "stock indicators" – the total number of international standard 20 foot equivalent units (TEUs) handled at individual container ports; and the amount of international freight or international passengers handled by individual airports. Telecommunications flow data are available for countries but not for cities. Only for international air passenger flows are there city-pair data. Even then these are confined to the top-ranking city-pairs and there is no breakdown by type of passenger (e.g. business, full economy, or tourist). Further comparable data are restricted to the period between 1984 and 1992.

Concentrating on the "top 25" stock and flow indicators between 1984 and 1992, however, has not been a drawback. An analysis of the available data suggests that this was a critical period in moving from a triad economy featuring Asia, Europe, and North America to a truly integrated global economy. Before discussing this development, attention is focused on identifying a conceptual framework for studying transport and communications among world cities.

The hierarchy of city networks

The growth potential of cities in traditional central place theory is roughly proportionate to size. Population, scale economies, and transport costs have long been regarded as the keys to understanding national systems of cities featuring different-sized centres within functional urban hierarchies and variable orders of rank-size. A nested hierarchy of cities and markets, however, has long since been superseded in advanced capitalist countries first by the development of small, but specialized, cities with high-order functions and then by the more recent emergence of city networks. By recognizing that the logic of "firm networks" parallels and partly determines that of the city system, Camagni (1993: 77, 84) has accommodated specialization and networking by collapsing the traditional urban hierarchy into a tri-level hierarchy of city networks. As shown in figure 16.1, it comprises:

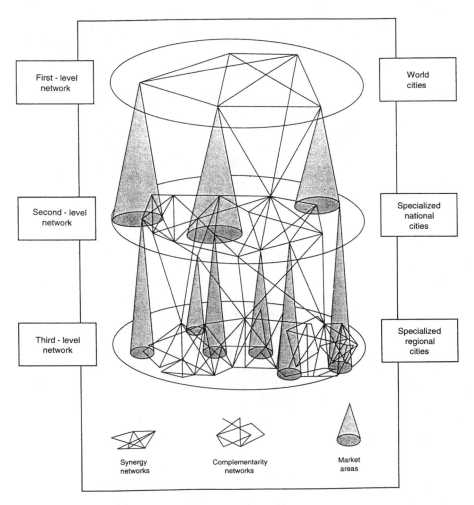

Fig. 16.1 **The hierarchy of city networks, showing world cities (information linkages), specialized national cities (input–output and market, and cooperation linkages), and specialized regional cities (input–output linkages and trade linkages) (Notes: synergy networks include first-level information networks; complementarity networks include input–output and trade linkages; and market areas include output, input of labour, and components. Source: Campagni, 1993: 78)**

1. the network of *world cities* – performing a complete range of functions – which compete and cooperate along "high-synergy" advanced transport and communications networks;
2. the network of *specialized, national cities* interconnected by input–output and trade linkages (e.g. Randstad Holland, and the Veneto area in Italy);

3. the network of *specialized, regional cities* also interconnected by input–output and trade linkages (e.g. Third Italy regions).

Upward and downward relationships and flows occur between the three levels (e.g. cities in lower-order networks may sell specialized products to world cities). Attention here, however, is concentrated on identifying the horizontal and non-hierarchical linkages among complementary centres within the network of *world cities* that offer externalities derived from cooperation, synergy, and innovation.

Camagni (1993) did not proceed to identify a set of world cities. This creates a problem. "World city" has been loosely used to apply to all urban centres with a major international component (Friedmann and Wolff, 1982; Friedmann, 1986).[1] The rationale for inclusion or exclusion has not been developed with any rigour. Multivariate analyses have been used to develop sets of cities based on population size, polarized employment and income structures, the number of headquarters of *Fortune Magazine 500* corporations and international institutions, openness to foreigners, and the number of conventions (see Rimmer, 1986, 1991).[2] Rather than repeat this exercise, I focus attention on analysing transport and telecommunications networks to assess if they are useful determinants of world city status. Gateway functions and sophisticated telecommunications are considered to be more important than mere population size.

Urban agglomerations

An examination of the world's "top 25" largest urban agglomerations listed by *World Urbanization Prospects: The 1992 Revision* (United Nations, 1993) reveals that in 1990 they ranged in size from Tokyo in first place, with a population of 25 million, to Chicago in twenty-fifth place, with a population of 6.8 million (fig. 16.2). Of these 25 agglomerations, 13 were in Asia (including Tokyo, Shanghai, Bombay, Seoul, Beijing, Calcutta, and Osaka – all of which have populations over 10 million); 4 in Central and South America (São Paulo, Mexico City, Buenos Aires, and Rio de Janiero, all with populations over 10 million); 3 in North America (with both New York and Los Angeles having populations over 10 million); 3 in Europe; and 2 in Africa and the Middle East. There was no representation in Oceania. The growth potential of central places as world cities is no longer necessarily proportionate to population size.

Essentially, world cities are groups of fragmented economic and social activities that are linked into external transport and telecom-

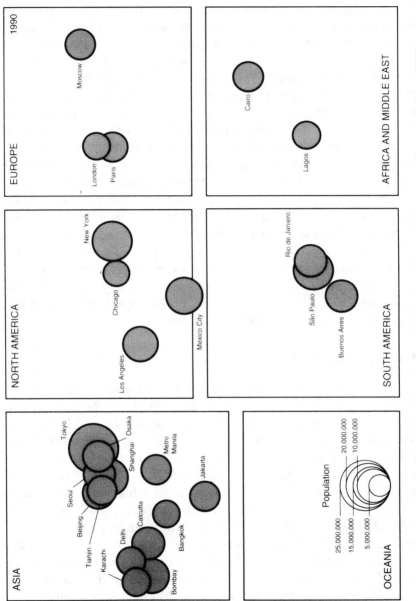

Fig. 16.2 The "top 25" largest urban agglomerations, 1990 (Data source: United Nations, 1993)

munications networks operating on continental and global scales. World cities should be seen as a "junction in flows" of goods, information, and people rather than as fixed locations for the production of goods and services (Harris, 1994). Competitive leadership depends upon the nodality, density, and efficiency of international transport and communications networks linking cities to the rest of the world. Hubs within these networks have accounted for a disproportionate share of urban development and have attracted firms engaged in transport logistics, telecommunications, and air passenger transport. For them to prosper, a higher share of the budget in freight, information, and passenger networks has to be invested in nodes – ports, teleports, and airports – rather than links (Batten, 1990). Initially, attention is focused on freight networks to recognize that network corporations are striving for global transport logistics systems, offering just-in-time methods, economies of scope, and an integrated approach to their economic activities.

Freight networks

Attention is centred primarily on container movements by sea because road networks and high-speed trains are beyond the compass of this study (see Hall, 1991). Since the late 1960s, container vessels have progressively supplanted break bulk shipping. Purpose-built container vessels now exceed 4,500 TEUs. In addition to scheduled liner and regional feeder services, round-the-world services have been introduced. Freight forwarders have become non-vehicle-owning carriers (NVOCs) – carriers without ships offering worldwide services. New working practices have been introduced and terminal operators and stevedores have made prodigious improvements in efficiency and faster turnaround times. Trucking companies have become highly flexible service providers and railway companies have introduced new methods on continental land bridges (e.g. double stack trains). Air freight has become more accessible and air–sea routes have been developed to obtain the optimum benefits of time and cost. These developments have facilitated the offering of door-to-door transport services (i.e. multimodal transport connecting sea and land) and specialized air freight services.

Sea–land services

Because large container ports are important international gateways, it is tempting to equate them with world cities. This proposition led to an examination of the world's "top 25" container ports derived from an annual survey by *Containerisation International Yearbook*, which provides details of the movement of intermodal containers at over 400 ports (CIY, 1984–1994). Whereas the amount of container-handling throughput of a port is essentially linked to the development of a country's economy, load centres or hubs in the three major container trades – transpacific, Far East/Europe, and transatlantic – have an additional advantage of increasing throughput beyond their national totals by attracting feeder traffic.[3] Transhipped boxes are double and even triple counted.

In 1984, the league of individual ports was headed by Rotterdam, handling 2,546,000 TEUs, and bi-state New York/New Jersey, handling 2,255,000 TEUs (fig. 16.3). Third-ranking Hong Kong and the combined Tokyo–Yokohama ports were the only other container ports to exceed 2 million TEUs. Reflecting the shift in the world's manufacturing production, 10 of the leading container ports were already in Asia. Six others were in Europe, six in North America (Los Angeles and Long Beach counting as two ports), and one each in Oceania, Central and South America, and Africa and the Middle East.

By 1992, Hong Kong (handling 7,972,000 TEUs) and Singapore (handling 7,560,000 TEUs) had moved up to first and second position, respectively, in the world container port traffic league (fig. 16.4). Rotterdam was the nearest challenger with 4,123,000 TEUs. Nine ports handled more than 2 million TEUs. Twelve of the "top 25" ports were in Asia, six in North America (Los Angeles/Long Beach and Seattle/Tacoma counting as separate ports), five in Europe, and one each in Central and South America (San Juan), and Africa and Middle East (Dubai). There was no representation in Oceania.

An analysis of changes in annual throughput between 1984 and 1992 highlights the emergence of major load centres (table 16.1). The most striking feature has been the growth of load centres in Asia (e.g. Hong Kong, Singapore, Kaohsiung, Pusan, Kobe, Keelung, and Tokyo/Yokohama), North America (e.g. New York/New Jersey, Los Angeles/Long Beach, Oakland, and Seattle/Tacoma), and Europe (e.g. Rotterdam). These changes have been brought about by the introduction of bigger ships (over 4,500 TEUs) and the greater scale and geographical scope of large carriers (e.g. American President Line, Evergreen, Hanjin, Maersk, Nippon Yusen Kaisha, and Sea Land). In a bid to stem financial losses from intensified competition, these carriers have entered into consortia and strategic alliances (e.g.

440

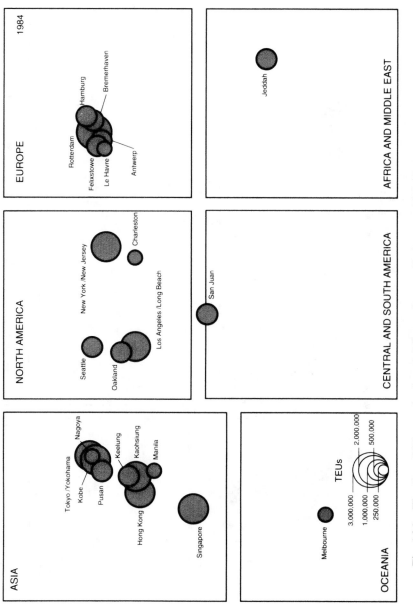

Fig. 16.3 The "top 25" ports in the world container traffic league, 1984 (Data source: CIY, 1986)

441

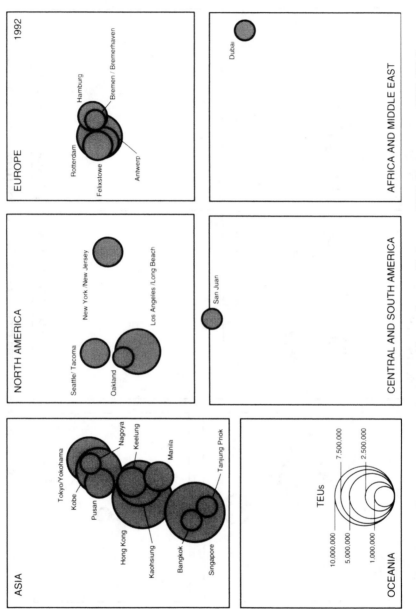

Fig. 16.4   The "top 25" ports in the world container traffic league, 1992 (Data source: CIY, 1994)

Table 16.1   **The "top 25" container ports, 1984–1992 ('000 TEUs)**

	1984	1985	1986	1987	1988	1989	1990	1991	1992
Hong Kong	2,109	2,289	2,774	3,457	4,033	4,463	5,101	6,162	7,972
Singapore	1,552	1,699	2,203	2,635	3,375	4,364	5,224	6,354	7,560
Rotterdam	2,546	2,655	2,870	2,839	3,289	3,603	3,667	3,766	4,123
Kaohsiung	1,785	1,901	2,482	2,779	3,083	3,383	3,495	3,913	3,961
Pusan	1,054	1,115	1,533	1,949	2,206	2,159	2,348	2,694	2,751
Kobe	1,826	1,857	1,885	1,997	2,233	2,459	2,596	2,635	2,608
Los Angeles	908	1,105	1,325	1,580	1,652	2,057	2,116	2,038	2,289
Hamburg	1,073	1,159	1,246	1,451	1,622	1,728	1,969	2,189	2,268
New York/NJ	2,255	2,367	2,340	2,089	2,096	1,988	1,872	1,865	2,104
Keelung	1,234	1,158	1,587	1,940	1,762	1,787	1,828	2,005	1,941
Yokohama	1,104	1,328	1,310	1,348	1,453	1,506	1,648	1,797	1,887
Antwerp	1,248	1,243	1,313	1,437	1,470	1,474	1,549	1,761	1,836
Long Beach	1,141	1,172	1,394	1,460	1,540	1,545	1,593	1,768	1,829
Tokyo	925	1,004	1,082	1,288	1,396	1,439	1,555	1,784	1,729
San Juan	918	882	963	1,004	1,136	1,289	1,381	1,584	1,577
Felixstowe	778	726	895	1,053	1,279	1,370	1,436	1,434	1,543
Dubai	NR	NR	NR	NR	NR	NR	916	1,255	1,482
Bremerhaven	975	983	1,000	1,043	1,121	1,204	1,198	1,277	1,315
Bangkok	NR	NR	511	650	792	924	1,018	1,171	1,303
Oakland	916	856	925	954	1,021	1,091	1,124	1,194	1,287
Manila	493	484	546	695	767	857	1,039	1,070	1,158
Seattle	1,050	845	851	1,026	1,024	1,041	1,171	1,155	1,151
Tacoma	NR	505	666	697	782	925	938	1,021	1,101
Nagoya	350	NR	NR	NR	666	815	898	1,001	1,098
Tanjung Priok	NR	NR	NR	NR	NR	NR	NR	NR	868
Le Havre	614	566	599	678	789	889	858	916	NR
Charleston	422	435	506	645	800	806	NR	NR	NR
Jeddah	805	678	605	597	NR	NR	NR	NR	NR
Melbourne	536	566	NR	NR	NR	NR	NR	NR	NR

Source: CIY (1984–1994).
NR = not ranked.

the joint Far East/USA/Europe trade venture established by Nippon
Yusen Kaisha, Hapag Lloyd, and Neptune Orient Line in April
1993). Although these developments have not altered the overall
number of ports or affected basic shipping schedules, they have led to
a rationalization of port calls and affected the viability of other port
cities.[4] Changing rates of port growth have also been affected by the
restructuring of the world economy. Rates of growth in New York,
Kobe, and Tokyo/Yokohama have begun to slow and even decline
(particularly as Japanese corporations have progressively shifted their

manufacturing activities to Asian countries).[5] Ports in the newly industrializing economies (NIEs), notably Hong Kong, Singapore, Kaohsiung, and Pusan, have maintained their growth – a reflection of their efforts to improve port facilities and service quality. The most significant developments, however, have been in South-East Asia with the rise of Bangkok, Manila, and Tanjung Priok (Jakarta). Although San Juan and Dubai do not appear to have strong geographical advantages, they have been active in inviting major container operators to use them as hub ports for transhipping cargo to feeder ports.

It is difficult to relate developments in container ports to world cities. Obviously, Hong Kong and Singapore have mega-hub status and serve several countries. So do Kaohsiung and Pusan, but they cannot be regarded as world cities because they do not host either the headquarters of large transnational corporations or the main branches of foreign transnational corporations. Rotterdam and Kobe are more plausible, but they have to be seen in the context of the wider Randstad and Kansai regions respectively, rather than in their own right. Los Angeles has a strong claim to world city status both as a hub in its own right and as a relay point for containers railed or trucked to the Midwest (Fleming and Hayuth, 1994). Further, New York/New Jersey has already plummeted down the rankings of the container league table; Tokyo–Yokohama is likely to follow; and London, a major centre for international shipping business, is no longer a major container port. Clearly, maritime accessibility can be one of the power bases of world cities but it is not necessarily the determining characteristic. Given that seaport gateways are often overemphasized at the expense of inland centres, attention now shifts to airports handling international freight to avoid discrimination against centres without coastal locations (e.g. Brussels, Paris, Seoul, and Zurich).

Air freight

The link between air freight hubs and world cities has been little studied. Yet the growth in specialized producer services located in world cities – banks, law offices, and computer and advertising services – has triggered an explosion in air freight services. These services are provided by both general cargo carriers handling high-value merchandise (e.g. clothing, office equipment, watches and clocks, and photographic equipment) and express cargo carriers handling high-price, time-sensitive documents, parcels, and packages (Schwieterman, 1993). General cargo carriers operate on an airport-to-airport basis in collaboration with ground handlers, such as local freight forwarders and trucking companies, providing door-to-door and global sourcing services. Most general cargo is carried in the "belly" of wide-bodied passenger aircraft, but there is a growing network of all-cargo flights (freighters). Express carriers or "integrators," typified by Federal Express, TNT Express Worldwide, DHL International Inc., and United Parcel Services, concentrate on scheduled, priority services. Unfortunately, the distinction between general air cargo and express air cargo is not reflected in the available data.

In 1984, New York (Kennedy), with 800,600 tonnes loaded and unloaded by commercial air transport, was the world's first-ranked international freight airport (fig. 16.5). It was followed by Tokyo (New Tokyo) with 714,100 tonnes, the combined London airports (Heathrow and Gatwick) with 671,200 tonnes, Frankfurt with 634,600 tonnes, the combined Paris airports (Charles de Gaulle and Orly) with 638,900 tonnes, and Chicago with 219,500 tonnes. Eleven of the world's "top 25" airports with the highest international freight traffic were located in Europe (London and Paris have two airports each), eight in Asia, four in North America, and two in Africa and the Middle East. Central and South America and Oceania had no representatives.

By 1992, Tokyo, with 1,288,000 tonnes of air freight (loaded and unloaded), had become the world's largest cargo airport (fig. 16.6). Frankfurt (with 989,000 tonnes) was ranked second, Hong Kong (with 957,000 tonnes) third, Seoul (796,000 tonnes) fourth, and New York (779,000 tonnes) fifth. If the combined London airports (Heathrow and Gatwick) with 936,000 tonnes and the combined Paris airports (Charles de Gaulle and Orly) with 808,000 tonnes are considered, they would displace Seoul and New York from fourth and fifth spots. Europe had nine of the "top 25" airports (including two each in Paris and London), Asia seven, and North America six. Africa and the Middle East (Tel Aviv), Central and South America (Bogata), and Oceania (Sydney) had one each.

The changes in international freight movements between 1984 and 1992 reflected the restructuring of the world economy (table 16.2). Its differential effects were reflected in Asia's marked growth rate, apparent in Hong Kong, Singapore, Seoul, and Taipei; Europe's slower growth rate, with all airports experiencing a pronounced downturn in 1991; and North America's equivocal trends. The decline

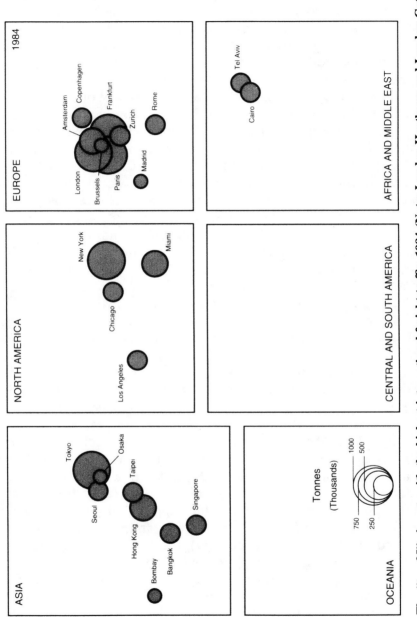

Fig. 16.5 The "top 25" airports with the highest international freight traffic, 1984 (Note: London-Heathrow and London-Gatwick, and Paris-Charles de Gaulle and Paris-Orly are combined. Source: ICAO, 1984)

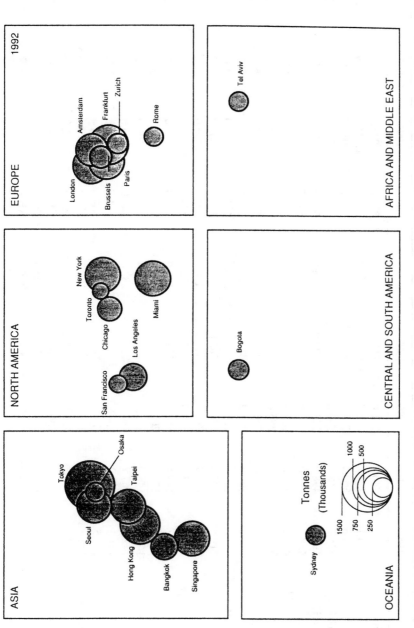

Fig. 16.6 The "top 25" airports with the highest international freight traffic, 1992 (Note: London-Heathrow and London-Gatwick, and Paris-Charles de Gaulle and Paris-Orly are combined. Source: ICAO, 1993)

Table 16.2   The "top 25" airports for international freight, 1984–1992 ('000 tonnes)

	1984	1985	1986	1987	1988	1989	1990	1991	1992
New York	800.6	740.3	771.0	900.0	925.0	1,035.0	945.3	796.4	779.0
Tokyo	714.1	726.2	858.8	1,018.6	1,194.0	1,319.1	1,341.0	1,339.7	1,288.0
Frankfurt	634.6	669.4	722.5	840.0	832.1	970.0	1,035.0	957.1	989.0
London (LHR)	535.6	518.7	530.8	568.4	635.3	678.4	710.0	648.0	748.0
Paris (CDG)	493.5	498.9	503.2	539.0	566.9	568.4	605.0	551.9	585.0
Amsterdam	438.1	436.0	450.9	513.7	575.3	582.5	592.0	630.3	695.0
Hong Kong	437.2	419.8	536.8	610.6	694.1	730.0	801.9	849.8	957.0
Miami	332.8	385.6	385.6	433.6	535.0	591.0	633.0	717.6	755.0
Singapore	294.4	299.0	352.1	418.3	511.5	577.4	620.7	642.0	719.0
Seoul	276.2	308.3	355.9	411.3	465.8	547.9	576.4	576.4	796.0
Los Angeles	249.6	241.4	280.0	325.0	390.0	404.0	400.0	404.1	470.0
Chicago	219.5	200.6	220.0	266.0	280.0	301.0	305.0	359.9	338.0
Taipei	213.0	222.9	290.0	345.6	450.0	394.4	396.0	613.3	702.0
Zurich	197.9	203.8	213.0	222.2	232.7	248.5	246.2	240.7	263.0
Rome	152.7	179.4	155.0	172.0	180.0	177.0	204.0	205.0	207.0
Bangkok	147.0	171.3	202.2	241.8	291.5	340.3	392.9	389.1	422.0
Paris (ORY)	145.4	148.0	155.7	165.1	174.4	188.7	200.0	216.9	223.0
Brussels	142.9	167.7	192.1	216.4	233.0	240.0	245.0	307.8	313.0
Copenhagen	141.1	137.2	NR	138.1	149.5	NR	NR	NR	NR
Cairo	140.5	NR	NR	NR	NR	NR	NR	NR	NR
London (LGW)	135.6	153.1	160.8	187.7	189.3	206.2	217.5	200.5	188.0
Osaka	129.7	NR	151.0	167.0	191.9	198.0	232.0	234.8	227.0
Bombay	120.5	129.0	130.6	NR	NR	NR	NR	NR	NR
Tel Aviv	118.5	142.5	145.0	178.9	165.0	179.2	195.0	207.6	200.0
Madrid	112.8	120.8	NR	NR	NR	NR	NR	NR	NR

San Francisco	NR	142.4	196.4	205.0	222.9	233.0	222.3	213.5	191.0
Sydney	NR	122.0	129.0	145.0	160.0	185.0	195.0	201.2	221.0
Manila	NR	NR	148.9	155.0	165.0	173.0	182.0	NR	NR
Toronto	NR	NR	NR	NR	NR	160.5	179.7	173.0	169.0
Bogotá	NR	NR	NR	NR	NR	NR	NR	202.3	250.0

Source: ICAO (1984–1993).
NR = not ranked.

of New York, Tokyo, and London (Gatwick but not Heathrow) associated with deindustrialization processes has occurred simultaneously with Asia's wave of industrialization (Markusen and Gwiasda, 1994). There was also the marked rise of Miami – a hub for South America. The net effect of these changes has been a slight relaxation of the stranglehold exerted over air freight by Asia, Europe, and North America, resulting in all regions being represented for the first time following the elevation of Bogotá (Central and South America) and Sydney (Oceania) to the "top 25" list.

Changes in the relative strengths of airports handling international freight between 1984 and 1992 have produced a distribution of nodes that approximates to a pattern of world cities. Essentially, it reflects the concentration of wealth, technology, and power in Asia, North America, and Europe. In particular, it pinpoints the core urban hierarchy in Europe playing central roles in the systems of world cities – Frankfurt, London, Paris, Amsterdam, and Zurich (Sassen, 1994). Some may argue, however, that air freight still puts too much emphasis on production and gives insufficient consideration to the technological revolution centred on telecommunications. More attention, therefore, has to be paid to the importance of information flows between business and financial centres that characterize a new economic geography (Castells, 1994).

Information networks

Telecommunications development has been seen as the means by which the world city system has emerged. It has allowed the selective reduction of space and time constraints and permitted new patterns of development between world cities. Telecommunication networks are interlinked in world cities because they interconnect headquarter functions, financial activities, and high-level tertiary institutions with multinational business and producer organizations (e.g. consulting and advertising) (Moss, 1991). Consequently, corporations in these dominant cities are better able to control the fortunes of peripherally located regions. Reflecting their extended reach, world cities can be further subdivided into: ordinary world cities, regional hubs (e.g. Singapore and Hong Kong), and global hubs (the "three-legged stool" comprising London, New York, and Tokyo) (Kellerman, 1993).

This proposition is an act of faith because appreciating the linkages between world cities and telecommunications networks as purveyors of *routine information* has proved to be extremely difficult. Analysing the new electronic spaces as being analogous to physical transport networks is misleading. Satellites and optical fibre routes carrying the instantaneous transmission of voice, data, and video signals are largely invisible. Consequently, it is difficult to conceptualize these fast, broadband digital systems, which transcend space barriers and create a more fluid capitalist society.

Many of the propositions on telecommunications and world cities have to be taken on trust. The data series on global traffic data did not commence until 1989 (Staple and Mullins, 1989; Staple, 1992, 1993, 1994). Attention, therefore, is restricted to telecommunications in 1992. Already by then major players in telecommunications had been affected by technical change and increased competition, which commenced with liberalization in the United States and other countries during the 1980s (e.g. Australia, Japan, and the United Kingdom) and lowered international tariffs. Major players had established strategic alliances and groups to meet the needs of an emerging global customer (presaging the switch from monopolistic, facilities-based, national "heavy carriers" to competitive, privately owned global light carriers that resell, repackage, or reprogramme their services) (Staple, 1992).[6] The effect of these developments on world cities cannot be traced adequately because the data on global traffic are restricted to the largest country-pairs, measured in millions of minutes of telecommunications traffic (MiTT) on public switched telephone networks.

In 1992, the "top 25" international routes with the largest two-way traffic volume linked the three core areas of the world – Asia, North America, and Europe – into a single axis (fig. 16.7). The only country-pair not incorporated in the axis was China–Hong Kong. Eighteen countries were involved in the "top 25" routes. Both the United States and Germany were in partnerships on eight international routes. The United States, however, was dominant. The country figured in six of the seven intercontinental routes and served as a "global junction" between the Atlantic and the Pacific. In comparison, Germany was essentially a continental carrier: it was engaged in only two intercontinental routes (including one with Turkey – a prime source of its migrant labour) (Tapia, 1995). Also the United States was involved in all three routes exceeding 1 billion MiTT (with Canada, Mexico, and the United Kingdom) and accounted for approximately one-third of the world's international telephone traffic (Staple, 1994). Of the other countries, France appeared in seven of the "top 25" routes, the United Kingdom in five, Italy in four, the

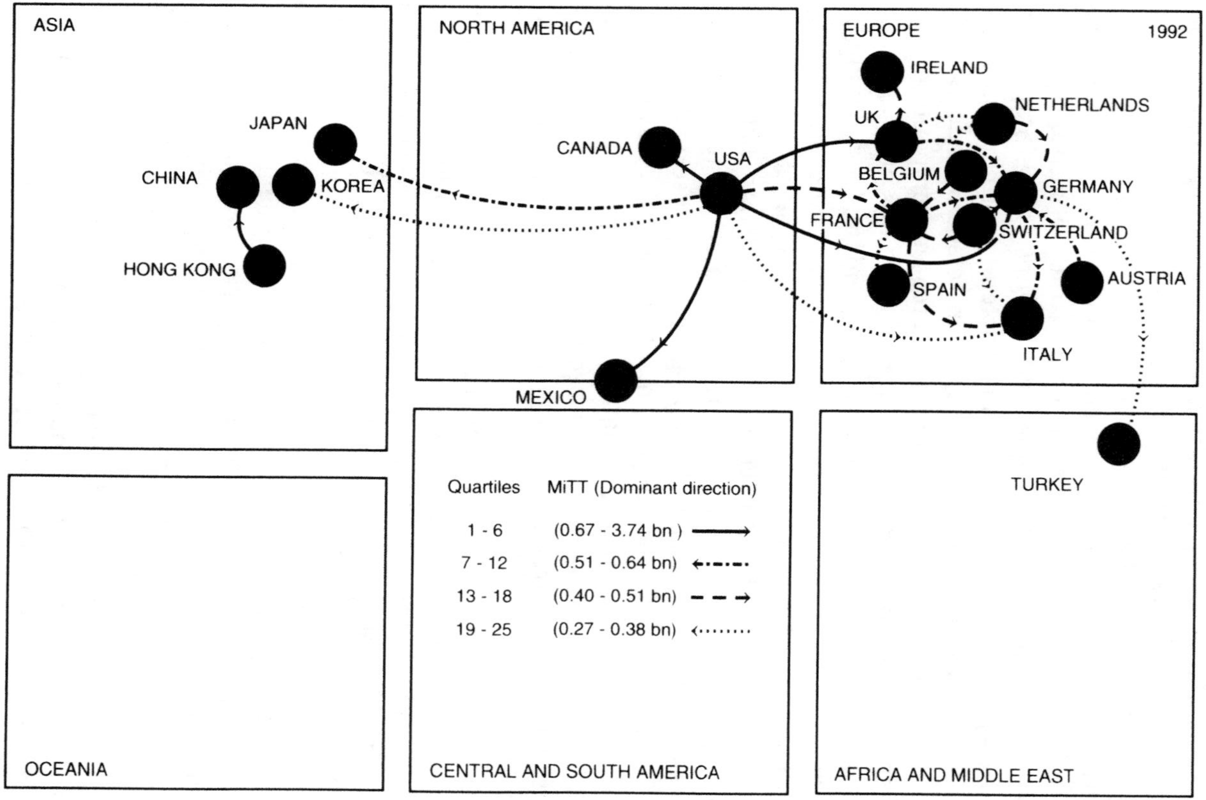

Fig. 16.7 The "top 25" international routes with the largest volume of telecommunications traffic, 1992 (Data source: Staple, 1993)

452

Netherlands and Switzerland in three each, and Belgium in two. Ten countries were involved in only one route. Central and South America and Africa and the Middle East had one connection with the core of the global economy, and Oceania none. The global contacts of Oceania and Africa and the Middle East were primarily through former colonial powers, and those of Central and South America through the regional power (Kellerman, 1990).

The most useful result of this exercise is to demonstrate the fact that telecommunications have welded Asia, North America, and Europe into a single axis. It is, however, more problematic to extrapolate from this information the importance of telecommunications among world cities. Assuming that world cities dominate economies, it may be possible to associate the data for European and Asian countries with major centres. More attention in interpreting their global role, however, has to be placed on the importance of national and local government and national production systems (Fujita, 1991; Keil and Lieser, 1992; Hill and Fujita, 1995). It is, however, more difficult to relate telecommunications and world cities in the more decentralized and multipolar urban system within the United States, particularly because intermediate service centres may be outperforming the highest-order centres (Hall, 1991). Presuming that the function of world cities is to provide advanced business services and access to information users (e.g. law firms, advertising firms, foreign banks), New York, Los Angeles, San Francisco, Washington D.C., Chicago, Boston, and Dallas would have to be investigated (Markusen and Gwiasda, 1994; Mitchelson and Wheeler, 1994). Such an investigation is obligatory given the claim that large metropolitan areas in the United States are more locally oriented than ever (Persky and Wiewel, 1994). However, without city-pair data, for both public switched telephone networks and international private leased lines, it is difficult satisfactorily to identify world cities in the United States that host concentrations of information activities and function as the headquarters of multinational corporations.

Generally, the international movement of information is associated with commodity flows, but for the United States (and the United Kingdom) it has been tied more to the movements of people (Kellerman, 1990). Because the bringing of people together by communications networks is enhanced by air travel, attention now shifts from telecommunications to the complementary development of air passenger networks. Furthermore, air travel is not affected by alternative service providers and foreign calling cards, which may not credit calls to their origin. Consequently, air travel offers a more accurate and sensitive gauge of international traffic involving world cities.

Air passenger networks

Air passenger travel contributes to economic globalization by bringing people together to acquire *complex knowledge* relatively unburdened by geographical constraints and national borders. International flights are regulated by bilateral aviation pacts between countries designating routes, loading capacities, and fares. These arrangements have been partly nullified by the expansion of deregulation worldwide. Some advanced capitalist countries are seeking less restrictive aviation agreements with their bilateral partners. Meanwhile, major airlines have adopted modern management methods and started to form strategic alliances to meet harsh competition (e.g. Delta with blue-chip carriers Singapore Airlines and Swiss Air). These methods include code-sharing, which provides access to the domestic routes of other countries (e.g. United Airlines with Ansett Australia). Expansion of airline networks is an industry trend. Without an efficient network, an airline operator cannot survive. The key to efficient networks lies in fully fledged hub airports that link both overseas and domestic flights. Attention here is focused initially on the number of passengers handled by the "top 25" international airports (i.e. a stock measurement) before examining the "top 25" city-pairs in international air passenger movements (i.e. a flow measurement).

Stocks

In 1984, the combined London airports of Heathrow and Gatwick, with 37,149,000 passengers, dominated international embarkations and disembarkations by commercial air transport (fig. 16.8). The combined total for Paris Charles de Gaulle and Orly was 19,434,000 passengers. Fourteen of the "top 25" international airports were located in Europe, with Frankfurt and Amsterdam also handling more than 10 million passengers; five in Asia; four in North America, with New York (Kennedy) handling more than 10 million passengers; and two in Africa and the Middle East.

By 1994, the combined London airports of Heathrow and Gatwick, with 56,947,000 passengers, had maintained their domination of international embarkations and disembarkations by commercial air trans-

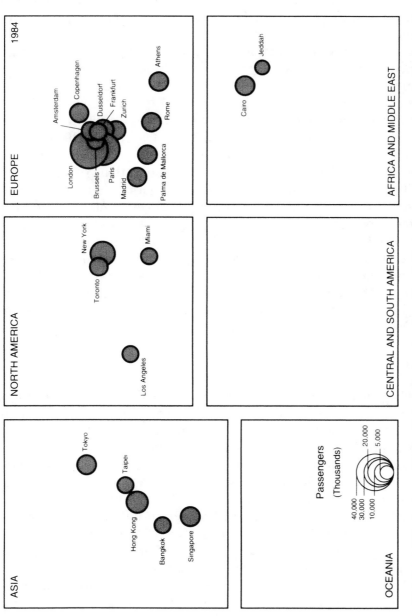

Fig. 16.8 The "top 25" airports with the highest international traffic, 1984 (Note: London-Heathrow and London-Gatwick, and Paris-Charles de Gaulle and Paris-Orly are combined. Source: ICAO, 1984)

455

port (fig. 16.9). The combined total for Paris Charles de Gaulle and Orly was 32,367,000 passengers. Fifteen of the "top 25" international airports were located in Europe, with Frankfurt exceeding 20 million passengers; six in Asia, with Hong Kong also exceeding 20 million passengers; and four in North America. New additions to the "top 25" were Seoul, Manchester, and Munich. Athens, Cairo, and Jeddah dropped from the rankings. Consequently, there were no representatives among the "top 25" from Oceania, Central and South America, or Africa and the Middle East.

Clearly, the pattern of the "top 25" airports as a guide to world city status is not unambiguous (table 16.3). A true hub pattern is prevented by the plethora of nation-states in Europe and, to a lesser extent, in Asia. There is also the vexed question that North America is underrepresented. In 1984, 16 North American airports were in the world's "top 25" ranked by total passengers embarked and disembarked on commercial air transport (domestic and international). Of these, Chicago, Atlanta, Dallas, Denver, San Francisco, New York (Newark), New York (La Guardia), Boston, St. Louis, Pittsburg, and Houston were not in the "top 25" international rankings.[7] Although no comparable data are available for 1992, this problem needs to be borne in mind in examining flows between the "top 25" city-pairs with the highest international traffic.

Flows

In 1984, an analysis of the "top 25" city-pairs reveals two major systems – the transatlantic and Asia/transpacific (fig. 16.10). There were also three isolated city-pairs: Copenhagen–Oslo, Cairo–Jeddah, and Miami–Nassau. Twenty-six centres were ranked in the "top 25" city-pairs. London and Tokyo were the dominant hubs, being involved in five city-pairs each. Hong Kong, New York, and Singapore were in four city-pairs, Paris and Toronto in three, Frankfurt, Bangkok, and Tapei in two. Sixteen places appeared in only one city-pair and cannot be regarded as major hubs (Kuala Lumpur, Amsterdam, Honolulu, Jakarta, Dublin, Seoul, Algiers, Cairo, Jeddah, Rome, Los Angeles, Miami, Nassau, Chicago, Copenhagen, and Oslo).

By 1992, an analysis of the "top 25" city-pairs shows that they were interconnected in a single system (fig. 16.11). This system functioned as the "Main Street" linking Asia, Europe, and North America. Conversely, Africa and the Middle East, Central and South America, and Oceania were *cul de sacs*. Twenty cities were involved in the "top

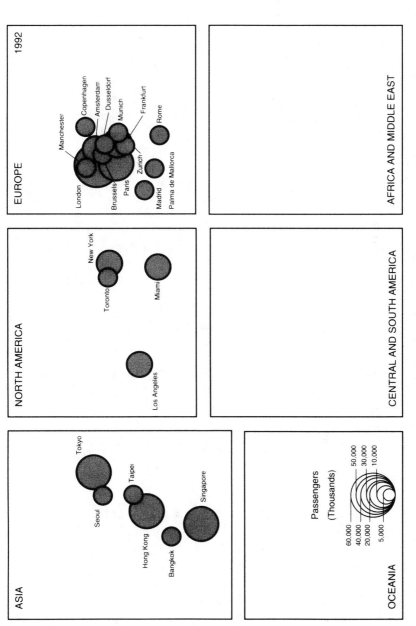

Fig. 16.9 The "top 25" airports with the highest international traffic, 1992 (Note: London-Heathrow and London-Gatwick, and Paris-Charles de Gaulle and Paris-Orly are combined. Source: ICAO, 1993)

Table 16.3 The "top 25" airports for international passengers, 1984–1992 ('000 passengers)

	1984	1985	1986	1987	1988	1989	1990	1991	1992
London (LHR)	24,353	25,867	25,734	28,615	30,659	32,472	35,070	33,531	38,257
New York	16,334	16,376	15,395	17,405	18,021	17,903	18,300	16,670	15,110
Frankfurt	13,348	14,393	14,544	17,147	18,398	19,502	21,750	20,861	23,271
London (LGW)	12,796	13,663	15,195	18,248	19,619	19,825	19,725	17,679	18,690
Paris (CDG)	12,123	13,130	12,899	14,450	16,172	18,282	20,700	19,384	22,444
Amsterdam	10,473	11,298	11,602	13,209	14,397	15,254	16,000	16,082	18,609
Hong Kong	9,539	9,856	10,610	12,667	15,277	16,204	18,688	19,158	22,061
Tokyo	8,522	9,203	9,555	11,397	13,893	16,127	18,385	17,743	19,022
Singapore	8,380	8,692	8,912	10,009	11,381	12,973	14,406	14,983	16,882
Zurich	8,248	8,676	8,767	9,603	10,194	10,999	11,585	11,185	12,007
Palma de Mallorca	7,504	6,786	7,785	8,827	8,979	9,400	7,966	7,676	8,265
Paris (ORY)	7,311	7,418	7,206	7,929	8,704	9,159	9,500	8,609	9,923
Miami	7,083	6,958	7,668	8,614	9,446	9,316	10,100	10,895	11,514
Copenhagen	7,025	7,481	7,824	8,437	8,793	9,098	9,268	8,742	9,699
Rome	6,863	7,559	6,550	6,962	7,250	9,086	9,660	7,987	9,873
Toronto	6,691	7,122	7,950	8,632	9,500	9,900	10,520	9,052	9,553
Cairo	6,442	5,124	NR	NR	NR	NR	NR	NR	NR
Athens	5,964	6,242	5,356	6,040	6,259	6,234	6,301	NR	NR
Dusseldorf	5,523	5,817	6,336	6,877	7,527	7,800	8,650	8,191	9,098
Los Angeles	5,323	5,935	6,520	5,517	8,065	9,244	9,980	9,971	11,456
Brussels	5,212	5,578	5,723	6,190	6,900	7,200	7,600	8,624	9,256
Bangkok	5,177	5,390	5,843	6,981	8,456	9,855	10,906	10,378	11,281
Madrid	4,921	5,164	4,959	5,403	6,007	6,550	7,330	6,465	8,477
Taipei	4,267	4,686	4,980	5,400	6,448	7,747	8,995	9,357	10,828
Jeddah	3,992	NR	NR	NR	NR	NR	NR	NR	NR
Manchester	NR	4,607	6,023	7,040	7,708	8,139	8,375	8,195	9,749

Munich	NR	NR	4,752	5,614	5,873	NR	NR	6,319	7,347
Stockholm	NR	NR	NR	NR	NR	6,086	6,555	5,978	NR
Seoul	NR	NR	NR	NR	NR	NR	NR	NR	9,800

Source: ICAO (1984–1993).
NR = not ranked.

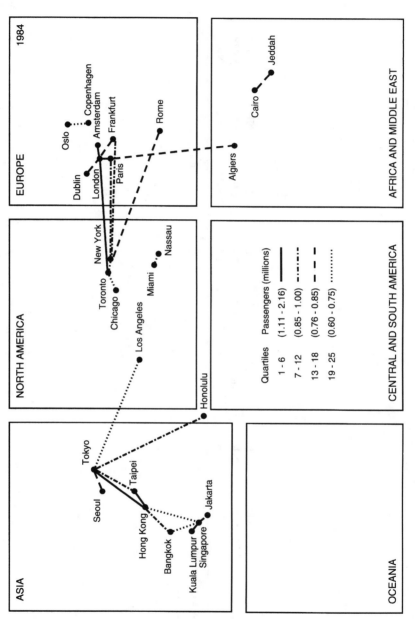

Fig. 16.10 The "top 25" international city-pairs with the highest scheduled passenger traffic, 1984 (Data source: ICAO, 1984)

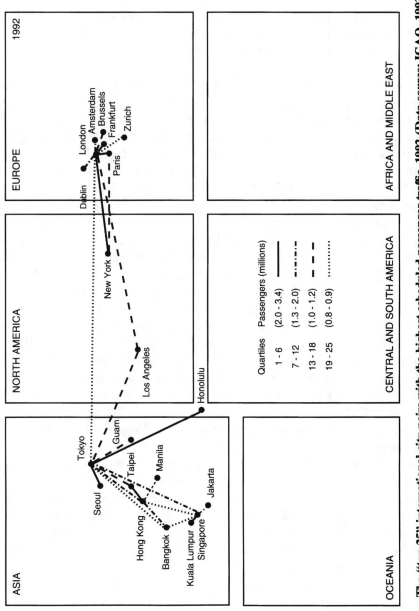

Fig. 16.11 The "top 25" international city-pairs with the highest scheduled passenger traffic, 1992 (Data source: ICAO, 1993)

461

25" city-pairs. London and Tokyo were the dominant hubs, featuring in nine city-pairs. Singapore and Hong Kong figured in five city-pairs, Bangkok in three, and Taipei, Los Angeles, New York, and Paris in two each. A further 11 cities have to be regarded as terminals because they featured in only one city-pair (Jakarta, Kuala Lumpur, Manila, Seoul, Guam, Honolulu, Amsterdam, Dublin, Frankfurt, Brussels, and Zurich).

Clearly, there had been an important shake-out of the air passenger network between 1984 and 1992. Thirty-five city-pairs had been recorded as occurring in the "top 25" between 1984 and 1992 – 16 of them being present throughout the period (table 16.4). Eight of the pairs recorded in 1984 had disappeared: New York–Toronto, Miami–Nassau, Algiers–Paris, Cairo–Jeddah, Copenhagen–Oslo, Chicago–Toronto, Frankfurt–New York, and New York–Rome. Eight new city-pairs had appeared by 1992: Hong Kong–Manila, Tokyo–Singapore, Tokyo–Guam, Bangkok–Tokyo, London–Brussels, London–Zurich, London–Los Angeles, and London–Tokyo. There were city-pairs with gaps in their records between 1984 and 1992, notably Hong Kong–Singapore, Hong Kong–Manila, Guam–Tokyo and Brussels–London. Single appearances in the rankings were made by Auckland–Sydney and London–Miami.

When these time-series are graphed for the period between 1984 and 1992, a series of features can be highlighted (fig. 16.12). Within South-East Asia, Singapore was the major hub, being involved in all major passenger routes. In North-East Asia, Tokyo was the dominant hub, with Hong Kong and Taipei playing minor roles. In movements between North-East and South-East Asia, Hong Kong played a more pivotal role, with Bangkok, Singapore, and Tokyo as the other hubs. In Europe, London was the dominant hub, being involved in six of the seven major routes. Surprisingly, in North America, Toronto was the only place involved in two major routes. New York's poor showing was countered by its apparent strength on major intercontinental routes, although two of them were no longer in the "top 25" city pairings in 1992, underlining New York's struggle to stay on top (Markusen and Gwiasda, 1994). The other key hubs were London, Los Angeles, and Tokyo.

The analyses of the "top 25" city-pair rankings in international passenger movements suggest that researchers have been overgenerous in designating "world cities." Only nine centres seem worthy of the sobriquet: London, Tokyo, Singapore, Hong Kong, Bangkok, Los Angeles, Paris, New York, and Taipei. There are a host of contenders

Table 16.4 The "top 25" city pairings in international passenger traffic, 1984–1992 ('000 passengers)

	1984	1985	1986	1987	1988	1989	1990	1991	1992
London–Paris	2,165	2,310	2,190	2,490	2,855	3,046	3,146	3,125	3,402
London–New York	2,115	2,334	2,067	2,332	2,413	2,356	2,534	2,215	2,276
Kuala Lumpur–Singapore	1,316	1,365	1,241	1,316	1,505	1,636	1,866	2,034	2,109
Hong Kong–Tokyo	1,243	1,306	1,255	1,623	1,799	1,770	1,984	1,922	2,020
Amsterdam–London	1,115	1,187	1,291	1,608	1,724	1,637	1,661	1,607	1,775
Hong Kong–Taipei	1,114	1,170	1,228	1,403	1,737	2,056	1,815	2,075	2,223
Honolulu–Tokyo	1,001	1,054	1,067	1,282	1,591	1,903	2,063	1,902	2,131
Taipei–Tokyo	981	1,021	1,024	1,143	1,288	1,342	1,073	991	1,090
Bangkok–Hong Kong	953	947	1,063	1,339	1,629	1,906	1,680	1,715	1,649
New York–Paris	892	893	786	1,030	1,137	1,163	1,235	1,237	1,217
Jakarta–Singapore	884	845	836	894	1,120	1,224	1,357	1,757	1,381
Frankfurt–New York	852	751	670	901	909	854	953	881	NR
Dublin–London	846	906	1,113	1,377	1,427	1,719	1,917	1,725	1,721
Seoul–Tokyo	837	943	1,018	1,131	1,519	1,890	1,965	1,319	2,023
Algiers–Paris	786	828	755	730	742	850	NR	NR	NR
Cairo–Jeddah	770	693	NR	NR	NR	NR	NR	NR	NR
New York–Rome	768	777	NR	NR	NR	NR	NR	NR	NR
Frankfurt–London	761	868	865	1,053	1,103	1,146	1,330	1,143	1,222
Hong Kong–Singapore	746	802	818	885	911	NR	952	1,006	997
New York–Toronto	720	826	940	1,068	1,131	988	964	880	NR
Bangkok–Singapore	685	757	778	949	1,073	1,162	1,156	1,058	981
Los Angeles–Tokyo	678	738	851	982	1,131	1,203	1,221	998	1,094
Miami–Nassau	668	668	686	NR	NR	NR	NR	NR	NR
Chicago–Toronto	656	667	794	912	931	910	934	818	NR
Copenhagen–Oslo	604	671	716	732	NR	NR	NR	NR	NR
Brussels–London	NR	NR	692	830	893	903	943	NR	NR
Hong Kong–Manila	NR	NR	650	742	NR	956	NR	938	998

Table 16.4 **(cont.)**

	1984	1985	1986	1987	1988	1989	1990	1991	1992
London–Zurich	NR	NR	NR	788	829	900	904	903	908
London–Miami	NR	NR	NR	NR	835	NR	NR	NR	NR
Auckland–Sydney	NR	NR	NR	NR	781	NR	NR	NR	NR
Singapore–Tokyo	NR	NR	NR	NR	NR	837	1,010	944	1,256
Guam–Tokyo	NR	NR	NR	NR	NR	819	862	NR	857
Bangkok–Tokyo	NR	NR	NR	NR	NR	NR	950	842	901
London–Los Angeles	NR	NR	NR	NR	NR	NR	NR	795	1,015
London–Tokyo	NR	NR	NR	NR	NR	NR	NR	NR	950

Source: ICAO (1984–1993).
NR = not ranked.

464

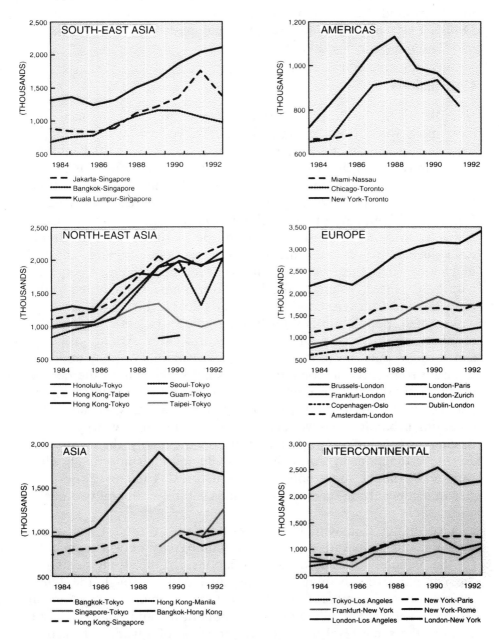

Fig. 16.12 **Trends among the "top 25" international city-pairs with the highest passenger traffic, 1984–1992 (Data source: ICAO, 1984–1993)**

– Kuala Lumpur, Manila, Seoul, Toronto, Amsterdam, Brussels, Frankfurt, and Zurich. None of these contenders is in Africa and the Middle East, in Central and South America, or in Oceania. Clearly, São Paulo and Sydney do not rank.

Conclusions

In 2010, all of the "top 25" urban agglomerations are expected to have more than 10 million inhabitants. Tokyo, with 28.9 million, is expected to have first ranking, whereas Moscow, with 10.4 million, will be in twenty-fifth position. (Lima, in twenty-sixth position, is also expected to have a population in excess of 10 million.) Asia will be home to 13 of the largest agglomerations; of the rest, 5 will be in Central and South America, 4 will be in Africa and the Middle East, 2 will be in North America, and 1 will be in Europe. These trends reflect urban growth rates anticipated in developed regions, and are much lower than those expected in less developed regions. Compared with 1990, Dacca, Teheran, and Istanbul will have been added to the "top 25" and Chicago, London, and Paris dropped from the list.

As noted, population is a misleading guide to identifying and determining the prospects and status of world cities. Attention has to shift from population to focusing on the accessibility of key nodes in separate transport and communications networks and on the degree of interactivity between them. The provision of advanced transport and communications networks between world cities – and other emerging urban forms – will enlarge cooperation and synergy among its components (i.e. network externalities). Inevitably, the location of advanced functions in world cities has affected their internal equilibrium and brought about polycentric structures. A major risk of policies that concentrate on critical functions is the creation of two-paced cities.

According to Camagni (1993: 79–80), the policy implications of the network and cooperative logic underpinning city networks include: (a) the planned inter-city division of labour; (b) the strengthening of the comparative advantage of individual cities through the *filière* integration of functions (e.g. the mechanical engineering *filière* in Brescia); and (c) the enlargement of cooperation and synergy among cities at the same level through the provision of advanced transport and communications networks, particularly by investment in nodes (Batten, 1990). Consequently, managers of an individual world city have a choice – depending on its competitiveness – between (a) developing priority functions in which they have a comparative advantage (e.g. by cooperating with other cities in airport provision); and/or (b) developing all possible synergies among selected functions at the level of the entire world city system (e.g. top management – transport – tourism/culture). In these policy debates, the network is a "club good" (Camagni, 1993: 72). Clearly, it enables firms and cities to obtain advantages by being members of the club.

Tangible transport and communications networks are not the sole arbiters of the future qualitative prospects of cities in the third millennium (Batten, 1990). A complete study would have to assess the importance of the strategic position of world cities in the system of intangible networks facilitating the global exchange of people, knowledge, money, goods, and services, and the ability to exploit the potential synergies (i.e. economies of scope) arising from the interactive character of different networks and collective knowledge permeating across them. As noted, these include headquarter information networks, personal networks of top managers, financial networks, and cultural networks.

More attention will also have to be given to the definition of urban agglomerations and world cities. At present their identification pays little heed to emerging urban forms: systems of cities (e.g. Cambridge–London, Stockholm–Uppsala, and Japan's Kansai); extended metropolitan areas (e.g. Tokyo–Osaka, Seoul–Pusan, Beijing–Tianjin, and Hong Kong–Guangzhou); and development corridors (e.g. the "blue banana" in Europe and the East Asian Corridor) (Rimmer, 1994). Obviously, such forms offer scope for economic synergies and the prospects for expanding knowledge within and between polycentric settlements. Also, consideration of their transport and communications networks cannot continue to be ignored.

Finally, the Janus side of changes in transport and communications networks among world cities needs to be considered. In highlighting some of the inter-urban inequities within the hierarchy of city networks, Harris (1994: 335) has posed some of the pertinent questions: what, for instance, are the social costs of containerization and relocation of dock facilities, and how have the disproportionate increases in air passenger movements (e.g. mass tourism) affected the high rate of growth in energy consumption and the production of toxic and other wastes? More fundamentally, how can a system of managing world cities be developed that accommodates both economic expansion and rapid movement with a reduction in threats to the environment?

467

Notes

1. Friedmann (1986) mapped 26 world cities. His hierarchy was: (1) primary cities in the core (Tokyo, Los Angeles, Chicago, New York, London, and Paris); (2) primary cities in the semi-periphery (Singapore and São Paulo); secondary cities in the core (Sydney, San Francisco, Houston, Toronto, Miami, Madrid, Milan, Vienna, and Johannesburg); and (d) secondary cities in the semi-periphery (Bangkok, Hong Kong, Taipei, Seoul, Manila, Mexico City, Caracas, Buenos Aires, and Rio de Janiero). Both Rotterdam and Zurich were also considered but omitted from the map.
2. Rimmer (1986, 1991) reported the results of an exhaustive study by Nomura Sogo Kenkyujo, which reviewed 345 cities by 20 attributes reflecting personal services, commodity and commercial transactions, information flows, and international finance. Of these cities 178 were eliminated as not reaching the threshold for international cities; 80 were recorded as third-ranking cities (*kokusai toshi*) specializing in commodity and commercial transactions; 56 were ranked in a second-ranking multinational group (*kojikokusai toshi*); and 29 were classified as first-ranking global cities (*chokokusai toshi*).
3. Singapore, Hong Kong, Kaohsiung, Keelung, Pusan, Kobe, and Tokyo/Yokohama belong to the group of hub ports on transpacific routes and the Far East/Europe trade; Rotterdam, Hamburg, Antwerp, and New York/New Jersey belong to the group of ports in the trans-atlantic trade; and Los Angeles/Long Beach, Oakland, Seattle, and Tacoma belong to the group of hub ports in the transpacific trade (Tanaka, 1994).
4. According to Harris (1994: 333), Los Angeles/Long Beach has superseded most West Coast ports in the Asia-Pacific trade and the Port of Rotterdam has marginalized competing North European ports.
5. The high cost of using Japanese ports has prompted Nippon Yusen Kaisha and Mitsui-Osaka Line to consider switching their activities to other hubs in East Asia (Mitsuada, 1995).
6. According to Staple (1994) the heavy carriers have responded to these developments by creating strategic alliances to provide "seamless global services" (e.g. Concert, ATT & World Partners, and Unisource) and adopting light carrier strategies to secure a global presence (e.g. Australia's Telstra).
7. A useful counterpoint to this analysis is *Fortune*'s first annual international survey of the world's best cities for business (Saporito, 1994). A key variable is the number of cities served with non-stop airline services. On this score New York (167), Chicago (164), London (150), Atlanta (135), Dallas (128), Detroit (122), Moscow (116), Pittsburg (116), Frankfurt (114), and Minneapolis/St. Paul (107) would be the leaders.

References

Andersson, A. E. and U. Stromquist (1989), "The Emerging C-society." In: D. F. Batten and R. Thord (eds.), *Transportation for the Future*. Berlin: Springer-Verlag, pp. 29–39.

Batten, D. (1990), "Network Cities versus Central Place Cities: Building a Cosmo Creative Constellation." In: *Cosmo-Creative '90: International Forum on Logistical Development and Its Regional Consequences in Osaka – Towards a Cosmo Creative City, Osaka*. Osaka: Prefectural Government, pp. 83–85.

Camagni, R. P. (1993), "From City Hierarchy to City Network: Reflections about an Emerging Paradigm." In: *Structure and Change in the Space Economy: Festschrift in Honor of Martin J. Beckmann*. Berlin: Springer-Verlag, pp. 66–87.

Castells, M. (1994), "European Cities, the Informational Society, and the Global Economy." *New Left Review*, March/April: 19–32.

CIY (1984–1994), *Containerisation International Yearbook*. London: National Magazine Co.

Fleming, D. K. and Y. Hayuth (1994), "Spatial Characteristics of Transportation Hubs: Centrality and Intermediacy." *Journal of Transport Geography* 2(1): 3–18.

Friedmann, J. (1986), "The World City Hypothesis." *Development and Change* 17(1): 69–83.

Friedmann, J. and G. Wolff (1982), "World City Formation: An Agenda for Research and Action." *International Journal of Urban and Regional Research* 6: 309–344.

Fujita, K. (1991), "A World City and Flexible Specialization: Restructuring of the Tokyo Metropolis." *International Journal of Urban and Regional Research* 15(2): 269–284.

Hall, P. (1991), "Moving Information: A Tale of Four Technologies." In: J. Brotchie, M. Batty, P. Hall, and P. Newton (eds.), *Cities of the 21st Century: New Technologies and Spatial Systems*. Melbourne: Longman Cheshire, pp. 1–21.

Harris, N. (1994), "Viewpoint: The Emerging Global City – Transport." *Cities* 11(5): 332–336.

Hill, R. C. and K. Fujita (1995), "Osaka's Tokyo Problem." *International Journal of Urban and Regional Research* 19(2): 181–193.

ICAO (International Civil Aviation Authority) (1984–1993), *ICAO Statistical Yearbook: Civil Aviation Statistics of the World*. Montreal: International Civil Aviation Authority.

Kellerman, A. (1990), "International Telecommunications around the World: A Flow Analysis." *Telecommunications Policy* 14: 461–475.

——— (1993), *Telecommunications and Geography*. London and New York: Belhaven Press.

Keil, R. and P. Lieser (1992), "Frankfurt: Global City–Local Politics." In: M. P. Smith (ed.), *After Modernism: Global Restructuring and the Changing Boundaries of City Life*. New Brunswick, N.J.: Transaction Publications, pp. 39–69.

Markusen, A. and V. Gwiasda (1994), "Multipolarity and the Layering of Functions in World Cities: New York City's Struggle to Stay on Top." *International Journal of Urban and Regional Research* 18(2): 167–193.

Mitchelson, R. L. and J. O. Wheeler (1994), "The Flow of Information in a Global Economy: The Role of the American Urban System in 1990." *Annals of the Association of American Geographers* 84(1): 87–107.

Mitsuada, H. (1995), "Harbor Business Is Drifting to Asian Ports." *Nikkei Weekly*, 5 June: 1 and 8.

Moss, M. (1991), "The Information City in the Global Economy." In: J. Brotchie, M. Batty, P. Hall, and P. Newton (eds.), *Cities of the 21st Century: New Technologies and Spatial Systems*. Melbourne: Longman Cheshire, pp. 181–190.

Persky J. and W. Wiewel (1994), "The Growing Localness of the Global City." *Economic Geography* 70(2): 129–143.

Rimmer, P. J. (1986), "Japan's World Cities: Tokyo, Osaka, Nagoya or Tokkaido Megalopolis?" *Development and Change* 17(1): 121–158.

——— (1991), "The Global Intelligence Corps and World Cities: Engineering Consultants on the Move." In: P. W. Daniels (ed.), *Services and Metropolitan Development: International Perspectives*. London: Routledge, Chapman & Hall, pp. 66–107.

469

—— (1994), "Regional Economic Integration in Pacific Asia." *Environment and Planning A* 26: 1731–1759.

Saporito, B. (1994), "The World's Best Cities for Business." *Fortune*, 14 November: 68–91.

Sassen, S. (1994), "The Urban Complex in the World Economy." *International Social Science Journal* 46(1): 43–62.

Schwieterman, J. P. (1993), *Air Cargo and the Opening of China: New Opportunities for Hong Kong*. Hong Kong: Chinese University Press.

Staple, G. C. (ed.) (1992), *TeleGeography 1992: Global Telecommunications Traffic Statistics & Commentary*. Washington: TeleGeography Inc.

—— (ed.) (1993), *TeleGeography 1993: Global Telecommunications Traffic Statistics & Commentary*. Washington: TeleGeography Inc.

—— (ed.) (1994), *TeleGeography 1994: Global Telecommunications Traffic Statistics & Commentary*. Washington: TeleGeography Inc.

Staple, G. C. and M. Mullins (1989), *Global Telecommunication Traffic Flows and Market Structures: A Quantitative Review*. London: International Institute of Communications.

Tanaka, N. (1994), "Container Shipping and Container Ports of the World in Recent Times." Unpublished paper. Tokyo: NYK (Nippon Yusen Kaisha) Line.

Tapia, S. de (1995), "Echanges, Transports et Communications: Circulation et Champs Migratoires Turcs." Unpublished paper presented at the 7th World Conference of Transport Research, Sydney, 16–21 July.

United Nations (1993), *World Urbanization Prospects: The 1992 Revision – Estimates and Projections of Urban and Rural Populations and Urban Agglomerations*. New York: Department of Economic and Social Information and Policy Analysis, United Nations.

17

Globalization and rural–urban relations in the developing world

T. G. McGee

Introduction

It is currently expected that during the first years of the twenty-first century, for the first time in human history, more than half of the world's population will live in urban areas and by 2025 this proportion will be nearing 58 per cent (United Nations, 1991). It would appear that the world is on a path of inevitable urbanization. Such evidence suggests that rural areas are becoming less important and that more attention should be paid to the problems and challenges of urbanization.

In fact, one may question this suggestion on the grounds that the rural–urban dichotomy is losing its utility as a heuristic concept and a policy paradigm. For almost 40 years I have been arguing that the concept of the rural–urban division based on spatial demarcation is artificial and needs to be restated within a broader theory of economic growth and urbanization. This assertion accepts that the new emphasis must be upon the ongoing analysis of the linkages between agricultural and non-agricultural activities and that particular attention should be paid to the flows of people, commodities, capital, and information (see McGee, 1971, 1972, 1975, 1979, 1982a,b).

Rather than thinking of a rural–urban dichotomy, it is more realistic to think in terms of a *mobility transition* in which the increasing capacity to move people, commodities, capital, and information through space is the major component of the process of development. Zelinsky has attempted to develop this idea into an evolutionary model of spatial behaviour, which argues that "[t]here are definite patterned regularities in the growth of personal mobility through space-time during recent history and these regularities comprise an essential component of the modernization process" (Zelinsky, 1971: 221–222).

Recently in my own work I have tried to avoid the evolutionary characteristics of Zelinsky's model with the concept of a constantly moving series of transactions flowing through national and international space. In a very general way these transactions can be grouped into four categories: (1) people, (2) commodities, (3) capital, and (4) information. Thus migration is a form of geographic action performed by people; the shipping of spices from Indonesia to Rotterdam is a commodity transaction; the transfer of funds from New York to Singapore is a capital flow; and news programmes broadcast on international TV to the world are an information transaction.

The major point to make is that the flow of capital and information is, in theory at least, unrestricted and instantaneous whereas the flow of people and commodities, though collapsing in time–distance terms, is still subject to the constraints of space. Most planners recognize that the processes have emphasized the centralization of urban systems and penetrated and transformed the non-urban areas of the globe, which are still defined as rural.

It must be stressed that, at a global level, the transactional revolution proceeds in leaps and bounds, producing a highly uneven impact in the pattern of urbanization and rural change at both the global and national levels. This makes the task of attempting to generalize concerning rural–urban dynamics quite complex.

In order to tackle this task, I have attempted to deconstruct the process of urban–rural relations within the framework of the urban transition in terms of three components: first, the geographic diversity of the developing countries; secondly, the effects of globalization on urban–rural relations; and finally the effects on the urban system. I then analyse rural–urban relations in three medium-sized countries of the developing world – Brazil, Indonesia, and Nigeria – over the past two decades. The final section discusses the need to develop new policies to facilitate rural–urban dynamics in developing countries.

Reconstructing the urban transition

The geographic diversity of the urban transition

As indicated in the introduction, the world seems set on the path to the creation of urban societies. However, this overall trend masks substantial differences between the world's major regions, particularly between more and less developed regions.[1] By 1990 the world's population stood at an estimated 5.3 billion, with 4.1 billion living in developing countries and 1.2 billion in developed countries. Approximately 45 per cent of the total population of the world lived in urban places, with 1.5 billion in developing countries and 0.9 billion in developed countries. Although the urban proportion in developing countries was only 37 per cent, their total urban population surpassed by a considerable margin that of developed countries, where the level of urbanization was 73 per cent. By 2025, the level of urbanization in the developing world will have risen to 61 per cent, implying that 4.4 billion people will live in the urban centres of developing countries, accounting for 80 per cent of the total urban population in the world (United Nations, 1991).

The contrast will be even greater for the global rural population, with rural populations increasing to 2.7 billion in 2025 from 2.5 billion in 1990. By 2025, almost 92 per cent of the world's rural population will be located in developing countries.

Thus, underlying all discussion of the urban transition in the developing countries is the fact that the population will continue to rise in both urban and rural areas for the next 10–15 years. Unlike the developed countries, the underdeveloped countries as a region will not experience an absolute decline in the size of rural populations in this period. This poses major challenges for policy formulation in the developing countries. As rural populations decreased in developed countries, policy strategies were designed to accommodate this process, but in developing countries similar policies may not be so easily implemented or even relevant.

Of course, this highly generalized picture of the less developed world needs to be further deconstructed because there are major contrasts between the three main continental regions. Table 17.1 shows that, over the next 30 years, divergent patterns will be exhibited by the three areas. Latin America, already the most urbanized, will increase its urbanization level to 84 per cent and continue to lose

Table 17.1 **Less developed countries: Main regions' urban and rural populations, 1990–2025 ('000)**

	Africa			Latin America			Asia		
	Urban	Rural	Total	Urban	Rural	Total	Urban	Rural	Total
1990	217,440	424,671	642,111	320,493	127,583	448,076	975,335	2,013,900	2,989,235
2025	911,735	685,120	1,596,855	637,541	119,850	757,391	2,821,647	1,963,342	4,784,989

Source: United Nations (1991).

rural population. Asia's urban population will grow by 1.9 billion to 59 per cent, while at the same time its rural population will decrease only slightly by 50 million.

Africa exhibits a completely different pattern. While its urban population levels will grow from 34 per cent to 57 per cent in 2025, its rural population will increase by more than one-third (261 million). Thus the dynamics of the urban transition and the rural–urban relationship need to be carefully analysed in each continental context.

The demographic components of these patterns are threefold: natural increase, migration, and redefinition of urban and rural territory. As table 17.2 shows, in Africa and Latin America the major component of urban growth in recent years has been natural increase, and this is expected to continue into the twenty-first century. However, there appear to be significant differences in the demographic impulses that lead to this common pattern. In Africa, the urban population is doubling every 12 years – a rate of urban growth that is among the highest in the world. This reflects high urban fertility and continuing high rates of rural–urban migration.[2] Latin America exhibits a different pattern, however, for the level of urbanization is already high and there is much more inter-city migration (see Roberts, 1992). As Gilbert points out, Latin America was transformed from a rural to an urban region by a combination of falling mortality rates, rapid internal migration, economic development, and changing technology. In the 1980s, fertility rates also began to fall and urban areas grew annually about 3.0 per cent, compared with 3.9 per cent between 1965 and 1980 (Gilbert, 1994a, 25–27).

In Asia, migration and reclassification are of much more importance in urban growth. However, the figures for Asia are greatly influenced in the period up to 1990 primarily by changes in the Chinese definition of urbanization. If China is excluded, natural increase for Eastern Asia accounts for two-thirds of the urban increase, although in the remainder of Asia rural–urban migration still contributes more than 50 per cent.

Sharp variations in population sizes underline the differences in the urbanization process experienced by Africa, Asia, and Latin America. Thus the prospects for Asia, with close to 3 billion people in 1990, differ in many ways from those for Africa (642 million) and Latin America (only 448 million). In each of these continents the population is also dominated by large population concentrations in a few countries. Thus in Latin America, two countries – Brazil (150 million) and Mexico (88 million) – made up 53 per cent of the total population

Table 17.2 **Components of urban growth, by country or area, 1980–2005 (%)**

Subregion, country, or area	1980–1985		1990–1995		2000–2005	
	Natural increase	Migration and reclassification	Natural increase	Migration and reclassification	Natural increase	Migration and reclassification
World	57	43	58	42	58	42
More developed regions	65	35	62	38	49	51
Less developed regions	45	55	50	50	54	46
Europe	45	55	34	66	26	74
North America	85	15	75	25	60	40
USSR (former)	54	46	79	21	56	44
Oceania	110	–10ᵃ	97	03	83	17
Latin America	67	33	73	27	77	23
Africa	60	40	61	39	65	35
Asia	40	60	44	56	46	54

Source: United Nations (1991: 27, table 6).
Note: The contribution of natural increase is calculated by assuming that the urban population has the same rate of natural increase as the national or regional population. The category of migration and reclassification is calculated as a residual.
a. Oceania experienced net out-migration from urban areas during 1980–1985.

in 1990; in Africa, three countries – Ethiopia (49 million), Egypt (52 million), and Nigeria (108 million) – accounted for 33 per cent; and in Asia, five countries – China (1.1 billion), Indonesia (184 million), Bangladesh (115 million), India (853 million), and Pakistan (122 million) – made up more than 80 per cent of the total population and two-thirds of the urban population. It can thus be argued that it is these "population giants" that present some of the major challenges to urbanization and rural–urban dynamics.

It is for this reason that I shall look at three case-studies from each of the continents: Nigeria in Africa; Indonesia in Asia; and Brazil in Latin America. By focusing on the rural–urban dynamics of the urban transition, we will be able to develop a more careful analysis and more valid generalizations.

Globalization and the rural–urban divide

It is now generally agreed that this is an age in which the "global imperatives" of production, trade, and investment are leading to an increasing integration and globalization of economic activity.[3] Most analyses of this process focus upon three facets: first, the role of technological change – telecommunications, computerization, containerization, and air travel – in facilitating this process (Dick and Rimmer, 1993); secondly, the changing features of the world order, which has seen the collapse and erosion of the communist bloc and attempts to free up the global regulatory environment, permitting greater mobility of labour, capital, and commodities; and, finally, an increasing "globalization" of information, labelled the "global cultural bazaar" by Barnet and Cavanagh – "the newest of global webs and nearly the most universal in its reach. Films, television, radio, music, magazines, T-shirts, games, toys and theme parks are the media for disseminating global images" (Barnet and Cavanagh, 1994: 15). Some writers have come to view these webs of information as some form of hyperspace. Castells, writing in *The Informational City* in 1989, says this:

The new international economy creates a variable geometry of production and consumption, labour and capital management and information – a geometry that denies the specific meaning of any place outside its position in a network whose shape changes relentlessly in response to messages and unseen signals and unknown codes. (Castells, 1989: 17)

Understanding the effect of this globalization on the rural–urban dynamics of the developing countries is difficult. However, it is possible to analyse the process of globalization at two levels – first at the level of the individual state and secondly at the level of the international system.

De Mattos (1994) has argued that the major effect of global developments has been to erode the entrenched Keynesian theories that argued it was possible to correct the problems of economic growth by rational state intervention. De Mattos suggests that one of the main goals of state policies was to achieve a more balanced spatial distribution of productive activities, employment, and population, influenced by such researchers as Hirschmann, Myrdal, Nurske, Robinson, and Rosenstein-Rodan.

[T]hree basic principles constituted the core of national development strategies adopted during the period: (a) the promotion of inward-oriented economic growth, so that internal markets would become the main support of productive activities, (b) the promotion of industrialization for import substitution, and (c) the establishment of a new mode of regulation which embodies the new theory of development planning. (De Mattos, 1994: 221)

De Mattos argues that these policies were successful in many parts of Latin America and Asia in the period between 1950 and the mid-1970s. Industrial growth rates in Latin America and Asia averaged 6.0 per cent per annum and were responsible for accelerating the penetration of rural areas by the capitalist mode of production and for increased migration and urbanization. Even Africa south of the Sahara showed similar tendencies in the 1950s and 1960s (see Becker et al., 1994). At the same time, in the capitalist or mixed economies of the majority of the states in the less developed world, these structural policies encouraged the focus of private capital in existing urban centres, thus "sustaining the process of concentration and the uneven territorial distribution of both capital and people" (De Mattos, 1994: 223).

Even in socialist countries such as China and Viet Nam where policies existed, attempts had been made to prevent migration from rural to urban areas; there is much debate on their success. Thus K. W. Chan's arguments for the need to economize on urbanization costs as a major element of China's determination to keep its population in rural areas in the period between 1953 and 1976 need to be modified by an understanding of the continuing concentration of the most productive economic activity in the more highly urbanized coastal zones (see Chan, 1992, 1994). In addition, this interpretation takes little account of ongoing rural–urban linkages, particularly in the extended metropolitan regions of Hong Kong, Guangzhou, the Sichuan Plain, Beijing–Tianjin, and Shenyang–Dalian (Tang, 1993). In a similar vein, Thrift and Forbes' (1986) paper on urbanization in Viet Nam between 1976 and 1986 argues for the success of containment policies of rural–urban migration. But, as Di Gregorio's (1994) probing study of the recycling of the refuse of Hanoi points out, many of the by-products of Hanoi's urban life, such as bicycle parts and organic waste, were collected by rural villagers from distances of up to 50 km away from the city. These materials were then recycled in various ways to aid the rural production process. Similar examples are used by Whitney (1991).

Indeed, the emphasis upon the persistence of rural–urban linkages in these socialist economies during periods of very active "rural containment" goes a long way to explain why the rural–urban nexus becomes so easily activated once these policies have been revoked, as in China after 1976 and Viet Nam after 1986. In China, numerous case-studies of economic activity in regions such as Guangdong (Lin, 1998), Jiangsu (Ho, 1994), the Shanghai region (Marton, 1998), and Liaoning province (Wang, 1998) show the manner in which rural–urban linkages are crucial to the resurgence of economic growth that has been associated with the transition to market economies.[4]

In the mixed and market economies of much of the developed world, structural policies encouraged continuing rural–urban migration and urbanization. In a few countries such as Malaysia, where a multiracial society was unevenly spatially distributed between rural and urban areas, vigorous policies of rural development were responsible for containing the rural population for short periods (Kamal, 1981). But generally these policies did little to slow urbanization.

By the 1970s, a grave structural economic crisis began to manifest itself in both developed and developing countries, which led to falls in productivity, increased political instability, and a development crisis in much of the third world. The response was to adopt "structural adjustment policies" designed to reduce the welfare role of the state, give priority to market forces, and foster an open economy with strong linkages to the global economy and the international division of labour. This structural aspect has exhibited significant differences in the developing world (Gilbert, 1994b).

In Asia, some writers have argued, these policies were effectively implemented in countries such as Korea, Taiwan, Hong Kong, and Singapore in the 1960s and have continued in the 1980s in Malaysia and Thailand (Dicken, 1993). In all these countries the rural population has fallen dramatically and urbanization levels have increased rapidly. In Latin America, on the other hand, the crisis had a different and much more dangerous impact. Already highly urbanized (64 per cent in 1980), city growth began to slow as the GNP actually declined. Faced with a debt crisis, governments that had previously been able to finance the provision of some essential services could no longer afford to provide comprehensive services. Inflation was rampant, unemployment increased, and the proportion of urban poor and numbers living in squatter settlements grew rapidly. Gilbert, citing Iglesia, reports that, "based on conservative estimates, the percentage of poor people rose from 41 per cent in 1980 to 44 per cent in 1989 – that is 183 million inhabitants," with an estimated 104 million living in urban centres. While this development crisis particularly affected urban areas, rural poverty remained high at 61 per cent (Gilbert, 1994a: 169). Gilbert sees some basis for optimism for some countries in the 1990s as growth rates have begun to increase with greater integration into the world economy, but the entrenched problems of highly unequal income, sizeable urban poverty, and ineffective government management still remain.[5]

In Africa, still the world's most rapidly urbanizing region, the majority of countries have experienced a decline or virtual stagnation in per capita output. Per capita food production fell in two-thirds of the countries and the absolute value of manufacturing declined in one-third of the countries in the decade of the 1980s (Becker et al., 1994). This was a consequence of virtual economic collapse and led to stern measures involving drastic devaluation, the removal of tariff and non-tariff barriers, and policies of reduction in state expenditure. These policies fell particularly hard on urban centres, where unemployment increased and poverty grew substantially. In such a situation the high level of rural–urban interaction of sub-Saharan Africa was reinforced in the overall increase in poverty (Simon, 1992). Whereas some commentators felt the effect of structural adjustment might slow urbanization in Africa (see Becker et al., 1994: 4–5), the growing precariousness of the state and continuing political instability in many states appear to have accelerated the flows of "refugee" migration to urban areas.

Globalization and the urban system

The introduction of the theoretical ideas implicit in the new globalism has important implications for the emerging urban system and urban–rural relations. As De Mattos argues: "under the new theories of rural–urban dynamics and ideological principles established by the neoclassical approach, the free play of market forces is assumed to be a necessary condition for achieving a more balanced territorial distribution of productive activities and population" (De Mattos, 1994: 228). Thus, whereas in the early stages of this approach primacy and centralization will occur, they will eventually be reversed as per capita income rises, leading to a reduction in regional inequalities and a more balanced urban system.

However, it is not clear that this new approach to public administration, which uses instruments such as fiscal incentives and improved transport and technological infrastructure, with the emphasis on communication and information networks, will necessarily result in spatial patterns that reflect a more equal population distribution. Because the major responsibility for investment is focused on the private sector, these strategies have emphasized the territorial mobility of capital, which has led to both concentration (of financial services) and decentralization (of productive activity) within large urban agglomerations.

However superficial, statistical analyses of the growth of the largest cities in the three continental regions do not support the view that excessive concentration is occurring in the major urban centres. Thus Lattes reports that "according to United Nations' estimates the concentration of the Latin America urban population in the largest city of each country reached a maximum sometime during 1945–1955, declined until 1980 and has remained constant since then" (Lattes, 1994: 151). Nevertheless, the figure is quite high at 27.8 per cent. This has led some writers, such as Portes (1990) and Gilbert (1994a), to argue that the slowing of the growth of large urban centres will continue, with an increase in the population in intermediate centres.

As tables 17.3, 17.4, 17.5, and 17.6 show, Africa exhibits a much lower proportion of people living in large agglomerations, and this proportion decreased in the decades between 1970 and 1990. However, Becker et al. (1994) report that the proportion living in the largest city of each country actually increased in the decade between 1980 and 1990. In Asia, the analysis of the growth of large cities of 2 million or more indicates three broad patterns. First, the number and volume of people living in these large urban agglomerations are growing rapidly. Thus Asia increased its global share of city agglomeration population from 42.0 per cent to 46.5 per cent despite the fact that the average growth rate was well below that in Africa (4.0 per cent)

Table 17.3 **Number of cities with 2+ million population, by main regions, 1960–2000**

Region[a]	1960	1970	1980	1990	2000
World total	54	61	88	116	157
Asia	17	22	36	49	71
Oceania	1	2	2	2	2
Africa	1	2	6	9	18
Latin America	5	8	13	19	23
North America	8	11	12	16	18
USSR (former)	2	2	3	4	4
Europe	12	14	16	17	21

Source: United Nations (1991).

a. These divisions follow *World Urbanization Prospects 1990* regional divisions: Africa (North, East, West, South), Latin America (Caribbean, Central America, Southern), Europe (Eastern, Northern, Southern, Western), Oceania (Australia, New Zealand, Polynesia, Melanesia), and the USSR.

Table 17.4 **Urban agglomerations with 2+ million population in 1985: Average annual growth rate, 1970–1990 (%)**

Region	1970–1980	1980–1990	1970–1990
World total	2.3	2.2	2.3
Asia	2.8	2.8	2.8
Oceania	2.0	1.3	1.6
Africa	4.3	3.8	4.0
Latin America	3.7	3.1	3.4
North America	0.5	0.6	0.5
USSR (former)	1.8	1.6	1.7
Europe	0.5	0.4	1.0

Source: United Nations (1991).

and Latin America (3.4 per cent) at 2.8 per cent per annum. At the same time, the proportion of the urban population living in the large urban centres fell quite dramatically from 30 to 23 per cent in the period between 1970 and 1990. Once again, as in the case of Latin America, it is tempting to see this pattern as being the result of the decentralization of economic activities and population to other parts of the urban hierarchy. Although this is occurring to some extent, it still seems likely that much of the increase in urban population is in districts adjacent to the major cities.[6]

Table 17.5 **Distribution by region of populations living in agglomerations with 2+
million population in 1985, 1970–1990 (%)**

Region	1970	1980	1990
World total	100.0	100.0	100.0
Asia	42.0	44.1	46.5
Oceania	1.4	1.4	1.3
Africa	3.9	4.7	5.5
Latin America	14.8	16.9	18.4
North America	16.3	13.6	11.5
USSR (former)	4.1	3.9	3.7
Europe	17.5	15.4	13.1

Source: United Nations (1991).

Table 17.6 **Urban agglomerations with 2+ million population in 1985 as a percentage of each region's total urban population, 1970–1990**

Region	1970	1980	1990
World total	25.5	24.7	22.7
Asia	30.1	28.3	23.5
Oceania	36.6	37.4	36.8
Africa	16.2	15.4	13.6
Latin America	31.2	31.2	31.1
North America	33.7	31.7	30.1
USSR (former)	10.3	10.2	10.5
Europe	19.7	19.4	19.4

Source: United Nations (1991).

Thus, in all three continents it is possible to argue that these macro
trends do not necessarily signal a reversal of urban concentration. It
can be argued that deconcentration is actually occurring in a zone of
agglomeration much larger than that covered by the UN definitions
of urban agglomerations. The processes of residential outward movement (suburbanization) and industrial decentralization into new
industrial estates, the creation of transportation networks, the consumption needs of the élite and middle classes, and the deterioration
and changing land use of the inner cores of many of these regions all
precipitate the creation of what I have described as extended metropolitan regions (EMRs) (McGee, 1991).

The EMRs are extremely important locations for the generation of
national income. Although figures for the largest urban areas are not

easily accessible in Africa, Becker et al. (1994: 27, table 2.1) estimate "that although 29 per cent of Africa's population live in urban areas, some 42 to 62 per cent of the GDP is generated in urban areas." In Latin America, with a much higher proportion of population in urban areas, up to 80 per cent of the GDP is generated in urban areas. In Asia, up to 40 per cent of the GDP of some countries is produced in the large EMRs.

Several studies recently published in McGee and Robinson (1995) provide evidence on the increasing concentration of population in the large urban agglomerations. Thus the Bangkok Metropolitan Region increased its share of Thailand's urban population by 6 per cent in the decade from 1980 to 1990. Jabotabek has followed similar trends, as has the Manila metropolitan area. The proportion of the population engaged in non-agricultural occupations in these regions has also grown dramatically and they dominate their nation's industrial production.

Of course, these arguments of increasing mega-urbanization based upon Asian evidence are difficult to extend to the entire third world. Gilbert has mounted a vigorous argument that "polarization reversal" is occurring in many Latin American countries. "Certainly in Latin America while the major cities have continued to grow and large numbers of people have joined the urban population due to the twin forces of migration and natural increase, there are strong signs that the overall pace of metropolitan growth is slowing" (Gilbert, 1993: 726).

Gilbert's arguments, however, rest upon a conflation of "cities" and "metropolitan regions." In enumerating the factors behind the slowing of growth of the largest cities in Latin America, he suggests this is due to "the impact of employment dispersal within the metropolitan regions" (Gilbert, 1993: 727). But surely this is part of the process of metropolitanization, which he argues is slowing. Indeed, the decentralization of employment opportunities from the urban centre to the cities' peripheries is a major factor attracting continuing rural–urban migration. For instance, it is estimated that some 60 per cent of the workers in industries located within the Bangkok Metropolitan outer ring are predominantly from rural areas of Thailand (Greenberg, 1998).

Thus, although there may be variations between various regions of the third world, it can be argued that generally the effect of the growth of these central subsystems on rural–urban dynamics is profound. First, the expansion into surrounding regions of agriculture leads to rapid changes in these areas, with an increase in cash-cropping and a loss of agricultural land. Secondly, within the wider national context, it is the EMRs, where household income is sometimes four times as much as rural incomes, that create significant pull factors for migrants from agricultural households. Finally, the growth of these central urban subsystems acts as a major focus for the acceleration of rural–urban flows of people, money, and commodities. The city and the countryside are no longer separated but are increasingly integrated in a "web of transactions" that break down and reinforce long-established rural–urban relations. Elsewhere I have suggested that these patterns will vary dramatically between the three continents. In the next section I explore the operation of rural–urban dynamics in the case of Brazil, Nigeria, and Indonesia.

Contextualizing the urban transition: Rural–urban dynamics in Brazil, Nigeria, and Indonesia

If rural–urban dynamics need to be analysed carefully within the context of individual countries and regions, then it is valid to look at this issue in a cross-country perspective.[7]

Brazil, Nigeria, and Indonesia have several features in common. They are big countries with large populations (table 17.7) that make up the biggest territorial and demographic component of the geographical region in which they are located – Latin America, Africa, and South-East Asia, respectively. All three countries exhibit a highly uneven population distribution (fig. 17.1). In the case of Brazil, a high proportion of the population is resident in the south and south-east part of the country, which incorporates the two major urban regions of São Paulo and Rio de Janeiro. In Nigeria, almost two-thirds of the population is concentrated in the southern region (although there is a large concentration in the northern states); the central region is comparatively lightly populated. Indonesia exhibits a similar pattern,

Table 17.7 **Area and population of Brazil, Nigeria, and Indonesia, 1988**

	Brazil	Nigeria	Indonesia
Total population (million)	144.4	110.1	174.80
Total area ('000 km²)	8,512.0	924.0	1,905.0

Source: World Bank (1990).

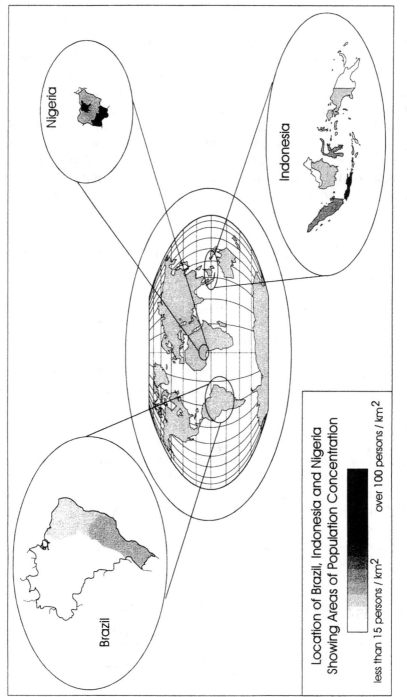

Nigeria

Indonesia

Brazil

Location of Brazil, Indonesia and Nigeria
Showing Areas of Population Concentration

less than 15 persons / km^2 over 100 persons / km^2

Fig. 17.1 **The location of Brazil, Indonesia, and Nigeria, showing areas of population concentration**

with over 60 per cent of its total population located on the island of Java, which occupies some 6 per cent of the land area.

The uneven distribution of population is further complicated by linguistic and ethnic differences. Thus, in Brazil, there are sharp differences between the Indian peoples, who inhabit frontier regions such as the Amazon, and the Mestizos and Brazilians of European origin, who inhabit the coastal regions. In Nigeria, in the north the Hausa people, together with other linguistic groups, are primarily Muslim. In the south, the two important groups are the Yoruba and Igbo. Indonesia also has marked ethnic and linguistic diversity, particularly between the dominant Javanese population and the many different linguistic and cultural groups of the Outer Islands.

Historically, these countries experienced a common pattern of incorporation into the world system, which involved the shaping of their economies in such a way as to make them major suppliers of raw materials for the developed countries. In the fifteenth to eighteenth centuries, Nigeria and Brazil were intimately linked by the involvement of the Portuguese in the slave trade. In the case of Brazil, coffee, sugar, and rubber were major products. Indonesia exported spices, tea, rubber, and kapok. Nigeria exported cacao, oil palm, and rubber. Minerals such as tin, gold, and gems were also important exports. This pattern of colonial development set up an agrarian structure characterized by a sharp division between the regions in which cash-cropping dominated and the frontier regions dominated by subsistence farming. In all countries the colonial organization of the agrarian economy involved the use of taxes to force subsistence producers into cash-crop production, the establishment of plantations for the extensive production of crops such as sugar cane, and the increasing penetration of capitalism into the rural areas, particularly those most extensively integrated into the colonial network.

Simultaneously with the development of agriculture, a system of colonial towns and ports grew up to act as the conduits for these products. Thus cities such as Rio de Janeiro, Lagos, and Jakarta emerged as dominant centres, although secondary cities such as Recife, Kano, and Medan were also important parts of the colonial system of administration and trade.

The political dismantling of this colonial relationship began much earlier in Latin America than in other parts of the world. Brazil became an independent state in 1822, whereas Nigeria and Indonesia became independent in 1960 and 1949, respectively. The longer history of Brazilian independence and the efforts of the various governments to establish an industrial base precipitated an earlier growth of industrialization and urbanization. By 1970, Brazil had reached a level of urbanization of 31 per cent (Gilbert, 1994a: 26) at a time when the urban population of Nigeria and Indonesia would have not exceeded 15 per cent. In Brazil these developments precipitated rapid rural–urban migration, and falling mortality rates associated with continuing high fertility accounted for high rates of natural increase in both rural and urban areas, which pushed the level of urbanization to 75 per cent by 1990. After independence, Nigeria's and Indonesia's urbanization rates also accelerated, but by 1990 they had reached only 35.2 per cent and 30.5 per cent, respectively.

In all three countries, however, the rural areas had begun to experience rapid changes. Table 17.8 shows the proportional contribution of various productive sectors to GDP, indicating the decreasing contribution of agriculture and the increasing importance of industry. In all three countries, the increase in income earned from the exports of fuels, minerals, and metals played a major role in the increase of the industrial contribution to GDP (notably petroleum in the case of Indonesia and Nigeria).

Reflecting Keynesian influences, all three governments attempted to redirect population from heavily populated parts of their country to frontier regions, adopting policies involving land development schemes, the opening up of the Amazonian region, and "transmigration" in Indonesia from Java to the Outer Provinces, as well as attempts to intervene in the urban system with the creation of new capitals. The most successful effort as regards the last policy has been in Brazil, where Brasilia, created in 1960, has now reached a population of 2.1 million. In Nigeria, the decision made in the 1970s, when the country was riding high on oil royalties, to create a new capital, Abuja, in the Central Plateau has still not been fully implemented.

In all three countries the existence of large territories with more regionally diverse economies has created a more developed urban system. Thus in Nigeria there are 9 cities over 1 million in size; Brazil has 14 and Indonesia has 7. This has the effect of reducing the proportion of the total population in the largest urban centre, but it has a limited effect on the increasing numbers of people located in the central urban subsystem of these countries. In Brazil, 45 per cent of the urban population now live in nine metropolitan regions (Fernandez, 1992: 230); in Nigeria some 50 per cent live in the nine largest metropolitan regions (Taylor, 1993: 6); and in Indonesia 30 per cent

Table 17.8 **The structure of production in Brazil, Nigeria, and Indonesia, 1963–1988 (% contribution to GDP)**

	Brazil		Nigeria		Indonesia	
	1963	1988	1963	1988	1963	1988
Agriculture	19	9	54	34	56	24
Industry	33	43	13	36	13	36
(Manufacturing)	(26)	(29)	(6)	(18)	(8)	(19)
Services	48	49	33	29	32	41
Size of GDP (US$ million)	5,850	29,370	19,450	323,610	3,840	85,220
Per capita GNP, 1990 (US$)		2,160		290		440

Source: World Bank (1990).

live in the four largest centres (National Urban Development Strategy, 1985: 60). In all these countries, this concentration of population has resulted in a series of major challenges. First, although formal employment opportunities have increased, they are insufficient to absorb all the growing populations and as a result the populations have been absorbed into the informal sector. There is also an ongoing crisis (aggravated in the 1980s) in the provision of housing and collective consumption services and facilities, while large areas of land lie unused in inner cities awaiting redevelopment. In Brazil alone, some 30 per cent of the metropolitan population live in slums and 30 per cent in squatter areas (illegal land divisions).

The rural–urban dynamics of each of these states have to be set against this background of a growing concentration of urban living, structural adjustment policies, and increasing globalization (Roberts, 1992) of the national economies. Given the diverse pattern that has been described it is possible to tease out only general features. First, it must be stressed that the central feature of the rural–urban dynamics in these countries is integrally linked to the historical experience of incorporation into the world system, the pattern of economic development, and the evolving agrarian structure of these three countries.

Perhaps the most useful way of encapsulating the common experience of rural–urban dynamics is to utilize Richard Morse's concept of Latin American urban development and apply it to the rural–urban dynamics of the three countries (Morse, 1962). In this essay, he argues that between 1500 and 1900 Latin American cities were characterized by a centrifugal stage in which their major function was to act as stages for the economic exploitation of the hinterland. One could certainly argue that this was true of cities such as Lagos and Ibadan in Nigeria, Jakarta in Indonesia, and Rio de Janiero in Brazil. The cities were the core of a colonial economy primarily serving an urban élite made up of colonial administrators, merchants, collaborating indigenous élites, and institutional groups such as the church and army. Within these three countries this relationship between urban centres and the surrounding countryside was subject to destructive regional variations. For example, in the Yoruba areas of Nigeria and in the intensive rice-growing areas of Java, in Indonesia, rural–urban linkages were much closer than in north-east Brazil, where sharp class distinctions separated the urban élite from the Negro rural workers.

As the countries became independent, so the cities have become more centripetal, involving increased rural–urban migration (beginning in the early twentieth century in Brazil and from the mid-twentieth century in Indonesia and Nigeria). As Roberts says of Latin America: "the cities grew relative to rural areas as industry became an important source of job opportunities. Economic modernization went hand in hand with political centralization and pro-urban development policies leading to a rapid expansion of urban infrastructure and urban based state bureaucracy" (Roberts, 1992: 52). Much the same can be said of Indonesia and Nigeria.

This process was associated with significant changes in the agrarian structures of all three countries, which fuelled this movement. The reasons are not identical in the three countries. In Nigeria and Brazil, as "peasant" agriculture has stagnated and the numbers in poverty have grown, the push factors have been of major importance. In Indonesia, particularly in Java, the "green revolution" has led to greatly increased productivity but also encouraged labour displacement. In all countries the proportion living in rural areas engaged in wage-earning activities has increased, whether in agricultural labour or in non-agricultural activities. In Indonesia (McGee, 1994a) and Nigeria, these populations are highly mobile, engaging in a form of circulatory migration between village and town.

This mobility is further enhanced by increased access because of improved transportation and the growing demand for urban-produced consumption goods that is created by the networks of communication such as television. In such a situation, the distinction between rural and urban becomes blurred as a network of mobile relationships and

490

flows in established income earned in urban areas is used to subsidize rural households, while food produced in rural areas is taken to urban households.

Thus, despite the significant differences between these three countries, they all share a process in which rural–urban differences are being reduced. In the final section, I discuss the policy implications of these conclusions.

Developing policies for the "new" rural–urban dynamics of the developing world

The realization that the rural–urban distinction is of only limited validity and needs to be replaced by the idea of networks of transactions is fundamental. This has important implications for policy-making. It is important to stress that, in suggesting policy initiatives, one has to see them within the prevailing neoclassical paradigm, which was discussed above. Thus there is no doubt that government policies will affect these networks of transactions between cities and countryside.

In general, the findings of this paper support the view that the processes of economic growth released by the neoclassical policy paradigm encourage the continuing growth of central urban subsystems. Although there is evidence that the immediate impact of structural adjustment policies may slow down growth (Becker et al., 1994: 226; Gilbert, 1993: 729–730), it is not conclusively shown that this will be a persistent trend.

Indeed, the growing investment in the components of the transaction environment (roads, telecommunications, etc.) greatly increases linkages between the city and the countryside and the importance of the central urban subsystems. Although many governments in the developing world are still supporting the agricultural sector by subsidized prices for agricultural products, structural adjustment policies advocate the removal of agricultural subsidies; the consequent reduction in agricultural income further accelerates rural labour dislocation.

The "agricultural question" therefore remains a central issue for all policy-making in developing countries, particularly as the urban transformation occurs. Given the estimates of the persistence of rural populations in Africa and Asia as the urban transition proceeds, governments will have to be particularly innovative to prevent a widening income and welfare gap between the two sectors. In Latin

America, the declining rural population is still almost two-thirds in poverty, and poverty alleviation measures will be needed.

In the present *laissez-faire* mood of development practice it seems that the rural–urban divide will continue to collapse. The policy intervention will have to be directed at alleviating the worst aspects of this transition: reducing poverty, improving deteriorating urban environments, and trying to facilitate the movement of people into urban areas with the least social and economic problems.

On the face of it, however, the most intractable problem of the urban transition is centred on the issue of creating viable employment opportunities. In all three regions, there is a continuing problem of absorption of labour into productive employment. As is well known, this leads not to high rates of unemployment but to underutilization of labour in generally less productive sectors of service and household industry. Thus, in Latin America, whereas in the 1970s underemployment was concentrated in the agricultural sector, by the early 1980s it had declined in that sector but grown dramatically in urban-based activities. In Asia, however (with the exception of the newly industrialized countries), the major absorption of labour into non-agricultural activities has been in areas defined as rural. The dominance of China, India, and Indonesia in this trend is significant but it can be asserted that a very high proportion of this absorption is occurring in the large extended metropolitan regions (McGee, 1994b). In Africa, the growth of employment in the non-agricultural sector of urban and rural areas has been accelerated by the decline of employment in the formal sector in both government and the private sector in the 1980s (Becker et al., 1994: 135–179).

Throughout the developing world, then, the problem of creating viable employment still remains. Given the increasing numbers of the potential labour force, it is unlikely that all employment creation will occur only in areas defined as urban. Instead, it will be spread over large regions that are functionally integrated with a central urban subsystem.

Thus, there is a need to think of new paradigms that break away from the rural–urban dichotomy. The collapse of time and space and the blurring of the boundaries between rural and urban point to a new focus on the flows of people, commodities, and capital through space that is neither urban nor rural, but often a mixture of both. As I have argued, in developing countries it is in the large extended metropolitan regions surrounding the large city cores that this mixture is most intense. These changing conditions throw up major policy challenges for the management and development of population policy and the provision of infrastructure and welfare. These will be much more successful if they are formulated within the paradigms of rural–urban dynamics rather than the rural–urban dichotomy.

Notes

1. In this paper the term "more and less developed regions" is used interchangeably with "developed and developing regions." According to current United Nations practices, the less developed regions include Africa, all of Asia (with the exception of Japan), Latin America and the Caribbean, and Oceania (excluding Australia and New Zealand). The more developed regions include Canada, Australia, Japan, New Zealand, the United States, the former USSR, and all of Europe.
2. Some of these high rates may be due to statistical definitions, but the most careful analysis by the French demographer Jean Marie Cour using a consistent definition of urban residence suggests that the UN and World Bank statistics may be underestimates (cited in Becker et al., 1994: 33).
3. For a popular account of this process, see Barnet and Cavanagh (1994).
4. For a much fuller treatment of these issues on China and Viet Nam, see Yeung and Hu (1992), Chan (1994), and McGee (1995).
5. Two excellent analyses of urbanization and the structural crisis in Latin America are Gilbert (1990a,b) and Portes (1990).
6. This is well illustrated in Firman's analysis of the spatial patterns of urbanization in Indonesia (Firman, 1993).
7. This section relies heavily on Morse (1962) and Roberts (1978) for Brazil, Metz (1992) for Nigeria, and National Urban Development Strategy (1985) for Indonesia.

References

Barnet, Richard J. and John Cavanagh (1994), *Global Dreams. Imperial Corporations and the New World Order*. New York: Simon & Schuster.

Becker, Charles M., Andrew M. Hamer, and Andrew R. Morrison (1994), *Beyond Urban Bias in Africa. Urbanization in an Era of Structural Adjustment*. London: Heinemann.

Castells, Manuel (1989), *The Informational City. Information Technology, Economic Restructuring and the Urban–Regional Process*. Oxford: Basil Blackwell.

Chan, Kam Wing (1992), "Economic Growth Strategy and Urbanization Policies in China, 1949–82." *International Journal of Urban and Regional Research* 16: 275–305.

———— (1994), *Cities with Invisible Walls: Reinterpreting Urbanization in Post 1949 China*. Hong Kong: Oxford University Press.

De Mattos, Carlos Antonio (1994), "The Moderate Efficiency of Population Distribution Policies in Developing Countries." In: *Population Distribution and Migration. Proceedings of the UN Expert Meeting on Population Distribution and Migration*. New York: UN Population Division, pp. 220–240.

Di Gregorio, Michael (1994), "Urban Harvest: Recycling as a Peasant Industry in North Vietnam." East West Centre Occasional Papers, Environmental Series, No. 17. Honolulu: East West Centre.

Dick, Howard and Peter J. Rimmer (1993), "The Trans-Pacific Economy. A Network Approach to Spatial Structure." *Asian Geographer* 12(1&2): 5–18.

Dicken, Peter (1993), "The Growth Economies of Pacific Asia in their Changing Global Context." In: C. Dixon and D. Drakakis-Smith (eds.), *Economic and Social Development in Pacific Asia*. London: Routledge, pp. 22–42.

Fernandes, Edesio (1992), "Juridico-politico Aspects of Metropolitan Administration in Brazil." *Third World Planning Review* 14(3): 227–244.

Firman, Tommy (1993), "The Spatial Pattern of Urban Population in Java 1980–1990." *Bulletin of Indonesian Economic Studies* 28(2): 95–100.

Gilbert, A. G. (1990a), *Latin America*. London: Routledge.

——— (1990b), "Urbanization on the Periphery: Reflections on the Changing Dynamics of Housing and Employment in Latin American Cities." In: D. Drakakis-Smith (ed.), *Economic Growth and Urbanization in Developing Areas*. London: Routledge, pp. 73–124.

——— (1993), "Third World Cities: The Changing National Settlement System." *Urban Studies* 30(415): 721–740.

——— (1994a), *The Latin American City*. London: Latin American Bureau.

——— (1994b), "Third World Cities: Poverty, Employment, Gender Roles and the Environment during a Time of Restructuring." *Urban Studies* 31(415): 605–633.

Greenberg, Charles (1998), "Capital Accumulation and Its Impact on Bangkok's Outer City." In: T. G. McGee and R. Casinader (eds.), *Deconstructing Desakota: Analyzing Processes of Peripheral Urbanization in Asia*. Vancouver: University of British Colombia, Institute of Asian Research (in press).

Ho, Samuel P. S. (1994), *Rural China in Transition*. Oxford: Clarendon Press.

Kamal, Salih (1981), "Rural–Urban Transformation and Regional Underdevelopment in Malaysia." In: Fu-chen Lo (ed.), *Rural–Urban Relations and Regional Development*. Tokyo: Maruzen Asia, pp. 109–145.

Lattes, Alfred (1994), "Population Distribution in Latin America. Is There a Trend towards Population Deconcentration?" In: *Population Distribution and Migration. Proceedings of the UN Expert Meeting on Population Distribution and Migration*. New York: UN Population Division, pp. 139–167.

Lin, George (1998), "Exploring the Transactional Economy of the Desakota: Spatial Reorganization in a Suburban County of Zhujiang Delta." In: T. G. McGee and R. Casinader (eds.), *Deconstructing Desakota: Analyzing Processes of Peripheral Urbanization in Asia*. Vancouver: University of British Columbia, Institute of Asian Research (in press).

McGee, T. G. (1971), *The Urbanization Process in the Third World. Explorations in Search of a Theory*. London: G. Bell & Sons.

——— (1972), "Rural–Urban Migration in a Plural Society. A Case Study of Malays in West Malaysia." In: D. J. Dwyer (ed.), *The City as a Centre of Change in Asia*. Hong Kong: University of Hong Kong.

——— (1975), "Malay Migration to Kuala Lumpur City. Individual Adaptation to the City." In: B. M. du Toit and H. Safa (eds.), *Migration, Models and Adaptive Strategies*. The Hague: Mouton, pp. 143–178.

——— (1979), "Labour Mobility in Fragmented Labour Markets, Rural–Urban Linkages and Regional Development in Asia." United Nations Centre for Regional Development Working Paper, No. 79, pp. 1–27.

—— (1982a), "Labour Mobility in Fragmented Labour Markets. The Role of Circulatory Migration in Rural–Urban Relations in Asia." In: H. Safa (ed.), *Towards a Political Economy of Urbanization in Third World Countries*. Delhi: Oxford University Press, p. 47–66.

—— (1982b), "Labour Markets, Urban Systems and the Urbanization Process in Southeast Asia." Paper of the East–West Population Institute, No. 81. Honolulu: East West Centre, pp. 1–28.

—— (1991), "The Emergence of Desakota Regions in Asia: Expanding a Hypothesis." In: N. Ginsburg et al. (eds.), *The Extended Metropolis: Settlement Transition in Asia*. Honolulu: University of Hawaii Press, pp. 3–25.

—— (1994a), "The Future of Urbanization in Developing Countries. The Case of Indonesia." *Third World Planning Review* 16(1): iii–xii.

—— (1994b), "Labour Force Change and Mobility in Extended Metropolitan Regions of Asia." In: Roland Fuchs et al. (eds.), *Mega City Growth and the Future*. Tokyo: United Nations University Press, pp. 62–102.

—— (1995), "The Urban Future of Vietnam." *Third World Planning Review* 17(3): 253–277.

McGee, T. G. and Ira M. Robinson (eds.) (1995), *The Mega-Urban Regions of Southeast Asia*. Vancouver: University of British Columbia Press.

Marton, Andrew (1998), "The Local versus the Regional in the Desakota: The Case of Kinshan County Jiangsu, People's Republic of China." In: T. G. McGee and R. Casinader (eds.), *Deconstructing Desakota: Analyzing Processes of Peripheral Urbanization in Asia*. Vancouver: University of British Columbia, Institute of Asian Research (in press).

Metz, Helen Chapin (ed.) (1992), *Nigeria: A Country Study*. Washington, D.C.: Library of Congress.

Morse, R. M. (1962), "Latin American Cities: Aspects of Function and Structure." *Comparative Studies in Society and History* 4(4): 473–493.

National Urban Development Strategy (1985), *Final Report*. Jakarta: Directorate of City and Regional Planning.

Portes, A. (1990), "Latin American Urbanization during the Years of Crisis." *Latin American Research Review* 25: 7–44.

Roberts, B. (1978), *Cities of Peasants*. London: Edward Arnold.

—— (1992), "Transitional Cities." In: Richard M. Morse and Jorge E. Harcloy (eds.), *Rethinking the Latin American City*. Washington, D.C.: The Woodrow Wilson Center Press, pp. 50–65.

Simon, David (1992), *Cities, Capital and Development. African Cities in the World Economy*. London: Belhaven Press.

Tang, Wing-shing (1993), *A Critical Review of the English Literature on Chinese Urbanization*. Hong Kong: Hong Kong Institute of Asia-Pacific Studies, The Chinese University of Hong Kong.

Taylor, Robert W. (1993), *Urban Development in Nigeria. Planning, Housing and Land Policy*. Aldershot: Avebury.

Thrift, Nigel and Dean Forbes (1986), *The Price of War Urbanization in Vietnam, 1954–85*. London: Allen & Unwin.

United Nations (1991), *World Urbanization Prospects 1990*. New York: UNO Sales No. F 91 XIII 11.

Wang, Yao-Lin (1998), "Invisible Urbanization in China: Village Case Studies in the Shenyang-Dahlian Region." In: T. G. McGee and R. Casinader (eds.), *Deconstructing Desakota: Analyzing Processes of Peripheral Urbanization in Asia*. Vancouver: University of British Columbia, Institute of Asian Research (in press).

Whitney, J. B. R. (1991), "The Waste Economy and the Dispersed Metropolis in China." In: N. Ginsburg et al. (eds.), *The Extended Metropolis: Settlement Transition in Asia*. Honolulu: University of Hawaii Press, pp. 177–192.

World Bank (1990), *World Development Report 1990*. New York: Oxford University Press.

Yeung, Yue-man and Hu Xu-wei (eds.) (1992), *China's Coastal Cities: Catalysts for Modernization*. Honolulu: University of Hawaii Press.

Zelinsky, Wilber (1971), "The Hypothesis of the Mobility Transition." *Geographical Review* 61: 219–249.

18

Feeding the world's cities

Hal Kane

Introduction

The current rapid growth of the world's cities leaves the international community with the challenge of feeding far larger numbers of urban dwellers than ever before. This challenge is made far more difficult by the fact that growing cities are consuming cropland at a rapid pace as they pave over it to build new roads, new residential areas, and new factories. Not only will these cities need large increases in their food supply, but their growth will make it more difficult to maintain that food supply.

These trends are of paramount importance to the well-being of cities. Not only will urban dwellers need adequate supplies of food, they will also need that food at low cost, especially since cities contain large segments of the world's poor. Rising food prices due to scarcities of cropland converted to urban use, and due to rising demand, would lower the quality of life in urban areas, would pose political problems, and might destabilize cities.

Changes in East Asian economies have become particularly important to this subject. There, industrialization and urbanization have already taken large areas of cropland out of production, and turned several nations from grain exporters to massive grain importers.

497

These countries include Japan, South Korea, and Taiwan. Now other countries are following. Most notably, China has suddenly gone from being essentially self-sufficient in grain to being an importer for the first time in history.

These trends tie together every city with the cities of faraway continents; they have major implications for the whole world. For example, the need of 1.2 billion people in China to import grain has the potential to raise prices in the world grain markets because all countries bid together in those markets. All countries would be affected. Thus, the poorer segments of the world's cities, even in wealthy countries, may have their food prospects affected by the loss of grainland and the rise in food consumption in China's booming cities and special economic zones.

Urbanization makes the production of food for growing populations difficult in other ways as well. As cities pull rural workers from the countryside by enticing them with higher wages or diverse opportunities, farmland is left uncultivated in many countries, reducing production and sometimes leaving the land in disarray. In addition, tastes among the prosperous in cities for diets rich in meat demand large amounts of grain as feed for cattle, and take a toll on the land as those cattle compact the soil during grazing.

These issues can be addressed, however. Additional research into the kinds of agriculture needed in some of the poorer parts of the world, directed at grain, the most important food for the poor, would supply additional food in the future. Policies to conserve farm soils and irrigation water will help. And population policies will affect the overall population growth of many countries and the migrations under way today in many populations. Those subjects might not at first seem relevant to the topic of urbanization, but in fact they are crucial – even if much of their implementation must take place in rural areas.

The limits of the plough

From the beginning of agriculture in the Middle East until the mid-twentieth century, cropland area expanded as agriculture spread from valley to valley and then from continent to continent. Throughout this period, growth in food output came largely from expanding the cultivated area. This era ended in the mid-twentieth century as the frontiers of agricultural settlement disappeared. From then until 1981, there were some modest gains in harvested area, but four-fifths of the growth in output came from raising land productivity. The method of expanding food output had shifted dramatically almost overnight. In 1981, grainland area peaked at 735 million hectares (ha). Then it began to shrink, dropping to 695 million ha in 1993 (USDA/ERS, 1993a). Thus the history of agricultural yields divides neatly into three periods: a time of expanding area until around the mid-twentieth century, a time of mostly expanding yields with some modest growth in area until 1981, and a time when all additional output has come from raising land productivity (USDA/ERS, 1992).

There are still occasional increases in cropland area here and there. Brazil, for example, more than doubled its area in grain between 1960 and 1980. Since then, however, its grainland has not expanded significantly. A few countries are expanding grain-harvested area by multiple cropping – combining, for example, winter wheat with a summer rice crop. On balance, however, these gains are offset by losses as cropland is converted to non-farm uses or abandoned because of severe degradation (USDA/ERS, 1993a).

Worldwide, gains in cropland area from year to year are the result of various cropland expansion initiatives, including the conversion of forest, new irrigation projects that permit the farming of land otherwise too dry to farm, and drainage of wetlands. Forest conversion is concentrated in such places as the Outer Islands of Indonesia (part of a long-term resettlement programme of people from densely populated Java) and the Amazon regions of Brazil and other Latin American countries. Some of these gains are illusory, because this land will often sustain cultivation for only a few years before losing its natural fertility.

Some of the most important gains have come from the adoption of high-yielding, early-maturing wheats and rices, which spurred the spread of multiple cropping. Traditional geography texts contained agricultural maps with a line drawn across both India and China, separating the wheat- and rice-growing regions. Modern maps do not make that distinction: wheat has extended into rice-growing areas and vice versa, with rice being grown in the summer and wheat in the winter. Earlier-maturing varieties of both grains, combined with the spread of irrigation, which facilitated dry-season farming, helped increase double-cropping. For example, of the 130 million ha of rice land in Asia, 12 million ha now also produce a winter wheat crop (Brown and Young, 1990).

Between 1972 and 1981, farmers responded to sustained high prices by expanding the world grain area from 664 million to 735 million ha, a gain of nearly 11 per cent (USDA/ERS, 1993a; USDA, 1993). Much of this increase came in the former Soviet Union and the United States on land that, unfortunately, was highly erodible and not capable of sustaining cultivation. After peaking at 123 million ha in 1977, the Soviet Union's grain-harvested area has declined almost every year, dropping to 99 million ha in 1993 as fast-eroding land was either planted to soil-stabilizing forage crops, fallowed, or abandoned (USDA/ERS, 1993c). In the United States, some 14 million ha of the most erodible cropland were converted to grass or trees between 1985 and 1992 under the Conservation Reserve Program (USDA/ERS/RTD, 1993). In an emergency, some of this land could be farmed in rotation with forage crops or by using other appropriate conservation tillage practices.

All grainland held out under commodity supply management programmes in the United States was released for production in 1994. European countries may be holding out up to 3 million ha.[1] But even bringing all this land back would expand the world grain area by only 1.6 per cent, not half enough to get it back to the historical high reached in 1981. The continuing abandonment of severely eroded land and the conversion of cropland to non-farm uses mean that net gains in the world's cropland area will not come easily (USDA/ERS/RTD, 1993).

Land will also be lost from soil erosion, much of it in Africa. Waterlogging and salinity will take a toll in the Asian republics around the Aral Sea and in the Middle East, India, China, and the south-western United States.

Some of the world's cropland is plagued by political problems rather than agronomic ones. These areas might be brought into production sometime in the future. Wars, ethnic conflicts, and discrimination that prevent farmers from working the land are no less real than problems of soil fertility or lack of water. Southern Sudan is one example of a food-deficit region that could feed itself if given the opportunity. But it has suffered from almost unbroken war in recent years.

With 3.6 billion people slated to be added to world population between 1990 and 2030, the cropland area per person will continue to shrink steadily. From 1950 to 1990, it fell from 0.23 ha per person to 0.13 ha. If the total grainland area does not change, by 2030 it will drop to 0.08 ha per person (US Bureau of the Census, cited in Urban and Nightingale, 1993; USDA/ERS, 1993a).

Urbanization, industrialization, and loss of farmland

The shifting of land to non-farm uses is particularly pronounced in China, which is losing nearly 1 million ha (or 1 per cent) of its cropland a year. One result of the prosperity since economic reforms were launched in 1978 is that literally millions of villagers are either expanding their houses or building new ones. And an average annual industrial growth rate of more than 12 per cent since 1980 means the construction of thousands of new factories. Sales of cars and trucks, totalling 1.2 million in 1992 and projected at close to 3 million by the end of the 1990s, will chew up cropland for roads and parking lots. Since most of China's nearly 1.2 billion people are concentrated in its rich farming regions, new homes and factories are of necessity often built on cropland. This loss, combined with a shift to more profitable crops, has reduced the grain-harvested area in China by roughly one-tenth from the peak in 1976 (USDA/ERS, 1992, 1993a; United Nations, 1991; Onishi, 1993; PRB, 1993).

Urban sprawl is also claiming cropland. In Thailand, the expansion of Bangkok, driven by both prosperity and population growth, has claimed an average of 3,200 ha each year during the past decade. Similarly, in Egypt, new building invariably comes at the expense of cropland, since the nation's 58 million people live on the thin ribbon of irrigated cropland along the Nile River (Dowall, 1991).

The requirements of some 90 million additional people each year for housing, schools, and transportation reduce the area available for crops worldwide.[2] Land claimed by expanding transportation systems is particularly extensive. For example, the growth in the world automobile fleet means cropland is paved over for streets, highways, and parking lots. Some $200\,\text{ft}^2$ is needed merely to park an automobile. If a car is to be widely used, parking spaces must be available in many different places – near residences, workplaces, shops, and recreation areas. Assuming a minimum of two parking spaces per car, the land required to park 100 cars could easily produce 1 tonne of grain per year, enough to feed five people.[3] Observing the difficulty in reversing this process, a US government official once remarked, "Asphalt is the land's last crop" (Cutler, 1980).

Cropland is also being lost indirectly through the growing diversion of irrigation water to cities in desert areas. In Arizona, for example, Tucson and Phoenix have purchased the irrigation rights to large areas of cropland, letting it go back to desert. Even this may be dwarfed by the diversion of irrigation water to cities in northern China (Checchio, 1988; Postel, 1992).

The loss of cropland can be seen clearly in East Asia, particularly in countries such as Japan, South Korea, and Taiwan that were densely populated before industrialization began. In Japan, the loss was already under way by 1960, when the nation harvested 5 million ha of grain. That figure now stands just above 2.5 million ha. South Korea's grain area grew during the early 1960s to more than 2.3 million ha, and then fell steadily, dropping to just 1.3 million ha in 1993. Taiwan experienced a similar drop, from 850,000 ha in 1975 to only 500,000 today (USDA/ERS, 1993a).

As factories, roads, and houses eat up land, and as relatively high wages in manufacturing industries pull labour away from farms, these trends in falling grainland area can be expected to continue. Even countries such as Thailand that have had less success than South Korea and Taiwan at industrialization are seeing their grainland areas slip. Thailand's grew steadily until 1985, but it has since shrunk by more than 10 per cent. India, which is projected to pass China to become the world's most populated nation near the middle of the twenty-first century, has watched its grainland area shrink from a peak of 107 million ha in 1982 to 102 million in 1993 (USDA/ERS, 1993a).

Future cropland losses are likely to be concentrated in Asia, with gains in Latin America. Losses will likely be heavy in Asia simply because that is where most of the population growth and industrialization is expected to occur. Gains will come mostly in Latin America because that is the region where there are extensive areas of land – albeit marginal – to be brought under production. Unfortunately, the cropland lost in Asia will be highly productive for the most part, whereas that gained in Latin America will be marginal. The largest single area of cropland loss will likely be in southern China, where much of the land is now being used to double-crop rice. In effect, land producing 8 tonnes of milled rice per ha annually will be replaced with marginal land in Brazil that will produce at most 3 tonnes of corn per ha (USDA/ERS, 1993a).

Grainland projections

Projecting future grainland availability per person in the more populous countries to 2030 is revealing (see table 18.1). In 1990, the

Table 18.1   **Grain-harvested area per person, by country, 1950 and 1990, with projections to 2030 (ha)**

Country	1950	1990	2030[a]
China	0.17	0.08	0.06
United States	0.53	0.26	0.22
India	0.22	0.12	0.07
Former USSR	0.57	0.35	0.27
Bangladesh	0.20	0.10	0.05
Pakistan	0.18	0.10	0.04
Indonesia	0.07	0.07	0.04
Iran	0.21	0.17	0.06
Egypt	0.08	0.04	0.02
Ethiopia & Eritrea	0.24	0.07	0.02
Nigeria	0.23	0.09	0.03
Brazil	0.13	0.14	0.07
Mexico	0.20	0.11	0.06

Source: Brown and Kane (1994).

a. Assumes no change in total grain-harvested area from 1990 to 2030; reductions in area per person due entirely to population growth.

smallest areas of grainland per person were in Egypt, with 0.04 ha per person, and in Indonesia and Ethiopia, each with 0.07 ha. Even though all of Egypt's grainland is irrigated, Egypt imports half its grain supply. Indonesia, with a large proportion of irrigated land, is nearly self-sufficient. Ethiopia, with the same land area per person, almost all of it rainfed, is struggling to keep its people alive, even with an annual food aid allotment of 1 million tonnes of grain (US Bureau of the Census, cited in Urban and Nightingale, 1993).

In 2030, if the countries are able to maintain the same total grainland area, only one of the developing countries listed in table 18.1 will have as much as 0.07 ha per person. All the others will have less, with Egypt and Ethiopia dropping to 0.02 ha. For Egypt, this will undoubtedly translate into even greater dependence on imports. For Ethiopia, a grainland area per person of 0.02 ha – less than a third of that today – can only be described as catastrophic. The same can be said for Nigeria, with only 0.03 ha per person.

This reduction in cropland per person argues strongly for individual country assessments of population carrying capacity in growing cities and in the countryside. Faced with such a threatening shrinkage of grainland, people living in these countries may opt to shift much more quickly to smaller families, and will want to ensure that the rural labour force is adequate and that urban growth does not consume any more land than necessary.

The fertilizer fall-off

When German chemist Justus von Liebig demonstrated in 1847 that all the nutrients that plants removed from the soil could be returned in mineral form, he set the stage for an explosion in world food production a century later. At the time of his discovery, the frontiers of agricultural settlement were still being pushed back. The US Homestead Act, designed to encourage settlement of the West, was still to come. With many opportunities to expand the cultivated area, there was little pressure to increase soil fertility and raise land productivity ("Justus von Liebig," 1976).

Several trends converged a century later to launch the steep climb in world fertilizer use. By mid-century, the frontiers had largely disappeared, and, almost overnight, population growth shifted from low gear to high. Faced with record growth in world food demand and little new land to plough, farmers responded by pouring on fertilizer to raise land productivity, boosting their grain yields from 1.1 tonnes to 2.4 tonnes per ha within four decades (USDA/ERS, 1993b). Thus, fertilizer has been at the centre of advances in world food output during the past four decades. In a sense, other technologies have been designed to facilitate its use. Irrigation, for example, permits the heavy use of fertilizer, resulting in high yields. Similarly, the new varieties have high yields precisely because they are much more responsive to fertilizer than traditional ones are.

The trend in world fertilizer use since mid-century divides into three distinct eras. From 1950 to 1984, annual use climbed from 14 million tonnes to 126 million tonnes, expanding ninefold or nearly 7 per cent a year – one of the more predictable global economic trends. From 1984 to 1989, growth continued, climbing to 146 million tonnes, but at a much slower pace – roughly 3 per cent a year. Then from 1989 until 1993, fertilizer use dropped each year, falling back to 120 million tonnes in 1993.[4]

The new trend in fertilizer use has two components. One is agronomic: the declining response of grain yields to additional fertilizer at higher levels of use (Chapman and Barker, 1987; USDA, 1991; IFA, 1993). The second is economic, specifically the decision by governments in major food-producing countries to reduce or eliminate fertilizer subsidies. The drop in the agronomic response to additional fertilizer slowed the rise in use in the late 1980s, bringing it to a near standstill. But the actual decline in use since 1989 is largely the result of reducing subsidies in key food-producing countries such as the former Soviet Union, India, and, most recently, China.

As grainland area per person has shrunk since mid-century, fertilizer use per person climbed from 6 kg to the historical high reached in 1989 of 28 kg per person. As long as production could be expanded by substituting fertilizer for land, farmers could easily stay ahead of population. But this period has ended, at least for now. The overriding dilemma facing humanity today is how to maintain rapid growth in grain production now that the use of additional fertilizer is having little effect on production where yields are high.

As more and more countries turn to imported grain, the nutrient cycle is disrupted. The United States, which exported close to 100 million tonnes of grain a year during the 1980s, suffered a heavy loss of soil nutrients. The nutrients in the wheat from Kansas and in the corn from Iowa were ending up in the sewage discharges of St. Petersburg, Cairo, Lagos, Caracas, and Tokyo. In order to maintain soil fertility, there was no alternative but to replace the lost nutrients with mineral sources (USDA/ERS, 1992). One consequence of these trends was a steady increase in the intensity of fertilizer use throughout the world. In 1950, fertilizer use per ha of grainland totalled some 24 kg. When it peaked in 1989, it was 211 kg.

The formula of using more fertilizer to raise land productivity was phenomenally successful in the period 1950–1984, when fertilizer use climbed to a new high nearly every year. During this time, each additional tonne of fertilizer applied boosted grain output 9 tonnes. (see table 18.2) (USDA/ERS, 1992, 1993a).

But 1984 was the last year in which a large increase in fertilizer use led to a comparable gain in world grain output. During the next five years farmers continued to use more fertilizer, but their crops did not respond much. Each additional tonne of fertilizer raised grain output by less than 2 tonnes. By 1989, the United States, Western Europe, the former Soviet Union, and much of Eastern Asia, including Japan and China, had raised yields to a point where adding more fertilizer had little effect on production.

Given such a weak response, applying more fertilizer was clearly not a money-making proposition. Farmers' reaction, both predictable and rational, was to use less. Between 1989 and 1993, they cut fertilizer use some 12 per cent, to roughly 186 kg per ha. Even excluding

Table 18.2 **World grain production and fertilizer use, 1950–1993 (million tonnes)**

Year	Grain production	Increment	Fertilizer use[a]	Increment	Incremental grain/fertilizer response[a] (ratio)
1950	631		14		
1984	1,649	1,018	126	112	9.1
1989	1,685	36	146	20	1.8
1993	1,682	−3	120	−20	–[b]

Source: Brown and Kane (1994).

a. Assumes that all fertilizer is used for grain; although this is obviously not the case, it provides a broad picture of the changing response.

b. Incremental ratio cannot be calculated because fertilizer use declined.

the precipitous drop in the former Soviet Union following economic reforms that removed subsidies, usage elsewhere dropped by 3 per cent. Fertilizer use per person has also reversed in recent years, dropping from the historical high of 28 kg in 1989 to less than 23 kg in 1993. This drop of 19 per cent helps explain why grain production per person has fallen in recent years.[5]

The decline in the crop response to fertilizer use was not a surprise to everyone. In a 1987 analysis of trends in Indonesia, Cornell economists Duane Chapman and Randy Barker (1987) noted that, "while one kilogram of fertilizer nutrients probably led to a yield increase of 10 kg of unmilled rice in 1972, this ratio has fallen to about one to five at present."

Unless someone can design new strains of wheat, corn, and rice that are much more responsive to fertilizers than are those now available, future gains in grain output from rising fertilizer use are likely to be modest. It is difficult to visualize any conditions evolving that will lead to rapid, sustained growth in fertilizer use similar to the one that occurred from 1950 to 1984. If large gains in food output cannot be achieved from using more fertilizer, where will they come from?

Struggling to raise yields

Countries that have doubled or tripled the productivity of their cropland since mid-century are the rule, not the exception. But with many of the world's farmers already using advanced yield-raising technologies, further gains in land productivity will not come easily.

Some sense of the future potential for doing so can be gleaned from looking at yield trends for wheat, rice, and corn in countries with the highest yields – for example, corn in the United States, wheat in the United Kingdom, and rice in Japan.

Yields of corn, a cereal widely used for feed and food, are highest in the United States, which accounts for 40 per cent of the world harvest. Data for US corn yields from 1866 to 1993 divide into three distinct periods. During the seven decades from the Civil War to World War II, yields were essentially unchanged, averaging about 1.6 tonnes per ha. From 1940 to 1985, the average yield jumped more than fourfold, reaching a phenomenal 7.4 tonnes per ha. But, in the eight years since then, the rise has slowed to a near standstill (Brown, 1963; USDA/ERS, 1992).

A similar situation exists for wheat in the United Kingdom, which has the highest yield of any major wheat-producing country. From 1884 until 1940, yields were remarkably stable. From 1940 until 1985, they more than tripled. But, since 1985, UK wheat yields have fluctuated around 7 tonnes per ha, showing little evidence of a continuing rapid rise (Brown, 1963; USDA/ERS, 1992, 1993a).

The rise in wheat yields in other parts of Europe with similar growing conditions is slowing as yields approach the UK level. This includes Germany and France, the latter a wheat exporter. The rise is also slowing in the United States and China, the world's two largest wheat producers. Since wheat in these two countries is grown in largely low-rainfall regions, the slow-down is occurring at yield levels one-third to one-half those in Western Europe. In China, the big jump in wheat production came immediately after the economic reforms in 1978, as yields climbed 81 per cent from 1977 to 1984. During the following nine years, however, they rose only 16 per cent (USDA/ERS, 1993a).

For rice, the key to understanding the yield potential is Japan, a country that has worked hard to raise its rice yields for more than a century. After an extended climb, the rise in Japan came to a halt in 1984. Since then, yields have actually fallen slightly. Yields in China, the world's largest rice producer, now approach Japan's and have been stable since 1990. In India, however, the second-ranking rice producer, the yield rise is slowing at a much lower level. In Japan and China, 99 and 93 per cent, respectively, of the rice is irrigated; in India, the figure is only 44 per cent, making it far more difficult to achieve high yields (*AsiaWeek*, 1993). The yield rise has also slowed in other major rice-producing countries, including Indonesia, Pakistan, and the Philippines (USDA/ERS, 1993a).

A similar trend exists in other high-technology rice-producing countries, such as South Korea, Taiwan, and Italy. In each case, once rice yields pass 4 tonnes per ha, they rise quite slowly or level off, suggesting that dramatically boosting rice yields above this level may require new technological advances (USDA/ERS, 1993a). Agricultural economists Duane Chapman and Randy Barker (1987) point out that "the genetic yield potential of rice has not increased significantly since the release of the high yielding varieties in 1966."

These recent slow-downs in the rise in grain yields are sobering. Between 1950 and 1984, the world grain yield per ha more than doubled, rising 118 per cent (2.3 per cent a year). But from 1984 to 1993, yields rose only 1 per cent a year. Since 1990, a year of exceptional growing conditions worldwide, grain yield per ha has actually declined slightly (USDA/ERS, 1993a).

This slow-down is a worldwide phenomenon afflicting industrial and developing countries alike, largely because all countries now draw on the same international pool of technology. Unfortunately, the slower yield increase raises questions about the earth's carrying capacity and, specifically, about the ability of the world's farmers to feed an ever-growing population.

The systematic application of science to agriculture has permitted a regular increase in yields for nearly two generations, making it difficult to imagine a situation in which yields will not continue their steady rise. None the less, a study published in 1993 observes that rice yields on experimental stations in Asia have been stagnant now for many years. In the absence of any new yield breakthroughs, a future of slowly rising or static yields may now be in prospect for many rice-growing countries (Pingali and Rosegrant, 1993).

Also of concern, many Asian rice farmers who have boosted output by continuously cropping rice with two or three harvests per year are experiencing a decline in yields. Scientists testing this cropping practice report that efforts to intensify agricultural production by continuously cropping rice with two or even three crops per year have actually led to a decline in yields on test plots in the Philippines, India, Bangladesh, and Thailand (Pingali and Rosegrant, 1993). At the International Rice Research Institute in the Philippines, plots producing three crops a year from 1963 to 1993 now show a decline in yields of more than 1 per cent annually. After 89 consecutive rice crops, with inputs held constant, yields are slowly declining. Apparently, the continuous flooding of the plots alters soil microbial activity, the physical structure of the soil, and its chemistry in ways that adversely affect yields. The only viable alternative is to replace one of the rice crops in the three-crop annual cycle with a crop that does not need to be flooded (Pingali and Rosegrant, 1993).

As early as 1986, Robert Herdt, senior economist at the Rockefeller Foundation, observed that the backlog of unused technology available to farmers appeared to be dwindling. He noted that, in some farming communities, crop yields on the best farms approached those on experimental plots (Herdt, 1986).

Rising grain yield per ha, like any other biological growth process in a finite environment, must eventually give way to physical constraints. Where farmers supply all the nutrients and water that advanced varieties can use, cereal yields may now be pushing against various physiological limits, such as nutrient absorption capacity or photosynthetic efficiency.

For those who remember biology class experiments that involved measuring the growth in a petri dish of an algae population with an unlimited food supply, this deceleration will not come as a surprise. With algae, it is the build-up of waste that eventually checks growth, bringing it to a halt. For grain with unlimited fertilizer supplies and abundant soil moisture, the plant's physiological limits will ultimately restrain the rise in yield. Grain production per ha is a process that relies on photosynthesis to convert solar energy into biochemical energy. Albeit modified by human intervention, it is – like all natural processes – subject to the limits of nature. These boundaries have been pushed back with great success during the past several decades, but that does not mean this can continue indefinitely.

More and more analysts are beginning to realize that the trend of steadily rising yields over recent decades may not continue in the future. Identifying the need for raising the genetic yield potential of a crop and being able to do so are not the same. In the United States, for example, corn yields have more than tripled since mid-century. Soybean yields, meanwhile, have gone up by roughly half, or only one-sixth as much as corn. Even though the crops are produced by the same farmers on the same land, farmers have not been able to raise soybean yields much at all, even though a bushel of soybeans is worth more than twice as much as a bushel of corn. Despite a powerful economic incentive to raise soybean yields dramatically, no one has been able to do so (USDA/ERS, 1993a).

Contrary to popular opinion, biotechnology is not an agricultural panacea that will end hunger. Perhaps the best assessment of the potential contribution of biotechnology is by Donald Duvick, former

509

director of research at the Pioneer Seed Company. He points out the two main ways to use biotechnology. One is to map the genetic structure of crops, such as wheat, rice, and corn; linking specific genes to specific traits can be an invaluable aid to plant breeders. The other, a unique contribution of biotechnology, is the transfer of germplasm from one species to another (Duvick, 1994).

Biotechnology can be used to breed resistance to diseases and insects or to raise the genetic yield potential of the crop. The new technology is likely to make its earliest contributions in the former, either in reducing the need for pesticides or in lowering crop losses. In either case, these are likely to be local solutions, because plant diseases and insects tend to be location specific (Duvick, 1994).

In the all-important area of raising the genetic yield potential of major crops, nothing is in prospect. Nor would it be wise to count on any major contribution on this front, simply because so much of this potential has been exploited using conventional plant-breeding techniques. Despite the astounding gains in molecular biology, which provides the foundation for harnessing the potential of biotechnology, expansion of food output through this new technique thus far has been limited. Duvick (1994) notes that, although we have had great hopes for contributions from biotechnology for the past 20 years, the projected date when this new research tool would make a meaningful contribution to plant breeding has "receded annually, staying always five to ten years in the future."

In summary, no prospective breakthroughs in plant breeding are likely to lead to dramatic jumps in food output similar to those resulting from the hybridization of corn or the dwarfing of wheat and rice. Minor incremental gains in raising the genetic yield potential of major crops will continue, but many of these will be localized, the result of breeding efforts tailored to specific local conditions.

In semi-arid Africa, where yields have risen little, the prospects for sharply increasing output during the next four decades are no better than they were for Australia's farmers, who boosted wheat yields by less than half between 1950 and 1990. Every country that has multiplied its yields has relied heavily on the same basic combination of water (either from relatively generous rainfall or from irrigation), fertilizer, and grain varieties that are highly responsive to fertilizer. Those that lack water are severely handicapped in efforts to raise yields dramatically (USDA/ERS, 1993a).

A further troubling element is the declining public support for agricultural research both within individual countries and at the international level. Research played a major role in developing the fertilizer-responsive grain varieties that have helped double and triple yields. It also helps maintain yield gains in the face of new insect, disease, and environmental threats. Declining investment has recently extended to the international research centres, such as the International Rice Research Institute in the Philippines and the International Maize and Wheat Improvement Centre in Mexico, both part of the network known as the Consultative Group on International Agricultural Research (CGIAR). Overall CGIAR funding dropped in 1993 and again in 1994; this decline was largely driven by a sharp drop in the US core contribution – from US$43 million in 1992 to US$28 million in 1994, a cut of 35 per cent.[6]

Turning the tide

Elements of a global food and population strategy are beginning to emerge. In April 1994, the United Nations Population Fund (UNFPA, from its original name) sketched the outlines of a bold effort to stabilize world population at 7.8 billion by the year 2050. This plan is a broad-based one that includes filling the family planning gap, raising the level of female education, and pressing for equal rights for women in all societies. There is no reasonable alternative to such an effort (UN General Assembly, 1994).

UNFPA has presented a budget for the family planning part of this programme. It includes providing counselling and services not only to the 120 million women who want to limit the size of their families but who lack the means to do so, but also to an additional 230 million couples who will need to plan their families if population is to stabilize by 2050. In the early years, the budget also provides for the training of family planning workers, which is one of the keys to the rapid expansion of services. But the programme does more than just provide family planning services. It includes information activities for public education, such as working with the mass media and schools, and the expansion of reproductive health care. It also has a component to control sexually transmitted diseases, including, importantly, the spread of the HIV virus. And, finally, it covers the population data collection, analysis, and dissemination needed for public education and policy formulation.

Implementing the proposed UNFPA Programme of Action requires an estimated US$11.4 billion in 1996, gradually rising to US$14.4 billion in 2005 (see table 18.3). Of this total, roughly two-thirds is

Table 18.3   **Global food security budget, 1996–2005 (US$ billion)**

Year	Family planning	Primary education	Adult literacy	Soil reforestation	Agricultural and conservation	Forestry research	Total
1996	11.4	3.0	2.0	2.4	4.5	1.0	24.3
1997	11.8	4.0	2.5	3.2	9.1	2.0	32.6
1998	12.3	5.0	3.0	4.4	13.6	3.0	41.3
1999	12.7	6.0	3.5	5.2	18.1	4.0	49.5
2000	13.2	6.5	4.0	5.6	24.0	5.0	58.3
2001	13.4	6.6	4.0	6.0	24.0	5.0	59.0
2002	13.7	6.7	4.0	6.4	24.0	5.0	59.8
2003	13.9	6.8	4.0	6.4	24.0	5.0	60.1
2004	14.2	6.9	4.0	6.8	24.0	5.0	60.9
2005	14.4	7.0	4.0	6.8	24.0	5.0	61.2

Source: Brown and Kane (1994).

to be mobilized within developing countries themselves. The complementary resource flows from donor countries would increase to US$4.4 billion (1993 dollars) in 2000, rising further to US$4.8 billion in 2005 (UN General Assembly, 1994; Brown and Wolf, 1988).

Achieving the UNFPA's fertility reduction goals will require substantial increases in female education. Although this would contribute simultaneously to economic progress and lower fertility, in many countries, such as Nepal, Ethiopia, and Senegal, fewer than half the girls of primary school age are in class. Almost all governments have adopted universal primary education as a goal, but many have seen their educational system overwhelmed by the sheer number of children entering school. The governments of high-fertility societies cannot realistically hope to rein in population growth without broadening access to education and thus providing women with options beyond childbearing (World Bank, 1993).

Fulfilling this social condition for a more rapid fertility decline will require a heavy investment in both school building and teacher training. Providing elementary education for the estimated (UN General Assembly, 1994) 130 million school-age children not now in school (70 per cent of whom are female) would cost roughly US$6.5 billion per year (Summers, 1992). Providing literacy training for those men and women who are illiterate and beyond school age (UNDP, 1993) would require an additional estimated US$4 billion per year.

On the food side of the equation, we at Worldwatch have focused in table 18.3 on protecting the soil and water resource base and increasing the investment in agricultural research. At the root of food scarcity in many developing countries is the loss of vegetation from deforestation, overgrazing, and overploughing. As vegetation is destroyed, rainfall run-off increases, reducing aquifer recharge, increasing soil erosion, and, in turn, lowering the inherent productivity of the ecosystem.

Where firewood is scarce, crop residues are burned for cooking fuel, thus depriving the soil of needed organic matter. Adding trees to the global forest stock is a valuable investment in our economic future, whether the goal is to satisfy the growing firewood needs in the third world or to stabilize soil and water regimes. Accordingly, we have included in our global food security budget a massive reforestation plan – totalling US$5.6 billion a year by the end of the 1990s (FAO, 1983).

More than 1 billion people live in countries that are already experiencing firewood shortages. Unless corrective action is taken, that number will nearly double by the year 2000. An estimated 55 million ha of tree planting will be needed to meet the fuelwood demand expected then. In addition, anchoring soils and restoring hydrological stability in thousands of third world watersheds will require tree planting on some 100 million ha (FAO, 1983). Considering that some trees would serve both fuelwood and ecological objectives, a total of 120 million ha might need to be planted. An additional 30 million ha will be needed to satisfy demand for timber, both local and for export, and for paper manufacturing. If this tree-planting goal is to be achieved during the next decade, the effort would need to proceed somewhat along the lines outlined in table 18.3, with annual plantings gradually expanding during the next several years.

Estimating the cost of reforesting an area equivalent to 150 million ha varies widely, according to the approach taken. Numerous studies by the World Bank and other development agencies show costs ranging from US$200 to US$500 per ha for trees planted by farmers as part of agro-forestry activities, and up to US$2,000 or more for commercial plantations (World Bank, 1992; Spears, 1983). Farmers' costs are lower, mainly because the labour to plant, maintain, and protect the trees is contributed by the family. The effort is seen as an investment in family welfare, much as home gardening uses family labour to reduce food expenditures.

In estimating the cost of establishing tree cover, it is assumed that the great bulk of the 150 million ha will be planted by local villagers and that the average cost will be US$400 per ha, including seedling costs (Anderson and Fishwick, 1984). At this rate, tree planting expenditures would total some US$53 billion, just under US$6 billion per year during the next decade.

Planting trees to restore watersheds, thereby conserving soil and water, complements the expenditures on soil conservation by farmers. To calculate the cost of a global effort to stabilize soils, data are used from the United States (USDA, 1992), from which Worldwatch estimates that roughly US$3 billion a year would be needed to stabilize soils on US cropland. First, it is assumed that one-tenth of the world's cropland cannot sustain cultivation with any economically feasible soil-conserving agricultural practices (WRI, 1994) – roughly the same proportion as in the United States. This would equal some 128 million ha worldwide. Applying the cost of converting such land to grassland or woodland in the United States, at US$125 per ha as a first approximation, the global cost would be US$16 billion per year (USDA/ERS/RTD, 1993). If expenditures to conserve topsoil on the remaining erosion-prone cropland (another 100 million ha) are comparable to these – disregarding, for the purpose of illustration, the vast differences in land tenure and farming methods that characterize farming in different regions – a global programme of conservation practices enacted by 2000 would cost an additional US$8 billion annually.

By 2000, when both the cropland conversion programme and the full range of needed soil-conserving practices are in place, global expenditures to protect the cropland base would total some US$24 billion per year. Although this is obviously a large sum, it is less than the US government has paid farmers to support crop prices in some years. As a down-payment on future food supplies for a world expecting at least 2 billion more people, US$24 billion is an investment humanity can ill afford not to make (USDA/ERS/RTD, 1993).

As mentioned earlier, at a time when the backlog of yield-raising technologies is shrinking, international expenditures on agricultural research are diminishing. The urgency of reversing this trend is obvious. A remarkably successful international network of 17 agricultural research institutes, ranging from the International Maize and Wheat Improvement Centre in Mexico to the International Rice Research Institute in the Philippines, identifies gaps in global agricultural research and systematically fills them. Tied together under the Washington-based Consultative Group on International Agricultural Research, this network has been the source of many agricultural advances of the past few decades.

Despite its widely recognized success, funding of this network, which climbed from US$20 million in 1972 to US$319 million in 1992, dropped to an estimated US$285 million in 1994 – a decline of more than one-tenth.[7] Worldwatch is proposing that investment in the international network of 17 research institutes be increased to US$500 million by 2000. At a time when every technological advance, however small, is needed to help buy time to slow population growth, investment in these centres should be rising, not falling.

Beyond the funding of this key network, there is a need to expand agricultural and forestry research broadly in the effort to boost food production on a sustainable basis. Among the more pressing research needs are deforestation, soil conservation, and the adaptation of internationally available technologies to local conditions. The World Bank (1992) estimates that filling this gap would take US$5 billion per year.

In summary, the food security budget outlined here, including needed expenditures on both sides of the food/population equation, would start at US$24 billion in 1996, increasing rapidly to just over US$58 billion in the year 2000, and then grow much more slowly, reaching US$61 billion by 2005. At the 2005 level, this would amount to less than one-fourth of current US military expenditures. Although the budget is described as a food security budget, it is also a political stability budget – an investment in an environmentally sustainable, politically stable future (Schmitt, 1993).

The growth in food output is also being slowed by the decline in public investment in agriculture in developing countries, particularly in building the physical infrastructure needed to support agricultural progress. This includes farm-to-market roads, improved local grain storage facilities, and maintenance of irrigation systems. At the institutional level, there is a need for an extension service not only to disseminate new technologies from the research stations but also to help farmers adopt soil-conserving farming practices and increase irrigation efficiency.

Aside from the global food security budget, which involves public expenditures, there are several needs that are best satisfied by reforming economic policies, especially those that deal with water efficiency. With water becoming increasingly scarce, future gains in irrigation depend heavily on the more efficient use of irrigation water. The key to this is to remove the subsidies that provide farmers with free water or water at a nominal cost. Only if farmers pay market costs for water will they make the needed investments in irrigation efficiency (Postel, 1992). Such policies may seem like environmental or agricultural policy, rather than urban policy. But if the world's cities are to be fed, then such policies sit squarely among the priorities of urban planners.

Notes

1. European land set-aside from Dan Plunkett, USDA, Washington, D.C., private communication, 20 October 1993.
2. Annual population increase from Center for International Research, US Bureau of the Census, Suitland, MD., private communication, 26 March 1993.
3. Calculated using yield data from USDA/ERS/RTD (1993).
4. Unless otherwise indicated, data in this section are taken from FAO, *Production Yearbook* (various years), FAO, *Fertilizer Yearbook* (various years), and IFA (1992).
5. Center for International Research, US Bureau of the Census, Suitland, Md., private communication, 2 November 1993.
6. Private communication from Heinrich Von Loesch, Information Services, Consultative Group on International Agricultural Research, Washington, D.C., 7 April 1994.
7. Private communication from Heinrich Von Loesch, 13 April 1994.

References

Anderson, Dennis and Robert Fishwick (1984), *Fuelwood Consumption and Deforestation in African Countries*. World Bank Staff Working Paper No. 704, Washington, D.C.

AsiaWeek (1993), "Thirsty Fields: Asia's Rice Lands," 26 May.

Brown, Lester R. (1963), *Man, Land, and Food*. Washington, D.C.: US Department of Agriculture.

Brown, Lester R. and Hal Kane (1994), *Full House: Reassessing the Earth's Population Carrying Capacity*. New York: W. W. Norton.

Brown, Lester R. and Edward C. Wolf (1988), "Reclaiming the Future." In: *State of the World 1988*. New York: W. W. Norton.

Brown, Lester R. and John Young (1990), "Feeding the World in the Nineties." In: Lester R. Brown et al., *State of the World 1990*. New York: W. W. Norton.

Chapman, Duane and Randy Barker (1987), *Resource Depletion, Agricultural Research, and Development*. Ithaca, N.Y.: Cornell University.

Checchio, Elizabeth (1988), *Water Farming: The Promise and Problems of Water Transfers in Arizona*. Tucson: University of Arizona.

Cutler, M. Rupert (1980), "The Peril of Vanishing Farmlands." *New York Times*, 1 July.

Dowall, David E. (1991), "The Land Market Assessment: A New Tool for Urban Management." Paper prepared for the Urban Management Programme of United Nations Centre for Human Settlements, World Bank, and United Nations Development Programme, University of California, Berkeley.

Duvick, Donald N. (1994), "Intensification of Known Technology and Prospects of Breakthroughs in Technology and Future Food Supply." Johnston, Iowa: Iowa State University.

FAO (Food and Agriculture Organization) (various years), *FAO Production Year-book*. Rome: FAO.

———— (various years), *Fertilizer Yearbook*. Rome: FAO.

———— (1983), *Fuelwood Supplies in the Developing Countries*. Forestry Paper 42, Rome: FAO.

Herdt, Robert W. (1986), "Technological Potential for Increasing Crop Productivity in Developing Countries." Paper presented to the meeting of the International Trade Research Consortium, 14–18 December.

IFA (International Fertilizer Industry Association) (1992), *Fertilizer Consumption Report*. Paris: IFA.

———— (1993), *Fertilizer Consumption Report*. Paris: IFA.

"Justus von Liebig" (1976), *Encyclopaedia Britannica*. Cambridge: Encyclopaedia Britannica, Inc.

Onishi, Norimitsu (1993), "Japanese Pass US Automakers in Race for Chinese Ventures." *Journal of Commerce*, 31 August.

Pingali, Prabhu L. and Mark W. Rosegrant (1993), "Confronting the Environmental Consequences of the Green Revolution in Asia." Paper presented at 1993 AAEA International Pre-Conference on Post-Green Revolution Agricultural Development Strategies in the Third World: What Next?, August.

Postel, Sandra (1992), *Last Oasis: Facing Water Scarcity*. New York: W. W. Norton.

PRB (Population Reference Bureau) (1993) *1993 World Population Data Sheet*. Washington, D.C.

Schmitt, Eric (1993), "$261 Billion Set for the Military." *New York Times*, 7 November.

Spears, John S. (1983), "Replenishing the World's Forests – Tropical Reforestation: An Achievable Goal?" *Commonwealth Forestry Review* 62(3).

Summers, Lawrence (1992), *Investing in* All *the People*. World Bank Working Paper No. 905, Washington, D.C., May.

UNDP (United Nations Development Programme) (1993), *Human Development Report 1993*. New York: Oxford University Press.

UN General Assembly (1994), "Draft Programme of Action of the International Conference on Population and Development" (draft). New York, April.

United Nations (1991), *World Economic Survey 1991*. New York: United Nations.

Urban, Francis and Ray Nightingale (1993), *World Population by Country and Region, 1950–90 and Projections to 2050*. Washington, D.C.: USDA, ERS.

USDA (US Department of Agriculture) (1991), *USSR Agriculture and Trade Report*. Washington, D.C., May.

———— (1992), *Agricultural Statistics 1992*. Washington, D.C.: US Government Printing Office.

———— (1993), *World Grain Situation and Outlook*. Washington, D.C., April.

USDA/ERS (US Department of Agriculture, Economic Research Service) (1992), "World Grain Database." Unpublished printout, Washington, D.C.

———— (1993a), "Production, Supply, and Demand Views." Electronic database, Washington, D.C.

———— (1993b), "World Grain Database." Unpublished printout, Washington, D.C.

———— (1993c), *Former USSR, Situation and Outlook Series*. Washington, D.C., May.

USDA/ERS/RTD (US Department of Agriculture, Economic Research Service, Resources and Technology Division) (1993), *RTD Updates: 1993 Cropland Use.* Washington, D.C., September.

World Bank (1992), "The Costs of a Better Environment." In: *World Development Report 1992.* New York: Oxford University Press.

——— (1993), *World Development Report 1993.* New York: Oxford University Press.

WRI (World Resources Institute) (1994), *World Resources 1994–95.* New York: Oxford University Press.

Contributors

Tarek Abu-Zekry
Faculty of Engineering,
Zagazig University,
Egypt

Keith Beavon
Department of Geography and
Environmental Studies,
University of Witwatersrand,
South Africa

Sang-chuel Choe
Graduate School of Environmental
Studies, Seoul National University,
Seoul, Korea

Salah El-Shakhs
Department of Urban Planning
and Policy Development,
Rutgers University, New Brunswick,
USA

Alan Gilbert
Department of Geography,
University College London,
London, UK

Peter Gordon
Department of Economics, School of
Urban Planning and Development,
University of Southern California,
Los Angeles, USA

Peter Hall
School of Planning, The Bartlett,
University College London, London,
UK

Masahiko Honjo
Former Director, International
Development Center of Japan, Japan

Hal Kane
Formerly of the Worldwatch Institute,
Washington, D.C., USA

Klaus Kunzmann
School of Planning, University of
Dortmund, Dortmund, Germany

Fu-chen Lo
United Nations University, Tokyo,
Japan

519

Contributors

T. G. McGee
Institute of Asian Research,
The University of British Columbia,
Vancouver, Canada

David R. Meyer
Department of Sociology, Brown
University, Providence, USA

Carole Rakodi
Department of City and Regional
Planning, University of Wales, Cardiff,
UK

Harry W. Richardson
Department of Economics, School of
Urban Planning and Development,
University of Southern California,
Los Angeles, USA

Peter J. Rimmer
Department of Human Geography,
The Australian National University,
Canberra, Australia

Saskia Sassen
Graduate School of Architecture,
Planning and Historic Preservation,
Columbia University, New York, USA

Ellen Shoshkes
Department of Urban Planning,
College of Architecture and Planning,
Ball State University, USA

Hamilton C. Tolosa
Department of Economics, Conjunto
Universitario Candido Mendes,
Rio de Janiero, Brazil

Yue-man Yeung
Hong Kong Institute of Asia-Pacific
Studies, The Chinese University of
Hong Kong, Hong Kong

Ahmed M. Yousry
Faculty of Urban and Regional
Planning, Cairo University, Cairo,
Egypt

Mahmoud Yousry
Faculty of Urban and Regional
Planning, Cairo University, Cairo,
Egypt

Index